1987

Edward F. Keefe

1986

Passionate Pilgrims

Passionate Pilgrims

The American Traveler in Great Britain, 1800–1914

Allison Lockwood

NEW YORK • *Cornwall Books* • LONDON
RUTHERFORD • MADISON • TEANECK
Fairleigh Dickinson University Press

© 1981 by Associated University Presses, Inc.

Cornwall Books and
Associated University Presses, Inc.
4 Cornwall Drive
East Brunswick, N.J. 08816

Cornwall Books
69 Fleet Street
London EC4Y 1EU

Associated University Presses
Toronto M5E 1A7, Canada

Library of Congress Cataloging in Publication Data

Lockwood, Allison, 1920-
  Passionate pilgrims.

  Bibliography: p.
  Includes index.
  1. England—Description and travel—1801-1900.
2. England—Description and travel—1901-1945.
3. Travelers—England. 4. Travelers—United
States. 5. Americans in England. I. Title
DA625.L8   914.1'048   78-68808
ISBN 0-8386-2272-0 (Fairleigh Dickinson)
ISBN 0-8453-4725-X (Cornwall)

Printed in the United States of America

To all the "passionate pilgrims"
so long ago embarked on that last journey
from which no traveler returns.

Contents

Acknowledgments

Thanks must go to my husband, Paul Lockwood, whose aid in practical matters involving time and space made my work possible; also to my son John for help in proof-reading. Thanks also to those kind Britons so prompt with answers to questions, especially Christopher Hewer, Assistant Librarian of the London Library; N.H. MacMichael, Keeper of the Muniments, and H.M. Nixon, Librarian, both of Westminster Abbey. Thanks to Wiley Boyd and Arletta Kolarik of the Library of Congress and to the librarians of Montgomery College; to my colleagues, Professors Marjorie Edwards, Bernard LeBeau, and Bob and Peg Miller whose friendly encouragement has meant so much; to Professors (Emeritus) of Smith College, Charles and Ruth Hill, who welcomed an old student and provided information as if nearly four decades had not passed; and to my former teachers, Anna Brewster, Alice McCulloch, and Anna Thayer who long ago inspired in me a love of literature, history and learning in general. Thanks to Houghton Mifflin Company for permission to quote at length from Joseph Ballard's *England in 1815 As Seen by a Young Merchant;* to Ohio State University Press for permission to quote from *Our Old Home,* Vol. 5 of the Centenary Edition of the Works of Nathaniel Hawthorne, edited by William Charvat, Roy Harvey Pearce, and Claude M. Simpson; Fredson Bowers, textual editor. Copyright © 1970 by the Ohio State University Press. All rights reserved. And last but not least, thanks to our friends, the Thaxtons of London, and to Elma's mother, Lady Janet Wright, for sharing with us so much of London and the lovely English countryside.

Allison Lockwood

London
Washington 1980

*It takes passionate pilgrims,
vague aliens, and other disinherited
persons to appreciate the "points" of
this admirable country.*
                              —Henry James, *English Hours*

Introduction

"If we had been brought here blindfolded from America, and were now after two day's visit, sent back again, we should feel well rewarded for the long passage," wrote young Frederick Law Olmsted in his journal shortly after arriving in Great Britain for a thirteen-week walking tour with a couple of friends in the summer of 1850.[1]

"If we were to stay a month," he continued, "we should scarcely enjoy less than we do now, rambling about among the relics of our old England. We cannot keep still, but run about with boyish excitement. We feel indeed like children that have come back to visit the paternal home, and who are rummaging about in the garret among their father's playthings, ever and anon shouting, 'See what I've found! See what I've found!' "[2]

This youthful sentiment of the man destined to become America's foremost nineteenth-century landscape architect and urban planner symbolizes the mother country mystique that for more than a century following the Revolution haunted British-American relations. Political independence was one thing, cultural independence another. Strong ties of history, religion, language, and literature bound the new nation to the old and even today are not totally severed.

Like most child-parent relationships, this one manifested a curious ambivalence, nowhere more clearly revealed than in what British poet-critic Stephen Spender has called "that comedy of manners and stereotyped patterns of love-hate which forms the *commedia* of a whole literature written by Englishmen visiting America, Americans visiting England."[3]

This mutual compulsion of Englishmen and Americans to survey, analyze, and assess each other throughout the century following American independence spawned so much commentary, in fact, that in reviewing in 1870 the latest British delineation of the United States a London critic estimated that "upon a modest computation, since the beginning of the century, a waggonload of books has been written by English travellers about the United States, and probably not one of those books has appeared thoroughly satisfactory to the natives of that country."[4] Fifty years later, in a bibliography he considered by no means "absolutely exhaustive," American historian Allan Nevins listed nearly three hundred titles of such books in his scholarly *American Social History as Recorded by British Travellers*.[5]

Never a people to be outdone, and indeed angry over the thoroughly "unsatisfactory" books written by Britons about the United States, Americans—both professional authors and, as befitted a democratic republic, amateurs of every ilk—responded in kind all through the nineteenth century, each considering his

11

or her reflections on the "parent nation" as worthy of preservation in print as those of a James Fenimore Cooper, Ralph Waldo Emerson, Nathaniel Hawthorne, or Henry James. Thus the nineteenth-century "invasion" of Britain by Americans became one of the best recorded such phenomena in history, thanks to these Yankee pilgrims—earnest, energetic, indefatigable journal keepers, letter writers, and readers of travel books by others that spurred them to embark on travels and books of their own.

"It is not true that everyone who goes abroad writes a book," remarked the Reverend John Edwards in the preface to his own *Random Sketches* published in 1857. "Not one in a thousand does. Yet everyone," he added democratically, "has the right to do so if he chooses."[6] So many did so choose that, in preparing this book, I encountered almost five hundred Yankee veterans of this great century-long literary confrontation, while many others doubtless went undiscovered.

"Books by visiting English about America, Americans about England, show that each sees the other as the 'production' of English or American circumstances," says Spender. "Moreover, each is seen as a kind of negative shadow of, or sum subtracted from the other. It is as though the earth were to describe the moon in terms of its being a fragment torn off it, or the moon the earth as the mother figure from which it was torn."[7]

Comparisons, contrasts, and competition between Britons and Americans were inevitable; and their attitudes toward each other over the years thus ranged anywhere from positive, friendly, or fawning to negative, hostile, or phobic. Both were quick to take offense when criticism grew caustic, particularly the Americans, who viewed satirical comments on their appearance, manners, or customs as attacks on the great republican experiment itself. Cooper concluded that both peoples were oversensitive, but, while the British were "thinskinned," the Americans were positively "raw."[8] Both criticism and oversensitivity lessened as time wore on, but it was close to the end of the century before American historian Reuben Thwaites would remark good-naturedly, in the preface to an account of his bicycle tour of England in the summer of 1891, that "American books about England are apt to be quite as amusing to Englishmen as their books about America are to us."[9]

Scrutiny of the Mother Country, as so many Americans continued to call Britain through the nineteenth century, was undertaken by three main classes of writers, beginning with prominent authors of the day: Washington Irving (*The Sketchbook of Geoffrey Crayon, Gent.*, 1820); James Fenimore Cooper (*Gleanings in Europe. By an American*), 1837; Ralph Waldo Emerson (*English Traits*, 1856); Nathaniel Hawthorne (*Our Old Home: A Series of English Sketches*, 1863); Henry James (*English Hours*, 1905); and William Dean Howells (*London Films*, 1905; *Seven English Cities*, 1909; and *Seen and Unseen at Stratford-on-Avon*, 1914). Accounts of their experiences in Great Britain by other authors widely popular in their day, like Catherine Sedgwick, Lydia Sigourney, Caroline Kirkland, Harriet Beecher Stowe, and Helen Hunt Jackson, further swelled this body of American commentary.

The second type of American commentator on nineteenth-century Britain consisted of editors, journalists, and professional travel writers, among them

Nathaniel Parker Willis, who enjoyed great popularity in the forties and fifties. Others included Horace Greeley, Grace Greenwood, Joel Headley, Kate Field, Curtis Guild, William Winter, William Rideing, Louise Moulton, Theron Crawford, Richard Harding Davis, and George Smalley, to mention a few. While their accounts are less reflective and perhaps not as profound as those of Emerson, Hawthorne, or James, they do provide far more contemporary detail and often radiate a kind of vitality lacking in the works of the major writers. Reports on the Great Exhibition of 1851, for example, sent from London as newspaper dispatches and later published in book form by both Horace Greeley, editor of the *New York Tribune,* and William Drew, editor of a popular religious weekly, the *Gospel Banner,* as well as commissioner for the exhibition from the state of Maine, preserve on-the-spot views of one of the great events of the century. To read their books is to wander through the Crystal Palace gazing on the artifacts displayed at this "first grand cosmopolitan Olympiad of Industry," as Greeley called it.[10]

The third, and by far the largest, class of American traveler-writers consisted of hundreds of less celebrated Americans who also toured the motherland, painstakingly recording their observations and experiences with an eye toward

BAYARD TAYLOR, 1844.
In his Traveling Costume.

Young Bayard Taylor, whose account, *Views Afoot,* **of his 1844 European walking tour inspired American travelers throughout the nineteenth century.** *From the author's collection.*

publication. Many of these literary hopefuls ended up publishing their works themselves, as indicated by the "privately printed" or similar label so often found on the title pages of their books. A few even went so far as to market their books themselves, as did youthful Charles Williams of Salem, Ohio, who toured Britain in 1861 for seven weeks at a total cost of $220, including his sea passage, by sleeping in model lodging houses and often dining on little more than tea, herring, and a bun. For a dollar a copy, Williams offered, "postpaid upon receipt of price," to mail out copies of his own lively, well-written *Old World Scenes.*[11]

Possibly the most influential travel book of the nineteenth century, and one that may well have inspired other young men like Charles Williams, was *Views Afoot,* future author-diplomat Bayard Taylor's youthful account of a walking tour of Europe that was first published in 1846. Into twenty editions in the nine years immediately following its publication, and still being reprinted as late as 1902,[12] *Views Afoot* motivated several generations of young Americans to set out for the Old World with knapsacks and hiking staffs, as well as others who had to postpone their adventure until sedate middle age and settle for a quick Cook's tour instead.

Following Bayard Taylor's example, many other travelers persuaded local newspaper editors to accept periodic travel letters describing their peregrinations abroad as a means of covering their expenses. So many were seized by this *cacoëthes scribendi,* or "irresistible urge to write," that in 1875 magazine editor and travel writer Moses Sweetser warned against seeking this means of financing a trip abroad. "So thoroughly written up by skillful pens for over a century" was the pilgrimage to the Old World, he pointed out, that most amateurs could now reasonably expect their proposals for foreign correspondence to be "consigned to the limbo for Spring poems."[13] Nevertheless, such travel dispatches continued to appear in hometown papers and later came out as books, as in the case of Eliza Connor, whose reports to the *Cincinnati Commercial* during her Cook's tour of Europe in the summer of 1883 were published later that year as *E. A. Abroad: A Summer in Europe.*[14]

In terms of social history, the observations of these common travelers possess far more value than those of noted authors and professional writers, for, as Roderick MacLeish has pointed out, "it is the jottings and ruminations of the uncelebrated that give reality to the past."[15] Historian Robert Spiller also reminded readers of this fact in his *The American in England during the First Half Century of Independence* (1926), with his opinion that the relatively obscure Unitarian clergyman Orville Dewey "expressed the state of mind of the average American traveler much more truly than did the Reverend Ralph Waldo Emerson, with whom he made part of his trip" in 1833–34. "There is less reflection of the actual state of thought of the two nations in the *Sketchbook* of Irving or the diplomatic correspondence of Jefferson than there is in a series of composite pictures drawn from the records of each group of Americans who were guided by more or less common motives," wrote Spiller.[16]

As a matter of fact, Protestant clergymen outdid all other groups of nineteenth-century Yankee travelers in Britain. "Sore throats and liberal congregations" was how one of their number explained his profession's possession of both time and money for their journeying.[17] This phenomenon, together with the fact that throughout the century it was primarily the white Anglo-Saxon Protestant American who had the means and leisure to go abroad, resulted in such a patently Protestant monopoly of the travel book genre, that in 1855, Father John Donelan of Rock Island, Illinois, finally rebelled. Protesting, as he said, "the characteristic slander of all I hold dear in religion," by all these Protestant writers, he took himself to a proper Catholic country and produced *My Trip to France (1857)* on his return.[18] Almost two decades later, Father Eugene Vetromile likewise complained that "Catholics have no other books of travel than those by Protestant tourists," and so he brought out his own *Travels in Europe* (1871).[19]

Close on the heels of all the Protestant preachers followed lawyers, doctors, businessmen, educators, students, housewives, schoolteachers, actors, health seekers, society women, youthful wanderers, torch bearers for various causes such as peace, abolition and temperance, and even "free thinker" DeRobigne Mortimer Bennett, fresh out of jail, who paid for his trip by selling subscriptions in advance for the book he cranked out on his return from his travels.

"The development of an American travel literature with England as its subject is," as Spiller pointed out, "a singularly revealing index" to the vast economic, social, political and technological changes that occurred in both countries during the nineteenth century.[20] Thus are preserved in these American travelers' accounts glimpses of Britain's recurrent Napoleonic war crises, her booming industrial revolution, the rehabilitation of the monarchy under Victoria and Albert, the excitement attending the passage of the Reform Bill in 1832, the social unrest reflected in the Chartist movement and demonstrations of the forties, the Irish famine, the Fenian terrorism of the later decades, and the inevitable cost of empire tabulated in the ubiquitous memorials to young heroes buried in foreign fields around the globe. As for the Americans themselves, they reveal the ever-increasing stress and strain stemming from their own inevitable industrial growth, the opposing and divisive interests leading to their tragic Civil War, and, in the later decades, what was to them the stunning and disturbing impact on their society of massive waves of immigration.

So extensive is this record left behind by generations of American travelers in Britain that it resists classification and even chronological ordering. Subjects and periods tend to overlap; stereotypes persist; stray anglophobes or anglophiles pop up when least expected; and occasionally an individual's crotchets uniquely color his or her reactions, as in the case of the self-styled "Hon. Wm. A. Braman of Ohio," who ran all over England in the summer of 1900 complaining that everything was "too old," including Westminster Abbey itself, which he labeled asymmetric, grimy, and gloomy.[21] Despite such factors, these hundreds of nineteenth-century commentaries finally sort themselves out into three major periods based on the types of travelers and their motivation; their itineraries and modes of travel; the nature of their observations; and, above all, the tone and mood of their responses to their experiences.

The first phase, from the century's start and lasting into the 1840s, involved primarily individual, ambitious, serious, often young, and usually male sojourners with a purpose. Motivated by a desire for self-improvement, professional advancement, material for a book, and sometimes all three, they sought knowledge and experience in a country far more advanced and sophisticated than their own. Thus, they made long, extensive tours of the parent nation to observe its fast-developing technology, advanced agricultural methods and highly structured society; they visited its great universities and sought out its men of accomplishment, especially its writers. With equal drive they made pilgrimages to those historical and literary shrines symbolizing the culture they still shared in common with the Britons. Despite their youthful nationalism and critical tendencies, they tended to be awed by this society so far ahead of their own in many respects. As young Isaac Jewett marveled in 1836, "How wonderfully advanced are these people! How far on are they toward society's highest point! How largely are they developed!. . . *Our* epochs are all in the future."[22]

Starting in the 1830s, the American traveler-writers began to write in response to caustic commentaries on the United States by British travelers whom they believed had concentrated on the cruder and more bizarre aspects of life in the young republic, thus holding them up to ridicule before the world. As time went on, the Americans grew increasingly defensive, querulous, caustic, and polemic. Not only were men of learning and refinement angry at being lumped with frontier bumpkins, but all Americans moving about Britain in these years had their noses rubbed in the dirt of their "peculiar institution," slavery, which Britons had finally abolished in the West Indies in the forties. It was as if British critic Sydney Smith's pronouncement on the Yankee habit of tobacco chewing and resultant spitting into and outside of brimming spittoons was being applied to the American institution of human servitude as well. Smith had declared that "all claims to civilization are suspended till this secretion is otherwise disposed of."[23]

This second period, consisting of the forties and fifties, thus throbbed with a relentless, continuous, angry dialogue between visiting Yankees and their British hosts on the subject of slavery, each side earnestly considering the other guilty of enormous hypocrisy. Britons considered it illogical for a people boasting so loudly of liberty and equality to hold over three million human beings in bondage. To this charge, outraged Southern slaveholders and New England abolitionists alike reacted angrily, some of the former claiming that they were actually lifting a barbarous people up to a state of civilization and treating them to a far more comfortable life than that lived by Britain's hordes of paupers. Antislavery Americans, equally angry, charged Britons with pharisaically closing their eyes to social evils in their own land, as well as in India and Ireland, as awful as the evil of slavery in America. To back up their arguments, traveling Americans in these years thus spent considerable time nosing about in the shadows of British society for examples of poverty, vice and exploitation of factory operatives and miners to fling in the face of their tormentors. This bitter slavery-versus-poverty dialogue pervades, or invades, all the books of this period and simply cannot be ignored. The Reverend John Mitchell spoke for all American travelers to Britain in those two decades before the Civil War when he wrote home that "they made me talk beyond my strength on that prolific and convenient topic, American Slavery; for it is often resorted to as a convenient diversion from sins and blemishes nearer home."[24]

A brief interlude of relative good will was provided through the excitement generated by the "Great Exhibition of the Works of Industry of All Nations," held in London in 1851, although even here the specter of American slavery raised its head briefly. During the exhibition, however, the head of steam built up between the two competing nations found a healthy release, and in the acclaim accorded the McCormick "reaping machine," and the victory of the yacht *America* in a racing event staged by the Royal Yacht Squadron off the Isle of Wight to enhance the exhibition, the Yankees found balm to soothe their wounded pride.

During the Civil War, most Americans, but by no means all of them, stayed at home. Once it was over, however, and despite the fact that the victorious advocates of the Union cause long remained bitter over the official British attitude during that struggle—allegedly neutral but in their eyes overtly pro-Southern—back again they trooped, in ever-increasing numbers, to the land that for most of them still represented their cultural and historical heritage—now in search of their own lost past.

During this second half of the century, and lasting up to World War I, the American traveler-writers manifested a new image. Weary of war, sadder, wiser, and notwithstanding the brash self-confidence with which the victorious Unionists had emerged from the conflict, Americans now sought diversion and escape in what was for them their own and Britain's romantic past. In pilgrimages to its historical, literary, and religious shrines they could forget—at least briefly—their own growing industrialism and the vast and unsettling impact on their culture due to continuous surges of immigration that between 1860 and 1920 brought 28 million emigrants from all over Europe to the United States. As if trying to reassure himself, lawyer-inventor John Latrobe declared in 1869: "The Anglo-Saxon blood is the leaven of the mass, and it is to this Anglo-Saxon origin that the American present is due."[25]

In place of the onetime youthful awe of "the old country," followed by their guilt-ridden, defensive carping in the decades leading up to the Civil War, the Americans now displayed a new spirit of kinship characterized by fervent declarations of Anglo-Saxon solidarity, and they actually sought to strengthen rather than weaken the old ties. Journalist Richard Grant White's *England Without and Within* of 1881 fairly glows with approval and enthusiasm for everything British.

"Tourists have gone about in both countries seizing upon the peculiar, the strange, the startling; and this they have set forth as portraiture," observed White. "Ignorance and . . .dislike have been fostered and kept alive by writers. . .to pander to the feeling of a day." He would, he vowed, use his pen "in the interests of truth and of kindly feeling," reminding his readers that "England is still the motherland, the 'Old Home'."[26]

Underlying all their more obvious motives—such as self-improvement, status, adventure, and escape—involved in this century-long "rummaging about in the garret" of their forefathers (as young Olmsted put it), these energetic, sentimental, seemingly naive and often annoyingly self-righteous nineteenth-century Americans appear to have been searching for their identity. Perhaps by comparing the new nation with the old, they might arrive at a negative definition of themselves. The quest for self-definition by the people of a new nation, or even of a newly self-conscious ethnic minority within an older nation, is no new thing today. But in the nineteenth century this was a uniquely American concern. During the first half of the century Americans sought to establish their differences from the parent nation; during the second half, as they dug for their once eagerly-discarded roots in the old country, they now rejoiced in the similarities. The old parental ties the Americans had once so earnestly sought to cut still held fast.

America's last king, George III, in his speech before the House of Lords on December 5, 1782, had expressed the hope that "religion, language, interests and affection may, and I hope will, yet prove a bond of permanent union between the two countries." Neither the monarch nor one of the Americans present that day, young Elkanah Watson—whose "every artery beat high, and swelled with my proud American blood," as he heard the former colonies at last acknowledged as "free and independent states"—could then have predicted the strength and durability of that bond.[27]

Throughout the nineteenth century, when history was still deemed a subject worthy of children's attention, little Yankee minds were stuffed with British history right along with their own. "The history of England is the history of our ancestors," Samuel Goodrich, prolific author of young people's books and editor of countless school texts, assured them, reminding them also that "in government, religion, manners, customs, feelings, opinions, language, and descent, we are wholly or partially English. We cannot, therefore, understand ourselves or our institutions, but by a careful perusal of English history."[28]

As for religious ties, the image of the United States as primarily a Protestant nation, like nineteenth-century Britain, persisted in the minds of Americans long after the facts had changed and continued to change as each boatload of immigrants brought people of other faiths to this country. Along with the influence of the King James Version of the Bible on their thought and language, the leading American Protestant sects shared British roots that included an abhorrence of Catholicism and well-tended memories of religious persecution. Long a special tourist site for American travelers, for example, was London's Smithfield Market. It was then the city's wholesale meat district, but three centuries earlier it had been the scene of religious persecution. This fact was kept fresh in their memories by Foxe's Book of Martyrs and also by a well-remembered illustration in their "old New England primer" of the death at the stake there of John Rogers in 1555. Thus, amid the bawling cattle, squealing pigs and bellowing butchers of Smithfield Market, droves of Yankee tourists struggled to reach the gaslight in the center, and there to meditate upon the faith of their fathers on the reputed site of religious martyrdom of long ago. The Reverend Stephen Tyng, rector of St. George's Church in New York, stood there in 1842, seeing the flocks of doomed animals around him as symbols of those "suffering saints of God" who "won the final conflict with Satan on that very spot."[29]

As possessors of a common tongue, Britain and the United States enjoyed, moreover, a unique position among the babel of nations. Despite irritable wrangles over pronunciation, usage, and regional dialects, which inspired George Bernard Shaw's paradox of two nations divided by the barrier of a common language, Americans and Britons understood each other well enough—at least when they wanted to. Crawling off their Channel boats, returning from tours of the Continent in the later decades of the century, most American travelers expressed their relief and a sense of homecoming on touching British soil once more. "It took us three hours to make the run," remarked one Yankee at the turn of the century, "and we were truly glad to reach here, and to feel ourselves once more in 'God's country,' or something akin to it: it was delightful to hear the English tongue!"[30]

The strongest bond of all, in the long run, especially for Americans blessed with the benefits of a vast system of free public education, was the treasure hoard of literature written in the English tongue. For thousands of Yankee travelers, particularly as the century wore on, their tour of Britain became primarily a literary pilgrimage to the birthplaces, homes, and graves of favorite British authors, as well as sites associated with their work, especially in the case of their beloved Sir Walter Scott. In the 1890s one Londoner remarked that if she wanted to locate an American known to be headed for that city she herself would simply head for the Poets' Corner in Westminster Abbey and wait for him to show up. "There are rows of Americans there," she said, "all sitting, looking mournful, and thinking up quotations. If I wanted to find an American in London, I should take up my position there until he arrived."[31]

This anglicization of the American mind began in early childhood, observed Ehrmann Nadal, a friend of President Grant and for over a decade a secretary with the United States Legation in London.

> A point which I have not seen much made of is the hold which English tradition and fable and fiction get upon the mind of infancy in this country [U.S.]. Scenes of English life come upon us from a hundred sources. In my day the pictures in the reading books were all English even if the books were of American production. The lessons were mainly English and had to do with English things. I was ten before I knew that the skylark was not an American bird . . . the bird about which so much was said in the McGuffey's Second Reader.[32]

Even before they went off to school, nineteenth-century American children learned from their Mother Goose rhymes about kings, queens, counting houses, English heroes, the names of English cities and towns, and even the sounds of the various London church bells. Early in the century youthful George Putnam, destined to become one of the foremost publishers in the United States, observed on reaching London: "We remember London as far back as the days when we rode ahorseback on father's best knee. Whittington and his cat lived there; and we thought, poor children, that everybody in London sold dolls and picture books, as the country boy imagined everybody in Boston sold gingerbread because his father always brought him some home on market days."[33]

"I have been followed all over England by scraps of nursery rhymes," Kansas lawyer Noble Prentis wrote home to the *Topeka Commonwealth*, his hometown paper, during the summer of 1877.[34] In the same decade Curtis Guild, a writer of travel books, reported that a replica of the long-vanished Banbury market cross—so familiar to his countrymen from their childhood verse, "Ride a Cock Horse to Banbury Cross"—was restored to its former place as so many Americans had gone away "disappointed at not seeing what they had set down in their minds as one of the leading features of the town, and thinking that they had in some way been imposed upon by not finding anyone who knew of it or cared to show it to them."[35]

Little wonder, then, that for many Americans of the previous century their sojourn in Great Britain was haunted by a sense of déjà vu, a singular sense of having been there before. In the fifties a young New England clergyman, whose account of his travels was published both anonymously and posthumously, remarked that "we seem to have been here before. Memories of the past come forth to greet us in familiar tones as if welcoming us to some former home."[36] A decade later Nathaniel Hawthorne, in *Our Old Home,* described this same sensation. The reason, he realized, was that "history, poetry, and fiction, books of travel, and the talk of tourists had given me some pretty accurate preconceptions . . . and these, being long ago vivified by a youthful fancy, had insensibly taken their place among the images of things actually seen."[37]

"The American in Britain," observed George Calvert in 1866, recalling his first youthful visit in the 1820s, "is filled with a filial reverence. He is like a wealthy heir, sent from home a bantling, come back at twenty-one to take possession. He runs about refreshing, verifying, and rectifying his vague memories. His rights are deep . . . they descend to him through the books he has read, and the plays he has seen, and the history he has learnt, and the language he speaks, and the prayers he breathes, and the imaginations he has fondled."[38]

As if symbolizing this American concern about one's identity, as well as this sense of homecoming, a curious recurrent note sounds on and off down the years in these Yankee traveler books. While some Americans proudly proclaimed their nationality—like William Drew of Maine at mid-century, claiming that "the announcement always commands attention and respect,"[39]—others seemingly would have preferred to pass as Englishmen. Thurlow Weed observed this trait in 1843 and scorned what he termed "the custom of temporary denationalization . . . among Americans in Europe," calling it "a pitiful affectation."[40]

In any event, many visiting Americans throughout the century were both puzzled and frustrated by their almost instant identification, by Britons, as Americans. No matter where they went, even if dressed in English clothes, and long before they opened their mouths to speak, their nationality was known at once. Arriving at Stratford-on-Avon in 1832, Charles Stewart wrote that "our nationality soon became known in the streets, and as we walked about the town, we were gazed on as two Indians, or something of the kind, just broken loose from the forest."[41]

Almost half a century later a ragged Irish urchin, peering through a hedge at Mary Wills and her party in a jaunting car, turned to his little companion, and informed him loudly enough for all to hear, "*American* all through!"[42] What *was* it about themselves, they wondered, that so quickly telegraphed their origin.

In the last century's first decade the youthful scientist, Benjamin Silliman, donned his London-made suit, tried to "strut and look brave and knowing like a Londoner," and still they found him out, he confided to his journal.[43] In answer to their often-asked question at different times and places, Britons informed them it was their hats that gave them away; or their sharp features, leaner bodies, and paler faces—as well as the cut of their hair and beards. One Briton claimed it was all a matter of the nose, while another declared it was those monstrous "iron-clad" trunks they dragged after them. A Londoner boasted that he could spot an American at any distance solely by his manner of walking. John Higinbotham solved the problem for himself, at least, in 1910, declaring that "an American is immediately recognized by his shoes."[44]

Pondering this mighty question in the 1830s, the American journalist Nathaniel Parker Willis studied two young countrymen seated at their dinner in a Liverpool hotel dining room one evening. It was their curiosity, lack of reserve, and tendency to look about them that initially differentiated them from the Englishmen seated at the other tables, Willis concluded. Added to this was their exaggerated, "ambitious" way of conversing, ordering too much wine with their dinner, and openly displaying their amusement at the little chambermaid performing her customary duty of "lighting" them to bed.[45]

Visiting Britain about 1880 Charles Wood observed:

Americans live in the delusion that they can talk English, and that by the aid of a high hat and a silk umbrella, they can pass unnoticed in the crowd. One or two hours in London are sufficient to convince any reasonable-minded American that he is mistaken. The "beef-eater" knew us for Americans, but for that matter so did everybody else. If in America there is an American ashamed of being known as such, there is but one thing for him to do—stay home![46]

These passionate pilgrims from nineteenth-century America, "always on the go, tearing up and down our little island"—as an English villager remarked to cyclist Reuben Thwaites in the nineties—may not have been quite sure who they were.[47] We of the twentieth century are, for in their hundreds of written records of their restless searching in the garret "among their father's playthings"—as Frederick Olmsted wrote—they left us a vast composite portrait—not so much of their intended subject, Britain and the Britons, perhaps, as of themselves.

Passionate Pilgrims

PART I

1800–1845

How wonderfully advanced are these people! How far on are they toward society's highest point! How largely are they developed! And when I contemplate these developments, and with the same eye, those in my own land, I see between them chasms wide, very, very wide. How much we have to achieve. . . . Our epochs are all in the future!
                                    —Isaac Jewett, *Passages in Foreign Travel,* 1836

1

Early Pilgrims to Britain

"There are three species," observed Margaret Fuller of travelers in *At Home and Abroad*—an account of her own 1846 European tour—in a classification of the various attitudes of Americans approaching the old world during the nineteenth century. "First, the servile American, a being utterly shallow, thoughtless, worthless. He comes abroad to spend his money and indulge his tastes. His object . . . is to have fashionable clothes, good foreign cookery, to know some titled persons, and furnish himself with coffeehouse gossip, by retailing which among those less traveled and as uninformed as himself, he can win importance at home."[1]

"Then," continued Miss Fuller, "there is the conceited American, instinctively bristling and proud of he knows not what. He does not see, not he, that the history of Humanity for many centuries is likely to have produced results. . . . He thought it was all humbug before he came, and now he knows it. . . . This is Jonathan in the sprawling state, the booby truant, not yet aspiring enough to be a good schoolboy."[2]

"The thinking American," the class in which Margaret obviously included herself, "recognizing the immense advantage of being born to a new world and on a virgin soil . . . is anxious to gather and carry back with him every plant that will bear a new climate and a new culture. . . . He wishes to gather them clean, free from noxious insects, and to give them a fair trial in his new world. And that he may know the conditions under which he may best place them in that new world," she concluded, "he does not neglect to study their history in this."[3]

American travelers in the early decades of the nineteenth century, at least those who left records of their endeavors, belonged in large measure to Miss Fuller's third category. Eager young men for the most part, they were serious, well-educated, and equipped with the then all-important letters of introduction from prominent American achievers to their British counterparts. Specific purposes motivated these sojourners—if not educational, professional or commercial, at least those of self-discovery and improvement through the maturing experiences of foreign travel. They were also dedicated to recording their experiences and impressions in the detailed journals they kept, not so much, as Yale professor Benjamin Silliman pointed out in his case, to provide "a review of some of the scenes of one's life" as "affording amusement, or . . . imparting information" to one's friends.[4]

"Business was my only object in visiting England," Boston merchant Joseph

27

Ballard announced candidly in 1815. Yet he, too, "endeavoured to associate as much as possible with Englishmen," attended the theater and opera in London, visited historical and literary sites as well as the cutlery mills at Sheffield and the Cloth Hall at Leeds, and, above all, kept a detailed and well-written account of his activities and observations, concluding that although he saw "much to dislike" in England, "if I were not an American I should wish to be an Englishman."[5]

Scholars and scientists like Silliman, John Griscom, and Jacob Green concentrated on highly valued meetings with leading British scientists, including Scottish engineer James Watt, inventor of the modern condensing steam engine; the astronomer Sir William Herschel; the chemist-physicist Michael Faraday; the botanist Sir Joseph Banks, who had circumnavigated the globe with Captain Cook; and the chemist Sir Humphry Davy, discoverer of twelve chemical elements. Proudly they recorded their attendance at meetings of the Royal Society, and, even more proudly, their invitations to visit the Royal Institution itself in Piccadilly, the so-called "workshop" of the Royal Society, where Davy, Faraday, and others actually achieved some of their greatest discoveries.

Educator Emma Willard, interested both in philanthropy and pedagogy, survived an encounter with social reformer Robert Owen and a visit with the poet Coleridge; had tea with the saintly Quakeress Elizabeth Fry, who served the female convicts of Newgate prison; and on leaving Britain regretted that she had been unable to tackle Lord Brougham on "the subject of public schools for females."[6] With great industry the self-styled "practical tourist," inventor Zachariah Allen, pursued "the useful arts" everywhere in Britain, touring cotton mills, visiting farms, exploring coal mines, and observing new methods of road construction.

Charles Stewart and Alexander MacKenzie, both naval officers at the time of their British sojourns in the thirties, produced books notable for detailed, lively delineations of British life in that period. Stewart, introduced at Court to King William by the American minister and entertained in upper-class homes in both Scotland and England, left a unique record of a long-vanished way of life. MacKenzie, less the guest and more the tourist, possessed a curiosity and energy leading to escapades like his private tour—with a young British officer friend—of the exotic Pavilion at Brighton, which was built by the Prince Regent (later George IV) and at the time of MacKenzie's visit was the summer residence of King William and Queen Adelaide.

The patrician, well-connected George Ticknor raced about, armed with letters of introduction to Britain's great and near-great, collecting celebrities—even the elusive Lord Byron—as if they were butterflies. William Henry Seward, future prominent politician and secretary of state in Lincoln's wartime cabinet, eagerly studied proceedings in the House of Commons and himself got to see the old "sailor king" by lying in wait one day for the royal carriage. So startled was Seward at the monarch's sudden appearance that he stood bolt upright in his own hired hack to stare, bowed low with embarrassment when he himself was noticed, and was then astonished to see King William, "not to be outdone in courtesy," stand and bow "equally profoundly to me."[7]

The noted surgeon, Dr. William Gibson, who for over thirty years occupied a chair in surgery at the University of Pennsylvania and who had actually been on the scene at the Battle of Waterloo, returned to Britain in 1839 to revisit scenes of his youth where he had studied medicine at Edinburgh and London. Now he was kindly received by the top medical men of both cities, who opened to him the doors of all the leading hospitals to observe surgical techniques and courses of treatment. Curious, lively, and even-tempered, Gibson was a good traveler, and in his book he was a fine reporter of the social scene as well as of his professional observations.[8]

Among the many clergymen touring in that period was the Unitarian Orville Dewey, a friend of Emerson and one who reveled in Britain's "antiquity," thus anticipating the rest of his countrymen by several decades. The Reverend Heman Humphrey, president of Amherst College, together with his colleague John Codman, combined a tour of Britain with their attendance at a London conference designed to establish a union between the dissenting faiths in the "old country" and the Congregational and Presbyterian churches of America. Their combined Puritan consciences enabled them one Sunday, they proudly re-corded, to make the proper choice against heading for Windsor to catch sight of King William at his prayers and instead attend church at one of the dissenting chapels. Seizing another opportunity to strike a blow at the established Church of England, a favorite pastime of Yankee clergymen in this period, Humphrey told his readers how the evangelical churches, called "chapels," were once actually denied steeples and bells. "The American traveler cannot think of it without his blood moving quicker in his veins," thundered Parson Humphrey. "We claim the *liberty* of attaching them to our *barns* even, if we please!"[9]

The Reverend Calvin Colton, sent to Britain in 1831 as correspondent for the *New York Observer,* spent four years traveling widely, surviving one of the earliest train wrecks, sniping at the monarchy and aristocracy, ranting at the "abuses and evils" of the established Church, and devoting a long chapter to the British system of "feeing," or tipping, entitled the "Extortion of Menials." Even at Westminster Abbey a fee was extracted from the visitor. "The only place in Great Britain worthy of a stranger's attention, that is free to all," grumped Parson Colton, "is the British Museum," and even there one had to pay for "the custody of one's umbrella which can never be dispensed with six months of the year."[10]

The Methodist minister Wilbur Fisk, first president of Wesleyan University, toured Britain in 1838, with a close eye on the penny and with warnings to future travelers against certain establishments to be avoided such as the Ship Hotel at Dover. Focusing on the evils of Catholicism in Ireland, he perspicaciously perceived "the fruits of Romanism" in the wretched beggars of Drogheda and deplored the mere 1,500 Protestants in a town of 20,000 souls. Fisk also found food for thought in the burgeoning industrialism he surveyed in the Birming-ham region.[11]

For some reason in these early decades it was primarily these prim, puritanical preachers who did all the carping and complaining. In later decades this carping was to be developed into an art form by querulous female tourists from America. The Reverend Nathaniel Wheaton, an Episcopalian, and rector of Hartford's Christ Church, on the other hand, thoroughly enjoyed his contacts with the Church of England clergy, reveled in attendance at London's famed churches, and mightily appreciated his brief but kindly reception by the Archbishop of

Canterbury at Lambeth Palace. He saved his fire for "the Duke of W——"
[Wellington] who passed by him in his carriage. "Here was vice, without doubt,"
grumbled Wheaton of the war hero who would be so admired in his old age by
visiting Yankees twenty years later. "The reception of Lord Nelson, when he
attempted to introduce the profligate Lady Hamilton into society," declared
Wheaton, "ought to have assured the victor of W——[Waterloo], that there are
moral delinquencies which will not be overlooked by the community."[12]

Authors Washington Irving and James Fenimore Cooper traveled in and
commented on Britain in these years. The former wrote romantically, almost
reverentially, while, in contrast, Cooper—convinced that "the English do not like
the Americans"—addressed himself more to an invidious comparison of the
relative merits of the two nations.[13] Other figures, less well known today, who
also undoubtedly had much to do with stimulating their countrymen both to
travel and write, were Andrew Bigelow and Nathaniel Carter in the twenties and
Henry McLellan and Fanny Hall in the thirties.

Last but not least, one of the most popular and prolific of all these American
correspondents in the early decades was Nathaniel Parker Willis. Over a five-
year period starting in 1831 Willis, one of three editors of the *New York Mirror*
and *Ladies Literary Gazette,* contributed 139 letters or travel essays that appeared
in 500 newspapers throughout America and were later collected and published
in book form.[14] Full of vitality, intelligent, cheerful, and likeable, Willis was a
first-rate journalist with an eye for detail, the ability to draw people out, and a
writing style that appealed to a broad spectrum of the public. Although Willis
may well have been that "servile American" dispensing "coffeehouse gossip,"
referred to by Margaret Fuller, he probably did more to inspire Americans to
travel in Britain than other more notable authors. Bayard Taylor himself was
first motivated to travel, he recalled later, "when [as] a boy of ten I read Willis's
Pencillings By The Way as they appeared from week to week in the country
newspaper."[15]

Coming to Great Britain primarily to learn, as they did in the early decades of
the nineteenth century, most Americans concentrated their sights on
phenomena of Britain's present, "the age of utility and invention," just as
Hezekiah Wright, fresh out of Harvard and full of advice for humanity, advised
them to do about 1837. It would be all too easy for Americans to wrap themselves
in romantic notions stemming from their reading of English literature, Wright
thought, and thus feed themselves on "a more exciting aliment in the history of
the past."[16] This he warned against.

> Whether as a nation our example shall shine gloriously upon the pages of
> history, or whether our Experiment shall be recorded but as a beaconlight to
> warn the world, the dim ages of futurity will display. We will not anticipate:
> our business is with the present. If we shine, it must be by pursuing those Arts
> and Sciences (cradled in the lap of old Europe, and fostered upon her
> maternal bosom), which by elevating the moral tone and condition of man, are
> alone worthy of his intellectual endowments.[17]

Young Wright's serious, worshipful tone anticipates that of Emerson, who, in
his *English Traits* of 1856, advised readers that in Britain "we are met by a

civilization already settled and overpowering. The culture of the day, the thoughts and aims of men, are English thoughts and aims."[18] Wright had one further word of advice for prospective American sojourners in the Old World. The American arrives, he observed, prepared "to gaze about . . . on the 'foreign slaves' with a kind of 'Sum Romanus Civis' expression. This feeling is usually rather an ephemeral plant. . . . We find the mass of people scarcely acquainted with our national existence; or, if they are aware that there is such a country as the United States of America, usually unenlightened as to whether our color be black or white." For the proud American, Wright concluded, this experience was well "calculated to stifle in the bud the passion of vanity."[19]

2

Voyage

"Now comes a splendid place to skip—the ocean voyage," steel magnate Andrew Carnegie wrote in 1881, starting an account of a summer holiday trip to Britain. "Everybody writes that up on the first trip." By then a veteran of twenty-odd crossings of the Atlantic, Carnegie thought no more of it, he said, than of a rail trip from New York to Chicago, adding that he had no intention of boring his readers with details of either.[1]

For most nineteenth-century Americans, however, their trip abroad was a once-in-a-lifetime experience for which the 3,000-mile sea voyage constituted the prelude not to be omitted from their written account. Confinement aboard ship, moreover, offered ample time for journal writing, and many travelers began their labors at once. "While I am scribbling," wrote Nathaniel Wheaton aboard the packet *Cortes,* one afternoon in 1829, "one of my fellow passengers is practising the gamut with a flageolet, the other is dozing over a review, and altogether we exhibit a very edifying spectacle of idleness and ennui."[2] The captain of the *Plymouth Rock* entered the cabin, wrote James Clarke in 1849, "to find us sitting at the table all at work on our journals and remarked, 'I should like to see all these journals published!' " The writers were not quite sure whether this was meant as a compliment or intended as sarcasm.[3]

Hundreds of detailed descriptions of these trans-Atlantic voyages provide us today with an informal maritime history of the previous century, beginning with the sleek sailing packets of the early decades and ending with great steamers so immense and so luxurious that passengers could almost ignore the sea altogether.

In 1818 regularly-scheduled sailing packets took over the New York-Liverpool run. These were well-built ships of about 500 tons, with quarters for the crew in the forecastle, berths for immigrants amidships, and luxurious accommodations for cabin passengers. Fares for the passengers were thirty guineas or about $154 for the voyage over, and thirty-five guineas or about $164 for the longer return trip in the face of prevailing westerly winds. Crossing time ranged anywhere from an optimum twenty-four days to six weeks or longer, depending on vagaries of wind and weather.[4]

Youthful George Putnam crossed the Atlantic in 1836 in nineteen days—very good time indeed.[5] Blessed with favorable winds and with vast amounts of canvas spread—"tier after tier, four or five tiers high, reaching up to a dizzy height"— the *Orpheus,* with the Reverend Robert Breckinridge aboard in 1836, actually exceeded ten miles an hour at times, and thus on the twentieth day out of New York was at the mouth of St. George's Channel heading up to Liverpool. Ships could lay becalmed for days, however, during which time passengers fretted away the hours—some of the hardier ones taking brief dips—or the captain might order the jolly boat launched for a bit of fishing.[6]

Voyagers were fond of describing their elegant accommodations aboard packets that bore proud names like the *George Washington,* the *New England,* the *Washington Irving,* the *Corinthian,* the *Daniel Webster,* and the *Silas Richards.* Zachariah Allen depicted a saloon sixty to seventy feet long, paneled in varnished mahogany, with white marble columns topped with gilded capitals framing the latticed doors of the staterooms, seven on each side. Huge mirrors at each end of the saloon provided seemingly endless vistas and also reflected the glittering brass fixtures. A separate cabin for ladies on some of these ships provided sofas, along with a piano and other musical instruments for passing time.[7] The *New England* boasted a library and the luxury of a real bathroom; otherwise, ablutions were performed out of the washbowl in one's stateroom. In the case of the men, a cold, saltwater shower could be had on deck by arrangement, according to the Reverend James Clarke, who thus indulged himself aboard the *Plymouth Rock* one morning after coming on deck in his "bathing clothes" and asking the seamen "to throw some buckets of salt water over me."[8] If American river steamboats were termed *floating palaces,* concluded Allen, "these American ships may be called floating hotels."[9] Liverpudlians, said Fanny

The famed Boston packet ship the *Daniel Webster,* as depicted in the *Illustrated London News. Illustrated London News,* January 18, 1851, p. 33. *Courtesy the Library of Congress.*

Hall, in 1836, told her that these packets were "decidedly among the 'lions' of Liverpool and great numbers of people go to see them as a matter of curiosity."[10]

Provender for first-class cabin passengers matched the luxury of their quarters. "Eating makes the greatest item in the daily business," observed Jacob Green in 1828, going on to describe "an inexhaustible larder supplied with almost everything. . .all kinds of poultry, even peacocks to eat; young pigs, fresh veal, and divers other kinds of meats; wines, including the best Madeira, champagne, and all other choice French liquors, porter, ale, cider, etc. After the ordinary dinner every day we have oranges and apples, raisins, figs, filberts, almonds, and other dried fruits."[11] A St. Andrew's Day feast prepared for some Scottish passengers on one vessel included "real turtle soup, fine salmon preserved as if just caught, a rich cake made on board. . .also fine desserts, puddings tarts, preserves, fruits and nuts. . .choice red and white wines, and champagne."[12]

Hosts at these well-appointed and overloaded tables were tough, urbane Yankee sea captains, equally able to preside over the conversation as to deal with their brutish, hard-driven seamen who often stumbled on board far gone in drink—ready to "prove each other's pugilistic attainments," as one passenger put it—and sometimes ended up lashed to the rigging or put in irons until the ship was at sea and they had simmered down.[13] One of these captains, a perfect gentleman at the dinner table, was known for his habit of smoking out stowaways by burning sulfur under the closed hatch, with the crew standing by to daub them with tar as they emerged like "stifled bees" from their hiding places.[14] One youthful stowaway was allowed to work his passage back home aboard Alexander MacKenzie's vessel in the thirties. MacKenzie described him as "a white-headed ragamuffin" in an old cut-off coat, who drudged away the days washing dishes, creeping in and out of the longboat to milk the cow. The only time MacKenzie saw the boy smile was on his first glimpse of Portsmouth.[15]

Fresh meat, milk, eggs, and poultry were provided by animals housed on deck, often in the longboat with a jolly-boat inverted over their heads for a shed. Passengers thus awoke each morning to comfortable barnyard sounds, the crowing of cocks, the cackling of geese, to say nothing of the sheep and the cow. The passengers on one ship headed for home were disturbed all the way over by a rooster which persisted in "crowing by Liverpool time," recalled a voyager, and which "thus broke us of our night's rest."[16] Occasionally, one of these beasts got loose, as did a pig aboard John Griscom's vessel in 1818, which in panic ran over the side. "The poor animal continued swimming in the tossing waves as long as we could see him," wrote Griscom.[17]

Voyagers in these days often referred to their ships as a miniature world and sometimes itemized their fellow passengers as did Calvin Colton aboard the *Silas Richards* in 1830. His shipmates included a Philadelphia merchant and his family; an English lady going to visit her family; the captain's wife; a Scottish merchant; a "sprig of the English nobility"; a commercial traveler from Bristol; a "hypochondriac" who never left his cabin; "a cross-eyed flute player from London who occasionally entertained us"; and "some other persons quite agreeable but not particularly important enough to be specified."[18]

Traveling in the steerage of these outward-bound vessels were usually some forty-odd disenchanted, homesick, or desperately ill emigrants trying to get back home. "I were a happy man in England, and I were an unhappy man in America," declared a Yorkshireman.[19] Often they were tubercular Irishmen wanting to die at home, like the tall, gaunt man "far gone with consumption, friendless, hoping once more the see his native land and those he had left behind," who boarded Colton's vessel in New York. Twelve days out the ship's bell summoned all on board to his funeral. Colton never forgot that burial at sea and the sound of the corpse plunging into the deep. "Four years since, it even now rings in my ears . . . I cannot cease to hear it. To be buried in the ocean! Nature shrinks though religion may whisper 'tis all the same."[20]

Voyagers on these packets passed their time pacing the deck, in conversation, reading and writing in the cabin, and playing endless games of chess and backgammon. A special amusement through most of the century was a mock court "where offences against the dignity of the ship were tried,"—as Ballard described it in 1815—"and the culprits fined in sundry bottles of wine."[21] Considerable amounts of spirits were consumed on these voyages, according to the Reverend Robert Breckinridge, who declared, "I never saw more steady drinking amongst respectable people. There are four kinds of wine, and nearly as many liquors constantly before us."[22] Another amusement was the production of little shipboard newspapers sometimes read aloud after dinner. Fanny Hall praised "the nautical wit" of the *Roscoe Herald* aboard the packet *Roscoe* in 1836.[23]

Sorting the trans-Atlantic mail, to assist the captain in his role as postmaster, also helped to pass time. Seven thousand pieces were brought on board one ship at the last minute in New York, in rawhide bags, carried in wagons rushing up to the dock. William Henry Seward, sorting mail in 1833, found that by "far the largest portion had very circumlocutory addresses for parishes in Ireland."[24] Another passenger took down some of these addresses: "Mitchelltown, Ireland, Andy O'Brien with speed"; "To Widow Connors Fox-Fork Barusha P. Offis. Tipperaree"; "To the care of Mr. John Clark, Cow Bag, London derry, Ireland."[25] One mail sorter was shocked to see some of his companions take to reading letters that "accidently" came open.[26]

Another pastime was watching the heaving of the log, by which the speed of the ship was ascertained. Scientist Jacob Green explained, "[I]t is done every two hours at the ringing of the bell. . . . A triangular piece of wood, loaded with lead on one side is attached by its three corners to a cord of known length; a sand glass which discharges itself in a given time is then prepared; the triangular piece of wood, or log, is thrown into the water, while the ship is under way, and sinking below the surface, in the direction of its loaded side, remains nearly stationary, and presents sufficient resistance to unwind a certain length of the cord, which is on a reel, in the time marked by the glass."[27]

Maritime phenomena provided hours of enjoyment for those new to the sea, such as the strange phosphorescence sometimes seen in the fog at night off Newfoundland, or groups of whales that came spouting and sporting alongside sometimes for up to two hours at a stretch. Watching porpoises gamboling, the Reverend Nathaniel Wheaton of Hartford observed how half a dozen of them would place themselves under the ship's bow, then shoot away "with the velocity of arrows and join us in another quarter."[28] Professor Cornelius Felton, future president of Harvard, read aloud to his captain the passage from *A Midsummer Night's Dream* about a mermaid riding a dolphin's back. " 'Humbug!' snorted that old salt. " 'The dolphin's back is sharp as a razor, and no mermaid could possibly ride the beast unless she saddled him first!' "[29]

Besides the confinement and inevitable boredom of shipboard life, there were real discomforts and genuine perils to face. These early voyagers aboard the packets made less of seasickness than did their descendants aboard the steamers, for some reason, confining their treatment of the subject to a few brief comments like Ballard's "I suffered more than any other from seasickness, the horrid disagreeable sensations of which I think I shall ever remember. In four days, however, I was perfectly hearty and well."[30] Zachariah Allen said merely that after weeks of "disheartening malady," and at last tired of his narrow berth, "hemmed in by boards as if in a wooden trough," he dragged himself up on deck where he promptly recovered.[31]

The awesome perils of the deep were well known to all travelers, the fates of maritime disasters having become legend through detailed newspaper reports and even prints. Many a good ship never made port, and as late as 1886 Dr. Oliver Wendell Holmes, nearly eighty years old and nervous as a cat, was told by his captain that the best way for a fearful voyager to sail was "under opiates until he wakes up in the harbor." Rejecting this course, the old man sat up each night, nursing his chronic asthma and contemplating the lifeboats with dreadful speculation. "No man," he wrote, "can find himself abroad over the abysses, the floor of which is paved with the bones of the shrieking myriads whom the waves have swallowed up, without some thought of the dread possibilities hanging over his head."[32] His fears were shared by many throughout the century.

The five dangers of the Atlantic crossing were fog, icebergs, fire, storms, and mechanical failure. Of these five, fog was perhaps the most dreaded. Icebergs could be watched for and avoided; fires could be put out or got under control; storms could be weathered; and repairs could be made even at sea. But the fog was simply there, and in its soft, silent gray depths lurked other blindly-groping ships, plunging icebergs, and rockbound coasts capable of pounding a ship to pieces. All these ingredients for tragedy were amply supplied by the northerly route taken—the shortest distance between the two continents—which involved heading up the Canadian coast, skirting the southeastern tip of Newfoundland, past the dreaded rocks of Cape Race, and then traversing the frequently fog-shrouded Grand Banks region dotted with small fishing vessels and in summer with icebergs drifting down from the north. Before the days of fog "whistles" or horns, the ship's bell was rung at regular intervals, sounding like the knell of death to frightened landlubbers, to warn other ships. Icebergs looming out of the fog, as Benjamin Silliman wrote in 1805, appeared like great, white, ruined palaces of marble with many jagged edges capable of piercing the hull of a wooden vessel on contact or joining forces with another iceberg to crush a ship. Almost half a century later, crossing to see the Great Exhibition, Silliman would find himself remembering the terrors of that night long ago, "spent among these floating masses," in a sailing ship.[33]

This same youthful voyager and his shipmates on that crossing aboard the ship *Ontario,* early in the century, were at first amused by a storm as they huddled

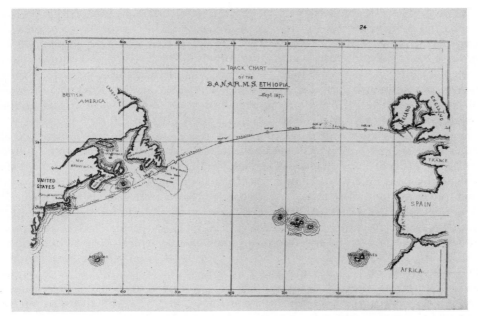

Typical northerly route across the Atlantic. Drawing by Augustus Hoppin. *Courtesy the Library of Congress.*

grotesquely on the floor of the cabin trying to eat, bracing each other foot to foot, plates between knees, one holding the wine decanter, others supporting a gravy bowl or soup bowl. As the storm increased in violence, persisting into the second day, the novelty waned as they found themselved flung from one side of the cabin to the other. Suddenly the helmsman was thrown from his station, and the rudderless ship "lurched," as the sailors called it, or "fell into the trough of the sea," Silliman wrote. Only desperate action at the helm by a sweating, cursing captain just roused from sleep put her before the wind and righted her again. Silliman had "no particular dread of the water," he maintained, but he was "astonished that any machine, constructed of such frail materials as those of a ship, could withstand such shocks as those we received every moment from the waves, and which caused every timber to tremble."[34]

Fear of fire that could burn a wooden ship to the waterline was another source of anxiety. Voyagers remembered the fate of the *Poland,* struck by lightning that set fire to the bales of cotton in her hold. On one voyage a sadistic cabin boy set fire to the ship's cat; and as it raced about the deck in its agony, passengers and crew were more frightened of the possibility of fire than moved by pity for the poor beast, which the sailors finally chased over the side.[35]

Mechanical breakdowns, such as the loss of a rudder, could leave a helpless ship to founder in high seas or be driven to its doom against rocky shores. Nathaniel Wheaton's return voyage in 1824 stretched over seven weeks as Captain Sprague and his valiant crew struggled to keep their ship afloat in never-ending rough weather, managing somehow to jury-rig a makeshift rudder to replace one smashed in a storm. Wheaton pitched in as ship's surgeon, setting sailors' ribs, patching skulls laid open to the bone, and lancing "internal infusions of blood," all suffered "in the dangerous business" of that awful voyage. Little wonder that one Sunday he chose to read from the 107th Psalm.[36]

Voyagers who survived such experiences at sea saw considerable evidence of other ships that had not. Pieces of wreckage and derelict hulls often were spotted from the safety of their own decks and chilled the heart. "This morning the mate saw a long-boat, filled with water, sweeping over the waves. Where is the crew that once manned this boat?" a frightened voyager asked in his journal.[37] Another spied the wreck of a schooner "consisting of little more than the keel and the ribs from which the planks were already stripped."[38] George Catlin, aboard the *Roscius* in 1839—taking his paintings and American Indian artifacts to London for exhibition—reported the rescue of twenty-eight men from a jolly-boat, their only possession a keg of rum which Captain Collins promptly tossed overboard saying, " 'This you will not want now, my boys.' " The rescued captain fell to weeping over his dinner as he recalled how he had forgotten his dog tied to the mast when they abandoned ship. " 'My God,' he moaned, 'I never thought of poor Pompey.' " They had made eighteen voyages together, and Pompey always " 'scented land before anyone else,' " he said.[39]

Ever at risk were the lives of the seamen, and many a poor sailor aloft in the rigging in foul weather hurtled to his death on the deck or in the cruel sea. "It being very dark, there was no chance to save him," observed George Rapelje, matter-of-factly, concerning one such incident.[40] Cornelius Felton described what happened aboard the *Daniel Webster* when a rescue was attempted under such circumstances. A first boat with four men aboard was lost almost immediately, and only after two hours did a second boat of four would-be rescuers manage to return, empty-handed, to the ship. "I need not say that this spectacle . . . was the most terrible ever witnessed by me," wrote Felton.[41]

On one of his voyages Samuel Prime endured a similar experience. It was near midnight when he heard "the agonized cries of a seaman" and came on deck, where he watched the frantic efforts to launch a boat to try to rescue the man. "Never shall I forget the look of the Mate as he screamed, 'Give me a knife—a KNIFE!' and taking one from a sailor he passed it through the ropes. 'In men, in'—and four stout fellows leaped in with him, and down it went upon the ocean, a little shell of a thing, sent forth to seek and to save that which was lost. . . . The little boat was soon out of sight," observed Prime. But it was all in vain. Finally,

a dark spot rose on the wave: the flash of dripping oars in the moonlight met the eye, and we knew they were coming. The mate was soon seen standing at the helm. . . . We sent out the cry, "All well?" Our hearts stood still for the answer—a half-spoken "No" murmered [sic] along the waters, and we knew the brave fellow was among the dead. The following morning we docked at Portsmouth and were taken off in a small boat and set ashore in a pouring rain. A dreary and dismal time we had.[42]

The loss of a sense of motion, or of covering distance, bothered some voyagers. "I lay down and rose up in the same place," complained the Reverend Humphrey. "It was the same great circle, and the same great vault over our heads which I left the night before. I seemed to myself . . . no longer in time but in eternity."[43] Observed another traveler, "We seem to be sailing in a deep, circular basin with its broad rim surrounding us, though we are never able to reach its border. . . . Perhaps others have experienced the same."[44]

About the time the travelers despaired of ever seeing land again and were starting to feel "exiled completely from the rest of mankind"—as Silliman put it—"confined to a floating prison," the first signs of their reentry into the world of men began to appear.[45] First was a change in the color of the sea from the deep blue, indicative of great depth, to green, meaning that they were "in soundings" and nearing land; and then came blessed glimpses of the Irish coast. Not infrequently the ships were hailed, as was Jacob Green's, by "cunning sons of Erin" lurking aboard tiny fishing boats in the mouth of St. George's Channel, seeking to exchange a few fresh cod and "pratees" for rum, pork, bread, and tobacco. " 'Your honors won't forget the backey,' they called out, and we gave them two or three pieces from our stores."[46]

From there it was on past the Old Head of Kinsale on the left, scene of the wreck of the *Albion* in 1822—when hundreds of helpless voyagers were dashed to their deaths, within sight of land, against those pitiless rocks. Jacob Green thought of his old friend, Professor Fisher of Yale, as did Samuel Goodrich, who eulogized the twenty-eight-year-old mathematics scholar who perished there. Fisher was last seen in his berth calmly studying, with the aid of a small compass in his hand, the course of his vessel, Goodrich informed his readers. A moment after he was never seen again as the ship struck rock. "The struggles of the sufferers, clinging to ropes, yards, and points of rocks, in the very sight of persons on shore were fearful and rendered the event one of the most agonizing on record."[47]

On up through the Channel, then right round Holyhead, and soon "the little pilot boat, with its single tapering mast, and its three queer-looking sails, all set, coming right off the shore, upon our beam, in utter contempt of wind and waves, hove into view," recalled Robert Breckinridge. He observed that the pilot boat came around under the stern, "saluted the captain by name and passed up the lee side upon which was cast off a little dark-looking boat, which danced on the waves like a nutshell; our pilot was in it, and in five minutes he stood on our quarter deck, a short, broad, tough-looking little fellow," whose job it was to direct the final hours of careful navigation along the cliffs of the Welsh coast and over the treacherous shoals into the great harbor of Liverpool.[48] The sturdy presence of these pilots brought assurance of a safe arrival, along with news of recent events and sometimes fresh newspapers, all three symbolizing the end of another voyage.

The mighty stone docks and basins of the port of Liverpool struck American travelers with awe, so different were they from the wooden, unsubstantial docks and wharves of American ports. "What docks are these my countrymen!" enthused young George Putnam in 1836. "Substantial, spacious, well covered and well paved. What a contrast to those in New York! But hush! I will not abuse

my home on my first day in Europe."[49] These docks were, according to Calvin
Colton, "stupendous works of solid masonry," occupying in these earlier years of
the century about 111 acres, appearing as firm as the natural rocky base of the
hills. Since the swift tide of the Mersey varied by some twenty-five feet, the
problem was to maneuver vessels in and out of the great gates of the docks
during the brief hours of high tide. The quays, Colton wrote, "afford pleasant
promenades and are often thronged with multitudes of well-dressed people,
especially when anything extraordinary is to be seen on the river."[50]

The most extraordinary thing to be seen on the river Mersey at the time of
Benjamin Silliman's landing in 1805 was a large "Guinea ship," a slaver, into
whose awful depths he descended to examine "the cells where human beings are
confined under circumstances which equally disgust decency and shock humanity. . . . *Our* country, so nobly jealous of its own liberties, stands disgraced in the
eyes of mankind and condemned at the bar of heaven, for being at once active in
carrying on this monstrous traffic, and prompt to receive every cargo of
imported Africans. I did not come to England to see Guinea ships because there
were none in America," Silliman admitted, "but accident had never thrown one
in my way before. Liverpool is *deep, very deep* in the guilt of the slave trade. It is
now pursued with more eagerness than ever, and multitudes are, at this
moment, rioting on the wealth which has been gained by the stripes, the groans,
the tears, and the blood of Africans. There will be a day," he warned, "when
these things shall be told in heaven!"[51]

"We reel as if intoxicated with wine," groaned John Griscom after disembark-
ing, expressing the sensation that overcame many of his countrymen all through
the century as their feet touched solid ground after weeks at sea.[52]

Passing through customs was even then a process about which few travelers
had much good to say. In 1823 Nathaniel Wheaton chose to pass over "the
vexations and delays of the Custom-house, and the rapacity of drunken under-
lings, which every passenger has experienced, and every journalist described."
New arrivals apparently had the choice of submitting to a scrupulous examination of their luggage, with long waits involved, or of offering "a husher" or
"douceur" to the examining official and being passed through quickly.[53]

Passports as such seem not to have been required in the century's early
decades, but at moments of national crisis, during the Napoleonic wars, for
example, both Silliman and Ballard mention having to register at the Alien
Office in London. Letters of credit on British banks provided a source of cash
much in the manner of the traveler's check of today, while the other essential for
visiting Americans consisted of letters of introduction from American professional men to their British counterparts that led to meetings with the leading
scientists, scholars, artists, and authors of the day. Silliman was at first embarrassed to deliver his letters of introduction, feeling that he was "imposing on
strangers an obligation to be civil to me," but finally he hired a coach and went all
over London to complete the business in a single day.[54] The result, as all readers
of his journal know, was that he met many of Britain's brightest and best during
his stay in their country. He must have realized the value of such letters, for
twenty-seven years later it was just such letters from "Professor Silliman of Yale
College" that opened so many doors for his countryman, Charles Stewart.[55]

**The "Rows" at Chester—small booths and shops "not bigger than a nutshell," accord-
ing to Orville Dewey.** *Illustrated London News,* **October 9, 1869, p. 352.** *Courtesy the
Library of Congress.*

Just south of Liverpool lies the ancient town of Chester—once a Roman camp,
and even today still surrounded by its fine Roman-medieval wall providing a
splendid promenade around the ancient city. For Americans all through the
nineteenth century, a brief sojourn at Chester was often their first objective after
landing at Liverpool. The Reverend Orville Dewey's first taste of "antiquity in
every structure and stone" struck him "with wonder and delight," and then he
proceeded to describe the town's famous "Rows," the double tiers of shops and
raised footways under cover, dating back to the fourteenth century. "The streets
are channelled out of the freestone foundation rock. This makes the basement
story, used mostly for shops. The first story above this retreats back from the
street, leaving a planked sidewalk, of six to eight feet wide, while the second story
again comes forward to the line of the first, thus making a covered walk over the
whole town. These little recesses," observed Dewey, "are full of queer-looking
little booths or shops, not bigger than a nutshell. The town itself looks as if it
were made for 'hide and go seek' or something worse—full of corners and
crannies, of a most suspicious appearance—full of narrow passages and blind
alleys leading away into darkness and obscurity."[56]

Dewey then made the four-mile trip out to Eaton Hall—throughout the
century the Yankee visitor's first exposure to ducal splendor. Today all but
demolished, in the previous century it was a luxurious retreat that was constantly

being rebuilt. An early reference to it is by Ballard, who walked out one day in 1815. "I cannot do justice to the description of this fairy structure," he wrote. "It is but finished. The house is of the gothic order and finished both interior and exterior in a superb manner. The furniture corresponds to the buildings. . . . If the ancient buildings, the ruins of which still remain visible," he continued, "were at their erection as truly beautiful as Eaton House, one must sincerely deplore that barbarism which tempted the destruction of these ornaments to Britain."[57]

Eaton Hall's proprietors maintained a guest album, in which Nathaniel Carter on his 1825 visit was pleased to observe that "the United States furnished quite a list for one day," as he added his name below those of "a party of ladies from Boston." He informed his readers that the structure had cost two million dollars, with another two million spent on the furnishings, and still the owner had an income of $600,000 a year. "Such," moralized Carter, "is the inequality of wealth in this country, between the thousands of beggars who ask an obolus [small coin] and the noblemen, wallowing in luxury. Happy, twice happy is our Republic which yet knows not. . .any of these extremities."[58]

The various accounts by Americans viewing Eaton Hall trace its development from what must have been a charming expression of the early Gothic Revival into what appears, oh a postcard pasted in Lily Rust's handwritten journal of 1903, to be something resembling American "City Hall Grandiose" of the gay nineties.[59] There are frequent references to the "rage for building" of the various owners as well as to their steadily-rising fortunes over the years, which may explain this architectural evolution.

In the 1830s Charles Stewart had found "a structure of light free-stone, in the richest style of the florid Gothic, presenting a facade of 450 feet, exclusive of a long range of offices, coach-houses, and stabling, on a line with the main building, adorned with tracery and sculptured heraldic emblems, and surmounted by numerous pinnacles, clustered turrets and embattled towers."[60] The Reverend Wilbur Fisk and his wife, during their visit, were also charmed by their glimpse of the owner himself, "the Marquis of Westminster," and even more by the marchioness just leaving for "an airing in her phaeton drawn by two elegant ponies" driving herself "in the graceful and horsemanlike style as became an English marchioness," with her footman perched behind "much at his ease." Mrs. Fisk was, moreover, presented "with a choice bouquet and a specimen of fruit" upon their departure, he bragged.[61]

Jacob Green was altogether overwhelmed by the grandeur of "this residence of the nobility," as well as by the extensive grounds "in a high state of culture— every part of it seemed to have been beaten or rolled, and continually dressed so as to present an even and smooth surface" with hundreds of freely roaming deer to complete the picture of pastoral perfection. He was less impressed by the "noisy chatter of a thousand rooks, much prized by the nobility, which an American farmer would shoot off his grounds as a parcel of worthless crows which," snorted Green, "they very much resemble!"[62]

3

Travelers with a Purpose

Leaving Liverpool, Chester, and Eaton Hall behind to set out for their various destinations, American travelers in the first three decades of the nineteenth century embarked upon a mode of travel that was "perfectly novel" to them and to other foreigners as well because of its speed, efficiency, and comfort. "There is nothing in the world of the same kind equal to the English stagecoach system," declared Calvin Colton in 1831, "if that may be called system which is the accidental result of the enterprise of thousands of individuals, each of whom is opposed to all the rest in the way of competition."[1]

Setting out for London in the early thirties, Alexander MacKenzie studied the coach then loading and climbed aboard himself. He was enchanted with "the neat, graceful form of the pretty toy, the mettled and important air of the shiny and well-groomed horses, the high polish of the harness, and admirable order and neatness of the whole affair."[2] These coaches, some of which transported the Royal Mail as well as passengers, carried four travelers within and twelve up on top, the latter seats being considerably cheaper but much preferred in good weather. Considered the best place of all was that seat beside the driver. Behind the driver sat four more, with another four on the third seat, and one or two next the guard on a rear seat just over the "boot" or storage box for luggage. Additional luggage and packages were stowed in a boot under the driver's seat.

MacKenzie was equally impressed by

the stately and consequential air of the portly and well-muffled coachman as he ascended to the box with the mien of a monarch seating himself on his throne. . . . When, however, the guard mounting behind, called the characteristic "All right!" and the stable boys who held the horses had abandoned them to their impatience, the whip cracked, the wheels began to spin round and the pavements to rattle, while the veils of the fair occupants of the top of the coach streamed out from the rapid motion, and the whole presented an array of excited and happy faces,

then, thought MacKenzie, the scene was "one of the most spirited and striking it was possible to behold."[3]

"We sped onward," he wrote, concerning a later journey, "at a tearing rate over hill and valley. The road was as smooth as if laid with rails and nothing impeded the rocket-like rapidity of our course. Indeed, if my memory does not mislead me, *The Rocket* was the ambitious yet not ill-worn name of our con-

43

Giving them a Start.

Coach leaving an innyard with the hostler and stableboy "giving them a start." *The English Illustrated Magazine*, **vol. V, 1887–88, p. 233.** *Courtesy the Library of Congress.*

veyance."[4] Other names, all beautifully painted, as on a ship, were recorded by other travelers: *Magnet, Venture, Perseverance, Wonder, Excelsior, Dart,* and *Comet.* At all periods of the nineteenth century Americans marvelled at the quality of the English roads—hard, smooth, well-maintained gravel surfaces in the first two decades, and, after 1820, macadam highways.

Average speed of the coaches ranged from seven to ten miles per hour, including the fifteen-minute stops, about every eight to ten miles on main roads and twelve to fifteen on others, for refreshment and changing horses. "Frequenters of the bar-room and idle fellows" would gather around at these stops, wrote Nathaniel Wheaton, just like "a posse of long-legged Jonathans gathering about a stage at a tavern in America." He recalled one hasty stop at an inn for a breakfast consumed "amidst a great confusion of cloaks, umbrellas, fowling pieces, and pointers. Such cutting and slashing a huge round of beef, and swearing, and blowing of fingers, and bawling for waiters and clamours of the coachman—'Coach ready!' and twanging of horns! Indeed the breakfast of such a coach party as ours was no very orderly matter."[5]

Another feature of coach travel, noted by Joshua White, was the children who ran alongside at slow places in the road, holding up little bouquets attached to sticks, which they thrust in at the windows until rewarded with pennies. Some were able to chase the coach as far as a mile.[6]

On the shorter runs, the coaches continued on through the night, and there are numerous anecdotes concerning these nocturnal journeys. Joseph Ballard watched a young woman exchange her bonnet for a nightcap and then compose herself for sleep—"quite an interesting picture."[7] Another traveling Yankee was quite content to support the young, convalescent soldier, "home from India," who clutched at him and groaned in his sleep.[8] One old gentleman amused the others by calling in his sleep for his dogs "Sweetheart" and "Tray."[9] Occasionally an American resented what seemed to him the intrusion of a sportsman loaded down "with game bags and guns . . . in an ostentatious display of the wonders he had performed."[10] Altogether, such complaints are rare, and most of the travelers, like Jacob Green, found the company in these English coaches "vastly more communicative and agreeable than it is in America—a circumstance directly the reverse of what I had been led to expect."[11]

"These English coachmen form a class by themselves," remarked the Reverend Heman Humphrey in 1835, "and I am inclined to think quite a respectable class . . . civil and intelligent. After being in the country a few weeks, you can hardly mistake one of these sons of Nimshi, wherever you happen to meet him. His broad-brimmed hat, his drab-colored, quaker-like coat and small clothes, his white-topped boots, his air, his gait, and his goodly-keeping and his plump, weather-beaten face, all tell you to what caste he belongs."[12]

Coachman Joe Walton of the *Star,* which ran between Cambridge and London in the thirties, was much admired by Calvin Colton, who conversed with him all the way up to London. Walton drove his round trip of 108 miles every day except Sunday, Colton learned, with one eye on the brass clock secured to the dashboard, generally making the fifty-four-mile run each way in about five to five and a half hours. "He has a responsibility which he feels, and which weighs on him, the lives of his passengers . . . their comfort, and their pleasure, their luggage and parcels, besides verbal messages and errands, in great variety and number, committed to his charge at Cambridge, picked up enroute, stowed away in his brain, to be discharged at London and replaced by others. Joe Walton's task is by no means trifling," concluded Colton, "and yet he works it out, apparently without fatigue, by resting on the Sabbath." Accustomed to Yankee travelers, and noting Colton's thirst for detail, Walton remarked upon their parting, "I suppose you will put it in a book when you get home to America."[13]

"Every coach that carries the royal mail is required to have a guard," Humphrey explained. The guard

> has his box behind the passengers, and wears a scarlet uniform, goes armed with a kind of bugle swung over his shoulder. . . . He sees to putting on your baggage (though you must pay for that service), takes in and throws out small packages on the road, and blows his horn most vociferously when you approach the stand for changing horses; and also when he sees any cart, wagon, man or beast in the way of your swift coursers.[14]

The guards were usually armed with pistols fixed in holsters attached to the top of the coach, although—as Silliman advised readers early in the century—once armed, the coaches were seldom attacked. The guard's duties also included opening and closing doors at stops to enable the driver to keep control of the reins.

On one trip, young MacKenzie competed with one of these guards for the attentions of five ladies' maids en route to London. "He was a gay Lothario, this guard of ours," MacKenzie observed, noting that his technique consisted largely of "complaining with an air of affected sentiment that nobody would have him. He did not stay long enough in one place; he was here today and gone tomorrow; one night sleeping in Dover, the next in London; there was no time for love-making." Then, thought MacKenzie, "pray what are you about now?" He also recorded a pastime of young schoolboys on their way home for the holidays. "Full of merriment they began to shoot peas, through long tubes which they had for the purpose, into the faces of everyone we met. There were other coaches similarly blessed, and when we passed each other, urchins would mutually prepare to fire a volley."[15]

At the inns along the twenty-seven coach routes were landlords and landladies, waiters, porters, barmaids and chambermaids, and even bootboys, all devoted to the traveler's comfort for the anticipated "fees," or tips, of course, but whose ministrations nevertheless made a stranger feel almost like arriving at his own home as one recalled. "The English inn is as close an imitation as can be made of a private house," concluded Jacob Abbott in 1847.[16] "We can add our testimony to that of other travellers," affirmed Emma Willard, "to the general excellence of English inns."[17] If the traveler arrived by himself in one of the more expensive post chaises, he would hear as he pulled up, " 'A chaise is come!' " throughout the entire establishment. "So many came trooping to our aid we could hardly get out of the carriage through the crowd of arms raised for our assistance," one American recalled.[18]

So many are the references to bustling landladies, plump and rosy maids, soft beds, tidy rooms, neat parlors, cheerful fires, mugs of foaming ale, and huge

"Can I have a night's lodging"

From a Drawing by Hugh Thomson.

Coach traveler seeking a night's lodging at an inn. *The English Illustrated Magazine*, vol. V, 1887–88, p. 696. *Courtesy the Library of Congress.*

rounds of beef that one has to conclude that the comfort of these inns was real and not just the romantic recollection of Washington Irving.[19] Colton copied down the names of some of the inns: Swan with Two Heads; Saracen's Head; Hen and Chickens; Pig and Whistle; Old Red Heifer; Crab and Lobster; Bag of Nails; Ship and Shovel; Bolt-in-Tun; Labour in Vain; Three Foxes; Four Awls; Pickled Egg; Hog in the Pound; Hog in Armour; Bear and Ragged Staff; Cock and Bottle; Cat and Boot; and the famous Bull and Mouth of London opposite the General Post Office.[20]

Even as these visiting Americans savored the delights of English stagecoach travel at the height of its glory, the whole institution was rapidly galloping toward extinction, its fate sealed on that day in 1825 when the first puffing little passenger train chugged from Darlington to Stockton. Another line to cover the thirty miles between Liverpool and Manchester was already under construction. Americans had heard of steam power used for hauling coal wagons, and in 1825 Nathaniel Carter was taken by his English host at Leeds "to witness the operation of steam carriages upon rail-roads" a mile outside town.

> After waiting an hour we had the satisfaction to see twenty-five wagons, containing three tons of coal each, impelled or rather drawn along a horizontal rail-road by a steam-engine possessing a six-horse power . . . a most novel and interesting spectacle. The steam-carriage is placed in front, and the whole apparatus is not much larger than an ordinary Jersey wagon. To this the

Coachyard of a typical inn, this one the *Tabard*, Southwark, London. *From the author's collection.*

twenty-five four-wheeled cars are appended by chains and follow in obedience to the self-moving power. One man, whose services are required to regulate the machinery is the sole navigator, and even he has little to do. . . . We mounted one of the carts and rode a considerable distance. The ordinary speed is four miles per hour, but of course it may be greatly accelerated if necessary. There are several engines upon this railway which ply regularly between extensive collieries and the town, a distance of three or four miles. It is odd enough to see the smoke arising, like that of a steam-boat, and the carts moving with no visible agent to move or govern them. The experiment here has been fairly and successfully tried, and I see no reason why transportation by steam is not as practicable upon land as upon water . . . which evinces in a striking manner to what extent the control of mind over matter may be carried.[21]

Five years later Carter's countryman, Henry McLellan, boarded the regularly-scheduled Liverpool-Manchester Railway, a few months after its opening in 1830. "We scarce seemed to touch the earth," he marveled,

while the passing objects appeared to whirl by with dizzy swiftness. Occasionally, carriages from the other direction shot by us with their sparkling furnaces, leaving a train of smoke and fire behind them. We had scarce time to take note of their presence before they had passed us with the *whir* and speed of a rocket; *a mist of wagons and faces,* visible for a moment, then gone! . . . We completed the thirty miles in about ninety minutes, including twelve or fifteen stoppages.[22]

That same year Calvin Colton paid his five-shilling fare for this same thrilling ride and experienced the added feature of a train wreck. Observing "great irregularity in the degree of speed" from the start, they were halfway to Manchester when, watching nervously out of the window, Colton to his horror spied "the engine off the rails, staggering, pitching and plunging down the bank! I drew in my head," he recalled, "and as my friend who sat opposite me afterward said, though I have no recollection of it, exclaimed three times, 'We are gone! We are gone! We are gone!' Crash! Crash! went the whole concern— one car against the other—with tremendous violence, and we were all at rest in a heap." Only the engineer was injured, dragged out from underneath the overturned engine, he reported, but all were badly shaken—"their senses half driven out of them by the shock, particularly the females."[23]

"If I were called upon to select any single physical feature of modern times, which more widely than any other distinguishes them from the ancient," observed Isaac Jewett in 1836, "I should make choice of that which in the last two hours I have, for the first time, seen. I mean the Railway between Liverpool and Manchester, with its machinery of engines and cars, all the diversified apparatus that belongs to it." He could think of nothing, he declared, "whose influence is to be more wide, more direct, more permanent than that of the railway and the steam engine." He went on to describe the little engine he had seen, "rather a small laborer to perform so great a work . . . not larger than two good oxen, and yet there is about it a certain bull, or bull-dog expression of energy that promises much. . . . It backs up, the foremost car, and you learn with pleasure that its name is 'Lightning'!"[24]

"Look around you," Jewett continued. "England has 300 miles of railways completed, and has 500 more contemplating. As an American I am anxious to see converts made to the railroad system. In our country," he predicted, "it will be an agent well able to facilitate our very distant communities, and to help in developing and distributing our immense resources. It seems to me that the vast extent of our territory, makes it more desirable with us than in England." Foreseeing the inevitable, he prophesied that "the coach shall no longer gather a merry company of voyagers around its top, and the coachman and guard, fat and perdurable as they now seem, shall vanish into things only for remembrance."[25] And he was right. Less than a decade later Caroline Kirkland would remark that "railway travelling will soon supersede all other."[26]

By 1845 many travelers lamented the passing of English stagecoach travel, as did Henry Colman. "They have spoiled the pleasure and benefit of journeying. We wished for the old post-coach that we might travel as in old times, but no such vehicle is known; the former celebrated post horses and coachmen have disappeared before steam, and you are compelled to take 'the rail'." Colman thought the railroad

> an execrable mode of traveling: hurrying and driving like madmen . . . seeing ordinarily nothing but two high, gravelly banks; shooting through tunnels miles long and dark as midnight . . . unable to converse for the clattering of the rails; convulsed every once in a while by that unearthly shriek of the railroad whistle; afraid of being smashed . . . to say nothing of sleeping at Land's End, dining in London, and taking tea at Johnny Groat's house the same day. . . . If there were any other means of locomotion, I should renounce all railroads.

He was honest enough to admit, however, that he "accomplished almost as much in six weeks as could ordinarily be done in six months" traveling by stagecoach.[27]

Itineraries of these American travelers in the nineteenth century's early decades varied as did their personal interests and professions. Unique among those interested in practical matters was inventor Zachariah Allen, whose encyclopedic tour of Britain about 1830 resulted in a book that is virtually a survey of the industrial revolution in that country. Labeling himself "The Practical Tourist," Allen visited manufactories, farms, and mines; observed industrial processes, including steel making, and Telford's method of road construction; surveyed England's canal system; studied working conditions and wages; and reported on new parliamentary labor laws. He was witnessing Britain's rise to industrial and commercial greatness, and he knew it. "From the concentration of so many advantages of nature and improvements of art within the range of a few hours of travel," he wrote, "the stranger in England is remarkably impressed with the spectacle of wealth and resources of this little island, which physically and intellectually exercises more important influence on the destinies of civilized man than one whole continent."[28]

Other Americans, less concerned with technology and commerce, coming from what was still primarily an agricultural country, too, were drawn to Britain's industrial centers, which seemed alternately to fascinate and repel them. It was one thing to visit the Herculaneum Pottery just outside Liverpool, there to observe "a great many genteel-looking men and women drawing the landscapes upon the china," as did Boston housewares merchant, Joseph Ballard in 1815, and quite another to enter a cloth mill at Leeds where he observed child laborers at their work, "about fifty wretched boys and girls, the eldest not over ten years of age." They were, he went on, "all besmeared with grease and dirt arising from the wool. The proprietor observed in reply to my asking him if they never went to play, that they were there at six in the morning and never left off work, except for dinner, until seven at night. Thus, these poor little wretches are confined in these hells—for I cannot find a more appropriate name—deprived of education and buried in these dark, noisy and unwholesome dens. They either pass a quick, miserable existence or furnish turbulent, ignorant and vicious members of society."[29]

As early as 1815 the first view of Manchester was of "quite a smoky place." Ballard reported that on "walking a little way out of town I found it was quite fine weather, and what I had supposed was a foggy day was only an accumulation of smoke from their manufactories."[30] A decade later Wilbur Fisk observed that "the entire environs and neighboring villages are filled with *monumental towers,* running upwards toward the clouds, from one to three hundred feet. . . . A black cloud of smoke is rolling from the top of them." Standing in one great shed housing 700 cotton looms, Fisk thought the sight "magnificent to see and deafening to hear," and then was told of another shed housing 1200 looms. Overhead transoms provided light, doing away with the need for conventional windows, and they so impressed him that he included a sketch in his book. Little mention is made of the operatives except their large numbers and that "by means of trades unions they compel their employers to pay them exhorbitant wages, for which they are none the better but rather the worse." They spent too much on drink, Fisk thought.[31]

Allen was conducted by the proprietor through "one of the most extensive cotton-spinning mills in Manchester, containing nearly 90,000 spindles." Beginning their exhaustive "ramble over his vast works," they entered through a guarded gate into a vast square created by four huge brick buildings set at right angles to each other, each 800 feet in length, the principal one in front being eight stories high. Within this square was "a sheet of navigable water," observed Allen, "bordered by a quay on which canal boats might be seen discharging their freights of raw cotton and coals in the heart of the works and receiving packages of yarns. A tunnel or arched passageway is made beneath the mill to connect this internal basin with one of the principal canals which traverses a considerable part of England."[32]

Allen, too, found the noise of the steam-driven machinery deafening but the physical condition of the workers better than he had been led to expect by earlier accounts. "The females in general were well dressed," he wrote, "and the men in particular displayed countenances which were red and florid from the effects of beer . . . rather than pale and emaciated." The children, he added, "also appeared to be healthy, although not so robust" as other children. Allen quoted recent parliamentary legislation prohibiting child laborers from working longer than twelve hours a day or between the hours of 8:30 P.M. and 5:30 A.M. He also set out a detailed comparison of American and British wages and prices, concluding that "with an equal amount of wages, the mechanic in the United

States may purchase nearly double the quantity of bread and other provisions
... that the English mechanics can purchase in England."[33] Visiting Manchester
several years later, the Reverend Humphrey concluded that "great fortunes have
been made and are in the making here."[34]

Sheffield, the great cutlery manufacturing center, was already, even in these
early decades, a region of "fire and smoke." Every American traveler knew of
"Mr. Rodgers's knife, razor, etc., manufactory," like Wilbur Fisk, who remembered the name from his boyhood penknife. He and his wife enjoyed a visit to
the famed showroom where Mrs. Fisk was presented with one of "the Lilliputian
toys" displayed there, "a pair of scissors about half an inch in length."[35] In 1836
Fanny Hall noticed a case of penknives, labeled "American Congress Knives,"
and was told that "the company 'had the honour of supplying our wise legislators
with this useful article.' "[36] Zachariah Allen, of course, went further and described the whole steel-making process for his American readers.

Approaching Birmingham in the thirties, most travelers noted again "dense
volumes of smoke rising up from numberless furnaces" as well as "the noise of
hammers and the rattle of machinery." Green said that it reminded him of "the
abode of the Cyclops family, for it smokes and fumes in every direction. Though
on a much larger scale, it reminded me of my first entrance into Pittsburgh."[37]
Fisk entered the region at night.

**Birmingham, c. 1840, showing the smoking factories already dominating that city's
skyline.** *From the author's collection.*

Suddenly we found ourselves in a region of fire. Flames were bursting out of the earth in every direction. Sometimes in a steady blaze, and sometimes in fitful, flashing alternations of flame and smoke. Here and there were vast piles of smouldering and gleaming embers; . . . extending as far as the eye could reach, and continuing through successive miles of our journey. The occasion of these phenomena we found to be the combined operation of working mines, and of roasting, smelting, and forging iron. In the coal districts the coal is raised from deep, subterranean pits by steam power; so also are the iron ore and the lime which are used for a flux in smelting ore, both of which are found in the same district of the coal, and in different strata of the same shaft or pit. The fires which generate the steam usually blaze out at the top of the flues, and the workmen also commonly have fires blazing at the mouth of the pit. Frequently large mass___ __f fine and unsaleable coal are set on fire to get them out of the way. All t____ ___s a good deal of fire; but the most vivid is from the roasting of the ir___ _____the furnaces and forges. Altogether, the scene was to us terribl_ _____ __re so, doubtless, because it was perfectly new to us, having _____ ____hibition until it burst upon us through the thick gloor___

Fisk w_____ _y a Mr. Bagnall, "one of the principal owne_____ _borhood," and in one area he observed "ra_____ _ Russia and the United States. "That all the _____ _, the coal for roasting and smelting, the lime _____ _ed precisely as they were wanted in the same _____ _nd Fisk as a true son of the industrial revolution, _____ _ our bountiful Creator."[39]

_____rd, visiting Thomason's showrooms, considered "one of _____aam," saw "exposed for sale almost every article which is _____ he rooms are fitted up in great taste, and the style in which t_____ _isplayed tempts almost everyone who visits here to be a pu___ ____ added. Once again he was appalled, on being shown through a pin fa_to. _o see "more wretched little boys and girls" at work.[40]

The effects on human bodies of long hours of factory toil—sallow complexions, sickly and misshapen bodies, ignorance and alcoholism—were noticed by Humphrey. "They are," he said of the operatives, "the servants, and to a great extent the *slaves* of that mighty steam-power to which no limits can be prescribed and which is extending its dominion so fearfully, as well as usefully, over the face of the Island." Concerning cheap, child and female labor, he suggested that it might be better if Americans were willing to pay "a cent or two more for our prints and fine bleached cottons." Quoting from government reports, he informed his readers that a child, tending a pair of No. 40 spinning mules in a Manchester cotton mill, "must walk 35,200 yards or twenty miles per day" apart from his journey to and from work. Parliament's more enlightened members, as well as medical authorities, were, he said, crying out for reform in both working hours and wages.[41]

The coal mines supplying the fuel for Britain's booming industry were likewise magnets to these visiting Americans. Old Samuel Curwen, an American loyalist who spent nine years of exile in Britain, and who in many ways was the first American tourist, went down into the Duke of Bridgewater's famed coal mine in 1777, found it "a dismal abode," and confessed he was glad to get out of it.[42]

Manchester cotton mill at night, c. 1840, where operatives—men, women, and children—toiled in shifts around the clock. *From the author's collection.*

Silliman proposed to descend into a mine at Newcastle in 1805, but on learning the process would take a whole day he abstained. Two decades after this, Nathaniel Carter resisted the invitations of the colliers at Wallend—four miles from Newcastle—to enter their mine with them, finding a "peep" into its depths quite sufficient. "Brimstone, and smoke, and every other horror came up from the abyss," he observed, adding, "this very mine once blew up and killed fifty-two men."[43]

Margaret Fuller in the forties insisted on entering a coal mine and did. She expressed much pity for the horses, "who see the light of day no more once they have been let down into these gloomy recesses but pass their days in dragging cars along the rails and their nights in eating hay and dreaming of grass." But she never did reach the men at their work after finding it meant a walk of a mile and a half underground. "Besides the weariness of picking one's steps slowly along by the light of a tallow candle, it was too wet and dirty an enterprise to be taken by way of amusement; so after proceeding half a mile or so," she wrote, "we begged to be restored to our accustomed level, and reached it with minds slightly edified and hands and face much blackened."[44]

Seemingly torn between revulsion at the effects of industrialism on the one hand, and on the other the realization that the United States was on the same path and might as well compete, the travelers' reactions are mixed. Ballard, in the second decade, observed that, if those at home could see the human misery attached to manufacturing, "they would not so strenuously argue that it is for our national welfare."[45] Child labor in particular struck him as evil, but for others it was evidences of alcoholism and sexual promiscuity that most concerned them. Allen claimed that "the most highly colored sketches of the moral depravity and vices of many of the laboring classes of Manchester, fall short of the reality."[46] In 1810 Joshua White of Georgia came out with a declaration, interesting not only because of its anti-industrial tone, but also because it symbolizes the great split in interests and ideology that was to plague American society for decades and finally to end in the Civil War a half century later. Railing against "the plague" that was infecting England through the cotton trade," he added, "I have noticed how many of my countrymen are now sighing, and longing, and striving to have manufactories erected in the United States. Even in the hall of congress has the power of eloquence been exerted in favour of this policy." Let Rhode Island, Connecticut, and Massachusetts manufacture the cotton from South Carolina and Georgia, his own state, he advocated. But "for the security and preservation of those principles which will give strength and prosperity to our representative institutions, let us be careful how we foster a snake in our bosoms or translate to our fertile regions and happy shores the depravities of such places as Manchester, Sheffield and Birmingham."[47]

With respect to English agriculture, Americans of all periods refer, as did scientist Jacob Green in 1828, to "the universal and high state of cultivation" of the land as well as "the neat appearance of the farm houses" set off by hedges and flower gardens. "One feature, common all over the country," wrote Green, "is the number of windmills. The graceful motion of their wings, as they slowly revolve, gives an animation to them which might well provoke the ire of a knight like that of La Mancha."[48]

A detailed agricultural investigation in this period was made by Henry Colman of Salem, Massachusetts, who spent three and a half years in Britain, beginning in 1843, collecting data on agricultural education, animal husbandry, fertilizers, farm management, marketing, soils and soil cultivation, and seeds, for his book *European Agriculture and Rural Economy From Personal Observation*. A second volume followed—*European Life and Manners*—which was based primarily on informal letters he had written to family and friends describing scenes, objects, persons, and places. His investigations took him especially to the great landed estates where agriculture was being carried on with advanced and experimental methods made possible by the wealth of the owners. On one such estate—Sir Charles Morgan's estate, Tredegar, in Wales—the actual work was performed by a corps of over 500 tenant farmers, he said.[49]

Colman himself reveled in the luxurious life led by the owners of these vast domains, one of which employed over sixty servants in the house alone, and he described the daily routine, in all its particulars, of life in these great country houses. On one occasion he actually tried hare coursing, and, after surviving a jump over a ditch and hedge so wide as to terrify him, he declared that he did not know why he had not broken his neck—unless he was "destined to have it broken some other way." Joining the gentlemen at one estate for a battue, he could think of only one improvement on this method of shooting—"to have an arm chair placed in the poultry yard, and then hens and chickens tied by the legs and shot at leisure."[50]

A high spot was his visit at Woburn Abbey, seat of the Duke of Bedford, and "next to the royal palace . . . the acme of elegance and grandeur." Bedford, said Colman, was

> the largest improver in England next to the Duke of Rutland, his estates at Woburn Abbey being no less than 20,000 acres in one body, and his redeemed land in the Bedford Level, all cultivated land, exceeding 18,000 acres. His farm . . . is deemed the most extensive and complete of any in the kingdom. So that my visit there, beside affording me the pleasures of the most refined society, in the house, and all the delights of pictures, statuary, and books, gave me out of doors, in his gardens and cultivated grounds, workshops and plantations, the highest gratification and improvement.[51]

Colman continued, "To give you some idea of his operations upon his own farm, under his own management, he pays more than four hundred laborers weekly, through the year, and in his home park which, to be sure, is thirteen miles in circumference, he has laid pipe drains, for several years last, to the extent of fifty miles each year."[52]

Unlike Colman, whom he considered to have directed his attention primarily to "the exceptional, improved modes of cultivation which prevail only among the amateur agriculturalists and the bolder and more enterprising farmers," Frederick Law Olmsted would set forth seven years later to learn more about "the prevailing, ordinary, and generally-accepted practices of agriculture than I could learn from Mr. Coleman's [sic] book." Himself a farmer on Staten Island for a number of years, Olmsted was, he claimed, seeking information "for farmers and farmers' families," and accordingly he concentrated on such mundane matters as English dairy farming, fruit growing, seeding, haying, and horse and cattle breeding practices. He was especially interested in crop rotation, tillage, and drainage, and interested to find bones being used as manure.[53] Whereas Colman had spent his evenings in the elegant drawing rooms of great country houses, Olmsted and his two companions would join a farm family at their supper or sit over pewter mugs of ale in a village alehouse to talk of the weather and the crops with the local inhabitants. The large class of agricultural workers who toiled for wages on land owned by others Olmsted compared to domestic animals—a dull, slow, passive, brutish folk. One of them he spoke with "had heard of America and Australia as countries that poor folks went to. He did not well know why but supposed that wages were higher, and they could live cheaper. . . . We advised him to emigrate by all means, not so much for himself as for his children. I scarcely ever saw a man of so limited information." Olmsted thought him dulled by hard labor, lack of education, and also by the three quarts of cider or beer a day, six at harvest time, provided him by his master.[54] At the end of his account, speaking of these farm workers, Olmsted remarked that "it is a melancholy thing there are so few yeomen now in England; that is, farmers owning the land they till, independent of landlords."[55]

Scholarly American travelers could scarcely return to America without having visited Oxford and Cambridge. Silliman had only time for a brief stay at the former, where he marveled at "the unrivalled air of magnificence and dignity" of the place. But he reserved most comment for an academic institution apparently not yet in vogue in his own country of "a loose black gown [worn] over their dress, which is like that of other gentlemen. They wear a black velvet cap . . . destitute of a rim or border. . . . On the very pinnacle of the cap is fixed a square board, covered also with black; it looks as a thin book would do, if laid on the crown of the head. From the middle of this, a tassel falls over on one side of the head. This is usually black, but in the case of noblemen, it is of gold." Like many an academic since, Silliman found that "the effect of the whole is somewhat ludicrous at the same time that it is grave and solemn."[56]

Wheaton gave his readers a long, loving description of the various colleges but also studied the students, deciding that they had "an appearance of greater muscular strength and capability of bodily exertion" than their American counterparts. "They use far more vigorous exercise than the pallid students of our American colleges; are in consequence much less frequently the victims of debility, dyspepsia, and all the abhorred train of ills, mental and bodily, which result from a too sedentary life."[57]

With more time at Cambridge, or perhaps better introductions, Silliman "took the liberty of making numerous inquiries concerning the university, its courses of instruction, its police and discipline, and other interesting circumstances." He found students left more to their own discretion concerning behavior, with none of the "personal inspection into the habits of every individual member of the colleges" as in his own country, and he also noted a far less formal relationship between the faculty and their students.[58]

Invited to dinner by a group of "masters or presidents, professors and fellows," Silliman was less amused than provoked to be complimented on his use of the English language, a recurring phenomenon with many of the American travelers during the earlier decades of the century. After theorizing on the types of linguistic changes caused by time and separation, and asserting his belief that British men of letters used the language "with more purity and correctness" than their American counterparts, Silliman then declared—that *The English language is more correctly spoken, at this time, by the mass of the American than by the mass of the British nation*"—italicizing his remarks for the benefit of his readers.[59]

Later that evening, the male scholars rejoined the ladies upstairs for tea, where young Professor Silliman was shocked to his puritan roots when "invited to join in a rubber at whist! . . . It is somewhat remarkable," he sputtered, "that I should be invited to play at cards, for the first time in England, with academic gentlemen; they were so polite as to excuse me, however, nor am I inclined to judge them with severity, only, it struck me as somewhat unfortunate that the usual instruments of gambling should be found in the hands of the guardians and instructors of youth."[60]

Surgeon William Gibson headed for London, in 1839, where he was well received by leading surgeons and professors of medicine at such hospitals as Guy's, St. George's, St. Bartholomew's, Westminster, North London, and Charing Cross Ophthalmic Institution. In addition to brief mention of consultations in which he joined, saving his technical material for professional purposes, he provides pen sketches of certain leading British physicians of the period, such as Mr. Liston of North London Hospital, "seemingly of robust frame and of great strength," who, "having fractured his pelvis and nearly broken his neck hunting,

A youthful Queen Victoria and Prince Albert out riding in Hyde Park with their retinue. *Illustrated London News*, **April 12, 1845, p. 232.** *Courtesy the Library of Congress.*

now took his exercise by rowing every morning seven miles before breakfast" on the Thames. He lavished his passion for domestic animals on his "enormous black cat, Tom, almost as well known in London," Gibson observed, "as Liston himself, being not unfrequently, mounted alongside his master in the splendid chariot, and a constant guest at his hospitable board, where I had the honour of forming his acquaintance, by finding his foot in my soup before aware of its proximity to my plate."[61]

In his nonprofessional moments Gibson enjoyed Mr. Wardrop—a favorite physician of George IV—because of the man's infatuation with horses. When they were strolling together in Piccadilly near Hyde Park Corner one afternoon, observing the usual splendid turnout of elegant equipages and well-mounted equestrians, Gibson was fascinated by Wardrop's manner of identifying people primarily in terms of their horseflesh. "That is the Marquis of Douro—there's blood for you!—look at her legs—examine her withers—observe her red hot eye! Zounds! what a pair of ears, like the fingers of a glove—did you ever see such a back! ... There comes the Queen!' he exclaimed, 'and that awkward Russian Prince. Look at his long legs, like a pair of tongs. She rides beautifully. See how easy she sits her saddle and how she plays him off. That's not her best nag, either. Her little grey mare has more action, but she has nothing so fine since she lost her black Arabian *Beauty*.' " The Queen, of course, was the young Victoria out riding in Hyde Park as was her custom in the early days of her reign.[62]

Gibson also wrote a spirited defense of Sir James Clarke, Victoria's court physician, who was involved in the unfortunate Lady Flora Hastings affair. This young woman, falsely believed to have conceived a child out of wedlock, finally died, undoubtedly the victim of a tumor; and all at court were considered by a sympathetic public to have mistreated the victim shamefully and no doubt hastened her demise. "That he may have been deceived by appearances, failed in his diagnosis, and suffered his judgement to be misled, by the fear of his responsibility ... or erred from other causes, is probable," judged Gibson of his British colleague. "But that he lent himself and his reputation to the vile purpose of blasting the character and ruining the happiness of an unfortunate woman, to secure for himself ... favours and rewards ... is an assertion I am sure his most violent professional or political enemy can never seriously believe."[63]

On leaving London, Gibson headed north to Scotland to visit the world-famed medical school of Edinburgh University, where, like so many young Americans of this period, he had learned his profession. He recalled "a score of Virginia lads—most of whom, poor fellows, have since passed away." Engaging rooms at the Waterloo Hotel, he then headed off across the North Bridge for the college, no longer a stripling but "a grey-haired sire," to experience the same sensations of Rip Van Winkle in familiar surroundings where few were left who remembered him. He found the college greatly built up, but one thing remained quite the same—his old room where he had lodgings. "I looked about and found that here, at least, I was home; for I saw the hooks I had driven into the wall to support my anatomical preparations, and above all, what can nowhere be found, except in Scotch country, the same pane of glass upon which I had scratched with a flint, my name, thirty years earlier!" Gibson then sallied forth in search of his "preceptor and friend, Sir Charles Bell," the famed pioneer neuro-surgeon, in whose company he had served British wounded on the field following the Battle of Waterloo twenty-four years earlier. Soon they were reunited, wrote Gibson, and "from that moment, I was a daily, almost hourly, visitor at Sir Charles's."[64]

4

Cultural Shrines

Despite the serious professional purposes that drove most of these early nineteenth-century American sojourners in Britain, they did not neglect that aspect of travel which later on, especially as it became more perfunctory, would be called "sight-seeing." Guided primarily by their reading, they made pilgrimages to Britain's literary, historic, and cultural shrines, seeking out living authors wherever and whenever possible.

To the Lake District in the northwest of England thus trooped the Americans to tour the region James Russell Lowell would one day dub "Wordsworthshire," because of the poet whom so many of them managed to visit during his lifetime at his various residences in that region.[1] George Ticknor, in 1819, found Wordsworth to be "a man with a tall, ample, well-proportioned frame, and a grave and tranquil manner." Surprised at the simplicity of the poet's conversation until he touched upon poetry and reviews, Ticknor then observed that "he was the Khan of Tartary again, and talked as metaphysically as ever. . . . In the evening he showed me his manuscripts, the longest a kind of poetical history of his life which he has brought to his twenty-eigth year." Ticknor, on a later visit in 1835, thought the poet's political views now "very gloomy" since, in expressing his growing political conservatism, he held "strongly and fondly . . . to the old and established in institutions, usages and pecularities of his country, and he sees them all shaken by the process of change." Ticknor informed his American readers that Wordsworth "made many shrewd, as well as kind, remarks about us; but he is certainly not inclined to augur well of our destinies, for he goes upon the broad principle that the mass of people of any country cannot be trusted with the powers of government."[2]

Unitarian Orville Dewey, visiting in 1833, too, was disturbed by what he considered Wordsworth's relentless pessimism and disbelief in the perfectibility of man. "He has no confidence in the people," complained Dewey, referring to the well-known conservatism of the poet's later years. "They are not fit to govern themselves, not yet certainly. Public opinion, the foolish opinion of the depraved, ignorant, and conceited mass ought not to be the law. . . . He says the world is running mad with the notion that all its evils are to be relieved by political changes, political remedies, political nostrums—whereas the great evils, sin, bondage, misery, lie deep in the heart, and nothing but virtue and religion can remove them." Dewey was far happier, after tea, when Wordsworth pro-

The poet William Wordsworth (1770–1850), who greeted his American guest in "a grave and tranquil manner," according to George Ticknor. By Daniel Maclise. *Courtesy the Library of Congress.*

Harriet Martineau (1802–1876), "full of anecdotes and a brilliant talker," according to
Orlando Wight. By Daniel Maclise. *Courtesy the Library of Congress.*

posed "a walk to Grassmere Lake, to see it after sunset . . . that loveliest of all scenes I ever witnessed on earth."[3]

Still receiving Americans in 1846, Wordsworth would welcome Margaret Fuller, who was pleased to report that he spoke "with more liberality than we expected of the recent measures about the corn laws," and that he charmed his visitors by his evident passion for hollyhocks, "a partiality scarcely deserved by the flower but which marks the simplicity of his tastes." He had, she observed, "made a long avenue of them of all colors, from the crimson-brown to rose, straw-color and white, and pleased himself with having made proselytes to a liking for them among his neighbors."[4] George Calvert was impressed by the poet's fondness for birds as well. "I like birds better than fruit," Wordsworth told the young American. "They eat up my fruit but repay me with their songs."[5]

Harriet Martineau, another Lake District dweller—by then in her old age— would be visited in 1853 by Orlando Wight in her little cottage at Ambleside, not far from Wordsworth's. "She put into your lap a tin-pan connected with her ear by a long, thin tube," recalled Wight, describing the old lady's hearing device, "into which one directed his conversation. She was full of anecdotes and a brilliant talker. She had become a firm believer in mesmerism, and gravely told me how she had broken the cow of the bad habit of kicking over both the milk and the milkmaid by mesmerising the animal only once." Miss Martineau had also been the recipient of a visit by Margaret Fuller. Her aged mother adored Margaret, Miss Martineau recalled, but was startled one day when, looking straight at her, the famed New England bluestocking "discoursed at length on 'the unloveliness of old age.' 'Alas!' the old woman exclaimed, astonished. 'The poor creature is stark mad!' "[6]

Chatsworth, seat of the Dukes of Devonshire—located in Derbyshire, south of Sheffield—was another establishment whose owners, like those of Eaton Hall, were possessed by "a rage for building." Nathaniel Carter, in 1825, called it "a sumptuous pile in bad taste."[7] But Orville Dewey, both more curious and more discriminating, described "an immense castle, of the ionic order, the oldest part built round a hollow square, the new part, a continuation, one story lower, of the rear block or portion . . . so extensive that when finished, there is to be a suite of rooms, through the whole of which the eye will range at a single view, six hundred feet." He was impressed by the Gibbons carvings but shocked by paintings of mythological figures on the ceiling of the great entrance hall, which, to his "simple American taste," appeared "a very improper exhibition—the forms being, generally, represented without any costume. The housekeeper, however, observed," he assured his titillated readers, "that these rooms were never *used* on any occasion."[8] Carter, on his earlier visit, had been much embarrassed on this same spot to have as his guide "a pretty, well-dressed, genteel-looking girl of twenty, with her white silk stockings and kid gloves in keeping with her gold chains and bracelets . . . well educated," and obviously, he thought, "qualified for a more appropriate and higher sphere than that of a cicerone . . . conducting strange gentlemen through galleries of undraped statues."[9]

Like many a guest at Chatsworth before him and after, Samuel Cox would be victim of a practical joke in a bosky dell in the extensive gardens. "A New Haven gentleman, a wag, wished me to examine the bark of a certain tree," the Ohioan recalled. "I was going up for that purpose when I observed the tree bleeding water-drops; and before I could look again . . . every part and pore and twig and branch spurted its jet, and the turf under my feet became suddenly alive with subtle fountains. I, of course, retired and was the food for merriment."[10] He had been the victim of "the spouting tree," as another visitor called it, judging it "a very cute affair quite worthy even of a Yankee's inventive genius."[11]

Lord Byron's grave in the church at Hucknall Torkard, north of Nottingham, was sought out by the more romantic American travelers. Wanting to be alone with his poetic reveries, Benjamin Moran was not a little perturbed by the levity of a group of English tourists visiting at the same time and was pleased when they left. Then, a lovely blond girl "with a face expressive of sinless purity," showed him around and told him, as he remarked on the many American names in the visitors' book, that "more of them visit Hucknall than any other foreigners." She also informed him that many recited poetry standing beside the poet's grave and that some were "affected even unto tears." As a relic, or memento of his pilgrimage, Moran was given a piece of oak left over when repairs were made to the pews not long before.[12] So infected with "Byromania" was another young Yankee visitor from Vermont that he left a poem of his own dedicated to his hero whose tracks he had followed all through Europe and finally to his grave.[13]

On her visit to Byron's onetime home, Newstead Abbey, Sophia Hawthorne and her son Julian busied themselves tearing up violets in the park for souvenirs and then also requested leaves from "the storied oak planted by Byron in an open lawn near the house." Aware that Colonel Wildman, the present owner, was watching them from an upper window, Sophia attributed it to her husband's fame as a writer. Could it have been, instead, his concern for his garden so dear to every Englishman?[14]

South of the Peak District, two miles southeast of Bakewell, on the river Wye, lay Haddon Hall. "Scott has woven its history into several of his absorbing tales," wrote one traveler, thus explaining its lure for Americans.[15] Today, quite restored, Haddon Hall was in the previous century a desolate and empty place, an old manor house built on the foundation of a Norman stronghold. Still, for Yankee devotees of Scott, it was alive with the ghosts they carried in their heads, and Orville Dewey started at the sound of a viol until told by the elderly caretaker that he "occasionally gave liberty to the young people of Bakewell to come and dance there." Remembering Sir John Manners and Dorothy Vernon and their romantic elopement, Dewey was "glad to feel this strange mingling together of death and life, of the past and the present, of ruins and revels."[16] Andrew Jackson Downing in the fifties wrote of the "*realness* and the *rudeness* of these halls of ancient grandeur . . . a veritable antique castle."[17]

Another obligatory stop for Americans was York, site of the great cathedral. "From the first moment the traveler arrives within sight of the mountainous form," wrote Zachariah Allen, about 1830, "which becomes perceptible at a distance of twenty miles, with its massy outlines raised above the edge of the horizon, he becomes impatient at the tardy progress of the coach and even at the necessary delay in securing lodgings, and hurries forward to view the edifice. . .the pride of England."[18] Not even the cholera epidemic of July 1832 could keep away Charles Stewart, who assured his readers that "but for the magnificent Minster we should never have slept within its walls." Once checked in at the Black Swan, he "lost no time in repairing to the Cathedral," whose west front he found "indescribably beautiful," as well as "the great eastern window of richly painted glass, seventy feet in height and of proportionate breadth."[19]

Jacob Green kindly quoted for his readers those lines from Scott's "The Lay of the Last Minstrel," which so many of these American visitors claimed ran through their heads while gazing up at the east window.

> The moon on the east oriel shone
> Through slender shafts of shapely stone
> By foliage and tracery combined;
> Thou wouldst have thought some fairy's
>   hand
> 'Twixt poplars straight, the ozier wand
> In many a freakish knot had twined;
> Then formed a spell, when the work was
>   done.
> And changed the willow wreaths to stone.
> The silver light so pale and faint
> Showed many a prophet—many a saint.
> Whose image on the glass was dyed.[20]

Several decades after Green's visit, Nathaniel and Sophia Hawthorne pored over the visitor's album at the Black Swan, noting the many American signatures there—"two or three hundred Americans in it—the Nortons of Cambridge, the Quincys and Wares and Waterstons, Mr. Frank Peabody of Salem, and multitudes of New York people and others."[21]

At mid-century Andrew Dickinson found York Minster twice as large as he had expected, stared with amazement at the stained-glass windows and elaborate carvings, and concluded that, "after a deliberate survey, our famous Trinity in Broadway would just about fill the choir." Artist George Catlin told Dickinson that he had taken a party of his Indians through the cathedral. "You know they never express surprise, and yet, when they entered, all instinctively lifted up their hands in aweful astonishment. . .and on coming out they said to me, 'We never thought anything of the white man's religion before!'[22]

Visiting Britain in this same period, Caroline Kirkland observed that "nothing charms the American more than the relics of old times, but Time is fast obliterating these precious relics, and they become, like the books of the sybil, more and more precious every year."[23] The region around York had changed rapidly from the time when Allen drove through the countryside in his stagecoach. By the 1850s it was "checkered with railroads so completely that it is impossible to look out upon the landscape," as one traveler remarked, "without seeing the swift-rushing car. . . . These vehicles are every moment darting, freighted with coal and coke, iron and humanity. The country after night seems alive with fires from furnaces and coke-ovens; while by day deep, dark holes. . .open on every side like entrances to Hades, out of which machinery is shelling coal by the ton."[24]

Moving up into Scotland, the hills, wynds, closes, and tall old tenements of

**Edinburgh, c. 1840, "a city of a most singular, romantic . . . and beautiful appearance,"
in Benjamin Silliman's eyes.** *From the author's collection.*

Edinburgh—"a city of a most singular, romantic. . .and beautiful appearance," as
Benjamin Silliman aptly described it—drew the tourists all through the century
as one of their essential stops. But Dr. Johnson had been right about that city's
"effluvia," declared Silliman, visiting in the century's first decade. "The nuisance
exists in the streets before the very doors of the houses, and in the more obscure
streets it is not removed till a later hour in the forenoon." The poverty of the
inhabitants of the "old town," or historic section, most visited by these Yankee
travelers, also struck his eye. The people appeared "less comfortable than in
England," he concluded. "Even now, in winter, some of the female servant girls
in Edinburgh walk about the streets without shoes or stockings; in London I
never saw girls in service so destitute."[25]
   During his stay in Edinburgh Silliman learned that two young American
medical students, of the many who flocked to that city's world-famous medical
school in this period, were the object of considerable disapproval regarding their
determination to fight a duel over some alleged injury. They went south to
England to carry out their plan after the Scottish magistrates interfered. "The
conduct of too many of our young men abroad is such as to give no very
favourable impression of our social refinement or national morals," Professor
Silliman observed. "Nor can we wonder at the disadvantageous opinion of the

The bloodstain of the murdered Rizzio at Holyrood Palace. *The Graphic*, vol. XIV, August 19, 1876, p. 176. *Courtesy the Library of Congress*.

American character which prevails too generally in Europe. It is not long since," he added, "that a young man originally from the West Indies, but educated at a New England college, killed a fellow-student here, a youth from Ireland, in a duel."[26]

Generally, these tourists of the early decades conducted their visit in much the same way as a modern American sojourner. The hardy hiked up Salisbury Crag to Arthur's Seat, strolled through the old part of the city, as did Orville Dewey, in search of "as many spots mentioned by Scott as I could find,"[27] and, above all, rambled through the then mouldering and lonely palace of Holyrood, there to gaze on bits and pieces of her life left behind by the star-crossed Mary, Queen of Scots. It was virtually mandatory to shudder over the alleged bloodstain on the floor left from the murder of her secretary, David Rizzio, perforated by over fifty stab wounds on that spot. "It has, they say," Silliman told his readers, "resisted every effort to wash it out."[28]

Even as early as Carter's visit in 1825, the vandalism committed by souvenir gatherers was glaringly evident, and the American noticed that he was carefully watched by "the aged portress" guarding Mary's bed "lest the example of others should be followed in clipping a shred of the tapestry."[29] By the time Fanny Hall arrived there ten years later, "scarcely a thread of the rich satin counterpane" remained intact, although now a strong cord surrounded the royal bed. "Apparently she has acted upon the principle of locking the door after the horse has been stolen," observed Mrs. Hall of the aged cicerone who showed them the historic rooms.[30]

Exploring famed Edinburgh Castle atop the crag overlooking the town, Mrs. Hall was thrilled by a military review of the 42nd Regiment she watched there, many of whose participants had fought at the battle of Waterloo. She described their costume, "unlike anything else under the sun," consisting of "a scarlet jacket; a very short and full plaid frock called a *philabeg;* long white stockings, with a plaided top [of] scarlet and white; a cap or bonnet . . . ornamented with a broad band of scarlet and white, nearly covered with a profusion of black ostrich feathers. The knees are left quite bare. . . . They seem to be of an uncommon height and remarkably fine-looking fellows."[31] Mrs. Hall's reaction to the "philabeg," or kilt, was far more positive than that of her fellow countrymen, most of whom had unkind things to say about that garment.

Edinburgh's high street would fairly echo to the tramp of American feet by the middle decades of the century. Their particular objectives did not take them up into the elegant "new town," and consequently their descriptions tend to focus on the poverty then blighting the "Royal Mile" between the castle and Holyrood Palace. "When the sun pours down," observed a visitor in the forties, "an immense number of children are brought out from these damp tenements, and scattered along the sidewalks of the high street to bask . . . squirming and crawling with delight, like snakes just thawed from frozen torpidity."[32]

Looking down on this teeming street one afternoon at mid-century was George Catlin—now working up in Edinburgh "as an agent for a British land company, delivering able and popular lectures on emigration to Texas, illustrating his lectures by large transparent paintings of American scenery"— according to his friend Andrew Dickinson who visited Edinburgh in 1850. "You see this long, dingy-looking street below," mused Catlin. "Here the kings and queens, nobles and noblesse, lived in the splendours of olden time. Up and down these narrow streets, where a decent mechanic would now refuse to live, their processions marched. . . . Edinburgh throws all you have seen into the shades."[33]

Holyrood Palace continued to draw fascinated Americans to the haunted chambers of Mary Stuart, but fewer of them, as time went on, were inclined to accept the "bloodstain" as genuine. Young Benjamin Moran would receive "a round lecture from the ancient dame" showing him around, so shocked was she by his "infidelity."[34] Nathaniel Hawthorne, however, would conclude, "I do not see why it may not be the genuine, veritable stain"—not an odd remark from the author of tales like *The House of Seven Gables* or *The Scarlet Letter*.[35]

Teetotaler Yankees were, or pretended to be, mightily shocked at the consumption of spirits in the northern kingdom. "Scotland smells of whiskey as England does of mutton," Samuel Young would remark in 1855.[36] John Mitchell assured his readers that he believed "their cold wet climate has much to do with the habit. It enables them to bear more without inebriation. . . . They drink even more than the English."[37]

Leaving Edinburgh, the Yankee travelers headed next for "Scott-land"—as young Bayard Taylor named it in 1844—the region endeared to them by Sir Walter Scott's *Lady of the Lake* on which they based their itinerary.[38] "What did Walter Scott write without stint?" asked Emerson scornfully, "A rhymed travellers' guide to Scotland!"[39] Generally they headed, by way of Stirling Castle, for the village of Callandar. Once an obscure Highland village, Callandar, after the publication of Scott's work, became the starting point for excursions to the Trossachs and Loch Katrine, and it expanded rapidly. "What a benefactor was Scott to his country," observed George Putnam in 1836, who attributed the original tourist boom to English holidaymakers kept home from the Continent by Napoleon's blockade who went instead up into Scotland, attracted by the writer's romantic descriptions of the scenery. "New roads, hotels, and even villages have sprung up in hitherto solitary places among the hills and valleys of which he has written," recalled the American, "supported almost entirely by inquisitive visitors."[40] Henry Colman observed in 1843 that "Scotland actually swarms with tourists attracted by Scott's descriptions."[41] Scott himself was well aware, according to Washington Irving, that his writings were attracting travelers, and he even expressed concern that this influx might have "injured the old-fashioned Scottish character." A woman who kept an inn at Glenross had begged him, Scott told Irving, to write of her region as he had of Loch Katrine where his book had, in her words, done the inn "a muckle deal of good."[42]

The tour route took visitors some ten miles along the banks of Loch Vennachar, Loch Achray, through the Trossachs, or "bristly country," to the banks of Loch Katrine. There they proceeded by boat to Stronachlachar at the foot of the nine-mile-long loch, and then it was overland to Inversnaid on the banks of Loch Lomond. In the early decades this pilgrimage involved long hikes on foot and treks on the backs of rough Highland ponies pulled along by wild-haired, Gaelic-speaking girls "in tartan duds," as Gibson described their colorful, ragged attire. Sturdy oarsmen rowed them in small boats over Loch Katrine with the head boatman reciting line after line of Scott's poetry in English, although conversing with his fellows only in the Gaelic. "These merry grigs," as Gibson called them, "although they could neither read nor write, managed to recite with great beauty and emphasis some of the finest passages of *The Lady of the Lake*."[43]

Nathaniel Carter alone really perceived what had happened to the Gaels and their Highland culture after their tragic defeat under Prince Charles at Culloden in 1745. He wrote:

> The lofty spirit of the clans has been broken down by conquest in war, and the oppressions of the government; and though inroads have been made upon their language and habits by the establishment of English schools among them, and the commercial intercourse of modern times: yet a sort of twilight of national manners still lingers upon their hills, and in some of the remoter glens, the original cast of character is preserved in its pristine simplicity.

Carter listened to the "wild sweet airs" of songs in the Gaelic and noted their pathetic efforts to retain something of the Highland mode of dress.[44]

Calvin Colton entered one of the so-called "black houses" of the region (the term deriving from the effects of peat smoke in these chimneyless structures), as did Zachariah Allen a few years later. Low, one-room cottages they were, built of stones, and covered with roofs of turf held in place by rocks. They were not much more than thirty by fifteen feet, with the family occupying one end and the few beasts they owned the other, with a low partition between.[45] Colton and Allen both noted how their eyes stung from the peat smoke from the fire, which was laid on the earthen floor and whose only escape was a hole in the roof. Allen was served buttermilk by an old woman who had reddened eyes and blackened skin and yet who was "truly hospitable" despite her circumstances. "All her worldly gear," so far as he could see, consisted of "a sort of bunk built of boards. . . a few earthen dishes, tubs and pots, with a crudely made case of drawers. The floor was of earth or mud, hardened by frequent tread."[46] Frequently, in these years, American visitors were offered oatcakes by these poverty-stricken Scots—cakes too coarse and unpalatable for refined tourist palates—but Orville Dewey actually unbent and sampled some proffered usquebaugh (water of life), or whiskey, which his boatman told him was "the only thing and the *only* thing indispensable." The whiskey was not, Dewey admitted, the "usual bilious" stuff he had expected.[47]

Unlike Fanny Hall, American males were shocked by the kilt. Silliman labeled that garment "indecorous and uncomfortable," also expressing surprise that it was sanctioned in a country where "decency of personal appearance is so commonly regarded."[48] Dewey likewise was horrified, almost thirty years later, at the sight of soldiers "parading about naked from above the knee to the middle of the calf of the leg."[49]

Yankee reaction to the music of the bagpipe was also mixed, but prim Calvin Colton, of all people, sensed its power to stir the blood and touch the heart. Seated at his breakfast one morning in the thirties at the inn in Dunkeld, Colton heard the sound of pipes out on the road. "I jumped up and ran to the window," he recalled, "and by that time every window and every door in the street was full of heads; everybody in the street, horses and all, stopped, and other people came pouring in from adjacent streets as the music passed. There were two pipers." It was merely a party of reapers heading for the fields, he learned, adding, "I had often heard the bagpipe before, but never with a power to be compared to this." It seemed to him that the pipers were unconscious of the power they exercised over the villagers. "There is a subduing plaintiveness in the bagpipes skillfully played which few hearts can resist," observed Colton. "There is a world of poetry and the deepest soul of song in the best music on the bagpipes."[50]

By mid-century the tour through Scott's magic land would follow much the same route as earlier, only now comfortable hotels awaited the tourists at various points, and their modes of conveyance were more sophisticated. Instead of rough-coated little ponies, heavy wagons now trundled them over roads once trod as paths by the bare-footed Highland girls; tiny steamers paddled them over the lochs once dominated by strong-armed rowers. Shortly before his visit in 1844, Taylor was told, one of the new little steamers had been towed out in the middle of Loch Katrine and sunk by boatmen "jealous of their privileges."[51] It was, of course, in vain. Even the recitation of the poetic passages from Scott was taken over by wagon drivers, who now merely read aloud from battered copies of *The Lady of the Lake*. A blind fiddler or ragged piper provided music for pennies on board the steamers, and they quickly learned to play "'Yankee Doodle."

Like Putnam twenty years earlier, educator Henry Tappan at mid-century was "reminded of the wealth Sir Walter had caused to flow into the country and the number of persons for whom he had indirectly provided employment. Villages have been enlarged, hotels have been built, roads have been opened and improved, lines of steamboats and coaches established. And so it is," he wrote, unknowingly describing the advent of "tourism," that "Stratford-on-Avon will forever be indebted to the grave of Shakespeare. . .and the Trossachs to the pen which wrote *The Lady of the Lake*."[52] Another American observed that the Scots seemed to look upon Scott "not only as an author but as a sort of patriot."[53]

Despite all this American interest in and adulation of Scott, Harriet Beecher Stowe was surprised in London, in 1853, to discover almost none of it among the literati she met there. "We discussed this among ourselves," she wrote, "and rather wondered at it. The fact is," she finally concluded, "Scott belongs to a past and not to a coming age. He beautified and adorned that which is waxing old and passing away. He loved and worshipped in his very soul institutions which the common people have felt as a restraint and a burden."[54] Perhaps Mrs. Stowe had indeed put her finger on it. While Americans flocked to Britain with their heads full of dreams spun by "the wizard of the north," Britons themselves were at that moment finding escape in the excitement of Mrs. Stowe's own *Uncle Tom's Cabin*—a world and situation as remote from their own as Scott's was to the Americans. Meanwhile, both nations marched steadily toward tragic wars that sapped their mid-nineteenth-century optimism and killed hundreds of thousands of young men—for the Britons the Crimean War, and for the Americans their Civil War.

Any American who could gain an invitation to Abbotsford to be entertained by Sir Walter Scott achieved a kind of immortality of his own. Washington Irving, of course, was so honored, but author Samuel Goodrich bragged that he had gotten to see Scott even before the years of his great renown, when the latter was still at

Sir Walter Scott (1771–1832), who "made it a rule never to turn his back on good company," according to Edward Everett. By Daniel Maclise. *Courtesy the Library of Congress.*

work as clerk of the court of sessions at Edinburgh. "Three full-wigged judges were seated upon a lofty bench," recalled Goodrich, "and beneath them at a little table in front, was a large man bent down and writing laboriously . . . it was Sir Walter himself!" In one of those "pen portraits" of which people in the nineteenth century, before photography, were so fond, Goodrich described him as "very nearly six feet in height, full-chested, and of a farmer-like aspect. His complexion seemed to have originally been sandy, but now his hair was gray. He had the rough, freckled, weather-beaten face of a man who is much in the open air; his eye is small and gray and peered out inquisitively beneath a heavy brow, edged with something like gray-twisted bristle—the whole expression of his face . . . being exceedingly agreeable."[55]

Invited to Abbotsford, Edward Everett never forgot how, upon his arrival, he was taken outside to meet the author in what the Scotts called the "Mushroom Park." There, recalled Everett, "we soon fell in with Sir Walter, who though he had been on his feet all morning, said he made it a rule never to turn his back on good company, and joined us. We had a scramble as to who should pick the best mushrooms and the most." During his visit, Everett wrote, "Sir Walter poured out all the treasures of his memory, in traditions of border times, anecdotes of celebrated characters, interspersed with sallies of quiet pleasantry." Although Scott is today remembered primarily as a lover of dogs, his deerhound Maida, a spaniel, a terrier, and a greyhound, Everett recorded how, after dinner, "a favorite cat placed herself upon the table near him. As I sat next, Scott begged me not to be disturbed. He caressed the animal, who was evidently a pet, and said that if cats were as well treated as dogs, they would be as gentle and faithful." Twenty-six years later Everett would stand in that same room, by then known as the room in which the author died, remembering that happy evening and depressed by the sad emptiness of a house which had become another tourist mecca.[56]

George Ticknor was a house guest of Scott's the night the latter was seized by an attack of the illness that eventually killed him, and in 1832, knowing that Scott lay mortally ill at Abbotsford, Charles Stewart traveled to the estate simply for a glance at the exterior of the great house in which he knew Scott was even then "sinking into the arms of the ruthless conqueror to whose power all living flesh must yield."[57] Arriving there shortly after Scott's death in 1832, Henry McLellan was shown around by a "Mistress Alice," whom he prevailed upon to give him "some of Sir Walter's handwriting and a seal from one of his letters." He also took, he admitted, "a number of flowers from her mantel shelf."[58]

A year later Orville Dewey shared his almost religious ecstasy with his readers. "I have seen it! The study—the desk at which he wrote! In the very chair, the throne of power from which he stretched out a sceptre over all the world, and over all the ages, I sat down—it was enough! My homage was silence until I had ridden miles away from that abode of departed genius."[59] Dr. Gibson, a few years after this, was, he claimed, permitted to touch "the last garments worn by the friend of the human race" and also honored with a momentary "sit" at the author's desk.[60] Later tourists were to find this last feat rather more difficult, as their numbers increased and efforts were made to protect the house and its contents from the ravages of over-eager "relic" hunters. Over 500 Americans

THE STUDY, ABBOTSFORD, WITH SIR W. SCOTT'S CHAIR AND WRITING TABLE

THE LIBRARY, ABBOTSFORD, WITH PORTRAIT OF SIR W. SCOTT'S ELDEST SON

BUST OF SIR WALTER SCOTT IN THE LIBRARY AT ABBOTSFORD

Scott's library and study (upper left), where travelers all wished to seat themselves in the author's desk chair. *The Graphic,* vol. IV, August 15, 1871, p. 23. *Courtesy the Library of Congress.*

had signed as visitors to Abbotsford in the summer of 1845, according to Margaret Fuller who came a year later.[61] "Such is the influence of a name," mused Briton Charles Greville, who considered Abbotsford "a miserable humbug of a place" and expressed surprise that "crowds of traveling pilgrims repair to this habitation of Sir Walter Scott."[62]

Abbotsford indeed became a shrine for visiting Americans, and there were frequent complaints about a sharp-tongued old woman who showed the place, rushing them through too fast, and occasionally nicking one of them with her verbal weapon as in the case of Ohioan Samuel Cox. Instead of waiting meekly at the entrance to be admitted with the next group of visitors, he had strolled down to the riverbank of the Tweed. "So!" she greeted him when his time came to enter. "You're the party that have been wandering over the grounds where you've no business—none at all!" "I did not like to spoil our visit," Cox wrote, "so I kept my teeth clenched and my tongue in prison, and we all marched in like whipped and naughty children."[63]

To sit in the author's chair eventually became a duel of sorts between the tourists and the custodians. In the chair where Orville Dewey had luxuriated in the thirties, by mid-century no one was permitted to sit, and Benjamin Moran was allowed to touch it only.[64] Another young American was stared at sternly and roundly scolded by the elderly guide when he asked permission to seat himself for a moment. "We hold that chair too sacred for anyone to sit on," he was informed.[65] Yet in this same period Mrs. A. E. Newman would claim she was not only permitted to sit in the chair but also to examine books lying on the table just as Scott had left them and "to handle the pen and ink stand . . . sacred relics . . . at which thousands will look mournfully and sigh that Scott ever was born to die."[66] Bayard Taylor, the romantic young hiker, walked all the way to Abbotsford and actually forded the Tweed, which seemed to him the only proper manner in which to approach the abode of departed genius. Taylor claimed that his visit to Abbotsford inspired in him the same feeling of awe "which impressed me before the grave of Washington."[67] Another visitor found himself oppressed by sadness and thoughts of mortality. "All must die—all must die," sighed Henry Tappan. "It comes to this at last. The man of genius no less than the most insignificant creature. There is no escape."[68] Journalist Grace Greenwood, in a similar mood at mid-century, would mourn: "Gone, gone forever—dust, dust, these twenty years."[69]

After Abbotsford followed the visit to Melrose Abbey and then the author's grave at Dryburgh Abbey. "If thou wouldst visit fair Melrose aright," Scott had written, "go visit it in the pale moonlight."[70] William Dana did just that, while Bayard Taylor settled for a brief daylight meditation on the broken pillar Scott himself always used for a seat when he visited there. At Melrose Henry Colman was mortified to be known as an American when the guide pointed out that "many Americans who had been there had broken off and plundered" much of the ornamental stonework.[71]

To make the pilgrimage to Scott's grave at Dryburgh Abbey, youthful Benjamin Moran dutifully walked the nine miles from Melrose. "I will remember the scene to the last hour of my existence," vowed Moran, "a scene for a pilgrim and a double glory for one who had come so far. I waited for an hour contemplating the ruin and the splendor of the setting sun."[72]

Few of these travelers looked beyond the pages of Scott's romantic descriptions to study the flesh-and-blood Scots who labored for their comfort, driving the heavy coaches and wagons, lifting their heavy luggage, and striving hard in inns and hotels to meet American standards. Jacob Abbott was one of the few to notice the empty desolation of the Highlands in 1848, due to the Clearances, and remarked that "the whole land is given up to sheep, cattle, and grouse, and to sportsmen and tourists; the sole occupation of the cottagers being to take care of one and that of the villagers to provide the other."[73] Less Gaelic was heard now, but Taylor related how a Scot told him that they reserved English mostly for their dogs, along with their English employers, and the tourists. "Very few dogs understand Gaelic," a boatman solemnly assured him. "But they all understand English. . . . Indeed, I know some persons, who know nothing of English, that

Birthplace of Robert Burns. Tourists eventually had to be restrained from jumping into the old bed in the corner where the poet was born. *The English Illustrated Magazine,* **vol. IV, 1886–87, p. 325.** *Courtesy the Library of Congress.*

speak it to their dogs."[74] Something of the poverty in the Hebrides would be recorded by William Cullen Bryant in 1849, when he observed on the docks at Wick, on Scotland's northeast coast, "some strapping fellows in blue Highland bonnets" and was informed that they had walked over three hundred miles from the islands for six or seven weeks' employment in the herring fisheries for about six pounds in wages.[75]

The humble birthplace of Robert Burns, some thirty miles southwest of Glasgow, was to become another literary shrine for Americans in Scotland. Passing through Alloway in 1817, Andrew Bigelow bribed the driver of his "dilly," or public stagecoach, to stop while he and his companion took a quick look at the rough cottage with a simple marker: "Burns Cottage—the Ayrshire poet was born under this roof on the 29th January, 1759." Inside, Bigelow found two plain rooms inhabited by "an elderly sawney-looking man, who seemed never to have been particularly abstemious in the use of whiskey."[76] The youthful traveler took a quick look at the recessed bed in which the poet was born and then resumed his journey. In later decades a veritable industry grew up around this simple dwelling, and it would become an all but obligatory stop for the American tourist throughout the nineteenth century.

Visiting Alloway a decade later, Carter was shocked to see that souvenir or "relic" hunters had chipped away at the gravestone of Burns's father until the inscription was illegible, while the old kirk [church] of Alloway itself was a "roofless ruin" with only the walls standing, "and even these are dropping away piecemeal." Unlike many future pilgrims, Carter was pleased with the newly-completed neo-classical "Grecian temple" erected as a memorial to the poet, and at the old "brig o' doon," the bridge immortalized in Burns's poem, *Tam O'Shanter,* he bought a walking stick made of sweetbriar for "a highly prized relic." At Dumfries he enjoyed a brief visit with Burns's widow, whom he was pleased to find "retaining lineaments of beauty which the poet found in his bonny Jean."[77]

If Scott was good for business, so was Burns. "The lands celebrated by Burns are now included in the European tour," Benjamin Moran would inform his readers in 1851, "and the one who does not visit them is considered deficient in taste." Moran "passed a half hour under the straw-thatched roof, where pilgrims from every section of the world have been to pay homage to the genius of the Ayrshire ploughman." He found the frame around a portrait of the poet all "cut and carved full of the names of visitors," and was thrilled to come upon, in the pages of the signature album, "the name of 'A. Tennyson' written in a hand as delicate as the breathings of his own muse."[78]

No self-respecting nineteenth-century American tourist could fail to honor the English trinity consisting of Stratford-on-Avon, Warwick Castle and the ruins of Kenilworth Castle, the last two recommended and endorsed by their beloved Sir Walter Scott. In the early days of the century, Stratford was little more than a coach stop for travelers, but even then Americans, like Elkanah Watson in 1782, were "stimulated by an ardent and deeply excited enthusiasm" to view the birthplace of Shakespeare. He called it "a little, old and dilapidated dwelling," where an old woman claiming to be a descendant of the poet showed him "the remnant of an antiquated armchair" almost chipped away by the knives of

Shakespeare's birthplace at Stratford-on-Avon as it appeared c. 1840. *Illustrated London News,* **September 18, 1847, p. 180.** *Courtesy the Library of Congress.*

visitors in search of relics.[79] Silliman, whose coach stopped there at midnight in 1805, could say little more than that "we supped in the town of Stratford-on-Avon" and that "all the inhabitants were asleep and I could not visit Shakespeare's monument which is still standing in the church."[80] Ballard, a decade later, also stopped in the town to change horses, and his curiosity led him to the alleged birthplace, which he called "one of the most wretched hovels I ever beheld . . . now used as a butcher's shop."[81]

It was Washington Irving, in his *Sketchbook* essay entitled "Stratford-on-Avon," who made the town the obligatory shrine it soon became for Americans and still is today. Many tourists would insist on trying to reenact the solitary evening Irving described, depicting himself as a wayfarer, meditating for hours late at night, before a fire in a little parlor of the Red Horse Inn.

Let the world without go as it may; let kingdoms rise or fall, so long as he has the wherewithal to pay his bill, he is, for the time being, the very monarch of all he surveys. The arm-chair is his throne, the poker his sceptre, and the little parlor, some twelve feet square, his undisputed empire. . . . The words of sweet Shakspeare were just passing through my mind as the clock struck midnight from the tower of the church in which he lies buried. There was a gentle tap at the door, and a pretty chambermaid, putting in her smiling face, with a hesitating air, inquired whether I had rung. I understood it as a modest hint that it was time to retire. My dream of absolute dominion was at an end; so abdicating my throne like a prudent potentate, to avoid being deposed, and

putting the Stratford Guidebook under my arm, as a pillow companion, I went
to bed, and dreamt all night of Shakspeare.[82]

By 1855 Samuel Young was to find the walls of Irving's bedchamber at the inn
literally covered with signatures of tourists like himself, many of them American.
All his countrymen, he was told, "were desirous of sleeping in Washington
Irving's room."[83] They had scarcely to ask now to see the famous "sceptre," for it
was proudly brought forth for their inspection once it was known they were
Americans. Now it was in a silk case, then wrapped in red plush, and, on one
tourist's visit, wrapped in a towel. At mid-century, a visitor claimed to have seen
it folded in an American flag. The old poker had become virtually an object of
veneration. "All the Americans wish to see *that,* but I have to lock it up to
preserve it," the landlady told Stephen Massett in 1854.[84]

The day following his midnight reverie at the Red Horse Inn, Irving, too, had
visited Shakespeare's birthplace, the same "small, mean-looking edifice of wood
and plaster" seen by Ballard, and still presided over by a "garrulous old lady."
More satisfying to Irving was Shakespeare's tomb in Trinity Church on the banks
of the Avon. "His idea pervades the place," Irving thought. "The whole pile
seems but as his mausoleum. . . . As I trod the sounding pavement, there was
something intense and thrilling in the idea, that . . . the remains of Shakspeare
were mouldering beneath my feet. It was a long time before I could prevail upon
myself to leave the place; and as I passed through the churchyard, I plucked a
branch from off the yew trees, the only relic that I have brought from Stratford."[85]

On their visits to the Red Horse Inn both Charles Stewart and Nathaniel
Parker Willis were told by the landlady of her encounter with Washington
Irving, whom she remembered fondly for "his modest ways and timid look."
Stewart said she told him that she knew *he* was an American at once, as "so many
Americans visited the tomb of Shakespeare."[86]

Nathaniel Carter, who stopped at the inn after Irving's time, observed "a copy
of Washington Irving's sketch of Stratford-on-Avon upon the table of the
parlour." Carter, too, enjoyed "the pleasure of occupying the author's bedchamber." He found the Shakespeare birthplace still with the downstairs front
room being used as a butcher shop, all "lighted and hung with meat." He was
shown upstairs to "the chamber in which the favored child of genius was born,"
where he came on a large album filled with the names of those for whom no
room was left on the walls, which by now were covered over with signatures. "A
large proportion were from our country," Carter observed as he examined the
album, "and the names of several of our friends were recognized."[87] He does not
mention signing the book himself, but eleven years later young George Putnam
copied an inscription he found written there "by the esteemed and lamented
Carter," by then in his grave.

> Think not, Britannia, all the tears are thine,
> Which flow, a tribute to this hallowed shrine;
> Pilgrims from every land shall hither come,
> And fondly linger round the poet's tomb.
> 1825   Nov. 18.
>   N. H. Carter
>   H. J. Eckford[88]

Washington Irving (1783–1859), as the young man remembered by the landlady of Stratford's Red Horse Inn for his "modest ways and timid look." By Daniel Maclise. *Courtesy the Library of Congress.*

Warwick Castle attracted Americans who had read Sir Walter Scott's enthusiastic endorsement of it. *The Graphic*, **vol. IX, May 9, 1874, p. 453.** *Courtesy the Library of Congress.*

At the birth chamber of Shakespeare in 1850 the Reverend Henry Ward Beecher went into ecstasies and announced in one of his dispatches home to the *New York Independent* that he had made arrangements "by which I have free use of the room where I now write. . . . Two hundred and eighty-six years ago, in this room, a mother clasped her new-born babe to her bosom—perhaps on the very spot where I am writing."[89]

Another romantic Yankee pilgrim, reported Nathaniel Parker Willis, had taken the notion to sleep in that room and did so on a make-shift pallet on the floor. Two-thirds of the visitors were Americans, so the custodian claimed, and the visitors' album proved her correct.[90] Hawthorne, unlike Beecher or his other countrymen, when he visited a few years later was "conscious of not the slightest emotion . . . nor any quickening of the imagination".[91]

Conveniently near Stratford, for pilgrimage purposes, was Warwick Castle—still inhabited—dating from the fourteenth century, and open to the public through the nineteenth century, as it still is today. Sir Walter Scott urged his readers to experience it as "the fairest monument of ancient and chivalrous splendour, which yet remains uninjured by time."[92] A Puritan stronghold during

England's Civil War in the seventeenth century, it had been spared by the Cromwellians—unlike its neighbor Kenilworth, which was all but reduced to ruins. Here at Warwick, as at Chatsworth, certain Yankee travelers enjoyed grousing about the fee they had to pay to view a nobleman's treasures. "I am told on good authority," confided Charles Stewart in 1832, "that a late housekeeper of this castle, left, by will, to a younger son of the family . . . a fortune of many thousands, chiefly accumulated in this way."[93] Allen assured his readers he was told that the sum was "above 10,000 pounds."[94] The Reverend Robert Breckin-ridge grumped, "In England everything is kept for show and all at a price." But he felt reimbursed by his glimpse of two members of the family, "a feeble-looking lad and a stately and rather handsome middle-aged female . . . the first of this proud aristocracy upon whom our democratic eyes had ever chanced to light."[95]

While waiting for entrance to the castle, George Putnam was first taken into the lodge there to view the great one-hundred-gallon iron kettle known as "Sir Guy's Porridge Pot," his armor and that of his horse, and his halberd and lance. This enormous pot was long a tourist favorite, and one Yankee would recall how his guide popped "a little fellow, reminding one of Tom Thumb"[96] into its depths while another claimed that "five of our party got into this pot and there was room, like a 'bus' for one more."[97]

Once into the great house itself, Putnam was charmed by "that magnificent range of apartments, extending 330 feet in a line, on one side, only, overlooking the river, and furnished in a style of which the epithet *superb* scarcely gives you an idea, as we apply it, to things insignificant in comparison. And what is more," he added, "they looked *comfortable*; a bright coal fire in each room, with ottomans, and every modern elegance." He was shown, he said, all the rooms "save that at the moment occupied by the earl's family," and, as a "special favor," so he thought, he was led through the armory, "a long hall: about six feet wide, *actually cut out of the thickness of the castle walls* . . . with ancient armor of all sorts." The modern tourist, Putnam informed his readers, is met, instead of by "warriors bold . . . a pretty blue-eyed damsel who will:"

> Bow him through donjon-keep and hall
> For three and sixpence sterling.[98]

Warwick Castle would elicit Andrew Jackson Downing's enthusiastic and unqualified approval as the mid-century arbiter of architecture and landscape design in the United States. Whereas Eaton Hall was "meretricious," Warwick combined "perhaps more of romantic and feudal interest than any other actual residence in England. All was entirely harmony. Still a castle, as real in its character as a feudal stronghold and yet as complete a baronial residence as the imagination can conceive," Downing wrote.[99] Reverend Beecher was overcome at Warwick. "It opens upon the sight with grandeur," he gushed. "I stood for a little and let the vision pierce me through. Who can tell what he feels in such a place!"[100] Visitors in these mid-century years would complain of being rushed through too rapidly by an officious housekeeper "inexorable with her bunch of keys and rustling silk dress." One traveler told how he "tried to soften her hard heart by telling her I was from America and had never seen such fine pictures before. 'Yes,' she responded, I knew you were from America. We have a great many Americans here!' "[101]

Leaving Warwick, the Yankee pilgrims headed for Kenilworth, where Putnam was "set down amidst a swarm of juvenile sellers of guidebooks at the entrance" when he visited the castle in the 1830s. " 'What a pity,' " he remarked to his guide, " 'that the walls of the castle should have been so battered down.' 'Yes,' said my ancient guide, 'you may thank Cromwell for that.' " Altogether pleased at the end of his day's sightseeing, Putnam returned to his inn "filled with excitement enough to make one speechless for the rest of the day," and he promptly recorded his impressions in his journal instead.[102]

To Americans with sensibilities as tender as those of the Reverend Orville Dewey, their visit to the ruins of Kenilworth sent them into raptures equaling those they enjoyed in Scott's study, where he wrote the novel *Kenilworth* that had so captured their youthful fancies. "Alas! the feast and the song are gone," mourned Dewey, gazing on the ruined walls. "The gatherings of nobles, and the flourish of trumpets are here no more. . . . Here and there in the courtyards I saw picnic parties, carelessly seated on the grass, as if in mockery of the proud and guarded festivals and grandeurs of former days. I thought with myself, that they must be more familiar with the spot than I was, to be able to sit down, and 'eat, drink and be merry.' "[103] Stewart found Kenilworth "beautiful indeed," but, unlike the puritan Dewey, he was pleased to see families enjoying their modest lunches and young ladies with sketchbooks busily at work.[104]

With his penchant for romantic moonlight visits to Britain's literary shrines, Dana came back to Kenilworth at night for a second view. "I seemed to be treading on enchanted ground. That silent hour . . . that pale moon, shining behind ruined towers . . . I can never forget it."[105] Caroline Kirkland simply proclaimed it a place "to make one forget breakfast, dinner and supper."[106] Once again, the Reverend Beecher lost all control, trembling, weeping, meditating there for three hours, so he claimed. "I had never in my life seen an *old* building. I had never seen a *ruin*. I hastened back to my inn with a strange sadness of spirit which I did not shake off all day. I was glad I had visited the place *alone*; no one should go except ALONE!"[107] Even sensible Grace Greenwood declared that the place was "enough to make one in love with ruins."[108] For many decades the Americans continued to prowl the precincts of Kenilworth, clutching their guidebooks, dreaming their fantasies out of Scott's novel, some of them even purchasing copies to read right on the premises.

Tours of Blenheim Palace, built by the first Duke of Marlborough, were fewer than those to either Eaton Hall, Chatsworth, or Warwick Castle and usually occurred in conjunction with a visit to nearby Oxford. Again, there were the usual complaints about the fee extracted by the owner's servants—a whole half crown, complained scientist Jacob Green in 1828, "paid to the crusty old housekeeper who conducted me over the whole. I cannot let her go without a slap," he wrote. "The surly pride and affected importance of the menials of His Grace of Marlborough are well known to most travellers and one is apt to lose before leaving the house half the complacent feelings with which he may have entered it."[109] The magnificent neoclassical chapel, serving also as the family tomb, elicited Yankee admiration, but at Blenheim there were more of those "indecent" pictures so offensive to delicate American tastes. Young Dana, who so enthused over the ruins of Melrose Abbey and Kenilworth in the moonlight, was embarrassed on being shown pictures in the Titian Gallery "of the most gross and indecent character," particularly as he was "with a large party of ladies that happened to arrive just after me." They were, he concluded, "evidently at a great loss to know which way to look," but he added that "American ladies would have been more so." Apart from its great size, he said of Blenheim that he found "nothing at all imposing in its exterior."[110]

Stonehenge attracted American travelers, although in limited numbers, from the earliest decades of the nineteenth century and even before. Old Samuel Curwen, for example, the American loyalist who spent nine years of exile in Britain during the Revolution, made his way out to the Salisbury Plain in 1776. At first he thought that the strange mass of stones off in the distance "resembled a company of men."[111] Zachariah Allen's first glimpse of them in 1830 reminded

Stonehenge as it appeared early in the nineteenth century. Henry McLellan and friends chipped off pieces for souvenirs in 1831. *From the author's collection.*

him of a clump of cedars "rising above the edge of the horizon . . . some leaning, others standing erect, with heavy blocks of stone lying horizontally upon their tops." As an inventor, he was curious as to the methods of construction, seeing how readily such great stones could be lifted by "the present mechanical engines" but mystified as to how it was done in ancient times. "Unaccountable," he concluded at last.[112] In these years a mallet actually hung there on a peg to assist visitors in their efforts to chip off bits of stone to carry away as relics. Henry McLellan and his friends, in 1831, labored "until nearly dark, making our observations and endeavouring to splinter off some pieces from the rock . . . very difficult as they were of a hard species of quartz. But we persevered until we were rewarded by getting a few small pieces," he reported.[113]

Few American travelers at mid-century pushed farther northwest to Bath, but earlier, when it was a fashionable resort, a number of Yankee visitors reported on its sophisticated wonders. Abigail Adams, the American minister's wife, for example, had spent "a fortnight in amusement and dissipation" there in 1787, gazing with disapproving New England eyes on the doings not only of invalids ostensibly there for health reasons but "the gay, the indolent, the curious, the gambler, the fortune-hunter."[114] Her young countryman, Elkanah Watson, who had preceded her there by a few years, thought the King's Bath "a most singular and ludicrous spectacle; old and young, matrons and maidens; beaus and priests, all promiscuously wading and splashing . . . a band of music the while playing some solemn march or exhilarating dance."[115]

Silliman studied the same scene in the first decade of the new century, terming this same King's Bath a "warm sea," luxurious and well managed, "accessible to all decent people."[116] Young oats-sower George Rapelje actually achieved a solitary swim, so he claimed. "They told me if I would come early in the morning before anyone came, I might have a swim; but must quit the moment anyone came. The water is delicious," he wrote. "Everything is prepared in the greatest comfort; a small room with a fire; a man waiting to assist you in putting on a bathing gown, which they have ready when you come out; your clothes are hung round the fire airing . . . stockings, shirt, drawers and flannels." The water was pleasantly warm, he found, but too warm if one got one's feet near the hole where it "boils up in the center of the pond."[117]

All the "fine, light-coloured free stone" that his countryman Benjamin Silliman so admired in the houses and buildings of Bath in the first decade had, by 1828, when Jacob Green arrived there, turned "greyish" in color, stained "dark and ugly with the coal smoke." Green's republican sympathies were, moreover, shocked by the spectacle of "sedan chairs in which the lazy citizens are transported from one place to another," as well as by "a kind of go-cart on three wheels which is dragged along by one man. The persons who sat in these chairs, some of them young and healthy, seemed, to my notion, very ridiculous," snorted the Yankee chemistry professor.[118]

Brighton, successor to Bath as the favored resort of the fashionable—due to the patronage of the Prince Regent, later George IV—was visited by a number of American travelers in its heyday. John Griscom, in 1818, studied the Prince's famed "Pavilion" and thought "its architecture extremely whimsical, if not ridiculous, having more the appearance of a Turkish mosque, than of a habitation. It has been undergoing almost constant change during the last twenty years," he added, "and is not yet completed to the satisfaction of its Royal owner. But 'Great Princes' have great playthings," he concluded, "and the Pavilion has probably answered its purpose of a useful hobby."[119]

"The tide of prosperity is already beginning to ebb," observed Nathaniel Wheaton of Bath, about 1824, "since the king [George IV] has diverted his attention to reforming the architecture of Windsor Palace [*sic*]. Since his accession to the throne his visits to this place have been few and far between. . . . It will probably sink into oblivion when he ceases to live." Judging Brighton "a haunt of dissipation, both high and low, a vanity fair for pleasure-hunters and gamblers, and whatever else is worthless in society," Wheaton nevertheless admired "the fine complexions" of the ladies he saw there.[120]

Sailor MacKenzie was shown about the Pavilion—"the most eccentric building I have ever seen, like some gorgeous Indian encampment"—by a young military officer-friend attached to the household of George IV's successor, his brother William IV, the old "Sailor King." Since the Royal couple was in residence, a bit of dodging about was required on the part of the two trespassers so as not to interfere with the domestic arrangements. MacKenzie appreciated William's comment that "while he would not himself have built such a place, now it was here he would enjoy it." The American thought "the paintings and ornaments were in a rather tea-chest taste and yet not destitute of grace." What impressed him most was the huge airy kitchen where "there was quite an army of joints turning by means of machinery before a coal fire and quantities of cooks and scullions, and women preparing pastry. They were scrupulously neat in their appearance, and everything in the place looked nice, clean and decidedly English." At one point MacKenzie and his "guide" had to duck out of sight "as the royal family were likely to be returning from the breakfast room and our proceedings were not exactly in order."[121]

One other English region—the Isle of Wight—drew substantial numbers of American travelers right through the century. The Reverend Heman Humphrey was among the first, however, to head there. The island was not yet, in the summer of 1835, strongly related to royalty as it would one day be upon the acquisition of land and the building of Osborne House by Victoria and Albert as a private summer residence. Humphrey's visit involved a pilgrimage to the shrine of a popular Protestant "saint" of the period, Elizabeth Walbridge, subject of the Reverend Leigh Richmond's *The Dairyman's Daughter*—an account issued as a religious tract in 1809, which eventually reached over two million copies. Journey Humphrey must to the little village of Arraton to seek out the humble cottage where this long-suffering young woman died. Reverently, the American thumbed through her Bible and touched the old armchair in which she had sat, when able, during her last days. Since his visit, he reminded his readers, that same chair had been "purchased by a benevolent countryman of our own . . . and exhibited, with all the vouchers in due form, at a late anniversary meeting of the American Tract Society, as a present and a memorial, to be sacredly kept, and to be occupied by the President of the Society, on all similar occasions." Humphrey admitted that he thought "it was a thousand times more in keeping by the side of Elizabeth Walbridge's little table than it ever can be in the Broadway Tabernacle." Her grave in the little churchyard, a mile and a half a way from the cottage, he finally located with the help of some "squalid children" whom he judged "old enough to be at work and all of them to be at school. Little did they think of anything," complained the clergyman, "but the pennies for which they were ready to scramble at my departure."[122]

5

London

"It resembles Boston in its tortuosities; New York in its activity; Philadelphia in its magnificence," wrote Henry McLellan, seated before his journal, pen in hand, trying to sort out his impressions at the end of his first day in London in 1831, and he concluded, "I am quite overwhelmed with its magnitude, activity and splendor....Passed through many a noted street. Walked over Tower Hill where I had a good view of the close pent city."[1]

McLellan soon learned—as had Silliman before him—to navigate the world's greatest metropolis with some preparation. "A stranger," Silliman warned, "should not trust himself in London without a guide or ample directions. A method we soon found it necessary to adopt was to plan every excursion with the aid of a map, and to make out on a pocket card, in their proper succession, a list of the streets through which we wished to pass."[2] Street maps could be had, Joshua White learned on his arrival in 1810, "at almost any of the stationery or print shops." Polite and civil shopkeepers, he added, "always cheerfully give information in their power, in a manner which seems characteristic of Englishmen."[3]

Despite their initial confusion, London was to Americans of every period the fulfillment of childhood dreams to minds crowded with echoes of nursery rhymes, snatches of songs, legends, passages from literature, remembered facts, and even pronouncements by Dr. Johnson. Like George Putnam, they "remembered London" from the days when they "rode a-horseback on father's best knee." But even in this frame of mind, and equipped with their street maps, the clamor, bustle, and surging traffic of the great city at first overwhelmed these Yankee pilgrims.

"The first night in London I heard everytime that I awoke a rushing sound which at first I thought was the river," recalled a traveler. "It sounds like the Falls of Niagara. This was the noise of the streets; the steady flow of carriages along the streets around you, rises and falls, swells and sinks, but never ceases day or night."[4] Henry Colman observed that "there is no night in London."[5] Joseph Battell, some years hence, would conclude that "more than any other city, London satisfies an American's craving for bigness."[6]

"Do all these persons know what they are after, or where they are going?" asked Wilbur Fisk in amazement in the thirties, as he stood in a London·street, jostled by the flow of people pushing past him.[7] "I have stood two or three times," remarked Colman, "in situations where I had the opportunity of looking up a long line of street, and the carriages and people seemed absolutely piled one upon the other."[8]

"What shouts of drivers! What crying out of pedestrians! What cracking of whips! What rattling of vehicles!" marveled Isaac Jewett in 1836.

> Here are cars drawn by dogs, and cars drawn by men; omnibuses with two horses, gigs with one horse, and coaches with four; and every now and then shall you see one of those enormous vehicles, only to be found in London, whose body reminds you of Noah's ark, drawn forward by animals whose stature and prodigious muscular development proclaim the antediluvian—the veritable horse-mammoth. The confusion seems to be inextricable; and yet this little world of counter and cross interests moves on, slowly to be sure, but yet harmoniously and quite surely.[9]

Sometimes a traffic jam would nonetheless occur, such as one observed by Alexander MacKenzie in the 1830s aboard an omnibus, when an intersection was totally blocked. "The scene approached its climax of confusion," he noted.

> Just then a policeman stepped up and looked into the matter and . . . without asking leave, very quietly took a pony by its head and drew pony, gig and gentleman high and dry upon the sidewalk . . . caused an omnibus to advance to the left, and made room for a clamorous drayman to pass us, a stout fellow in blue frock, breeches, and hob-nailed shoes, with a well-fed, florid beer-drinking physiognomy who addressed the policeman in a somewhat threatening tone, "Why arn't you made that homnibus keep back? Theys want smashing," and seeing me smile with delight at the comic oddity of the scene, "and them as rides in um as well!"

This was not the first nor would it be the last time an American marveled at the calm, civil efficiency of London's policemen.[10]

Feelings of helplessness and loneliness often overpowered these arrivals from the new world in a city unlike any they had ever seen. "Peculiar feelings took possession of my mind on my first arrival," admitted Georgian Joshua White in 1810. "Placed amidst a population of nearly a million people, to all of whom I was a stranger, I seemed a solitary being, though in the midst of an incessant bustle." Through friends at Hoxton Academy, "a seminary for indigent young men, who are destined for the pulpit," he was put in touch with an acquaintance from Savannah. "I need not say how much I was gratified to meet a friend and countryman, amidst the *wilderness* of London."[11]

Once these dazed Americans discovered the miracle of London's public transport system, however, their troubles were over, as, to their mingled surprise and delight, they found the great maze of London easier to get about in than many a smaller city at home. Whether they were traversing the Thames by boat, trotting about in the cozy comfort and privacy of a hansom cab, or sailing through the streets in a brightly-painted omnibus, their praise for the city's transit system—and for the diligent, quiet policemen who kept everything moving in an orderly manner—runs through their accounts all during the nineteenth century.

In these early years the Yankees took to the Thames in light wherries, "skimming fleetly under the influence of a single pair of sculls—a most agreeable

A view of the Thames showing the small "wherries," with their single oarsmen, used as river taxis. St. Paul's Cathedral in the background. *From the author's collection.*

conveyance," as MacKenzie described these river "taxis." Himself a sailor, he thought them "indeed among the most beautiful boats I have seen. . .somewhat between our Whitehall skiffs and a Greek caique—they have much of the beauty and grace of both." The watermen, he said, eyeing a prospective fare, would cry out " 'Sculls, sir! Sculls!' "[12]

Americans were delighted also with what was originally called the "Hansom Patent Safety" cab and quickly shortened in true English style to "hansom"—the two-wheeled London taxi of these years. Isaac Jewett whirled all over London in one of these describing it as "an easy, cushion-like vehicle, the lower part of whose body rises not much more than six inches from the ground, and whose driver is perched right over your head."[13] The safety element apparently derived both from the low center of gravity and the fact that the passenger was fastened in behind low doors closed on hinges after he was seated. Communication with the driver was through an opening in the roof. Eventually, these perky little vehicles were dubbed "the gondolas of London," and little imagination is required to see a comparison with the sleek but roomy London taxi of today, scampering in and out of traffic and making turns with incredible (to an American) ease in the narrowest of streets.

MacKenzie was charmed by the omnibus, as yet a one-level vehicle. He watched the conductor, called a "cad" in these early days, "who stood like a parrot on his perch at the side of the door at the back where passengers entered and left, chattering a set of phrases in a style of cockney eloquence. He seemed to know our object ere we were quite sure of it ourselves; and, beckoning in a coaxing and winning way with his forefinger very politely invited us to get in." But once his quota of passengers was reached, MacKenzie observed, the "cad" quickly underwent a change of manner and would call out to the driver, " 'All right!' " whether his passengers were seated or not. Thus did "an elegant lady come down with violence" upon another woman already seated, he noticed, "clawing her bonnet in an effort to save herself. I felt sure there was going to be a fight and," he confessed, "was grieved to the heart to find there was to be no scattering of ribbons and false hair."[14]

Even with the aid of wherries, hansoms, and the omnibus, the American visitor soon discovered that enormous physical stamina was required to explore the endless city. "This business of sightseeing is hard work," one of them would observe. "You must walk, walk, walk until your nether extremities ache [Americans were loath to use the "vulgar" word leg in this period]—and you must look until your eyes ache—and think until your brains seem on fire. And when you are asleep, you are still 'going.' You must be systematic," he concluded, "and know how to organize your time. I have therefore laid out my work methodically."[15]

The Americans came to London with three basic goals: one, to see the time-honored "lions" of London, as tourist objectives were called in the nineteenth century; two, to absorb as much as possible of the ambience of London life itself; and three, to visit or observe as many famous Britons as possible. The Yankees usually went after their "lions" first, beginning with Westminster Abbey, the Tower of London, St. Paul's Cathedral, and, in these early decades, the famed Thames Tunnel that was under construction between Wapping and Rotherhithe. Many also included a visit to the House of Commons, but even with these objectives out of the way their "work" was just begun.

Steeped in the Abbey meditations of Joseph Addison and their own Washington Irving, certain of the early travelers seemed bent on recapitulating these authors' experiences. "I was, when a boy," recalled Silliman, "strongly impressed by some of the papers of Addison, with a wish to behold Westminster Abbey, and it is no small addition to my pleasure here, that I was contemplating the same objects which had long before excited in him those reflections with which he has instructed and delighted mankind."[16]

Nathaniel Carter, twenty years later, found himself unable to roam at large as Silliman had done, as he was confined instead to a group of travelers led about by a guide. "This rigid prohibition," he explained, "has been adopted in consequence of the mutilations which have been committed by visitants. Mary Queen of Scots. . .has lost nearly all her fingers. Some of the monuments have been treated still worse. In that to the memory of Major André, the relief statues of Washington and Putnam have been beheaded."[17] James Fenimore Cooper, noting this same phenomenon a decade or so later, was told by a verger, " 'Oh, sir, there are plenty of evil-disposed people get in here. *Some American* has done it, no doubt.' "[18] The American reputation for reckless relic-hunting was already well established and not without reason.

Westminster Abbey, c. 1840, as seen from the Poets' Corner. *From the author's collection.*

Carter sought "a dispensation of the rule" that he must tour only with the guide, "with assurances that no depredations would be committed, but he [the guide] was inexorable, and after paying two shillings for walking twice round the circuit, I was compelled to leave the royal groups to their repose." The Coronation Chair itself was "less guarded, and a republican may sit down and rest in it if he desires."[19] From the century's earliest years the Poets' Corner held special meaning for Americans, as seen in Mordecai Noah's comment on the literary memorials. "These, in part, were the ancestors of our nation," thought Noah, "and while we should endeavour to produce parallels, advance science and literature, reward merit of our own, there is much to admire and imitate."[20]

The Yankee clergymen—mainly Methodist, Congregationalist, and Presbyterian in this period—took little pleasure in their visits to the Abbey, due most likely to their innate prejudice against the established church, but for other travelers it was a great event. Emma Willard, even though she considered the Abbey "less sublime" than some of the Gothic edifices she saw on the Continent, nevertheless admitted that "it is rich in fine monuments, and interesting in its associations, especially to an American, beyond any other spot on earth." On one visit, she claimed, she was "shut up by accident in the vault, next the body of the church; but my companion and myself found our way out through a back court."[21] Young Allen, after viewing all the countless tombs in the Abbey, confessed that he could not leave "without forming renewed resolutions to become a better if not a wiser man."[22]

The Tower of London inspired Silliman to an entire chapter in his book. He traced its history briefly and provided a description of its appearance, adding, "[T]he principal uses to which the tower is now appropriated are for the mint, as a state prison, as a menage, as a deposit of some ancient records, of arms, and of the regalia of England." He was shown its "principal curiosities," armor, weapons, and torture instruments, by one of the yeomen of the guard whose costume he thought "a curious and ludicrous remnant of antiquity." What Silliman called "the jewel office" was then located in "a strong, stone room which appeared to have no windows, for the regalia were exhibited by candlelight, by an old woman who presented the articles to our view without permitting us to touch them; she remained within the grate and we without. This was indeed a splendid display," Silliman admitted, adding that "on leaving the tower one of us was required to write his name and address in a book in case anything should be missing."[23]

Something about these "Crown Jewels," as we now call them, brought out some of the worst traits of the tourist mentality even in these early travelers. One of them, in 1830, labeled as "an old hag" the elderly custodian who "presided like a high priestess over their glories," and then went on to mock her mechanical performance. "Placing an arm akimbo, and stretching the other forth towards the glittering baubles, she began in a most solemn, measured tone—'Ladies and gentlemen, please to attend the explanation,' but the ladies were somewhat overcome by the pompous manner . . . and laughed outright."[24] Another visitor thought her "sing-song" solemn tone amusing, and added that "another waggish person present, would ask her a great many questions as she went on." This forced her "to go back again and start anew, again and again, to the great amusement of her tormentor."[25]

Even Alexander MacKenzie, normally a fairly civil traveler, had to have his fun with this old lady on his visit by suggesting "the very American idea of selling 'the uncut ruby of inestimable value' for the purpose of completing the Thames Tunnel. As I expected," he recalled, "the old woman was struck with horror, opening her eyes, and lifting her hands with a lackadaisical manner which was irresistibly ludicrous. Yet she spoke not." Still not satisfied, MacKenzie remarked to her, " 'How happy you are, to be able to see all these fine things for nothing everyday.' To which she only replied with unexpected sprightliness, 'An hi honly got that for my pains, hi should be badly hoff!' " He was a little ashamed a few moments later, when, on overhearing him say he was thirsty, "she kindly undertook to procure me some water."[26] Scientist Green, seriously endeavoring

London 95

to ask her a question on his visit, realized that interrupting her was useless, and so he "let her talk on to the end."[27]

Visitors liked to lay their heads on the block, "once wet with the blood of brave men and fair women,"[28] or to try screwing up their own thumbs "in a little trinket contrived for that operation,"[29] and to shudder at "The Scavenger's Daughter," a torture device designed to compress its victim's head, hands and feet simultaneously. It was pleasanter to view the animals in the menagerie, especially the serpents—monsters like the boa constrictor, "who lie coiled up in boxes, with blankets thrown over them, and the temperature of the room artificially raised to form a suitable climate." They are "so far domesticated," wrote a traveler, "that the keeper plays with their spotted necks and permits their forked tongue to come into contact with his hands."[30] One visitor "provoked the keeper to wrath," or so he thought, "by telling him the animal he was showing off as an American fox was a racoon."[31]

Looking back at the Tower as he emerged from its gates in the 1820s, George Rapelje decided it wasn't much, really. "It is now tottering, and is not held in respect, either for its form, masonry or commemorations, and will probably be pulled down before many years. It looks now as if it was about to fall on the head of the traveler . . . an old and clumsy building, and fit only for the abode of wild beasts, although some noble fellows have been imprisoned here."[32]

Atop Ludgate Hill "a huge, dark object broke through the smoke," wrote MacKenzie. "Presently it assumed the shape of a dome, and its colossal proportions told that it could only be St. Paul's."[33] Jacob Green asked his readers to imagine Philadelphia's Bank of the United States in Chestnut Street "to be daubed all over with a thin coating of mud and black paint—the white colors of the marble, here and there, towards the top of the building making its appearance."[34]

"What a pity it should be thus obscured," remarked George Putnam—noting the structures crowding around the great cathedral—"and smoked, too, as black as a stovepipe." Yet, like MacKenzie, he had to admit that St. Paul's not only presented "an impression of grandeur, but also of extreme beauty."[35] A century-long complaint began upon their entrance, for here at the door they encountered that first of a host of black-gowned vergers confronting them with requests for fees to see each and every part of the cathedral, "each particular part having its price set on it," as MacKenzie explained, "the whole altogether about five shillings." MacKenzie, like many others, noted a decided military emphasis in the myriad of memorials, many "representing land or sea officers in the act of dying in battle. Some had their uniforms and epaulets," he noted, "and others were naked; all, however, were encouraged by Britannia or some other female genius who stood over them in the act of crowning them with laurel, but having more the air of being bent on the merciful errand of taking them out of their pain by knocking their brains out with a powerful fist, armed with a great stone." He liked the inscriptions, however, confessing that that of Nelson "pleased me greatly," and then, like a good sailor, he headed for "the rigging" to climb the 627 steps inside the layers of the great dome up into the Golden Ball itself.[36]

"Making my way upwards . . . I did not pause until I found myself at the very summit in the ball itself, into which I dragged myself," wrote MacKenzie,

with somewhat more difficulty than in going through the lubber's hole, by perpendicular steps. This ball . . . constructed of copper, is very ingenious, and, no doubt, very strong, also, although the wind rushed through it and around it with a noise not unlike that of split canvas, or when whistling through the blocks and rigging, and the whole swayed and vibrated sensibly. I indulged in speculations concerning the probable result of an aerial voyage in this copper balloon should it detach itself, and how one would feel while on the journey to the churchyard at the bottom.[37]

Pausing on his descent, he clung to the iron ladder in the lantern to survey the city of London spread out on all sides below, "the station from which the most extensive and complete view of London is commanded . . . bounded only by the limits of the horizon." It was overwhelming—"the whole of this immense space was covered with the habitations of man. Roofs of tile and black slate, chimneys, steeples, tall smokestacks, vomiting forth from manufactories as far as the eye could reach." The river was, he decided, "the most conspicuous object in the scene . . . like a huge artery serving to entertain health and cleanliness, and to furnish a ready and convenient communication. Many bridges, some of them beautiful, and all of them picturesque, spanned the stream, and opened a passage for thronging multitudes from bank to bank, while trim wherries, borne quickly by the tide and the efforts of the glancing oars, were seen shooting the bridges." Coal boats and steamers plied their way up and down, MacKenzie observed, and near the docks he saw "a forest of masts and yards," as well as great ships putting out to sea or just arriving. In its animation and activity the scene reminded him of the thronging streets below to which he now must at last descend.[38] A young New Englander, who was traveling for his health and who died on returning home, said of his own trip up to the Golden Ball, "Never have I felt so entirely secluded as in that copper ball on top of St. Paul's."[39]

"The annual celebration of the charity schools of London at St. Paul's Cathedral is the most magnificent sight in London," declared an American traveler who got to see it in 1847. "It has been a great annual occasion for more than a century: how much earlier, I am not able to say."[40] Rapelje described "six thousand boys and girls . . . all neat and cleanly dressed, and sitting round the church in rows, one row above another, about twenty rows high, making forty-five feet in height, the whole number singing at one time, hymns and psalms, adapted to the occasion. What a sublime and magnificent scene."[41] Colman, several decades later, noted the girls' white caps trimmed with ribbons of red, white, or blue, and depicted the children, seven to ten thousand of them, ranged on three sides of a great oval created in the center of the cathedral and stretching along the nave. He went up into the Whispering Gallery, the better to observe the spectacle from two hundred feet above. "We could hear them distinctly," he recalled. "They resembled a beautiful bed of variegated flowers, and indeed it seems to me nothing on this earth ever appeared one half so beautiful."[42] So carried away was he by their singing that he felt himself close to fainting and, indeed, a few years later an American clergyman did swoon and

"Charity Children" of London holding their annual celebration in St. Paul's Cathedral in June, 1850. *Illustrated London News*, June 8, 1850, p. 408. *Courtesy the Library of Congress.*

Brunel's famed Thames Tunnel, one of London's greatest tourist attractions in the first half of the nineteenth century. *From the author's collection.*

have to be carried out, thus missing "the grand hallelujah chorus in which the children united at the close."[43]

The Thames Tunnel, planned in 1823 by M. I. Brunel and completed, finally, in 1843, is all but forgotten today, although it still serves as a conduit for London's underground system since it was taken over for the purpose in the 1860s. Throughout the first half of the nineteenth century, however, the tunnel was one of the greatest attractions in all of London, especially for Americans who had first read about it in Jacob Abbott's *Rollo in London* and Samuel Goodrich's *Peter Parley* series, favorite nineteenth-century children's books in America. Although not formally opened until March 25, 1843, with Brunel knighted by Victoria the day previous, the tunnel was open to visitors in those periods when construction work permitted or was halted due to lack of funds. The Duke of Wellington, one of the subscribers, was occasionally seen conducting a party of friends to the tunnel, as observed by Zachariah Allen one day in 1830.[44]

Scientist Jacob Green attended lectures by Michael Faraday at the Royal Institution in 1828—three years after the work began—during which the two recent "irruptions" of the river into the tunnel and the ensuing chaos were described. "Numerous diagrams and models, so as to make the operation of tunnelling perfectly intelligible to everyone," convinced Green and most of those in the audience of the practicality of this engineering feat. Visiting the site itself, about 150 feet under the bed of the Thames, Green declared that he was "as much gratified with my visit to this magnificent work as . . . by anything since I left home."[45]

Three years later Henry McLellan visited the tunnel—by then about half completed—and was "forced to stop by a mirror which threw back a thousand lamps and our own persons on us."[46] Fright-prone Calvin Colton, survivor of a railway accident as well as a brief nocturnal incident on Waterloo Bridge which he convinced himself was an attempted robbery (the only one mentioned by any American traveler in the nearly 500 books consulted for this one), now entered the Thames Tunnel to be terrified again as he thought he detected mysterious whispers and even laughter directed at his person from some unknown source. "Horrible!" he exclaimed. "It was earnest, impassioned! and it was near enough to lay a hand upon me! It seemed at my ear! but nothing visible but darkness. A freezing chill ran through all my veins. . . . The assault of the previous night was play to this!" Colton made for the lamps at the far end where he discovered two men chatting amiably and smoking. Something about their "savage looks," however, told him, that they were not gentlemen and that he had better depart, which he did. If ever he realized it was merely echoes he had heard, he never let on.[47]

Less skittish, Alexander MacKenzie thoroughly enjoyed his tunnel visit a few years after Colton's, finding the work still half finished. He noted "the dripping of the water, the sense of dampness and chilliness, and the hoarse panting of the steam-engine and the valves of the huge pumps, the only sounds which disturb this solitude. . . . You more than half expect to see some great anchor, dropped from the bows of an Indiaman come crashing through, letting in the river itself and everything in it—a deluge with all its consequences of desolation and death." MacKenzie, too, mentions the great mirror "placed at the extremity of the work," still only half finished, which prevented his "seeing the iron machine in which the excavators worked, and which was pushed forward as they made room for it." Money and money alone "is wanting to complete this labour of surpassing magnificence and unquestioned utility," concluded MacKenzie.[48]

Fanny Hall took a quick look at the tunnel in 1836 but confessed "no fondness for passing through these lamplighted passages under any circumstances."[49] Reverend Humphrey complained about his entrance fee and having to buy a guidebook "at twice its value," but he was impressed despite himself. "Some even now doubt," he wrote in 1835, "whether this Tunnel will ever be finished but . . . our English kinsfolk [*sic*] are commonly much less in a hurry than we are. They possess the virtue of perseverance, and I have no doubt some half-a-dozen years hence, they will be passing under the bed of the largest river, with as much composure as they now pass over London Bridge."[50] He was off by only two years. "There is something majestic and Roman in the workmanship," said

Charles Stewart of the Thames Tunnel, "as well as in the design. One's ideas seem to expand in the very contemplation of it."[51]

Parliamentary sessions interested the more serious and scholarly Americans, who gained access to the gallery either by the introduction of a member or by payment of a fee—as did Silliman in the first decade, of "from half a crown to half a guinea, according as the occasion is more or less interesting." The House of Commons then met in St. Stephen's Chapel of the old Palace of Westminster, which was destroyed by fire in October 1834. The chapel was connected to Westminster Hall, which then housed the courts of law, and which still stands today. Silliman thought the parliamentary quarters ordinary indeed, "merely neat . . . no appearance of splendour . . . and really unequal to the dignity of this great nation." It was, he also decided, too small for its more than 600 members, but he added, "[T]hey are never all present. The side galleries are fitted up for use of the members, and it is only the gallery at the end of the House which is devoted to strangers. The floors are covered with carpets, and the seats with green cloth, besides a matting or cushions."[52] In this first decade a young American law student, William Austin, also visited the House of Lords, tucked away in the same ancient "labyrinth," and finding it "rather ornamental than useful," jeered at the satin seats as "well calculated for lounging."[53]

Silliman watched Castlereagh, Windham, Sheridan, Fox, and Pitt intently, providing his readers with pen sketches of the latter two. "Tall and spare" was how he saw Pitt. "He has small limbs with large feet; his features are sharp; his nose large, pointed, and turning up; his complexion sanguine; his voice deep-toned and commanding, yet sweet and perfectly modulated, and his whole presence . . . when he rises to speak [is] full of superiority and conscious dignity." For six hours he watched Pitt in operation and observed that, whenever he rose to speak, "the House became so quiet that a whisper might have been heard from any part." The contrast with Fox was notable, the latter being "very lusty" in appearance. "His neck is short,—his head large, round, and now quite grey,—his chest is broad and prominent, and his body and limbs vast and corpulent, even for England. His complexion is dark,—his features large—eyes blue, close together and of uncommon size, and his whole appearance peculiar, noble, and commanding." Fox seemed "very uneasy," Silliman thought, "and changed his place many times. He walked about, went out and came in—went up gallery and down, and was almost constantly in motion. He spoke a few minutes on a petition from a person imprisoned in Ireland for treason. His remarks were very pertinent to the case; his manner flowing, easy and natural, but without the dignity and impressiveness of Pitt. The caricatures of both him and Mr. Pitt are correct," decided Silliman, "with the usual allowance for the extravagance of this kind of print." Tiring of his long vigil sometime after midnight, and finding that he was not permitted to enter the members' coffee room, Silliman took tea in the lobby and made for his lodgings, "without meeting any adventure," concluding that "London is as safe by night as a village."[54]

Twenty years later Cooper surveyed the same scene, now peopled with different politicians, and took away a quite different impression of the House of Commons. Piqued at unfavorable descriptions of his own nation's House and Senate, Cooper observed M.P.s sprawled in "attitudes a good deal resembling those which your country buck is apt to take in an American bar-room." Was there a tendency, he wondered, for the "Anglo-Saxon race to put the heels higher than the head." Two members he saw "stretched at full length asleep" behind the speaker's chair, and two others on the benches. Only fifty or sixty members were present,—"not a few of whom were coming and going pretty assiduously between Bellamy's and their seats." Bellamy's, he informed his readers, "is the name of the legislative coffee-house, and it is in the building." He expressed amusement at the range of reaction exhibited by the members with their cries of "Hear, hear, hear," and also told his readers of "a member or two, just now, that are rather expert in crowing like a cock, and I have known an attempt to bleat like a lamb." As for Peel, "there is too evident an effort to insinuate himself into the good opinion of the listener," decided Cooper. "One rather resists than yields to persuasion so very obvious." Besides, observed Cooper, he pronounced "opinion as 'o-pinion' " and "occasion as 'o-casion.' "[55]

Quite a contrary view of Commons was recorded by young William Henry Seward, who perceived "dignity, decorum as well as earnestness of attention. . . . Neither then, nor at any time since, when I visited the House of Commons, have I witnessed such listlessness as generally prevails in the House of Representatives when the subject of debate is uninteresting, or such confusion as prevails there when debate becomes loud and vehement. "The reason," he concluded, was that "in England the Government is actually carried on in the House of Commons. Its measures are opened and decided there. The spectators, as well as the press, go there, to learn what the Government proposes to do, and to see it done. But, in the United States, the government is carried on by the Executive Department."[56]

"A stranger in the metropolis is surprised at nothing more than the extent of the parks which skirt the western and northwestern borders of the town," observed Nathaniel Wheaton early in the century. One could, he pointed out in 1823—

> taking the Horse-Guards as his point of departure, and proceeding in a northwesterly direction along St. James's Park, either through Green, or Queen's, into Hyde Park and Kensington Gardens:—walk a distance of three miles almost in a straight line, with green turf or gravelled walks under his feet, and his head overshadowed by oaks and elms. The first three enumerated cannot consist of less than 500 acres. . . . One can imagine himself transported far from the busy and overgrown metropolis, and dropped down in the midst of delightful rural scenery. . . . Man pent up in the city has still a longing for something rural on which to feast his eyes.[57]

Strolling in St. James's Park one fine day, MacKenzie was as much taken by the beauty of the children playing there as by the trees and flowers. The youngsters were close-guarded by "comely nursery maids, who seemed to have time not only to watch over their charges, but to exchange words of kindness with tall and well-dressed footmen, whom a happy accident had led there; and sometimes with others whose costume and air announced a higher station." There were plenty of "redcoats," too, in the vicinity, he noted. In fact, a "regiment of them, in admirable equipment, and moving with consummate steadiness, were marshaled along the main avenue, enlivening the groves with the inspiring strains of their military music."[58]

"Who has not heard of the promenade in Hyde Park?" Wheaton asked his readers, having strolled there himself between the fashionable hours of three and four.

> The whole distance between Oxford Street and Hyde Park Corner. . .was thronged. . .[with] wealthy shop-keepers, in whose rotund persons were displayed the substantial qualities of "the roast beef of old England"; firm-stepping matrons and mincing maidens; the old, the shrivelled, the young, the beautiful, and the fair; privates of the guards with their military strut and rusty mustaches; thriving green bachelors in their frog-buttoned frock coats; corinthians and exquisites from Bond-street, sporting an eye-glass. . .waiting men in laced coats and plush unmentionables of yellow, green, blue, red. . .and a multitude more of pedestrians not so readily classified all elbowing their way amidst the throng, in the gayest and most talkative humour imaginable.[59]

George Putnam rented "a nice little saddle-horse" and rode in among the gorgeous carriages and ladies and gentlemen on horseback on the other path. There he could inspect the carriages and "the pretty faces of my lady this and the dutchess of that—for many of these great ladies are really pretty," he discovered, "and with what exquisite neatness and elegance some of them dress! The ladies on horseback invariably wear men's hats—literally—and without the least alteration, except that a black veil is appended. This is the fashion at present. What a luxury these parks are in such a city as this," enthused the young American. "To have a fine space of three or four hundred acres, kept in the nicest order, with footpaths, and carriage paths, groves and ponds, surrounded by a collection of palaces! I can well believe Willis's remark that the West End of London is unequalled in Europe!"[60]

With Presbyterian prescience, the Reverend Humphrey realized in 1835 that, in a land where space was so widely available, the Americans were neglecting this aspect of urban life—the need for open spaces. "One would judge, from the extreme compactness," he wrote, "of such new towns as Utica, Geneva, Oswego, Rochester, Buffalo, Cleaveland [sic], Chicago, and Cincinnati. . .that they were to be fortified." He could not understand why, when "thousands of acres of cleared land, or primitive forest lie all around," trees and grassy space could not be incorporated into the new cities instead of crowding buildings one upon the other. "This strange want of taste," he predicted, "this unaccountable disregard to health and comfort and beauty, will be matter of the deepest regret to those who come after, some two or three hundred years hence, when many of our towns which are just now springing into existence will have become great cities and when it will be too late to remedy the evils of our absurd and contracted policy What a pity," he declared, "that in fifty growing towns, which I might name, no open squares, of any extent, were left, in laying them out, and that as far as they have been extended, almost every rod of ground is covered with brick and mortar."[61]

Among other pastimes for visiting Americans in these years were visits to London's famed charitable institutions, such as the Foundling Hospital in Guilford Street—"and a delightful sight it was," wrote Fanny Hall in 1836, "to see about one hundred little girls, between the ages of three and thirteen, seated at a long table enjoying their comfortable repast. They were dressed in a uniform of a brown stuff dress, and neat white cambric cap; and the little things appeared so clean, rosy and happy that it was quite a pleasure to look at them."[62] Others observed the foundlings during their attendance at Sunday worship in their chapel. Silliman had watched the children singing during the service he attended thirty years earlier. He was much interested also in Hogarth's splendid portrait of the hospital's founder, Captain Coram, whose name is now remembered in the park where the hospital stood—until it was pulled down, with only the entrance gate left standing, where it is even today. Silliman saw also some of the collection of paintings that Hogarth, one of the governors, collected there, including his own "March to Finley."[63]

Abigail Adams had described the chapel as it appeared on her attendance there in 1784, comparing it in size to Old South Church in Boston.

> There is one row of galleries: upon the floor of this chapel there are rows of seats like Concert Hall, and the pulpit is a small, ornamented box near the centre. There were about two thousand persons. . .who attended. In the gallery, opposite to where I sat, was the organ loft; upon each side an alcove, with seats, which run up like a pyramid. Here the foundlings sat, upon one side the boys, upon the other the girls, all in uniform; none appeared under five, nor any older than twelve. About three hundred attended the service. The uniform of the boys was a brown cloth, with a red collar, and a red stripe up the shoulder. The girls were in brown, with a red girdle round the waist, a checked stomacher and apron; sleeves turned up, and white cloth caps with a narrow lace, clean and neat as wax. They performed the vocal music.[64]

Equally popular as a place of worship and also of curiosity for visitors was the Magdalen Hospital. It was "about as large again as Braintree Church," said Mrs. Adams, a lovely place, "surrounded by weeping willows." She was happy to observe "the great decorum and decency observed" with respect to "the unhappy beings who are the subjects of this merciful institution" and who were confined to two small galleries high above and screened from the view of the other worshippers. "You can discern them through the canvass," Mrs. Adams observed, "but not enough to distinguish countenances."[65] Silliman quoted figures of his day to demonstrate the success of this institution in reclaiming "fallen" women for respectable society. "Out of 3370 who have been discharged. . .since its founding in 1758, 2230 have either been restored to their friends, or placed in service," he reported, "while only 476 have been discharged for improper behaviour. . .by far the greater number are *under twenty years of age.*" Many emerged to make respectable marriages, he wrote, "and now form virtuous and useful members of society." Their singing he found as moving as Mrs. Adams, who had wept. About fifty voices emanated from behind that veil, Silliman estimated, adding, "Alas! you may meet more than this number in walking fifty rods by night in any great street of London, and even before the door of the Magdalen itself!"[66]

Since the American visitors did not usually get behind the scene at the Magdalen Hospital, there are none of the typical descriptions of the uniform dress of the inmates of this famed charity The best description is by the Reverend William Drew of Maine, who was in London for the Great Exhibition

Christ's Hospital schoolboys hold one of their public suppers. *The Graphic*, vol. I, April 9, 1870, p. 433. *Courtesy the Library of Congress.*

of 1851 and who was one Sunday asked to help with the preaching there. Following the service he was invited by the matron, Mrs. Cooper—"a good, hearty old English lady"—into her sitting room, where she startled her teetotaling Yankee guests by offering decanters of wine and brandy. Drew thus got to see some "magdalens," however, and described them as dressed in a uniform of checked calico with a white apron, with chocolate-colored merino cloaks, and on their heads "a Quaker cap with plaited lace in front." Quiet and orderly as the women were while one of Drew's ministerial friends addressed them, he observed that there was "hardly one that seemed to pay attention."[67]

"One cannot be long in London," observed William Coombs Dana, "without occasionally meeting in the streets one or more boys, always *without a hat* and a long, oddly-shaped coarse blue frock-coat, drab small clothes, with large buckles at the knees, yellow worsted stockings, yellow vest, and a leather girdle around the waist. This quaint attire distinguishes the elves of one of the noblest benevolent institutions in London, Christ's Hospital, founded by Edward IV."[68] Americans of every decade in the nineteenth century took themselves, if possible, to the public suppers held on Sunday evenings during certain months of the year. It was a kind of ceremonial meal beginning with "three strokes of a hammer, intended to enforce silence," explained Grant Thorburn in 1833.

> One of the senior boys reads a chapter, after which prayers are read, a hymn sung—all the boys standing and pronouncing *Amen!* together. The company are seated at one end of the hall, and the steward, master, matron, etc., occupy the other. When the supper is concluded, the doors of the wards are opened, and a procession formed in the following order: the nurse, a boy carrying two lighted candles; several with breadbaskets and trays [all of wood], and the others in pairs, who all bow as they pass the company.[69]

Travelers with strong stomachs, or curiosity concerning human misery, found their way to Newgate Prison. One way to recognize the pile, Calvin Colton told his readers in the thirties, was to look down Skinner Street in the direction of Ludgate Hill certain mornings about 8:15. "He will perhaps see two, three, or half a dozen human beings hanging by the neck to a beam thrust out for the occasion from this wall; and many thousands of spectators literally crammed and piled into every inch of space which might afford a view of these suffering victims, as they struggle with death for offences lighter, probably, than the conscious guilt of half the multitude who are looking on."[70] Silliman, in 1805, described for his readers an earlier type of scaffold as it actually functioned once executions had been relegated to Newgate. It consisted of

> a stage erected on runners, and furnished with a gallows, beneath which is a trap door, that falls from under the culprit; when an execution is to take place, the machine is dragged out from the yard into the street and placed before one of the prison doors through which the prisoner is conducted to the scaffold. There he is suffered to hang, sometimes for an hour. Although several executions have happened since I have been residing in London it has not been my misfortune to pass Newgate to see a kind of tragedy of which I would not willingly be a spectator.

Just the day before his visit in 1805, he was told that a girl of sixteen was condemned to death for forgery.[71] Stewart just missed seeing an execution as he was hurrying to a friend's house one morning for breakfast in 1826. He passed Newgate

> just as the door of death was opened in the walls, and four youthful victims were brought forth, the eldest was scarce four and twenty years of age, and the youngest not yet seventeen; and housebreaking the highest crime for which any of them was about to suffer. A single glance at these pallid and trembling wretches was sufficient to hurry me from the sight, with a sickness of horror, which caused me ever afterwards to shun the same street. For years I have never heard or thought of Newgate without an emotion of horror.[72]

Colton insisted on entering Newgate where he was shown groups of female prisoners, all of whom were quick to rise from their dinner and curtsey to the gentlemen. "The countenances of some of them," Colton said, were "good, even pleasant. It is uncertain how many of them will be convicted and transported," he was told, "all in the hearing of these poor creatures." Another group of female convicts were actually awaiting transportation to Australia. "They did not appear particularly unhappy," Colton observed. "They knew their fate, and had probably resigned themselves to it." He was also shown a printseller from Bond Street, "committed for exposing obscene pictures in his shop window," and considered a test case and "an experiment." In another room were fifteen males under sentence of death, "most of them young men, some mere youths." Two or three of the worst cases would go to their deaths, he was told; the "rest will be transported." In the prison chapel Colton examined the legendary pew, in front of the pulpit, where sat convicts awaiting execution. Large enough to hold fifty men, it was painted black and defaced by carvings done by prisoners themselves, several of them consisting of gallows with occupants hanging therefrom.[73]

Elizabeth Fry, the Quakeress, who ministered to the female prisoners of Newgate, was sought out by a number of visiting Americans in this period. Emma Willard took tea with her one afternoon, during which they talked "in a mingling of souls": Mrs. Fry about her favorite subject, "the reformation of prison discipline," and Miss Willard about hers, "that of female education."[74] Lydia Sigourney actually entered Newgate with Mrs. Fry to observe her ministering to a group of female convicts destined for Botany Bay. "She was a lady of commanding height and of plain garb and countenance," wrote Mrs. Sigourney of Mrs. Fry.

> Every eye was fixed on her, and the dignity of calm benevolence seemed felt by all. With a peculiar melody of voice and that slow intonation which usually distinguishes that sect to which she belongs, she read from the Bible, and after a few simple remarks, and touching admonitions, knelt in prayer. But neither in her comments, nor in the solemn exercise of devotion, was there a single allusion which could harrow up the feelings of the unfortunate beings who surrounded her. Over the past a veil was drawn. It was to the *future* she urged them to look, with newness of life.

Besides spiritual sustenance, the Quakeress brought the women little necessaries to help them on their long voyage to Australia, Mrs. Sigourney noticed—combs, soap, needles and thread. Most of all, it would seem, what Elizabeth Fry brought to the female convicts of Newgate was hope.[75]

Visits to Greenwich Hospital four miles down the Thames, from London, were somewhat happier occasions. There, amidst the architectural glories created by Sir Christopher Wren, Silliman observed the old naval pensioners spinning out their last voyages, "quietly counting the last sands of life as they run." He found it a quiet place; indeed, almost too quiet, in 1805. "Their minds seemed to be vacant," he observed. "They were lounging, walking, or playing cards, or sitting in listless silence. Some of them had but one leg; others none. They were dressed in coarse blue cloth and seemed well provided for."[76] It was very affecting, the Reverend Humphrey remarked on his visit, "to stand in the midst of them at their meals, and to see them hobbling along the walks, or sitting

Old army veterans at the Royal Hospital in Chelsea always did, and still do, like to chat with visitors. *The Graphic,* **vol. XXVIII, November 24, 1883, p. 513.** *Courtesy the Library of Congress.*

John Wesley's chapel, in City Road, today is little changed from the time of its building by the founder of Methodism. *Photo by Paul Lockwood.*

Bunhill Fields burial ground, across from Wesley's Chapel, contains graves of many famous "Dissenters," including that of John Bunyan, author of *Pilgrim's Progress*. *Illustrated London News*, January 27, 1866, p. 96. *Courtesy the Library of Congress.*

helpless in their rooms, one having lost an arm, another a leg, another an eye, and some both legs or both arms in the murderous battles. How much they have suffered in every sea."[77]

On his visit to Greenwich in 1815 Joseph Ballard noted the pensioners' "blue clothes and cocked hats" and peered into some of their rooms, "each fitted up like the stateroom of a ship," he wrote. "These are kept perfectly clean and neat, and many of them are ornamented with little pictures. One who had been in the Battle of the Nile had Nelson's portrait and a picture of the action."[78] Reverend Humphrey was conducted about Greenwich in the thirties by Admiral Brenton, lieutenant governor of the hospital—"an American by birth, a native of Rhode Island: and though he left the country fifty years ago, or more, he still cherishes the kindest feelings towards the United States." Humphrey reported 2,500 pensioners then in residence, and he deemed their battered bodies a living testament to the wickedness of war. Humphrey also managed a tour of nearby Woolwich Arsenal—not always open to Americans, to the anger of some—where he was stunned at the sight, in an artillery park, of 27,000 cannon including some taken at Waterloo.[79]

The old military pensioners, in their red coats and cocked hats, at the Royal Hospital in Chelsea—founded by Charles II—were a more gregarious lot than the old salts of Greenwich. Less isolated and freer to move about, they were fond of chatting with the tourists. They always made a special point of showing

Americans certain battle flags (now in glass cases), which had been captured at Bladensburg and Washington, among "the long ranges of tattered banners that hang from their staves all round the ceiling of the chapel." Silliman found about 500 old soldiers in residence. Standing in their dining hall, he watched the long tables being set by veterans. "Many of them are hoary and bowed down with years," he observed, and he regretted that he had not time to inquire more "into the private history of individuals and learn what hairbreadth escapes each one had met with."[80] Nathaniel Hawthorne had more time, in the 1850s, and was quite taken with his guide, "a meek-looking, kindly old man, with a humble freedom and affability of manner that made it pleasant to converse with him. Old soldiers," mused Hawthorne, "I know not why, seem to be more accostable than old sailors. One is apt to hear a growl beneath the smoothest courtesy of the

Wesley Chapel interior (today) where many an American preacher climbed up into John Wesley's pulpit in search of inspiration. *Photo by Paul Lockwood.*

latter. This mild veteran, with his peaceful voice and gentle, reverend aspect, told me that he had fought at a cannon all through the Battle of Waterloo."[81]

Religious impulse drew large numbers of the Yankee pilgrims to Wesley's Chapel in City Road—founded by John Wesley, the father of Methodism—and also to his nearby house. Directly across the road, convenient for visitors, was old Bunhill Fields, "Burial place of Dissenters." It contained the grave of John Bunyan, author of *Pilgrim's Progress*—a book almost as familiar to these nineteenth-century American Protestants as the Bible itself. Humphrey told his readers "that had it pleased God to bring me to my last bed of sickness in London, there is no spot in which I should have esteemed it so great a privilege to be buried as Bunhill Fields." Then, like a good Presbyterian, he added, "It is not necessary for a person to abjure Calvinism, or even to be influenced by the slightest methodistical bias, to admire such a man as Wesley." He finished up in style, too. "When the trumpet shall sound and the dead shall awake, where will the greater number rise to be crowned with glory and honor and immortality? in Westminster Abbey, or in Bunhill Fields?" Across the road in the chapel, he permitted himself to stand—as did so many preachers—in Wesley's pulpit, where a "thrill" ran through him.[82]

Charismatic preachers, so much in vogue in the United States through the nineteenth century, had their London counterparts—although perhaps fewer in number. During the 1830s one really determined American, Grant Thorburn, fought his way into the chapel of the popular Reverend Edward Irving. Thorburn was all but crushed by the mob, he said, "with women fainting, men cursing, boys swearing; some bawling for their hats—canes, and umbrellas; some singing out 'take care of your money, pocketbooks, etc.' In the meantime I was in danger of suffocation." Once inside, Thorburn found the famed preacher's discourse "a rambling incomprehensible, harangue of high-sounding and great-swelling words, bombast and jingle . . . for upwards of two hours." When at last he emerged, Thorburn swore that his first exposure to the Reverend Irving would also be his last.[83]

Some years later Irving was observed by author Samuel Goodrich, "in the full flush of his fame," still drawing great crowds—"people of all ranks, literary men, philosophers, statesmen, noblemen, persons of the highest name and influence." Goodrich was first taken by Irving's appearance, which he concluded was nothing less than

> very remarkable. He was over six feet in height, very broad-shouldered, violently cross-eyed, with long black hair hanging in heavy twisted ringlets down upon his shoulders. His complexion was pallid, yet swarthy, the whole expression of his face—half sinister and half sanctified. . . . He wore a black silk gown, of rich material and ample, graceful folds. His hair was sedulously parted so as to display one corner of his forehead which a white hand, and a very pure linen handkerchief frequently wiped, yet so daintily as not to disturb the love-locks that enclosed it.

Something about the preacher's strange manner of speaking puzzled Goodrich.

A feeling crossed my mind that I had heard something like it, but certainly not in a church. There was a vague mingling in my imagination of the theatre and the house of worship; of footlights, a stage, a gorgeous throng of spectators. . . . Suddenly I found the clew; Edward Irving in the pulpit was imitating Edmund Kean upon the stage. And he succeeded admirably—his tall and commanding person giving him an immense advantage over the little, insignificant, yet inspired actor.[84]

As one of the "lions" of London, the newly-constructed Exeter Hall in the Strand was shown to Charles Stewart in the thirties—an "edifice erected within the last few years, principally for the celebration of anniversaries of the religious societies of London—built by subscription."[85] Various philanthropic and benevolent organizations maintained offices on the ground floor, while the large public hall on the second floor could seat up to 5,000 persons. Many an American clergyman would enter that hall, none more eagerly than Reverend Humphrey in May of 1835 to attend the "London Anniversaries" that included representatives "from all the important and dissenting denominations." He himself was pleased to announce that he represented the General Associations of both Massachusetts and Connecticut, the American Temperance and Peace Societies, and the American Sunday School Union. The meetings were more lively and excited than those in America," he found, "with cries of 'Hear, hear, hear!' " and loud applause which served to relieve the tedium. Still, he judged all this enthusiasm "questionable." For himself, he preferred "the silent attitude of a great assembly—the serious and deeply interested look—the sparkling and tearful eye a great deal better."[86]

Secular amusements in this period included the theater, and Nathaniel Carter treated himself to an evening at Covent Garden, "a magnificent building, finished much in the style of the Italian Opera House, with splendid furnishings, decorations, and scenery," where he saw Kemble "personate the character of Charles the Second in *The Merry Monarch*." At Drury Lane, "by far the handsomest theatre in London, and probably one of the finest in the world, with its arches, pillars, and saloons, its crimson curtains, and gilded decorations," he watched *The Wager, or Midnight Hour*.[87] Alexander MacKenzie observed "the enthusiastic admiration of the female leg" to be a decided taste in England, and thus he was not surprised at Covent Garden one evening to observe a young female singer noisily acclaimed—not so much for her singing, he decided, as for her costume, that of a page. "Each theatre is obliged to provide for this taste by having, if possible, a pair of fine legs in the troupe."[88] Scientist Jacob Green went to Drury Lane "to see Matthews perform *Jonathan in London*, a most ridiculous and contemptible caricature. I left the place early and resolved not to go to another theatre in London." Doubtless this is a reference to the famous comic actor Charles Mathews (1776–1835) who, in addition to countless dramatic roles, also satirized Americans whom he had observed on a trip to America in 1822. One such entertainment he actually entitled *A Trip to America*.[89]

Other popular entertainments included "pantomimes, rope-dancing, and other feats" at Sadler's Wells Theatre, which—as Silliman told his readers—was erected on the site of a spring once celebrated for its curative powers but which was stopped up at the Reformation. There Professor Silliman watched the antics of a clown and ogled the dancers who had "laid aside the petticoat and appeared

The Coliseum in Regent's Park where visitors were treated to a panoramic view of London taken from the top of St. Paul's Cathedral. *From the author's collection.*

in loose muslin pantaloons, white silk stockings, and red slippers ... with an open short frock, hanging loose like a coat. Such facts need no comment," he observed sternly, but he admitted that "they danced with much spirit and elegance."[90]

The Coliseum in Regent's Park attracted Charles Stewart to marvel at this great

> panoramic painting of the city, taken from the summit of St. Paul's, so true to nature and arranged with such skilful distribution of light, as to produce one of the most perfect illusions I ever witnessed. You insensibly draw back from the balustrade ... as from the fearful parapet, from which on the Cathedral itself, you cast a glance into the terrific depths around. And you are almost obliged to reason with yourself to be persuaded that it is not nature but a work of art.[91]

Many Americans were similarly dazzled by this showcase. At Astley's Amphitheatre patrons enjoyed still more illusion as they witnessed various equestrian acts, one simulating a fox hunt, another a chariot race.[92]

One of the most exciting spots in London for visiting puritans from America

Vauxhall Gardens, a pleasure park "splendid beyond description," according to Benjamin Silliman in 1805. By George Cruikshank. *From the author's collection.*

was Vauxhall Gardens, a popular pleasure garden from about 1732 to 1859, which was situated on the south bank of the Thames in Lambeth. Silliman went there in the century's first decade and found it "splendid beyond description, almost beyond conception, exceeding all that poets have told of fairy lands and elysian fields." Tall trees arched their branches over long passageways "crossing each other in geometrical figures"; alcoves and recesses, some of them covered over, presented comfortable spots for resting and eating. Ten thousand little lamps twinkled everywhere, forming designs on trees and shrubbery. Silliman explained the very simple but effective form of these lamps—simply colored spheres, suspended from wires, open at the top, and lighted by a wick floating on oil.

An orchestra installed in a Greek "temple" in the center provided music, and on tables were set out "cold collations, confectioneries, and other refreshments." The rotunda was "a magnificent room . . . finely carpeted, its walls covered with mirrors and gilding." Transparent paintings, lit from the rear, were seen at the end of each walk. From ten o'clock on "thousands of well-dressed people thronged the gardens," Silliman observed, and at eleven a bell announced the fireworks. Following this, he and his party sat down to supper, where he said he finally learned what "a Vauxhall slice" meant from the thinly-cut ham they were served.

As the hour grew late, and people began to dance on the raised platforms or "floors" provided for that purpose, another feature of Vauxhall Gardens appeared—"young courtezans . . . many of considerable beauty and elegance, and some of them could not have been more than fifteen or sixteen years of age."[93] Jacob Green and a friend had themselves rowed to this same spot two decades later, and in an obvious slap at his countryman, Silliman, whose book he must have read, Green said that he found nothing of "fairy scenes or Elysian fields," but rather a place "calculated to excite the admiration of the young and inexperienced, and admirably fitted to seize and carry away the senses . . . therefore, no doubt, a most successful school of corruption and misery."[94]

Greenwich Fair, an annual holiday celebrated on Easter Monday—down river at Greenwich near the foot of the naval observatory hill—presented these Americans with another dilemma of combined delight and disapproval. George

Greenwich Park on Easter Monday showing the traditional race of lads and lasses down the hill from the Observatory. Note the old naval pensioner in foreground who has wandered over from Greenwich Hospital to observe the festivities. By George Cruikshank. *From the author's collection.*

Putnam, at age twenty-two, gave up a day to the Thames Tunnel and the Greenwich Fair, discovering the latter to be far more amusing, with "thousands of country beaux and lasses cutting up all sorts of capers. Some were running down the steep hills with dangerous velocity, and many a poor girl fell sprawling in the attempt"—apparently the object of the sport. There were strolling singers and booths with cheap novelties for sale. But what struck Putnam's fancy were the "kissing rings," an adult version of "drop-the-handkerchief" which children play. Just as he had joined with the "swells" in the vanity fair of Hyde Park, now Putnam joined these country and working-class young people at their game. "There were many well-dressed and passably pretty girls in the collection," he noticed. "I took my place in the circle without ceremony, determined to make the best of the sport. It was marvellous what a sensation I produced!" he crowed, sounding not unlike a young Boswell or Samuel Pepys. "The girls threw the gauntlet as fast as I could overtake them, and merry chases they were!" To this little account he felt obliged to attach a footnote, explaining that he presumed *our* village damsels would scarcely take part in such *unfeminine* amusements."[95] Even the Reverend Orville Dewey made it to the Greenwich Fair—not to enjoy himself but to complain that "there was a publicity and grossness about it to which I am sure no young country girls of ours, though of the humblest class, would submit," which, of course, may explain why his young countryman Putnam enjoyed it so.[96]

Both Hampton Court and Windsor Castle in this period were visited as day trips out of London, much as they are at present, but sometimes these hardier travelers made the journey on foot. Silliman caught only a glimpse of Pope's villa at Twickenham—not open to the public—and he missed seeing the interior of Walpole's Strawberry Hill by not receiving a requested ticket of admission in time. He decided his experience at Hampton Court made up for it. Although he and his companion were conducted through the apartments "in a manner much too rapid," he was still "much gratified," never having seen the inside of a palace before. In addition to the splendid structure itself and its rich furnishings and works of art, his principal satisfaction came from "the consciousness that I was in a *palace*, and that kings, queens, and illustrious men, had trod the boards that were then beneath my feet." At Windsor, sometime later, he was "civilly conducted" through the castle and declared its magnificence too great for his pen. He was surprised to learn that the reason he was deprived of his umbrella—a fact which annoyed many a traveler—was that the custodians of Britain's treasures, royal, public, and private, had long since learned that "if visitors in such places have anything in their hands with which they can deface pictures by pointing out the parts that please them, they will almost invariably do it."[97]

On his visit to Windsor Castle in 1818, John Griscom said he was informed that in a room below poor old King George III was spinning out his days in seclusion, "quite blind . . . his beard extended to his breast; that his constant delight is playing on the piano; that he is seldom spoken to except on subjects relating to his personal comfort, as conversation more than anything excites and disturbs him. He is said to be particularly averse to the Prince Regent and will not suffer him to be in his room."[98] It was a far cry from that summer in 1802, when William Austin had journeyed to Windsor to see the royal family on their

Windsor Castle, c. 1840, a favorite "day trip" out of London for American visitors during the nineteenth century. *From the author's collection.*

evening stroll upon the terrace—much admired by their subjects and visiting Yankees alike—with the King himself "frequently bowing to the spectators."[99]

Letters of introduction proved particularly valuable to Americans in London, where they opened doors to Britain's famous figures in the fields of literature, art, and science. Such an introduction enabled George Ticknor to meet Lord Byron, who was one of the most elusive of Britain's great. Byron expressed in Ticknor's presence, at news just brought of Napoleon's defeat at Waterloo, a decidedly unpatriotic sentiment: " 'I'm d——d sorry for it. I didn't know but I might live to see Lord Castlereagh's head on a pole, but I suppose I shan't now.' " Ticknor informed his American readers that Byron "talked a great deal about our literature, how many universities we had, whether we had any poets whom we much valued, and whether we looked upon Barlow as our Homer. He certainly feels a considerable interest in America; and says he intends to visit the United States."[100]

A friend living at the Temple, in London's Inns of Court, invited Nathaniel Parker Willis to meet essayist Charles Lamb—"a gentleman in small-clothes and gaiters, short and very slight in person, his head set upon his shoulders with a thoughtful, forward bent, his hair just sprinkled with gray, a beautiful deep-set

Michael Faraday (1791–1867), British chemist and physicist, "exceedingly affable and communicative" to American scientist Jacob Green, who visited him at the Royal Institution in 1828. By Daniel Maclise. *Courtesy the Library of Congress.*

eye, aquiline nose, and a very indescribable mouth. Whether it expressed most, humor or feeling, good-nature or a kind of whimsical peevishness, I cannot in the least be certain," wrote Willis. Lamb spoke admiringly of Webster's speeches but expressed a distaste for Cooper's novels—a distaste which was not shared by his sister, Mary, who, he said, " 'devoured them with a ravenous appetite.' " Declared Lamb, "the only American book I ever read twice was the *Journal of John Woolman,* a quaker-preacher-tailor. He tells a story or two about negro slaves that brought tears to my eyes. I can read no prose now, though Hazlitt sometimes to be sure—but Hazlitt is worth all modern prose and writers put together." Willis found Lamb "querulous and aged," but "wreck as he certainly is ... I would rather have seen him for that single hour than the 101 sights of London put together."[101]

Michael Faraday, "exceedingly affable and communicative," welcomed Jacob Green in 1828 to the Royal Institution, where he displayed "some of the original instruments in electro-magnetism which he had invented and which had first turned my attention to that curious subject." Green also had the honor of dining with the Royal Society "at the head of the table, next the president, with a nobleman below me. Gilbert, the president, successor to Sir Humphry Davy, was highly curious about everything relating to America," Green wrote, and much ashamed of the "wanton destruction of our publick property at Washington, during our late, unhappy war."[102]

John Griscom trekked out to Slough, in 1818, to the home of the famed astronomer, Sir William Herschel, who invited him to stay to tea, talk astronomy, and examine the great 8,500-pound telescope "erected in the yard immediately back of the house."[103] Another Yankee traveler, finding Herschel absent, was nevertheless permitted to inspect the telescope and was told how parties of ladies sometimes assembled there, "not so much for telescopical observation, but to take tea in the air, and then as evening comes on, to gaze at the stars through the largest telescope in the world."[104]

Benjamin West, the expatriate American painter who was a special favorite of George III, often invited American visitors to dinner and to see his studio. Silliman, one of these, was told a story by West about an experience at Windsor Castle, involving the King, during the American Revolution. A courtier sought to embarrass the American artist by speaking in his hearing of a British victory in South Carolina. Turning then to the painter, he remarked, " 'This, I suppose, cannot be very pleasant news to you, Mr. West!' " Seeing the trap laid for him, West responded, " 'No, Sir, this is not pleasant news to me, for I can never rejoice at the misfortunes of my countrymen.' " The King, who had appeared not to notice the conversation up to that point, suddenly spoke to West. " 'Sir, that answer does you honour!' " To the now-embarrassed courtier, he said, " 'Sir, let me tell *you,* that, in my opinion, any man who is capable of rejoicing in the calamities of his country, can never make a good subject of any government!' "[105]

George Ticknor, visiting West a decade later, was told

a singular anecdote of Nelson while we were looking at the portrait of his death. Just before he went to sea for the last time, West sat next to him at a large entertainment given to him here, and in the course of the dinner Nelson expressed to Sir William Hamilton his regret, that in his youth he had not acquired some taste for art and some power of discrimination. "But", said he, turning to West, "There is one picture whose power I do feel. I never pass a printshop with your 'Death of Wolfe' in the window without being stopped by it." Nelson went on to ask why he had painted no more like it. "Because, my lord, there are no more subjects." "D—— it", said the sailor, "I didn't think of that", and asked me to take a glass of champagne. "But, my lord, I fear your intrepidity will yet furnish me with such another scene; and if it should, I shall avail myself of it." "Will you?" said Nelson, pouring out bumpers, and touching his glass violently against West's,—"will you, Mr. West? Then I hope that I shall die in the next battle." He sailed a few days after, and the result was on the canvas before us.[106]

Mortally wounded by a French musket ball lodged in his spine during the Battle of Trafalgar on October 21st, 1805, Nelson endured a three-hour death agony, lying in the cockpit of the *Victory,* waxen, sweaty, staring into eternity—as that legendary engagement drew to its close. "Thank God I have done my duty," he is supposed to have murmured over and over as the mists closed around him.

The spirit of the Utilitarian philosopher Jeremy Bentham glows brightly from the pages of a journal kept by Aaron Burr during the period of his penny-pinching, half-starved exile in London after killing Hamilton in their famous duel. Bentham apparently was kind to the wretched American refugee. "Received in the most affectionate manner. How inexhaustible is the goodness of Bentham," wrote Burr after his arrival at Bentham's house in Queen's Square Place, during one of his hours of need.[107] Dr. Gibson heard an anecdote concerning Burr while he was dining with Lord Jeffrey, the famed Edinburgh judge who knew Scott and had dined with him and Burr one evening in 1808. "Burr had that kind of face one could never forget," remarked Jeffrey, and "Scott, who dined with Burr at my house remarked that Burr had the eye of a black snake."[108] Sometime after this, in the 1840s, Margaret Fuller would view the famous wax-encased skeleton of Jeremy Bentham, who bequeathed his remains to the University of London—still to be seen today, upon special request. "The figure leans a little forward, resting the hands on a stout stick which Bentham always carried," she observed. "The attitude is quite easy, the expression of the whole quite mild and winning." The figure is, of course, properly clothed. "Bentham," Fuller explained to her readers, "while quite a young man, had made a will in which he had given his body after death to be used in the name of science. 'I have not yet been able', said the will, 'to do much service to my fellowmen by my life, but perhaps I may in this manner by my death.' "[109]

William Wilberforce, remembered for his work toward the abolition of slavery in the British dominions, was sought out by Silliman, Ticknor, and Wheaton. The latter conversed with him as he was "putting up and arranging his books" and described him as "apparently about seventy, small in person, and extremely lively and active in all his movements."[110] Ticknor found his way to Wilberforce, of course, and termed his conversation unusual. "His voice has a whine in it, and his conversation is broken and desultory. In general, he talks most and is most attentive to those who talk most to him, for his benevolence has so long been his governing principle, that he lends his ear mechanically to all who address him. Yet now and then he starts a subject of conversation and pursues it with earnestness, quotes Horace and Virgil. . . . But, in general, he leaves himself much in the hands of those about him, or, if he attempts to direct the conversation, it is only by making inquiries to gratify his curiosity."[111] Several decades later Hawthorne would remark on the curiously-alive memorial statue of Wilberforce in Westminster Abbey. "His exceedingly homely and wrinkled face, held a little to one side, twinkles at you with the shrewdest complacency," observed Hawthorne, "as if he were looking right into your eyes and twigged something there which you had half a mind to conceal from him."[112]

Reformer Robert Owen, founder of the industrial utopia New Lanark in Scotland, and whose son, Robert Dale Owen, created the utopian colony of New Harmony in Indiana, made a poor impression on certain American travelers, Emma Willard for one. "Never did I meet a man with a smoother face or a smoother tongue," she snorted. They met one evening at a social gathering of a friend of Mrs. Willard's. Although determined "to avoid, if possible, controversial matters," she soon found herself locked in an argument with Owen on the subject of education. When Owen laid down certain premises, including the one that "man was the creature of circumstances," she wrote, "I saw the conclusion to which they were leading." Despite her resolve she jumped in, and there followed a lively 1830 version of what is today called the "Nature versus Nurture" educational controversy, with Owen insisting that environment "is all" and Mrs. Willard stoutly maintaining that heredity, too, is a vital factor in intellectual development. "You do not even allow man the dignity of a vegetable," she told Owen, "which, though it has its changes, is yet something of itself; and is always the same, whatever may be the soil or culture by which it is modified. The hawthorne may be stunted or expanded in its growth, but no skill of the gardener can make it a rose." Owen persisted, and Mrs. Willard, trapped until her son returned with their carriage, fought on. "Mr. Owen said that his opinions were prevailing,—the governments of the world would be *obliged* to yield to them. He was then on his way to meet delegates at Liverpool from 600 societies formed on his plan. In short, the world had heretofore gone on from error to error, both in philosophy and morals. Sir Isaac Newton, and others whom I had mentioned, had guided the opinions of the multitude, taught ten errors to one truth." Finally, Emma Willard blew up and demanded of Owen if he claimed "to be favored with direct revelations from the only sure fountain of truth." This question silenced the whole company. "Mr. Owen reddened, and stammered out with an indirect reply, like a man that spoke in pain. I at once changed the conversation," she said, "and after a while my son arrived and I took my leave."[113]

At New Lanark in company with Owen a decade earlier John Griscom, too, had found him something of the zealot. "As it is impossible to listen to him without objecting to some of his fundamental positions," Griscom discovered,

argument becomes unavoidable. We sat up till twelve, engaged in a wordy warfare upon the best means of correcting the abuses of society, and making the whole world a band of brothers. He is confident that this would be the result, were his measures universally adopted. Pauperism would become unknown. . .wars would cease. . . .Idleness would vanish. . . .The turbulent and angry passions would subside. . .the pursuit of gain and the thirst for

S. T. Coleridge

Samuel Taylor Coleridge (1772–1834), British poet and critic who won Emma Willard's heart with his praise for the "intellectual woman." By Daniel Maclise. *Courtesy the Library of Congress.*

riches would disappear. . . .Ambition. . .would die a natural death. . . .In short, such would be the just and equal balance between the wants of mankind, and the means of supply, between rational desire and the power of gratification, that discontent and stress would become unknown.[114]

Emerson, unlike his fellow Americans Emma Willard and John Griscom, was quite taken with the British reformer, finding him "an excellent lecturer." His "vinous face is a powerful weapon. He has a surgical smile," Emerson went on, "and an air of virility that penetrates his audience, a perfect self command. . .stepping securely from stone to stone."[115] Emerson's countryman, agriculturalist Henry Colman, would no doubt have quarreled with this critical judgment, for, in listening to one of Emerson's own speeches in London, Colman concluded that

> his lectures seem to me very much like a kaleidoscope, full of everything beautiful, and a constant succession of most brilliant changes, but vanishing suddenly before the eye, and leaving it difficult to recall the combination of distinct images, or to retain any strong impression of some single great point. They somewhat resemble Champagne wine—sparkling, delicious, exhilarating, but evanescent, and as far as practical results are concerned, insubstantial.[116]

Mrs. Willard also got to meet Samuel Taylor Coleridge, "with all the poet in his dark eye," but whose conversation she found difficult to follow. "You look intensely for his ideas as you look. . .for the outline of the distant mountain. Sometimes you think you have caught it, but then comes another cloud,—and the view was too evanescent to admit of your making a sketch. Yet the clouds themselves are beautiful. . . .The subject of his conversation was nature— intellectual and material—the animals and the vegetables—the heavens, and man with his noble faculties, looking with faith to his God and Redeemer. And last of all, the angelic figure. . .Heaven's best gift, beautiful, refined, intellectual *woman*!"[117] Coleridge may have been a cloudy talker, but he knew how to charm feminist Emma Willard.

Despite their rampant republicanism these liberty-loving Yankees were absolutely fascinated by British royalty. Almost every account includes a detailed pen portrait of the reigning monarch; it is a standard item. So eager was young Benjamin Silliman for a glimpse of his country's last king that he bought tickets for *The School for Scandal* at Drury Lane in order to view George III, whom he found "a noble-looking old man, fleshy, yet not oppressively corpulent," who appeared "years younger than almost any man of his age I have ever seen." The King was long and enthusiastically applauded by his people, Silliman noted, and obviously enjoyed not only the play itself but a comic interlude—at which he laughed heartily—satirizing one of Napoleon's many threatened invasions of England.[118]

Joseph Ballard stood in the street in 1815 for a glimpse of the Prince Regent but reported that his carriage went by at a fast clip and that he was not fond of showing himself to the public. The crowd had an annoying habit, Ballard observed, of chanting, " 'You damned rascal, where's your wife?' "—a reference to his unlovely spouse, Caroline, whom they seemed to favor so as to annoy him.

They had even done this the previous year, Ballard was told, when the Prince Regent had to appear in public with his royal guest, the Emperor of Russia.[119]

"A plain-hearted and generous-spirited sailor" was how navy officer Charles Stewart described old King William IV, George IV's successor, when he was taken along to Court by the American minister to meet that monarch. "In manner and dress he was the least formal of the assemblage," observed Stewart.[120] Emma Willard, on another occasion, found William "very florid" and deplored poor Queen Adelaide's plain white silk hat.[121] Young Oliver Wendell Holmes, abroad to study medicine in 1834, observed William one night at the theater, "tapping his white-gloved hand on the edge of the box when he was pleased with the singing." The monarch was accompanied, he noted, by a tiny, fresh-faced young woman, Princess Victoria.[122]

This same small figure was observed by another traveler one day at the Ascot races, seated in the royal box, "listening to a ballad-singer and leaning over the front of the box with an amused attention, quite as sincere. . .as any beggar's in the ring."[123] George Putnam observed her at the theater with her mother, the Duchess of Kent. "The princess is now seventeen, pretty, dresses with a neatness and simplicity which would be a pattern for New York belles. She appears to be very intelligent, sensible and unaffected, and is doubtless thoroughly educated. They say she can speak nearly all the languages of Europe. She is evidently the darling of the people, and deservedly so; but she must be a very fine girl," he concluded, "if she can wear all her honors and sip all the flattery which is paid to her, and not yet be spoiled."[124]

On May 24, 1837, although mortally ill at Windsor, old King William gave a sumptuous birthday ball for Princess Victoria and this time the chairs of state were occupied by Victoria and her mother. There to observe the future monarch was Henry Wikoff, the adventurer who later turned up at the White House during the Civil War as a favorite of Mary Lincoln, and who acted as a sort of social "spy" for the New York *Herald* of James Gordon Bennett. Wikoff, an admirer of ladies' bosoms, enthusiastically judged that of the Princess to be "strikingly handsome." Most of all he admired her "quite remarkable self-possession" on this occasion with all eyes upon her.[125]

Less than a month later, Victoria was indeed Queen although not yet crowned, and a gimlet-eyed Yankee preacher studied her in the Chapel Royal at St. James's during the Sunday service. "There is nothing at all queenly in Victoria's appearance," declared the Reverend John Clark. "She is short, and not re-markably sylph-like in her form, with a round, blooming face. She wore a light pink bonnet with the dress of a genteel lady." Apparently unaware that one of royalty's primary obligations is to be *seen,* the preacher complained that the young monarch "manifested no disposition to veil her charms or screen her person from the views of the hundred eyes that were directed towards the Royal Gallery. After having offered up silent prayer, she stood up and looked very deliberately around the Chapel as though willing to gratify the eager eyes that were gazing upon her. I cannot say that Victoria appeared devout," complained Clark. "Although she followed the service, she appeared very little interested in it. Upon the whole, I can think of Victoria only as a young, cheerful-minded girl; and seeing as I do, this whole nation bowing down to do her homage, I am led to

QUEEN VICTORIA IN 1839.

(From a Drawing by R. J. LANE, A.R.A.)

Queen Victoria in 1839: "only a young and cheerful-minded girl," in the eyes of the Reverend John Clark from America. *From the author's collection.*

admire the majesty of British law which has the power to sway so many millions of minds and bind them in unwavering loyalty to the throne."[126] Most Americans were far kinder to Victoria than Clark, and so assiduously did they follow her about London during her active, happy years at the side of the handsome young German prince she married in 1840 that their pen sketches amount almost to a pictorial history of her reign.

Sooner or later during their sojourns in London the Yankee travelers turned their attention to that city's weather. In these early decades they did not yet routinely describe or complain about the heavy impenetrable fogs that would shroud the metropolis in later decades. More often in this early period they complained of rain. "Every man except myself was the bearer of an umbrella," wrote MacKenzie who slunk back to his hotel, The Colonnade, one day, drenched to the skin, and "determined if I live to see another day, that I would become what I have never yet been, the possessor of an umbrella!" In England, he concluded, "a man without an umbrella is as incomplete as a man without a nose."[127]

Americans also had to learn to put up with the soot pouring from thousands of chimney pots. "The more respectable classes," observed Reverend Fisk, "have learned to adjust themselves to circumstances, but the labouring classes appear unwholesome; their clothes often look as though they were glazed over with dirt. . . . This is understandable, owing to the impossibility of attending to business without contracting a share of the soot, smoke and mud, which adhere to everything they touch, and as it ceases to be offensive, no pains are taken to avoid it."[128] Reverend Humphrey declared that he missed "those clean, airy and painted dwellings, shops and warehouses" he was accustomed "to see and admire in Baltimore, Philadephia, New-York, or Boston," and how grand it would be on his return to stroll up Broadway "to see everything so fresh and new and clean."[129]

Fog was, however, fast becoming a problem in the London winter. Richard Rush, the American minister, recorded "a remarkable fog" in 1818, "a day when carriages ran against each other and persons were knocked down by them . . . it was of an opake [sic], dingy yellow. Torches were used at mid-day."[130] Nathaniel Carter complained of no more than four or five hours of imperfect daylight in the autumn of 1825. "The lamps are lighted in the shops by about three o'clock."[131] "Thick smoke," together with the dampness, wrote the Reverend Wheaton, caused him and his companion to be "seized with a violent catarrh."[132] November was the month that brought on all these phenomena.

Seated at his breakfast one morning at The Colonnade—the coffee room "as still and solemn as some deathbed scene"—in the quiet English manner MacKenzie picked up his morning newspaper. "One of the first paragraphs that struck my eye was a list of suicides . . . no fewer than three, in which the weapon had been a razor, and two of the self-murderers were women." When at last he went out, the upper stories of buildings were half hidden "by a canopy of smoke, fog and rain," and even newly-printed placards "shed big, inky tears and seemed about to dissolve in grief." It did not rain as it did at home, he noticed, "with that earnestness and energy common in our climate, which conveys the idea of a thing to be done . . . despatched with business-like rapidity, but in a deliberate, cold-blooded way, as if it might continue on forever."[133]

Foul weather or fair, Americans were fascinated by the endless variety of London street life. "There is never a dearth of novelty to a stranger in the streets of London," observed Ballard early in the century. "Numerous ways are resorted to by the beggars to attract attention and gain a half-penny. One poor fellow who had lost both his legs, has a board before him upon which he chalks in so elegant a manner that it would not disgrace a copper-plate engraver."[134] Silliman too observed a sidewalk screever, as did Joshua White, "seated on the pavement, writing and making various figures with red chalk, thus for a moment to arrest the passer-by and get a penny." Other mendicants sang, played violins, or a small "barrel-organ" for the same purpose.[135]

"In almost every place where there is a pathway across the street," wrote Jacob Green in the 1820s, "a man or woman stands, like Macbeth's witches, with a broom with which some of the dirt from the path has been swept, and you are accosted with 'Sir, remember *the sweeper.*' "[136] Travelers in the know carried pocketfuls of coppers for this purpose, as well as for the ragged men and boys who leaped forward at hotel entrances or the doors of cabs, sometimes even running after the latter so as to be first to open the door. After handling heavy luggage they would humbly ask, "Anything y'r honor pleases." Joshua White found the demands upon his purse incessant but wrote that "it afforded me happiness when I could relieve."[137] Wheaton went so far as to buy dinner for a threadbare young man, "shivering with cold," who presented himself as an out-of-work actor to the American departing one day from Westminster Abbey, but not without first delivering a lecture on the evils of the theatrical profession to the recipient of his charity.[138]

Other Americans, less kindly spirited than White or Wheaton, ranted about the constant "feeing"—not only to the street people but to porters, waiters, coachmen, guards, guides, and minor officials of every description. Humphrey even tried to do one man out of his earned and expected "tip."[139] Others, like Emma Willard, resigned themselves to observing the customs of the land they were visiting. "There is no use in performing with a bad grace what one is obliged by the customs of the country to do," she wrote.[140] Silliman found that the pennies he dispensed actually produced a sort of willing, efficient service, "*cheerfully* rendered, and not with that *sullen salvo for personal dignity*, which we so often see in America."[141]

The beggars were another matter, some aggressive and seemingly professional, others obviously in dire want and heart-rending in their helpless passivity. Silliman maintained that some of the blind men he saw were veterans of the Egypt expedition and suffering "from the Egyptian opthalmia." Former sailors he saw, too, on crutches, "singing in concert." Then there were countless other wretched beings, seemingly too far gone even to beg, "sunk down in the streets—under the eaves of the houses—on the steps of doors, or against the corners, apparently asleep, but there is much reason to believe, that, they are, in some instances, finding a refuge forever from hunger and the repulse of pride, pleasure and affluence."[142] MacKenzie said that he would never forget a man he

The Chimney Sweeps' annual holiday. "No one can grudge a penny to such an applicant," thought one American traveler. By George Cruikshank. *From the author's collection.*

saw stalking up Regent Street—"tall, graceful, and distinguished in his appearance" but gaunt, unshaven, emaciated, and shirtless, in greasy, threadbare but once respectable clothes, "a picture of consummate misery and woe . . . doubtless ashamed to beg, though evidently starving."[143]

Chimney sweeps were everywhere but were little noticed except on their one holiday, the first of May, when, "fantastically dressed," they paraded about the streets "dancing to their own music on the brush and shovel."[144] Another traveler described them toting about "a chimney of green things, nearly or quite concealing the occupant who gave it motion," a sort of "moving obelisk of green. Their game seemed to consist in pausing before certain doors and soliciting a gratuity. Certain it is that no one can grudge a penny to such an applicant, or behold the one day's sport of the poor climbing boy without wishing he may succeed in trying to make the most of it."[145]

With an obvious desire to be shocked, a few Americans made their way to Billingsgate, London's wholesale fish market, noted for its salty and uninhibited language. Headed there one morning, George Rapelje was suddenly confronted by "a large woman, with a broad-brimmed hat, and broad, high-flushed cheeks," of whom he inquired the way to the market. "Putting her arms akimbo and raising herself on her toes, in a harsh angry, discordant tone, she replied, 'This *is* the market, and I am one of the Billingsgate fishwomen; what the d——l do you think of me?' I was almost struck dumb at her size and speech," confessed the youthful sport, "But I decided to make the most of it by saying, 'Why I really think you a fine-looking woman, with a basket of excellent fish!' This, with the present of an English shilling saved me," he concluded, from "a torrent of abuse."[146] A prim preacher who went to the market some years later was advised by a pert young lady, " 'If you do not like our talk, why clear out!' "[147]

The Sunday morning Rag Fair, still another of London's curiosities, drew American travelers to watch—usually with disapproval—this display of Sabbath commercialism. Henry Colman observed "about 20,000 Jews, Irish, and vagabonds, all collected in a few streets and open buildings for the sale of every kind of old clothing." The police "are always at hand in strong force," he was well assured, but nevertheless he was admonished to look out for pickpockets.[148]

London's ingenious and all-pervasive advertising caught the eye of almost every Yankee visitor—apparently not yet accustomed to it at home. "Immense ambulatory advertisers, like huge skeleton houses, covered with handbills," were observed by MacKenzie in the thirties.[149] "An enormous one-horse vehicle" caught Jewett's eye in the same period, "a sort of house twenty feet high . . . all over whose sides were notices of departing coaches and sailboats into every quarter of the kingdom. And from morning till night does this travel through the principal streets of the city."[150]

Ragged men stalked the streets with placards in their battered hats bearing such messages as: "To Paris, 30 shillings," while others "slyly insinuate toward you a bit of paper on whose top are the words, 'To the afflicted.' "[151] MacKenzie thought that it degraded men to walk about in such a state as he saw two of them—in a single comical garment with one aperture for both their heads, advertising "the street number of Dr. Eddy, the infamous curer of an infamous disease."[152]

Fascinated by all these advertisements, Isaac Jewett copied down a few for his readers. "Sold, *on oath*, the pure grease of a fine large bear," read one sign. Proclaimed another: "The industrious fleas, patronized by their Royal Highnesses, the Duchess of Kent and the Princess Victoria, may be seen at No. 10, Picadilly." Still another read: "Repair your tailor bills by going to the cheap Clothes Warehouse, No. 15, Strand." Over a picture of a priest choking a woman, on an another ad, were the words: "Awful disclosures of what was done in the Charlestown Convent, Massachusetts, have just been published." One poor, soiled and shabby creature advertised baths: "Warm baths at reduced prices—vapor, sulphur, shampooing,—all for two shillings."[153]

Having read *The Cries of London*, in their "infant hours," as one traveler put it, Americans watched and listened for the street cries of London. Jewett was one morning wakened as a strange cry, "gutteral . . . like the solitary note of your hoarse bullfrog" came from the throat of a man hailing the world on the "subject of worn-out garments." Another cry "of three syllables . . . clocklike . . . hoarse and grating, like a wheel, moaning as it were for relief," proved to be an announcement for lobsters. "Two other notes,—two deeply bass, followed by two piercingly tenor, proceeded from a little woman who would fain have one buy

"Peeler," or "Bobby," a member of the Metropolitan Police, founded in London by Sir Robert Peel in 1829. *From the author's collection.*

her watercresses." And behind her, he observed, "stormed a boy with a huge basket on his shoulders, ringing a little bell continually, and crying out with most money-making impatience, 'hot muffins, muffins all hot.' "[154]

The streets of London themselves astounded these visitors, with their cleanliness and good lighting. Silliman observed in 1806 at a chemist's shop a single gas light which he described to his readers as a kind of novelty.[155] By 1823 Wheaton was telling his readers that "England is now lighted with gas. Every village has its line of leaden pipes twisted about underground, creeping up the corners of houses, and spurting out their jets of flame for the convenience of the public. Churches, halls, dining rooms, shops, streets,—all are now made luminous by carburetted hydrogen gas."[156] Double rows of lights on city streets seemed to turn night into day for the astonished American travelers.

The safety of the streets was, moreover, insured by "a most remarkable body of men," wrote Grant Thorburn of the newly-formed, blue-coated, metropolitan police, who were "very polite and obliging. I have frequently been accompanied by one of them for nearly a quarter of a mile to show me the street I wanted."[157] Wilbur Fisk gave his readers something of the origin of the London police in 1829, attributing the institution to Sir Robert Peel. He described them as "youngerly-looking men, of a fine and sober character, and gentlemanly manners. Every few rods you meet one of them . . . and if you have any occasion to make inquiries for persons or places . . . you are sure to receive a civil and intelligent answer. Their manner is quiet and unostentatious," he continued, "and to see them moving about in the city, you would hardly think they, of all men, had least authority to intermeddle with the affairs of others; but if occasion require, you find them very decided and efficient." Fisk was most impressed, he concluded, by the ability of "this unarmed city guard" to assert moral over physical power "with not even a stick in their hands to enforce their authority."[158] And thus began the long love affair between American visitors and the London constabulary.

When it came time for these Americans to leave London, "fairest of cities all," they did so with mingled regret and pleasure—regret that they had not seen and done more than they did, but swelled with pride and satisfaction at what they had managed to accomplish in their limited time in the capital of the world. "The picture is too complicated and vast ever to be examined fully, or copied correctly by anyone," decided scientist Jacob Green.

As a place of residence, if it were my own country, it would be delightful. There are so many literary, benevolent, religious and scientifick institutions, and the distinguished personages in each are all, as far as they fell under my observation, so easy of access, that it seems to me I should never tire with them; yet none of these could induce me to reside here, for it is not *home*. I feel greatly mortified that I have gained so much less real, substantial information here than I expected; yet from morning till night, and day after day, I have been as busy and inquisitive as man or yankee could be.[159]

Concluded Mordecai Noah about 1819: "On the whole, an American who visits London with the desire to be pleased with the people, and the city, will not come away disappointed."[160]

6

Great Events

Although some American travelers in the early decades of the nineteenth century manifested a studied indifference to the foreign affairs of the "motherland," as one called it, few were unaware of that nation's life-and-death struggle with Napoleon, nor later on were they unaware of internal turmoil as the movement toward political and social reform began.

Silliman devotes several anecdotes to the ever-present threat of invasion from the Continent by the French. At dinner one evening in London at the home of a friend—a clergyman of the Church of England—the company talked of this danger. A venerable parson who had dozed off, woke suddenly to hear a snatch of the conversation. " 'What? Bonaparte come to invade England? he invade this country-a d——d lamp-lighting scoundrel!' " Less than a month later Bonaparte was reportedly poised at Boulogne with "vast armies and with his flotillas in a state of unexampled preparation." All England was on the alert, Silliman observed, "all officers and soldiers . . . to be ready at a moment's warning. . . . The whole land is in a state of . . . unexampled preparation, while most of the Channel fleet is drawn off in pursuit of the combined squadrons of France and Spain."[1]

Silliman was in Portsmouth on September 14, 1805, the day Horatio Nelson sailed to meet those squadrons and achieve immortality at Trafalgar. In company with Admiral Coffin and a few other officers, Nelson seemed wanting to get away to sea quietly, as he dodged round some of the back streets leading to the quay. Once he discovered the crowd waiting to see him off, however, he submitted cheerfully. "I stood on one of the batteries near which he had to pass," recalled Silliman. "He was elegantly dressed, and his blue coat was splendidly illuminated with stars and ribbons. As the barge . . . pushed away from the shore, the people gave him three cheers which his lordship returned by waving his hat." In a footnote the American reminded his readers that "this was the last act of respect Nelson ever received, while living, from his countrymen. It is well known that he then left England forever, and lost his life on the 21st of October, at the great battle of Trafalgar." Although "his private life was not without its faults," admitted Silliman, "his public character was all that is splendid and commanding. He was the very idol of this nation and the terror of its enemies."[2]

Half a century later Nathaniel Hawthorne would stand before a case at Greenwich Hospital, staring at the same "splendidly illuminated" blue coat that had made Nelson so easy a mark for the French sharpshooter whose bullet entered at the collar and tore into the Admiral's spine. Although Hawthorne tried to be cool about the British hero, his American heart was nevertheless touched by that small coat, along with other leftovers from its owner's life—a hat, a shirt, a single glove, his "foul weather" cap, a spyglass, a combination knife and fork for a man with one arm, and his prayerbook. Nelson, concluded Hawthorne, had "expressed his life in a kind of symbolic poetry." And for a moment, at least, he felt the spirit of the "frail, ardent man . . . quivering here and there about the room like a blue, lambent flame."[3]

A decade after Trafalgar Bonaparte was ravaging the continent of Europe once more, and Joseph Ballard was in London when the city celebrated Wellington's victory at Waterloo. "London," he recorded on June 22, 1815,

> is one continual scene of uproar and joy in consequence of the total defeat of Bonaparte at Waterloo by Lord Wellington. This is announced by the Park and Tower guns and by placards upon the gates of the Mansion House. . . . Friday and Saturday night all the public buildings and many private ones were illuminated. Many fanciful and beautiful devices were exhibited . . . [at] the Excise office, the Bank, Post-Office, Somerset House, Admiralty, Horse Guards, Carlton House, Foreign and Home Department (here the eagles taken from the French were displayed) . . . One house in St. James's was particularly fine. The whole front resembled a fortress with cannon, flags, etc., formed by colored lamps. A publican who keeps a tavern with the sign of a cock, had a large transparency representing a game cock strutting over his fallen combatant with the inscription, "England, the cock of the walk!"

Surging crowds celebrated in the streets, and Ballard did not get home till one o'clock in the morning and found himself "a little indisposed on Saturday morning."[4] In the years to come the Duke of Wellington would become almost as much a revered London "lion" for visiting Americans as the Tower itself.

"Since my residence in England, some of the most important events in modern history have occurred," rightly concluded Joseph Ballard of Boston in 1815. At that moment, in early August, Bonaparte himself was a prisoner aboard the Bellerophon at Plymouth, awaiting exile on St. Helena. Over 2,000 small boats a day, reported Ballard, were carrying curiosity-seekers out into Plymouth harbor "to catch a glimpse of the disturber of the world."[5]

A third major event in these early decades of the nineteenth century in Britain, of which visiting Americans became aware, was the passage of the Reform Bill in 1832. Breckinridge devoted a chapter to it, describing it to his American readers as a "fundamental revolution in the British Constitution." The effects of its passage, or rather its momentum, would continue for many years to come, he predicted. "It may provide for general education; it may modify the questions growing out of the religious establishments; it may provide a better system of taxation, expenditure and revenue; it may simplify the jurisprudence of the country. But all these improvements," the Reverend Breckinridge concluded,

> will only more and more coerce the extension of the basis of representation; and make more constantly indispensable such a revolution to come, as will place the real power, intellect, and property of the community finally in possession of the constitution. This will consummate that moral impulse which

forced the Reform Bill through the House of Peers—and over and through the British Constitution; and when this event arrives, a revolution from the present to future, far greater than that from the past to the present, will have occurred.

Gradually over the centuries, power had been wrested from the monarch and extended to the clergy and to the nobility, he wrote, and now finally to the middle classes. "There remains but one more partner to admit into the state; the great class of labour. When they come, new changes must occur."[6]

Something of the tension of this era was observed by Charles Stewart when he arrived in England in June 1832.

> The last year. . .has been replete with tumult and popular dissatisfaction. . .and, the passing month has witnessed a degree of national excitement without a parallel in the history of the kingdom. Had we arrived, even ten days earlier, we should have seen. . .the very verge of open revolution. All parties admit the retirement of Earl Grey as premier, and the resignation of the ministers consequent upon it, to have been a most fearful crisis to the empire; and nothing but the speedy recall of that statesman, and triumph of reform, of which it was the royal pledge, saved the nation, at the time, from the horrors of a civil war.[7]

Not long after this, in Birmingham, Stewart learned of the unpopularity of the Duke of Wellington, stemming from his opposition to the Reform Bill. The young man who conducted him through one of the manufactories showed Stewart a magnificently-wrought Wellington "Shield of gold," created when he was the idol of the nation. "Were this to be exhibited from our windows for a few moments just now, gentlemen, I can assure you it would soon receive a *finishing touch* from the workmen of the town." Still to be seen in the city's streets, noted Stewart, were men "wearing blue and tricoloured ribands; and flags of the same signification are flying from many houses on which are placards with the inscription 'NO TAXES PAID HERE TILL THE REFORM BILL IS PASSED!', while every corner is covered with calls to public meetings." Before he got back to his hotel that day Stewart wrote,

> An express arrived, with the intelligence that the important bill had passed the House of Lords. . .The streets are now thronged with crowds, wearing joyous and triumphant faces; the royal standard is floating gaily from the towers of all the churches; almost every window shows its tri-coloured banner; guns are beginning to be fired, and huzzas to fill the air; while unnumbered bells are sending forth, on every side, their peals of joy.[8]

Shortly after this Stewart was in London, watching King William and Queen Adelaide, who were greeted with mingled hisses and cheers as they entered Hyde Park for a military review with the Duke of Wellington at the head of his own regiment. The same evening, however, they were cheered enthusiastically, he saw, as he watched them arriving at Wellington's residence, Apsley House, at Hyde Park Corner. "The gloomy blinds of sheet iron, by which the windows have been screened, since the glass of the whole front was broken by a mob, some weeks ago," were opened, Stewart observed, and "floods of light were now pouring from the mansion and triumphant and joyous strains of music filling its courts and rooms." Wellington himself then pulled up, having just come from a dinner at nearby Buckingham Palace, in time for his own reception, and he, too, now was greeted "with enthusiastic cheers, continuing till long after he had alighted, and entered his mansion."[9] The iron shutters remained in place for several decades after this—the stubborn old Duke of Wellington, who gained thus his nickname of "The Iron Duke," not willing to forget the action of the mob at the time of the Reform Bill. Visitors to Apsley House today, now a museum, can see, if they look carefully, certain indications in the stonework where these blinds were installed.

In this same period of social and political agitation, MacKenzie took himself to hear reformer Robert Owen speak before a group of London working men—

> their faces, hands, and bodily conformation indicating their peculiar line of labour. Some were in their holyday clothes; others had just evidently escaped from their benches, having their aprons twisted up and stuck through the drawing string. . . . Their conversation was of trades' unions, initiation of nobs and dungs, that is, recusant individuals of their fraternities who refused to affiliate. They spoke very angrily of the *Times* newspaper, as being against the working men, and the partisan of rich persecution.[10]

"A little shoemaker," smelling of wax and leather, marked by the pox and a disfiguring scar—"which had rendered him blear-eyed and scarified on one side of his face, [and] showed how neglected had been his childhood"—attracted MacKenzie's attention with his excited comments. " 'We had a famous meetin' last night; we filiated up to ninety. If we could unite with the tailors we'd be main powerful; but the darn stitchlouses are too ristocratic; they're worse, all hollow, nor the Ouse o' Lords. They think they're better nor hus; and undertakes to turn their noses up at a cobbler.' "[11]

"Here Mr. Owen made his appearance, and was received with unbounded applause." Owen, after he had spoken for a few moments, affected MacKenzie much as he had Charles Stewart and Emma Willard—"filled with self-complacency and tickled at the reception which the tatterdemalions gave him." His style of eloquence, MacKenzie observed,

> consisted of all the startling truisms which have been uttered at various times. . .by cleverer men. . .and which he now strung together with as little art as might be, his language being vulgar and slovenly. When he fancied he had made a good hit, he would stop for applause; and when it came, grin back a responsive recognition. . . . In the course of his address he was saying, what is indeed very true, that the power was all wielded by the rich in England. "But," Owen declared, "we will take it away from them." Here he was interrupted by overpowering applause. When he could be heard he added—"But peaceably, not forcibly." This qualifying statement was not so well received. I noticed, however, one starved, thin-legged conspirator. . .who seemed mightily to approve of the peaceful mode of redress,. . .for he cried "hear! hear! hear!" at the top of his squeaking voice.[12]

MacKenzie expressed a lack of respect for Owen who, he claimed, has "mismanaged his own affairs. . .and failed notoriously in all his undertakings. . . . I must confess that a benevolent and philanthropic fool always seems more dangerous to me than a roguish one. A roguish fool may steal, and allow himself to be quickly caught . . . but the other, being left at large, may lead astray others yet simpler than himself." There can be no doubt, the American decided, "that the poor are insufficiently paid in England. . .that in the presence of a development far exceeding whatever the world has hitherto seen, the profits of it are concentrated in the hands of a few, while they who mainly contribute to it by their labour are left to languish in destitution of what mere animal wants require." What irony, MacKenzie thought, "that while property has for its mercenary champions the genius and learning of the country, the claims of labour are unrepresented and unsustained; its cause. . .abandoned to the advocacy of rogues like Cobbett, and idiots such as Owen. . . . Overweening vanity is at the bottom of all his extravagances," he concluded.[13]

The social effects of Britain's already well-advanced industrialism were observed several years later by Heman Humphrey on his visits to manufactories: "millions of men, women, and children. . .the slaves of that mighty steam power."[14] And Joshua White, in 1810, had already advised his nation to remain an agricultural society. Even as they expressed such sentiments Americans seemed to realize the inevitable, as in Fisk's remark at Sheffield that "steel is beginning to be made in the United States, as are also many other Sheffield products."[15] Nevertheless, Humphrey declared, "It is certainly high time to inquire, whether those inventions and discoveries, which threaten to break up domestic manufactures, throughout the civilized world, and to subject, to so vast an extent, human bones and muscles, and minds, even, to the power of water-falls, and steam-engines, are likely in the hands of over-grown capitalists, to bless or curse the nations."[16]

Britain's class structure took many a knock at the hands of these professional republicans from the New Jerusalem across the Atlantic. Early in the first decade young Austin claimed, in fact, that one could determine a man's station in life by the number of knocks he applied to one's front door: once for a servant, for example, while a gentlemen knocked thrice.[17]

MacKenzie observed that in London "the races are most distinctly marked. It was not necessary to observe the cut of a coat, or the fashion of a nether garment, to tell in an instant who was the bramin [sic] and who the pariah. The gentleman was easily distinguishable by his superior height, his air of generous feeding, his pride of step, and a certain erect, elevated, confident, contented, and—I may add a qualification which applies to most of our native-born population in America—independent republican freedom and nobleness of carriage."[18]

"The trader," opined MacKenzie, "had a very different air though he struggled to make it the same; for it was the effect of imitation . . . a blending of haughtiness and humiliation . . . [which can] soften at once into a complacent simper and cringing obsequiousness." The humbler classes he perceived marked in various ways by their trades, thus suffering "a general physical deterioration." As a sailor himself he particularly noticed the American sea captains in the London Exchange—"well-dressed respectable-looking men, in nowise distinguishable in their air and manners from the best people around them; while the British captains were coarse, rugged, rough of speech, not unfrequently dressed in round jackets." The difference stemmed, he decided, from the fact that the former had "something to lose or gain. He is probably part or the whole owner of the noble ship he stands upon . . . he is not toiling for a pittance."[19]

Despite their rather complacent diatribes against Britain's class system, the Americans nevertheless fairly reveled in the endless services and physical comforts the British class of trained and willing domestic servants provided—both at inns and hotels and in the homes they visited. Either the Americans failed to make the connection between the two factors in the social equation or chose not to. Agriculturalist Henry Colman actually enumerated the types of servants, their number, and their duties in the stately homes in which he was a guest, marveling at the serene and luxurious existence their labors made possible for their masters and mistresses.[20] Zachariah Allen and William Austin faulted British servants for being "obsequious" but still commended them for their efficiency.[21] Humphrey, in describing the role played by household domestics in England—who were in service for life and were unashamed of that fact, so far as he could tell—remarked, "How much better, for all parties, is this system, than the perpetual changes and sore destitution and embarrassment, to which we are doomed in *our* domestic arrangements. . . . I confess I do not quite like the word *servant*," Humphrey admitted, "and I never use it, either in speaking to or of domestics in my own family." Then this Yankee parson added: "But then I can see no harm in it where it is customary, especially as this use is so abundantly sanctioned in the Scriptures."[22] Upward social mobility, which MacKenzie praised at home as "the perpetually raising to competency and distinction of the industrious,"[23] was all very well, but these Americans in the early decades of the nineteenth century were not perceiving the dichotomy between that concept of which they were so proud and their own lack of a dependable servant class. And as long as they had an ever-fresh supply of immigrants, or slaves, they did not have to.

Joshua White went so far as to compare English servants with those he was accustomed to back home in Georgia.

> The English servants are also greatly superior to ours; and those who have been accustomed to the management of slaves and negroes, will not fail to mark the difference. Without the disgusting filth, habitual carelessness, and general depravity which too generally distinguish the Africans and their descendants, English servants are withal civil, obliging, active and obedient. They are and must be industrious for few families keep more than a maid-servant, boy, cook, and sometimes a nurse where there are children. Even with a less number the domestic affairs are conducted with ease and regularity. . . . In the inns and coffee-houses, they are prompt and wonderfully active in their several stations.[24]

There are interesting, stray references by these Americans to blacks they observed during their travels in Britain—particularly when they observed them enjoying the same social privileges as the whites around them. Silliman, who was horrified by the "slaver" he inspected at Liverpool, also observed that

> the prejudice against colour is less strong in England than in America; for, the few negroes found in this country, are in a condition much superior to that of their countrymen anywhere else. A black footman is considered as a great

acquisition, and consequently, negro servants are sought for. . . . An ill-dressed or starving negro is never seen in England, and in some instances even alliances are formed between them and white girls of the lower orders of society. A few days since I met in Oxford-street a well-dressed white girl: walking arm in arm, and conversing very sociably, with a negro man who was as well dressed as she, and so black that his skin had a kind of ebony lustre. As there are no slaves in England, perhaps the English have not learned to regard negroes as a degraded class of men, as we do in the United States where we have never seen them in any other condition.[25]

Attending church in Edinburgh, Isaac Jewett, however, was appalled to observe two black men seated right in the middle of the congregation at St. Giles one Sunday. "Now as I am an American, and not an abolitionist," he declared, "a host of what are called early prejudices, instantly arose within me, and I queried by what right the men of color were there. " 'Why, sir, they are human beings and good citizens,' said a tailor beside me. This is not the first instance I have witnessed in Scotland," continued Jewett, "of such familiarity between the races. I do not speak of the dark, elegant East Indian ladies, who may be seen walking daily, arm-in-arm, with the fashionables of Edinburgh. It is the crispy-haired, flat-nosed, thick-lipped, and ebony black gentleman, whom you shall see in fraternal confab with the polished sons of this modern Athens, to whom I allude. But the prejudices of early education do not exist here, and your negro is deemed nearly as much of a human being as a white man." He was further much offended at the theatre one evening at the sight of a young black man

> right in the centre of the pit filled with ladies and gentlemen. . . . I turned my eye inward to contemplate that feeling which I possess in common with most of my countrymen, which abhors the hand-in-hand companionship of the negro, that feeling which is associated with all our thoughts and sympathies and which, if able here, would have instantly elevated into a higher atmosphere the youth so cordially associated with, by an apparently respectable portion of a theatrical audience, in one of the most refined and intellectual cities of Europe.[26]

Studying law at Lincoln's Inn in London in 1802, William Austin was ashamed at the difference in racial attitudes he perceived in England, where "a negro is as free as a Briton." How can it be, he wondered, "that in the United States, a country where triumph the purest principles of legislation which ever adorned civil society: that in such a country you can find a 'Slave to be sold'? What unheard of inconsistency!" remarked the young man. "I blush for my country; and I have been made by Englishmen, to blush for my country!" It was nothing to how his countrymen would be taunted in the decades just before the American Civil War.[27]

Britain's harsh criminal code did not go unnoticed. Besides touring Newgate prison, or observing, or just "missing," executions, some Americans actually entered courtrooms to observe the stiff sentences handed down for such crimes as breaking and entering, petty theft, or robbery. In the forties, observing the Old Bailey Assizes, Thurlow Weed said that he saw a young woman sentenced to "a year's imprisonment for stealing a handkerchief, and to another girl for a petit larceny, it being the second offense, twelve year's transportation."[28]

Abigail Adams in 1784 had felt pity for the youthful highwayman she saw being dragged into London on foot by a man on horseback. "Ghastly and horrible: he looked like a youth of twenty only, attempted to lift his hat, and looked despair [sic]. You can form some idea of my feelings when they told him, 'Ay, you have but a short time; the assize sits next month; and then, my lad, you swing.' "[29] Austin declared that "they have very humanely abolished torture— but they have accepted death. Their humanity cannot endure the broken arm, the lacerated body, the quivering flesh of the criminal; but a simple hanging affects them as little as the loss of a sheep, a sorry horse, or forty shillings."[30]

Those convicts condemned to transportation were seen in the holding pens at Newgate and some even aboard ship already on their way to Australia. MacKenzie, coming up the Thames, spotted one of these convict vessels, "a large black ship, whose open ports displayed gratings of stout iron bars . . . bound with convicts to Botany Bay. . . . They were going into exile to the fertile fields of a distant colony," he mused, "which, however it may be, and indeed must, become one day great, can never wholly escape from the stigma of its origins." The convicts, MacKenzie thought, were much like "prisoners of war captured in the battles of that perpetual contest . . . between property and poverty."[31]

Still another manifestation of the law in this period was an object the travelers spied from their comfortable stage coaches racing over country roads—the gibbet. From atop a coach en route to visit the caves of Derbyshire about 1830 Allen saw "on the top of a distant hill. . .a post about thirty feet high with an arm stretching horizontally from its top, like the arm of a tavern signpost in New England." Drawing closer, he perceived suspended from that arm "a sort of iron basket or cage, of the exact outlines of the human form, and filled with the white bones of the criminal." Allen, with his always practical approach to everything, made it his business to learn precisely how the corpses of executed criminals were installed in these contrivances and described the process in detail to his readers. This particular gibbet, the postboy told him, would probably last five or six years longer until the wooden shaft had rotted away, as it had been there about nine already. "During this period," wrote Allen, "it is intended to operate as a terror to evil-doers," adding "[T]hey are usually erected in the vicinity of the spot where the crimes that give occasion for them are perpetrated." As he contemplated this curious sight, "a gust of wind swept by. . .the sound of it rushing between the crevices of the iron frame actually produced the 'sighing through the gibbet'—a phrase which I had always considered a figurative expression."[32]

Evidences of the mass migration that would in time depopulate both Scotland and Ireland, as well as carry many Englishmen to America, were already in evidence in these early decades. At the start of the century Austin wrote on the poverty in both Celtic lands, but of Scotland especially, where the welfare of cattle was put before that of human beings, and he remarked that "Scotland, reduced far below a state of nature, and weary of the sight of her dear, native hills, banishes herself forever to the frontiers of America."[33] The great Irish migration had not yet begun in these early decades, but the desperation of her people was seen even in Britain where they came as laborers to help with the harvest. "These poor fellows come over to get a little money to pay their rents," wrote Fisk in the 1830s, "and as the harvest is ripe in the south soonest, they land there and work up until they *reap their way through the kingdom*. The number surprised us; we met hundreds on hundreds in addition to those who were in the fields."[34]

Crossing the Irish Sea with some of these migrant workers on their way back home, Stewart watched them making the best of a rough passage, staked out on the open decks of the vessel, shivering and cold, on a wet and windy crossing, "apparently as hungry as they were poorly clad." Some of them sought refuge in empty hogsheads, he observed, while the rest simply made the best of it.

> They soon became sportive and jovial, bandying from one to another no little of the wit and repartee for which their nation is so proverbial, and which was sharpened by an occasional glass of *"the mountain dew"* of Scotland, circulated by one and another, from the bar of the boat. At length, one. . .brought out an old, squeaking violin, and by striking up a jig, set the whole company to dancing and merry-making which continued till I had fallen asleep in my berth below.

Stewart had seen Irish workers along the canals in the United States and recalled the miserable sheds and "shanties" put up for their shelter; but after seeing how they lived in Ireland, when he got there, those Yankee "shanties" seemed more like "palaces of comfort" for the poor emigrants of the Emerald Isle.[35]

Many inquiries were made of traveling Americans, including John Griscom, of the possibilities of emigration to America, "and the probable advantages of a removal to that country." In his replies, he said, he endeavored to discourage them unless they possessed "some capital, and sufficient enterprise and good conduct to manage it prudently" or unless they were "mechanics and labouring men skilled in their professions, and of moral and industrious habits."[36] Allen was questioned closely by an Irish drover, "well dressed and of respectable appearance," who had saved several hundreds of pounds in cash and was especially interested in matrimonial possibilities upon his arrival in America.[37]

Americans voyaging over the Atlantic in these years were well aware of the ceaseless migration traffic. One recorded the panic of steerage passengers aboard his vessel during a storm in a sea so terrible they could not have lived a minute. "The poor Irish emigrants, stifled between decks, were busy supplicating the Virgin for their safety, or infuriated with fear, were endeavoring to get on deck and throw themselves overboard, rather than go down in a prison."[38] Some of these wretches were surveyed on their arrival in the United States, by an American embarking for England, aboard "a large emigrant-ship, the deck of which was literally crammed with miserable and squalid beings from the old world."[39]

Some of those who yearned for a better life in the new world, and actually made the break with the old, never got there. Leaving for home aboard the comfortable, speedy packet *Roscoe* in 1836, Fanny Hall described how they were hailed in Liverpool harbor by Captain D. of the *Mexico*, "having on board a large number of immigrants." He wanted the *Roscoe* to report his ship on their arrival in New York. " 'Oh, yes,' replied one of our passengers jestingly, 'and *if you get there first,* report us, will you?'" It all seemed amusing at the time, aboard the *Roscoe* with its good speed and safety record. Later, Mrs. Hall told her readers that, one week after they had safely landed, she read in the newspaper of the fate of the *Mexico,* "wrecked a few miles from New York; and out of one hundred and sixteen persons who were on board, one hundred and eight perished!"[40]

PART II

1845–1865

No one likes to be ridiculed; and when it proceeds from those whom we respect and look up to, as Americans naturally did to the country from which they sprung, it is doubly painful and offensive.

—Oliver P. Hiller, *English and Scottish Sketches by an American,* 1857

7

Voyage

That steam was the conqueror of both time and space Ralph Waldo Emerson and his contemporaries were fully convinced. Man "no longer waits for favoring gales but by means of steam, he realizes the fable of Aeolus's bag, and carries the two and thirty winds in the boiler of his boat."[1] Beginning in the 1840s, steam thus made it possible for ever-larger numbers of Americans to set out across the Atlantic, which some now patronizingly began to call "the duck pond."

"The travel to England is immense now," the popular *Home Journal* for May 1856 informed its readers. "On ocean-bound steamers state rooms are engaged as far in advance as September." The excitement generated by the Great Exhibition of 1851 in London, together with the advent of the steamship, had so swelled the number of American travelers that by 1855 between thirty and forty thousand of his countrymen were turning up in London each summer—to the point where George Dallas, American minister to Great Britain (between 1856 and 1861) referred in July 1856 to "a steady stream of American travellers" and "book-making tourists" badgering him at his office for various forms of aid and favors.[2]

"A voyage to Europe is, in these days, so common an occurrence that its mention slips into conversation almost unnoticed," observed Margaret Sweat in 1855. "Travelling seems to be the rule for Americans—and staying at home the exception."[3]

Samuel Cox of Ohio acknowledged in his preface to *A Buckeye Abroad,* an account of his honeymoon trip to Europe and the Great Exhibition in 1851, that "a book of travel is no longer a book of marvels." He nevertheless kept a painstaking record of his tour for that very purpose just as did his countrymen of earlier decades.[4] Another traveler in the same period remarked that "England, for many reasons, is more familiar to Americans than any other part of Europe," attributing this fact in large measure to the many books written on it by Yankee travelers. "Delightfully painted in part by our Washington Irving, and retouched every year by crowds of eager travelers, it has scarcely a noble structure, or city, or landscape, or view, whose image has not been distinctly brought out,"—a realization that stopped neither Dr. John Corson nor any other American traveler who was obsessed by this urge to record and publish his or her adventures in Britain.[5]

"The press has teemed of late with the words of American tourists," observed Benjamin Moran at mid-century.[6] And the Reverend John Choules also ob-

served that "books of travel have multiplied of late with fearful rapidity, but still
the vast amount of readers in our country creates a steady demand for such
publications."[7] Apparently, it was their awareness of this demand that kept these
scribblers going.

One of these enthusiastic diarists was described in action by Orville Horwitz in
1853 as

> a specimen of a pure traveling Yankee. . . . He scarcely arrived at a town
> before, with the dust of the road still on him, he would start out, purchase a
> book and map of the place, and run, without intermission, to every spot
> named. Worn out, scarcely able to sit up, he would return at nightfall, looking
> for all the world as if his thirst for information was about to be his quietus! In
> this half-alive condition he would take notes of what he had seen.[8]

Many of these traveler-writers complained of the fatigue that came upon them
by evening, which was their only time to write. "When the eyes of my friends are
asleep, and when my own are heavy" it was hard to settle down to work,
discovered Hiram Fuller in the fifties.[9] Certain travelers also went to considerable lengths to assure readers of the verisimilitude of their work, the freshness
and honesty of their impressions, with no recourse to professional guidebooks.
The Reverend John Edwards, for example, boasted that he wrote as he traveled
and not "in the quietness of my study at home, from notes taken while away. I
carried a book in my pocket and often sat down amid the ruins of old palaces,
and ivy-mantled castle walls, and under the shadow of crumbling arches . . . and
wrote out my impressions of what was before me."[10]

At mid-century the American travelers were still intensely curious, energetic,
and earnest about their travels in "the Motherland," Britain, but, viewed all
together, they were more of a mixed lot than their predecessors of the first four
decades. For one thing, more women made it across the Atlantic, both professional authors and ordinary female travelers. They included Grace Greenwood,
the journalist; authors Catherine Sedgwick, Lydia Sigourney, Julia Ward Howe,
and Harriet Beecher Stowe; the famous Mobile society belle, Octavia LeVert; a
cranky Yankee named Margaret Sweat; and Nathaniel Hawthorne's querulous
Sophia.

Two young men with thin wallets and strong legs hiked their way about in
these years, both of whom later ended up in the American diplomatic service—
Benjamin Moran and Bayard Taylor. American college presidents, just as in
earlier decades, came to make their customary diligent observations: John
Durbin of Dickinson College; Cornelius Felton, a future president of Harvard;
and Edward Thomson of Ohio Wesleyan. Also making a visit was educator Jacob
Abbott of New York, author of over two hundred books—including the popular
"Rollo" series for children, such as *Rollo in London*. Artist George Catlin went
over in 1839 with a collection of paintings, Indian artifacts, and even a group of
"Ojibbeway and Ioway Indians," who were introduced to the young Queen
Victoria at Windsor Castle, for his exhibition in London's Egyptian Hall in
Piccadilly. In 1850 both Frederick Law Olmsted and Andrew Jackson Downing
arrived, the former to study English farm practices, the latter architecture and
landscaping. Dr. Andrew McFarland, superintendent of the New Hampshire

George Catlin's Indians take time away from their exhibition in London's Egyptian Hall to visit Queen Victoria at Windsor Castle where they mistook a liveried minor household official for royalty. *Punch*, **vol. VI, 1844, p. 28.** *Courtesy the Library of Congress.*

Asylum for the Insane, and Dr. Walter Channing of Boston represented the medical profession. Randal MacGavock of Tennessee and Henry Maney of North Carolina were lawyers who traveled together, and each wrote his own account of the trip. Father George Haskins of Boston and Father John Donelan of Rock Island, Illinois, produced books of travel suitable for Roman Catholic readers, because they were so discouraged by the Protestant domination of the travel-book genre.

Journalist Thurlow Weed, one day to be a power in American politics, wrote of his British travels, as did his colleagues in the news profession, Joel Headley, George Wilkes, Hiram Fuller, and, last but not least, Horace Greeley, editor of the New York *Tribune*. Black abolitionist William Wells Brown, technically a fugitive slave, produced a remarkable account of his experiences in Britain as a lecturer and writer, paying his own way, as he insisted. Samuel Young, a self-styled "Wall Street Bear" as in his title, followed the time-honored practice of dispatching a series of letters home to a local newspaper—in his case *The Saratoga (N.Y.) Republican*—as did Charles Fairbanks to Boston's *Saturday Evening Gazette.*

A sizeable number of clerics made the scene, among them the great Henry Ward Beecher himself—not yet soiled by the Tilton adultery scandal; Arthur Cleveland Coxe, rector of Baltimore's Grace Church and later bishop of western New York; Stephen Tyng, rector of St. George's in New York; William Ware, formerly pastor of the First Unitarian Church in New York and at the time of his journey head of the *Christian Herald;* Nicholas Murray, a virulent anti-Catholic convert to Presbyterianism; and the Reverend John Choules, who enjoyed his first trip to Britain shepherding a group of American schoolboys at the Great Exhibition and his second as a kind of resident chaplain aboard the fabulous steam yacht, *North Star,* pride and joy of Commodore Vanderbilt.

A particularly interesting account is that of young John Mullaly, who was involved in the laying of the Atlantic cable and who also served as a newspaper correspondent for the New York *Herald.* William Cullen Bryant, Herman Melville, and Nathaniel Hawthorne also recorded their British experiences in this period, the latter concentrating, in *Our Old Home,* more on his travels about the country than on his professional work as American consul at Liverpool from 1853 to 1857.

Unlike Benjamin Silliman's sober, descriptive title of 1810, *A Journal of Travels in England, etc.,* the travelers in the decades before the Civil War began to strive for trendy, catchy titles as seen in the flood of *Glimpses, Glances, Dottings, Jottings, Lingerings, Loiterings, Sketches, Vignettes, Notes* and *Memoranda,* along with a dependence on alliteration: *Aboard and Abroad; Bubbles and Ballast; Glimpses and Gatherings; Haps and Mishaps; Over the Ocean; Random Rambles; Rambling Reminiscences; Rambles and Reveries; Random Recollections; Rambles and Reflections; Shore to Shore;* and *Trials and Triumphs.* One title marked the triumph of technology—*Sparks from a Locomotive,* in 1859.

Quite evident is a change in mood and tone in the two decades leading up to the great American civil conflict. Its beginnings are perceived during the early decades, primarily in the works of Protestant preachers lambasting the Church of England and the British Establishment in general. But by the 1840s most Yankee traveler-writers had become downright assertive, aggressive, chauvinistic, and polemic—all of which was rooted in guilt-ridden self-defense. They were, in short, angry. First of all, they believed that their country had for decades been held up to ridicule before the world by British traveler-writers. Secondly, in these decades before the Civil War, Britons chastised Americans relentlessly, both personally and in print, for their institution of slavery, almost as if inspired by Dr. Johnson's riposte: "How is it that we hear the loudest yelps for liberty among the drivers of negroes?" Believing the best defense to be a good offense, the American traveler-writers in these decades thus spent considerable time and energy rummaging about in the shadows of British society for evils to offset their own. This resulted in frequent, and often very labored, odious comparisons rather than candid observations. Certain books, such as Ralph Isham's *The Mud*

The *Britannia*, one of the first four small, side-wheeler steamships of the Cunard line, founded by Samuel Cunard in 1840. *Illustrated London News*, October 23, 1847, p. 272. *Courtesy the Library of Congress.*

Cabin, for example, or Matthew Ward's *English Items*, are not really travel books at all—although classified as such—but actually polemic tracts aimed at putting John Bull in his place once and for all.

"I enter England," announced the Reverend Robert Breckinridge of Baltimore "under the full belief that every American who comes to this country ought to tell the world, especially his own countrymen, what he thinks of John Bull. No man speaks of all others so freely. . . . Of America, especially, he has never ceased to speak . . . in a way calculated to do us undeserved harm, and create in the minds of all Americans well-merited offense."[11]

With the formation of Samuel Cunard's shipping line in 1840, a whole new epoch in sea travel began aboard his first four sturdy little steamships, which were named *Acadia, Britannia, Caledonia,* and *Columbia.* Wooden "paddlers," as they were sometimes called, with a tonnage of about 1,150, they were 207 feet long on the keel, with a beam of 34.2 feet inside the paddles. Their side-lever engines were capable of 400 or more horsepower and proceeded at about eight and a half knots on thirty-eight tons of coal per day, with handsteering aft.[12]

There were two decks, the upper one housing the officers' cabins, galley, bakery, cow house and poultry coops, while on the main deck were two saloons and staterooms for 115 passengers who paid fares of about $190. As no emigrant quarters were built into these vessels, they carried about 225 tons of cargo. No smoking was permitted except on deck, although later it was allowed in a rough, cramped space off the engine room, called "the fiddley." Owners and devotees of the now-threatened sailing packets took to calling these first steamers by such names as "steam wagons," "tin kettles," and "tea kettles."[13] But the steamship was here to stay, as time would tell.

Competition would grow fierce as new lines were established to compete with the canny Canadian Cunard, who had got a head start in 1840, aided by a British government subsidy. Beginning in 1849, the American E. K. Collins company gave Cunard a run for his money with a fleet of ships noted for their speed and sybaritic passenger accomodations—the *Arctic, Baltic, Atlantic,* and *Pacific.* Unfortunately, their wooden hulls were not equal to their powerful engines, which wracked them to pieces—resulting in considerable trouble and expense to the company. Collins quickly amassed a history of wrecks and lost ships and after nine years went out of existence.[14]

Cunard had kept on, adding larger and faster ships—the *America, Niagara, Canada,* and *Europa*—still without a single passenger lost to mar his safety record. The 1850s brought the development of iron construction and screw propulsion to replace the side wheels or "paddles." More and more travelers turned to steam, and the packets were relegated to carrying the immigrant trade.[15] By 1868 a traveler noted "more than 100 steamers engaged in the fast-growing commerce between the Old and New World" and smugly referred to the Atlantic as "the pond."[16] By 1875 the American voyager would have a choice of eleven different shipping lines from which to choose,[17] in addition to Cunard, who, except for the Crimean War years, when engaged in transporting troops, kept a firm grip on trans-Atlantic travel. While many Americans considered it their patriotic duty to sail in an American vessel, exhorting others to do likewise, Cunard nevertheless continued to attract Yankee voyagers because of his firm's stout seamanship and proud record of never having lost a passenger's life. There also seems to be some evidence that female American voyagers, some of them now traveling alone, were drawn by all those sturdy British officers, so reassuring, as one young lady wrote, to any woman "who requires the protection of a gallant English captain."[18] American men liked the no-nonsense approach of Cunard voyages, and one of them even found an added benefit. "You get there ten days earlier," he wrote, meaning to Britain, "for when you step on deck in New York, aboard a Cunarder, you are in Great Britain already. It's all British from the keel up!"[19]

The passengers aboard the early steamships were making maritime history, and they knew it. Lovingly they recorded their own voyages and each new development. The Reverend Robert Breckinridge, mightily impressed with his twenty-day crossing aboard the packet *Orpheus* in 1836, added to his manuscript before its first publication in 1839 a description of the arrival of the first experimental steamship, the *Sirius,* in New York harbor on April 23, 1838. He rightly concluded, "We may consider the problem of navigating the ocean by steam fully solved; and so solved as to afford a certainty and rapidity of intercourse between distant nations before unparalleled, nay, almost incredible."[20] The *Sirius* had beat her way over in 19 days—a record broken almost immediately by the brainchild of the renowned Victorian engineer Isambard Kingdom Brunel, the *Great Western,* which had performed the same feat in 14½ days.[21]

The inevitable death of the sailing packets is seen in the contrast between two voyages in 1851 by two newspaper editors, both headed for the Great Exhibition in London: Horace Greeley of New York City and William Drew of Augusta, Maine. Greeley set out aboard the steamer *Baltic* on April 16, "in the teeth of a Northeaster that clung to us like a brother." The auxiliary sails proved useless, so "for days together, stripped to her naked spars, she was compelled to push her bowsprit into the wind's eye by the very force of her engines alone." Despite these conditions, the *Baltic* made it to Liverpool in twelve days. "Her wheels," boasted Greeley, "never missed a revolution from the time she discharged her New York pilot until she stopped them to take on his Liverpool counterpart. She needs but good weather to make the run in ten days from dock to dock."[22]

Two months later, William Drew, appointed a commissioner for the State of Maine at the Great Exhibition, also set out across the Atlantic. As a loyal Maine man, determined to prove the superiority of the sailing vessel, he booked passage aboard the packet *New England,* "one of the best that was ever launched upon our own Kennebec." Drew had read Greeley's newspaper account of his storm-tossed passage, and focusing on that writer's descriptions of seasickness, while ignoring his praise for "the steadiness and the perfection of the accommodations" of the *Baltic* labeled the account and steamship travel itself as both "nauseate and lachrymose."[23]

"See the sails fill; behold her move," rhapsodized Drew, on setting out aboard the *New England.* "Witness the grace with which she salutes the waves; mark the stillness of her decks; the sweetness and quietness of the cabins, but Brother Greeley went in a steam packet. He knew not the quiet dignity of a sailing ship. The steamship must expect the thumping sound, the tiresome jar of the heavy piston, and the stench of burning grease and oil. A steamer," he continued, "paws her way through the waters like some enraged animal on land, insulting the face of old ocean with every dash of her unnatural wheels! our ship *sails*—she goes of her own accord 'like a thing of life.' "[24]

The only drawback was that, after bad weather and a period of being becalmed, Drew's trip to London consumed altogether six weeks, including twenty-eight days between the ports of Quebec and London, whereas Greeley's crossing took but twelve. The "noble ship" *New England* was already an anachronism, and in his heart William Drew knew it. In a single sentence he finally acknowledged that fact, as well as the all-important time factor in the travel equation, when he found his days running short at the Great Exhibition. "Six weeks consumed on my passage was a loss of three weeks here."[25] Emerson, by his own admission not the best of travelers, found another plus for steam, although he chose a packet, the *Washington Irving,* for his own crossing in 1847. "Hour for hour, the risk on a steam boat is greater; but the speed is safety, or, twelve days of danger, instead of twenty-four."[26]

Watching the side wheels of his "paddler," as she made "suds of the briny deep," George Fisher of Illinois exulted over "this wonderful rapidity of motion annihilating space, and this whirling, eddying, lashing water foaming as if enraged." Almost as if echoing Drew, he termed his steamer "a sea monster bounding over the waves 'like a thing of life.' "[27] Another voyager in this period compared his three earlier crossings under sail with the ten days the trip took him now. "My first bondage to Neptune lasted seventy-seven days [the ship was becalmed]; my second voyage thirty-five; and my last one twenty-one days. I was now but ten days performing the same distance."[28]

Boston's Dr. Walter Channing recalled with distaste his own previous voyage "in the good ship *Nancy*," fifty years earlier. "For forty-seven days altogether I saw and felt the unmitigated horrors of sailing ship life, bracing yards, furling and unfurling, springing this, breaking that, tearing into ribbons every sail. Never, never will I try the experiment again." In contrast was the steady, relentless progress of his steamship. "On, on goes the steamer. She never goes out of her way. She shows not the slightest ceremony to the waves. She cuts through them as with a knife, and away flies the salt sea all over her, now in the whitest of foam, and now in every color of the rainbow; and few visions do I remember more sublime."[29]

It was the speed of steam, however, not its poetry, that attracted both travelers and the lucrative mail contracts awarded to the shipping companies with the best time records. Caught up in the mania for speed, the travelers boasted of their vessel's record as though it were some personal achievement of their own. George Fisher doubted if his nine-day and thirty-minute crossing in Cunard's *Persia* in 1857 could ever be topped, but a hand-written note by some long-ago anonymous reader in the margin of Fisher's book boasts—"1889—now do it in *six* days!"[30]

Passenger life aboard these early steamships was not entirely unlike that of the packets. Livestock still were carried on deck to supply fresh meat, milk, and eggs. The dining saloon with its long tables, benches, and overhead rack for condiments and bottles—that could be raised and lowered—likewise doubled as a lounge between meals and as a makeshift church on Sundays. Hardworking stewards swiftly and quietly cleared and set tables and otherwise learned to work around the passengers at their games, conversation, and reading.

Staterooms, or cabins, were small—usually with two berths and a little sofa that could be converted into a bed at night. There was just room left for a small trunk or valise and the washstand. "Almost too small for the healthy respiration—breathing—of one full-grown person" was the opinion of Boston's Dr. Walter Channing. *"Take a whole stateroom to one's self*, no matter what the cost," he advised.[31] So cramped were the little cabins that another voyager decided that "the process of dressing was a severe practical joke."[32]

Grace Greenwood was at first amused by "a queer little utensil of painted tin, a sort of elongated spittoon," until she learned its use during seasickness.[33] Another bodily function was provided for in the chamber pots, always swiftly collected while passengers were at breakfast and dumped to leeward with precision. A small port, covered over in dirty weather, let in such daylight as there was in these "sea-coops," as Harriet Beecher Stowe referred to these cabins.[34] At night illumination came from a small, gimbal-mounted lamp in an

aperture that opened into both the cabin and the passageway outside, where it
could be extinguished, for safety reasons, by the steward at an appointed hour,
usually about eleven o'clock.

For some reason voyagers aboard these early steamships devote far more
space to seasickness than did their predecessors aboard the sailing packets.
Unlike many females, Mrs. Stowe refused to give in to it and "become one of the
ghosts below," and thus she spent most of her daytime hours on the upper deck,
huddled out of the wind, against "the old red smoke stack, the domestic hearth
of the ship." From her refuge she observed the endless labors of the ship's cook,
"a tall, slender melancholy man with a watery blue eye, a patient, dejected visage,
like an individual weary of the storms and commotions of life and thoroughly
impressed by the vanity of human wishes." From the depths of her own
depression—one of the many symptoms experienced by the seasick—she
watched him "mournfully making little ripples in the crust of a tart, resignedly
stuffing a turkey," and hopelessly hanging utensils only to have them all knocked
down again by the next roll of the ship. That cook became the symbol of her own
mental and physical misery, and she felt that she shared his "state of philosophic
melancholy."[35]

Mrs. Stowe did not know it, but another passenger aboard the *Africa* was
watching *her*. "She is certainly a woman of moods," observed Martha Coston in
her journal, "at times affable and entertaining, and again disagreeably reserved
and almost morose. . . . Perhaps it is hardly fair to judge anyone's disposition on
shipboard."[36] For her part, Mrs. Stowe found unbearable those few women
immune to seasickness who "always greet you with 'What a charming run we are
having! Isn't it delightful? and so on.' It is really amusing," she observed.

to watch the gradual progress of this epidemic. To see people stepping on
board in the highest possible feather, alert, airy, nimble, parading the deck,
chatty and conversable, on the best possible terms with themselves and
mankind generally; the treacherous ship, meanwhile, undulating and heaving
in the most graceful rises and pauses imaginable, like some voluptuous
waltzer; and then to see one after another yielding to the mysterious spell.[37]

"First a feeling of dizziness, then a prickly sensation extending over the whole
body, succeeded by an indescribable nausea so severe as to cause me to seek my
stateroom and throw myself upon my berth, followed by the most disagreeable
heavings and vomitings" was the brief, clinical description provided by youthful
Jacob Frazee—en route in the 1840s to study medicine abroad—of the seasickness that seized him on the first night out.[38]

The symptoms usually appeared soon after the passengers' first gala dinner
aboard, shortly after setting out. Then, as the vessel reached open sea and began
to roll, one by one passengers disappeared hastily from the saloon—some not to
be seen again until the ship docked at Liverpool. "A few hours before," journalist
Joel Cook wrote, "the first duty of the passenger was to get even with the
steamship company by eating everything in the larder—but the company has
conquered."[39] An elderly woman was heard to groan that "this business of
carrying passengers across the ocean is the money-makingest business I ever

Gala dinner the first night out; soon passengers would depart hastily as the ship began to roll in the open sea. Drawing by Augustus Hoppin. *Courtesy the Library of Congress.*

seen, because they don't hardly hev to feed 'em atall."[40] Dr. Clement Pearson recalled a colleague's remark: "First the ship hove up; then the passengers hove up."[41]

Strange and startling cries would be heard the first night out as symptoms of seasickness made their appearance. Excited stewards and stewardesses rushed along the narrow passageways as if the safety of the ship depended on their movements. The ship's doctor usually tramped fore and aft giving hints and suggestions, as well as required prescriptions, until the scene resembled a hospital. One voyager asked his readers to "imagine three hundred people all sick at the stomach at the same time."[42]

Apart from the common denominator of nausea, each victim believed his symptoms particularly horrible if not unique. "Like being lowered headfirst into a barrel of moderately warm and very dirty water," wrote a midwesterner.[43] "Sick as a cow with hollow-horn," observed Buffalo Bill Cody of the Indians he transported to London in the eighties for his "Wild West" show.[44] A young Texan was all right until he spotted "the first puker," he wrote, and from then on it was all downhill. "Spit-spit-spit-spit-all day long. Why the water runs from my mouth like the drip under an ash barrel," he complained.[45] Samuel Young said that it felt "as if a can of lamp oil was struggling to get down your throat while your inner works come and endeavor to repel the invader. The fight takes place in the neighborhood of your palate, so that you have a taste of the whole affair."[46] Sick babies could be seen sprawled across the bosoms of mothers too ill to care for them. "They can be seen tugging at their bottles, when not sick, but others of them taste only to turn their heads away."[47]

Some passengers discovered odd articles of diet they thought alleviated their symptoms. In 1843, Julia Ward Howe's bridgroom fed her on brandy and cracked ice with beneficial results, while their friend, Jacob Abbott, she said, kept busy "compounding various 'soft' drinks for convalescent lady friends."[48] Others swore by champagne, and some mothers even offered it to their children. For some, fruit stayed down when nothing else would. One young woman recommended her own diet of "lemons, sour-balls, mint-drops, ginger-nuts and apples."[49] A physician observed, "I have eaten but one cracker in twenty-four hours. The company are saving money!"[50] Another passenger realized that his "sustenance yesterday was one cup of tea and two bits of dry toast; today a glass of ice-water and a cracker."[51]

An intensification of all the senses was reported by many sufferers, including burning eyes, severe headaches, tight chests and aching, heavy limbs. Sounds of the other passengers and of the crew going about their duties seemed designed to torment the sufferers' ears. Skin was extra sensitive; noses were tortured by

Seasick females. Drawing by Augustus Hoppin. *Courtesy the Library of Congress.*

A seasick preacher. Drawing by Augustus Hoppin. *Courtesy the Library of Congress.*

odors of oil and grease, steam, and even their own effluvia, in the stuffy little cabins. The Reverend Beverly Carradine of New Orleans worked out an analysis of the smells aboard a steamship:

Bilge water	10%
Rats	.05%
Musty, wet carpets	.25%
Old oilcloth	10%
Dining room smell	30%
Kitchen odor	15%
Indescribable	.05%[52]

Dr. Walter Channing, who recommended the restorative effect of ocean travel to his patients, actually admitted to having seen a nonexistent man in his cabin during the hallucinations accompanying his own illness.[53] In the depths of their suffering, travelers often said and did unusual things. Numerous vows of permanent residence in Europe were made—if they ever got there. One old gentleman declared that he would stay there four years if a railroad could be built across the Atlantic in that time. A United States minister to Britain was heard to say that anybody who would "go to sea for pleasure would go to hell for amusement." One voyager swore that he would be perfectly all right "if they would only stop the ship for five minutes."[54]

A smug young man who had boasted that he never got seasick was suddenly discovered with his head in the scuppers begging someone please to take his life.[55] After several days of agony below in his cabin, one sufferer was dragged on deck by the steward, groaning that he would like to shout a few " 'G—d——s!' but there were too many G—— D—— preachers aboard!' "[56] One woman passenger vomited incessantly and would cry out that the ship had hit a rock, or was on fire. Her physician husband finally knocked her out with "a full dose of hydrate of chloral" and finally got some peace.[57]

Generally, it was the poor stewards and stewardesses who bore the brunt of the seasick syndrome; tough but civil, they tended the sufferers' most intimate physical needs, cleaning up after them, bringing odd little delicacies from bar or galley to tempt them, cheering them up in their depression, and even dragging them on deck for the fresh air that often finally revived them. These devoted creatures, hoping to be rewarded with proper fees or tips at the end of the voyage—which a few passengers actually resented giving them—watched over all the stages of seasickness: the desire to hide; oblivion; a vague, returning interest in life; the ingestion of tea and toast and gruel; a crawl to the deck for air and a tentative peek through the skylight over the dining saloon; and, finally, the recall to life with the stomach an aching void, a yawning chasm to be filled.

And then began the gargantuan eating for which the ship's cooks were ready. One woman celebrated her recovery by tying into a breakfast of "coffee, beefsteak, boiled eggs, hot biscuits, buttered toast, fried potatoes, a tumbler of punch and one of cider."[58] The tradition of lavish meals carried over from the packet ships, and, aboard a Cunarder, in line with the British custom of frequent nourishment throughout the day, one could eat at least six times daily, and oftener, if desired: coffee or tea at seven in one's cabin; breakfast at eight-thirty; lunch starting at noon; dinner at four-thirty; tea at seven-thirty; and supper at nine. Scarcely were the remains of one meal removed when covers were laid for the next. "Under these circumstances," wrote Jacob Abbott, "the saloon is kept in a constant state of movement and change from morning to night."[59] An American traveler aboard a Cunarder in 1865 wrote: "I spent twenty-three days at sea, and I have no hesitation in saying that I have never breakfasted and dined so well."[60]

Competing for all they were worth, an American steamer of the Collins line offered as its dinner bill of fare in 1856: "Oyster and Julienne" to start; "Beef, Ham, Tongue, Chickens, and Oyster Sauces, Stewed Brisket of Beef, Veal and Ham pies, Baked Halibut and Lobster Sauce; Beef, Lamb, Goose, Turkey; Ducks, with onions; Mutton with Baked Potatoes; Sausages, Pigeon Pie; Fried Oysters; Stewed Steaks, Macaroni with Cheese; Assorted Vegetables; Tomatoes; Radishes and Cucumbers; Huckleberry Pudding; Cranberry Pie, Apple Pie, Squash Pie, and Tarts."[61]

Another voyager remarked, "The cuisine is perfect—as if a richly furnished market were just around the corner. We had everyday fresh vegetables, fruits, etc., in the finest order; the whole ration being packed in ice."[62] In the steward's larder aboard the *Baltic* in 1851, reported Thurlow Weed, was loaded:

2,000 lbs. of Crew Beef; 1,500 lbs. Prime Beef; 250 lbs. Veal; 250 lbs. Pork; 400 lbs. Mutton; 200 lbs. Lamb; 100 lbs. Sausages; 25 Sweetbreads; 6 Pigs; 12

Nothing killed the commercial traveler's appetite—not even a storm. Drawing by Augustus Hoppin. *Courtesy the Library of Congress.*

Kidneys; 50 lbs. Tripe; 6 Livers; 12 Ox Tails; 6 Calves' Heads, 12 Calves' Feet; 30 Turkeys; 30 Geese; 60 Ducks; 170 chickens; 60 Pigeons; 24 Grouse; 24 Rabbits; 12 Hares; 4,000 Eggs; 600 quarts Milk; 100 lbs. Codfish; 50 Haddock; 136 Lobsters; 100 bushels Potatoes; 2 barrels Turnips; 100 heads Cabbage; 200 Celery; Onions, Cauliflower, Horse radish, etc; 70 lbs. Figs; 40 lbs. Prunes; 6 Wiltshire, 4 Stilton and 2 Cheshire Cheeses; 6 kegs Butter; 25 barrels Flour, etc.[63]

The greatest consumers of all in this age of heavy eating were businessmen and commercial travelers who crossed the Atlantic often, who were never seasick or alarmed by rough weather, and some of whom acquired reputations as extraordinary gourmands. There seemed to be at least one of these aboard every ship, and artist Augustus Hoppin immortalized the type in a drawing that shows a line of poor waiters, barely able to keep their feet, hauling dish after dish to a lone and busy glutton.[64] George Wilkes, aboard the *Niagara* in 1851, found himself seated next to one such and missed several meals himself for staring. Stunned at the prowess of the eater—"a man who had gained some notoriety a few years ago for having won wagers in eating against heavy odds"—Wilkes watched whole trays of food vanish in a matter of minutes. "Rounds of beef dwindled under his hands; dishes of hash disappeared before him like magic, while cataracts of coffee passed through a line of sweating waiters to wash the solids down. When done, he would walk up and down, slapping himself on the belly in order to drive up the wind, exclaiming, 'Oh, that's good! That's comfortable!' as it came up in offensive installments. In offset for the disgust which he thus excited," recalled Wilkes, "he became the stock joke of the ship and whenever he appeared, the cry of 'pig, pig, pig' could be heard."[65] The gourmand aboard Edward Thomson's vessel would eat in installments, going on deck for a smoke before "returning to the engagement, which, with most of us, was protracted to two hours or more." Not content with the lavish dinner menu alone, this indefatigable glutton himself always conjured up a salad consisting of cold potatoes, onions, cucumbers, hard-boiled eggs, the whole seasoned with plenty of mustard, pepper, vinegar, and olive oil. "He often presses me to take some of his extra dish," wrote Thomson, "which I decline, thinking that if I have to bear the sight, I ought not to tempt Providence further. He generally orders at the onset a bottle of champagne and a bottle of brandy."[66]

Rough weather, while it usually cut down on the number of diners, added another dimension to eating for those still able to come to the table. A midwesterner wrote that the tables were, under these conditions, divided into "little pens with fences to keep things from sliding off, and each passenger ate out of his own pen." He said that the sight reminded him of "the Chicago stockyards."[67] As the vessel rolled, it would cause the two opposing rows of diners to appear as if "engaged in a children's game of see-saw," as one voyager described it. "One moment my side of the table would be elevated, and we would look down from a superior height on our friends, while we straightened ourselves back to keep our balance. The next minute, down we go, and the line of people on the other side would suddenly rise before us as if they were going to go through the ceiling. And so we see-sawed our way in great gravity through breakfast."[68]

In really bad weather the tables became a shambles. "Away goes the milk into the ham and eggs. The coffee pot upsets and floods the leg of mutton. . . .While you look aghast at the lump of butter that has nestled in your lap, the molasses jug makes a dart, falling off the table, lands in your neighbor's silk hat, standing on the floor. The potatoes roll about the table as though at billiards."[69] This chaos was usually accompanied by the sound of breaking dishes, sliding silverware, and feet, as discouraged diners departed quickly for safer ground when conditions reached the point where it was a case of "whether you will be thrown onto the table, or have its contents thrown onto you."[70]

Although it seems to have come close to it, eating did not consume all of the voyagers' time, and such free moments as remained were filled with holding mock courts, reading, card playing, and the publication of little shipboard newspapers. Shuffleboard made its appearance on the steamers, and young men quickly learned that it was a most practical way to make the acquaintance of young women. "They look well handling the clumsy cues," one observant gentleman remarked, "and as the vessel lurches, they fall readily into your arms. It is a curious fact that I did not see a young lady fall into the arms of another young lady during the entire voyage." Considerable flirting was observed by the same voyager on the part of "married men whose wives were many leagues away, determined to have a good time once more. . .with all sorts and conditions of

Deck scene. Queasy passengers take the air while sailors prepare to "heave the log" to ascertain the ship's speed. Drawing by Augustus Hoppin. *Courtesy the Library of Congress.*

women."[71] Passengers aboard the steamship *Lafayette* in 1851 long remembered their moonlight dances on deck, with music by an elderly German gentleman from Baltimore who obligingly played the flute.[72] Two-mile footraces, consisting of eight laps around the deck of the *Great Eastern*—itself "one of the wonders of the modern world," with a deck an eighth of a mile in length—enlivened the homeward voyage of Charles Williams in 1862.[73] Charles Fairbanks remembered his voyage in the fifties as "a maze of books, backgammon, bad jokes, cigars, crochet, cribbage, and conversation."[74]

A regular feature aboard the Cunard ships was the "concert" on behalf of the Sailors' Orphans' Home of Liverpool, with passengers and sometimes certain ships' officers providing the entertainment. Any stray member of the British aristocracy aboard was always asked to preside as master of ceremonies and usually did so with enough aplomb and grace to charm even Yankees. Celebrities aboard were often invited to perform, and there are references to Jenny Lind, Adelina Patti, Ellen Terry, Henry Irving, and Tony Pastor. One unnamed captain won all hearts with his rendition, in a deep baritone, of " 'I'm afloat, I'm afloat, and the rover is free.' "[75] The British crews were more than patient with certain Americans who were inclined to celebrate their Independence Day with far more energy in the face of their captive audience than at home. "We kicked up quite a smoke with a big procession around and about the ship," one voyager recalled, "with men with horns, pans, trumpets, tin cans. . .hoisting and cheering the flags, firing crackers, toasts, songs, and such."[76] Another traveler recalled that "we had some Freagle of Edom speeches, and closed the day by singing patriotic hymns, including 'God Save the Queen.' "[77]

The single source of irritation for most Americans aboard the Cunarders centered around the Sunday worship service traditionally conducted on British vessels, by the captain, from the Book of Common Prayer. First of all, the numerous evangelical clergymen usually on these ships resented the use of the liturgy of the Church of England, followed by what seemed to them too staid and quiet a sermon, read rather than "preached" by the captain. Secondly, some of them simply saw it as an affront that they themselves were not asked instead to preside. The Reverend Joseph Cross, author of *The American Pastor in Europe*—a dull tome published in 1856—spoke for all his brethren when he wrote that

Church of England services in the main saloon aboard the Cunarders riled many a Yankee preacher who thought he should replace the captain as leader of devotions. Drawing by Augustus Hoppin. *Courtesy the Library of Congress.*

the Sabbath day dawned. Worship according to the ritual of her majesty's church was performed on board her majesty's ship. But where is the clergy-man? There is none, so the captain must officiate. All hands are summoned by the tolling of the ship's bell to the long dining saloon. Most of the passengers are present, and as many of the sailors and stewards as can be spared from duty, making in all about three hundred persons. . . . We are all funished with prayer books, the service is solemnly read, and the responses are general and hearty. . . . But no one can deny that Captain Judkins prays better than he preaches; and I flatter myself that, all ungowned as I am, I might have read that sermon quite as well myself.[78]

Caroline Kirkland thought the prescribed Church of England service just one more instance of "English impertinence which ought to be steadfastly resisted by all Americans."[79] Others said that it was ostentatious, or lacking in feeling, and one voyager was disturbed that he had seen his captain at a champagne supper just the night before. Still another complained of the sound of corks popping "as an accompaniment" to the worship service on board his vessel.[80] According to legend, Cunard's famed Captain Judkins, preparing one morning to read the service, had trouble finding the prayer book, and, turning to a steward, was overheard to rasp, " 'Damn it, why wasn't this put where it belongs!' " On those occasions when a captain's duties kept him occupied, the ship's surgeon would take his place, and Dr. William Taylor was startled one Sunday to find his "professional brother" conducting devotions "with an impressiveness not to be expected from so nimble a swearer."[81]

Less querulous travelers, like Jacob Abbott, found these English services quite satisfactory.[82] There was dignity, solemnity, and even a kind of reassurance in those rows of starched and polished British seamen standing at the rear, swinging to and fro like pendulums, dressed, as one voyager recalled, "in clean linen trousers, wide blue turned-down shirt collars, bright tarpaulins with broad black streaming ribbons, in hand, held by their side."[83] One Yankee admirer of Captain Judkins thought that he conducted services "in a style and manner befitting the Archbishop of Canterbury."[84]

The evangelical preachers soothed their ruffled feathers and consciences with additional prayer meetings on board the British ships, and on American vessels they apparently took over the services altogether. During a fierce storm one Yankee parson riled up a whole cabin of uneasy voyagers by using as his text "Be ye reconciled to God"—at the very least, judged one irate observer, showing a "sad want of taste."[85] On another stormy Sabbath one of these volunteer preachers "supported his body with one hand and his Bible with the other and reeled like a drunken man," only to announce suddenly, "[B]ecause of the troubled condition of the sea, we will dispense with the sermon."[86]

During another storm a preacher "talked a great deal about the dangers of the sea," recalled a passenger, and "while the waves were dashing wildly against the ship, reminded us there was only 'a thin board between us and eternity.' " A steward broke the tension for everyone by exclaiming loudly, " 'Thank God it's a thick plank!' "[87] On the whole, most Americans were quite content to listen to a calm English captain read:

O, eternal God, who alone spreadeth out the heavens and ruleth the raging of the sea. . .be pleased to receive into thy Almighty and most gracious protection the persons of us thy servants and the ship in which we sail. . .[88]

On one voyage a newly-ordained, young Church of England clergyman horrified the Yankee preachers on his ship. "He soon became the most popular man aboard," reported Edward Thomson, president of Ohio Wesleyan, who was en route to England in 1851 to visit libraries, purchase books for his own institution, and also attend the Great Exhibition.

He preached well; he sang well; he played cards and chess and checkers well; he ate, and drank, and smoked well; and as to shuffleboard he could beat us all. . . .Moreover, he was lucky. When he made a bet he generally won, and pocketed the money. . . .While throwing the dice he represented a most perfect picture of animal delight; extending himself at full length upon the table, he threw up his heels like a kitten, and when it was announced he was the winner, he ran off with his prize in a perfect ecstasy of joy.[89]

Thank God this young man was not on board with evangelist Phoebe Palmer and her husband in 1859. She railed against all the drinking, gambling, and flirting she observed but had particularly harsh words for certain preachers she saw enjoying themselves. She had "actually seen a duly accredited Congregational minister and a Baptist minister together at a game of *chess* in the presence of a score of beholders!"[90] Another Yankee puritan informed a brother of the Church of England, "I do not believe that Saul of Tarsus ever traveled with a chess board in *his* luggage!"[91] Still another was highly indignant when a tipsy Briton seated near him at dinner offered him a drink, remarking, " 'I do like a parson,' " and, tapping him on the shoulder as he prepared to uncork another bottle, adding, " 'I *do* like a parson that is hail fellow, well met.' "[92]

These Pharisees would have been good company for the Reverend Nicholas Murray, who, when asked to comfort a young Irishman dying in the steerage, and trying to get back home, instead exploited him as a kind of visual aid to the rest of the wretched inmates huddled about him. "I suggested," recalled Murray,

that if our voyage should be protracted. . .he might not live to its close. The thought seemed new and overwhelming, and he turned away and wept. I asked him as to his preparation for eternity and saw at once the need for a protracted visit; and taking my seat on a greasy trunk by his side, I sought. . .in a variety of ways to impress him with a sense of his own sinfulness. . .I committed him to God in prayer, and especially implored that the ocean might not be made his grave. The effect upon him was not such as I desired. . . .Feeling that he was beyond my reach, I addressed myself to those around me—the profane swearer, the card-player, the infidel, the Papist.

When the corpse was later brought up on deck for burial at sea, the Reverend Murray recorded that he spoke from an appropriate text: "And the sea gave up the dead which were in it."[93]

Famous passengers were stalked and cultivated whenever possible. Orlando Wight thus met Nathaniel Hawthorne crossing on the steamer *Niagara* in 1853 and found the "usually so taciturn" author "one of the most brilliant talkers I ever listened to," as they enjoyed the typical late-evening shipboard repast of

"Welsh rabbit and porter."[94] Aboard the *Persia* in the fifties was Tom Thumb—"as diminutive in intellect as in stature," snorted an observer.[95] Margaret Fuller, on her trip over in 1846, was amused at the deference paid, "by the English on board, and the Americans following their lead as usual," to the wife of Nova Scotia's governor who came on board at Halifax—an illegitimate daughter of William IV and his mistress, the actress Mrs. Jordan. Too much attention, in fact—decided Margaret—went to this lady who was merely the product of a "left-handed alliance with one of the dullest families that ever sat upon a throne."[96]

Inmates of the steerage were viewed with a mixture of pity and disgust by some passengers, with one of them referring to this section of the ship as "that Dante's Inferno for the poor immigrants."[97] Another described "the dirty (I use the word advisedly) steerage passengers trooping out from their kennels to wash up their dirty tins and foul crockery at the pumps."[98] The men were "haggard and pale," observed another, "with long beards and unwashed faces while the women had a wretched helpless, squalid appearance like chickens with the pip."[99]

Stowaways made their unwelcome appearance more often in these years. "With the departure of almost every vessel poor wretches without the means to pay their passage, secrete themselves aboard till fairly out to sea when they creep forth," observed Joel Headley in the 1840's.[100] Returning to the United States in 1854, William Wells Brown reported that on his ship no less than five stowaways came forth one by one.[101] Half-starved men and boys, without work, and wanting only to get to "Ameriky," most were allowed to work for their passage over, which was probably what they had hoped for.

Headley befriended a young Scot, "Robert S. of Greenock, a dirty, ragged boy of seventeen with a certain honest expression on his face which was covered with tears." He had been laid off from his job as a baker's helper and was starving on the Liverpool docks, when he "determined, all alone, to cross the Atlantic to a land where a man is allowed the boon of working for a living," wrote Headley. "He seemed to have but one idea, and that was *work*." Headley watched over Robert during a shipboard illness, after paying his passage, and kept in touch with him after landing, reporting that he was well on his way to prosperity and independence.[102]

The career of Cunard's famous Captain C. H. E. Judkins can be traced in the pages of these American travelers' books. One of the earliest references to him was in 1846, when Margaret Fuller crossed with him aboard the *Cambria*. She judged him "an able and prompt commander," and she further identified him as the captain who insisted upon Frederick Douglass's being admitted to equal rights upon his deck with "the insolent slaveholders." Judkins mentioned with pride, she said, "that he understood the New York *Herald* now called him 'the nigger captain.' "[103]

Occasionally Judkins's forthrightness irritated passengers, as it did aboard the newly-launched *Persia* in February of 1856. He had just brought her safely into New York after a harrowing, ice-buffeted run from Liverpool, during which he had been expected to race the American ship *Pacific*, which never showed up in port. On his way back, disgusted at the betting and wagering of the passengers

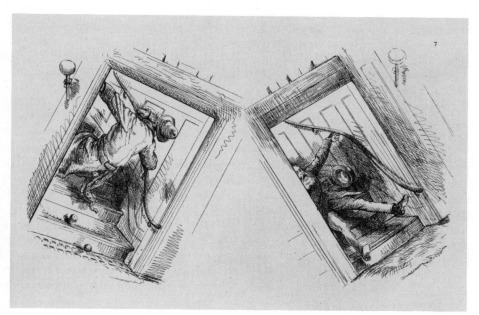

Equilibrium was hard to maintain in rough seas. Drawing by Augustus Hoppin.
Courtesy the Library of Congress.

about the fate of that ship, Judkins refused to post the daily run in nautical miles of the *Persia,* as was the custom, and was generally dour. John Edwards sensed that Judkins was revolted by this wagering on life-and-death matters, with some of the passengers actually laying bets on whether or not the *Pacific* would *ever* turn up. By the end of the voyage, however, tension let up, and Judkins was toasted for his seamanship. In his response he alluded to his own lack of sociability, charging it to his concern for the safety of the *Persia*—"all iron, the largest in the world"—in the rough and stormy weather they had passed.[104]

On this same voyage, nearing its end, the pilot, to his discredit, got them lost in the fog proceeding up the Mersey. Captain Judkins, according to Edwards, "lost his temper and called the pilot *stupid* with a prefix that need not be named" and then ordered him off the bridge "in no very complimentary terms to his professional skill." The captain brought his blindly-groping ship in himself, and, as they neared Liverpool, ordered the ship's cannon fired again and again. "Till I tell you to stop!" he roared at the officer who questioned this command. "It was affecting," recalled Edwards, "to hear the anxious inquiry from every vessel as we came into port,—'Any news from the *Pacific?*' and to witness the sadness in every countenance as the answer 'None!' rang over the waters like the knell of a lost ship."[105]

By 1865 an American voyager reported that Judkins had admitted to him that, although he was "never seasick, he was 'sick of the sea' and talked of giving it up."[106] But in 1867 this ancient mariner was still afloat and was now the captain of the *Scotia.* Judkins was, according to John Forney, "as good a specimen of a British seaman as ever was sung by Dibdin, painted by Lawrence, or described by Marryat. Some odd stories are told of his brusque deportment and not a few contend he prefers to be rude to his passengers." Claimed Forney, "[W]hat I have seen impresses me favorably, and as he has a great and perilous responsibility, his guests should gladly compromise by accepting his superior and vigilant fidelity to his trust as a fair set-off to any reticence of speech or roughness of manner."[107] It mattered little to that "imperturbable Captain that the sea swept his decks," recalled Mrs. E. A. Forbes. "He ruled his floating world, and carved his beef, and read the church service all the same."[108] The Reverend Edwards summed him up as "a blunt, unvarnished man—but a skillful seaman."[109]

The lot of the ordinary seaman had improved but little over that of those on sailing vessels. Many a poor sailor still fell to his death from the rigging of the auxiliary sails on these early steamers, or was washed overboard during a storm. "I have lost three of four poor fellows in that way," confessed a mid-century captain. "We could hear their cries between the roaring blasts, but we were driving at such a fearful rate it would have been madness to attempt their rescue. It is a dreadful sound, and it seems to ring in one's ears for days afterwards. It is a cruel death."[110]

Passengers had less contact with the crew now, except for the little programs of "games" the latter were permitted to stage for the voyagers' amusement, in the hopes of thereby gaining a few dollars to share for drinks with their mates. These games were rough, childish affairs, depending mainly on being thrown off balance by a roll of the ship, such as sack races, steeplechases, and so-called cockfights, even footraces aboard the gigantic *Great Eastern,* as a passenger first observed in 1862.[111] Another pastime permitted the seamen was "chalking" the male passengers, which merely involved the drawing of a chalk circle around an unsuspecting victim, who was expected to cough up a shilling. " 'Why that's not a circle—that's only a semi-circle,' " protested one voyager. " 'Faith, and sure it isn't the likes of yer honor'll be gettin' off in that way,' " was the sailor's quick Irish response.[112]

One unfortunate seaman let go of the wheel to save a young woman from being thrown overboard by a lurch of the ship and had half his teeth knocked out by a blow from one of the handles as the wheel spun around. "It looked as if part of his jaw must have gone with the teeth," remarked a passenger. " 'But,' said he, 'I care only for the lady, because on my return to Boston, Dr. Bliss will make me a new set of teeth, and a jaw, too, if needed, better than the old ones.' "[113]

Several stewardesses were immortalized by ladies they served. Caroline Kirkland's Mary, aboard a Cunarder in the 1840s was a faithful and tireless creature, who seemingly never slept "until every woman, sick or well, reasonable or unreasonable, is fast asleep. And after the last call has died away in an inability to conjure up another want, Mary sits down to read for an hour before she curls up on a sofa to play sleep for awhile till the most restless lady chooses to wake up and desire the aid of the sea-maiden in untying her night-cap strings, or some matter of equal importance." Alas, poor Mary! She was arrested at Liverpool for smuggling "a very paltry lot of cigars and brandy and thrown at once into jail. Our good Captain did all he could for her, but there is no evading penalties in England."[114]

Julia Ward Howe, future author of *The Battle Hymn of the Republic,* put her poetic talent to work on a rhyme—sung to the tune of "God Save the Queen"—in honor of her stewardess at the captain's dinner their last night out:

> God save our Mrs. Bean,
> Best woman ever seen.
> God save Mrs. Bean.
> God bless her gown and cap,
> Pour guineas in her lap,
> Keep her from all mishap,
> God save Mrs. Bean.

Mrs. Bean, by now embarrassed and not knowing how to respond, bobbed a curtsey and murmured: "Good ladies make good stewardesses—that's all I can say."[115]

A traditional shipboard adventure for male passengers was a visit to the Plutonian regions of the "Stokehole" to observe the furnaces that provided the power for the engines. In 1847 Jacob Abbott saw "the glow of fires and piles of coal, and black, Vulcan-like-looking men, replenishing and stirring the fires with enormous implements of iron seemingly too ponderous for human strength to manage."[116] Aboard his vessel at mid-century Henry Tappan counted thirty firemen and stokers, each of whom, he was told, worked an eight-hour day in "turns," as they called their shifts. "The temperature in which they worked was terrible," he observed. "Hence they drink freely of ice water, and come aloft once in a while to enjoy the cool air. They eat little for want of appetite, and consequently become emaciated. They seldom remain longer than a year."[117] Dr. Channing, in this same period, noted the "sixteen furnaces all in a row, to be kept at the same temperature with fifty tons of coal per day. The men never stopped stoking and clearing out ashes in a temperature of 120 degrees. Working in woolen shirts and pantaloons, they carried waste cotton in their shirts to mop their faces frequently. I asked how long the stoker could hold out, and learned it was for a few years only."[118]

George Wilkes, aboard the *Niagara* in 1851, noted that "the sweat poured from their laboring frames like rain, and every few minutes each would be obliged to pause and stand under the wind-sail to regain his breath and strength. I wondered as I inhaled that stifling air, and as my nerves shrank from the deafening crash of the machinery, how these beings existed in such an atmosphere and what was the allurement which tempted them to shorten their lives by such a process." He asked a "furnace-fiend" about their pay and was told that "we gets three punds a month, but in the Yankee ships they gets six punds, and has more men."[119]

Suicides sometimes occurred among both crew and passengers. A young "coal passer" leaped to his death in the sea from the *Baltic* in 1851, as witnessed by Weed.[120] In 1857 a French cook aboard the *Vanderbilt* chose the same escape route from his troubles.[121] Former seaman Herman Melville actually went over the side on a rope to save a passenger who leaped from the deck of their ship in 1849 and was "struck by the expression of his face in the water. It was merry. . . . The man drowned like a bullock. It afterwards turned out, that he was crazy," had declared he would jump, and "had tried to get possession of his child in order to jump into the sea with the child in his arms."[122]

Funerals were a common event on the steamships just as on the packets— usually for some poor Irishman trying to reach home before "the consumption" killed him. En route to the Great Exhibition in 1851, the Reverend Arthur Cleveland Coxe, an Episcopal priest from Hartford, aboard the *Arctic*, conducted the burial service for a young assistant engineer, William Irwin, who fell while oiling machinery and was struck by a lever on one of the engines.[123] Coxe himself alludes only briefly to the incident, but it is described in considerable detail by the Reverend John Choules, as well as by Aaron Willington, who were both on the same voyage—the latter sending home a series of travel letters to the *Charleston* (S.C.) *Courier*.

As if to offset these intimations of mortality, births sometimes took place— usually in the steerage—although Martha Coston, aboard the *Great Eastern* in 1863, was rudely awakened early one morning by the ship's cannon, certain they had been attacked by the Confederate raider the *Alabama*, only to discover that the furor marked the birth of a son to the captain's wife who was on board. Since a young, titled Englishman had died on that same voyage, this birth rather evened things up, she thought, "so that the *Great Eastern* went into port with the same number of passengers that she had started with."[124]

The same dangers that haunted sailing vessels imperiled the steamships, but with the added factor of greater speed involved. Collision with icebergs and other vessels was thus more to be feared than ever, as shown in the fate of the *Arctic* when she struck a French vessel in the fog off the Grand Banks in September, 1854. Her few survivors provided graphic accounts of the horrors they endured in the gray silence, as the ship went slowly under—their captain cradling his child in his arms only to see its head smashed by floating wreckage, a young crewman vainly firing his signal gun in the eerie stillness until he died, and survivors freezing and falling off a makeshift raft into the icy sea. Accounts of the tragedy were widely published, and Nathaniel Currier promptly brought out a print of the *Arctic* in her death agony. So terrified was one elderly gentleman aboard Caroline Kirkland's vessel that she observed "he has not lain down for several nights but stood most of the time, holding fast by the top of a door."[125]

Collisions and near-collisions were many and grisly. Most of them involved small fishing vessels. "At daybreak we ran through a fleet of fishermen off Newfoundland," reported E. H. Derby of Massachusetts, a friend of Samuel Cunard, in 1843, "taking them quite by surprise and exciting no little alarm."[126] So close were some of these near-misses that passengers caught glimpses of the terror-stricken faces of fishermen as they swept past.[127] On another voyage in 1851 fourteen men were saved off the *Florence* out of Wellfleet, but her hard-won 250 barrels of mackerel were lost. "Her only boat was smashed at the onset," recorded an observer aboard the steamship, "and one of her men had

Sinking of the *Arctic* in 1854, a tragedy known to all travelers through this famous Currier print. *Courtesy the Library of Congress.*

already disappeared."[128] On another such occasion, only one man out of a crew of eleven was saved.[129] When a preacher aboard one steamer objected to his captain's efforts to rescue some fishermen, the captain advised him to "go down to your cabin and pray that God may endow you with more charity."[130]

A most gruesome collision occurred on one voyage, which involved passengers awaking in the night and rushing on deck to see what had taken place. All they could see was that their own ship's bowsprit was damaged and pieces of wreckage trailed across the bow. Not until they came on deck in the morning did they perceive among the tangled rigging "a human body crushed to death, bloody and frightful to look upon—so dreadfully mutilated was he that no one had the heart to take him on board. The ropes were drawn up which held him, and he sank into the deep to rise no more until the morning of the resurrection."[131]

A happier meeting, between the *Great Western* and one of these small fishing vessels, a schooner named *Love*, occurred in July of 1838. "Her sunburnt crew seemed to look with astonishment on our gallant ship as she glided over the waves," recalled a passenger. "The Captain . . . mounting aloft, with sharp bony features peering out from under a slouched, weather-beaten hat, called out in shrill and clear tones, 'Please report the schooner *Love* of ———, out seven weeks, has taken 23,500 pounds of cod!'" Occasionally, in these early years of steam, a ship would stop, as did this one, to buy fresh fish from one of these small fishing vessels.[132]

Aboard the ship *Lafayette* in the summer of 1865, G. H. Mathews observed the rescue of survivors from the *William Nelson*. "The Captain suddenly disappeared from our table, and our attention was arrested by the exclamation of 'a wreck!' 'a wreck!'" A small boat made its way toward them, "rising and sinking again in the swell of the sea." Soon a second boat was spotted, and then a third, as Captain Bocande cruised the area, firing rockets and the ship's cannon at intervals. Finally, forty-three wet, famished, cold, and frightened survivors, all that were left out of 500 souls aboard the lost ship—which had burned the day before—were gathered on board the *Lafayette*, where they were ministered to by passengers and crew alike. "Among those saved," wrote Mathews, "was an entire family, father, mother, and four children. The father said, in his own simple way, that he did not know what he had done to God that he should be so good to him. Why were these few the only ones saved?"—Mathews pondered quietly. "It may be they are to fulfill a destiny," he concluded.[133]

Icebergs were thought to have caused the loss of both the *President* in 1841 and the *City of Boston* in 1870, both of which simply disappeared at sea. Nothing more was ever seen of the *Pacific*, either, except some wreckage floating in a sea of ice. The monster icebergs, drifting with wind and weather, possessed a locomotion of their own. Underwater melting made them top-heavy, and thus off balance they would reel and plunge, "rolling and tumbling like porpoises," recalled Charles Fulton. "Woe to the luckless boat or vessel that may be in too close proximity when the monster makes one of these lunges."[134]

Returning home aboard the *Great Western* in 1841, Lydia Sigourney devoted an entire chapter to the night they made their way through a fleet of icebergs. The terrified passengers had felt an ominous chill in the air before retiring—a sure sign of ice in the region—and at three A.M. they were wakened

> by harsh grating, and occasional concussions which caused the stronger timbers of the ship to tremble.... The Captain ... reported between three and four hundred distinct icebergs visible to the naked eye ... of all forms and sizes, careening in every direction.... The engine of the Great Western accommodated itself at every moment, like a living and intelligent thing to the commands of the Captain. "Half a stroke!" and its tumultuous action was controlled: "a quarter of a stroke!" and its breath seemed suspended: "stand still!" and our huge hulk lay motionless upon the waters, till two or three of the icy squadron drifted by us; "let her go!" and with the velocity of lightning we darted by another detachment of our deadly foes. It was then that we were made sensible of the advantages of steam, to whose agency, at our embarkation, many of us had committed ourselves with extreme reluctance.[135]

If the speed of steam increased hazards of collision with other vessels, the power and responsiveness of the engines also enabled a captain to maneuver his ship more readily in an ice field. But the danger was ever there, as the fate of the mighty *Titanic* would illustrate many years later.

The rockbound coastlines of both North America and the British Isles still presented dangers even to steamships. Vermonter Zadock Thompson, returning home from the Great Exhibition, experienced the terrors of Newfoundland's dreaded Cape Race, whose awful rocks his steamship just missed in the fog. "Awakened by a violent concussion of the ship," he recalled, "I hastened up on deck and found our ship with her starboard side towards a long line of precipitous rocks, rising abruptly out of the ocean, and but a few rods from us. But this time the engine was in motion again, and we were moving forward nearly parallel to the cliff. . . .The lifeboats on board were not sufficient to carry one half of the passengers and crew, and the scramble for places might have rendered even these useless."[136]

Mechanical breakdowns could be terrifying still, just as with Wheaton's rudderless ship back in 1824. Sweating engineers and mechanics aboard an Ohio landlubber's steamship at the end of the century struggled to repair a damaged steering gear in the middle of a storm. In the meantime, the voyager from Elyria, Ohio, vowed that he would not go down to the sea in a ship ever again.

> Walls were converted into ceilings . . . rails which in still water were twenty-four feet from the level of the sea, dipped into the foam, first on one side, then on the other; when the spray reached the smokestacks, everything in the ship became alive. . . . Trunks left staterooms and went tumbling up and down halls. . . . Crockery by the bushel was being smashed. . . . Every joint of our boat creaked and groaned as if in agony; and every passenger who attempted to move about was injured by falling . . . and the ship's surgeon was kept busy binding up wounds.[137]

At such times most passengers remained stoical, according to accounts. "No outcry, no complaints, no weeping were heard," reported newsman James Matthews of a fearful storm in 1866, "but every face wore a grave and anxious expression. . . . The roar of the tempest drowned all other sounds. Shouts became as whispers. Men tried to talk; and most wished to say something cheering to each other; but it was almost as difficult to speak as it was to hear—and more difficult than either was it to appear cheerful."[138] At such moments voyagers could be seen clutching Bibles, sitting on "gripsacks" as if they would save these on abandoning ship, grasping life preservers, and quietly praying.

The fear of fire was as much a terror as ever, "a living and abiding horror," according to Henry Morford, even aboard the steamships. "Storms are nothing, icebergs are trifles, fogs are endurable . . . but the fire-fiend, he is terrible always."[139] How foolish, then, of the rude and testy Reverend Mark Trafton, to actually boast about having "an abundance of matches and a candle," against all rules, in his cabin aboard the *Asia* in 1850.[140]

One elderly Yankee, mightily relieved at the sight of land after a rough crossing, crawled off his ship at Liverpool, remarking: "These steamship fellows call it 2,800 miles to Liverpool do they? Wal, that's measuring on a flat millpond. When your ship has to climb up and down all them waves, it measures about three times as fur!"[141]

In 1847 Jacob Abbott had a kind word or two for the customs officials at Liverpool, who usually received rough comments at the hands of his fellow travelers. In over sixty examinations in which he was involved, or observed, Abbott claimed, he saw not one "fee or bribe offered or received," and he added that "in every case the officer has seemed to me to desire only to do his duty, and to endeavor to make his discharge of it as little inconvenient to the traveler as possible. I have, in fact, never seen anything wrong, except the unworthy efforts of ladies and gentlemen . . . to throw obstacles in the way of an examination of their effects, or to contrive in some way to elude fair application of the laws."[142]

The luggage of black abolitionist William Wells Brown was passed through in 1849 without further examination once the customs officer came upon the heavy iron collar once worn about the neck by a female slave in Mississippi and brought along as an exhibit. "This democratic instrument of torture became the center of attraction," Brown recalled, "and closed the examination of my luggage. No sooner was I on British soil," he concluded, "than I was recognized as a man, and an equal."[143]

8

London

"Here we are in London!" crowed youthful Theodore Witmer in 1852, author of *Wild Oats Sown Abroad,* "and our money is flowing like water from the rock!"[1] He had just settled himself at Morley's Hotel, long a favorite with Americans and which was situated in Trafalgar Square on the site today occupied by South Africa House. Henry James, in the years to come, would never forget his own arrival at Morley's on a wet, dark night. "Morley's proved indeed to be a ruddy spot," James recalled. "Brilliant in my recollection, is the coffee-room fire, the hospitable mahogany, the sense that in the stupendous city, this, at any rate for the hour, was a shelter and a point of view. My remembrance of the rest of the evening—I was probably very tired—is mainly a remembrance of a vast four-poster."[2]

"How well I remember the night I first arrived in the metropolis," recalled Charles Fairbanks, writing under the pen name "Aguecheek," in the fifties in Boston's *Saturday Evening Gazette.*

> It was after ten o'clock, and I was much fatigued, but before I booked myself into my hotel, or looked at my room, I rushed out in the Strand. . . . I pushed along, now turning to look at Temple Bar, now pausing to take breath as I went up Ludgate Hill. I saw St. Paul's and its dome before me and I was satisfied. No, I was not satisfied; for when I returned up Fleet Street, I looked out dear old Bolt Court, and entered its Johnsonian precincts with awe and veneration. . . . And then I posted down Inner Temple Lane, and looked at the house where Charles Lamb and his companions held their "Wednesday nights", and going still farther, I saw the river—I stood on the banks of the Thames, and I was satisfied.[3]

"I looked," continued Fairbanks,

> and all the associations of English literature and history which are connected with it filled my mind, but just as I was getting into a fine frenzy about it, a watchman hove in sight, and the old clock chimed out eleven. So I started on, and soon reached my hotel. I was accosted on my way thither by a young and gayly-dressed lady, whom I did not remember ever to have seen before, but who expressed her satisfaction at meeting me, in the most cordial terms. I told her that I thought it must be a mistake, and she responded with a laugh which very much shocked an elderly gentleman who was passing.[4]

Although the first night in London was always an event to the American

Morley's Hotel in London's Trafalgar Square. Long a favorite of the American traveler, today it is the site of South Africa House. *From the author's collection.*

traveler, a more sedate arrival was that of the Reverend John Edwards on March 3, 1856.

> The clock on St. Paul's . . . has just struck eleven, and though weary with a day's travel I must write up my notes before I retire to rest. I can scarcely realize that I am in the very heart of London, the largest city in the world, and one that exerts an influence upon all nations of the globe! In London! About which we have all heard . . . even in the songs of the nursery, in the riddles that puzzled our childhood, in the primers that we read . . . and in the jingling rhyme that strangely clings to the memory,

he wrote, reminding one of Orwell's Winston Smith trying to recall such rhymes of a lost London in *1984.* "I can scarcely believe that Paternoster Row is only a minute's walk from my hotel," continued Edwards, "that Cheapside, Haymarket, Piccadilly, Charing Cross, and the Old Bailey are within a half hour's ride; that Temple Bar, London Bridge, the Tower, and old Westminster Abbey, may be seen tomorrow. Yes, tomorrow, should I live, I may see them all."[5] Even the less ebullient Nathaniel Hawthorne experienced similar sensations as he hastened to "all the objects and renowned localities that I had read about, and which had made London the dream-city of my youth."[6] It was almost as if these Americans of the mid-nineteenth century were coming home. Armed with their maps and guidebooks, off they went, just as had Benjamin Silliman and Alexander Mac-Kenzie before them, and they were as awed as their predecessors by London's booming traffic and swarming humanity.

In 1846 Dr. John Corson studied the scene on London Bridge.

> Vehicles of every kind; coalmen with broad canvass hats, blackened faces, and linen frocks dyed with soot, and driving heavily-laden wagons, with broad tires, drawn by elephant horses in single file; stout servant girls; spruce clerks; splendid coaches with footmen outside; old clothes men; red-faced market women; portly gentlemen, with large noses and whiskers; children of all sizes; tall, civil policemen—the best in the world—with glazed crowns to their hats, and blue coats ornamented with white numbers; stately women with fine complexions; foreigners with moustaches, staring at the crowd like ourselves; and omnibuses, with the figure for a sixpence and a noisy man behind.[7]

"We began to form an idea," continued Dr. Corson, "of the currents and eddies of human beings ever rushing through the streets of this vast capital. Detachments of the multitude on foot wheel round at the ends of the bridge," he observed, "and embark from the different stairs on board the little iron steamers, like toy-boats, plying incessantly on the Thames and crowded worse than the streets."[8] The beautiful wherries, so admired by sailor MacKenzie in the 1830s, only two decades later were virtually a thing of the past, having been replaced by small, sturdy, open-to-the-air steamers that "flew about on every side in the most funny manner imaginable, as if worried to death," wrote one visitor. "They shot hither and thither, flying along as if possessed by the power of will." Their names were so pretty, he thought, *Daylight, Starlight, Moonlight, Sunbeam,* etc. . . just fitted for such wee bits of things."[9]

Thurlow Weed also recorded river steamer names, in 1843: *Primrose, Pink, Bride, Tulip, Snow Drop, Bridesmaid, Lilly, Sweetbrier, Rose, Falcon, Victoria,* and *Naiad.*[10] An illustration in the *Illustrated London News* for April 3, 1847, showing Easter Monday festivities on the Thames, depicts the steamer *Naiad* hovering in the background. These small vessels were about ten feet wide, with an engine of eighteen horse power; the crew consisted of five men and boys. "The river is thronged with these steamers'. . . and you may sail in them from one end of London to the other for four pence, or eight cents in our money," observed Elias H. Derby, who proudly identified himself on his book's title page as "A Railroad Director of Massachusetts." Derby noted that they had "no guards, or promenade deck, and the boilers and the engine occupy the principal part of the hold. The passengers stand or sit in the open air, exposed, of course, to the wind and rain. In speed they do not generally exceed eight to ten miles per hour, and being painted black, have a dull appearance. These riverboats are altogether inferior to the American. Not so the English sea-steamers," Derby hastened to add, being a friend of Cunard himself, and having just crossed the Atlantic on the latter's *Caledonia.*[11]

One fussy Yankee, Henry Morford, denigrated these "diminutive ungainly, shelterless boats, with a single deck and no awning against the sun that seldom shines and the rain likely to fall at any moment . . . ricketty, crank little

Thames river steamers crowded with holiday-makers on Easter Monday. *Illustrated London News*, **April 3, 1847, p. 217.** *From the author's collection.*

conveyances . . . over-loaded two thirds of the time and always ready to drop someone overboard."[12] But most tourists liked them, as did George Wilkes, who praised them for the view one had from their decks "of the panorama of the shores—Lambeth Palace on one side, Somerset Palace on the other, and the new Houses of Parliament, the Tower, the dome of St. Paul's and the Monument [built 1671–77] to commemorate the Great Fire, looming in the air above the fungi of smokey warehouses and pinched dwellings."[13]

On one of his trips Wilkes watched as "a lank Tennessean with his eyes fixed on the tall smoke-pipe, in the wake of which he sat, and comparing it with the arch of the bridge, inferred that the boat could not go under in that direction." As the steamer came closer and no one made the slightest move, the Tennessean's anxiety mounted until he could contain it no longer, Wilkes observed. Unaware that the smokestacks bowed on hinges to pass under the bridges on the Thames, he suddenly roared out, "For God's sake, look out for yourselves!" He then sprang to the side and would have gone overboard if he had not been seized by two or three persons who had been watching his motions on the supposition that he was crazy. "He looked sheepish enough," concluded Wilkes, "when he saw the pipe rise gracefully to its position after we shot the arch, and bore with good nature the general roar."[14]

"The excellence of the pavements is another thing that must continually be present to Americans, at least to the people of New York, who are accustomed to pavements inferior to those of Pompeii laid two thousand years ago," remarked Caroline Kirkland in 1848. "The streets of the great cities in England are either paved with granite or macadamized so that one rolls for miles without a jolt or tilt. Their cleanness is another feature very striking to us; and it comes upon us with a certain surprise, from our notion that old streets must be dirty. Philadelphia is, physically, the only city in the United States as clean as London."[15] William Cullen Bryant watched one means by which London streets were kept clean, "the patent street-sweeper." It was, he wrote, "a machine drawn by one of the powerful dray horses of this country, and consisted of brushes turning over a cylinder, sweeping the dust of the streets into a kind of box . . . wet or dry, dust or mud, it is all drawn into the receptacle provided for it; and the huge horse stalks backward and forward along the street until it is almost as clean as a drawing room."[16]

The hansom cab still charmed Americans, but more and more they came to value the omnibus as one of the central institutions in the city's life. Charles Fairbanks recalled author Leigh Hunt's speculation that "if there were such a thing as metamorphosis, Dr. Johnson would desire to be transformed into an omnibus, that he might go rolling along the streets whose very pavements were

London omnibus, c. 1847. "What better place is there to study human nature?" asked an American visitor. *Illustrated London News,* May 1, 1847, p. 288. *From the author's collection.*

"**A Scamper Through Westminster Abbey**" satirizes the haste with which vergers conducted visitors through in order, so the victims claimed, to earn more fees. *Punch*, vol. 9, 1845, p. 178. *Courtesy the Library of Congress.*

the objects of his ardent affection. And he was about right," concluded Fair-banks.

> What better place is there in this world to study human nature than an omnibus? All classes meet there; in the same coach you may see them all—from the poor workman, to the genteely dressed lady who looks as if she disapproved of such conveyances but must ride nevertheless—from the young sprig, who is constantly anxious lest some profane foot should dim the polish of his boots, to the urbane old gentleman, who regrets his corpulence, and would take less room if he could. And then the top of the omnibus . . . what a place is that to see the tide of life which flows unceasingly through the streets of London![17]

By 1851, when hordes of American visitors to the Great Exhibition bore down on London, the omnibus had acquired its upper deck (carried over, of course, in the great red motorized conveyances of today), and it now carried twelve in and the same number outside. The only fault David Bartlett could find, frustrated as he was by cockney speech patterns, was the difficulty of understanding the conductor. They "have a wretched way of abbreviating the names of places," he complained.

> The stranger finds it impossible to understand them. We were at a family party where George Catlin, of Indian renown, arrived an hour late. He had been carried miles out of his way by trusting to the voice of an omnibus "cad." As an example, we will give the genuine omnibus pronunciation of "Kingsland," a

district adjoining the city. The conductor going there generally sings out "Ins-la! Ins-la!" Other names are murdered in a still more atrocious manner.[18]

The best place aboard a bus, for the stranger, was up on top and beside the driver if possible. "Have you ever occupied a front seat atop a London bus and tipped the driver a sixpence, and listened to his amiable dissertations en route? If not, you have missed a treat," observed one Yankee London bus fan.[19] Still another traveler remarked that "an omnibus driver, as far as he drives, is worth a dozen guidebooks."[20]

The American tourist rounds at mid-century varied little from those of earlier times: first Westminster Abbey, then the Tower, St. Paul's, and the Thames Tunnel, now in its finished state. Journalist Joel Headley tried to outdo Addison and Irving on the Abbey, but his best phrase was his last. Leaving "this great charnel house," with its eerie quiet, he said that he felt as if returning to the confusion "of some great battlefield . . . but none of it reached the ears of the mighty sleepers within."[21] The Reverend Stephen Tyng, rector of St. George's in New York, experienced the tension of being rushed through too rapidly, a complaint common enough to arouse a comment in *Punch* in 1845. A cartoon shows a little band of tourists tearing at breakneck speed in the wake of a verger and is entitled: "A Scamper Through Westminster Abbey."[22] The Reverend Mark Trafton, in 1850, found a number of items to offend him—first John Gay's little epitaph, which struck him as "both blasphemous and foolish."

> Life is a jest & all things shew it:
> I thought so once, and now I know it.

"Pretty stuff for Westminster Abbey!" growled Trafton, whose daughter Adeline would herself come over in the seventies and exhibit much of her father's anglophobia. "Why is not Charles Wesley here?" demanded the irate preacher. "A finer poet never lived. Why is that Southey here? A onetime *red republican* and *a socialist!*" He also did not like the memorial to Mrs. Siddons. "A full-length statue in white marble. And who was Mrs. Siddons? An *actress!*" By the time Trafton got to the Coronation Chair he was really warmed up. "I suppose all the John Bulls who saw this long, lean Yankee gazing about your solemnities supposed he was thinking, 'what a speculation I could make of this in Yankee-dom!' No; I mused on greatness, glory, ambition and change, grew sad, and departed. But I will tell you what I *did* think in the great chair of state," Trafton concluded. "If the people of this realm were wise, the last monarch has occupied it who will do so!"[23]

Horace Greeley took a whack at the Abbey as well, grousing about all the "lofty ceilings, stained windows, and barbaric profusion of carving, groining, and all manner of costly contrivances for absorbing money and labor. Surely," grumped Greeley, "Westminster Abbey ought to afford a place of worship equal in capacity and fitness to a modern church edifice costing $50,000, and surely it does not. I think there is no one of the ten best churches in New York which is not superior to the Abbey for this purpose."[24]

"An Englishman cares nothing about the Tower, which to us is a haunted castle in dream-land," thought Nathaniel Hawthorne.[25] True or not, Americans continued to flock there and to make snide comments on the Crown Jewels. On hearing them valued at $15,000,000, Alonzo Tripp, self-styled "Traveller and Teacher," exclaimed, in 1847: " 'How much good might not that do in relieving the miseries of poor starving Ireland,' whereupon my stalwart guide bridled up to me, and in a tone swelling with wounded pride, ejaculated, 'Yes, and we have spent double that sum on the miserable people within a few years!' " This is one of the very few recorded instances of these sorely-tried guardians talking back to a loudmouthed tourist.[26] An American lady in 1851 announced to the crowd, as she turned away, "Well, I'd rather have the crown than be queen," and was stared at, recalled George Wilkes, "by the English who were present as if they regarded her as some nondescript with a diseased imagination."[27] The Reverend Trafton, of course, did his bit by asking an Englishman near him, "Why is this waste treasure lying here useless and lost, and so many of your paupers sent over for us to support in the United States?"[28]

At St. Paul's, "clearly organized for the extortion of shillings and sixpences," as Julia Ward Howe complained, she and her party tramped through the cathedral, "spilling our small change at every step."[29] Wilbur Fisk, too, protested about the shilling extorted "at almost every angle we turned" and further deplored "dirty stairs and passages not decent for a lady with a respectable dress to pass over."[30] John Forney echoed Fisk three decades later, remarking on "the apparent carelessness and lack of cleanliness."[31] Reverend Trafton, eternally vigilant in his search for things to complain about, said that St. Paul's ought to be called "The Temple of Mars" because of all the emphasis on martial glory. He was particularly offended by all the attention paid to Nelson, lying quietly below in the crypt, calling him "that great butcher," and he further castigated him for "carrying off another man's wife—a disgrace to the race!" Jeering at the intoned Anglican service, he described "twelve boys with soiled white frocks" and thought, "so many monkeys would be an improvement," concluding, "How I longed to stand up in that little wine-glass pulpit and pour out my soul!"[32]

Authoress Caroline Kirkland, upon dragging herself up all those stone stairs, and then "after toiling up perpendicular ladders for half an hour," to the Golden Ball at the top of the dome, warned other ladies against "that gigantic humbug." For upon her arrival she discovered that she could see nothing, as "the smoke of London obscured most of the prospect."[33] Americans still attended the annual celebration of the charity children, and it was the Reverend Stephen Tyng, who literally had to be carried out, so overcome was he by emotion and the beauty of their singing.[34] One American, viewing the now legendary scene from high above in the Whispering Gallery, wrote that "the multitude of infant voices" suggested to him "the fancy of an immense concert of insects on a summer night, all singing marvelously in tune."[35]

The Thames Tunnel was indeed completed, finally, just as the Reverend Humphrey predicted it would be, and it was opened as a public thoroughfare in 1843. By mid-century it had become, however, little more than a powerful tourist attraction. Sufficient land at either end, in Wapping and Rotherhithe, was never acquired, and consequently the steep entrance stairways discouraged Londoners from making any great general use of it as a practical means of crossing the Thames; nor was its use as a carriageway ever effected.

In London for the Great Exhibition, William Drew nevertheless put a high priority on the tunnel as one of the great sights of the city and admired its construction, which involved "two beautiful arches, each containing a roadsted fourteen feet wide and twenty-two feet high, and pathways for pedestrians, three feet wide . . . and well ventilated." What captured his attention next was the partition between the double arches, itself divided into about fifty transverse arches, all fitted out with little "gilded shelves, and mirrors that make everything appear double. Ladies, in fashionable dresses and with smiling faces, wait within and allow no gentleman to pass without giving him an opportunity to purchase some pretty thing to carry home as a remembrance of the Thames Tunnel." Drew himself bought a china kaleidoscope with a view of the tunnel, a shoe made out of clay taken from the river bed during construction, an ivory hourglass, a gutta-percha inkstand, and several "other little matters to gratify my little friends."[36] One of the most popular mementos available was a collapsible, cardboard stereoptican view of the tunnel, several of which are today in the possession of The London Museum. One young American, Henry Maney, was so taken by a blond young lady at one of these sales booths in the tunnel that he vowed that his "first visit would not be the last."[37]

Music enlivened this underwater bazaar—strolling musicians, a "steam organ," a Welsh harper. And Joel Headley on his visit became alarmed by a humming sound he thought might be the tunnel giving way—only to discover the sound came at the opposite end from a man and a boy playing a harp and a violin.[38] One could have his silhouette cut down in the tunnel, hop on a weighing machine, or buy an account of the tunnel's history fresh off a printing press, which Thurlow Weed persuaded the operator that he knew how to operate and did.[39] Octavia LeVert observed "eating houses, exhibitions of dioramas and panoramas; an organ played by steam filled the moist air with music to which many couples were gravely dancing the polka."[40]

In this tourist heyday of the Thames Tunnel reaction was mixed. Some American visitors still recognized it for the great engineering feat it was, and one of these emerged shouting, or so he claimed, "Huzza for Brunel! And truly he is worth a shout."[41] But another Yankee concluded that "it is merely a bazaar under the river—that is all."[42] One remarked that "to see it degraded to a miserable show, scarcely paying for its keeper, and serving only to enable the visitor to say he has walked under the Thames, is enough to justify one in naming it a folly.[43] *Punch* agreed, for in 1842 a writer in that magazine called it "a large bricked tube—the purpose for which has never been clearly ascertained," and suggested that it could be filled with boiling water in winter to warm the Thames or used as a powder magazine in the event of invasion.[44] But in 1867 American politician John Forney labeled the tunnel "a great achievement as a work of science" and reported that he had heard it was about to be taken over by the "Directors of the Underground Railroad" as a conduit under the Thames, in which capacity it still serves today. Forney added that New York, "always over-running her cluttered highways, will be finally forced to tunnel *her* streets; but before doing so, she should take a leaf out of London experience which has cost so much brains and money."[45]

The "new" Houses of Parliament—built between 1840 and 1852 (the clock

The New Houses of Parliament, c. 1857. Many Americans thought the Gothic style unsuited to public buildings and said so. *Illustrated London News,* **April 11, 1857, p. 355.** *Courtesy The Library of Congress.*

tower completed in 1858 and the Victoria Tower in 1860) to replace the old Westminster Palace that had burned down on the night of October 16, 1834—underwent intensive scrutiny by Americans. The visitors were more attuned to the neoclassical splendors of their own public buildings and actually were looking in this period for things British to knock. "The Houses of Parliament stretched along the banks of the Thames look from the river like some gigantic toy in terra cotta," wrote Mrs. Kirkland, "be-pinnacled and befrittered until all grandeur is lost in endless detail, and the only thought that strikes you is of the enormous cost thrown away. . . . There is no grand thing in London so entirely out of harmony with surrounding objects."[46] Grace Greenwood thought "the new parliamentary palace beautiful and magnificent in the extreme, but the splendid unsuitableness of this edifice for the theatre of grave legislation can scarcely be questioned. Infinitely more suitable, surely, would have been the pure and severely simple Greek architecture, strong and calm, and cold, like government and law, rather than the elaborate, fantastic, poetic forms of the Gothic."[47]

Ralph Waldo Emerson and Maunsell Field together visited the new buildings one day in 1848, and although, according to Field, they were received by the architect, Sir Charles Barry, "stiffly and with but scant courtesy," nevertheless they were provided a complete tour around the premises. "Most remarkable" was their joint assessment, but "in its entirety very inferior to our National Capitol at Washington."[48]

The poetic Gothic, was, of course, firmly defended by its leading American proponent, architect Andrew Jackson Downing, who spent an entire morning with his fellow architect Barry, "examining every part in detail." Downing judged the building "quite the masterpiece of modern Gothic architecture, perfect and harmonious in every detail, and even the very complexity in keeping with the intricate machinery of a government that rules an empire extending over half the globe."[49]

Mrs. Kirkland was also much displeased with Sir Christopher Wren's magnificent Greenwich Hospital—now in its last years as a residence for naval pensioners, as it would be phased out of that capacity in 1865. "The place is far from clean," she grumped, "and the show-men are generally sulky and rude." Furthermore, she complained, there was no proper place for a lady to sit down.[50] Another Yankee female was observed by George Mathews embarrassing her companions in accosting an old sailor who was walking with a stick in his hand. "Are you blind?" she asked him. "Yes, Ma'am," he replied. "But your eyes look bright," she persisted. "Yes, Ma'am, too bright, too bright," answered the old veteran and went on his way.[51] Ella Thompson and her six traveling companions, all women, enjoyed their visit to Greenwich, even sampling the tea, which they pronounced satisfactory, and inquiring after the quality of the tobacco supplied to the inmates. They chatted at length with one "lean and withered old fellow," recalled Mrs. Thompson, "who hopped with us on his wooden leg through several rooms, chirping out like a superannuated cricket that he was ninety-two." She fired one round before leaving Greenwich, however, at the honor paid to "an old pair of Nelson's stockings on display, while they left his beloved Lady Hamilton in want."[52]

The parks of London continued to show Americans that they were neglecting such amenities in their own rapidly growing cities, just as Humphrey had observed several decades before. Even Greeley had to admit that "the Parks, Squares, and Public Gardens of London beat us clean out of sight."[53] A most exhaustive survey was made by Downing, which he attributed to his "park-omania." The 2,250 acres of Richmond Great Park stunned him. "Its solitude and seclusion, within sight of London, are almost startling. . . . Is New York," he asked, "really not rich enough, or is there absolutely not land enough in America to give our citizens public parks of more than ten acres?"[54] It was, of course, his countryman, Frederick Law Olmsted, who studied these same parks even more closely, and together with Calvert Vaux laid out New York City's famed Central

Park. Downing was not above studying the parade of female and equine grace in Rotten Row, either. Noting "a young woman of extraordinary beauty driving a pretty phaeton drawn by two beautiful blood horses, quite alone, behind her a footman with his arms folded," he remarked on the sight of this "lady" to a London friend, who replied, " 'Yes, but she is *not* a lady!' "[55] Americans were much amused by the so-called "quizzing glasses," used by so many in the parks and regarded as "utterly indispensable to both ladies and gentlemen to enjoy the pleasure of gazing and being gazed upon" as they paraded past each other.[56]

At Apsley House on Hyde Park Corner David Bartlett noted "the iron shutters over all the windows fronting on the Park," still in place in 1851, dating back to the riots at the time of the passage of the Reform Bill two decades before. The old duke was himself now one of the great and familiar sights of London. During his visits to the Great Exhibition, Bartlett watched for him. "Yonder you see the carriage of the Field Marshall, Duke of Wellington, and in it sits an old man with white hair, and a back bent with age, and a nose never to be mistaken—the Roman nose of the hero of Waterloo:" Still another view of Wellington was recorded by this same admirer. "We saw him one day at the Admiralty Office," wrote Bartlett. "He mounted his steed and rode away, and we were astonished to see so old a man mount his horse and gallop off like a young officer. He wore his favorite Hessian boots and overcoat of blue, a white neckerchief, and a common English hat. There is something grand in his stately old age."[57]

About this same time, the Reverend Arthur Coxe attended Sunday services at the Chapel Royal of St. James's. "There was no one in the Chapel but the beadle and one other person, in the seat next me, at my right. There, in a dim corner, quite crouchingly drawn together, eyes shut, and white head bowed down, Roman nose, and iron features . . . sat in silence the hero of Waterloo." The duke, admitted the clergyman, "was certainly not as eminent for sanctity as for his many other qualities . . . but at the name of Jesus, the great captain of his salvation, he bowed down his head full low, as if he were indeed a soldier of the cross."[58]

Another American, young Witmer, whose *Wild Oats Sown Abroad* title rather belies the book's contents, also viewed the Duke of Wellington in this last year of his life. "It is time," declared this young sprig, "for the hero of Waterloo to die. He belongs to the past, and the commander of the present age must be *steam!*"[59] Wellington complied, for, even before the youthful traveler's book was in print, the old warrior was in his grave in the crypt of St. Paul's—not far from Nelson.

In London at the time of Wellington's passing, Henry Tuckerman of New York—who at the time of the Civil War would become so enraged at British policies—was astonished to find, only a few weeks after the funeral, a representation at Madame Tussaud's of Wellington lying in state—a scene mentioned by many subsequent visitors. "The illusion was so complete as to be shocking; it was difficult to realize that the livid wax was not the honored chieftain's clay. . . . In spite of the wish to do him reverence," observed Tuckerman, referring to that favorite device of cartoonists for so many years, "the question would suggest itself—what substitute for his *nose* can *Punch* discover?"[60]

Most Americans, regardless of how they viewed Wellington's sexual morals as a young man, or his politics as an old one, reflected in their references to him the

Sam.ᵉ Rogers

"The poet Rogers" (1763-1855), as the Americans always referred to him. "A breakfast with [Samuel] Rogers is among the much-courted . . . pleasures of the traveler," boasted Caroline Kirkland. By Daniel Maclise. *Courtesy the Library of Congress.*

attitude of one of the Reverend John Choules's school boys, who were in London for the Great Exhibition. "We shall always be glad that we came to England in time to see the 'the duke', and if we live twenty or thirty years, it will be pleasant to say, 'I have seen the Duke of Wellington!' "[61]

The town house at 22 St. James's Place, home of "the poet Rogers," as he was invariably called, until his death at ninety-three in 1855, was well known to visiting Americans with any sort of literary credentials, or pretenses, even. There they were welcomed, handsomely entertained, and introduced to the literati and other artistic achievers of London. "A breakfast with him is among the much-courted and long-remembered pleasures of the traveller," boasted Mrs. Kirkland. Attending one of his famous breakfasts, she eyed "the service partly of gold," and, indeed, "the refreshments mingled with flowers, were fit for Ganymede to have served."[62] But it was primarily the company that drew everyone there.

Samuel Rogers, who entered the literary world of London in 1792 with a slim book of poems entitled *The Pleasures of Memory*, inherited his banker-father's fortune and settled early into a luxurious and pleasant life at the center of a salon made highly attractive by his excellent cuisine and service, the art and literary treasures he collected, and his own talent as a host. He was noted for his wit, which sometimes had a cutting edge—as Washington Irving observed, in his remark that Rogers "served up his friends as he served his fish, with a squeeze of lemon over each . . . very piquant, but it set my teeth on edge."[63] Yet Rogers is remembered for his acts of kindness to people in need, and Fanny Kemble summed him up, saying that "he certainly had the kindest heart and unkindest tongue of anyone I ever knew."[64]

Part of Rogers's attraction was his vast store of lively anecdotes acquired over his long life. He told Richard McCormick several stories of acts of humanity by Lord Nelson on behalf of British sailors, adding, " 'I have seen him spin a teetotum with his one hand a whole evening for the amusement of some children.' "[65] Another traveler met Rogers "as a charming old man of eighty-seven years, and except for a little deafness, as active in body and mind as ever. He recited poetry and reminisced about dining 'sixty years ago with the Duke of Rochefoucault and twelve others', and how in a single year, 'nine of them had died by the guillotine or some other violent death.' "[66]

Mrs. Charles Dickens accompanied Harvard professor Cornelius Felton on a visit to Rogers in 1853. They found him "in good condition of mind and ready to converse although excessively feeble." Mrs. Dickens herself thus showed Felton through the house.[67] Although unable to rise from his chair to greet Harriet Beecher Stowe that same year, Rogers chatted with her at length, "sparkling out now and then," and on her departure presented her with the little book of his poems, illustrated by Turner, and autographed with his "still firm, beautiful hand."[68] In 1856 traveler James Wall spoke sadly in the past tense of that famous house where the poet Rogers "gave those delightful entertainments so much sought after."[69]

Julia Ward Howe had met Dickens at Rogers's, as well as the fashionable painter Landseer.[70] But the greatest "lion" of all Britain's literary figures for visiting Americans in these years was Dickens, his *American Notes* and *Martin*

Charles Dickens (1812-1870), reading from his novels in St. Martin's Hall as described by several American travelers. *Illustrated London News*, July 31, 1858, p. 99. *Courtesy the Library of Congress.*

Chuzzlewit notwithstanding. They sought eagerly to meet him, and so eager for a relic of the famous author was Mrs. Kirkland that she admitted to pinching one of the pens right off his desk, "hoping there might be something inspirational in its touch."[71] Grace Greenwood boasted of dining with Dickens, at which time she also met Walter Savage Landor, Charles Kemble the actor, and his daughter Madame Sartoris. During the evening, she wrote, "Mr. Dickens spoke to me with much interest of Mrs. Stowe and Mr. Hawthorne"—which gratified her national pride no end.[72]

At least two Americans were in the audience the night Charles Dickens gave his first public reading in St. Martin's Hall on the evening of April 15, 1858, the Reverend Henry Field and actor Stephen Massett. The latter was particularly impressed.

> Precisely at eight . . . Mr. Dickens stepped on the platform. . . . His hair was of an iron gray color, he wore a pretty full beard, a sort of goatee, he had on a very white waistcoat, and a very large bouquet attached to the left lapel of a black dress coat. After adjusting the lamps on either side of him, and not once looking at the audience, or in the slightest degree acknowledging the storm of applause with which upon his entrance he was greeted—and opening a large book, which appeared to me to be printed on one side of the leaf, in very large type . . . and first moistening his lips with the inevitable tumbler of water, he commenced to read his celebrated "Christmas Carol". Dickens, without any exception, is the finest reader I have ever heard.[73]

The Reverend Field, remembered today for his defense of and marriage to Mademoiselle Laure Desportes, the young governess tried for murder in Paris, and acquitted, in the Choiseul-Praslin case, noted the extraordinary nervous energy and physical intensity of the man before them on the platform. "Mark the figure. It is slight and slender, but all quivering with life. That agile form seems to be set on springs. The man has the same elasticity of body as of mind. In age he looks to be just what he is, forty-seven, but time has touched him lightly. Notwithstanding his long literary career, and immense activity, he still seems as fresh as ever."[74]

Catherine Sedgwick "captured" Thomas Carlyle in the early forties, and Grace Greenwood repeated the feat a decade later. Carlyle's head "would throw a phrenologist into ecstasies," asserted Mrs. Sedgwick, reflecting the contemporary interest in that popular pseudoscience of the period. "It looks like the forge of thought, and his eyes have a preternatural brilliance." Several years before, Carlyle had been himself much impressed, she told her readers, with the "celestial nature" of Ralph Waldo Emerson when he visited him. Daniel Webster, so the Carlyles informed her, had caused quite a sensation here. "They have given him the sobriquet of 'the Great Western' " (after the British ship of that name). Carlyle, she said, compared Webster's eyes to "dull furnaces that only wanted blowing to light them up."[75]

Grace Greenwood and Carlyle talked of Margaret Fuller, now dead, having perished in a shipwreck off Fire Island en route home from her European adventures. "Margaret was a great creature," Carlyle assured Miss Greenwood, "but you have no full biography of her yet. We want to know what time she got up in the morning and what sort of shoes and stockings she wore."[76] Carlyle would not learn until 1856 what Margaret had thought of him, when her At Home and Abroad was posthumously published. Carlyle, Miss Fuller, wrote, "does not converse—only harangues . . . allows no one a chance but bears down all opposition, not only by his wit and onset of words," but also, she indicated, "by actual physical superiority, raising his voice and by rushing on his opponent with a torrent of sound."[77]

Bayard Taylor, the prototype youthful wanderer of the nineteenth century, was entertained by both of the Brownings, Robert and Elizabeth. Of them he wrote that "he over-runs with a boyish life and vivacity, darting out continual

Yours faithfully,

T. Carlyle

Thomas Carlyle (1795-1881), whose "head looks like the forge of thought and whose eyes have a preternatural brilliance," so Catherine Sedgwick thought. By Daniel Maclise. *Courtesy the Library of Congress.*

Queen Victoria, with Prince Albert beside her, and the old Duke of Wellington at her left in the rear, reads the "Speech from the Throne" at the opening of Parliament in 1846. *Illustrated London News*, **January 24, 1846, p. 57.** *Courtesy the Library of Congress.*

flashes of wit and imagination, like the pranks of heat lightning in a summer cloud; while his wife, with her thin, pale face, half hidden by heavy brown ringlets, shines between, with the mildness and steadiness of moonlight." He judged the two poets ideally mated—"both great, yet respecting each other's individuality, each proud of the other's fame." Browning confided in him, he said, that much of his poetry was "composed mentally, while riding daily to the City in an omnibus."[78]

Besides tracking down their literary stars in London, American visitors, always fascinated by the British royal family, devoted considerable energy to catching glimpses of Queen Victoria in these middle decades of the century with Albert still at her side to share and shoulder responsibilities. From their first views of her as a young princess in the train of old King William, they recorded her development in a cavalcade of pen sketches or "portraits" that record the progress of her reign. She was seen before her marriage riding in Hyde Park with Lord Melbourne, her mentor during her first few years as monarch; then as a radiant, self-possessed young queen, resplendent in white satin, diamonds, and royal robes, opening Parliament, reading her speech from the throne in a voice so melodic and with diction so precise that it charmed her American listeners especially. Soon the tall, handsome Albert took Lord Melbourne's place at her side, and they would be seen together gracefully performing their state duties as well as relaxing at the theater. Victoria, one observer noticed, always leaned forward when Albert spoke to one of the ladies-in-waiting so as to join in the conversation herself.[79] She was never actually referred to as pretty, but much praise went to her kindly expression and gracious manners. She was seen at the dull and stately "Drawing Rooms," a tiny figure in bouffant crinolines and off-shoulder gowns, performing her duties with energy and sensitivity, responding to each person presented. Standing in the street to observe the queen en route to a state function, William Drew was surprised to note that "she had the art which all reviewing officers cultivate, of catching the eye of everybody in the line of march. Every person where I stood really thought the Queen looked directly at him and bowed personally to himself." So positive was he in his own case that at once he snatched off his hat and returned her bow.[80]

Charming little glimpses of the royal family now included the children. "There's no doubt but the poor doomed little things are well trained," observed Dean Dudley of the little Prince of Wales and his sister, the Princess Royal, the former destined to reign as Edward VII and the latter to bear Kaiser Wilhelm II of future fame.[81] William Brown was much amused, during the royal visit to Ireland in 1849, to observe little Prince Arthur resolutely refusing to doff his cap to the crowds even at the order of his older brother, and when urged by an adult, clapping both small hands to his head to prevent the cap being removed by anyone else.[82] Several of the younger children, having been taken to the theater one evening by their royal parents, made the mistake of joining the audience in clapping their hands for the "Royals" until Albert hushed them.[83] On another occasion the little Prince of Wales and his sister tried hard not to stare at the crazy American tourist who forced his hired hack driver to overtake and pass the queen's carriage in Hyde Park for his look at royalty in 1851. "To our utter amazement and mortification," wrote Ohio lawyer Samuel Cox, who pulled this stunt, "the Queen herself turned round and gave us a good-natured look and a full view."[84]

Having trudged through the rain to watch the royal couple leave St. James's in the fifties, a well-soaked Mrs. A. E. Newman was at last rewarded. As the carriage came out, she saw the queen "giggling and laughing just as we do sometimes when we cannot help it" before she perceived the wet little crowd of people gathered to see her and quickly resumed her composure to smile and wave properly.[85] Early in 1862, evangelist Phoebe Palmer, in Britain for soul-saving, observed the country draped in mourning for the prince consort who had died on December 14, 1861. "Many weeks have passed since the Queen of England became a widow," wrote Mrs. Palmer, adding with what now seems like grim Presbyterian prescience, "she is still feeling her widowhood as if it were but

"A London fog cannot be described; it must be seen, or, rather, felt," according to William Wells Brown. *The Graphic*, vol. VII, November 9, 1872, p. 347. *Courtesy the Library of Congress.*

yesterday."[86] Seven years later little Agnes Claflin of Massachusetts, doomed herself to die shortly, when she reached Rome, had to content herself with a view of "Her Majesty in wax" at Madame Tussaud's, as Victoria was still in mourning. Agnes noticed placards at various prominent spots in London:

VICTORIA!

Modest lamentation is the right of the dead;
Excessive grief is the enemy of the living.

—Shakespeare

"And beneath these cards," noticed Agnes, "appears some advertising. I think it is a pretty broad hint, and I wonder at its toleration."[87]

The fog of London, commented on by earlier visitors, by mid-century, had apparently increased in intensity, as had the size of the city, the number of its inhabitants and their chimney pots. "A London fog cannot be described," declared William Wells Brown in 1850. "It must be seen, or, rather, felt, for it is absolutely impossible to be clear and lucid on such a subject. It is the only thing which gives you an idea of what Milton meant when he talked about 'darkness visible'."[88] Brown then proceeded to give a clear and lucid description of a mid-century London fog:

It was on Monday morning, in the fore part of October, as the clock on St. Martin's Church was striking ten, that I left my lodgings, and turned into the Strand. The street-lamps were yet burning, and the shops were all lighted, as if day had not made its appearance. This great thoroughfare, as usual at this time of day, was thronged with business men going their way, and women sauntering about for pleasure or for want of something better to do. I passed down the Strand to Charing Cross, and looked in vain to see the majestic statue of Nelson upon the top of the great shaft. The clock of St. Martin's Church struck eleven, but my sight could not penetrate through the dark veil that hung between its face and me. In fact, day had been completely turned into night; and the brilliant lamps from the shop-windows almost persuaded me that day had not appeared.[89]

"There is a kind of light to be sure," continued Brown,

but it only serves as a medium for a series of optical illusions; and, for all useful purposes of vision, the deepest darkness that ever fell from heaven is infinitely preferable. A man perceives a coach a dozen yards off, and a single stride brings him among the horses' feet; he sees a gas-light faintly glimmering (as he thinks) at a distance, but scarcely has he advanced a step or two towards it, when he becomes convinced of its actual station by finding his head rattling against the post; and as for attempting. . .to distinguish one street from another, it is ridiculous to think of such a thing.[90]

On "a foggy, melancholy day," November 25, 1849, young Herman Melville found Westminster Abbey itself "full of fog."[91]

London's rain elicited something of the same sort of negative reaction as that of Alexander MacKenzie twenty years earlier, but without his humor, from Margaret Sweat in 1855. Comparing the "sweet influences of sunshine" she experienced in Paris with London's moisture, she complained that "in London, though it is only the first week in September, the weather is very cold and wet, and certainly London, on a wet day, is the dirtiest, dreariest and most disagreeable of places. . . . Anything short of a positive storm passes, it seems, for good weather." She made fun of the sensible clothing and sturdy walking shoes favored by Englishwomen, which permitted them to get about in bad weather, and which American men praised for their practicality and the mobility they provided their wearers. Before she was through, Miss Sweat had compared London to "a huge black spider toiling away forever in a cobweb of smoke and fog, looking at the cold, damp, ground for worms and flies, heedless whether the sky be blue or no; while Paris is like a gay butterfly rejoicing in the sunshine, thriftless but happy."[92]

American clergymen of the various evangelical persuasions, continued to lambaste the Church of England, as did the Reverend John P. Durbin, a Methodist cleric and president of Dickinson College, in 1844. "I gave as much attention as possible to the condition of the Church of England during my stay," he assured his readers, as if this was his bounden duty. Then, after a sort of pro forma assurance as to a onetime respect and affection for that institution, he proceeded through the catalog of evils and abuses made familiar by his predecessors Colton and Humphrey: political control by the party in power through appointments and patronage, oppression of the poor through compulsory tithing, and various forms of persecution of the dissenting sects. Charts and tables were produced to show the Church's holdings and wealth.[93]

This would be about the last of these detailed condemnations of the established Church, for these Yankee Protestants now had a far deeper concern, and one "much closer to home," than concern over the state church of England. What now really started their blood "moving quicker," as the Reverend Humphrey once put it, was their detection of what were, to them, unmistakable signs of "popery" that had infiltrated the Church of England in the form of the controversial "Ritualism" or "Puseyism," under the influence of Edward Pusey, John Henry Newman, and John Keble of Oxford, beginning in the 1830s. This new American concern now far outshadowed their former one and grew increasingly urgent as the decades wore on.

Pusey himself was observed at Oxford by the Negro abolitionist and historian William Wells Brown in 1851, who went out of his way to seek out that cleric at Christ Church Chapel, "where the reverend gentleman officiates," and described Pusey's "thoughtful and somewhat sullen brow, firm and pensive mouth, a cheek pale, thin, and deeply furrowed. A monk just fresh from the cloisters of Tintern Abbey in its proudest days," continued Brown, "could scarcely have made a more ascetic and solemn appearance."[94] Unlike Newman, whose convictions ultimately led him into the Roman Catholic fold, Pusey and Keble remained Anglicans, seeking to revive an emphasis on the liturgy of the Church of England and on the sacramental system as a whole. In their efforts to retrieve some of the beauty and dignity of the service lost at the time of the Reformation, "Puseyism" encouraged the use of vestments, crosses, candles, incense, and the intoned or chanted service. Even more than such visible signs of "popery" as candles and crosses, it was the intoning of the service that seemed to rile these Protestant pilgrims from America almost to a frenzy. Their complaints first began to appear in the thirties, and by mid-century they had really warmed up and continued loud and clear through most of the century. "The medieval miasma originated in the bogs and fens of Oxford," thundered geologist Hugh Miller in the fifties, "and has blown aslant over the face of the country: and not only religious, but scientific truth is to experience ... the influence of its poisonous blight and rotting mildew."[95]

"I am filled with disgust," the Reverend Mark Trafton announced in 1850, concerning the service at St. Paul's Cathedral. "The priests chant the service from beginning to end. It is *not* music nor *dancing* before the Lord; it is nonsense, the whole of it, and I cannot well conceive how common-sense men can bear it. It seems to me to be a feeble attempt at imitating the *Catholics*."[96] As late as 1891, attending a service in the Abbey, the Reverend Beverly Carradine would be similarly offended by intoning, which he defined as "a rising and falling voice, confining itself to two notes, with a sound that is composed of a whine and moan. I would have supposed that I was in a Catholic church."[97] It was apparently this flavor of "Catholicism" that enraged and frightened them.

An explicit clue to the fear hiding behind these expressions of disgust on the part of visiting Americans concerning "Puseyism" or "Ritualism" in the Anglican church is found in some comment by Choules. "Popery," declared the Reverend Choules, "has lost its hold upon the continent, and is seeking to regain its influence in England and plant it in America. The people of England are Protestant to the heart's core. The folly of a few scholars at Oxford has . . . invigorated the hopes of Rome."[98]

Choules believed that he had it all figured out in 1851. "Popery in America must be spread by immigration, and we have Ireland virtually in America. But," he reassured both himself and his readers, "the Irish will gradually merge into Americans, and the power of the priesthood will be less and less regarded by their children. I have no apprehensions from the coming of Catholics to America. Let them come, and we must get our *Bibles* ready for them, and *Bible* readers to visit them, and schools to teach their children."[99]

The Reverend Stephen Tyng of New York had been even more explicit in a speech he gave in London in 1842. Informing his listeners that Roman Catholics had "increased one hundred-fold in America within his own recollection," he urged all Protestants to unite against popery and confessed "that in America we look to Britain and the British Church as the grand bulwark of the Reformation. The most discouraging thing we have ever heard of is the spread of popery here."[100]

9

"Battle of the Books"

The attitudes and responses of American travelers in Britain during the last two decades before the Civil War must be viewed against the backdrop of that "battle of the books" referred to by Stephen Spender in his *Love-Hate Relations: English and American Sensibilities*. Thoroughly aroused and irritated by decades of querulous British comment on their infant nation, the Americans, now "decidedly adolescent, brash and self-assertive," began to fight back.[1] In order to understand their mood, one needs to trace its development.

Concerning the books by British traveler-writers, 142 such books were published *before* 1850 according to Nevins's bibliography for his *American Social History as Recorded By British Travellers*.[2] From about 1789 to 1825 these accounts were the fruit of "utilitarian inquiry," as Nevins put it, books by men of the middle or working class, motivated largely by the purpose of gathering facts, figures, and other information concerning immigration possibilities in the United States. Although not always flattering, these accounts were usually basically favorable or at least untinged with airs of superiority or scorn.

Americans found these books not at all to their liking, however, and there are caustic references to the works of these British travelers in the books by the American travelers to Britain from the first decade on. Silliman complained in 1806 of "a very vague and incorrect notion of our geography, institutions, political divisions, and state of society and manners" in the British accounts and said that they "listen, apparently, with incredulity and impatience, to any accounts of the country which exhibit a favourable representation of it." Even acknowledging "the *flatulency* of national vanity" with which Americans were cursed, the "turgid and bombastical" quality of much Yankee literary effort, and the "pompous declamation" so common in American speech, much of the negative British attitude toward the United States, Silliman believed, stemmed from "the *petulant* volumes of European travellers in America."[3]

Only a few years after this Joshua White also complained of the distorted impressions of the United States fostered by British writers, "without the means of enjoying a general and familiar intercourse with the inhabitants, but whirling rapidly along in the mail stages from New England to Georgia. . . . Foreigners," he continued, "who visit the United States to acquire information concerning their topography and geography; to learn what is the physical and moral state or condition of the people; to gain a knowledge of their habits, manners, and dispositions; of their literature, arts and manufactures . . . should not confine

Sydney Smith (1771-1845), British clergyman, wit and writer, who angered generations of Americans with his "Who reads an American book, etc., etc.?" By Daniel Maclise. *Courtesy the Library of Congress.*

themselves to sea-ports or Atlantic towns and cities. Such a traveler was Weld," declared White, in an obvious reference to Isaac Weld's *Travels through the States of North America, 1795-1797,* published at the turn of the century.[4]

Several other American writers also made similar caustic references to Weld, although George Ticknor, who was entertained by him in 1835 on a visit to Ireland, assured Americans that the writer by then looked on his book as "a youthful production . . . for the opinions of which, touching the United States, he expressed his regret as mistaken."[5] This may have been Ticknor's effort to reward a kindly host; unfortunately, such books as Weld's were widely read by Americans and never forgotten.

Also playing their part in this international squabble, fought in printer's ink, were certain leading British periodicals of the day, particularly the English *Quarterly Review* and the *Edinburgh Review.* The former publication, founded in 1809, published in November of that year a harsh review of *American Annals,* a book written by Abiel Holmes. Holmes was an ancestor of Dr. Oliver Wendell Holmes, the physician-author, and his equally famous son, Justice Oliver Wendell Holmes. The review of his book, consisting largely of an attack on American institutions and manners based on information out of the writings of Weld and others, aroused considerable ire in the United States.[6] Even those British writers who sought to present balanced, fair portraits of the new republic, the American critics claimed, only opened the door to more of these scathing British attacks often under the guise of book reviews.

The *Edinburgh Review* provoked still further angry response in the United States with the publication of its January-May issue of 1820, in which Sydney Smith, in a review of Adam Seybert's *Statistical Annals of the United States,* demanded:

> In the four quarters of the globe, who reads an American book? or goes to an American play? or looks at an American picture or statue? What does the world yet owe to American physicians or surgeons? What new substances have their chemists discovered? or what old ones have they analyzed? What new constellations have been discovered by the telescopes of Americans? What have they done in mathematics? Who drinks out of American glasses? or eats from American plates? or wears American coats or gowns? or sleeps in American blankets? Finally, under which of the old tyrannical governments of Europe is every sixth man a slave, whom his fellow creatures may buy, and sell and torture?[7]

This so-called review threw down the gauntlet as far as the Americans were concerned: they *never* forgot it. All during the nineteenth century—and even into the twentieth—it was quoted and referred to. It was quoted by H. L. Mencken himself in his book *The American Language,* first published in 1919. Smith had, however, at the very end of his remarks put a sturdy finger on the one weak spot in the American moral armor: slavery. No matter what else Americans might achieve, they were still, just as Smith charged, buying, selling, and torturing their black brothers. This confrontation of Americans with their national shame would become a persistent, in fact, the leading, subject of dialogue between visiting Americans and their British hosts in the two decades during which the United States marched steadily toward its Civil War and the final reckoning.

In the meantime, certain cooler and more rational heads, perceiving this growing acrimony between the two English-speaking nations, had tried to sound a note of conciliation. One of the first of these peace-makers was Washington Irving. Said that genial, sentimental anglophile: "We attach too much consequence to these attacks." Writing in one of his *Sketchbook* essays, published in 1819 and called "English Writers on America," he declared that "they cannot do us any essential injury. The tissue of misrepresentation attempted to be woven round us are like cobwebs round the limbs of an infant giant. Our country continually outgrows them. One falsehood after another falls off of itself. We have but to live on, and every day we live a whole volume of refutation."[8] When Emma Willard met with Irving in England some dozen years after this, she said that he told her Americans were still "too militant, and were sometimes too prompt for battle, if any question, however innocent or trivial, was made touching the superior excellence of anything and everything American."[9]

In the books of the American travelers up to 1840 the tone is, for the most part, fairly amicable, despite denunciations of the Church of England by evangelical preachers and repeated criticisms of the more glaring manifestations of British class and rank. MacKenzie, for example, acknowledged in his preface that his perusal of some of the English writers had led him "to feel some measure of ill-will towards England in return," but this, he went on, "has yielded almost entirely to personal observation." In his own account he said that he had tried "to forget that any books before his own had ever been written . . . and to see each thing as his own eyes might convey its picture to his mind . . . and to take as accurate notice as he might of all his impressions."[10] Even the Reverend Humphrey tried, so he claimed, to set aside "the snappish vituperations" of English travelers, and he urged Americans to keep their temper and to "return good for evil, by doing justice to the nation from which we sprang."[11] Henry McLellan assured himself and his readers that "notwithstanding the severe and oftentimes coarse manner in which we have been treated by British travellers, and which has produced much ill feeling on each side of the Atlantic, it will be perceived that a most kindly and cordial sentiment towards this country prevails, among many of our well-informed transatlantic brethren."[12]

The worst was yet to come in this battle of the books, however. Following the publication of works by three Britons—Basil Hall, Frances Trollope, and Charles Dickens—these writers became, in fact, a sort of unholy trinity to thin-skinned Yankees, whose diatribes against them persisted over several decades, and they even elicited an occasional burst of fire right up to the end of the nineteenth century. These writers came from a different class than the early British travelers, being drawn from the middle class or professional level. The attitude of these travelers was, as Nevins has said, one of "Tory condescension toward the United States."[13] They were primarily writers and opinion molders in search of material to interest and amuse their readers, and thus they were far more likely to focus on novel or exotic sights and customs. It might even be suggested that, during these years, those conditions in British society which led up to the passage of the Reform Bill in 1832, and the resultant agitation and fear of social and political change on the part of certain British writers, may have affected their interpretations of life in the great republican laboratory across the water. Another factor is simply that these travelers got around more, traveled farther west, saw something of frontier life, and indeed did observe much crudity and vulgarity that any proper Bostonian, for example, would very much resent if it were presented as a picture of life in America as a whole.

Captain Basil Hall, first of this unholy three, published his *Travels in North America in the Years 1827 and 1828* with the expressed intention of treating his subject in a fair and objective way and in a friendly spirit.[14] An experienced traveler and a Royal Navy man from the age of fourteen, Hall was no mere hack but a lively and sophisticated person with a keen eye. Primarily he contrasts the British and American forms of government, coming to the conclusion that an inherent danger in the American system is the tyranny of the majority, and that thus it is no proper model for his own country. There are some descriptions of crudity and discomfort suffered on their trip (his wife and little daughter accompanied him), but these are not unduly emphasized. His "mistake" was that he dared to touch on details of American slavery, although frankly admitting that he had observed plenty of examples of man's inhumanity to man in British schools and military institutions.[15] Possibly a flaw in Hall's makeup was revealed to American Jared Sparks in a meeting in London with Sydney Smith in 1828. When Hall's name came up, Smith remarked that he was a friend and inquired after his welfare. "Basil is as honest and straightforward a man as there is in the world," declared Smith, "but he wants tact."[16]

Frances Trollope was really rather harsh on the United States and Americans, and thus she was far more resented and vilified than the "terrible Captain Hall." Her two-volume *Domestic Manners of the Americans,* published in 1832, led even to attacks based on her own last name. "Her name is so peculiarly illustrative of her book that one feels half inclined to suspect that it was assumed for the occasion," fumed one angry-as-a-hornet Arkansas reader, Matthew Ward in 1853.[17] Mrs. Trollope, having failed in a business venture in Cincinnati, was charged with being motivated by bitterness over this experience. Whatever the cause, her depictions of prudery, ignorance, and lack of manners and civility in general, as well as poor speech and posture, inflamed American readers. The irony, of course, was that those guilty of such faults did not in all likelihood read such books, while those who were not probably did.

A British traveler, Edward Coke, arriving in New York when Mrs. Trollope's book first appeared, verified Irving's claim that Americans were a nation of readers. The attention of the public at that moment, he reported, was about equally divided between the latest outbreak of cholera and Frances Trollope's book.

At every corner of the street, at the door of every petty retailer of information for the people, a large placard met the eye with "For sale here, with plates, *Domestic Manners of the Americans,* by Mrs. Trollope." At every table d'hote, on board of every steamboat, in every stagecoach, and in all societies, the first question was, "Have you read Mrs. Trollope?" And one half of the people would be seen with a red or blue half-bound volume in their hand, which you might vouch for being the odious work, and the more it was abused, the more rapidly did the printers issue new editions.[18]

Irving had observed this same phenomenon over a decade earlier. "There is nothing published in England on the subject of our country that does not circulate through every part of it. . . .Over no nation does the press hold a more absolute control than over the people of America; for the universal education of even the poorest classes makes every individual a reader."[19]

The third member of the three most resented British commentators was Charles Dickens, who fell into that role in 1842 on the publication of his *American Notes* following his first visit to the United States. Idolized by American readers of "pirated" editions of his novels, there being no international copyright law as yet, Dickens was welcomed as a well-liked and respected celebrity. He got off on the wrong foot, apparently, at Boston, where he chose the opportunity of an after-dinner speech to try to promote the concept of an international copyright law to benefit both British and American writers. "Mr. Dickens brought with him letters and petitions to individuals, to Congress, and to the American people— from eminent British authors, some of them couched in offensive terms," claimed American author-editor Samuel Goodrich, "demanding copyright on the principle of absolute justice. In order to carry the point at a blow, the whole British press burst upon us with the cry of thief, robber, pirate, because we did precisely what was then and had been done everywhere—we reprinted books not protected by copyright! We resemble our ancestors, and do not like to be bullied!" declared Goodrich.[20] In any event, Dickens had advanced an idea whose time had not yet come, and he was much resented for it. It was not until 1891, when the Platt-Simmonds Act was passed, that the United States accepted the principle of international copyright and such protection came about.

Dickens's other sins were all in the *American Notes*—some cold-blooded depictions of cruelty to slaves, further elucidation upon the copyright problem, a chilling description of a Philadelphia penitentiary based on the humane and uplifting principle of solitary confinement, and colorful descriptions of crudity in western frontier towns. No matter that he had found Boston agreeable, praised New England's factories, schools, charitable institutions, beautiful scenery, and the manner in which he was received there. It was the "crimes" in the *American Notes* that were remembered. And he then proceeded to compound these by the harsh satire in his novel *Martin Chuzzlewit*, some scenes of which also were based on his observations in America.

In London shortly after that novel appeared, and planning to effect a meeting with Dickens, journalist Thurlow Weed abruptly changed his plans on reading "the latest number [installment] of the novel." Demanded Weed: "Was ever such malice or ribaldry perpetrated? Dickens has actually out-Trolloped Fidler and Hall!"[21]

Other British traveler-writers who were also detested for their accounts, besides the above-mentioned Isaac Fidler, were Captain Frederick Marryat, Thomas Hamilton, and Charles Augustus Murray, all of whose names run in and out of the various Yankee rants directed at their ilk. Miss Harriet Martineau, author of *Society in America* (1837) and *Retrospect of Western Travel* (1838), better withstood the inspection of American readers, as she portrayed a more favorable view of the young republic—except that she found the status of women not all that it should be and also criticized the great national embarrassment, slavery. She retained the good will of Americans for the most part, however, and some of them in their tours of her country stopped to call at her home in the Lake District.

Americans, Canadians included, now began to satirize the more sensational and superficial of the British travelers' books. Judge Thomas C. Haliburton of Nova Scotia, who wrote under the pen name "Sam Slick," satirized both American and English travelers in a pair of fictitious letters—ostensibly written by an American en route to Britain and an Englishman headed for America—in his book entitled *The Letter-Bag of the Great Western* (published in 1840). The American is all fired up, even before his arrival in Great Britain, to depict the decay of the British Establishment and the imminence of revolution. Meanwhile, the Briton plans, on his arrival in the United States, "to scour the country in eight weeks" so as to be able to claim that he has seen the locations that he has already written up, and he now needs only to fill in the gaps with "jests and anecdotes." The Briton's pre-determined subject matter includes:

> Lynching—spitting—gouging—steamboats blown up—slavery—sales and breeding of slaves—licentious manners of the South—slang expressions of the East and West—border doings in Canada—Clay—President Webster—ignorance of the fine arts—bank frauds—land frauds—stabbing with knives—dinner toasts—flogging in the United States navy—voluntary system—advantage of excluding clergymen from schools—Girard's College, etc.—cruelty to Indians—ravenous eating—vulgar familiarity—boarding houses—lists of names of drinks—watering places—legislative anomalies and tricks of log-rolling bills—anecdotes of Papineau—Sir John Colborne and Sir John Durham—and some few of women, perhaps the most attractive of all. These I can gather from travellers and from party-men, who, in all countries, never spare their opponents; and from country journals, and the speeches of mob-orators. It will spice the work, afford passages for newspaper puffs and paragraphs, and season the whole dish. All this can be accomplished in eight weeks, easily. The Americans live in steam boats, rail-cars, stage-coaches, and hotels, so that I shall see them at home while travelling, and of their domestic manners, ask freely of anyone I meet. It is not necessary to give dates; no one will know when I arrived, when I departed, or how long I was in the country. . . .I will give the whole a dash of democracy of the new school, being both anti-church and anti-tory in my opinion. I will talk of general progression—of reform measures—of the folly of finality, and so on. It will take—it will do. I shall go down as well as any ultraliberal of the day. I think I see the notices of it already:—"This is decidedly the best book ever written on America.—*Sunday Times*."[22]

In several different ways the Americans had begun to respond directly to their British critics; first, in certain of their own periodicals, such as the *North American Review,* and through individual writers such as Robert Walsh and his *Appeals From the Judgements of Great Britain Respecting the United States of America* (1818); James K. Paulding's *The United States and England* (1815) and *John Bull in America or the New Munchausen* (1824), and in James Fenimore Cooper's *Notions of America, Picked Up By a Travelling Bachelor* (1828). One especially amusing and interesting of these literary rebuttals is a book by Grant Thorburn, a British immigrant who rose to success in New York, returned to his homeland for a visit in the 1830s and wrote an account entitled *Men and Manners in Great Britain; Or, A Bone to Gnaw for the Trollopes, Fidlers, etc.* Every few pages he directly challenges Mrs. Trollope, as, for example, when he visits the Tower of London and recalls the botched-up execution of the old Countess of Salisbury, wild and disheveled, who was literally chased around the block by her executioner in his effort to complete his commission. "Well, Mrs. Trollope," demands Thorburn, "where was now your champions of England, your gallant knights, your men of refinement; there they stand in martial array to witness the brutal murder of their *grandmother!* Why, woman, you never heard of such soulless meanness among the red savages in the western wilds of America."[23]

By 1835, even the famed *Quarterly*, a chief British offender in this preposterous international literary quarrel, tried to soothe the troubled waters. In its September issue for that year an editor wrote: "Let us hear no more then,—at least, let us hear nothing in harsh, contemptuous or arrogant language about the petty circumstances which may happen to strike an English eye—as offensively characteristic of the people of America in their interior domestic intercourse among themselves."[24] But the damage had been done, and for the next two decades, and even beyond, the Americans took their revenge in the most satisfactory way of all—in kind. For all the printed insults they believed their nation had so long suffered, they would now inspect John Bull just as mercilessly and write books equally derogatory.

Briton Alexander Mackay, author of *The Western World* (published in 1849), understood better than most what had happened. "The feelings of the American people have been wantonly and unnecessarily wounded by successive travellers who have undertaken to depict them, nationally and individually, and who, to pander to a prevailing taste in this country, have generally viewed them on the ludicrous side. It is a mistake," pointed out Mackay, "to fancy that the Americans are impatient of criticism. They will submit to any amount of it that is fair, when they discover it is tendered in an honest spirit. What they most wince at is the application to them and their affairs of epithet tending to turn them into ridicule."[25]

"England has her fixed position in the great family of nations and at the head of civilization—a position which she has long occupied," Mackay observed, "and from which it will be some time ere she is driven. . . . The desire of America is to be at least abreast of England in the career of nations; and every expression which falls from the Englishman, showing that in his opinion she is yet far behind his own country, grates harshly upon what is after all but a pardonable vanity, springing from a laudable ambition."[26] Mackay also sensed that the affections or feelings of Americans were more involved with "the social and political system with which he is connected than with the soil which he inhabits," and that therefore criticisms of his manners and customs were often taken by the American as criticisms of his republican government which was still on trial and had yet to prove its durability.[27]

British newspapers, particularly the *Times* of London also created much ill will among American readers. O. P. Hiller, in 1857, devoted an entire chapter of his travel book, *English and Scottish Sketches, By An American*, to "the Thunderer," as the *Times* was familiarly known, labeling that newspaper a great mischief maker. It has bred more ill-blood between England and America than all other periodicals together (always excepting the outrageous *Quarterly*) .... In treating American affairs they come out, one day, with threatening, contumely and war. Then, finding they have gone too far, they will creep out, a day or so after, with a very humble look, never have the nobleness to make a frank apology, but trying to make up for their previous abuse by sneaking and partial praise.

Hiller chose to believe that the *Times* was not, in fact, the paper most respected by "the wise and good" people of England, but that it held its sway, in much the same manner as Bennett's New York *Herald,* through its extensive coverage and strong establishment. "The presses of England and America," Hiller concluded at mid-century, "seem to conceive that they say their best things when they say their worst, of the two countries. ... Why cannot something be done to bring this mischievous war to an end?"[28]

The precise nature of the ridicule to which Americans believed they had been subjected by the British writers and press can best be seen in a book by a well-known Arkansas journalist, Matthew Ward, *English Items* (published in 1853), obviously written for one purpose alone—that of cutting John Bull down to his proper size. Although ostensibly an account of English manners, customs, institutions, and the established Church, it is in effect a relentless, vituperative, diatribe, laced with heavy-handed attempts at humor, and designed to get back at British writers for their depictions of the following: Americans' tobacco chewing and the resultant spitting; their tendency to talk primarily of business matters and money; gobbling of their meals both in public and private; "angular attitudes"; curiosity; heavy drinking; political demagoguery; slavery; suicides; railway accidents; swindles and frauds; provincial linguistic oddities; poorly constructed bridges; and pompous-sounding classical names like Athens for mud-streeted villages.

Castigating what he called "Anglicized Americans" for their subservience to British critics, Matthew Ward concluded that "mutual enmity is the only feeling which can ever be maintained with sincerity between the two nations."[29] Orville Dewey, several decades earlier, had listed a catalog of grievances fairly similar to this one, pointing out that "we *read* everything that is written about us ... but *our* productions do not obtain the same currency with them."[30] Matthew Ward's indictment was obviously an attempt to rectify this situation:

> The mercenary bookwrights, including Mrs. Trollope, as well as the "Quarterlies, Monthlies, Weeklies and Dailies" unite in heaping contumely on America. ... Spitting? Let us spit fearlessly and profusely. It becomes a duty in the presence of an Englishman. Let us spit around him, above him, beneath him, everywhere but on him, that he may be perfectly familiar with the habit in all its phases. I would make it the first law of hospitality to an Englishman that every twist of tobacco should be called into requisition and every spittoon flooded. ... Leave no room for his imagination to work. ... Give each hurrying tourist who lands on our shores, inflated by preconceived notions for an abusive work on America, his fill of spitting.[31]

Equally furious in 1853 was Samuel Young. "We can easily see what England is, but she does not know us. She will not hear the truth, for her conceit and jealousy will not permit it. She gets her notion of America from Marryat the tippler, Trollope the bawd, Fanny Kemble the female rowdy, and Dickens, toad-eater to the aristocracy. Must we," Young demanded, "be compelled to take the conceit out of her for the *third* time?"[32]

According to George Train, an eccentric American businessman residing in London before and during the Civil War who would make speeches on behalf of his country and the Union cause, the popular image of the American as fostered by the British press was a creature

with a slouched hat, lank hair, sallow face, striped pantaloons, swallow-tailed coat, quid in mouth, whittling a stick, no spittoon on floor, brandy masher on table, bowie knife and *parish* [communal] toothbrush in pocket and revolver in belt. Add a peculiar nasal twang, and place his feet on the mantelpiece, and you have the type of my poor fellow-countrymen as portrayed to the people of England—a caricature even worse than the Frenchman's burlesque of John Bull.[33]

"As sands make mountains," continued Train,

drops oceans, so do little cuts of ridicule create large wounds of irritation. Old customs, like old shoes, wear too easily to be readily thrown away. . . . So this constant representation of everything American settles in the mind of the child, and manhood refuses to dispel it. Neglected in infancy, oppressed in youth, ridiculed in manhood, yet we are accused of over-sensitiveness, of ingratitude, our faults exaggerated, but our virtues are unextolled. This is not right. America and England must be friends or foes—like married life, either heaven or hell.[34]

By the time of the Civil War another American, and far more of an opinion molder—journalist Henry Tuckerman—had lost all patience in this continuing battle of print. Now, like all supporters of the Union cause, he was further enraged by the British government, which announced its neutrality while it was in actuality pro-Southern in sentiment. In a chapter entitled "English Abuse of America" in his book *America and Her Commentators* (published in 1864), Tuckerman proclaimed that "the long-continued gnawing of the tooth of detraction [has] at a momentous crisis, let in the cold flood at last upon the nation's heart, and quenched its traditional love."[35] For every human folly or social evil in the new nation, he pointed out, there was a British equivalent or counterpart quite adequate to "counterbalance in English civilization, . . . those so constantly proclaimed as American":

Deans and poachers, snobs and weavers, sempstresses and governesses, convicts, pretended lunatics . . . poor laws, costly and useless governmental arrangements; the ravages of gin and beer, the pressures of taxation, the inhumanity of rank and fashion, the cold egotism of the social code, the material routine of life, the absurd conventionalities, the servility of one class and the arrogance of another, the law of primogeniture, ecclesiastical abuses, the hopeless degradation of labor, and numerous kindred facts and figures in the economic and social statistics of the British realm, not only offer ample range for relentless and plausible defamation, akin to that which has been so bitterly indulged by English writers on America. . . . Let John Bull beware.

War or no war, he has made an enduring enemy of us. I am startled to hear myself say this, but England is henceforth to me only historical—the home of *our* Shakespeare, and Milton, and Wordsworth; for all her best writers are ours by necessity and privilege of language: but farewell the especial sympathy I have felt in her political, social, and total well-being. With her present exhibition and promulgation of jealousy, and selfishness, and heartlessness and ungentlemanly meanness, she has cut me loose from the sweet and cordial and reverent ties that have kept her so long to me a second fatherland.[36]

This American mood of resentment had been a long time abuilding and is here expressed at its apex, by Tuckerman, during the Civil War. Its growth can be traced from the start of the century, but it became really heated in the two decades before the War as the Americans were harassed about slavery—the problem they and their system of government proved unable to sort out or solve in a peaceful manner. Understanding the American bitterness does much to explain the querulous attitudes and negative comments of Yankee travelers in the prewar decades and even after. That Britons were not unaware of its existence is seen in casual remarks of ordinary people, like that of an English-woman at a party for author Samuel Prime in 1854. "Now you will be writing a book when you go home to pay us for all the wicked things that our travellers have reported of your country!"[37]

The whole struggle narrowed down, in the decades just before the war—as far as American travelers in Britain were concerned—to direct and often heated little personal encounters with Britons on the one enormous flaw in the great American experiment in government to which fault-finders and humanitarians alike could point: slavery. One could argue down a Briton on subjects like manners, customs, and institutions, but how to rationalize the fact of human servitude in the New Jerusalem? Cooper had shown them a way, back in 1837, in a chapter entitled "The Poor," in which he equated wretched British "female servants of all work, in the families of those who keep lodging-houses, trades-men, and other small house-keepers" with "Asiatic slaves." These English servants, he maintained, manifested "an air of dogged sullen misery that I have never seen equalled, in any other class of human beings, not even excepting the beggars in the streets. . . . The comparison between the condition of the common English house-servant, and that of the American slave, is altogether in favour of the latter, if the hardship of compelled servitude be kept out of view."[38] This sort of comparison, then, strongly backed with statistics and descriptions of urban poverty and pauperism in Britain, consumed much time and effort on the part of Americans visiting Britain between 1845 and 1865 and played a prominent part in their written accounts of travels in that country. It even intruded momentarily into the brief interlude of good will and international euphoria created by the Great Exhibition, as we shall see. For the one thing Britons most definitely would *not* keep out of view, as Cooper put it, was "the hardship of compelled servitude."

Despite all this acrimony, it is a tribute to the basic good sense and decency of individual, ordinary Britons and Americans that most of them could still deal with each other so civilly, and that so many Americans traveled in Britain so pleasurably, enjoying pleasant relationships with Britons whom they met or who opened their homes to them, and then came home to write, even in these years, primarily enthusiastic accounts of their sojourn in "the Mother Country." Henry McLellan found himself and his English hosts "all laughing heartily at the silliness of Mrs. Trollope's book which had just appeared."[39] John Mitchell concluded that, while "the upper classes too commonly regard us with dislike," having "gathered a rich treasury of prejudices from their tourists [i.e., their books], the common people of England are well disposed to us."[40] Frederick Olmsted wrote that "altogether, considering the exceedingly queer company English travellers seem to keep when in the United States, and the atrocious caricatures in which with few exceptions, they have represented our manners and customs to their countrymen, I was surprised at the general respect and the degree of correct appreciation of us."[41] Charles Stewart found that his aristocratic Scottish host had hidden his copy of Mrs. Trollope's book so as not to offend his American guest, an act unknowingly disclosed by his young son Arthur, seeking to amuse their guest before his father could appear. He had looked everywhere for the book, the boy said, and could not find it. "It is full of the funniest stories and the funniest pictures! Someone must have it in their room." At dinner Stewart learned that his host, "feeling that it would be no compliment to an American to find such a book on his table, had ordered that it be removed."[42]

Certain of these American traveler-writers actually met with their British counterparts. Mrs. Sedgwick recounted the extensive and kindly hospitality provided her by Captain Hall.[43] And Bayard Taylor was most warmly received by none other than Mrs. Trollope herself. "That lady," wrote Taylor,

> whose famous book on America is no gauge of her cordiality towards Americans, received me in a manner which must always command my gratitude. It must be remembered that her speculations in Cincinnati were unsuccessful, and that she left the United States chagrined and embittered at her heavy losses. Her book which, spiteful and caricaturesque as it was, did us no real harm, was written under the first sting of her failure, and she regretted it sincerely in later years. We can afford now to be friendly again towards a witty, cheerful, and really warm-hearted woman—who having forgotten what she lost, remembers only what she admired among us.[44]

Not for nothing was Bayard Taylor heading for a career in the diplomatic service. As for Charles Dickens, David Bartlett admitted, as if speaking for at least some of his countrymen, "Perhaps we were the more deeply hurt from the fact that some portions of his book were unpleasantly true."[45]

10

American Slavery

" 'Sir, you have some strange anomalies in America,' " remarked a Briton to youthful Henry McLellan when he was touring Britain in 1831. " 'There is no country where there exists greater personal freedom, door by door with the most insulting tyranny. Pray how can you call yourselves a free and equal people, and boast as you certainly do of it, whilst two million slaves are retained in captivity in your midst? I cannot understand it. . . . There is your treatment of the Indians also.' He then made particular inquiries about the Choctaws and the Cherokees. 'I do not see how you can answer to God or conscience for your treatment of those friendless people.' "[1]

Thus began one of those typical British-American dialogues on the personal interchange level, on that one subject, "so mortifying to a Yankee," as one traveler put it, that would plague most Americans in Great Britain in the decades before their Civil War toward which they were steadily drifting.[2]

"This is a standing topic here," observed the Reverend John Mitchell, in 1843. "In many cases it is treated in a candid and gentlemanly way; too often it is introduced in an unamiable spirit, in great ignorance of facts, and as a fair occasion for the indulgence of national antipathy and philanthropic railing."[3] Mitchell found it amusing, so he said, "to see their eagerness on the subject of slavery, our great national iniquity, (as it truly is),—all leaning toward me, and talking with an earnestness that made them interrupt one another." This occurred in a stagecoach, he wrote, where "they made me talk beyond my strength on that prolific and convenient topic, American Slavery; for it is often resorted to as a convenient diversion from sins and blemishes nearer home."[4] At mid-century, Henry Tappan likewise found the subject of slavery brought up whenever "any American appears rather boastful of his country's freedom and prosperity: it is a missile levelled at him to dash his pride."[5]

Until the Emancipation Proclamation of 1863 no American could, apparently, travel far in Great Britain without having the subject of slavery raised by people who had ended it in their dominions by an act of parliament and who wondered why their liberty-loving American cousins could not achieve something similar. "Of course he touched upon slavery," young George Putnam had reported from Scotland in 1836, writing of his interview with "Dr. Dick, the author of *The Christian Philosopher*. He did not understand why blacks should not be admitted into society and considered as equals in intellect with the whites."[6]

"They are so elated with the abolition of slavery in the British West Indies," observed John Durbin, president of Dickinson College, touring in the forties, "that they can hardly look with patience upon any system that holds men in bondage, however mild and *patriarchal* may be its character." Another cause was, he continued, that "a number of the most fanatical of our anti-slavery lecturers have been among them, and fed the public appetite for horrors to satiety."[7]

What particularly bothered the American travelers was that they were all badgered equally, as if all were either responsible for, or advocates of, slavery. "Whether you come from a Free State or a Slave State, it is all the same," the frustrated Mitchell complained.[8] Caroline Kirkland in 1848 found the subject immediately "thrown in the teeth of Americans who venture to have opinions on any subject in England. . . . The mere abolition of the legalized slave-trade, which it took Wilberforce, Clarkson, and their associates twenty years to worry Great Britain into," she fumed, "is considered a counterbalance for all the grinding and desolating oppression allowed in India because it fills the pockets of impoverished nobles and needy soldiers, who might else prove troublesome at home."[9]

Educator Henry Tappan reproduced in his travel book of 1852 a sample British-American dialogue on the slavery topic, possibly to get even or to warn future travelers what to expect. "After some courteous remarks on commonplace topics," warned Tappan, sooner or later, the Briton would introduce that "one subject which holds the British mind by a sort of fascination . . . American Slavery."[10]

Generally, the conversations began with a few words of praise for "Brother Jonathan" and his accomplishments, but inevitably there would crop up some such remark as "it is very inconsistent for a free country to keep so many of their fellow-beings in bondage." Tappan was in the habit of retorting that it was the British who first introduced slavery into the colonies. "But why did you not abolish slavery when you declared your independence and established your republic?" was the inevitable British rejoinder, logically based on the fact that Britain had, by an act of Parliament, abolished the slave trade in 1808; likewise emancipated all slaves in her dominions in 1833, save for India and St. Helena; and finally freed slaves even in these places in 1843.[11]

"The *political* relations of American Slavery the English seem at a loss to comprehend and are equally at fault in regard to other difficulties involved in its removal," Mitchell had discovered.[12] Tappan, too, lectured his British listeners on the nature of the American political system, which, he claimed, Englishmen did not understand.[13] After diligently explaining the concept of "sovereign states" united in a federal union under the Constitution, which permitted each state to handle the slavery question as it deemed fit, the American was then more than likely to hear, as Tappan pointed out, that in this case the Constitution should be altered so as to give it the power to prohibit slavery. All the American disputant could do then, said Tappan, was to point out the lengthy procedure involved in altering the Constitution and that efforts along these lines could well "create an agitation that might dissolve the Union." His British opponent was likely to end up with: "All we have to do is determine whether slavery be right or wrong. If it be wrong, then it ought to be abolished. To my mind there is but one side to this question. Slavery is clearly wrong, and therefore ought to be abolished. No nation or individual can be justified in perpetuating a wrong."[14]

The American reaction to this relentless baiting by Britons came to be the one first exploited by James Fenimore Cooper: the best defense is a good offense. By way of counterattack, Americans began charging Britons with hypocrisy in countenancing forms of servitude and misery in their own country that were, the Americans tried hard to demonstrate, at least as horrible in effect as Negro slavery in America. As if echoing Cooper, the popular travel writer Samuel Prime, as late as 1855, would call English working women "the white slaves of Europe" and claim that "Virginia negroes were better dressed for church than English peasants."[15]

"If you look at the people who labor in your manufactories, in your fields, in your mines, and at the relation between them and their employers," argued John Mitchell, "you will find a slavery not less real, and far more odious, if not more miserable, than the other," he argued. "You see labor unrequited; physical wants imperfectly relieved; personal liberty taken away, in fact, if not in form; abject dependence; humiliating fear; in short, all the elements of deepest servitude."[16]

"You may challenge a comparison in every respect," continued Mitchell,

> physical, and moral, between your form and grade of slavery and ours. You will find the negro working fewer hours, better fed, better clothed, better lodged, more instructed in religious truth, if not in letters, exhibiting a better physical condition, and a happier face, than your English, Scotch, and Irish operatives, hands, colliers, and domestics. And the bondage is not less hereditary and perpetual, descending from the fathers to the children, and perhaps is more hopeless, as to any prospect of its speedy termination, here than there.

"This, of course," Mitchell had to add to his argument, "is no justification of negro slavery; it is by no means urged as such; but it is fact, and it ought, we say, to temper British feeling and language in reference to transatlantic servitude.[17]

Such an argument might not be intended as a justification of slavery, but it was taken that way by Britons who heard it, and thus the debate continued irritably on. A few Southern travelers actually tried to make out a positive case for Negro slavery, such as the argument offered by E. K. Washington in the account of his travels in Britain. "American slavery elevates the subject of it," he declared, "from an inferior to a superior condition. The slave is many degrees higher— socially, intellectually, morally, industrially—than his ancestor in Africa. . . . American slavery elevates, by a practical impartation, by contact with a superior race, who impart civilization to the blacks—Christianity in return for manual labor. It gives the results of centuries of civilization." Washington further maintained that while

> the slave receives no immediate or stipulated or nominal wages, [he] gets protection, interested care, and familiar, kindly, benevolent support in old age, infancy, sickness. His wants are all provided and guaranteed to him. He has no thought for the morrow; what mind he has is free—free from the tyrants of want, debt, apprehension, poverty; for no slave *can* be a poor man—having an assurance of abundant support, no matter what may befall his master—who, if unable to keep him, disposes of his right to his labor to

Scene of many antislavery demonstrations, London's Exeter Hall lent its name to a phrase used by Americans to describe British hypocrisy concerning their own social ills: "Exeter Hall morality." *Illustrated London News*, February 7, 1863, p. 153. *Courtesy the Library of Congress.*

another who can keep him. He never can have an annoyance or uneasiness about support for wife or child. His condition is the natural relation of a superior and inferior race, when in contact, where both have found their level according to laws impressed on their being.[18]

Traveling aboard a train from Liverpool to London in 1851, lawyer Henry Maney of North Carolina listened in on one of these arguments between an Englishman and a young man from Virginia, the conclusion of which, in a very real sense, symbolized the impending split to which the American nation itself was drawing ever nearer as all efforts at communication and compromise failed. "As the Englishman condemned, in no measured terms, the slaveholding portion of our country," reported Maney, "he found himself suddenly picked up by the warm-blooded Southerner, and quite a sharp controversy ensued. The debate grew warmer still, yet neither would be convinced, until the Virginian, wheeling off, remarked in his wrath to his opponent, that he hadn't the brains to comprehend nor the candor to confess the truth, and he therefore declined all further discussion with him."[19]

A quite different view of American slavery was being presented to Britons in these decades before the Civil War by that host of "anti-slavery lecturers," referred to by John Durbin—some of them white abolitionists like William Lloyd Garrison, and others black abolitionists like William Wells Brown and Frederick Douglass. Exeter Hall in the Strand, at No. 327 on the north side, was the primary auditorium in London not only for religious and benevolent conferences but for antislavery meetings as well. As a matter of fact, the first meeting of the Society for the Extinction of the Slave Trade was held there on June 1, 1840, with Prince Albert presiding at his first public meeting in England on that occasion.[20] "Exeter Hall morality" and other epithets were applied by guilt-ridden Yankees to such gatherings when their own "peculiar institution" was the subject of discussion.

On an evening in 1843 agriculturalist Henry Colman sampled one of these antislavery meetings in the British capital. "I saw advertised a meeting of an anti-slavery league and that Garrison, Douglass, etc., were to hold forth. I thought I should like to hear some familiar and accustomed voices, and to shake hands with some old friends," Colman wrote. "The meeting was well attended, and Douglass was exceedingly entertaining and was received and heard with a tempest of applause continually bursting about his ears. Wright was very caustic. Garrison, whom I believe to be honest and disinterested, and certainly to be admired for his consistency and perseverance, was violent and virulent beyond precedent. The speeches were a continued attack upon the United States." Colman would not, he maintained, deny to any fugitive slave, "knowing by his own experience the miseries of the condition . . . the right to be plain-spoken, denunciatory and severe," but he was put off, he said, by the

> unqualified and malignant attacks upon my own country, which seemed to give such malignant pleasure to those who heard them. . . . Shoals of Americans, abolitionists, temperance agents, propagandists, and end-of-the-world men are here now, trying to kindle a fire, and they find here and there a pile of fagots which will burn. The audience last night seemed delighted beyond measure, to hear the United States abused, as they were so severely. It was not for me to enter the lists and advise "those who live in glass houses not to throw stones"; and I leave these matters to take their course, in the confidence that truth and right will ultimately prevail.[21]

Years later, William Henry Seward, Lincoln's secretary of state, looked back and remarked that

> one of the social enigmas which has always puzzled me is the proclivity which political reformers in our country have to go to England to promulgate their theories and develop their measures. I suppose that they have two reasons for this: one is, the greater safety with which a subject, unpopular at home, can be discussed there; and the other, that reformers who find fault with the Government of their own country can easily enlist followers in a foreign and unfriendly land.[22]

A Baptist minister, the Reverend Daniel C. Eddy of Massachusetts, was far more outspoken in 1851 in his criticism of these lecturing Americans making "almost every week the walls of Exeter Hall ring with some declamation upon the wrongs of American bondage." The British approach to the subject, he complained, "consists of a curious compound of national spleen and spite, prejudice and revenge. The speeches which are made upon the subject are generally in a taunting, bitter spirit which no American, however strongly he may be disposed to oppose slavery, can but resent. The citizen of the States is expected, when he makes a speech to cast some slur back upon his country; and if he does not do it, he is not applauded." He himself was asked to preach at a London church one Sunday, he related. " 'But understand,' " his British colleague added, 'I invite you on the condition that you have no love of the fugitive slave law, and no fellowship with those who have.' 'I shall not preach for you on any such conditions,' " Eddy says he replied. " 'You know me to be from a free state and opposed to slavery; and your "condition" is a thrust at my country.' Perhaps I exhibited some Yankee obstinacy, but I could not help it."[23]

"Almost every negro who goes from this country is caught up, hugged with desperation, and almost loved to death," continued Eddy.

> If he can show a scar on his back, his fortune is made; and if he can tell a few, vulgar, silly stories, he is a wonder of wonders. I would give a negro his due. If he has intellect, goodness, and piety, I would so far respect him, and treat him as kindly as I would a white man under similar circumstances. But the idea of catching up a negro simply because he is a negro, and thrusting him into the pulpit, and on the platform, where a white man, with equal ability and goodness, would not be allowed to stand, is a great piece of folly, which the English just now are desirous of committing to any extent.[24]

American sojourners continued to writhe under what they considered to be hypocritical British claims to a moral superiority belied by facts, and thus they started to hammer hard on the pauperism so glaringly evident in Britain's cities. Randal MacGavock, a lawyer from Tennessee, declared in 1851 that

> Englishmen may write, talk and preach what they please about the horrors of our peculiar institution; they may send their abolition missionaries across the water with pockets well-filled to preach a crusade against our liberty and laws; but they had better consider the deplorable condition of their own population, one tenth of which is now supported by charity, and whose condition both in a physical and moral point of view is far inferior to that of the slave owned by the most cruel of masters. Our colored population are provided with everything calculated to render them comfortable, and life happy. They are worked moderately, clothed comfortably, fed abundantly, and provided for when they get old and decrepit—while the poor of this great metropolis [London] are devoid of all these blessings.[25]

Another American got a Scotsman to acknowledge the misery of many British factory operatives. "There are many things about the working classes, which are not what they should be," he admitted, but then he declared, "We are *no* slaves!"[26] Somehow these arguments always seemed to bog down on that one point.

Well qualified to answer reasoning like that of McGavock and of all others who tried to rationalize the ugly fact of slavery was abolitionist William Wells Brown, himself technically a fugitive slave. His account of five years spent in Britain is invaluable, no only for its record of the antislavery crusade and his interesting descriptions of British life in the 1850s, but above all for his disclosures of what it was like to come up from slavery to an environment in which at last he was "treated like a man." Brown left the United States in 1849 to attend the Paris Peace Conference and followed this with a five-year stay in Britain, during which he earned his living by writing, traveling more than twenty-five thousand miles, addressing over a thousand meetings, and lecturing to a wide variety of organizations, during which he met Britons of every class and condition.[27]

"The more I see and learn of the condition of the working class of England," he wrote, "the more I am satisfied of the utter fallacy of the statements often made that their condition approximates to that of the slaves in America. Whatever may be the disadvantages that the British peasant labors under, he is *free*," declared Brown, "and if he is not satisfied with his employer, he can make choice of another. . . . But how is it with the American slave?" he asked.

> He has no right to himself; no right to protect his wife, his child, or his own person. He is nothing more than a living tool. Beyond his field or workshop he knows nothing. . . . He has not the least idea of the face of this earth, nor of the history or the constitution of the country in which he dwells. To him, the literature, science and art, the progressive history and the accumulated discoveries of by-gone ages are as if they had never been.[28]

"The past is to him as yesterday," continued Brown,

> and the future scarcely more than tomorrow. Ancestral monuments he has none; written documents, fraught with cogitations of other times, he has none; and any instrumentality calculated to awaken and expound the intellectual activity and comprehension of a present or approaching generation, he has none. His condition is that of the leopard of his own native Africa. It lives, it propagates its kind; but never does it indicate a movement towards that all but angelic intelligence of man. The slave eats, drinks, and sleeps, all for the benefit of the man who claims his body as his property.[29]

Brown served as chairman of a meeting held in London on August 1, 1851, at the Hall of Commerce, to commemorate the liberation in 1834, by Britain, of the slaves in the West Indies and to give a number of fugitive American slaves the opportunity to publicize their cause. Among those Britons present, Brown observed, were the historian-stateman Thomas Macaulay and the poet Alfred Tennyson.[30]

Returning to the United States in 1854, Brown suffered pangs of homesickness for Britain, where he had begun to fancy himself "an Englishman by habit, if not by birth. The treatment which I had experienced at their hands had endeared them to me, and caused me to feel myself at home wherever I went. . . . I had partaken of the hospitality of noblemen in England."[31] He continued,

> I had looked from the strangers' gallery down upon the great legislators of England as they sat in the House of Commons; I had stood in the House of Lords when Her Britannic Majesty prorogued her Parliament; I had eaten at

the same table with Sir Edward Bulwer Lytton, Charles Dickens, Eliza Cook, Alfred Tennyson, and the son-in-law of Sir Walter Scott; the omnibuses of . . . Edinburgh, Glasgow and Liverpool, had stopped to take me up. I had often encountered the *Caledonia, Bayswater, Hammersmith, Chelsea, Bluebell,* and other omnibuses that rattle over the pavements of Regent Street, Cheapside, and the west end of London—but what mattered that?. . . . [Back in Philadelphia,] walking through Chestnut Street, in company with two of my fellow-passengers, we hailed an omnibus going in the direction we wished to go. It immediately stopped, and the white men were furnished with seats, but I was told that "We don't allow niggers to ride in here."[32]

In London to serve as a judge at the Great Exhibition in 1851, editor Horace Greeley entered the great American slavery versus British pauperism dialogue. Unlike those Americans who tried to make a "case" for slavery, and were unable, logically, to put down the British arguments against it, Greeley went on the offensive and sought out human degradation in London to use as ammunition.

Thus, on the evening before he was slated to appear at the Annual Meeting of the British and Foreign Anti-Slavery Society, Greeley went in search of evidence at the famous Field Lane Ragged School and spared no punches in describing what he saw there.

It was something past 7 o'clock when we reached the rough, old building in a filthy, poverty-stricken quarter, which has been rudely fitted up for the Ragged School—one of the first, I believe, that was attempted. I should say there were about four hundred pupils on its benches, with about forty teachers; the pupils were at least two-thirds males from five to twenty years old, with a dozen or more adults. The girls were a hundred or so, mainly from three to ten years of age; but in a separate and upper apartment.[33]

The teaching is confined, I believe," continued Greeley,

to rudimentary instruction in reading and spelling, and to historic, theologic, and moral lessons from the Bible. As the doors are open, and everyone who sees fit comes in, stays so long as he or she pleases, and then goes out, there is much confusion and bustle at times, but, on the whole, a satisfactory degree of order is preserved, and considerable, though very unequal, progress made by the pupils. But such faces! such garments! such daguerreotypes of the superlative of human wretchedness and degradation! These pupils were gathered from among the outcasts of London—those who have no family ties, no homes, no education, no religious training, but were born to wander about the docks, picking up a chance job now and then, but acquiring no skill, no settled vocation, often compelled to steal or starve, and finally trained to regard the sheltered, well-fed and respected majority as their natural oppressors and their natural prey.[34]

Greeley was much impressed by the fact that three-fourths of the "pupils" remained for a prayer meeting at the end, until he learned that this was their one hope of shelter for the night. Following prayers, he went down to see the quarters for these homeless wanderers.

O the sadness of that sight! There in the mens' room were perhaps a hundred men and boys, sitting up in their rags in little compartments of naked boards, each about half-way between a bread-tray and hog-trough, which, planted close to each other, were to be their resting places for the night. . . . And this is a very recent and blessed addition to the School, made by the munificence of some noble woman, who gave $500 expressly to fit up some kind of a sleeping room, so that those who attended the School should not *all* be turned out (as a part still necessarily are) to wander or lie all night in the always cold, damp streets. There are not many hogs in America who are not better lodged than these poor human brethren and sisters, who now united, at the suggestion of the superintendent, in a hymn of praise to God for all His mercies. Doubtless many did so with an eye to the shelter and the hope of food (for each one who is permitted to stay here has a bath and six ounces of bread allowed him in the morning); yet when I contrasted this with the more formal and stately worship I had attended at Westminster Abbey in the morning, the preponderance was decidedly in favor of the latter.[35]

Journalist Richard McCormick would visit this same Night Refuge in 1854 and report that, "while sheltered from cold and exposure, no luxury is provided for the night beyond a boarded berth and a rug. A small loaf and water are not strong inducements to deter the idle from work," he concluded. "The periodical reading of the Bible, the regularity of prayer, the washing night and morning, the baths, the cleansing of the Refuge by the inmates, the strict discipline enforced, the necessity of attending Bible and Secular classes to keep their ticket—these things are not attractions for the lazy and the vagabond!"[36]

The evening following his own tour of the Ragged School Greeley showed up at the Anti-Slavery meeting in Freemason's Hall,

very ready to accept the Chairman's invitation to say a few words. For while all that the speakers uttered with regard to slavery was true enough, it was most manifest that, whatever effect the course of action they urged might have in America, it could have no other than a baneful influence on the cause of Political Reform in this country. True, it did not always say in so many words that the social and political institutions of Great Britain are perfect, but it never intimated the contrary, while it generally implied and often distinctly affirmed this.[37]

Greeley proposed three courses of direct action as a substitute for all the hot air emanating from Exeter Hall and all the other halls in London where Britons met to deplore slavery in America. First, "energetic and systematic exertions to increase the reward of Labor and the comfort and consideration of the depressed Laboring Class here at home"; second, "determined efforts for the eradication of those Social evils and miseries *here*"; and third, "the colonization of our Slave States by thousands of intelligent, moral and industrious Free Laborers, who will silently and practically dispel the wide-spread delusion which affirms that the Southern States must be cultivated and their great staples produced by Slave Labor or not at all."[38]

The Reverend Eddy was in the hall that night to observe Greeley's performance, and he found it "very amusing to witness the effect upon the assembly. Those composing it were too polite to retire or hiss, but a freemason sitting on a hot griddle could not have been more uneasy than most of them."[39] A decade or so earlier Dr. William Gibson had gotten a similar rise out of a British audience firing questions at him "about Indian and African persecution in the United States," by suggesting to those English ladies in attendance that they "adopt Red Jacket's plan proposed to Mr. Jefferson, to intermarry the Indians and whites, and to set the example of sending out respectable spinsters from the British Isles to commence operations with."[40]

When editor Greeley finished, despite his audience's cool response, he thought that he had made some inroads against what he saw as "Phariseeism," and he reiterated his belief that "American, and especially Afric-American, lecturers against slavery" actually served to distract British listeners from attacking the social problems crying out for attention in their own country. "I think I did not speak more than fifteen minutes," he recalled,

> and I was heard patiently to the end, but my remarks received no such "thunders of applause" as had been accorded to the more politic efforts of the colored gentlemen. . . . I have a faint hope that some of the remarks thus called forth will be remembered and reflected on. I am sure there is great need of it, and that denunciations of Slavery addressed by London to Charlestown and Mobile will be far more effective after the extreme of destitution and misery uncovered by the Ragged Schools shall have been banished forever from this island![41]

Right up to the outbreak of their Civil War, and even afterwards, Americans in Britain made it a point to find evidence to offset their guilt over slavery. Long after the great purge of the war between the states some would still remember how relentlessly they had been hounded, and indiscriminately, as a nation of slave-beating hypocrites. As late as 1886 an Ohio lawyer named Charles Collins would harp on the same tired theme. "The condition of the lower strata observed in this night wandering about London seemed to me more a slavery than that of southern plantation slaves before the war."[42]

British sins other than pauperism were dragged into the light of day as ammunition in the great dialogue. "They are filled with a very virtuous indignation at the continued existence of American slavery," argued the Unitarian journalist, William Ware in 1848, "while at the same time they swallow without difficulty the slavery of one hundred and fifty millions of Hindoos." They liked to think of themselves, he went on, as the "most moral and religious, the most loving and peaceable, the most generous and magnanimous, the most self-sacrificing, pious, and Christian people in the wide world. . . . In England the very occupation of the people seems to be straining at gnats and swallowing camels."[43] Complained David Bartlett, "Exeter Hall resounds with eloquence directed against negro slavery—but India is passed over in silence."[44]

"The English anti-slavery societies are very much impressed with the wretched condition of the slaves in our Southern States, but, like many other philanthropists, they have a wonderful eye for suffering at a distance, but cannot see that at their own doors," wrote Benjamin Moran in 1851. He called upon his readers to perceive the irony of an old, half-starved man dragging himself about the streets of London, "under a pair of heavy, placarded boards, almost heavy enough to crush him, on which were pasted flaming bills printed with large letters, calling upon the humane to assemble in their strength, and express their opinions against 'the infamous system of American slavery!' " Asked how much he received for his day's labor, the old man's answer was eighteen pence for ten hours. " 'But I may not get so much!' " Concluded Moran, "A happy commentary upon the benevolence and sympathy of the anti-slavery societies of England and their practical philanthropy!"[45]

Behind all the British antislavery tirades against her country lurked a concealed contempt for the United States, Caroline Kirkland believed. Despite much kindness in private, personal relationships,

> England, social England looks upon her American children with contempt, only half veiled; prizes not their love, scorns their admiration, views their efforts at improvement with a lofty disdain, and studiously avoids recognizing their claims to respect. . . . The corner of our rock of offence, is of course, that old rebellion, so vexatiously successful. . . . We love England for her mighty ones, for her greatness, for being our mother. . . . But she does not love us.[46]

The great slavery-poverty debate, with both sides guilt-ridden and pharisaical over their respective social evils, came to a head at the time of Harriet Beecher Stowe's visit in 1853. Her recently published *Uncle Tom's Cabin* was enjoying phenomenal success in Britain, where it provided further proof of the "national iniquity" of the United States. And now the very symbol of abolition herself came over on what at first proved to be a virtual triumphal tour, but before it was over would provide some moments of acute embarrassment for Mrs. Stowe.

Those of her countrymen and countrywomen visiting Britain that same year were astounded, and some were annoyed as well, at the furor *Uncle Tom's Cabin* was causing in Britain. Authoress Grace Greenwood first became aware of the phenomenon at Liverpool, where she expected to pay duty on her copy as she went through customs. " 'O, we will pass *Uncle Tom's Cabin*,' " the officer remarked, smiling, handing the book back to its owner.[47]

Professor Thomas Cogswell Upham of Bowdoin College arrived in London in September, 1852, to find the book occupying

> to a considerable extent the attention of the British nation. It is not often that a literary work, whatever its merits, produces what may be called a national sensation. But such is the fact . . . it is universally read, and it has been asserted on what seems to be good authority, that the popular writings of Walter Scott and of Dickens have had at no time a circulation so general and rapid as *Uncle Tom's Cabin*. It is published by a multitude of booksellers in all forms, and with all sorts and degrees of decorations and prices, and is found in all book-stalls and booksellers' shops.[48]

By the end of 1852, the novel had, in fact, sold over one million copies in Britain. Ultimately, one and a half million "pirated" editions would be sold.[49] One American, profoundly irritated by the novel's success because it gave Britain's antislavery forces fresh new ammunition to lob at the Yankees, was Henry Tuckerman, who declared the two great "lions" of London in 1852 to be the Duke of Wellington—who had just died and whose funeral obsequies had aroused a great wave of patriotic emotion and excitement—and "Uncle Tom." He compared the overwhelming ubiquity of *Uncle Tom's Cabin* to the "infernal punishment" of the water torture, "single drops of water falling on the head at regular intervals. . . . The incidents were frequently exciting," he admitted, and "some of the scenes were cleverly drawn, and a very judicious mingling of humor and pathos introduced; some of the characters, too, were effectively modelled, and the narrative interest was well sustained. Such were the literary merits of the tale."[50]

"But," Tuckerman continued,

an additional *éclat* attended this novel, if such it may be called. To elevate negroes and negresses into heroes and heroines was a new experiment; and to expose to the world, as this book professed to do, a monstrous social evil, awakened the ardent sympathy of philanthropists and reformers. These effects were not diminished by the gross exaggeration and caricature displayed in the story, regarded as a picture of actual life. Indeed, the basis of truth was not examined among the partisans who adopted the work as an exposition of American slavery. The appeal it made to the pity and moral indignation of the public by the high-wrought and exceptional scenes of cruelty and degradation, found an immediate response; the intelligent minority alone, compared its revelations with facts, or applied to them the test of reason and charity. [Why did not *Oliver Twist* and *Mary Barton,* a picture of the misery of the English factory operative, become "lions" in the same way as Uncle Tom?] Why was this honor reserved for Uncle Tom? Because he was the type of an evil which England has had the good fortune to cast off, and because he is the symbol of reproach to America. Thus the national pride was doubly gratified by this canonization; and what rendered the apotheosis more delectable was, that its ostensible, and in part doubtless its real motive, was philanthropy. Thus, during my brief visit, Uncle Tom was the "lion."[51]

The Reverend Eddy claimed that he was told, on a visit to a "gin-palace," that *Uncle Tom's Cabin* offered one more opportunity "for John Bull to 'put his flippers into the peepers' of Brother Jonathan."[52]

Even before he was off the boat at Liverpool, Tuckerman encountered "Uncle Tom" in the newspaper brought aboard by the pilot, which contained "an account of a meeting of ladies to present a memorial to the authoress" of Uncle Tom. "Thus the initiative breath of English air was prophetic of this tenacious companion." Upon the tea table at his hotel rested a collection box with the announcement that it was "a savings bank for Uncle Tom." A street singer assaulted his ears with a number based on Uncle Tom's "Massa, I can tell you Nothing." On his washstand he found a cake of "Uncle Tom Soap," and, requesting a book at bedtime, he was brought Mrs. Stowe's novel. At the hairdresser's the following morning his eyes rested on a newly papered wall, to find that "the entire wall exhibited innumerable tableaux of Uncle Tom and Little Eva." Peering out of the window of his train to London, at every stop he perceived Uncle Tom's effigy and title emblazoned over each bookstall, even as he listened to an Englishman in the same compartment assuring a listener that "whipping blacks to death was a common sight in the streets of Boston."[53]

London theaters were making the most of the vogue, too, Tuckerman discovered on his arrival in the metropolis. The play *Uncle Tom's Cabin* reigned at Drury Lane, while other versions of the story were enacted in pantomime at a minor theater; in an act at Astley's Amphitheatre involving Uncle Tom's being hunted down by horsemen; and even in a kind of bawdy burlesque at the "Coal-Hole" off Fleet Street.[54] The Uncle Tom craze apparently reached even into the royal family itself, for, a decade later, visiting the elegant dairy at Windsor Castle, Elihu Burritt was amused to find cows named "Topsy" and "Eva."[55]

The lionizing of Mrs. Stowe herself began the moment she stepped ashore at Liverpool. "Much to my astonishment," she wrote home, "I found quite a crowd on the wharf, and we walked up to our carriage through a long line of people, bowing, and looking very glad to see us. . . . They stood looking very quietly, and looked very kindly, though evidently very much determined to look."[56] Mrs. Stowe was discovering that she was indeed a celebrity, for this welcome set the tone for her whole visit. Although she and her husband Calvin managed a bit of sight-seeing up in Scotland at the start, their trip soon took on the shape of a "state visit" much like that of visiting royalty. There were constant "appearances" before groups and societies, and public meetings in Liverpool, Edinburgh, Aberdeen, Dundee, and London all enlivened with numerous toasts to friendship between John Bull and Brother Jonathan, with Mrs. Stowe the recipient of numerous gifts and testimonials.[57]

Like most authors, Mrs. Stowe was charmed to meet people who had read her book, and during the early stages of her journey she faithfully recorded such little incidents in her letters home. She was introduced by the Duke of Argyle, for example, to "a broad-shouldered Scotch farmer, who stood some six feet two, and who paid me the compliment to say that he had read my book, and that he would walk six miles to see me any day."[58] Stopping one day at a roadside cottage for a bit of refreshment, she was told that all the household, "even the old grandmother, had read Uncle Tom's Cabin and were perfectly familiar with all the details."[59] The landlady at a hotel where they stopped presented her with a bead purse knitted by one of her daughters "during the winter evenings while they were reading Uncle Tom."[60] Mrs. Stowe found much in Scotland to remind her of New England, she said—the moral earnestness of the people, their respect for learning, and their necessary thrift. "The children of the Covenant and the children of the Puritans are of one blood," she decided. "It is because America, like Scotland, has stood for right against oppression, that the Scotch love and sympathize with her."[61] Following her tour of the Burns-Scott country, Mrs. Stowe made the obligatory pilgrimage to Stratford-Warwick-Kenilworth, expressing her hope that "the lover of the picturesque . . . is not sinning against the useful in his admiration of the beautiful."[62] Finally, she was ready to tackle London.

Here, with Calvin trailing tiredly in her wake, Mrs. Stowe was taken up by London society in a manner that soon left her close to exhaustion—beginning with an invitation to the annual dinner given the judges of England by the lord mayor at the Mansion House. Calvin, surprised to see so much "dirty lace" at the wrists of men otherwise resplendent in black velvet, asked her sotto voce, she said, " 'How can men wear such dirty stuff? Why don't they wash it?' I expounded to him what an ignorant sinner he was, and that the dirt of ages was one of the surest indications of value. Wash point lace! It would be as bad as cleaning up an antiquary's study." For her part she was dazzled, and a little shocked as well, by the bare shoulders and deep décolletage of the ladies. "This requirement seems to be universal, since ladies of all ages conform to it," she observed.[63]

Sitting opposite Mrs. Stowe was Charles Dickens, who surprised her by looking "so young," and she beamed to hear a toast proposed to both herself and Dickens as writers who "employed fiction as a means of awakening the attention of the respective countries to the condition of the oppressed and suffering classes." Her fate as a "lion" in London was now sealed. Recollecting the angry reception of her book by many of her own countrymen at home, she remarked: "Every thing here meets the very freest handling; nothing is too sacred to be publicly shown up; but those who are exhibited appear to have too much good sense to recognize the force of the picture by getting angry. Mr. Dickens has gone on unmercifully exposing all sorts of weak places in the English fabric, public and private, yet nobody cries out upon him as the slanderer of his country."[64]

The social pace of the London "season" quite stunned her, what with all the "breakfasts," luncheons, teas, dinners, and evening receptions at which she was invited to appear. "Yesterday. . .I was 'fairly knocked up,' " she wrote home to her family. "This expression which I find obtains universally here, corresponds to what we mean by 'used up.' " She found Londoners "under such a pressure of engagements that they go about with their lists in their pockets." Evening engagements, she discovered to her horror, began at ten o'clock. "People [are] staying out night after night till two o'clock, sitting up all night in Parliament, and seeming to thrive upon it."[65] At one point she wished that "one could have a relay of bodies, as of clothes, and go from one to the other. But we, not used to the London style of turning night into day, are full weary."[66] It was a complaint she was to make often as the invitations kept pouring in. "The city of London made a goddess of Madame Stowe for her 'Uncle Tom' misrepresentations," businessman George Williams of Charleston would remark two decades later.[67]

One morning, feeling too spent to go anywhere, Mrs. Stowe was nevertheless persuaded to attend "just for a little while" a meeting of the Bible Society at Exeter Hall. There at last she met the Earl of Shaftesbury, the famous philanthropist of the period. "He is quite a tall man, of a slender figure," she wrote, "with a long and narrow face, dark hazel eyes, and very thick auburn hair. His bearing was dignified and appropriate to his position. People here," she added "are somewhat amused by the vivacity with which the American papers are exhorting Lord Shaftesbury to look into the factory system, and to explore the collieries, and in general to take care of the suffering lower classes, as if he had been doing anything else for these twenty years past."[68] Noted both for his antislavery zeal and his efforts to end child labor in Britain, as well as to alleviate the miseries of London's poor, the famous philanthropist now became her personal guide on her tour of London's "model" lodging houses, washhouses, and the Ragged Schools.

At one of the washhouses Mrs. Stowe was amazed at the degree of mechanized efficiency. "We entered a large hall. . .divided by low wood partitions into small apartments, in each of which a woman was washing." Two or three wash waters were possible, Mrs. Stowe observed, through drains at the bottom of the tub and fresh water let in at the top from a spigot. Scalding steam could be directed into each tub by turning a stopcock, she reported. But most of all she was amazed at the drying process. The women's washes are "whirled in a hollow cylinder until nearly dry, after which they are drawn through two rollers covered with flannel which presses every remaining particle of water out of them. The clothes are then hung upon frames which shut into large closets, and are dried by steam in a very short space of time."[69]

It was not long before Mrs. Stowe discovered, like many a celebrity before and since, that individuals associated in the public mind with moral superiority, real or assumed, are highly vulnerable. First, there is the natural human tendency in those less perfect to sniff out flaws and failures in the object of admiration; second, the tendency for persons or groups with axes to grind to try to exploit them. Mrs. Stowe faced both situations—the first when she decided that she required a new silk dress for all the social functions she was attending. When it came time to publish the account of her *Sunny Memories of Foreign Lands,* she seized the opportunity to record her side of the brown silk dress story. "It always has seemed to me," she began,

> "that [English] newspapers tell a vast deal about people's concerns which is not our custom to put into print in America. Such, for instance, as where the Hon. Mr. A. is staying now, and where he expects to go next; what her grace wore at the last ball. . . .Could I have expected dear old England to make me so much one of the family as to treat my humbler fortunes in this same manner?· But it is even so. This week *The Times* has informed the United Kingdom that Mrs. Stowe is getting a new dress made!—the charming old aristocratic *Times* which everybody declares is such a wicked paper, and yet which they can no more do without than they can their breakfast! What am I, and what is my father's house, that such a distinction should come upon me?[70]

To use Mrs. Stowe's own words, a letter in the *Times* accused her of having a dress "made up piecemeal, in the most shockingly distressed dens of London, by poor, miserable white slaves, worse treated than the plantation slaves of America" Mrs. Stowe was startled, stunned and angry, and it shows in the self-conscious third-person manner in which she describes the event.

> Now Mrs. Stowe did not know any thing of this, but simply gave the silk into the hands of a friend, and was in due time waited on in her own apartment by a very respectable woman, who offered to make the dress; and lo, this is the result! Since the publication of this piece, I have received earnest missives from various parts of the country, begging me to interfere, hoping that I was not going to patronize the white slavery of England, and that I would employ my talents against oppression under every form. . . .[71]

"Let my case be a warning to all philanthropists who may happen to want clothes while they are in London," complained Mrs. Stowe. "Some of my correspondents seemed to think I ought to publish a manifesto for the benefit of distressed Great Britain, stating how I came to do it, and all the circumstances, since they are quite sure I must have meant well, and containing gentle cautions as to the disposal of my future patronage in the dressmaking line. . . .I verily never thought," she protested, "but that the nice, pleasant person, who came to measure me for my silk, was going to take it home and make it herself; it never occurred to me that she was the head of an establishment. And now, what am I to do?" Horace Greeley, she added, "would be delighted could his labors in this line excite a similar commotion in New York."[72]

A second round of embarrassment, and more explaining to do, would stem from Mrs. Stowe's association with the Duchess of Sutherland, a personal friend of Queen Victoria, onetime Mistress of the Robes, immensely wealthy, and famed for her public devotion to various liberal and philanthropic causes, especially, the antislavery crusade. Journalist Henry Stanton, who covered the World Anti-Slavery Convention in London in June 1840, recalled in later years his impression of the duchess and her associates. He summed them up in a single sentence. "In England the cause of Abolition wore golden slippers."[73]

The two women met at the house of the duchess' brother, Lord Carlisle, "the one English traveller who ever wrote notes on our country in a real spirit of appreciation," wrote Mrs. Stowe by way of establishing her host's pro-American credentials. "While the Halls and Trollopes and all the rest could see nothing but our breaking eggs on the wrong end, or such matters, he discerned and interpreted those points wherein lies the real strength of our growing country."[74] She was speaking of Carlisle's *Travels in America*, published in 1851.

"I observe," continued Mrs. Stowe, who obviously did not take criticism philosophically,

that American newspapers are sneering about his preface to *Uncle Tom's Cabin;* but they ought at least to remember that his sentiments with regard to slavery are no sudden freak. In the first place, he comes of a family that has always been on the side of liberal and progressive principles. . . .While Lord Carlisle was in America he never disguised those anti-slavery sentiments which formed a part of his political and religious creed as an Englishman, and as the heir of a house always true to progress.

Moreover, the Duchess of Sutherland, too, claimed Mrs. Stowe, "has always professed those sentiments with regard to slavery which are the glory of the English nation."

Flattering her subject, Mrs. Stowe described the duchess as

tall and stately with a decided fulness of outline, and a most noble bearing. Her fair complexion, blond hair, and full lips speak of Saxon blood. In her early youth she might have been a Rowena. . . .Her manners have a peculiar warmth and cordiality. One sees people now and then who seem to *radiate* kindness and vitality. . .the engraving by Winterhalter, which has been somewhat familiar in America, is as just a representation of her air and bearing as could be given.[75]

Mrs. Stowe's next contact with this fabled creature, after the first meeting at her brother's home, was at the duchess' own palatial London residence, Stafford House, on the edge of St. James's Park, where the American author was met at the door by "two stately Highlanders in full costume." Mrs. Stowe's name was repeated through the long corridors, from one to another, by "an innumerable multitude of servants in livery with powdered hair." The splendor of the rooms dazzled the American as did the duchess herself, "dressed in white muslin, with a drab velvet basque slashed with satin of the same color. Her hair was confined by a gold and diamond net on the back part of her head."

By her own account, Mrs. Stowe's first overture was an odd

> little private conversation with the duchess in her boudoir, in which I frankly confessed a little anxiety respecting the arrangements of the day: having lived all my life in such a shady and sequestered way, and being entirely ignorant of life as it exists in the sphere in which she moves, such apprehensions were rather natural. She begged that I would make myself entirely easy, and consider myself among friends; that she had invited a few friends to lunch, and that afterwards, others would call; that there would be a short address from the ladies of England read by Lord Shaftesbury, which would require no answer.[76]

Mrs. Stowe soon found herself meeting family members such as the Duke and Duchess of Argyle, Lord and Lady Blantyre, the Marquis and Marchionness of Stafford, and Lady Emma Campbell. Soon entered Lord and Lady Shaftesbury, Lord and Lady Palmerston, followed by the Marquis of Lansdowne, Lord John Russell, Mr. Gladstone, and Lord Grenville. The guest list reads like a list of Britain's leading and most influential statesmen, and one begins to suspect, as Mrs. Stowe must have realized, that this little luncheon had as much to do with politics as it had to do with advancing the cause of abolition.[77]

Seated next to the Marquis of Lansdowne, "one of those who, as Lord Henry Pettes, took a distinguished part with Clarkson and Wilberforce in the abolition of the slave trade," she conversed about "affairs in America." The elegant menu was in French, and she was much impressed by one of the dishes, a nest of plovers' eggs, "precisely as the plover made it, with five little blue speckled eggs in it," this particular dish and mode of service being "one of the fashions of the day." Once again, her Puritan conscience got in the way, for the nest reminded her of that of a New England robin, and "I had it not in my heart to profane the sanctity of the image by eating one of the eggs."[78]

Mrs. Stowe's appearance at this luncheon, and her acceptance of "the short address from the ladies of England read by Lord Shaftesbury," entreating the women of America to stand forth against slavery in their country, was to put her name once more on the front page of the newspapers, much to her chagrin. "Nothing can be more false than the insinuation that has been thrown out in some American newspapers that it was a political movement," she scolded. "It had its first origin in the deep religious feelings of the man [Lord Shaftesbury] whose whole life has been devoted to the abolition of the white-labor slavery of Great Britain." The meeting at Stafford House, she insisted, "was not a personal honor" to herself but

> the most public expression possible of the feelings of the women of England on one of the most important questions of our day. . . . The most splendid of England's palaces has this day opened its doors to the slave. Its treasures of wealth and of art, its prestige of high name and historic memories, have been consecrated to . . . the recognition of the brotherhood of the human family. . . . A fair and noble hand by this meeting has fixed, in a most public manner, an ineffaceable seal to the beautiful sentiments of that most Christian

document, the letter of the ladies of Great Britain to the ladies of America. That letter and this public attestation of it are now historic facts which wait their time and the judgment of advancing Christianity.[79]

Mrs. Stowe fails to mention that the Duchess of Sutherland also bestowed upon her noted American guest a bracelet of gold fashioned in the shape of a slave shackle.[80]

Led ever on by the attentions and flattery of the high and mighty, she had let herself be used, and Mrs. Stowe knew it. To save face she would have gone to great lengths to rationalize her association with the Sutherlands, and she did. The duchess' own background might be one of "liberal and progressive principles," as the American author insisted. That of her husband's family was far from it, for the duke's father was the one of the leading perpetrators of the Highland Clearances, in which cottagers were burned out and driven like animals to ships to make way for sheep.

"Imagine then," wrote Mrs. Stowe,

what people must think when they find in respectable American print the absurd story of her turning her tenants out into the snow, and ordering the cottages to be set on fire over their heads because they would not go out. But if you ask how such an absurd story could ever be made up, whether there is the least foundation to make it on, I answer, that it is an exaggerated report of a movement made by the present Duke of Sutherland's father in the year 1811.[81]

It was all "part of a great movement that passed through the Highlands of Scotland, when the advancing progress of civilization began to make it necessary to change from military to agricultural establishments," wrote Mrs. Stowe. By burning families out of their homes and forcing them onto boats for North America, Sutherland and his ilk, according to Mrs. Stowe, were bringing them forward into the nineteenth century. How very like the argument of the slave owner that he raises his African up to the level of civilization. And then for thirteen, long, mealymouthed pages, Harriet Beecher Stowe, the champion of the American slave, justifies the infamous Highland Clearances as just another of those "movements which, in their final results, are beneficial to society, at first vehemently resisted, and had to be carried into effect in some cases by force." To sum up her defense of her friend's family, Mrs. Stowe termed the Clearances "an almost sublime instance of the benevolent employment of superior wealth and power in shortening the struggles of advancing civilization, and elevating in a few years a whole community to a point of education and material prosperity, which unassisted, they might never have attained."[82]

Mrs. Stowe's hypocrisy and double standard of morality would be remembered in print over thirty years later by the American artist Joseph Pennell and his wife in their account of their visit to the Highlands and Islands of Scotland in the eighties. "Mrs. Stowe could write *Uncle Tom's Cabin* on behalf of slaves in the United States," they pointed out.

In Great Britain she saw only the nobility and benevolence of the slave-driver. From the plantations of the South there never arose such a cry of despair and sorrow as that which rang through the glens and straths of Sutherland when men were driven to the sea to make room for sheep. And yet to Mrs. Stowe, this inhuman chase was but a "sublime instance of the benevolent employment of superior wealth and power in shortening the struggle of advancing civilization and elevating in a few years a whole community to a point of education and material prosperity which, unassisted, they might never have attained." You might as well call the slavery of the negroes a sublime instance of the power of traders to shorten the natural course of human development, since if left to themselves, the blacks could not have advanced beyond the savage state in which they were found. I fear the American love for a lord is not exaggerated, if even Mrs. Stowe could be blinded by it."[83]

A far more honest and accurate account of the Highland Clearances was provided by John Mitchell in 1843:

The most oppressive instance that I have heard of, of such ejectments of small tenants as have been mentioned above,was that made by the Duke of Sutherland, in that county of his, at the northern extremity of the kingdom. I will state the facts briefly as they were related to me by a highly intelligent and philanthropic gentleman, who has often visited those injured people. About twenty-eight or thirty years ago, the Duke conceived the plan of turning his estate into large *sheep-farms*. To effect this, it would be necessary to clear off the numerous small tenants. They refused to remove: they denied the *exclusive* claim of the Duke to the country; alleging that it was obtained originally by conquest, in which the people (the ancestors of these tenants) assisted; and that, though the title was vested *nominally* in the chief, the people virtually had a joint title with him. After a year or two of resistance, the debate was terminated in a summary way. Soldiers were employed to effect their removal; and to do the business thoroughly, they fired their dwellings! What became of these poor people then? Retiring from their blackened, roofless dwellings, they went down to the wet and bleak coast, where the larger portion of them still remain—in deep poverty and dejection. A portion of them emigrated to America. One ship-load, after embarking, returned, in consequence of stormy weather and the bad condition of the vessel; and in their discouragement, concluded to remain. Numbers of them occupy small patches of ground about the coast, by the duke's sufferance. A sense of injury embittering their minds is not the least part of their calamity. They had long occupied the homes and farms from which they were driven: their fathers had occupied them. They had considerable possessions, particularly in cattle. They are now poor, and without adequate employment. Many of them can earn but sixpence a day at most; and a whole family, in some instances, can only earn that amount.
I fear God has a controversy with that Duke.[84]

11

British Social Ills

Paupers—evidence of human misery far beyond anything Horace Greeley shuddered over during his brief visit to the Ragged School—were not hard to find in Britain's larger cities in the nineteenth century. And one aspect in particular that much disturbed the visiting Americans was that those ragged, hungry, begging wretches "are our own near kin, and one's heart goes out to them with a pity which Italian beggars rarely call forth."[1]

"The hungry eyes of the beggars as they stared through the windows of the coffee-room at Sheffield, made us hasten from our breakfast to Rodgers' cutlery show-room," wrote Henry Tuckerman in the fifties, unable to bear their wolfish glare.[2] In London itself Gilbert Haven stood on Hungerford Bridge watching the spectacle forty feet below of "men and boys wading in the filthy knee-deep mire, and oft-times almost neck deep, searching for the pennies thrown to them from the bridge. Passers by were casting down the coins which sank into the oozy mud, and enjoying the sight of the fierce contestants who plunged pell mell after them. Many pennies were lost, but enough were found to make the sport sportful in a very melancholic way."[3]

Another traveler taking his breakfast in a poor man's coffeehouse observed by what means some individuals managed to acquire something resembling a meal.

One thin-faced, middle-aged man brought in a salt herring with him, which he gave to the waiter to get roasted, and the roasted salt herring, with a penny's worth of bread and a penny's worth of coffee, formed his breakfast. Another considerably younger and stouter man brought in with him an exceedingly small bit of meat, rather of the bloodiest, stuck on a wooden pin, which he also got roasted by the waiter, and which he supplemented with a penny's worth of coffee and but a halfpenny's worth of bread.[4]

Henry Colman remarked:

Every day I live I thank heaven that I am not a poor man with a family in England. In the midst of the most extraordinary abundance, here are men, women and children dying of starvation; and running alongside of the splendid chariot with its gilded equipages, its silken linings, and its liveried footmen, are poor, forlorn, friendless, almost naked wretches, looking like mere fragments of humanity. Is there any panacea for this evil? I know of no panacea. You must not think, because this misery exists that men's hearts are steeled against it. I do not believe there exists a country fuller than this of kind hearts or of charitable establishments for the relief of the distressed. A great

"Houseless and Hungry" depicted for Britons themselves the condition of paupers huddling in city streets at night. *The Graphic*, vol. I, December 4, 1869, p. 9. *Courtesy the Library of Congress.*

problem is to be solved, and the heart of humanity is reaching everywhere for its solution. I am often asked if I like England. Yes; very much, very much; but the inhabitants of New England, I fear, very imperfectly appreciate their own blessings.[5]

Colman continued: "Here in the midst of plenty men, women and children are dying of absolute starvation; and when you see these poor, shivering hungry creatures looking into the very window of a cook-shop, redolent with every savory perfume and crowded with viands, cooked and uncooked, of every description to tempt and pamper the Epicurean appetite, you are amazed that a thin, transparent pane of glass keeps them back from actual onslaught."[6]

Journalist George Wilkes, in London for the Great Exhibition, looked around until he found exactly what he wanted for a chapter entitled "London—Its Dens of Crime and Misery." He found it in a public lodging house. They came to a side door, he wrote,

which let us into an apartment some sixteen feet square, and about ten feet high. All was dark when we entered, but our lantern lit up such a sight as I had never seen before, and such a one as I pray God I may never see again. In that contracted lair laid thirty human beings, men, women, and children; yes, thirty white Christians of a Christian land, packed head and feet in layers, like the black cargo of a slave-ship under chase. . . . Some were families, some were man and wife, some were single lodgers at a penny a head. Some wore a few scanty patches, others were partly covered by a sheet, but many were thread-less and indifferent to exposure.[7]

"In the centre of the room," continued Wilkes,

stood a large tub or reservoir, which the comity of the apartment permitted to be used by two or three at once; and in the muck and gloom, and stench and vermin of that place, these larvae of a stifled and rotten *civilization,* crawled and groveled and profaned the rites of nature; and what seems most strange of all, bred souls for immortality. I deal with a repulsive subject, but surgery cannot be fastidious, and I dwell upon the features of this den, because it exists almost within a stone's throw from the palaces of nobles, and under the noses of the snuffling hypocrites of Exeter Hall, whose mock philanthropy com-missions emissaries to excite our slaves to insurrection, and who plunder well-meaning poverty to provide blankets and bibles for the happier heathen.[8]

Hawthorne seems actually to have gazed at slum dwellers not as cases or curiosities but simply as people. He noted dirty, gray-faced children whose only acquaintance with water appeared to be "the nearest mud-puddle"; and women with "wrinkled yellow faces, tanned and blear-eyed with the smoke"; and hopeless, dull-eyed men, some too drunk to stand. He recalled, he said, "the feeling with which, when a boy, I used to turn over a plank or an old log that had lain long on the damp ground, and found a vivacious multitude of unclean and devilish-looking insects." What touched him was the apparent resignation with which they accepted and bore their lot. "Forlorn, ragged, care-worn, hopeless, dirty, haggard, hungry, as they were, the most pitiful thing of all was the sort of patience with which they accepted their lot, as if they had been born into the world for that and nothing else. Even the little children had this characteristic in as perfect development as their grandmothers." He was concerned for the children, for in them he saw "the ill-omened blossoms from which another harvest of precisely such dark fruitage as I saw ripened around me was to be produced." And yet here and there he observed examples of "a courtesy and deference among these ragged folks, which having seen it, I did not thoroughly believe in, wondering whence it should have come," and . . . "sometimes again, I saw, with surprise and a sense as if I had been asleep and dreaming, the bright, intelligent, merry face of a child whose dark eyes gleamed with vivacious expression through the dirt that encrusted its skin, like sunshine struggling through a very dusty window-pane."[9]

There are many references, possibly tinged with romanticism but appealing nevertheless, to the indomitable spirit of the Londoners, especially the young, taking their pleasures where they could. There are numerous references to poor children romping in the Green Park, as well as playing and dancing in the wet and dingy streets. Stephen Massett, himself a London boy until his emigration to America in 1837, observed how boys swarmed wherever there is a sight, or an accident, or a water-cock turned on. They delight in everything dangerous. You may see them running their hardest along a parapet, or climbing over the spiked railings of the park. Keen sportsmen, they wander with an old tin shaving-pot, or a short stick, thread and hook, to enjoy a day's fishing for stickle-backs in the Hampstead ponds. They are the mortal enemies of butterflies and cockroaches. . . . Sent to fetch the beer, when other and more fortunate children are laughing gaily upon painted rocking horses—taught to look sharply upon the world, to see that they get good weight and full pints; cuffed for every fault, and rewarded for any service by permission to play about the streets—they are as wild as the offspring of the woods.[10]

Despite laws against begging, beggars were much in evidence in the larger cities and especially in London. Whether these were professionals, as some chose to believe, or people truly in want, it was often hard to tell. "One pleasant afternoon as I was strolling up Ludgate Hill," wrote Joel Headley in the forties, "I saw a sight I shall never forget; it arrested even the Londoners, accustomed as they are to all kinds of misery." What caught his eye were two children, about eight and six, who seemed

to have just been taken from some damp, dark cellar, where they had been for months deprived of light and almost of sustenance. Their clothes were in rags, black, damp, and ready to drop from their crouching bodies; their cheeks were perfectly colorless . . . and the little boy was evidently dying. How they came there, no one could tell; but there sat the sister . . . to whom someone had given a morsel of bread . . . crowding the food into his mouth. . . . The spectators . . . rained money into her lap; but she did not even deign to pick it up or thank them, but with her pale face bent in the deepest anxiety on her brother, kept forcing the bread into this mouth.[11]

William Cullen Bryant was similarly stunned one day in 1845, in Oxford Street, when "an elderly man of small stature, poorly dressed, with a mahogany complexion," said as he passed him, " 'I am starving to death with hunger.' These words and that voice sounded in my ear all day."[12] Cynical Alonzo Tripp, in the same period, devoted a section of his book to "Beggars in London," claiming that "the English authorities give it as nine to one—that is, out of every ten beggars, nine are mendicants or professional beggars that pursue the calling as a regular branch of business. I am inclined to think, however, that the statement is exaggerated, unless it be meant to include only street beggars; for many of the real cases of indigence are hidden from view."[13]

They were not hidden from the view of Britons themselves, it must be noted here, for the evils of pauperism were widely reported on and depicted in the British press, and there is no description of human misery in an American traveler's book that cannot be illustrated from the pages of the *Illustrated London News* and *The Graphic* of the period. More than a few Americans, moreover, had read, and refer to in their own books, that famous "diagnosis of London street life," as Henry Tuckerman called it, Mayhew's *London Labour and the London Poor.*[14]

Portrayals of London's open vice market required a kind of field work on the part of these professional puritans that both titillated and shocked them at the same time. It beat anything they had ever seen in wicked New York, they

"**The Haymarket, from twilight to daylight, swarms with these miserable angels of darkness,**" wrote Hiram Fuller of these London prostitutes. Drawing from Henry Mayhew's *London Labour and London Poor, 1861-1862. Courtesy the Library of Congress.*

claimed, and perhaps it did. Hiram Fuller, editor of the *New York Mirror,* informed his readers in 1859 that London had eighty thousand "women of the town," and he expressed his belief that in these "victims of sin and society . . . there is more real suffering in London in one week than in all the United States in a year. And yet, the sham philanthropy of Exeter Hall pours out its perpetual torrent of lachrymose sympathy for the imaginary woes of fictitious 'Topsys' and fugitive 'Uncle Toms' while this awful array of wronged and wretched women is parading nightly before its doors!"[15]

Attributing the women's choice of career primarily to poverty and lack of other employment, Fuller went on to describe the phenomenon.

The "Haymarket," from twilight to daylight, swarms with these miserable angels of darkness, in all conditions of attire, from the gaudiest satins to the wretchedest of rags; assuming every variety of manner, from the most bashful sentimentalism to the most brazen obscenity; and in all stages of tipsiness. . . . They will beg, weep, entreat, implore for money, or a drink, in every possible tone of seduction, and with the promise of every conceivable blessing in return. Failing to extort either, they will pray for the privilege of walking a block with you to tell you how they dare not, cannot, go home without money, to pay their daily or weekly rent. Ah, what terrible tales they relate; what awful tragedies they play, themselves being the heroines. In the gaudy glare of the "Argyle Rooms," or at the more aristocratic "Mott's," one sees these poor *Traviatas* of real life in both the earlier and later scenes of the fatal drama. Here is the spring chicken of fifteen, with a look of innocence still lingering about her—the faint blush of retreating virtue; and here, too, the carefully rouged cheek of the courtesan of forty, with death in her eye and contamination in her touch. It is altogether a sad exhibition; the most melancholy spectacle the world can show. . . . The evil cannot be eradicated in the present condition of society. *It must be recognized and regulated.* It is no use to legislate or preach against the enormous sin of prostitution. . . . In the meantime, let me remind the noisy negro sympathizers of "Exeter Hall" that these eighty thousand white female slaves of Poverty and Passion in London must and will live; while the vengeance due for all their wrongs will yet appear in the shape of some terrible Nemesis that will shake the social organism of the city to its centre.[16]

Other American male visitors reported on the same scene but less polemically. Herman Melville recorded that he experienced "a singular interview there for a moment one evening in 1849."[17] A young Southerner wrote that "the collection of loose women is absolutely wonderful. Some of the most beautiful women in the world with a large amount of decency for that class . . . [through] every grade to the lowest and most depraved of womankind, it presents a remarkable phase of London life."[18] Dr. Sinclair Tousey observed that some of the streets were "alive with unfortunate women whose importunities were not limited to words, but strong hands would be laid on the male traveler, and very urgent physical efforts made to force him along. This class of persons were more numerous, and more decided in plying their trade, than I ever saw elsewhere."[19] Crowed young Theodore Witmer, out on his *Wild Oats Sown Abroad* adventures, "Talk of the Turks and their slave market! Such eyes! complexion! hair! as I have seen offered for sale."[20]

Along with all the other social sins of Britain concentrated on during these years, Americans still hammered at the class system and sought for fresh metaphors or analogies to illustrate it to their readers. Just as William Austin in the century's first decade had seen the "caste" concept manifested in the ways of knocking on London's front doors, now Dr. Andrew McFarland, superintendent of the New Hampshire Asylum for the Insane, perceived manifestations of "caste" in 1850 in the behavior and treatment of English lunatics. "The difference between an American and an English lunatic strikes you immediately on entering any gallery of one of their institutions," observed McFarland.

Instead of the uproarious demeanor and impertinent address of the former, the Englishman of the lower class, sane or insane, never loses sight of the distinctions that birth, fortune and office establish between man and man. He always remembers that he was born to serve and to obey, and he must be far demented to violate a principle so strongly inherent. The medical officers walk through the wards with their hats on; and when, in obedience to a custom which I always practised and inculcated, I was about to remove my own, I was politely checked, and informed that such was the usage in Asylums in England, save those peopled by the upper and middling classes.[21]

Acknowledging his countrymen's unceasing rant against the British class system, or "caste," as they usually referred to it, Henry Field reminded Americans that, while Britons might worship noble birth, "is it much more honorable in us to make a god of money? ... We need to look well to it that we do not, in banishing a hereditary nobility ... supply in its place a more vulgar aristocracy."[22]

Americans still assumed that Britain's system of criminal justice had something to do with its civil order, and they were always ready to observe it in action. On November 13, 1849, young Melville trotted across Hungerford Bridge to watch a public execution, or, as he put it, "the last of the Mannings," a couple convicted of murdering a man under their own roof. "Paid half a crown each for a stand on a roof of a house adjoining," wrote Melville. "An inimitable crowd in all the streets. Police by hundreds. Men & women fainting. The man & wife were hung side by side—still unreconciled to each other. What a change from the time when they stood up to be married, together! The mob was brutish. All in all, a most wonderful, horrible & unspeakable scene."[23] Dean Dudley, another American present at the same event, recalled that there was "swearing, low jesting, fighting, hurrahing, fainting, laughing, crying, gambling, thieving, and, I hear, three persons were *pressed to death* by the crowd."[24]

A decade later, Stephen Massett was present at the hanging on April 26, 1858, of a young Italian, Giovani Lani, who was convicted of the murder of one of the women of the Haymarket. "We, the night before, took a cab to Newgate Street, and at the small tavern immediately opposite the jail, on the second floor, we secured two 'chairs,' " he wrote.

At the early hour of four ... even then, the streets were filled with people, and at the door-steps of the houses were seated, men, women, and even children, some eating and drinking, having passed the night in the open air, to be in readiness for the event. As daylight appeared, the excitement in the street below became more intense, and at about half-past seven, one mass of human beings jammed together so tightly that ingress or egress seemed impossible, swaying to and fro like the heaving of the sea, whilst the hubbub, noise, and din of voices ... resembled its roaring.[25]

Massett continued:

As the first stroke of the big clock of old St. Sepulchre's church fell upon the ear, announcing the hour of eight, it seemed to act like an electric shock upon the multitude: the sight beggars description: the roofs of the houses swarmed with human beings in the distance; from the railings of St. Sepulchre to the corner of Newgate, and Fleet Street, it was one moving mass of humanity; and from this teemful and excited mob, there rose a yell so demoniacal and appalling that the lookers-on from the windows seemed to shrink from the hearing of it, while the clock below was pealing its slow and solemn dirge—and the last note—the hour of eight had died upon the ear ... suddenly the head of the culprit appeared upon the black platform, accompanied by the Sheriffs of London, the clergyman, and Calcraft, the executioner, the yelling, tearing, and shouting ceased, and saving . . . a few cries of "hats off'—"that's him" and the like, all was comparatively still. The preliminaries over—the rope was placed around his neck, the black cap put upon his head, covering his face—the rope was cut—and the body dangled in the air—then ere the spirit had fled, arose the shoutings, hootings, and yellings of a thousand voices, some crying out, "Ere's the last speech and confession of Giovani Lani, hung just now, on'y a a'penny." In half an hour the crowd had dispersed.[26]

Prison reform was very much the vogue in these years, and, just as Dickens had done in America, Americans now wanted glimpses inside British penal institutions. In 1843, in London on their honeymoon trip, Julia Ward Howe and her husband were conducted by Charles Dickens himself to "the old prison of Bridewell," there to observe the treadmill in operation. "Every now and then a man would give out," Mrs. Howe observed, "and be allowed to leave. . . . The midday meal of bread and soup was served to the prisoners while we were in attendance. To one or two, as a punishment, for some misdemeanor, bread alone was given. Charles Dickens looked on, and presently said to Dr. Howe, 'My God! If a woman thinks her son may come to this, I don't blame her if she strangles him in infancy.' "[27]

Journalist George Wilkes took himself in 1851 to Pentonville Prison at Islington. Modeled after the Eastern Penitentiary in Philadelphia, involving the principle of silence and separation of the inmates from each other, it was often called "the Model Prison." Wrote Wilkes:

From the center of the building where you enter, five aisles branch off in rays as from the centre of a half circle. In the centre . . . of this fan is placed a keeper, who looks down all the aisles at the same time, from a jutting bow-window erected in the second tier for that purpose. Each tier, of which there are three, and each section, of which there are fifteen, has a special keeper; but the man in the centre overlooks them all. In the cells, which are very clean, and very finely arranged with windows that look out to heaven, instead of upon the gloomy inner passages, as in most of our prisons, the men pursue their regular trades, and perform in solitude the labor which is the penalty of crime.[28]

"An hour a day is allowed each of them for exercise," he continued,

and for this purpose they are taken into the grounds where there are three huge rosettes of brick and mortar, divided into wedge-shaped yards, each with an iron gate, where the prisoner paces or runs up and down, as suits his humor, like a tiger in a show. Each of these rosettes contains twenty yards, and to prevent the possibility of conversation, a keeper in a central tower, a little higher than the radiating walls, watches the motions of his beasts. . . . The prison contains about eight hundred convicts, and sixty may be exercised at a time. They never see one another's faces, and even when, for convenience, in turning them in and out of cells for attendance at chapel, or at school, they proceed in file, they are obliged to keep some ten feet apart, and the cloth in front of their caps is so cut it drops over the face and conceals it to the chin, in the style of a mask. They look through two small round holes cut in the cloth, and even through this can only see the back of the man who goes before. No danger here, therefore, of conspiracy, correspondence or revolt.[29]

Wilkes was impressed by the method of delivering food to each cell by a system of dumbwaiters between the tiers and a system of rails along which buckets of food could be slid down the corridors for delivery at each cell door. Carbonate of soda, to discourage "self-abuse," had replaced such old-fashioned devices as stocks, shower baths and spiked gloves, he observed, and he thought that its use should be introduced into American prisons.[30]

At Millbank prison, Wilkes' sharp reporter's eye caught another feature. "The prison throughout is lit with gas, a jet of which is introduced into every cell. This burns all night in every cell, as well as in the passages, and is kept up, not as an article of luxury, but as a rule of safety to prevent escapes. A man cannot skulk out of a passage that is continually in a glare of light."[31]

The American was much impressed with the fairness shown by a justice at the Bow Street police station who gave out ten days imprisonment to a Guards captain for speeding his horses, lashing a policeman with his whip when stopped, and trying to leave the scene. Back home in America, Wilkes believed, "the oil of influence and wealth" would have gotten such a young man off for a similar offense. "Captain Paulet Henry Somerset," to the contrary, "was consequently taken to the House of Correction, and forced to wear the convict livery, and undergo the prison discipline, and though a hundred and thirty noble families united in an application to Sir C. Grey, the Secretary of the Home Department, for the remission of the sentence, the noble Captain served his time out." Wilkes was amazed, for in New York City, he declared, "poverty . . . is trampled down in an instant" by the law, while "wealth may defy all its power."[32]

In the critical, polemical mood of these pre-Civil War decades, some Yankee visitors gathered evidence of human exploitation among the agricultural workers of Britain and her coal miners as well. Descriptions of Britain's urban paupers were not enough to even the score with the British critics of America. Misery among agricultural workers and factory operatives was sought particularly by propagandists like one Warren Isham, about whom no information can today be found but who produced a polemic called *The Mud Cabin*. Dedicated to "the working men of the United States," what purports to be a study of working conditions in Britain, on careful reading, appears to be a leading example of one of those relentless literary retaliations against British writers on the United States. Isham admits "that but one design pervades the book, viz., to furnish a test by which to estimate the value of the institutions of our own country."[33] The book thus consists of a series of overdrawn odious comparisons. English farm workers, for example, are equated with serfs, and Queen Victoria is charged with being the sovereign of a nation of paupers.[34]

In the same vein, Isham compares "lynch law" in America with the whipping of an apprentice. British police, so much admired by most American visitors, Isham advises, "are, in fact, equivalent to a military band" designed to oppress the people. The custom in Britain of requiring "testimonials" from job applicants indicates the low moral character of the nation. He includes a hymn of praise to

Cromwell, "wonderful man that he was, thus raised above all ordinary weaknesses of humanity!" [35]

In a chapter entitled "The Public Press Used by the Aristocracy to Blind the People in Regard to Our Institutions," Isham once more takes up the cudgel against British charges of Americans' spitting and fast eating that so shamed and annoyed readers in the United States. He is proud, moreover, of having stayed away from art galleries in Britain, which make so large a figure in the diaries of many American tourists—"not because I did not admire them as productions of human genius . . . but I have been thoroughly disgusted with the prostitution of these divine arts in these old countries, to the great work of human oppression . . . they have done more to *degrade* than to elevate and refine." He ends his book with the implication, although it is framed as a question, that British constitutional government, "far from dispensing blessings to the mass of people," is "as effectual an engine to crush them as the most despotic governments of Europe." He concludes that "the character and tendency of *their* institutions is to *produce* the evils of which I have spoken, while the character and tendency of *ours* is to *destroy* the evils with which they taunt us—quite a difference truly! In the one case the evils in question are the spontaneous growth of a vicious system, and in the other, they are but fungeous excrescences, which the healthful development of the system itself will shed off!"[36]

As in the early decades of the century, British coal mines were the objects of considerable American attention. The Reverend Stephen Tyng, having read in the forties "Lord Ashley's [later Shaftesbury] report to the House of Commons, of the appalling oppressions which are allowed and endured in these places," assured himself and his readers that "these histories of cruelty and suffering, practised upon the wives and children of British subjects, under the very eyes of legislators and landowners, put out of all comparative calculation the grievances which are alleged as connected with American slavery." He stayed above ground, however.[37]

It was educator Jacob Abbott, one of the very few Yankee travelers to come right out and acknowledge the sin of American slavery, who actually went down, in 1847, into a British mine and recorded his experience dispassionately. Dressed in miner's garb, "with a leather cap shaped like a bowl," Abbott entered the cage with his guide and waited for the signal to drop. "The sensation was precisely that of falling from a great height. It was down, down, down, until at last all daylight disappeared, and then down, down again in darkness." At the bottom he could see "nothing but a few luminous points, made by lamps and candles, and rows of white teeth and shining eyes, in the midst of black faces grinning here and there. 'Come here a bit,' said my guide, 'and sit ye doon . . . till ye get the sun oot of your eyes.' "[38]

Abbott was shown how to carry a miner's candle mounted in clay, the flame of which was kept from blowing out by the clay and his own hand. The din below astonished him, but it proved to be merely one of the little carts on rails that carried coal. In one section of the mine they came to a place too small for men and horses to do the work.

Their places were taken by boys and Shetland ponies. . . . We could see them very indistinctly on account of the dimness of the light. The little savages had

Coal miners at work. "These men had their frolics and jokes, their forms of etiquette and politeness, their pride . . . all the usual phenomena social life develops in man," an American visitor discovered. *The Graphic*, vol. XVIII, September 28, 1878, p. 309. *Courtesy the Library of Congress.*

no clothing except an apron and a jacket without sleeves. . . . They looked bright and active, and worked away with a hearty good-will. They seemed pleased to show off their ponies and their little trains of cars before us. . . . These boys are paid according to the number of "toobs" [wagons] which they get down from the extreme ends of the drift, where the coal is hewed out from the mine, to the place where the larger men and boys take them with horses. The ponies draw two tubs and the horses ten.[39]

At one point Abbott remarked that all this was new to him as he was a foreigner.

"Ah, indade," responded his guide. "Indade." "Yes, I am from America." He stopped suddenly in his walk turned round and faced me, and said with an accent of the greatest astonishment and pleasure, "*Indade!* from Ameriky! Then it is from Ameriky that ye'll be. Well, Ameriky will be the first-rate country of the world in somebody's day.". . . He continued extremely interested in this topic; made a great many inquiries, and received, perhaps, as much information from me, about the workings of our institutions, as he gave me about the mine. He liked Benjamin Franklin very much. "I have bought his life three or four times," said he, "I lend them and then they don't bring them back again, you know!"

These men, Abbott observed, "had their frolics and jokes, their forms of etiquette and politeness, their pride and love of display; and, in fact, they manifested all the usual phenomena which social life develops in man."[40]

Another American who actually went below with the men, President John Durbin of Dickinson College, also viewed the miners simply as human beings bravely performing dangerous, brutal labor.

We now approached the little companies of pickers on each side of the main avenue. The seams did not average more than four or five feet in thickness; of course the workmen could not stand erect, and we had to approach them in a stooping posture. . . . Their faces, arms and legs, from the knee to the ankle, were bare, but perfectly black, except the eyes and teeth. . . . Under the loose flannel shirt . . . I could see the strongly-developed pectoral muscles, which are unnaturally strengthened by their peculiar work. Their feet were uniformly well defended by yarn socks and heavy, iron-nailed shoes. The men were cheerful, even jovial at their work; and perhaps my sympathies were thrown away. Yet I felt, in looking at their wretched toil, that I would prefer to lay all my boys, while young, in one common grave than consign them to such a living tomb as this. . . . Yet the men seemed cheerful and contented; doubtless they are so. I talked freely with them. . . . An old man acted as a guide for us, and we had much conversation with him. He had been in the mines for thirty-five years, and was at this time overseer of the men employed below. I found that his name was Joseph, and that he was a Wesleyan Methodist. When informed that two of us were Methodist preachers from America, he was greatly pleased, and his old eyes almost lighted up the horrible darkness around. He shook us heartily by the hand, and insisted on making known to us the Wesleyan Methodist, the New Connexion Methodist, and the Primitive Methodist men, as we passed.[41]

A Manchester cotton mill was visited by Baptist minister Daniel C. Eddy at mid-century. The outside he found

Operatives leaving their work at a Manchester cotton mill seemingly healthier and better dressed, in this 1878 picture, than in earlier descriptions. *The Graphic,* vol. VI, October 26, 1872, p. 391. *Courtesy the Library of Congress.*

dingy and dirty, the bricks were of a very poor quality, and . . . begrimed with
smoke and coal dust. The inside was of unfinished brick or stone; the walls,
floors, stairs, all of one or the other of these materials; no woodwork seen
except in the window-frames, the doors, and in the machinery. The floors
were slippery with oil, the walls covered with dust and hung with cobwebs, and
the windows cracked, broken and shattered. The operatives were generally
younger than those employed in the mills in our own country, and would bear
no comparison with that industrious, cheerful, and intelligent class in our own
population. They were very poorly dressed, and very dirty. Many of them
were deformed, and seemed to groan as they moved about, as if in bodily
anguish. On the countenances of some there were the marks of crime and woe,
the contemptuous scowl, and the lewd, wanton smirk. On other countenances
were the deep traces of suffering and wretchedness; care and sorrow had
made youth look haggard and withered like age. The comparison between our
cotton manufactories and those in Manchester is altogether favorable to this
country. . . . The comfort and convenience of the operatives seem not to have
entered the mind of the employer . . . and as you see many of the operatives,
with bare feet and shivering limbs, gliding over the cold stone or brick floor,
you feel justly proud of the more enviable condition of operatives in this
land.[42]

As they pursued their investigations into Britain's social conditions, the
Americans returned ever and again to their contention that American slaves
were better off than British paupers, farm workers, miners, and factory operatives. "I had rather be sold at auction in Alabam' any day," declared journalist
Charles Fairbanks in 1859,

than to take my chance as a denizen of the slums of London, or as a worker in
the coal mines. I have no patience with this telescopic philanthropy of the
English, while there are abuses all around them. . . . It is, perhaps, all very
well, for ambitious orators to make the House of Commons or Exeter Hall
resound with their denunciations of French usurpations, Austrian tyranny,
Neapolitan dungeons, Russian serfdom, and American slavery; but thinking
men, when they note these enthusiastic demonstrations of philanthropy,
cannot help thinking of England's workhouses, the brutalized workers in her
coalmines and factories, and her oppressive and cruel rule in Ireland and in
India; and it strikes them that a country whose eyesight is obstructed by a
beam of such extraordinary magnitude, should be so solicitous about the
motes that dance in the vision of its neighbours.[43]

Jacob Abbott tried, as did many Americans, to explain to British listeners the
American federal system, which permitted the states to assume "all responsibility
for the local law of slavery," but, unlike the others, he pointed out that "this
would be a good and valid ground of defense" except for one major weakness.
"So long as the government retains the institution of slavery in the District of
Columbia, the government itself is a slaveholder, and all its constituents must
bear their share of the responsibility." Then he went further.

We may admit that slavery is morally wrong, and declare that we personally
would have it abolished in all the national dominions if we could . . . or we may
maintain that it is in itself a political evil, which cannot be eradicated without
bringing greater evils in its stead, and thus defend its present continuance; or

we may contend that in the case of a superior and inferior race, inhabiting the same country, and distinguished by strongly marked physical peculiarities, it is the right and proper relation to exist between them; but we cannot with propriety claim that we of the north have nothing to do with the question. To acknowledge that our national slavery is wrong, is candid. To maintain that it is right, is at least open and manly; but to deny our own concern with it, is an unworthy attempt to evade a responsibility to which the world at large justly hold us, and which we ought to acknowledge.[44]

Another one of these American visitors was able, like Abbott, to face the slavery issue squarely. "It is very humiliating indeed," observed George Fisher in 1857, "to have it [slavery] thrown into our teeth." But "we could not defend our country in this respect as we desired to, and could but confess that it was a system of unmitigated shame, cruelty, and barbarism, unworthy the age; despicable, beyond defense or justification. . . . We found that if we do not realize our position at home, we certainly do when we go abroad. . . . How," asked Fisher, "can we at this day and age of the world, excuse or justify American slavery, though it were formerly a colonial legacy from our British forefathers? We cannot; and it is a shame and disgrace that it still remains. . . . When every slave is unshackled and permitted to go free . . . then no great reproach will remain against any portion of our country, people or government; but we shall be more united at home and more respected abroad."[45]

History and time were, of course, bringing the Americans ever closer to the day when all such questions would at last have to be answered on the battlefields of the Civil War. Until then, the warning sounded by Benjamin Silliman back in 1805, as he inspected the depths of that slave ship docked at Liverpool, hung in the air! "There will be a day when these things shall be told in heaven!"[46]

Ireland, which the American travelers either "did" upon arrival in the Old World, or "picked up" before leaving it, was quite a different place in the early decades of the nineteenth century from what it was to become in the years of "the Hunger." Always, the inhabitants were poor, but what would change so astonishingly were their numbers. Ensconced in a jaunting cart, making his way from Cobh to Cork in 1825, Nathaniel Carter diverted his eyes from the gentle green countryside to the large numbers of human beings, "swarms" of them, in fact, all along the road, "passing both ways in troops. . .some on horseback, frequently riding double; women and girls with arms full of children, and crowds of a larger growth were seen at the door of every cottage." He took careful note of "the extreme meanness of their dress. . .tatters and rags. . .with bare heads and bare feet," but also their air "of extreme health, and in most cases, cheerfulness." The country, declared Carter, "is populous almost beyond what an American who has never seen it can imagine. It literally swarms with inhabitants. . .eight millions are crowded upon an Island three hundred miles long, and of an average breadth not exceeding 130."[47]

Visitors in this same period found Dublin an elegant city. "It resembles Philadelphia in two respects," decided Orville Dewey, "with its regular ranges of buildings and its fine, open squares." Like other Americans armed with the proper letters of introduction, he was entertained by the literati, one of them being the poet Mrs. Hemans, with whom he attended services at St. Patrick's Cathedral. His eye told him that there was plenty of human misery in this beautiful city, however, even apart from the professional beggars—one of whom he observed carrying a candle at night, the better to illuminate the face of the sleeping child she carried.[48]

Heading north to Belfast, Dewey discovered appalling misery en route at Drogheda, "decrepitude, disease, beggary, rags, presenting themselves everywhere in frightful masses." Along the road were cottages "with little light, nasty as pigstyes with ragged women and children about the door, and often the men lying down by their hovels, in laziness, filth and rags, with a horrible vile puddle always before the door."[49] Most of these Yankee travelers, especially the Protestant clergymen, were quick to blame the Catholic church for all of Ireland's misery. Even layman Andrew Bigelow had hit this note in 1819, writing that, "whatever may be the grievances under which the poorer classes in this country have for a long period laboured," they are "distinctly traceable to Catholic instigation. . . .They have uniformly resisted the most judicious schemes for the amelioration and improvement of their condition. . .simply on the ground of their protestant origin."[50] The Reverend Wilbur Fisk, ever on the outlook for signs of "popery," in the thirties attributed "the full and abundant harvest of degradation and want" directly to the Church. With respect to Britain's role in this sociopolitical drama, he said that it reminded him of "a man struggling with a cur—who wishes himself well out of the scrape but he dare not now relinquish his grip upon the dog's throat, lest, as soon as he is at liberty, he should turn and bite him."[51]

Agriculturist Henry Colman, touring Ireland in August, 1844, observed families subsisting only on "potatoes and milk, generally sour milk, for three hundred and sixty-four days out of the three hundred and sixty-five, yet they are on the whole an agreeable people, full of life and humor, of brilliant imagination, and dealing a good deal in fiction; ready to serve you with anything they have; grateful to an excess for any kindness, and making no whining nor complaints. The women," he added, "if they had the advantages of dress, would be uncommonly beautiful." He was also much impressed by a schoolboy, son of a Killarney shoemaker, "living only upon potatoes and milk, [who] bore a good examination in the Latin and Greek grammars and recited well in Virgil and the Greek Testament."[52]

Out in the countryside, Colman entered several cabins "dug out of the bog, with no walls but the peat in which they had been excavated, with the roof covered with turf and straw. . .without chimney, window, door, floor, bed, chair, table, knife, or fork; the whole furniture consisting of some straw to lay down upon, a pot to boil the potatoes in, a tin cup to drink out of, and a wicker basket to take up the potatoes in after they are boiled. . . .[They] eat their food with their fingers, sometimes with salt, and often without."[53]

In another cabin Colman spoke with "a beautiful little girl about fourteen, of sweet address and manners, with nothing on but a rag covering the upper part of her person, and a piece of flannel reaching not quite down to the knees, for a petticoat; and she told us she had no other clothes." She was caring for the family's three other children, "almost naked," while their parents cut peats for the fire "made upon the floor." And yet, wrote Henry Colman, "I never saw a more beautiful country. . .nor met with a more hospitable, generous, witty people."[54]

A year later Colman was writing home from London, about Ireland, that "the state of the crops is something quite alarming. The potato disease is much more extensive than at first was apprehended. . . .What is to become of the poor Irish without potatoes, Heaven only knows. Many are always on the borders of starvation for a great portion of the year, and the failure of the potato crop will finish them."[55]

"But, soberly," continued Colman, "when one travels in Ireland and witnesses the condition of millions of those naked, degraded, miserable beings, one is compelled to ask, what is the value of life to them?" The Irish, he concluded, "have been very harshly used, and their grievances are real and deeply aggravated."[56] Fanny Hall, visiting Ireland in 1836 had demanded, "I should like to be informed in what respect the condition of the Irish peasant is superior to that of our African slaves for whom the English profess so much sympathy!"[57]

Ireland at mid-century, devastated and depopulated by "the Hunger", which agriculturist Colman had foreseen, was not a place much visited by Americans. Black abolitionist William Wells Brown reached Dublin in 1849 and was appalled to see people fighting over "rotten fruit, cabbage stalks, and even the very trimmings of vegetables" near an open-air market.[58] Out in the desolate countryside, Andrew Dickinson sickened as he watched "half-starved tatterdemalions, with no covering but a few ancient rags dangling from knees to elbows," trying to run after and keep up with his train, "yelling cries for a pitiful brass farthing or two. . .but they were outdistanced. Poor fellows! Their voices are annihilated. We hear and see them no more."[59]

What drove so many Irish to America, "the Hunger", was seen and described at first hand in 1845 by a Quaker relief worker, Asenath Nicholson, who tried to relieve suffering and also to report to the outside world what she discovered there in order to stimulate more aid from "kind English or blessed Quakers." There were three stages to starvation, she quickly perceived, "and reader if you have never seen a starving human being, *may you never!*" At first, the sufferer is "somewhat clamorous," she noted. He begs, he calls attention to his plight, he tries to help himself. This is followed by a second stage characterized by "a patient, passive stupidity." The third and final stage, she noted, resembles "idiocy." In this stage, observed Mrs. Nicholson, "the head bends forward, and they walk with long strides, and pass you unheedingly." No more clamor, no more begging, and not even the vacant stare.[60]

Mrs. Nicholson tried to explain the initial resistance of the Irish to the yellow corn meal sent in to aid them—"the yaller," they called it—and at first they would have none of it. Some actually believed that "the Inglish intinded to kill them. . .with the tarin' and the scrapin'." They did not know how to properly prepare it, and indeed it apparently did tear and scrape the innards of someone already starving. " 'And have ye seen the yaller Indian, God save us awl?. . .Peel's brimstone has come over. . .to scrape the maw of ivery divil on us!' " This sort of

"Reader, if you have never seen a starving human, may you *never*," wrote the American Quaker, Asenath Nicholson, trying to help out during the Irish famine of the forties. *Illustrated London News*, December 22, 1849, p. 404. *Courtesy the Library of Congress.*

remark was heard often by Mrs. Nicholson, but, as their hunger progressed and their fear subsided, she noticed that "they cared neither what they ate or who sent it to them."[61]

Mrs. Nicholson lists the facts and figures of the hundreds of thousands of pounds in relief funds sent by both Britons and Americans, but what stays in the reader's mind is the image of her helping a father, too weak to do it himself, to dig a grave for his fifteen-year-old son. "I untied the cord, took the corpse from the father's back, and with the spade, as well as I could, made a grave and put in the boy." She described whole families so far gone that they could not stand to greet her as she entered their cabin, "crawling on all fours towards us, and trying to give some token of welcome. . .that heart-felt greeting they give to the stranger." She told of poor creatures found lying dead in front of undisturbed shop windows stacked with bread. Worst of all, she could not forget the little boy to whom she handed a biscuit. "And a thousand times since have I wished that it had been thrown into the sea; it could not save him: he took it between his bony hands, clasped it tight, and half bent as he was, lifted them up and looked with his glaring eyes upon me." And then, she said, he tried to smile.[62]

"God is slandered," wrote Mrs. Nicholson of the Irish famine, "where it is called an unavoidable dispensation of His wise providence to which we should all humbly bow, as a chastisement which could not be avoided." The Quaker lady's anger is there, hot on the page, even after 135 years.[63]

"Indeed, Ireland would empty herself upon us at once were the Great Ferry narrowed to a strait," observed John Mitchell of the ever-increasing emigration he was witnessing in 1844. "Their poverty is our protection." He described the despair of a young man hopelessly trying to raise the three pounds for his passage by trying to sell copies of last year's almanac. "Poor fellow, he was at that moment hungry for want of a pennyworth of bread." Mitchell was appalled by those who had sunk to beggary, swarms of paupers, "looking like animated bundles of rags. . .besieging and moving with you. . .like swarms of flies." English and Scottish beggars approached the traveler with "rueful" countenances, Mitchell observed, "but the Irish beggar accosts you with frankness and good humor. Not even begging itself subdues their native disposition to wit and merriment. Tell them you have not a penny about you, they 'will not object to a shilling.' "[64]

With some of the same prescience as had Silliman concerning slavery, Hawthorne at mid-century questioned the socioeconomic system of Britain, which he thought offered so much to a few and so little to so many. "One day or another, safe as they deem themselves, and safe as the hereditary temper of the people really tends to make them, the gentlemen of England will be compelled to face this question."[65] Overt protests against this system did not go unnoticed by Americans visiting in England in the 1840s and 1850s any more than did the public demonstrations at the time of the Reform Bill back in the thirties. The so-called "hungry forties," or decade of revolution in Europe, manifested itself in Britain in the Chartist movement and demonstrations that came to a head in 1848.

Ralph Waldo Emerson, in London on March 9 of that year, attended a Chartist meeting at National Hall in Holborn, where he heard the report of

The Departure of the Emigrants' Ship.

The emigrants at dinner amid-ships.

"Ireland would empty herself on us at once were the Great Ferry narrowed to a strait," observed John Mitchell. *Illustrated London News*, April 13, 1844, p. 229; July 6, 1850, p. 190. *From the author's collection.*

the Deputation who had returned after carrying congratulations to the French Republic. The *Marseillaise* was sung by a party of men and women on the platform, and chorused by the whole assembly. . . . The leaders appeared to be grave men, intent on keeping a character for order and moral tone . . . but the great body of the meeting liked best the sentiment, "Every man a ballot, and every man a musket!" Much was whispered of the soldiers,—that "they would catch it," i.e., the contagion of Chartism and rebellion.[66]

Mrs. George Bancroft, wife of the American minister in London at this time, actually went for an early morning carriage drive with her husband on April 10, "the day of the 'Great Chartist Meeting,' which has terrified all London to the last degree. The city and town is at this moment stiller than I have ever known it," she wrote in her journal. "Nothing is to be seen but a special constable (every gentleman in London is sworn into that office), occasionally some on foot, some on horseback, scouring the streets. . . . The Queen left town on Saturday for the Isle of Wight, as she had so lately been confined [by the birth of Princess Louise, March 18, 1848] it was feared her health might suffer from any agitation. . . . There is not the slightest danger of revolution in England," declared Mrs. Bancroft. "The upper middle-class, which on the continent, is entirely with the people, the professional and mercantile class, is here entirely conservative, and without that class no great changes can ever be made."[67]

Ensconced at Morley's Hotel in Trafalgar Square, American Maunsell B. Field was sworn in along with some twenty Yankee friends, he wrote, as special constables, each provided with "a formidable club . . . as ready as any of Her Majesty's loyal subjects to do battle in defense of law and order." His friend, Kendall, overcome by curiosity on the eve of the ninth, strolled off down Whitehall to the head of Westminster Bridge "where cannon were planted to rake the insurgents who were expected to come over on the morrow from their camping ground on Kennington Common. . . . Here he was pounced upon in short order . . . and only liberated next day upon establishing his identity and his harmlessness." The next day Field, along with all of London, awaited the expected march of the Chartists into Trafalgar Square. "About eleven o'clock, I noticed unusual indications of preparation among the police," wrote Field, "and shortly afterward a dense mass, composed of the lowest class of the populace, came straggling up Parliament Street and began to pour in upon the open area . . . singing and shouting, and seemed more impelled by the love of frolic than by anything more serious. In a moment about a dozen policemen charged at a full gallop, and the mob, by some remarkable power of elastic self-compression, instantly made way for them, laughing and hurrahing as they did so. . . . The Chartists themselves," Field reported, "did not attempt to cross the river, overawed, probably, by the reception which they knew was prepared for them." French revolutionary agents roamed London at this moment, Field claimed, and were treated "by the populace with anything but . . . consideration. I saw one unfortunate apostle of liberty, equality and fraternity so severely ducked in the basin of one of the fountains of Trafalgar Square, that I was afraid the poor Gaul was taking his last (and perhaps his first) bath."[68]

"The rest of the day," recalled Field, "was a sort of carnival. No one attempted . . . any business, and the shops remained closed. Fun was universal, and the special constables . . . paraded the streets with the consciousness that their valor had not been very severely tried. That evening the monster petition was rolled upon a barrow into the House of Commons and duly presented, by its godfather, Fergus [Feargus] O'Connor. The next day I happened to be at the railway station as Fergus was leaving the city."[69]

"The day of the Chartists passed off with most ridiculous quiet, and the government is stronger than ever," wrote Mrs. Bancroft, on April 14.[70] "One or two evenings afterwards, the Court having returned to Buckingham Palace," recalled Field,

> the Queen went in state to the opera. I took especial pains to be there, for I expected an extraordinary exhibition of loyalty. . . . Her Majesty entered while the orchestra was playing the overture [*Don Giovanni*]. In a moment the entire audience arose and cried with one voice for "God Save the Queen." The orchestra ceased playing, the prompter's bell tinkled, the curtain was drawn up and displayed all the principal artists ranged in a semi-circle upon the stage. . . . Grisi advanced to the footlights . . . sang the first verse, the whole house standing, Her Majesty included. The chorus was taken up by other singers, and by the entire pit. . . . I never saw such a scene of wild enthusiasm. It was so contagious that I am confident the Queen had no more loyal subject there that evening than myself. The boxes entirely forgot their usual frigid propriety, and marchionesses and countesses vied with each other in clapping their hands and waving their handkerchiefs.[71]

Mrs. Bancroft observed similar enthusiasm the night the Queen came to hear Jenny Lind sing. "Loyalty is very novel and pleasant to witness, to us who have never known it," she wrote.[72]

"The English are a staid, calculating, reflecting people," Henry Colman wrote home to Salem, Massachusetts, after viewing the Chartist disorders, which he considered "greatly exaggerated" in the press, "and do not act without deliberation . . . are strongly attached to their institutions . . . conservative in the highest degree. . . . All hopes of reform," he concluded, "are extinguished for at least the next quarter of a century."[73]

Arriving on the London scene a few months after the Chartist excitement, Caroline Kirkland found the city still

> full of fun about the 200,000 "special constables" who were sworn in on the occasion of the late anticipated attempt of that terrible British bugbear, the Chartists. The shop-window caricatures, the penny ballads, the minor theatrical pieces, and the spontaneous fun, generally, all turn upon this demonstration of alarm on the part of the government and the property holders. The alarmists still insist that, but for the protecting shadow of these two hundred thousand extempore heroes, all sober people would have been first murdered and then burnt in their beds, by a few half-starved weavers, whose grievances alone make them formidable; but the middle classes generally treat the idea with derision, and consider the smallness of the dreaded meeting a manifestation of the weakness of those who might have wished to disturb the peace.[74]

If Britain's day of reckoning was not yet at hand, that of the United States drew ever closer. Three years before the famous incident involving John Brown at Harper's Ferry in 1859, British historian Thomas Macaulay shocked Maunsell

Field with his prophecy that "slavery was certain to break up our Government within ten years from that time, and that in the no very distant future two divided confederacies would . . . drop into half a dozen broken states, with military despotisms ruling over them. This was an extraordinary prediction to an American ear in 1856," observed Field. "At that time none of us thought of the possibility of an impending crisis. Slavery brought us to a civil war, within less than the limit of Macaulay's prophecy. . . . I tried to persuade him to reduce what he had said to writing, and permit it to be read before the New York Historical Society; but he declined, excusing himself on account of his overwhelming engagements."[75]

Like a moment of calm in these two decades before Britain plunged into the Crimean War in 1854 and the Americans into their Civil War in 1861 stood the Great Exhibition of the Works of Industry of All Nations, held in London in 1851, the year Thomas Hardy aptly called "a precipice in time."[76]

12

Great Exhibition of 1851

"Was there ever anything like it?" wondered William Drew, commissioner of the state of Maine to the Great Exhibition of 1851 at the end of his first day's visit to the now legendary Crystal Palace. "Never," he assured his readers in the first of his dispatches home concerning the "Great Exhibition of the Works of Industry of All Nations," as it was officially known. "It is indeed the world daguerre-otyped," wrote Drew. "We have sat and feasted upon it for hours. Neither we nor others ever saw the like before, and shall never see the like again."[1]

The man from Maine was both accurate and prophetic. Nothing like the Great Exhibition had been seen before, nor has it ever been matched since in impact and excitement. "The first grand, cosmopolitan Olympiad of industry,"[2] as Horace Greeley called it, and in which more than forty nations took part, enjoyed an actual life span of a mere five and a half months between May 1 and October 15, 1851. But it was to live in history as the symbol of western man's confidence, energy, optimism, faith in the future, and belief in the dignity of work at the halfway mark of the nineteenth century.

"London was a miniature world during its continuance," observed Benjamin Moran. "Such a variety of the human family as was then assembled in the British metropolis was probably never before convened in the world's history. . . . It was in truth a congress of the great family of man."[3] Benjamin Silliman, now an elder member of the Yale faculty and a distinguished scientist, returned in the evening of his life to inspect this great brainchild of Prince Albert and of Henry Cole of the Royal Society of Arts. Silliman, too, spoke of the international character of the Exhibition. "Crowds of all nations throng this palace, sometimes 70,000 in a day. As you thread your way through the great masses of human beings that crowd the avenues you may hear half the languages of Europe and some of those of the Orient."[4]

Abolitionist William Wells Brown took time off from his lecturing and writing in Britain to visit the Exhibition and observed not only "Europeans, Asiatics, Americans, and Africans with their numerous subdivisions . . . and even the exclusive Chinese with his hair braided and hanging down his back . . . but also a goodly sprinkling of my own countrymen, I mean colored men and women, well dressed and moving about with their fairer brethren." This sight, Brown noticed, did not sit well with "some of our pro-slavery Americans" present.[5]

Yankees steamed across the Atlantic in large numbers, while others sailed aboard the beautiful clipper *Nightingale,* under Captain Miller, "so favorably known to the Public on both sides of the Atlantic as a noble Navigator and Gentleman," as the advertisements read. Moored at a London dock, the *Nightingale* served both to exemplify American shipbuilding skill as well as a hotel for its passengers during their stay at the Exhibition, which must surely make this trip one of the first tourist "cruises."[6]

"London is full of Americans at present," reported New York journalist George Wilkes, "and I am constantly meeting faces that I have been in the habit of confronting in Broadway, Nassau Street and City Hall."[7] Commissioner Drew checked the visitor's register book at the American department of the Exhibition one midsummer day and found 1,600 names inscribed therein, although, as he pointed out, "not half of our countrymen who visit the Palace call for the book or write their names in it. Running over the list," he concluded, "we notice more from New York and Boston than elsewhere."[8]

The Great Exhibition, before it closed, would have 6,201,856 attenders, resulting in a profit of £186,000 to be used as the genesis of the Victoria and Albert Museum, and other cultural institutions. The impact on London of the throngs of visitors was immense. "Along Fleet Street, the Strand and Piccadilly during the Exhibition," observed Zadock Thompson of Vermont, "there were from eight in the morning till ten at night, two continuous streams of omnibuses and other carriages, one stream running to and the other from the Crystal Palace; and the rattle and thunder of so many heavy carriages caused the very earth to tremble. These carriages succeeded each other so closely that a person was obliged to wait for a considerable time before he could cross . . . the street."[9] Drew observed that "before the summer was far advanced, there was no longer any green grass; footsteps going to the Palace have trod these many acres so constantly all over that the whole surface is as bare and smooth as a hard and level sea beach."[10]

The part played by the police of London—dressed in their blue coats, brass buttons, and glazed hats—not merely in maintaining order but in aiding these hordes of visitors with their many problems is stressed in the American accounts. "They were everywhere on duty," wrote the Reverend Arthur Cleveland Coxe, rector of Baltimore's Grace Church.[11] "You cannot go ten rods without finding a policeman," observed Commissioner Drew, "and when you ask for information on any subject in relation to streets, residences, places of business, public conveyances, or indeed, almost any matter of history, you will find him instantly serving you with a zeal that shows how deep an interest he takes in accommodating you."[12] David Dorr, another black American who made it to the Exhibition, found these London officers "intelligent men who seem to take an interest as well as pride in this great fair."[13]

"Ready eyes to the blind, wits to the stupid, path-finders to the stranger, and great annoyances to anyone disposed to transgress certain fixed rules and

The Crystal Palace housing the Great Exhibition of the Works of Industry of All Nations held in London in the summer of 1851. *Illustrated London News,* **May 3, 1851, p. 366.** *Courtesy the Library of Congress.*

boundaries" is how one grateful American lady described the London constabulary.[14] "The best-looking and most civil and intelligent set of officers I ever met with," declared a gentleman.[15] Youthful traveler Ralph Keeler, who found himself the prey of "all the sharpers in the city," solved his problem by taking the fatherly advice of a London policeman, who told him to replace the obviously American straw hat he was wearing, which made him an easy mark.[16] "So urbane, so ready to do anything for you," enthused another Yankee visitor, "you are almost inclined to lift your hat when you pass one of these London policemen."[17]

Like everyone else in London, the Americans were awestruck by the sheer, shimmering beauty of the Crystal Palace itself. It was designed by Joseph Paxton, whose great conservatory at Chatsworth so many of them had admired, and which they now realized had served as the prototype of the Palace. Words failed many of them but not all, as they gazed for the first time on what appeared to be an enormous greenhouse, on an incredible scale, with its great arched central transept soaring 108 feet in the air, and flanked on either side by immense outstretched wings to an overall length of 1,848 feet, resting on its site on the south side of Hyde Park between and parallel to Kensington Drive and Rotten Row.

"I shall never forget my first glance I got of it through those arching trees that bound the line of way as I entered Hyde Park under the triumphal arch near the Duke of Wellington's mansion, called Apsley House," recalled William Drew. "The wonder of the world," he labeled it, "covering eighteen acres of ground, three stories in height, with an arched roof in the center that embraces huge trees one hundred and eight feet high. It was worth a voyage across the Atlantic to behold."[18]

Architectural historians of the future would agree with young Benjamin Moran, who sensed that the structure itself, erected in only seven months, was "the greatest curiosity connected with the display, sublime in every feature and gorgeous in its grandeur. Harmony was blended in all its proportions and beauty and symmetry in its lines and airy form. It possessed magnitude without the power to weary, and magnificence with simplicity."[19] Even scientist Benjamin Silliman came close to poetry and in fact did borrow from the poet Milton and the Bible. " 'It rose like an exhalation', a magical illusion of the senses. The framework of iron, although strong enough to sustain weight and to resist the winds, is so little apparent to the eye, that the Crystal Palace appears a sea of glass, as in Revelations, 'A sea of glass like unto crystal.' "[20]

At least three visiting Americans perceived religious implications in the Crystal Palace as if it were a great temple dedicated to industry and technology. Brown actually compared it "in some respects to the cathedrals of the country," adding that "it is the greatest building the world ever saw."[21] Moran described "the great arch which sprang like a silver bow aloft, while the symmetrical naves swept softly away into the distance, and left its impress indelibly upon the soul."[22]

Equally entranced by the structure, Horace Greeley concluded that "the Crystal Palace is better than any one thing it contains; it is really a fairy wonder and is a work of inestimable excellence for future architecture. It is not only better adapted to its purpose than any other edifice ever yet built, but it contains remarkable cheapness with vast and varied utility." In the prefabricated cast-iron columns and girders, as well as the mass-produced panes of glass (49" x 10"), the largest available in this period, Greeley perceived implications for construction in the future. "Depend upon it," he wrote, "stone and timber will have to stand back for iron and glass hereafter, to an extent not yet conceiveable. The triumph of Paxton is perfect and heralds a revolution." Castle Garden, of which New Yorkers were so proud, "is but a dog kennel," opined Mr. Greeley.[23]

Conscientious Zadock Thompson gave his readers a detailed report on the specifications of the great glass wonder. "A parallelogram made entirely of glass and iron, the length of the building is 1,848 feet, the width 408 feet," wrote Thompson.

The height of the main building is 76 feet, but nearly midway it is crossed by a transept with a semi-circular roof, made 108 feet high for the purpose of enclosing a group of trees. The main parallelogram is formed, longitudinally into 11 divisions, which are, alternately 24 and 48 feet wide, with the exception of the central walk, or nave, which is 72 feet wide. The entire area of the ground floor is a little over 18 acres. The building is in three lofts, one behind the other, so that the end shows as a pyramid of steps.[24]

Thompson continued:

The columns are of iron, cast hollow, and for the most part stand 24 feet apart each way. The number of columns is stated to be 3,230. The number of cast-iron girders is 2,244 for supporting the galleries and roofs, with 1,128 intermediate bearers, besides 358 wrought-iron trusses. The roof, which consists of glass and iron is thrown into vallies [sic], eight feet across, and running transversely, and these vallies are directed to the heads of the columns so that the water which falls on the various sections of the roof is conveyed immediately into the heads of the hollow columns and through them to the earth beneath. The length of these gutters is 44 miles. There are in the building more than 200 miles of sash bars, and 900,000 square feet of glass.[25]

The forerunner of the Crystal Palace, the conservatory at the great country estate of the Dukes of Devonshire, Chatsworth, was described by agriculturist Henry Colman, who saw it in 1843, as a great glass house covering an acre of ground and "large enough to drive a carriage through." It was, he wrote, "three hundred and eighty-seven feet in length, one hundred and seventeen feet in breadth and sixty-seven feet in height, with 76,000 square feet of glass covering, and seven miles of pipes for water with which to heat it."[26] By 1849 this great greenhouse had developed into the so-called famous "Lily House," sheltering the giant water lily, the *Victoria Regia,* brought to England in 1847 from British Guiana. The famed American landscape architect and builder Andrew Jackson Downing studied the Lily House on his visit in 1850 and described it as "an immense palace of glass" with a "curved roof springing seventy feet high." Just as would the Crystal Palace, it enclosed whole trees, "some of which," Downing observed, "have already nearly reached the glass."[27]

The interior of the Crystal Palace itself, almost twice the breadth of St. Paul's Cathedral and four times its length, evoked an emotional response equal to that aroused by the shimmering beauty of the exterior. "The crystal roof showered a soft daylight over the immense interior," wrote the Reverend Arthur Cleveland Coxe. "The trees and curious plants gave it a cheerful and varied beauty. Musical instruments, constantly playing, bewitched the ear. . .fountains were gurgling and scattering their spray like diamonds and pearls."[28] Several visitors spoke of the freshness of the air and "uniform comfort" of the temperature within the Palace, which Paxton had provided for through multiple louvers in the ground floor wall. The air is as "sweet as it is in the adjacent Park," wrote Drew.[29]

Under the great arch of the transept, the first object to meet the visitor's eye was "the far-famed glass fountain flinging from its five tons of flint glass every hue in the prism in a flood of beauty," according to Ohioan Samuel Cox.[30] "The fluid is projected to a height of some thirty feet," observed Horace Greeley, "falling thence into a succession of regularly enlarging glass basins and finally reaching in streams and sprays the reservoir below. A hundred feet or more on either side stand two stately and graceful trees, entirely included in the building, whose roof of glass rises clear above them, seeming a nearer sky."[31] One

The crystal fountain in the transept of the Crystal Palace, a favorite meeting place for visitors attending the Great Exhibition. *Illustrated London News*, **June 7, 1851, p. 526.** *Courtesy the Library of Congress.*

afternoon, David Dorr watched as two birds "tried to light on a spray of water but could not make it go."[32]

The crystal fountain became the great meeting place at the Exhibition, according to William Wells Brown. "There you may see husbands looking for lost wives, wives looking for stolen husbands, mothers for their lost children, and townspeople for their country friends. Many people make the Crystal Palace their home," he added, "with the exception of the night. I have seen them come in the morning, visit the dressing room, then go to the refreshment room and sit down to breakfast as if at their hotel. Dinner and tea would be taken in turn."[33]

"The building was opened on the first day of May," reported David Bartlett who was present for the Inauguration, as it was called.

The morning was a chilly one, yet very nearly all the avenues leading to Hyde Park were crowded almost to suffocation with masses of enthusiastic people. Business was generally suspended throughout London, and all those parts not contiguous to Hyde Park wore an air of loneliness and desertion. The shops were all shut, few people to be seen, the streets silent—strange sight for London. But the Park itself was one huge sea of human faces all eager to and

Opening of the Great Exhibition—Entrance of Her Majesty and His Royal Highness Prince Albert. *Illustrated London News,* **May 10, 1851, p. 398.** *Courtesy the Library of Congress.*

anxious to get a sight of the Crystal Palace and the Queen who was soon to enter it.[34]

"The holders of the season tickets alone were admitted that day," recalled Bartlett,

and at an early hour they flocked to the doors of the building in such force that a company of Sappers and Miners were called in to enforce order. By half-past eleven o'clock, twenty-five thousand persons had arrived and were seated under the crystal roof; then the doors were closed. The view of these thousands in that wondrous interior was splendid beyond description. The elite of the world was there, the flower of England. Men of rank, intellect, and wealth—renowned on the field and in the workshop. There was the Duke of Wellington—it was his eighty-second birthday. There was the venerable Archbishop of Canterbury, Paxton, the designer of the beautiful structure, in the prime of manhood; there were beautiful women, too, from England, and France, and Russia and America.[35]

There also was the Reverend John Choules, shepherding his little group of

American schoolboys, who described the nasty weather that had plagued London in the week preceding the Exhibition's opening, mentioning that only the day before there had been a hailstorm. But now, on the first day of May, except for a brief shower of rain just before noon, the sun broke through and transformed the Crystal Palace into a "mountain of light." Choules overheard an Englishman remark that "it is the Queen's weather. It is always her luck."[36]

A few moments later, at about a quarter to twelve, another Briton remarked that "she will be to her time; she always is." And he was right, Choules observed,

for scarcely had he prophesied before a prolonged shouting told that the queen was coming. . . . Off went all hats. I wish you could have heard the cheering as she entered the wondrous building. It was like "the voice of many waters". Such a deep, hearty, prolonged shouting I never heard. As Victoria entered, up went the standard of England. This was the signal for the organ to play; the vitreous roof vibrates as the sounds fly along the transparent aisles; and we had musical glasses on a large scale.[37]

Another American present at this scene, Aaron Willington, described the royal procession around the Palace followed by speeches from Victoria, Albert, and the Archbishop of Canterbury. Heading the procession was the Queen,

who led by the hand her eldest son, the Prince of Wales [the future Edward VII], and Prince Albert with "Vicky", the little Princess Royal, then all the members of the Court and high officers of state, the Foreign Ministers, Royal Commissioners and Commissioners from the various countries, the architects, the contractors, etc. As the procession advanced, it was received with loud acclamation, and as it passed, each of the organs poured forth its powerful music, and this was followed by the bands of the Coldstream and Scotch-Fusileer Guards.[38]

"Everywhere . . . the cheering and waving of hats and handkerchiefs went on continuously," recalled Willington, "in which the foreigners present seemed to vie with Her Majesty's most loyal subjects. The Queen," thought Willington, "bore the excitement with her usual firmness and self-possession; but the Prince was evidently anxious, and exhibited considerable emotion when the ceremony was brought to a close which is easily accounted for when we remember that the project is one in which his name and reputation are to be forever hereafter associated."[39]

Characteristically, Horace Greeley pounced on one aspect of this Inauguration not to his liking. He found no fault with Prince Albert, acknowledging that "his labors in promoting the Exhibition began early and have been arduous, persistent and effective. Any Inauguration in which he did not predominantly figure would have done him an injustice."[40] Nor did Greeley knock the Queen herself except to suggest that "her vocation is one rather behind the intelligence of this age and likely to go out of fashion at no distant day." What riled Greeley's republican taste were the members of her court trailing after her, "the descendants of some dozen lucky Norman robbers, none of whom ever contemplated the personal doing of any real work, and any of whom would feel insulted by a report that his father or grandfather invented the Steam Engine or the Spinning Jenny. This," declared Mr. Greeley, "is not the fittest way to honor industry," adding that "the grandfathers of these Dukes and Barons would have deemed themselves as much dishonored by uniting in this Royal ovation to gingham weavers and boiler-makers as these men would be by being compelled to weave the cloth and forge the iron. . . . Patience, impetuous souls!" trumpeted editor Greeley. "The better day dawns, though the morning air is chilly."[41]

A proud moment for Samuel Cox of Ohio occurred when one of the Crystal Palace organs, a monster requiring "four men to blow and three to play," struck up "Yankee Doodle." "My heart beat hot and queer. I felt the Declaration of Independence and a couple of Bunker Hills in my bosom . . . it made the universe tremble!"[42]

In light of all the buoyant opening-day enthusiasm, and the phenomenal success the Exhibition was to enjoy, it is surprising how much skepticism, if not downright hostility, was directed at it during the formative stages. Most scoffers were Britons themselves, notably the eccentric Colonel Sibthorp, member of parliament, who was bitterly opposed to the construction of the Crystal Palace in that region of Hyde Park where the London aristocracy aired themselves and exercised their horses. Bartlett reported that Sibthorp's "hatred of foreigners, too, is intense, and he prophesied all manner of evils as the result of such an incoming of foreigners to see the Great Exhibition. He frequently called on God to strike the crystal building and dash it to pieces: The proper place for such an idiot," opined Bartlett, "is not Parliament but a Lunatic Asylum!"[43]

Visiting in England at the time of the Exhibition's preparation, Arthur Cleveland Coxe took on some of the skepticism of those around him and elected to skip the Inauguration—a decision he later regretted. "I supposed it was a mere toy of Prince Albert's," he confessed.

> I am astonished to remember the indifference of many Englishmen in differ-ent ranks of society, to the entire project until its success was demonstrated. From *The Times,* which was a great grumbler at first, and from old *Blackwood* which railed at the "Temple of Folly", down to the shopkeepers in Regent Street, there was a widespread feeling of contempt for "Prince Albert's Hobby", as likely to cost more than it would come to; while sincere apprehen-sions were entertained that something revolutionary and bloody might be the result of the collection of vast bodies of men, with a large proportion of foreign republicans among them, into the bosom of the Metropolis. How idle all this seems now![44]

With Londoners still remembering the Chartist disturbances of the forties, "riot and murder were the very least of the evil results predicted by some, and our American press," continued Coxe, "had anticipated nothing less than general pillage and insurrection." The only disorder Coxe personally observed on opening day, as he stood in the street to see the Queen pass, having failed to secure tickets for the opening, was considerable "good-natured pushing and thrusting, and the occasional squall of an infant whose mother was more engaged to save her tawdry finery than to secure the safety of her child."[45]

"And so," Coxe concluded, "having frankly confessed my prejudices against the Great Exhibition, I must now frankly own that I am ashamed of them. I was nicely punished for my folly at the outset in losing the pageant of the opening. The whole Exhibition was indeed strongly marked by the spirit of the age," he

"To depicture the furniture—no! no! It cannot be done," wrote Samuel Cox of Ohio, overwhelmed by items like this ornate bedstead. *Illustrated London News*, October 4, 1851, p. 417. *Courtesy the Library of Congress.*

realized, "and was, therefore, such as no one who sees and understands the faults of our own times can enthusiastically admire. Yet little by little," he admitted, "I saw so much in it which illustrates the better elements of that spirit of man, that . . . I rejoice in the complete success of that splendid experiment."[46]

The Reverend Coxe's ambivalence symbolizes our own reaction today—not to Paxton's wondrous palace of crystal, but to the 100,000 artifacts displayed there as the best of their kind. They were, in fact, a glorious mixture of the useful, the beautiful, the useless, and the ugly, and various combinations of these qualities. Certain objects on display seemingly managed to combine all four, such as "Count Dunin's Man of Steel," a robot composed of 7,000 pieces, and for which no particular purpose could be discerned but which nonetheless won a Council Medal.[47]

From our perspective today, the least impressive aspect of the Great Exhibition was the plethora of mass-produced and incredibly ornate articles of furniture and household objets d'art, some of which, to be believed, have to be seen in contemporary depictions in the *Illustrated London News*. Even the ever-ready pen of Samuel Cox, self-styled "Buckeye Abroad," failed when it came to a description of some of these exhibits. "To depicture the furniture, some elaborately carved and gilt; some formed of peculiar woods and arranged in perplexing uniformity and variety; to reproduce papier maché tables and ornaments with their gorgeous hues and dazzling beauties; to write down—no! no! It cannot be done."[48]

Few visitors failed to note such novelties as the "alarm bedstead," which also caught the eye of William Drew of Maine. "See that fellow lying on the bed. Soon the clock strikes; and if in precisely two minutes he does not arise, the head of the bed is thrown up, and he is pitched over the foot without ceremony!" When it came to the "air-exhausted coffin," invented by E. G. Tuckerman of New York, Drew was practical enough to point out that this same technique could be used to preserve "fruit, fish and flesh" as well as corpses.[49]

Most featured in Drew's exhaustive account of the Exhibition were useful, practical items, which, in the long run, received most of the attention and even a number of medals, such as ploughs, clod crushers and seed planters; a "family freezing-machine which will convert water into ice in the hottest weather"; a "self-propelling, portable chair for invalids with vulcanized india-rubber wheels"; sewing machines; screw-cutting machines; an electric telegraph; and an envelope-making machine that turned them out "as fast as a boy can seize and pile them up."[50]

Of the Great Exhibition's four main divisions—Raw Materials, Manufactures, Fine Arts, and Machinery, all displayed in over ten miles of frontage in the Crystal Palace—the Machinery Court proved the great focus of popular interest. There, under the north gallery, flocked visitors from all nations to observe examples of the fast-developing technology so drastically reshaping their lives in this period. "There were cotton mills in full operation," reported Bartlett, "printing presses striking off impressions of newspapers; and all kinds of curious machines requiring steam motive power."[51] This steampower was supplied, Mr. Drew ascertained, "by a huge boiler, underground, that supplied power the whole length of the Palace for all the machinery that is in motion in it. These

The Machinery Court. The public, in their wisdom, turned away from ornate furniture and Paris bonnets to crowd around the demonstrations of the machinery so rapidly changing their lives. *Illustrated London News,* **August 23, 1851, p. 248.** *Courtesy the Library of Congress.*

machinery rooms are a young Birmingham and Manchester under a glass roof," he declared. "This department is always filled with skillful or curious observers."[52]

As might be expected, editor Horace Greeley's attention was caught by "the great cylinder press on which *The Times* is printed. The cylinders revolve horizontally as ours do vertically," he observed, "and though something is gained in security by the British press, more must be lost in speed. Hoe's last has not yet been equalled in this island," he concluded.[53] This comparison of an American with a British model was, of course, the typical Yankee reaction at the Exhibition, for they always saw themselves in competition with others. One of them concluded that this spirit rather characterized the Exhibition as a whole. "This is the place where every country is trying to make a pigmy of some other," declared black American David Dorr.[54]

Greeley finally had to acknowledge the more advanced technology of the British, who made up over half of the 15,000 exhibitors. "I never saw one fourth so much machinery before. I do not expect ever to see so much again. Almost everything a Briton has invented, improved, or patented by way of machinery is here brought together. In Machinery, England has no competitor." But, he added, "I think the American genius quicker, more wide-awake, more fertile than the British. If our manufactures were as extensive and firmly established as the British, we should invent and improve machinery much faster than they do. But I do not wish to deny that this is quite a considerable country."[55]

For the competitive "Jonathans," as the British press often called the Americans, their primary concern was, of course, the American Exhibit in the eastern wing of the Crystal Palace. To early visitors, before the American minister got to work, along with the London-based Yankee financier-philanthropist, George Peabody of Massachusetts, their nation's meager display was a source of acute embarrassment. Randal MacGavock found the huge American eagle "spreading her wings over an immense desert, with only an oasis here and there to relieve the monotony. As my eye ranged round this comparatively unoccupied portion of the building, my ardor was a little cooled, for after making such a large demand for space, we had failed to occupy one third appointed to us. . . . In no one branch of industry is the United States fairly or adequately represented," he complained in the spring.[56]

"The question arises to the inquiring mind," MacGavock continued, "as to the causes of this magnificent failure. The main cause lies at the door of the committee in Washington who rather threw cold water upon the undertaking, and failed to infuse into our people the spirit of rivalry by acquainting them with the extent of the Exhibition." Secondly, the Tennessean went on, "Congress had made no appropriation to assist the exhibitors; and this has tended to strengthen the third cause, the remoteness of our scene of action. What we have is very good," he decided, "but the great difficulty is that we have so little that it makes comparatively no show at all. Powers' Greek Slave attracts more attention than anything else."[57]

"That splendid creation of genius, the Greek Slave, which will immortalize the name of Hiram Powers, is in sculpture, one of the two gems of the Exhibition," concluded the Reverend Choules, another of these early visitors.[58] "Perhaps if I were not from the United States I would say it was 'the gem.'" Commissioner Drew, less inhibited, pronounced the statue "the best specimen of sculpture in the Palace," and indeed, the Greek Slave did win a medal in its class.[59] Zadock Thompson, of course, was particularly proud of this creation of his fellow Vermonter. "Whoever thought, when they saw Hiram Powers playing his boyish gambols on the banks of the Ottaquechee at Woodstock Green, in Windsor County, that in him was that creative power which would one day call forth from the shapeless marble that perfection of grace and form which are exhibited in his Greek Slave? Certainly, I did not," Thompson confessed.[60]

Alas! This lush, pretty, rather sentimentalized representation of a naked young lady in chains on an auction block was to prove almost at once a far greater source of embarrassment to Americans than their quickly augmented display. In no time at all, the sharp tongue of *Punch* was asking, as Samuel Cox reported to his readers: "We have the Greek Slave in dead stone—why not the Virginia slave in living ebony?" British journalists never let the Americans forget

"We have the Greek Slave in dead stone–why not the Virginia slave in living ebony?"
inquired *Punch,* **an American visitor reported with embarrassment.** *Illustrated London*
News, **August 9, 1851, p. 185.** *Courtesy the Library of Congress.*

that they still held some three million human beings in bondage. "The satire is
well pointed," squirmed Cox. "We feel it abroad. The thing above all others
which I was proud to see in that palace—the nonpareil 'Slave' of Powers,
becomes the occasion of by-word and reproach."[61]

The meagerness of the American Exhibit was soon remedied when news of
this fact reached the United States. "Within a fortnight," Drew reported, "over
seventy packages arrived from America, which, with what we had before,
amounts to six hundred and fifty contributors from the United States. Our
Department now, large as it is, is quite well filled—as full as we could desire."[62]

A good idea of the kinds of American items finally on display can be seen in the list of prize medal winners published in the *New York Times* on October 29, 1851, just after the Exhibition's close. They included awards for cotton, wool, starch, tobacco, rice, wheat, corn, ham, and maple sugar; for steel, zinc, and iron—both sheet and cast; and for a wide variety of manufactures, including a buggy, an iron bridge, a sewing machine, a wagon, a nautical compass, a safe, a bookbinding machine, various musical instruments, harnesses and other leather goods, soaps, daguerreotypes and photographs, and rifles and pistols.[63]

Still unimpressed with his nation's offerings, one American declared that "one of our ordinary steamboats would have astonished the natives beyond all this trumpery put together!"[64] Professor Silliman realized that "the American department has been somewhat undervalued because it was not so splendid and was less full than the collections from some other countries." He referred particularly to the endless "bijouterie of the French," but he added that "even the *Times*, which has generally an unfriendly bearing in relation to our country has commended the American department on the score of utility."[65]

The *London Daily News*, too, reflected the growing respect for the American offerings and was quoted on September 25, 1851, in the *New York Times* as having admitted that

> a great change has taken place in the comparative attractiveness of the various departments. Formerly the crowds used to cluster most in the French and Austrian section, while the region of the Stars and Stripes was almost deserted—now the domain of Brother Jonathan is daily filled with crowds of visitors . . . trim mercantile men crowd round Hobbs' lock; right opposite the click of Mr. Colt's revolvers is increasing as the exhibitor demonstrates the facility with which they can be made to perform their murderous task; and in the rear, jolly, broad-shouldered farmers gather about McCormick's reaping machine and listen in mild stupidity to the details of its wondrous prowess at Tiptree Hall and at Leicester over smooth and rough ground, over ridge and furrow.[66]

The reference to Hobbs's lock acknowledged the triumph of the so-called "Yankee Lock King," Boston-born Alfred Hobbs, who had boasted that he could "pick any lock in England!" He startled lock experts and bankers alike by promptly opening a Chubb lock—the product of one of Britain's leading manufacturers, having three bolts and six tumblers—within twenty-five minutes, and then relocking it in seven. Hobbs would eventually open his own London firm, which supplied locks for the fabled steamship *Great Eastern* as well as for the Bank of England.[67]

Having observed his country's exhibit from the start, David Bartlett had to crow a bit as he saw Yankee stock rise. "America in May was the laughing stock of Europe; the journals of Paris and London went into convulsions of merriment at our expense; *Punch* jeered, and *The Times* thundered forth its sarcasm; and the people laughed. The same America in September was the envy of Europe. Then even *The Times* gave us the first position, in the Crystal Palace, and out of it; and Mr. Punch's wit was suddenly in our favor . . . Our reaping machine became the wonder of England."[68]

"Of more practical account than a Crystal Palace full of in-laid tables and Paris bonnets," observed Horace Greeley of the McCormick Reaper that became the star of the Exhibition. *Illustrated London News*, **July 19, 1851, p. 89.** *Courtesy the Library of Congress.*

Unlike much machinery of the period, the McCormick reaper was not, at first glance, particularly heavy or impressive. The first illustration of it in the *Illustrated London News* made it look something like a cross between a grasshopper and a praying mantis. It was ridiculed, according to Horace Greeley, "as a cross between an Astley's Chariot [a reference to the equestrian circus show in London], a treadmill, and a flying machine. Its uncouth appearance has been a steady butt for the London reporters at the Exhibition."[69]

When the reaper was put to a practical test on July 21st at the Mechi farm, Tiptree, Greeley was there. "The brown, rough, homespun Yankee in charge jumped on the box," reported Greeley, "starting the team at a smart walk, setting the blades of the machine in lively operation, and commenced raking off the grain in sheaf-piles ready for binding,—cutting a breadth of nine or ten feet cleanly and carefully as fast as a span of horses could comfortably step. There was a moment, and but a moment of suspense," continued Greeley.

Human prejudice could hold out no longer, and burst after burst of involuntary cheers from the whole crowd proclaimed the triumph of the Yankee "treadmill". That triumph has since been the leading topic in all agricultural circles. *The Times* report speaks of it as beyond doubt, placing the harvest absolutely under the farmer's control, and ensuring a complete and most auspicious revolution in the harvesting operations of this country. . . .One such, plain, odd-looking concern as McCormick's Reaper, though it makes no figure in the eyes of sight-seers in comparison with an in-laid table or a case of Paris Bonnets is of more practical account than a Crystal Palace full of those, and so will ultimately be regarded.[70]

The *Times* of London indeed admitted, as the Great Exhibition drew to its close, that the American department, "at first regarded as the poorest and least interesting of all the foreign countries, of late has assumed a position of the first importance, as having brought to our distressed agriculturalists a machine which, if it realizes the anticipation of competent judges, will amply remunerate England for all her outlay connected with the Great Exhibition. The reaping machine is the most valuable contribution from abroad."[71]

Cyrus McCormick's "reaping machine" thus won a Council Medal, or top award in its class; as did Gale Borden, Jr., for his "meat biscuit"; D. Dick for "various engineer's tools and presses"; William Bond and Son "for the invention

Currier print depicting Uncle Sam boasting to John Bull of the yacht *America*'s victory the speed record of a Collins Line steamship, the locks of the "Yankee Lock King," Alfred Hobbs, and last, but not least, the "American reaping machine." *Courtesy th Library of Congress.*

of a new mode of observing astronomical phenomena"; and Charles Goodyear "for India rubber goods" consisting of pontoons, buoys, life-boats, veneering, coats, hats and boots.[72]

American ambition and amour propre were further satisfied by the victory of the yacht *America* in the race off the Isle of Wight, instituted by the Royal Yacht Squadron to enhance and publicize the Great Exhibition. In September the *New York Times* ran a long poem on its front page, by "J.H.D.," extolling this maritime feat, the last stanza of which reads:

> So honour to the country which, upon a foreign strand,
> Has shown that it is destined to command:
> And let Great Britain vapor & vaunt as she may please,
> 'Tis not likely she will ever be the mistress of the seas![73]

Queen Victoria's efforts to promote the success of the Exhibition were both observed and admired by visiting Americans. Besides the royal pageantry she contributed on opening day, her frequent visits, dressed "in a rich but plain satin gown. . .with a circlet of diamonds, or a coronal upon her brow," lent interest and glamour.[74] MacGavock observed, too, how "she walks about the Palace with her suite and examines the articles with much interest, attended by no body-guard or soldiery, and moves about leisurely and gracefully, noticing things eagerly and making them topics of conversation. The stranger would fail to recognize her were it not for the great deference paid to her by her subjects who seem to idolize her."[75]

Stopping at the American Exhibit on one occasion, the tiny Queen caught sight of a group of busts of American historical figures sculptured in soap. "The Queen, hardly believing that the images were soap," reported an American observer, "was about to try them with a tiny metal bodkin but was prevented by the proprietor who exclaimed, 'No, your majesty; this is Washington!' " To which Prince Albert quipped, " 'O, it is Royalty picking at Liberty!' "[76]

Interesting political implications were perceived by some Americans in the nature of the exhibits displayed by the various nations. Drew concluded that "the articles exhibited in the several national departments offered a pretty good index of the freedom and independence of the people of the various kingdoms and states represented in the Great Exhibition. The Turkish, the East Indian, the Italian, the Austrian, and the Russian Departments show little or nothing adapted to the support and comfort of the masses," he noted.

Utility and cheapness constitute no merit in the mind of a Russian or an Algerine. But the nations which are free have proportionately more articles on exhibition that are of service to the common people. In England the free principle preponderates; there has evidently been more effort of the English mind to meet the wants of the greatest number, and yet mixed up with utility there is much that is useless and costly, adapted only to the means of the aristocratic few.[77]

"But go into the American Department," boasted Drew,

and there mere fancy matters are so few that at first even the English sneered at Uncle Sam for the plainness and simplicity of his appearance. He was too republican for his place among the nations; but republican as he was, he happened to have the strongest legs, and in due time, threw even John Bull fairly upon the Crystal Palace floor. All his articles were adapted to cheapness of production, greatest durability, and most general usefulness. It is all because Brother Jonathan is the freest boy on earth. The Emperor Nicholas had groups of human figures in solid silver as large as life, representing some of his victorious battles, which are of no use but as toys for despots. Jonathan had his Reaper and his Meat Biscuit which feed the people.[78]

In an argument overheard between a Briton and an American, a typical "Jonathan" declared to his opponent, a dignified "John Bull" type: "You are a scientific people, a religious people, a great people. All this we learn in the Crystal Palace. But," he added, "you are a haughty and arrogant people!" The elderly Briton responded quietly, "Ah, pride and arrogance often attend greatness. Beware you do not contract them yourselves."[79]

The Yankee chauvinism expressed by Drew and Greeley was more than matched, however, by enthusiastic expressions of human brotherhood and above all by typical mid-nineteenth century optimism concerning the future of mankind. "The assembling of the tribes of man was a grand event," declared Benjamin Moran, headed for a diplomatic career, and who, as assistant secretary at the American legation, together with Minister Charles Adams, would spend the Civil War years coping with the crises involving Britain and the United States during that conflict. "Its peaceful tendencies will be felt in all climes in coming ages," Moran believed, knowing nothing of what lay ahead for Britain in the Crimea, or for his own people in their fratricidal tragedy.[80]

Samuel Cox was enraptured by this vision of "the fruits of human progress, resulting from the common labor of all men, springing from the germs implanted within our common nature by our Creator." To him the Crystal Palace was "no ice-frolic of haughty power but a glowing enshrinement for the objects of mingled beauty and utility. I devoutly thank God that He has permitted me to view this common shrine among the nations—this crystal medium through which a better day doth glimmer."[81]

Horace Greeley, too, expressed this mid-century faith in progress, with a sunlit future ahead for all mankind. "Let us, taking heart from the reflection that we live in the age of the Locomotive and the Telegraph, cheerfully press onward. As we rejoice over these trophies of Labor's might and beneficence," he asked, "shall we not also perceive foreshadowed there that fairer, grander, gladder future whereof this show is a prelude and a prediction? Such is the vista which this edifice with its contents opens and brightens before me."[82]

"On a somewhat cheerless day of October, with few ceremonies and little circumstance, the Great Exhibition was closed," recorded David Bartlett sadly. "The trees of Hyde Park had begun to shed their leaves and there were approaching signs in every direction of the coming of winter....Upon every countenance there was a shade of solemn sadness. The world had tried its utmost and built a palace of wondrous beauty and filled it with its grandest and proudest achievements. The summer passed away in gloryings and rejoicings. . .and yet here was the end."[83]

Bartlett could not then have known that the Crystal Palace would be reerected outside London, at Sydenham, there to be visited and used as a pleasure dome by millions for over half a century, as well as for a naval depot in World War I and a demobilization station at that war's end, until it was at last destroyed by fire in 1936.

"It is a good thing. . .that the Crystal Palace, when it had served its purpose was taken utterly away," wrote the Reverend Arthur Cleveland Coxe. "It is now a thing of history. A bubble, like the world, it has glittered and vanished, but its memory will have a moral value till the end of time."[84] Ohioan Samuel Cox observed that "the year 1851 may truly be called *Annus Mirabilis*—at least so far as travelers were concerned. The Great Exhibition—that novel phase of our civilization—was enough to entitle the year to that honor, as a special wonder."[85] Benjamin Moran would never forget his own last day at the Crystal Palace.

I lingered until the close of day and felt reluctant to bid farewell. The great organ in the eastern nave was filling the magnificent pile with tides of melodious sound, and nearly seventy thousand souls listened to its tones. After performing a number of sacred compositions, the organist drew forth from his powerful instrument the thrilling tones of England's national anthem, "God Save the Queen"; and as the sounds quivered in the air, and began to roll in waves through the aisles of the vast edifice, the voices of seventy thousand human beings were blended with them and rang like a wild hallelujah of praise to heaven.[86]

"Each individual sang as if his soul were in the strain," the young American recalled, "and the enthusiasm of the throng heightened the grandeur and the sublimity. The chorus ceased with the words, but the sounds still waved and rolled through the transept until, like softly beating surges of a subsiding sea on a sandy shore, they died in gentle murmurs in the far distance; and then, as the assemblage departed, darkness and silence resumed their reign."[87]

13

Civil War Period

Taking up his pen on April 28, 1861, the American minister in London, George Dallas, confided in his journal that, at Cambridge House the previous evening, Lord Palmerston, recovered from the "tortures of the gout," informed him that he looked upon "the extraordinary report of the bombardment for forty hours of and from Fort Sumter, without anyone being hurt, as an absurdity which further news will clear up. Nothing else," observed Dallas, "engaged the conversation of the whole company. Italy, Poland, Hungary and Holstein all yield in interest to the drama thought to be now formally inaugurated in America."[1]

Three days later Dallas closed his account of six years spent as the representative of his government in London with a notation that his successor, Charles Francis Adams, was even then en route from Boston. "My poor country can henceforward know no security or peace," wrote Dallas prophetically, "until the passions of the two factions have covered her hills and valleys with blood and exhausted the strength of an entire generation of her sons. All Europe is watching with amazement this terrible tragedy."[2]

As the Civil War disclosed its horrors one by one, London became a hot spot indeed for the American minister, Charles Adams, accompanied by his son Henry, both sustained by the diligence and professionalism of careerist Benjamin Moran. First, there would be Britain's official proclamation of neutrality, issued on May 13, the day of Adams's landing at Liverpool. Northerners took this action as a blow to their cause in its tacit recognition of the Confederacy as an independent and sovereign state. Six months later followed the explosive, highly dangerous international situation in November 1861, precipitated by Captain Wilkes's seizure of the Confederate agents, Mason and Slidell, off the Royal Mail packet *Trent*. This situation was resolved only after considerable consultation and the intervention of cooler heads on both sides, culminating in Mason and Slidell's release. "One war at a time," Lincoln was said to have insisted as hawks like Seward advocated military action.[3] After the war the American politician John Pendleton Kennedy said that Lord Houghton had told him that it was really Lord Palmerston who had prevented the "break" between the United States and Great Britain.[4]

The depredations of the *Alabama* and other Confederate sea raiders—built, outfitted, and launched from British ports—on United States maritime commerce, despite Britain's alleged neutrality, provided a continual crisis for Minister Adams. On June 19, 1864 the sinking of the *Alabama*—after eleven months of action at sea—by the Federal cruiser *Kearsarge,* in the English Channel off Cherbourg, brought on another crisis, although not of the same caliber as the *Trent* incident. Claims for compensation by the United States for the *Alabama*'s ravages would be settled at last in 1872 with an indemnity of $15,500,000 paid by the British government.[5] History would credit Adams with the prevention of other British-built vessels, ordered by the Confederacy, from putting to sea. However, Adams seems to have been aided by special agents such as John Murray Forbes, sent over in 1863 to buy up Confederate-ordered vessels at Laird's Liverpool shipyards, if necessary, to keep them out of action. Forbes, armed with instructions from Navy Secretary Gideon Welles and credits of £1,000,000 sterling from Secretary of the Treasury Salmon P. Chase, later wrote that, when he and Adams met in London, the latter "wanted to know only what was absolutely necessary of our mission, so that he might not be mixed up with operations which we knew might not be exactly what a diplomat would care to endorse." Adams, however, was "very gracious to me," Forbes added, "and threw open his house to me on all occasions during my stay."[6]

Facing these crises in London, along with plenty of bad news from American battlefields pouring in during the first years of the War, Minister Adams's soul was further tried by the relentless vilification of the Federal cause and overt expressions of sympathy for the Confederates by the British aristocratic and mercantile classes in their organ the *Times*. Moran, now a career diplomat with seven years London experience—the same young man who had stood so enraptured that evening in the Crystal Palace back in 1851 as the Great Exhibition drew to its close—found both Adams and his son Henry a bit hard to take. Henry had been brought along to serve as a sort of unofficial private secretary, and his activities had the effect of displacing Moran as the minister's official secretary. "The two sit upstairs there exchanging views on all subjects," Moran fumed in his diary, "and as each considers the other very wise, and both think all they do is right, they manage to think themselves Solomons and to do some very stupid things."[7] Charles Adams is nevertheless credited by modern historians with having ultimately won the respect of the British officials he encountered and with success in preventing worse violations than there were of the alleged neutrality of the British.

Besides the legation staff and those sent over on special missions by the United States government, there were still a few ordinary American travelers making their way about Great Britain during the Civil War years. In their shock at the attitudes expressed by much of the British press, and by many Britons themselves, toward the Federal cause, one can trace the ever-worsening relations between the two nations, as well as the steadily mounting resentment of Unionists angered by all this overt British sympathy for the Confederacy. Tormented for so many decades by Britons over their American institution of human slavery, many Northerners had naively expected moral support for their side and against those condoning and maintaining that institution. Before the conflict broke out, some prominent British publications had manifested a positive interest in American antislavery forces trying to gain control on the political level, and Lincoln's election had been hailed by others as another milestone on the road to slavery's extirpation. Now, with the Civil War in progress—as the

Americans were to discover—these same publications, notably the *Times,* seemingly advocated the cause of the Confederate States of America.

While aware of the economic situation facing British cotton cloth manufacturers, cut off from their supply of raw material by the Northern blockade of Southern ports, the Americans were not so well informed concerning internal British politics. Thus the Federals judged British reactions to their Civil War as it widened and worsened, particularly as expressed in the *Times,* outrageously hypocritical as well as plain wrong-headed. Dean Dudley, a New England traveler-writer had predicted some years before the war that, "if the slavery question should ever cause a separation between the Northern and Southern states of our Union, this government [Britain's] would aim to retain its friendship with the South rather than the North; because the cotton and tobacco trade is of immense importance to England. But the interests of the North are directly opposed to those of this country."[8]

Moses Coit Tyler, who spent the war years in Britain and later became a distinguished professor of history at Cornell, confessed that it was

> hard to give an adequate picture of the terrible prostration of the Liberal cause in England between 1860 and 1865, in consequence of the prostration of the national cause in America. It was with a jubilant frenzy that the Tories contemplated the bursting of the bubble republic. Jeff. [sic] Davis and Stonewall Jackson were doing what the Tories had tried in vain to do: they were refuting the arguments of Cobden and Bright, and were unraveling that beautiful but dangerous tapestry of democratic success. . . . "Talk no more of popularizing the government of England; you see what popular government comes to,"

Tyler quoted as ruling-class sentiment.[9] All that most Americans knew at the time, however, was that the very people who had so castigated the United States for countenancing slavery, and who had so challenged American visitors to their country with the same charge, seemed now to have turned on them when they were involved in a bloody civil war in which slavery was one of the items being fought over. Bostonian George Train, in a series of pro-Union speeches in London in 1862, reminded his listeners that members of the chic Exeter Hall crowd, who had so concerned themselves over American slavery in the fifties, had refused even to attend a prayer meeting on behalf of peace between the United States and Britain at the time of the *Trent* crisis.[10]

The *Times* of London, long resented by Americans for depicting them as a nation of ignorant vulgarians, now "made a fool of itself over the American Civil War," as the modern British scholar Hugh Brogan put it recently. Whereas at the start of the conflict, "the Thunderer" had urged the North to accept Southern secession as irrevocable, suddenly it swung around full circle and began blasting the Union for its failure to reassert Federal authority. "It toppled from its pinnacle," said Brogan of the *Times,* in his preface to *The American Civil War: Extracts from the Times 1860–1865,* which was published by the *Times* in 1975. "It became in certain quarters a standing joke."[11] Until the final eight months of the war, when it appeared that the Union might survive after all, the great London newspaper appeared overtly pro-Southern. "Year in and year out, while the war lasted," continued Brogan, "*The Times* had insulted Northern patriotism, belittled Northern victories, gloried in Northern defeats, freely predicted Northern failure. It did all this at great length and at the top of its voice." And the North was "rightly resentful," concluded Brogan.[12] Sitting in London during those war years, reading the *Times,* as well as copies sent over from home of James Gordon Bennett's New York *Herald,* young Henry Adams, the minister's son, concluded that both papers seemed to be trying to outdo each other in falsity and manipulation of facts dealing with the war.[13]

It is against this background that one must view the American visitors in Britain during the Civil War years. Landing at Liverpool in November 1861, just following the *Trent* incident, young Charles Williams of Ohio—who carefully explained to his readers that he suffered from "a physical debility," apparently some form of lameness—recorded his surprise at the anti-American sentiment raging over the seizure of Mason and Slidell. "The feeling versus our government is stronger than we at home have been aware of," he discovered, "and has only been waiting for a pretext to crop out in public expression." On the train between Manchester and York he was informed, he said, by an Englishman, that the British soon would be "walking into the Yankees," to which Charles said he responded that it would prove "pretty deep wadin'." He also reminded his opponent that they had not done so well in 1776 or 1812, either. Fortunately, at that moment the train pulled into the station at York.[14]

Williams devoted a chapter of his book to this and similar adventures as a defender of the Union cause. "It is amusing to listen to the arguments which are so often advanced to justify the South," he wrote,

and the gross errors under which they labor with regard to the North. . . . The prevailing ignorance of the English respecting our country, its institutions and its customs, is greatly owing to the willful misrepresentation and malicious slander of the press, which, in this country, is generally under the control and servilely devoted to the interests of the aristocracy whose antipathy against our government is based upon the sure foundation of self-interest and self-preservation.[15]

"A large proportion of the press openly espouse the Rebel cause," Williams continued,

and nearly all treat the final success of the Rebellion as a fixed fact, declaring that the full triumph of the Federals is an absolute impossibility, while one of the leading journals, in a late issue, draws a parallel between the two sections of our country, in which it makes the rather startling disclosure that the Slave States are the bone and sinew, the strength and vitality of our nation; that the free States are not self-supporting, and could not subsist without the general aid of their abused sisters of the South. . . . A favorite theme for the witticism of the press is the conduct of the American war, the condition of American finances, and the principles of our American policy, not omitting an occasional intimation that the state of society among us is rapidly retrograding. Everything American is open to the wildest license of unfriendly criticism.[16]

"Would you have the strength of your patriotism tested?" demanded Williams.

Then go with me to what we have been accustomed to consider the friendly shores of old England when our country is grappling in a death struggle with a traitorous foe. . . . You will long to give vent to the pent-up bitterness of your mind and the burning indignation that will boil and rage in your blood when you find the press, as with one voice, ringing throughout the length and breadth of the land the basest misrepresentations and most ungenerous slander of our country. With what feelings will you read the morning papers, teeming with abuse of our government, with ridicule of our rulers . . . triumphing in the prospective destruction of our sea-board cities, and the total annihilation of our commerce. Can you retain your composure when you see Jefferson Davis extolled as one of the great leading spirits of the world, as "the creator of a new nation", . . . our glorious Lincoln, whose name is the touchstone of loyalty, denounced as a low buffoon, actuated by sordid motives, devoid of principle, with no administrative ability, and scourged forward in his career of folly by his restless but imbecile ambition?

In a footnote Williams advised his readers: "This was written before the murder of Lincoln."[17]

Not long after this literary explosion in his journal, Williams was overjoyed one morning to read the news of the capture of New Orleans "by the iron-clad navy of Farragut running contemptuously past the bellowing forts at the mouth of the Missisippi." He said that he could not hold back "an involuntary shout" as the *Times* now openly debated "the question whether London was safe."[18]

Evangelist Phoebe Palmer and her ailing husband, also in Britain at this time, further observed the effects of the *Trent* crisis. "Newsboys, by way of insuring a more ready sale for their paper cry 'War with America! War with America!' " she observed. "And how do Americans resident in England feel amidst such surroundings? We can only speak for ourselves," she declared, "and say that we feel more security cn this point than those around us. We cannot believe that our country would be willing to plunge itself into a war at present, and would prefer to make the *amende honorable* rather than to gratify the war spirit of England, or to give the advantage to the Southern States which would ensue in case England should join them in hostilities." Mrs. Palmer and her husband noted "warlike preparations on a gigantic scale" with the Cunard steamers *Persia* and *Australasian* readying to convey troops to Canada, plus arms, ammunition, and a field-battery of artillery.[19] She recorded her awareness of

the thousands here who are now out of employment, and thousands more who are on half pay . . . and the thousands of business men who are feeling the pressure occasioned by the dreadful conflict in America. Can we wonder that they are willing to throw in an ingredient which, though it may sharpen the conflict, may shorten it?[20]

How tempting must be the thought, mused Mrs. Palmer, that by "blowing away" the American blockade they could put the "suffering-working classes" back to work. . . . "If it might also be confidently affirmed that the results of this war would in fact be the ultimate and absolute extirpation of slavery," she continued, "then the manifest want of English sympathy were more inexcusable; but what are we doing," she demanded, "or what have we hitherto done, which may be regarded as a guaranty to England or any other nation, that the end of the war will be the wiping-away of the foul blot of slavery from the American nation?" Phoebe Palmer further reminded her readers that Britain had bought the freedom of *her* slaves, and noted also the prayer meetings called all over England, including Exeter Hall in London, to pray for peace "in behalf of poor, distracted America," and to "avert from us the curse of war."[21]

John Lewis Peyton, a Confederate agent in London for North Carolina, recorded the flap over the *Trent* from his point of view. "The excitement spread with electric rapidity," he wrote. "There was a spontaneous uprising of the whole people, as if a cord of indignation had vibrated in every heart. The honor and glory of the country seemed the first thought of all. . . . It was palpable that all was working admirably for the cause of the Confederate States." In the long run, however, Peyton claimed that he learned a harsh lesson of worldly wisdom. "I found that the English admiration of the South was a thing altogether separate and apart from anything like kindred love. They admired her endurance, her stubborn resolution, her indomitable pluck and gallantry," but that did not, he finally concluded, mean that Britain had any idea of drawing the sword in the contest.[22]

When news of the Emancipation Proclamation's going into effect on January 1, 1863, reached Britain, Mrs. Palmer recorded the results. First of all, Americans, long baited over their national shame, could at last hold up their heads! "We have never doubted but the God of battles would give us victory," she exulted on February 12.

> The policy of our excellent President, though at first doubted and cruelly maligned, is now securing unbounded praise. The news of the enthusiastic meeting at Exeter Hall . . . has already reached you. A large deputation of seventy gentlemen from many cities, towns, and villages in England recently waited on our American Minister, Mr. Adams . . . commending in strong terms the course pursued by President Lincoln, particularly his firmness in carrying out the Emancipation Act. The name of Lincoln, so much abused through Southern perfidy, and mistaken conservative politicians of the United States, is now being embalmed in the minds of thousands in England as one of the greatest benefactors of the age. The proposition and attempt to establish a nation on the basis of slavery is now looked upon by tens of thousands as infamous beyond parallel. . . . Arrangements are being made in every part of England for anti-slavery demonstrations on a large scale. The name of our good President bids fair to be immortalized in the public mind.[23]

She may have overstated her case, but some of the other American Unionists in England at this time also began to perceive new signs of sympathy for the Northern side.

Elihu Burritt, for example—the so-called "Learned Blacksmith," the all-purpose social reformer advocating abolition, temperance, and peace, who spent eight years walking the length and breadth of Britain, attending conferences, making speeches, and becoming well known and liked in the process—arrived in the little village of Ashburton on the edge of Dartmoor, just after the sinking of the *Alabama* in 1864. There Burritt came upon an American flag, "as large as life, suspended over the road," by the village blacksmith, he later learned, as an expression of sympathy for the Union cause in America.[24]

George Alfred Townsend—fresh from his adventures as a war correspondent following McClellan and Pope "over their sanguinary battlefields," as his posters read—arrived in Britain in October, 1862, prepared to pay his way by lecturing on the Civil War to British audiences, "as I could depict it fresh from the action." It was not to be; for, after facing too many evenings of empty halls, interspersed by fiery exchanges with audiences when they did show up, he finally admitted that "my itinerant profession lost its novelty as we steadily lost money."[25] Besides Southern sympathizers, his trouble may have been that he started out in Liverpool where secession was popular, and then proceeded to manufacturing towns in Lancashire, where people may simply have lacked money for lectures, due to the economic decline caused by the American blockade.

Another American, self-styled "Yankee Boy from Home," Joseph Battell, recorded his experiences in Britain during his nation's Civil War. In the Autumn of 1862, on hearing the news of the battle of Antietam, he remarked that "my English friends don't like McClellan; he is spoiling all their fun." Not all British papers were pro-Southern, he noted, as was the *Times*. He found the *Manchester Examiner and Times* "wholly liberal," as was London's *Daily News,* and a penny paper called the *London Star.* The *Leeds Mercury,* he thought, "takes a fair and honorable view of matters. . . . *The Scotsman,* too, is tolerably fair toward us." As he was preparing to leave for home toward the end of 1863, he referred to an American girl he had met in London who expressed, he said, "a strong doubt of my patriotism because I had not returned before this to get shot."[26]

An English-born printer, John Tobitt, having returned after twenty-four years in the United States to visit a dying brother, arrived in his native land shortly after the outbreak of the war. He stayed on a few weeks to see old friends and visit familiar scenes. Reacting to the anti-American feeling he perceived around him, much of which he felt stemmed from misinformation, he decided to serve in any way he could as an unofficial spokesman for his adopted country. "You may as well own your republican government's gone to smash!" one old acquaintance had told him.[27]

In London's Commercial Street Chapel one evening, attending a lecture entitled "The War—North and South," by "H. Vincent, celebrated Chartist leader of previous years," Tobitt sat quietly through that speaker's "tolerably impartial" lecture. But, when Vincent finished with a grotesque burlesque of Lincoln, Tobitt sought permission to set matters straight concerning the actual American regional accents "peculiar to the Eastern, Middle and Southern states." He also urged Britons to stay out of the American quarrel, to be honest in their proclaimed neutrality, and not to let the cotton accumulating at New Orleans, Savannah, and Charleston tempt them. "Oh, it was so manly for you to speak up for your country," he said one lady told him afterward.[28]

On another occasion, visiting down in Kent, Tobitt took on the local "squire" in a taproom, and at Bristol a Church of England clergyman, who told him that the war was God's vengeance "for your rebellion to British rule."[29] Still "proud of my connections with Shakespeare's countrymen," Tobitt wrote near the end of his visit in his former country, "I even indulged a belief that by prolonging my stay and speaking whenever and wherever asked, I could do good by dissipating prejudice and thus contribute toward cementing closer together two nations who, united, might rule the world." Preparing at last to leave for home, he met other Americans at Gun's American Agency in the Strand, preparing to do likewise, "all with a wonderful unanimity of desire to return home, even while hearing on every hand that our nation had gone to ruin." As he boarded his ship he overheard two Britons. "There goes a Yankee home to fight," remarked one. "Yes, and they'll want every one of them," responded the other. "But what a blarsted fool the fellow is to go!"[30]

Even on much higher social levels than that of John Tobitt, visiting Unionists could be provoked to speak up for their country at this time. Special agent Forbes sat quietly at dinner in London one evening while the upper-class guests, chewing over the news of the Federal defeat at Chancellorsville, deplored " 'the folly of protracting the useless struggle to save the Union' all meant for my especial benefit," wrote Forbes. "I listened with cold outside manners of good society to all the stuff . . . until my patience gave way. In one of the pauses which all dinner parties experience, our host appealed to me for information as to the truth of the sad, heart-rending rumor that the hero, Stonewall Jackson, had been killed by his own soldiers on the evening of the rebel attack, and at the most critical period of the whole battle." Seething by this time, Forbes snapped,

"I don't know or care a brass farthing whether Jackson was killed by his own men or ours, so long as he is thoroughly killed, and stands no longer in the way of that success upon which the fate of everybody and everything I hold dear depends!" Had a naked Indian in warpaint, with tomahawk and scalping knife, appeared at the dinner-table, the expression of horror and dismay at my barbarous utterance could hardly have been greater; but anyhow, we heard no more than evening about the wisdom of concession to the "erring sisters" and their "chivalrous heroes and lamented leaders."[31]

Not long afterward, on a visit to the House of Commons, Forbes was not surprised to note that "much diplomacy had been expended in arranging seats to keep ourselves and Messrs. Mason and Slidell separated."[32] Recalling those days, long after the war, Forbes said that "Bright, Cobden, W. E. Forster, the Duke of Argyle, and a few others were with us heartily, and took bold ground in our cause; but generally speaking, the aristocracy and the trading classes were solid against us. Gladstone, the magnificent old man of today, had not found out the merits of our cause, and Lord John Russell . . . sneered even in a public speech at what he called the 'once United' States."[33]

An attempt to sum up the attitudes and feelings toward Britain of the victorious Unionists at the end of the Civil War was undertaken by Stephen Fiske in a book entitled *English Photographs*, published in 1869. Ostensibly a travel book, based on his actual residence in London for a time, it proves to be primarily a harsh, uncompromising retaliation against the British for their stand during the American Civil War. "I liked England before I came," Fiske declared in his preface, "and I like it better than ever now that I have sojourned here for two years."[34] Nevertheless, his series of "photographs," or descriptions of many aspects of British life, are negative to the point of exaggeration: steamers, railways, climate, hotels, cabs, journals, theaters, sports, women, houses, Parliament, castes (the class system), and London itself. In his final chapter he winds up with what seems to have been his intent all along, a denunciation of Britain for her treatment of the United States, *both* North and South, during the War. In his view, Britain's alleged neutrality, proclaimed in May 1861, in effect permitted them to "play fast and loose with both sections; to stab the North in the back while professing to be neutral, and to encourage the Southern people just enough to render their ruin utter and complete . . . which has resulted in embittering both belligerents against England."[35]

The British press and the speeches of British statesmen, maintained Fiske, all served to spur on the South and cause them to persevere in their doomed struggle. Nor would Unionists ever forget how "the ravages of privateers built, equipped, and manned in England, assisted to fire the Southern heart and cripple and harass the North." Fiske claimed, moreover, that the war for the Union was actually changed into an antislavery crusade, as a bid for English support, by Massachusetts politicians who "thought that they could gain the countenance of the British government *via* Exeter Hall. The scheme failed," added Fiske, "but it incidentally freed the negro." He found it ironic that

> England, after repudiating all her philanthropic theories and siding with the slaveholders during the war, should have an indirect share in the abolition of slavery. . . . The Liverpool merchants broke our blockade to make money, but the Lancashire weavers cheerfully consented to starve from the cotton-famine rather than permit the English Government to intervene with France and assist to dissolve the Union. Surely this heroic sacrifice—grander than any the world ever saw before, because it was offered to secure the integrity of a foreign country—is more than a compensation for all pecuniary wrongs

—a reference, no doubt, to the Alabama claims then under discussion.[36]

Many Americans continued to press hard, however, for financial compensation for the depredations of the raider *Alabama,* and American travelers in England just after the war ranted about that issue even as British-American negotiations were carried on. In 1869 Thomas Jefferson Clayton attended the theater one evening where he listened to a sort of all-purpose song, lines of which a comic singer could apply to almost any contemporary situation or news event:

> But all is yet uncertain.
> I have no cause to doubt it.
> It may be yes. It may be no.
> That's all I know about it.

"The whole song was coolly received," recalled Clayton, "until the last verse was reached. . . . This verse was received with prolonged shouts of applause, encored two or three times."

> Now in the Alabama case,
> The Yankees want their bill.
> But will they get it? Not for Joe!
> I do not think they will.[37]

The *Alabama* claims were finally settled in 1872 with an indemnity of $15,500,000 in gold, but the post-Civil War mood of Americans visiting Britain, for at least a decade following the end of the War, was understandably ambivalent.

We had been somewhat boyish as a nation, a little loud, a little pushing, a little braggart. But might it not partly have been because we felt that we had certain claims to respect that were not admitted? The war which established our position as a vigorous nationality has also sobered us. A nation, like a man, cannot look death in the eye for four years, without some strange reflections, without arriving at some clearer consciousness of the stuff it is made of, without some great moral change. . . . It will take England a great while to get over her airs of patronage toward us. . . . Justly or not, we have a feeling that we have been wronged, not merely insulted.[38]

Writing thus in the *Atlantic Monthly* in 1869, James Russell Lowell summed up the mood of most Americans in the years just after the war. They had achieved some sense of identity at a high price in the bloodbath of their Civil War. Soon, however, they would be trooping back to Britain still questing—but now for their own lost past and roots in the "old home." So fast was their nation changing that it was as if they needed reassurance that the old Anglo-Saxon ties still held. Their anger over British attitudes toward their conflict faded remarkably fast, all things considered.

PART III

1865–1914

There is no country which contains so much of absorbing interest to a thoughtful American as Old England; finding there as he does the head-springs of the life and power of his own nation, and in almost every object that his eye rests upon, seeing that which (a short two centuries ago) formed part of his own history. He finds there the complement of the life of the New World.

—James M. Hoppin, *Old England,* 1867

14

A New Type of Traveler

In June 1866 the *New York Times* predicted that while "200,000 passengers from the Old World will be landed upon our shores during the present year, it may also be estimated that in the same time Europe will be visited by 50,000 travelers from the New World."[1] Charles Poston observed in 1867 that over one hundred "magnificent steam palaces daily plough the Atlantic,"[2] and former Confederate agent John Peyton remarked that "like shuttles in a loom ... these gigantic steamers flying to and fro between Europe and America are weaving nations closer and closer together."[3]

Scarcely was the Civil War over, and despite their resentment and anger at Britain's official stand during that conflict, back again flooded the Americans in larger numbers every year—victorious supporters of the Union as well as a few still feisty Rebels. Lists of dinner guests at the United States legation in these years include Major John Hay, Congressman James A. Garfield, Colonel Oliver Wendell Holmes, Major General Schofield, Richard Henry Dana, Kate Chase Sprague, James Gordon Bennett, William Lloyd Garrison, Henry Ward Beecher, and Julia Ward Howe.[4] Soon hundreds and then thousands of lesser-known, now long-forgotten Americans swarmed over the Atlantic, encouraged by postwar prosperity, larger and faster steamers, the Paris Exposition of 1867, the Vienna Exhibition of 1873, and, above all, the same strong American urge to visit the land of their historical and cultural heritage, Great Britain. The visit to Britain would become more and more a part of an extended, once-in-a-lifetime "trip to Europe," but it was a vital part.

Lest American travelers overlook or underestimate this need to touch the roots of their culture, Professor James Hoppin of Yale reminded them of it in his preface to *Old England,* a much-read book that by 1893 had gone through twelve editions. Writing in 1867, while Americans still cherished their anger at Britons, Hoppin admitted that "there have been heretofore, it is true, good reasons for this disinclination of Americans to remain very long in England; but these reasons do not now exist, or at least to the extent that they once did." Urging his countrymen "to spend more time in England ... to see that country more thoroughly, instead of making it a stepping-stone to the Continent," he reminded the American traveler in Britain that there he would sip "from the headsprings of the life and power of his own nation, and in almost every object that his eye rests upon, seeing that which (a short two centuries ago) formed part of his own history. He finds there the complement of the life of the New World."[5]

Professor Hoppin felt obliged to say, "I hold no special love for the English and have felt as deeply as anyone the sense of her blind and selfish injustice toward our country in the late war, but I have never lost sight of the principle that the two nations were essentially one, that they should acknowledge this unity, that they *will* do so in the final struggle between free and despotic peoples." Hoppin ended by quoting Lord Derby who remarked that "no other earthly event would conduce so much to the future of civilization as the union of these two countries."[6]

Advice like this from Professor Hoppin, and time itself, soothed the angry American spirit sooner than might have been expected. James Hoyt of Cleveland read Hoppin's book on his way across the Atlantic in 1871, aboard the *Wyoming*, and he was "much pleased with its healthful, breezy, manly spirit ... an admirable preparation for an approach to the shores of our old Fatherland—with all the faults of the English, still the home of the brave and the free."[7]

The mood of the American sojourner in Britain in the remaining decades of the nineteenth century, and up to World War I, thus consists of an ambivalent mixture of national confidence, plainly chauvinistic at times, along with a reverence for the old country where he hoped to find his lost past. As time marched on, the balance tipped ever more in the latter direction.

Still, the old wounds were picked at by various individual travelers for a decade or so even as they enjoyed themselves in the land of their ancestors. Author Henry Morford stood in the cathedral at Chester in the summer of 1865, gazing up at the old battle flags once borne up Bunker Hill by the 22nd Cheshire Regiment, and he recalled how "not many years before, Theodore Winthrop, then as little dreaming of his sudden immortality as an author, as of his death wound at Big Bethel, had stood before those flags." At Liverpool, even as Morford admired the mighty docks, "the wonder of the world," which he described at great length for his readers, he had taken careful notice of

> the colossal foundry and works of Laird—that Laird whose name through the building of the "rebel rams," has been nearly as well known in America as it ever was in Great Britain. Into this receptacle of the funds of "southern sympathizers" crept many hundred thousands of pounds ... that I opine many of the lenders who found themselves donors afterwards wished that they could have back in their broad purses; and out of it, as from a predal [sic] lair, crept not only the rams but many of those fleet blockade runners so well calculated to keep in flow the threatened life-blood of the Confederates.

Later, up in Scotland, he observed berthed in the Clyde many vessels "large and new in appearance," and he was told by a Scotsman that "they *are* steamers laid up; they *were* blockade runners not long ago!"[8]

In the summer of 1866, stopping at the Shakespeare house in Stratford-on-Avon, newsman James Matthews of Buffalo looked over the visitors' register. "Nearly a third of the names, I should think, are American," he wrote, noting that a clergyman from Norfolk, Virginia, just the day before had "added the initials C.S.A. in the largest Roman characters." He was obviously a man "unable to acquiesce in the logic of events," Matthews concluded.[9] Republican politician

The Langham Hotel, Portland Place—a favorite haunt for American visitors just after the Civil War. Today an office building for the BBC. *Illustrated London News,* **April 8, 1865, p. 5.** *Courtesy the Library of Congress.*

John Forney, also a prominent journalist, en route to the Paris Exposition the following summer, stopped for a time in Britain. At Liverpool he surveyed, as had Morford,

> the ship-yards of the Lairds at Birkenhead, opposite the city, where some of the corsairs were built; and I have seen much to indicate that the feeling against our country was intense among the commercial and manufacturing princes. Their sympathy with Slavery was a matter of business as well as of sentiment, and they gave enormously to the cause of our enemies. As I looked up on their lordly mansions and enduring warehouses, I could not forget the philippic of George Frederick Cooke, the eccentric British actor, nearly fifty years ago, "that the stones of their boasted edifice of trade were cemented by the blood of American slaves." But this is past, and it should be our study to forget it. A happy and a healthy change has taken place, and all over England the classes who were eager to plan and pray for our downfall are anxious to cultivate our friendship.[10]

Arriving in London, Forney checked in at the swank, new Langham Hotel in Portland Place [today an office building for the BBC]. Under the management of an American, a Civil War veteran, Colonel James M. Sanderson, the Langham fast became a favorite hostelry for the American in London.[11]

Meeting "with nearly all the liberal leaders" during his stay, Forney paid particular tribute to their chief, John Bright, a hero to Americans for his pro-Union stand during the war. "Indeed, Mr. Bright deserves the title of 'the champion of American liberty' in the British Parliament," declared Forney. Together they discussed the Fenian movement, and Bright expressed regret, Forney reported, "that Irishmen in America vote with the falsely-called Democratic party . . . the more painful when I tell you that the Liberal party in Parliament has never had so able and faithful a body of supporters as the majority of the members from Ireland. But time will cure all this."[12]

Bright and Forney agreed, so the latter recorded, that the correspondents in the United States for the *Times, Telegraph,* and *Standard* were still misrepresenting facts and "trying to revive and keep alive the bitterest animosities between England and America."[13] But Forney thought that he perceived them having less effect than formerly on the attitudes of their readers toward Americans. "The change in tone in regard to the United States among the English people is especially gratifying to Mr. Bright and his friends. They had a trying time of it during the rebellion, and nothing but their confidence in the right and their long discipline in contending with the aristocracy fortified them against the sneers and falsehoods of the enemies of their principles and ours."[14]

Forney reminded his American readers that "the English working masses everywhere sympathized with us during the rebellion, and although thousands of them were brought to want and beggary by the closing of the great manufactories, owing to the scarcity of cotton, very few could be seduced into sympathy with the slaveholders of America." One of these men, Forney was told, had "walked fifteen miles, almost without shoes on his feet, to assist in a meeting of congratulation on Mr. Lincoln's Proclamation of Emancipation." Forney had strong praise also for Charles Francis Adams and for his secretary of legation, Benjamin Moran, for their steadfast conduct "during the early period of their country's travail."[15]

Despite his obviously partisan political interests, and his jubilance over the Union victory, Forney appears to have felt something akin to pity for those exiled Confederate leaders he observed existing uneasily and all but forgotten in both London and Paris. Several times during his stay at the Langham he observed the comings and goings of John C. Breckinridge, "woefully changed in appearance, if not in opinions," and he learned that the exiled Confederate secretary of war was refusing to claim any rights "under the Constitution which they had repudiated and the Government they had vainly fought to destroy." Judah P. Benjamin, secretary of state for the Confederacy, was, Forney reported, practicing law with some success and was said to be the American editor for the *Telegraph* and "the writer of the articles, that now delight the Tory readers of that pretended Liberal paper, eulogistic of Jefferson Davis and 'the Lost Cause'." Other Confederate exiles sojourning in London, Forney noted were George N. Sanders, "the violent" Lewis P. Wigfall of Texas, and Robert Toombs of Georgia, "not less vehement than ever though greatly reduced in his physical proportions."[16] Even the Republican stalwart Forney was moved to say that

> men have never been so heavily punished for a causeless crime. I have not met one of them who did not look as if he had drained the cup of sorrow, if not of repentance, to the dregs. Bitterly indeed have they realized their offence, and in nothing so much *as in the heartlessness of foreign sympathy for men in distress.* A stranger in a strange land, without money, presents a feeble picture in comparison with these exiled secessionists. And if I were their most envenomed foe, I should say that they have been sufficiently punished.[17]

Forney encouraged his fellow Americans to take up their travels in Great Britain again and to let the past be buried.

> No more do we hear the American Union satirized and denounced; the poor Yankees are no longer ridiculed on the streets by traveling mountebanks, or caricatured on the stage by degenerate actors. The aristocracy, on the one hand, and the plutocracy on the other, are either silent, or openly confess that they were mistaken in their estimate of the American character. . . . Even the Tory journals confine their abuse of our country to the publication of correspondence from Philadelphia, Washington, and New York, so crowded with falsehoods that each succeeding letter is the unconscious correction of the fabrications of its predecessor.[18]

At the close of his book Forney urged his countrymen to follow a time-honored Yankee tradition. "From the beginning of the Government, our leading minds have regarded a knowledge of foreign habits and doctrines an essential part of political education. Franklin, Jefferson, and Adams spent a considerable period in Europe when the passage was long and dangerous," he continued. "Now that a sea voyage is much easier, cheaper, and quicker, there is hardly an excuse for any thoughtful American refusing to follow these illustrious examples." Further reassuring his readers, he told them that "the triumph of the Union arms has given our country a new influence. . . . We are now generally, if not universally, appreciated."[19]

Putting the war behind them at last, and no longer needing to dread being looked on as representatives of slavery, the Americans trooped back to all their old familiar haunts. But their mood had changed. Gone was that attitude of wonder with which the travelers in the early decades had savored the sophistication of an older civilization and beheld the advanced technology of the country that first experienced the industrial revolution. Gone, too, was the harsh, guilt-ridden, defensive querulousness of the decades just before the war. The old train compartment wrangles over American slavery and British pauperism were now replaced by half-joking conversational encounters, such as one Mary Wills enjoyed with a "jovial gentleman" who informed her that "the exultation of you Americans over your Declaration of Independence, and the subsequent results, always reminds me of the boasting of a child who has whipped his parent and was glad of it." She recalled another conversation with "a prominent merchant who told me that he had two good customers, Uncle Sam and the Prince of Wales; the former paid his bills promptly, but the latter did not."[20]

In place of thoughtful pedagogues, preachers and fact-finding polemicists came a new breed of American travelers to Britain, brimming with energy, with money in their pockets, and with a new pride in their country, but creatures very much weary of strife. Americans came to Britain in these years not to see a preview of the future, nor to study that nation's present. They came now in search of the past, Britain's past, which was also their own, and which they perceived through a romantic haze of British history and, above all, literature. Britain had become for the American, as Robert Spiller put it, "a romantic shrine worthy of reverential pilgrimage."[21] It was "ruins" the Americans wanted, and soon Britons would wonder at this American obsession with everything ancient. Writing home to the New York *World* in the eighties, journalist Theron Crawford observed, "I have found that the American visitor to England is more interested in what is old and relates to its past than in the modern and in its present life."[22] Some American travelers actually used the term "pilgrimage" in reference to their visit, and others called themselves "pilgrims," as did Gilbert Haven in his title *The Pilgrim's Wallet.*

Back in 1838 Hezekiah Wright had already perceived that Americans tend to romanticize the past. "A spirit of romance induces them to lose sight of the age of utility and invention and seek a more exciting aliment in the past."[23] And now this tendency took over indeed.

Somewhere along the way, through their first frenetic century of frantic growth, Americans had lost something, it seems, and they were searching for it. Or was it something they had never had? Whatever the cause, "there is an implicit idea in the books written a century ago by American visitors to Europe," as Stephen Spender has said, "that in reentering the traditional sources of their own country, they were piecing together their divided selves."[24]

Gnawing at the edges of their postwar pride and confidence was a new concern as well. Their once largely white, Anglo-Saxon, Protestant culture reeled under waves of immigrants flooding into the New World after the Civil War. Catholics and Jews with strange names and different customs swarmed into American cities some also bringing ideas new and strange as well to "native" Americans. Returning from his trip to Europe in 1900, Ohio politician William A. Braman contemplated the steerage of his vessel, fretting lest among the miserable occupants of that section there were more "outcasts of the old world . . . [to be] dumped upon us . . . enemies of all government, of all law, of education, of religion, of society and of everything good. . . . Their power for mischief should not be minimized," he warned his readers.[25] Thomas Bailey Aldrich hit the same key in his poem, "Unguarded Gates," warning his country against becoming "the cesspool of Europe."[26] William Hemstreet, in his book of travel advice, referred to American seaport cities as "the dumping grounds of the Old World's slough and where American society itself is degenerated by the infection of foreign fraud, vice, cowardice, and disloyalty."[27]

Flocking to "the Mother Country" in these later decades, Americans thus sought more than culture or even escape from the growing pressures and tensions of their changing society. They seemed in search of something very much like reassurance as to the strength and durability of their still primarily Anglo-Saxon heritage in the heart of that great empire on which the sun never set. Eagerly they now sought to identify with the nation symbolizing their heritage, and some of them even began to discover that they felt "more at home" in Britain than in their own country. "Never that I can remember did I find it so easy to harmonize with the environment," discovered Richard Grant White. "Never was I, a Yankee of eight generations on both sides, so much at ease in mind and body, never in one English word, so much at home as I was in England."[28]

Where once they had predicted that "a democratic republic shall gladden her shores," in reference to Britain—one even ending his book with "God bless the *Commonwealth* of Great Britain!"[29]—now they reveled in all those evidences of Britain's mighty empire and were among the most energetic celebrants of Queen Victoria's Golden and Diamond Jubilees. Once so self-righteously critical and shocked at Britain's class system, they themselves now evidenced signs of a lively class consciousness, not only with reference to their travel arrangements and those who served them, but in reference to their own traveling countrymen as well. This, too, was the period during which young American ladies with fortunes went hunting on the marriage market for Englishmen with titles, or, at the very least, sought the blessing of a "presentation" at the British Court.

In these later decades of mass travel, an even wider variety of Americans headed for the Old World. As always, there was a large flock of preachers, many of them now making trips to "The Holy Land" with a little European sightseeing en route. The Reverend Beverly Carradine of New Orleans, stopping off in New York in 1890 to hear the noted preacher Dr. Talmadge, only to learn that he was abroad, remarked, "What a kind congregation he has, off on a trip to the Holy Land with a vacation granted upon top of that!"[30] Some of these ecclesiastical embarkations assumed almost royal proportions, another traveler observed in 1878—with tugs full of handkerchief-waving, cheering parishioners following their clergyman's ship as it moved out through the harbor—and he was told by his captain that, "whenever there were any Brooklyn ministers aboard, such a company of steam vessels always followed them down the harbor."[31] Eight years later the Reverend Henry Ward Beecher, having nicely survived the disgrace of the Beecher-Tilton adultery trial, embarked on June 19, 1886, aboard the *Etruria*, with 3,000 wildly-cheering members of his congregation following him out of New York harbor aboard the excursion steamer *Grand Republic*, as a band played "Hail to the Chief," followed by a choral rendering of "Praise God from Whom all blessings flow."[32]

Politicians made equally grand embarkations, as journalist Benjamin Walker noted, himself leaving aboard the *Umbria* in 1889. There were at least 1,500 people assembled to wish bon voyage to a mere 500 travelers, he observed, with much of the attention aroused by "the presence of Mr. J. J. O'Donohue, evidently one of New York's famous Tammany magnates," whose adherents followed him as far as Sandy Hook, with "Mr. O'Donohue vigorously waving the American flag" the while.[33]

Businessmen, like Daniel F. Beatty of Washington, New Jersey, a piano and organ manufacturer, sometimes combined the status conferred by foreign travel with business. He was "innundated with floral offerings and wreaths" on his departure on August 2, 1878, from New York and was met with a procession led by the Washington brass band on his return home. "Already since my return have I begun to feel the effects of my travels," he boasted in his little book *In Foreign Lands*. "I am in receipt of orders, which, if it had not been for the persistency with which I have pushed and introduced my interests in Europe, some other enterprising house might have reaped the benefit. My export trade has become extremely large."[34]

In quite a different mood when he departed was the well-known journalist and Shakespeare devotee, Richard Grant White, father of architect Stanford White. Thirsty for culture, he left for England in 1876 to fulfill "one of the great unsatisfied longings of my life." Deliberately he avoided England's industrial towns and all evidences of her mercantile life. "I kept away from mills and mines and everything connected with them. . . . It is impossible not to see," he added, "that railways and mills and forges and towns are gradually . . . destroying rural England."[35]

Britons who had emigrated to the United States earlier in the century and gained a certain degree of prosperity now returned in their middle years to visit relatives and friends. Lucy Culler and her preacher-husband of Newton, Iowa, visited her birthplace at Cheltenham, where she stood for a few moments in the room where she was born in a house now owned by strangers. The "choice plants" given her from her cousin's garden were now, she wrote in her book, "blooming gaily" in her Iowa garden.[36]

Actor Stephen Massett, who had arrived in New York as a boy of seventeen in 1837, returned to England after several decades. Once in London he hastened to Salter's Chapel in Cannon Street, where he had attended services with his mother just before her death. Everything was unchanged, he found, except himself.[37] William Peberdy returned in 1888 to Mount Sorrell, near Leicester, after twenty years in America. His sister had died, so he trimmed and clipped her grave—"all I could do for her then." His former home had become a stable, he noted. As he said good-bye to his aged mother, he realized that "it was our final parting." Still, he congratulated himself that "at an early age I adopted a new country as my future home, under more liberal rule, a land of promise and plenty."[38]

A happier homecoming was that of Welshman William Whyte—now a portly official of the Anchor Line—returning in 1867 for a visit in Llanelly. He was still remembered, and there were even relatives "to gaze with wonder and admiration" at the stout and prosperous figure so unlike the youthful emigrant of their recollection. " 'Dear me! indeed to goodness,' " gasped one old lady who had sold him "sugar by the quarter pound, tea by the quarter ounce, and tallow candles by the twelfth of a dozen" from her tiny shop. " 'Dear me! Are you William Whyte?' " she asked. " 'And they tell me you can spake Welsh as good as when a boy!' "[39]

Charles Linskill, editor of the *Wilkes-Barre Telephone*, in 1887 kept a promise made to his dying father to visit the latter's old home in Whitby which he had left as a boy in 1830. " 'Aye, I knew 'im,' " chirped an old codger. " 'E was a tailor.' " Linskill's Uncle James, a man of eighty, remembered the day in the summer of 1815, he told his nephew, when Whitby had rejoiced in the downfall of Napoleon at Waterloo. "Here is the public house, named 'Nelson's Flag', near the pier where my father lived," marveled Linskill. "Here is the turnbridge, where the old draw-bridge of my father's time used to be, and where crowds used to collect while ships passed."[40] James Rusling likewise found kin at Winterton, in Lincolnshire, the place his grandparents had left in 1795. A cousin took him to Epworth to visit the birthplace of John Wesley, making the mistake of handing over the reins to the American. " 'Keep to the left, man keep to the left!' " he had to admonish his Yankee driver not yet accustomed to that rule of British roads.[41]

Other Americans digging for family roots had to settle for less. Physician Edward Thwing was satisfied, so he wrote. with merely locating a village of that name near York.[42] George Williams, who wrote that he "made a hasty run through Wales trying to find the home of my forefathers," but gave it up, concluded that trying to find a Williams in Wales was "like looking for a diamond in a coal pit."[43] In 1884 Leonard Morrison took himself to the land of the Morrisons, the Isle of Lewis in the Outer Hebrides. He gave up trying to find relatives, however, and settled instead for the boundless hospitality and kindness of the islanders. His other lasting memory was that of a Monday morning— following the austere Lewis Sabbath on which he attended both English and Gaelic church services—when he watched over 1,000 fishing boats that had moored there over Sunday, heading out of the harbor at Stornoway into the Minch. The harbor was black with their sails, he recalled—an extraordinary sight. "one which perhaps could be seen in no other place on the globe."[44]

Little Kate Murphy set out alone aboard the *State of Georgia* in 1885, "with only one suit besides the one I wore, a bag, and $140 in English money." Once in Belfast she set to work with "the Directory" and called on families named Murphy till she found the ones related to her. "In doing so," she wrote, "I was shown the same affectionate attention and was greeted with the same joyful welcome by all, as I was by my own relatives."[45] On the other hand, the Reverend Nicholas Murray, who had withheld even his particular brand of cold Presbyterian comfort from the dying Irish lad in his ship's steerage, found himself a virtual stranger on his visit to the village of his birth. "Nobody knew me, and I knew nobody . . . I became sick."[46]

Old Dr. Oliver Wendell Holmes decided in 1886 that, if he was ever going to revisit scenes remembered from his youthful years as a medical student abroad, he had best go now, at age seventy-seven, and wait no longer, despite his chronic and troublesome asthma. "For a whole week we lived under the shadow of the spire of the great cathedral," he wrote of his stay at Salisbury, his "first love among all the wonderful ecclesiastical buildings I saw during my first journey." He composed a poem, "The Broken Circle," after visiting nearby Stonehenge, where suddenly he realized how deaf he was, as the others listened raptly to the notes of the mounting skylark he could not hear. "The show is almost over," he wrote philosophically in his journal. The lionizing of him in London delighted him, and he reported to his readers what superb listeners were "the precious old dowagers" of that city. It astonished him to realize that his own parents had been "full-blooded subjects of King George III." He recalled much anti-British sentiment in his youth, he said, and again during the Civil War; but "a new generation is outgrowing that alienation."[47]

Besides these earnest searchers for roots were invalids of every description in search of health in an age that believed in the healing powers of travel and a change of scene. Mrs. E. A. Forbes repaired to Britain for her health's sake in 1863 and, strangely, was the only member of her party to make it up to the top of the dome of St. Paul's and even into the Golden Ball. "I feel rather proud of the exploit," she admitted.[48] Others sought health and did not find it, like poor consumptive Agnes Claflin of Massachusetts in 1868. Diligently she worked at her sightseeing and journal-keeping, but she reacted like the child she still was at London's Zoological Gardens. "Imagine me in the great garden of London, parading round on a camel's back," she wrote.[49] Less than a year later she died in Rome of tuberculosis. "A nervous disease which threatened to become troublesome to manage" took lawyer John Bender, a prominent citizen of Plymouth, Indiana, to Britain in 1874, where he gave the jitters to everyone he met but himself returned home, six months later, considerably improved.[50]

"All the 'shoddy', all the nouveaux riches"—complained journalist Kate Field in 1872—"began rushing across the Atlantic, once the Civil War was over, "for the purpose of spending their rapidly acquired and frequently-ill gotten fortunes, and stupidly imagining that fine feathers make fine birds." Frequently Miss Field was shamed, she said, by the ignorance and vulgarity that some English people took to be typical American traits. "When I tell English people that the most brilliant women I know never leave their quiet New England homes, they exclaim, 'Why, I thought all Americans travelled!' As a nation we do travel more than any other," acknowledged Miss Field, "but the proportion of culture is less than among European travellers. The European observer, especially if he be English, picks out the least attractive of our people and then and there concludes that Americans are the vulgarest and most ostentatious." Considering their great numbers, she concluded, "the marvel is not that there are so many uncouth Americans, but that there are so few." She was appalled at the growing mania of American women to be "presented" at the British Court, and she declared that they "deserve to be despised as the worst of flunkies."[51]

In the 1890s, one such lady, Sarah Maria Aloisa Britton Spottiswood Mackin—who entitled her book *A Society Woman on Two Continents*—enjoyed "the rare good fortune of courtesying before Her Majesty, the Prince and the Princess of Wales at one and the same time," concluding that "the cup of bliss is indeed full to the brim and running over." Bowing with her, she boasted, was Mrs. Cornelius Vanderbilt, resplendent in pink satin, white velvet, and yellow satin, with an astonishing array of diamonds. As an afterthought, Mrs. Mackin named a third American presented, young Lady Randolph Churchill, in "white brocade."[52]

Many other American women, less wealthy and less social than mighty Mrs. Mackin, enjoyed once-in-a-lifetime trips to Britain during these years—due largely to the genius of one Thomas Cook, the Englishman who conceived the idea, so common today, of the "package" or group tour at relatively moderate cost. In 1873, Messrs. Cook, Son and Jenkins of New York, in collaboration with Thomas Cook and Son of London, collected 148 Americans from twenty-seven states, "embracing a great number of the leading instructors from various sections, including professors of colleges, public and private school teachers, ministers, press representatives, and others engaged in various departments of educational work," packed them aboard the *Victoria* of the Anchor Line, and got them safely over to the Vienna Exhibition and back "with uninterrupted health." Britain was not overlooked en route, for there was a stop at Ireland's Giants' Causeway, a tour through Sir Walter Scott-land, and a stop in London where they were divided into four smaller groups before invading the Continent.[53] So successful was this first "educational" tour that a second took off the following summer, and thus began an institution. By 1880 Cook's would boast in their American brochure that they "have had the honour of conveying *many thousands* of the citizens of the United States to all the chief points of interest."[54] The age of "tourism" was here!

As the number of American travelers grew, so did the number of books they turned out on their return. "In these days of the Nineteenth Century," the professional society matron, Mrs. Mackin, observed, "to prove one's claim to fashion, and fashion rules the world, I am told that one must ride the bicycle and write a book."[55] Some of her enterprising countrymen indeed did both, like Alfred Chandler of Boston and Reuben Thwaites of Wisconsin, and they thus gained added points in the status race through their descriptions of their bicycle tours of England in the summers of 1879 and 1891, respectively. The urge to write accounts of their rambles in the mother country still burned in the hearts of these American pilgrims, even as some of them, like Mary Blake, wondered in 1890 "whether there is any room now for the journal of an enthusiast" and went ahead and wrote one anyway.[56] Even hard-pushed tourists on group tours managed to write books. Up in Scotland in 1900, one traveler observed flocks of "bright-faced Yankee school ma'ms, many of them with notebooks."[57]

In these years the writers scratched harder than ever for eye-catching titles, and as more women hit the trail titles like *An American Girl Abroad*, *A Girl's Journey*, and *A Woman's Vacation* began to appear. The speed-up of the whole travel process becomes apparent in such titles as *Rapid Transit Abroad*, *Sixty Days across the Water*, and *The Quick Traveler*—especially when compared with Calvin Colton's *Four Years in Great Britain* of 1835. Soon there were titles like *Three Weeks in the British Isles* and even *Ten Days Abroad*. Young men still under the spell of Bayard Taylor came out with books called *The Youthful Wanderer*, as did George Heffner, and Orrin Hubbell wrote *A University Tramp*, in which there is far more railway travel than there is tramping of any kind.

There were even books of travel for "stay-at-homes," like that by Mrs. E. H. Thompson of New Hampshire, a devout Methodist, who prepared in 1890, a complete "armchair tour" of Great Britain for members of the Epworth League. Using the typical American tourist's itinerary in Britain, which she referred to as "the mother of our mighty nation," she embellished each stop with appropriate passages from English literature or from American travelers' books on Britain.[58]

Interesting errors, both typographical and factual, crept into the accounts of these latter-day travelers. One Yankee scribbler had Mary Stuart buried at Holyrood Palace.[59] Another said that she was executed in the Tower of London.[60] Another tourist had Dr. Johnson interred at St. Paul's.[61] "Don't give up the ship" was solemnly attributed by one American to Lord Nelson.[62] Another writer informed his readers that British monarchs are crowned in "a rather insignificant chapel called Westminster Hall" and that "many nobles were executed there."[63] Edinburgh's famous Tron Church came out as "Torn" on several occasions, and Madame Tussaud appeared variously as "Tassaud," "Taussud," and even "Toussard."

How-to-travel books were no new thing after George Putnam's *The Tourist in Europe* of 1838, John Henry Sherburne's *The Tourist's Guide* of 1847, and Roswell Park's *Handbook for American Travellers in Europe* of 1853. But in the last decades of the nineteenth century, such books poured forth in response to the great boom in tourism. Boston newsman Curtis Guild produced *Over the Ocean* in 1871, *Abroad Again* in 1877, and *Britons and Muscovites* in 1888. William Hemstreet came out with *The Economical European Tourist* in 1875, a journalist's itemized account of three months abroad for $433, including Ireland, Scotland, England, France, Switzerland, Italy, Austria and Prussia. "There was no pinching economy," he assured his readers. "I ate and drank all I had a taste for, and lived, when halting, at respectable places."[64]

Most prolific of them all, with seven different guides for different parts of the world, was Thomas Knox, who began with a basic *How To Travel* in 1881. Other such books are Morford's *Short-Trip Guide to Europe* in 1874; Morris Phillip's *Abroad and at Home* in 1892; Moses Sweetser's *Europe for $2.00 a Day* in 1875; and an interesting little book published by the "Women's Rest Tour Association" of Boston, called *A Summer in England*, published in 1896. Giving American women advice on everything from what to wear at sea to social customs in Britain, that little book seems to bear the imprint of the much-traveled Julia Ward Howe, president of the association. It ends with a glossary of comparable British-American terms to aid the traveler.[65] May Alcott Nieriker, sister of Louisa May Alcott, and herself the "Amy" of *Little Women*, put out a little book of advice for impecunious American art students, based on her own experience. In it she advocated such economies as paper cuffs and taking old underclothes, because "the grime of London and the acid used by all Parisian blanchisseuses soon rot anything delicate," and they would then constitute perfect "paint rags."[66]

In order to get the most out of his trip, the American traveler headed for Great Britain was now actually advised, by Moses Sweetser, to brush up on the novels of Dickens and Thackeray for London; the romances of Scott and the poems of Burns for Scotland; the lives and poetry of Wordsworth, Coleridge, and Southey for the Lake Country; Lever's stories and Moore's poems for Ireland; and John Timbs's *Romance of London* and *Curiosities of London*, which "contain many valuable items." Add to this Hawthorne's *Our Old Home* and Washington Irving's *Sketchbook* and the American traveler was ready to embark;[67] except, possibly, for Dr. George Beard's *A Practical Treatise on Sea-Sickness* of 1880, highly recommended by one traveler as "a means by which sea-sickness may be entirely avoided."[68]

15

Voyage

How different was Henry Adams's passage across the Atlantic in 1892, aboard his comfortable steamship, from Benjamin Silliman's passage under sail in 1805, or even Adams's own first trip three decades earlier. "So big and so fast, and relatively so comfortable, that as I lay in my stateroom and looked out of my windows on the storm, I felt a little wonder whether this world were the same that I lived in thirty years ago," marveled Adams, referring to the time he and his father set out for Britain at the start of the Civil War. "In all my wanderings this is the first time I have had the sensation. All the rest of the world seems more or less what it was . . . but the big Atlantic steamer is a whacker!"[1]

In the decades following the Civil War, the "tea kettles" of the forties and fifties evolved rapidly into floating "hotels" or "palaces" where the passenger and his pleasures were the primary concern. "Not his comfort and safety merely, but his very whims are studied," observed the experienced traveler and writer, William H. Rideing, in 1890, adding that, "to his transportation from continent to continent all things are subordinated, except the sea and the wind."[2] Describing the Inman Line's posh *City of New York* and *City of Paris* steamers, Rideing remarked that "we do not seem to be in a ship at all but the palace of a voluptuary."[3]

The screw propeller, and then twin screws, had long since replaced the sidewheels or paddles. Antirolling chambers, electric searchlights, watertight bulkheads, electric communication systems throughout the ships, sufficient lifeboats and rafts, and lifebelts and buoys in every cabin, all added to the passengers' comfort, safety, and sense of security aboard these ships which Rideing also compared to "a great marine projectile."[4] The captain and his officers, now remote figures on the bridge above the main deck, presided over crews of 400 men manning a vessel of 10,000 tons, compared to the hundred or so able seamen who had pushed the 3,000-ton "steam kettles" across the Atlantic in earlier decades. As auxiliary sails disappeared, seamen became mere drudges—sweepers, painters, and cargo handlers. It took, instead, 200 engineers of various types, most of them Scots, to keep these "steam palaces" or "naval mansions" running.[5]

The aim seemed to be to make the voyager forget altogether that he was on a ship at sea. Describing the main saloon of ships like the *City of New York,* Rideing observed that "there is not a more beautiful dining-hall in any American or European hotel." Instead of an ordinary ceiling, he wrote,

THE "GALLIA" AT SEA

ON DECK

The Cunard Company's new steamship *Gallia*. **Larger, faster steamers (side wheels now a thing of the past) crossed what voyagers now patronizingly referred to as "the duck pond."** *The Graphic,* **April 19, 1879, p. 397.** *Courtesy the Library of Congress.*

there is an arch of rich stained glass, in which the colors of the turquoise, the amethyst, and the topaz are blended. This is fifty-three feet long, and twenty-five feet wide, and spans the centre of the saloon; leaving rows of alcoves on each side . . . which are lighted by windows opening on the upper deck. The arch springs from a molded cornice of ivory-white in which are delicately carved figures of mermaids, tritons, and dolphins. At one end of the arch, high above the floor, a music gallery is embayed.

Chairs of solid mahogany, "richly carved," provided the seating, along with lounges upholstered with "caressing cushions." The galleys and pantries were now located near the dining saloon, eliminating the old necessity for wind-buffeted, spray-drenched stewards having to career over open decks, hurrying great covered dishes to the waiting diners.[6]

Besides the palatial dining saloon there was now a spacious smoking room with "spongy divans, bookshelves and card tables" to replace the discomforts of the old, covered hatchway called "the fiddley," where men on the early steamers had to take their pipes and cigars and enjoy a few moments away from their ladies as well.[7] Women were catered to with "boudoirs of soft blue and gold where the lights admitted by the 'ports' became irridescent through many-tinted glasses and where flowers are blooming even when the sea is gray and sullen." Rideing described another such drawing room with "hundreds of incandescent lamps, costly fabrics used in the upholstery, the gleam of stained glass . . . even the pillars supporting the roof are covered with flowered silks of an exquisite pattern, reaching up to gilded capitals."[8]

Personal hygiene, too, had come a long way from the days when women usually settled for furtive washbowl ablutions in the tiny staterooms, while the men, if they so desired, could take cold saltwater showers on deck by arrangement with the stewards. Now there were, Rideing assured his readers, innumerable bath and toilet rooms in every section and on every deck. "Who does not remember," he asked, "in the old days what competition there was among the passengers for a few minutes in the only bathroom which the ship contained?" Now there were even self-contained suites, for those able to afford them, opening directly on the deck. Cramped and spartan staterooms, like the one Harriet Beecher Stowe called her "sea-coop," were also a thing of the past. Those small and often dark little cabins—in which voyagers struggled to dress and undress, hitting knees and elbows in the process, and where fearful contortions were required to get in and out of the narrow berths, particularly the upper when seas were rough—were now replaced by roomy electric-lighted "staterooms" convertible to sitting rooms while passengers sat at their breakfast. "Instead of a chamber of repose," wrote William Rideing, "we now have a charming little parlor."[9]

By 1875, travelers had a choice of eleven different lines in addition to Cunard, which, except for the Crimean War years when its ships were otherwise engaged, kept a firm grip on Atlantic travel.[10] While many Yankees considered it their patriotic duty to patronize an American line and even included exhortations to others to do likewise in their travel accounts, Cunard continued on with its proud record of never having lost a passenger, to attract both the more sophisticated and the more timid travelers who valued seamanship over silk upholstery.

"Think of it," observed Noble Prentis of Kansas in 1877, "fifty years of sending ships to sea, and never yet a vessel lost!" He was impressed, too, by the ships' officers aboard his vessel, the *Bothnia,* "big, bluff, red-faced fellows, with a width of shoulder, and a circumference of abdomen fearful . . . to contemplate. I do not suppose a cannon ball could knock one of these officers over . . . and they certainly know their business."[11] Theodore Cuyler remarked in 1882 that "this veteran line has earned its crown of supremacy for perfect discipline, staunch steamers, and the preservation of every human life committed to its charge."[12]

Another well-traveled American attested, "I have never seen steamers more carefully navigated than those of the Cunard company."[13] May Alcott Nieriker—who, as the daughter of Bronson Alcott, learned early to extract maximum value from every penny—urged even poor students to "take passage on a Cunard if the student prefers safety," even though it cost more.[14] William Dean Howells pronounced Cunard "an ark of safety for the timid and despairing," recalling an old maxim that voyagers on a Cunard ship "could sleep on *both* ears" as one was not needed to be kept cocked for sounds of impending disaster, as on other lines.[15]

Seasickness continued to plague voyagers even in these large, luxurious vessels, but now the malady had been studied exhaustively by the medical profession and there were preventions and cures far more sophisticated than Mrs. Stowe's stoic huddling on deck by the smoke pipe. The suggested treatments of "the celebrated George M. Beard, M.D.," as voyager James McClay dubbed him, today sound worse than the malady itself—dangerous, even.

In his *Practical Treatise on Sea-Sickness* of 1880 Dr. Beard, who termed the malady "a functional disease of the central nervous system," advocated, besides generous dosing with bromides of sodium and potassium, atropia by injection for severe cases, even though he admitted that swallowing became difficult when he tried it on himself, and he found also that it numbed certain muscles of the eye, thus making it difficult to read. Citrate of caffeine and *Cannabis Indica* were his recommendations for sick headache. He did warn, however, against the use of morphine or opium, in any form, as well as the use of nitrite of amyl, which, in one case he knew of, had induced "temporary paraplegia." Hydrate of chloral, or "knock-out drops," could be resorted to, Beard claimed, but it was "not recommended for daily or long-continued use."[16] Evangelist Phoebe Palmer always swore by "five drops of chloroform taken in a spoonful of water" and freely recommended this nostrum to others as her husband, "a physician of long-standing," endorsed it.[17]

One suggested way to avoid the suffering of seasickness altogether was to practice abstemiousness the week before sailing. J. M. Bailey, the "Danbury News Man," said that he knew of one such effort by a young man of his town.

> Born of Puritan parents and reared among the refining and wholesome influences of a New England home, he carefully dieted himself the week before sailing. He ate freely of oatmeal and bran bread, and eschewed greasy foods and stimulating drinks. The night before sailing he went down to New York in the flush of health and hope, and, stopping at a Norwalk clam-bake, filled up with roast clams and gin, getting to the city just in time to take the boat. For three days he pranced around on the edge of eternity, kicking up his heels, swinging his arms, and turning himself inside out.[18]

The conquest of seasickness was believed by some travelers to be all a matter of willpower and mental outlook. Editor Charles Linskill determined that "if the Cunard people could afford me a hammock on the billows, worth fifteen hundred thousand dollars, I might try to keep well and cheerful," which he did, aboard the mighty *Servia*, even though roughing it in second-class quarters. "I think if one stands on deck and watches the billows rise and fall and breathes the fresh air, he will see what rocks him, and expect it, and resolve to let accounts with Old Ocean rest as they are and keep well. I did not get sick," he proudly reported. "I liked the motion of the ship. It was like a swing, a cradle, a see-saw, a rocking-chair, and merry-go-round, but most of all it reminded me how, when a boy, I climbed a very tall and slender hickory tree in a high wind [where] I rocked to and fro."[19]

Once the symptoms of seasickness abated, just as in the old days, the same massive meals and gargantuan eating commenced, with refrigeration now aiding still further the gastronomic efforts of the chefs. In 1895, aboard the *City of New York* carrying 1,420 people, was loaded "17,500 pounds of dressed beef, 3,600 pounds of mutton, 500 pounds of lamb, 500 pounds of veal, 1,150 chickens, ducks and turkeys; 450 grouse and squab, 1,250 pounds of fish, 3,780 pounds of butter, nearly 700 dozen eggs, 12½ tons of potatoes, 280 heads of cabbage, 1,500 pounds of turnips and carrots, besides a large quantity of other vegetables, such as beets, cauliflower, beans, peas, lettuce, etc., 146 barrels of flour, 5,000 oranges, 15 barrels of apples, 400 pounds of grapes, dozens of boxes of pears, peaches, plums and lemons, 7,000 pounds of sugar. Added to this . . . 13,500 pounds of corned beef, nearly 3,000 pounds of bacon and ham, 300 gallons of fresh milk, and sixty gallons of condensed milk . . . on this particular voyage, 2,812 bottles of ale, 2,400 bottles of mineral water and 300 bottles of other kinds of drinks also disappeared," finished Lou Beauchamp who compiled this record of his vessel's larder. There was also a "permanent buffet" available in addition to seven meals a day. "I was afraid I'd bust before I reached Liverpool," he confessed.[20]

Aboard the *Egypt* of the National Line in 1882, Lucy Culler described "four simply wonderful meals a day with breakfast at half-past eight, lunch at half-past twelve, dinner at five, and tea at half-past eight in the evening." She listed "an ordinary bill of fare for dinner" for her readers:

Mock-turtle and spring soup
Pigeons on toast, and mushrooms
Mutton cutlets, curried chicken and rice
Dresden patties, roast beef and Yorkshire pudding
Boiled mutton and caper sauce
Roast lamb and mint sauce
Roast fillet of veal, corned pork and vegetables
Corned beef, roast turkey, sausages and cranberry sauce

Duck and green peas
Ham and tongue, pickles and asparagus
Plum and custard pudding, damson tarts, currant pies, Leipsig and plum cakes,
Genoese pastry, apple tripple, blanc mange, calves-foot jelly, Charlotte russe,
macaroni and cheese
Apples, oranges, raisins and several kinds of nuts.

"All of the China dishes bear this stamp," noticed Mrs. Culler: "National Steamship Company. 'Pro orbis utilitate' (for the use of the world). The tureens for meats and vegetables are of solid silver, and when the bell taps, the waiters take off all the covers at once, sometimes revealing the most unheard-of mixtures. Mr. Culler took four square meals every day, and did not indulge in seasickness. But alas! I was not so fortunate." She admitted, in fact, that at one point she felt miserable enough to jump overboard.[21]

"Although we do little else but eat," Eudora Lindsay South in 1884 was surprised to find that she and all her friends had lost rather than gained weight on their voyage. "This afternoon the Captain fastened to the rigging a pair of balances, then attached to them a short swing in which we would sit while he determined our respective weights. Despite our hearty and frequent meals, the sea air has taken from each of us several pounds of flesh."[22]

To travelers collapsed in deck chairs, digesting their heavy meals, the deck "walkers" on these larger ships were a source of amusement and curiosity. They "paced the deck from one end to the other, as though bent on some great enterprise," wrote one pilgrim of the perambulators aboard his ship; "among these a young Englishman walked bareheaded and resolute." There was also, he added, "a gentleman who had at one time some presidential aspirations. He could be seen at almost any hour from daylight until ten o'clock at night, hurrying along the deck, yet making as little progress as he did in getting to the White House."[23]

Female travelers gave considerable thought to their appearance in these years. "Do not be beguiled by those who would have you economize by wearing out your old clothes on board," advised Boston's Women's Rest Tour Association— headed by the well-traveled Julia Ward Howe—in its travel-advice booklet. "Plain, simple and comfortable attire you must have, but if you are to enjoy the voyage, forswear shabbiness." They suggested a stout, "simply-made serge or tweed dress," which could be brightened at the neck with a ruche, a silk kerchief, or lace scarf. "Flannel knickerbockers are more convenient than thick pet-ticoats," they maintained, and also suggested an ulster for deck wear that was heavy enough to keep one's skirts from blowing about. "A hood, soft felt hat or cloth cap" should replace the impractical bonnet, and stout but good-looking boots should be worn as they became "conspicuous" objects when one was stretched out on a deck chair. Beyond this, the voyager was advised to carry a pair of "colored glasses," to wear "a thick paper over the stomach for extra warmth" and to "keep the bowels open and avoid fatiguing the eyes."[24] Another experienced female travel adviser gave essentially the same pointers, though in far greater detail, urging in particular the wearing of warm flannel underwear, including "a pair of overall flannel drawers, bright turkey red, to be worn *over* the underclothing and slipped off on going below."[25]

The men, for the most part, were content, as of old, to don worn winter woolens that had seen better days and to top these off with cloth caps or soft, slouch hats as substitutes for the customary "stovepipe" of the day. Hemstreet, advising male travelers on matters of dress, suggested traveling light, and he boasted that his own luggage usually consisted of "six shirts and collaterals, a tooth-brush, a hair-brush, *Harper's Guidebook,* an opera-glass, and note-books—

that is all."[26] Knox suggested "the roughest clothing procurable" for shipboard wear. Woolen or "hickory" shirts were recommended, as was woolen underwear, it "being much safer against the skin than linen or cotten."[27] Some of the female travelers suspected that the males enjoyed their enforced sartorial sloppiness. "They positively seem to wring a kind of salt comfort out of this rough, scrambling, ungloved life at sea," sniffed Ella Thompson. "The taste for barbarism, latent in all of them, comes to the surface."[28]

Shipboard activities still included the little newspapers such as "The Daily Journal" aboard the *Gallia,* turned out now on the small presses used to print up the daily bill of fare. The Fourth of July was still the excuse for a raucous celebration, which far exceeded in enthusiasm those the passengers commonly indulged in at home—particularly if they were aboard a British ship. Some Yankees liked to think that this annoyed their patient British crews. "Her Majesty's subjects, with gold-banded caps and without, fringed the edges of the Yankee company," wrote Eliza Connor of Ohio, a member of a Cook's tour, aboard the *Circassia* in the summer of 1882, "with a look on their faces of mingled smile, sneer and curiosity. And didn't we make the American eagle scream!"[29] No matter that it was these same Britons who fired the guns, ran up the flags, supplied the "crackers," and responded to the toasts.

Traveling academics felt neglected if not asked to lecture on a given evening, and, aboard the *City of Berlin* in the eighties passengers heard "Dr. Gregory, president of Illinois University, read his paper on 'Antagonism of Labor and Capital',"followed by recitations from Grace Greenwood, nom de plume of the now middle-aged matron, Sara Jane Lippincott, taking her daughter abroad for voice lessons.[30] Voyagers aboard a ship in 1890 were treated to two lectures, one by "Mrs. Lockwood, the superintendent of the Peace Department of the Women's Christian Temperance Union," as well as an exposé by "Edith O. Gordon, the escaped nun," who was in the middle of her talk when "rudely interrupted by a Catholic priest who, thrusting in his head through a window, called the lady speaker a liar."[31] Actual libraries graced these later, larger vessels, and a voyager at the turn of the century reported that of her vessel well filled with good books such as Boswell's *Life of Johnson,* Hume's detective stories, and Strickland's *Lives of the Queens.*[32]

Aboard the British Cunarders, the traditional end-of-voyage "concerts" on behalf of the Sailors' Orphans' Home at Liverpool were still enthusiastically supported by American travelers. Jesse Johnson, aboard the *Umbria* at the turn of the century was told by a ship's officer that, "since the establishment of the orphanage at Liverpool, 85,000 seamen on English vessels had been drowned."[33] Passengers contributed most of their own entertainment, and one of them listed some items of the program on her voyage: "Overture on the piano, Mrs. Dr. Moore; 'Grandfather's Clock,' a song by Mr. A. H. Pilley; 'The Curfew,' a recitation by Miss Converse; an address by Reverend Dr. Morrell of New York; 'The Speech of Wolf Jim in the Missouri State Legislature' by Prof. Charles Whitney; 'The Sleighing Chorus' by the Young Ladies; a recitation of 'The Charge of the Light Brigade,' also by Prof. Whitney; and the song, 'Hannah at the Window Binding Shoes,' by Mrs. Anna P. Sears."[34] Florence Trail, on her voyage aboard the *Bothnia* in 1883, was "highly complimented" for her "rendition of Chopin's *Polonaise Brillante*," she boasted, and she told how all the ladies were charmed by the captain's gift of little vegetable corsages—"an oleander ingeniously made from beets and turnips." He was, she recalled, "the beau of the ship."[35]

The more serious shipboard pursuits were still drinking and gambling, which riled the Protestant preachers no end, although one of them was not above including a small joke on the subject. The Reverend Cross wrote that, upon his inquiring after the health of an acquaintance missing at breakfast one morning, he was told that the man had sat up all night watching for the boarding of the pilot. " 'And did he see him?' I asked. 'Oh, yes,' answered my informant. 'He saw *two!*' "[36]

Gambling was observed by the Reverend Zachary Taylor Sweeney aboard the *Umbria* in 1887. "After tea [the smoking room] is turned into a gambling hell, where dissipation of all kinds is freely encouraged," he thundered. "Thirteen of us wrote out a protest . . . and gave it to the Liverpool papers. It was copied largely by the London dailies, and also the American papers. On our return, I was gratified to see placards in the smoking room prohibiting gambling or indecent language."[37]

The attitude of the seamen toward all these traveling clergymen was observed about 1870 by the daughter of one, Adeline Trafton, child of the Reverend Mark Trafton who wrote of his own European trip two decades earlier. In her book, entitled *An American Girl Abroad,* she told how she overheard one sailor grumbling to another: "Always a headwind with a parson aboard!"[38]

An Englishman aboard a ship in 1882 achieved a reputation based on his willingness to bet on everything or anything and then bet another sovereign that he would win his bet! Another young Briton reached his homeland in 1884 "completely skinned," in his own words, and had to telegraph his brother-in-law for money to reach home. This was the same voyage on which "Father C.," a Catholic priest, "swept the card-table of its last sixpence," and he may well have been the downfall of that unlucky youth.[39] On Thomas Clayton's voyage in 1869 the story was the same: "the only amusement was drinking and gambling . . . One gentleman bet £80 . . . on the toss of a penny!"[40] By 1881 travel writer Thomas Wallace Knox had already begun to warn voyagers to shun "the adepts at cards" aboard the ocean liners. "The Atlantic is crossed every year," he wrote, "by men who boast they are able to cover their expenses by gambling."[41]

Eventually it became well known that "there are ocean tramps who live on ocean steamers," as Leonard Morrison put it in 1887, "whose business it is to gamble and bet. . . . The wine bill of some of these men, during a single voyage of ten days, would often be one hundred and fifty dollars." Morrison told the story of a transplanted Welshman, now a Texas rancher, who became the butt of considerable merriment, aboard the *City of Chicago* in 1884, because of his odd dress, peculiar manners, and his fear of the sea, which led him to stack twenty-seven life preservers in his cabin during a storm. Continually invited to join the sporting gentlemen at their games of cards in the smoking room, he steadfastly refused, claiming that he knew nothing of such games. Finally, as the ship neared Liverpool, he gave in, and in a single day he took them all to the cleaners. After that, Morrison wrote, he not only "commanded their respect [but] also won ducats enough to pay his expenses across the ocean."[42] Edgar Magness watched another gambling drama as a young man named Phillips, recently graduated from Harvard, got taken by a trio of cardsharpers just after landing. They relieved him of twenty-five dollars in twenty-five minutes, and he "smiled a sickly smile as his sovereigns were passed to the slick-handed shuffler."[43]

Certain card players became legends. Joel Cook told of a group of four Philadelphians "who for fourteen years past have been steadily playing euchre, never changing partners and have, on this ship, [the *Ohio*] according to the official record they keep, played their twenty-eight thousandth game." Probably commercial travelers, these men, Cook claimed, had, "since 1864, in all the ups and downs of American life . . . continued their games through weal and woe, with no break in their circle; no cheating at cards, and are now continuing with a vim that even sea-sickness cannot shake."[44]

Famous passengers were still cultivated, if possible, and, returning home aboard the *Java* in 1871, James Hoyt sought out the company of weary old William Henry Seward, Lincoln's secretary of state, returning home from his voyage around the world. "Though both of his arms are nearly helpless from paralysis," reported Hoyt, "he has lost little of his natural activity, and is every day on deck for hours, when the weather will admit." The young man who had once bowed to old King William in his carriage and enthusiastically observed the British House of Commons was now an old man himself. "His face is deeply scarred by the wounds inflicted by the assassin who attempted to take his life in Washington," reported Hoyt. (Seward was badly gashed on the face and throat by Lewis Payne, one of the conspirators whose task it was to kill Seward on the same night Lincoln was murdered but who was foiled by a male nurse and Seward's son Frederick.) "He is easily approachable," Hoyt continued, and delights "in conversation."[45] Poor Kate Chase Sprague—but recently divorced from Senator William Sprague after considerable scandal, who was the tragic daughter of Chief Justice Salmon P. Chase, and who herself played a large part in the drama of Civil War Washington—was observed on one of the many restless journeys that marked the downward spiral of her later years. She sailed aboard the *Gallia* with the James Bradleys of Asbury Park in 1883, but they record no conversations with that star-crossed lady.[46]

In 1884 the Reverend William Pratt Breed had ample opportunity to study P. T. Barnum's latest novelty, called Krao, "the missing link," who sailed aboard his ship, the *City of Richmond*. A rather hairy little girl of Siamese birth, she good-naturedly entertained the other children on board and "generally assumed a position somewhat of authority."[47] The diva Adelina Patti graced the decks of the *Oregon* in 1884, returning home with an assortment of pets that included "a dog, a rooster, and a parrot."[48] Returning in 1899 to America aboard the *Oceanic,* Julia Wilson was thrilled at her proximity to such personages as Andrew Carnegie, Lord Paunceforte, Mr. Alfred Arnold, M.P., and "many dukes, ladies and titled people."[49]

The inhabitants of the steerage were still a source of curiosity, sometimes mixed with compassion, for the voyagers on the upper decks. To "see something funny," Eudora South was urged by a companion to "go into the forward steerage." There she found three or four wretched steerage passengers "rolling on their part of the deck in an agony of sea-sickness."[50]

"Now and then for recreation," wrote Chicago society matron Adelaide Hall in 1896 "we lean over the rail of the aft upper deck and watch the steerage passengers eating their meals and playing games." One old man, she observed, would "untie an old, soiled rag, and take out some chunks of bread and a dried-up sausage, and with his battered clasp knife slice off portions to share with his toothless wife."[51] Another traveler remarked that it was "great fun to watch life in the steerage; they were a merry lot, although deprived of nearly every comfort."[52] Julia Wilson surveyed "the motley group quartered below . . . some strong and well, others pale and sickly," and became aware of the contrast between her own lavish, elegantly served meals and those of the emigrants— "soup taken in tin ladles, with large chunks of bread."[53]

One voyager, looking down on such scenes, referred to "these scarcely human . . . discordant and swarming masses" and regretted that they would soon be landing on the shores of his country.[54]

Wrote Marion Adams in 1872: "Try to find some amusement in the steerage and find a coffin making for a man just dead."[55] Another of her sex got into trouble with the ships' officers on the voyage for taking baked apples from her table to hand out to children in the steerage. "The children among us," she wrote, "pelt the little ones not so fortunate as they with nuts and raisins; and these look up . . . with such eagerness they remind me of a nest of little birds waiting for the food the faithful mother-bird will surely bring."[56] The Reverend Morton Wharton viewed the steerage of his vessel, the *City of Berlin,* packed with six hundred seasick emigrants, and termed it "a sickening sight . . . disgusting to behold."[57]

The woes of the steerage inmates were not over on landing, either, certain travelers observed. One American surveyed a scene at New York's Castle Garden in 1860 where the new arrivals waited for hours, harassed by a "rowdy-looking officer or fellow, in a caricature of a uniform, with a stumpy gun," swearing and cursing at his charges. "Having been a foreigner in other countries, and been treated with civility by their officers, I took occasion to note how foreigners who come to our country to settle . . . are treated on their arrival in New York; and I must say it is not calculated to impress the lonely, perhaps desolate immigrant, with a very favorable opinion of our 'free institutions.' "[58] A decade or so later kindly Charles Poston, equally concerned, urged: "Let us give them a generous welcome. They have wives and little ones to support and perhaps the old and decrepit at home. They are strangers in a strange land. We have all been the same."[59]

Still, some of these steerage passengers never made it to the other side. Sometimes it was a child, "hardly . . . a mouthful for some of these porpoises I have seen tumbling along," remarked "Freethinker" DeRobigne Bennett, aboard the *Ethiopia* in August of 1881.[60] On a voyage in 1884 a young Irish girl, dying of consumption, begged the captain not to bury her at sea if she succumbed on her way back across the Atlantic to her home. She was, nevertheless, committed to the deep, 1,500 miles from her homeland, upon her death. Passengers all over the ship heard the cries of grief from the mother who came on board via the mailboat out of Queenstown to meet the daughter she thought was coming home.[61]

A woman voyager would never forget the "tears rolling down the cheeks" of their stolid captain as he read the simple service from the Book of Common Prayer for one of his young seamen killed in an accident near the end of the voyage. On that same ship in 1884 a young Irish crewman complained of feeling ill. "The ship's doctor could see nothing wrong with him, so he was not excused from duty. The other sailors kept teasing him, calling him a lazy fellow. He grew more and more dejected every day, and finally . . . put an end to his miseries by jumping overboard."[62] In 1898, wrote Edward Temple, "our faithful deck steward, with a wife and children in Southampton, threw himself overboard, leaving a brief note and a little money with the purser."[63] Aboard the *Abyssinia* in 1877, William Hutton reported the disappearance of "Judge Doolittle of Utica, who came on deck at 9 o'clock last evening, and has not since been seen. It is supposed that in a state of mental depression, or melancholy, he cast himself into the sea."[64]

Kindly William Hichborn of Boston, aboard the *Servia* in 1896, got together with some other passengers to pay the passage of two homesick boys trying to get back home to Britain, rather than see them treated as stowaways.[65]

Psychotic passengers showed up from time to time, as they always had, and one enlivened considerably the adventure of a little group of Yale students bound for "a tramp trip" abroad, who elected to travel in steerage across the Atlantic. A fellow-passenger, far gone with both drink and delusions, was locked in a cabin for the night. "In the dead of night," wrote young Frederick Stokes, "we were aroused from our slumber by the sound of sudden confusion, and our blood ran cold as we heard that most horror-infusing cry that can strike one's ears at sea—'Fire!' " The imprisoned wretch had set fire to both berths, "calmly lying in one of them," when found, and had a bonfire blazing on the floor as well. Freed, he rushed on deck and "hurled himself headlong over the side," wrote young Stokes. "Those who saw him, horror-stricken, made no motion to have the ship stopped until it was too late; so, the fire out, she rolled on as calmly as though a fearful tragedy had not been performed."[66]

Journalist Theron Crawford wrote how a former British diplomat informed him that "there was hardly a ship . . . to England which did not bring some insane person from the United States . . . shipped over to Europe by their relatives, simply to get rid of them." These individuals, Crawford added, "constantly harassed" the United States Legation in one way or another.[67]

Although more remote figures than in the early days when they paced the decks with their passengers, the captains were still the focus of much attention. Some females seemed to think that the captain was there for the purpose of playing the role of father, brother, shipboard escort, confessor and friend, and they were quite put out if the poor man was "too absorbed" with his ship. Travel writer Curtis Guild observed that some of them expected the man entrusted with the lives of hundreds at sea to perform "like the skipper of an excursion steamer ... to walk-arm-in-arm with young ladies, stand about in nautical uniform, and hold a spy-glass for them to peep through."[68] Some female passengers were so desirous of a place at the captain's table that they would be seen "arranging and almost fighting for good places at table, either with or near the captain."[69] Wrote Lily Rust in her journal, "[W]e were highly relieved when the Chief steward asked us to sit at the Captain's table in future"—following her complaint about a first meal "at another table with rather unattractive people."[70]

The lot of the ships' stokers was not much different from that aboard the earlier ships. Now they made five pounds a month, but the toll on men's bodies was as great as ever. The *Servia* boasted "thirty-nine roaring furnaces where twenty-one sweating men" constantly heaved coal. "It was ... the most oven-like place I had ever seen," observed editor Charles Linskill of Wilkes-Barre. "The men stay down here four hours at a time, and then go up to rest for eight. When not really in front of the roaring furnaces, they stand under the ventilators, whose funnel-shaped mouths are turned to the windward, on deck, fifty feet above."[71] In 1871 James Hoyt, aboard the *Wyoming,* observed a stoker, who had collapsed in 136-degree heat, brought on deck: "a strong Englishman, laid on his back, half naked, on a bed made from tarpaulins. He was gasping for breath, and convulsed with sobs, was crying. Poor sufferer!"[72]

Edward Temple, taken with other male passengers on a tour of the stokehole aboard the *Westernland* in 1898, was shocked when the chief steward informed them as they viewed the half-naked, panting stokers, " 'Well, they don't last long.' "[73] Passengers aboard the *Britannic* in 1878 were startled to hear in the night the dreadful cry of "Man overboard!" Boats were lowered; nothing was found. The next day they learned that a stoker had been carried up on deck for air—"a green hand, working his way over. He sat for a moment, so the sailors say, with his head in his hands, and then without any warning, jumped upon the railing and plunged into the sea."[74]

Voyagers still spoke of their sensation of being at the center of a lake, "far below its depressed circumference, where the boat constantly tries to paddle up one of its sides, without getting any nearer the edge of it."[75] John Burroughs, the famous naturalist, observed:

Every night the stars dance and reel there in the same place amid the rigging; every morning the sun comes up from behind the same wave. ... The eye becomes a-hunger for form, for permanent lines, for a horizon wall to lift up and keep off the sky, and give it a sense of room. ... Is it the steamer that is moving, or is it the sea? Or is it all a dance and illusion of the troubled brain? Yesterday, today, and tomorrow, you are in the same parenthesis of nowhere. ... One understands why sailors become an imaginative and superstitious race; it is the reaction from this narrow horizon in which they are pent—this ring of fate surrounds them and oppresses them. They escape by invoking the aid of the supernatural.[76]

Often, an errant wave sweeping over the deck and drenching an astonished passenger relieved the tedium of a voyage. Buffalo newsman James Matthews, one such victim, found himself in a predicament in 1866. Hurrying below to his cabin to change his sea-soaked trousers, he could not find the key to his valise. "I was quite certain I had left my keys in Cork," he concluded. "I sat down on the sofa and gave myself up to despair. I could not go out again to borrow a pair, for the hall was full of ladies. My position was truly an embarrassing one." A further frantic search turned up the missing keys. "How hastily I opened the valise and put on the welcome things" he recalled later, "but I didn't trust the treacherous waves anymore during the voyage, for I now had on my last pair."[77]

Storms still provided a source of hair-raising anecdote. Few travelers could report a voyage as placid as that of Kansan Noble Prentis, aboard the *Bothnia* in July of 1877. "It was as uneventful as a trip from the corner of Sixth and Kansas Avenues to North Topeka," he recalled. "The ocean was, day after day, as calm as a duckpond."[78] Fewer still could claim as did journalist Charles Fulton in 1873, "We have crossed the Atlantic between America and Europe six times, and our ocean-traveling in other directions have been extensive, yet we have been so fortunate as never to have encountered a genuine storm, and very little rough weather, at sea."[79]

Aboard the *Circassia*, en route home in 1879, Adelaide Harrington described the effects on the passengers of a gale that hit them their second night out.

The trunks piled on each side of the passage-way where the second-class passengers took their meals, inaugurated a game of pitch and toss, and the thunder they occasioned in their attempts to break through the ship's sides, mingled with the crash of crockery, the creaking of timbers, the groans of the sick ones, and the cries of the frightened, made the night one of such horror that a life-time can never serve to obliterate. It was only by the greatest effort that I was able to keep in my berth as the ship rolled in spasmodic jerks from side to side, dashing me against the walls of the berth one moment, the next leaving me hovering over the edge, in momentary expectation of being hurled to the floor. Feeling that the last hour had certainly come, I rushed out toward the stairway, where some of the male passengers already were, and who expressed the belief that it would be but a few moments before we should all be at the bottom of the sea. At this moment a heavy sea came sweeping down the stairs, and I retreated to my room, giving all up for lost. To add to the horrors, there were horses on board which were distressingly sick; the sides of their stalls had to be padded, as the animals were valuable, and as the roughness increased, they were suspended to prevent their injury.[80]

If cabin passengers suffered during these storms, the steerage travelers endured far worse. Just as back at mid-century one voyager heard "poor Irish immigrants, stifled below decks, noisily supplicating the Virgin for mercy, while some of them, half mad with fear, were trying to get on deck to throw themselves overboard," so travelers in these later decades reported similar panic. In 1892, aboard Cunard's luxurious *Servia*, a traveler observed this same fear of steerage passengers confined below decks, during a storm so severe that even the ship's seaworthy old cat was injured when, "asleep on a chair, with all her twenty claws gripped into the cushion for safety, [she] was suddenly flung like a stone from a sling and went slap into a bunch of glassware on the sideboard."[81]

Greatly feared still were the legendary but seldom seen "waterspouts," which a full-powered steamship might avoid being drawn into but which were thought highly dangerous to other vessels. Laura Collins, aboard the *Adriatic*, at the turn of the century, saw "afar off in the water . . . encircling ranges of vast mountain—'Alps-upon-Alps'—capped with white foam. From these snowy cones, like the eruptions of volcanoes, burst forth in swift succession great columns of the seething mass that shot upward apparently to the very heavens and exploded."[82] Another voyager, John Barrows, was reminded of the tornadoes of his native midwest. He described

> a gigantic waterspout, a phenomenon the Captain said he had not seen for years. At first we saw on the surface of the sea, perhaps a mile away, what looked like a whirling pillar of steam. From the sky above there reached down a strange, snake-like cloud-finger, which may have been a half a mile in length. As the ship drew nearer, we saw that this cloud in the heavens was connected with the phenomenon on the sea. Had we struck it and the whirling vortex thus been broken, an immense quantity of water would have deluged our ship. A small vessel in a huge waterspout would have no chance. . . . Three other smaller waterspouts came into view. The first and greatest soon disappeared, doing no damage, becoming only a strange memory.[83]

In earlier days ships had fired their signal guns at these waterspouts in the belief that the shock would dispel them; sometimes this appeared to work, sometimes not.

When "fog-whistles" came into use, many passengers discovered that the incessant "satanic screech" tortured their nerves. Captain Land's passengers thus complained to him aboard the *City of Richmond* in 1884, but he informed them that his whistle would sound every thirty seconds whether they liked it or not. He had gone down with the *City of Brussels,* which had sunk within twenty minutes after being rammed by another vessel, fortunately with no loss of life, but with himself and his crew left "swimming about in the Channel like goldfish in an aquarium." He had no intention of repeating that exercise if he could help it, he declared. "From fogs and icebergs, good Lord deliver us!" he was heard to exclaim.[84]

Up early for a turn around the fog-shrouded deck of his vessel in 1879, Burr Polk suddenly heard "two shrill blasts, and in an instant a full-rigged sailing vessel . . . emerged from the fog like a phantom. . . . She came quartering, and in less than thirty seconds would have struck us amidships, but when the whistle blew, she luffed up and gave us her side, but as she passed . . . we could plainly see the faces of the few men astir upon her. In less than one minute . . . she had disappeared . . . and I notice the fog-whistle has since been blown with greater regularity."[85] A schooner "came gliding hard upon our larboard, so close indeed," recalled one anxious voyager, "that you might have tossed a biscuit upon her deck."[86]

In 1878 the Reverend O. R. Burchard's steamer ran down a fishing smack from Beverly, Massachusetts. "I can never forget how wildly the fishermen ran to the stern of their vessel," he recalled.

> Almost instant death threatens them, for in less than half a minute they expect to be run down by the steamer. But they are seen from our vessel, and she is instantly turned from her course so that only the bowsprit of the fishing smack

THE VICTIMS OF HIGH SPEED.
THE DREAM OF AN ANXIOUS CAPTAIN AFTER TEARING ACROSS THE FISHING-GROUNDS OF NEWFOUNDLAND.

"Victims of High Speed." This graphic cartoon in *Punch* needs no explanation. Fishing boats came second to speed records over the Atlantic, *Punch*, October 18, 1890, p. 183. *Courtesy the Library of Congress.*

is cut off . . . and the shattered vessel grates harshly against the iron side of the steamer as we pass along. Our steamer is stopped, the men taken off from their sinking vessel, and we are on our course again through the interminable fog.[87]

Aboard the *Anchoria* in 1881, Dr. Clement Pearson experienced a collision with an unknown vessel that left everyone shaken. "What kind of craft this was, or how many were on board, no one could tell; a cry was heard for help, that they were sinking. . . . A thorough search was made, [but] not a trace except a piece of spar could be found."[88] By 1890 so fearful had become this toll of fishermen's lives off the Grand Banks, at the mercy of the hard-driven steamships, that *Punch* published a drawing entitled "The Victims of High Speed," depicting the skeletons of a dozen or so fishermen, still clad in their oilskins and sou'westers, climbing up out of the sea onto the deck of an ocean liner to confront those who had held their lives so cheap.[89]

How the steamship passengers sometimes reacted to potential disasters at sea was related by Eliza Connor during the summer of 1882. Noting the absence from table of their captain, a jolly, handsome, English bachelor, she was told that he was up on the bridge "watching the fog." The diners then fell to discussing the collision of the *Anchoria* and the *Queen* several years before. " 'Some [passengers] tried to get upon the *Queen* from the other steamer,' " related one of the company, " 'but the captain of the *Anchoria* drew a pistol and swore he would shoot the first man that left the ship.'. . . 'But after all, how very rare such incidents are,' remarked someone. 'Yes,' said another, 'there is about one chance in ten thousand of such a collision.' "

The diners had just finished their meal and were picking at their grapes when the ship's engines suddenly ceased. "In an instant—it could not have been longer than while you drew in your breath," wrote Miss Connor, "an awful spectral shadow loomed up and glided by our windows, right past where we sat at dinner. In another instant the shadow took the shape of a great sailing vessel. . . . We saw sailors on her deck, heavily-bearded, foreign-looking men. There was a wild, bewildered look on their faces as they shot past. They stood as if utterly unmanned and demoralized, paralyzed with terror." When the now thoroughly frightened diners reached the deck, the vessel was gone, "swallowed by the fog as if she had never been."[90] Only later did they learn that the other vessel had actually grazed them.

By now everything came to life on board the great steamship. Crew members rushed about "like bees whose hive has been overturned," wrote Miss Connor. "With trembling hands [one] set about cutting a lifeboat loose. 'Get away! get away from here!' he shouted to the passengers racing about the deck." One terrified voyager broke into "hysterical laughter, and gave vent to shriek after shriek." Another gathered his wife and children about him, crazily took possession of a stairway leading to the upper deck, and kept up a steady roar of " 'Keep off here! Keep off here!' " Soon their level-headed captain "had reduced things to order again," wrote Miss Connor. The ship hovered for several hours in the region, watching for signs of life. No boats were lowered; they would have been swallowed up in the fog in an instant. Seeing and hearing nothing, they resumed their course.[91]

Turning the air blue as he related how the other vessel had sounded no other fog warning until it spotted the steamer almost on them, the captain told how "the blamed fool put his fog-horn to his lips and blew it just as we struck. That's the closest ever I was to a ship," he declared. "I saw her first when she was about a hundred feet away, coming right down on us bow to bow. I tried to get out of her way. Then the fool appeared to start right across our bows. Then I says to myself, 'If we must hit, I'll see which can hit the hardest.' " His veering to the right had apparently prevented a disaster for the steamship, but both vessels were damaged. Later they would learn that the smaller vessel had been able to reach port. " 'Captain,' said one of us, 'suppose you hadn't changed the steamer's course, and we had struck her as she crossed our bows, what would have happened?' 'If we had struck her broadside, we would have gone right over her in two minutes.' 'And suppose she had hit us?' 'Well, sir, if she had struck us amidships, you and I would be feeding the fishes now,' he said."[92]

"The vast number of icebergs which are borne past the shores of Newfoundland during the spring and early summer is almost incredible," wrote Charles Fulton in 1873, "and it is believed that all the missing ocean steamers have met their fate by coming in contact with them."[93] The *President* and the *City of Boston,* for example, had embarked in 1841 and 1870, respectively, and were never heard from again. The common assumption was that they had struck icebergs and sunk, just as the great *Titanic* would one day in the future.

Travelers wanted to believe that they were safer in the great steamers of the century's later decades. "The iron structures of the present almost insure them against the calamity of fire," Charles Poston assured himself and his readers in 1867.[94] This was not necessarily so. With combustible cargo, such as hay carried to feed the livestock she was transporting, the *Alsatia* gave her frightened cabin passengers a real run for their money in September of 1880. Leaving New York on a Saturday afternoon, the dozen passengers were told around noon on Sunday that their ship was afire and probably had been even before they embarked. The captain's intention was to keep to his course as usual, assuring his passengers that such fires sometimes smoldered "all the way across." Two hundred and fifty miles at sea, with the coal bunkers by now ignited, with smoke issuing around the stacks, and following two coal gas explosions, the captain, who by now, passengers were later to claim, had taken to the bottle, was at last persuaded to turn back to New York. Once on shore, the terrified travelers hastily booked passage on other vessels.[95]

On large, all-passenger ships the fear was just as great if not more so, because of the potential for mass panic. "Awful to realize, we find our ship is on fire," a frightened passenger—aboard the *City of Montreal,* under Captain Land—wrote in his journal in the eighties. "Our hearts almost faint within us at the horror that stares us in the face. . . . There were seven hundred and ninety-five souls on board," he added later, "and boats enough for possibly one third that number. Two hours after the initial alarm the fire was out, but this did not erase their recollections of the *City of Chicago* which had burned at sea and whose fate they had anticipated.[96] Peter Hamilton, of Mobile, on his honeymoon voyage in 1891 recorded how he, his bride, and other voyagers trembled for an hour until news came up from below that some tar barrels had finally burned themselves out. At this point the relieved captain treated all the ladies on board to champagne for keeping their nerves so well under control during the emergency.[97]

"It is a solemn thing for a Kansas man to land at Liverpool on a rainy day," wrote Noble Prentis in 1877.

> Coming from an open country full of brightness and lit up by a cloudless sun, the bigness and the blackness, the inner and outer darkness of Liverpool is well nigh appalling. A turbid river, foaming and tossing like the sea; steamers black as midnight plowing to and fro; miles of low-lying warehouses, their slate roofs gleaming dimly in the rain; spires and chimneys looming up spectrally in the mist; docks that seem the work of giants, skirting the stream as far as the eye can reach; ships' masts like the trees of a girdled forest; ship-yards a maze of timbers;—these are the outlines of Liverpool as seen from the steamer's deck.[98]

These mighty docks compelled George Williams to declare that "the wharves of New York are a disgrace to that great and prosperous city!"[99]

Liverpool dock scene, c. 1900. Some American arrivals rushed out "within twenty-fou
hours, and often within twenty-four minutes," according to William Dean Howells
Courtesy the Library of Congress.

This admiration for the ‘world's greatest docks sometimes soured a bit wher
ships dropped anchor in the Mersey about a mile out and voyagers had t
transfer to sturdy but hardly luxurious little steamers, open to the elements, t
be ferried to their dock. Frank Stockton, writing in *Personally Conducted* in 1889
warned his readers of this possibility, but this did not prevent negative reaction
on the part of a typical group of some three hundred keyed-up, sea-wear
travelers on the uncovered deck of one of these dingy, shabby, and clutteree

little workhorse steamers, seatless as well, making their way to the Liverpool customs officers awaiting them.

The experiences of travelers at the hands of these officials, according to their own accounts, ran the gamut from perfect civility, honesty, and efficiency to rudeness, dishonesty, and inefficiency. At various periods contraband had consisted of tobacco, daguerreotypes, and American reprints of British authors' books. Now, in the eighties and nineties, the Fenian terrorist bombings livened things up considerably. Certain querulous Americans were outraged, or pretended to be, at the searching of their luggage for dynamite. Such a one was Chicago society matron M. E. W. Sherwood in 1884. "All our trunks were examined for dynamite," she fumed, "and the officials evidently thought we brought it in our smelling bottles. Mr. McCormick of Chicago, the distinguished capitalist, said that such mismanagement would not be endured in the West if one was shipping goods!"[100]

"I found myself lurching from side to side in my walking for several hours after landing and steadying myself as when the steamer rolled," remarked James Bates in 1889, sounding very much like his countryman John Griscom eighty years before.[101] Once they regained their "land legs," however, these Yankee travelers were raring to go. Some took time to look around Liverpool, but others rushed out "within twenty-four hours," observed William Dean Howells, "and often within twenty-four minutes," speaking of the floods of Americans pouring forth "from every Cunarder" in the 1880s.[102]

A reminder of the fear of the deep still lurking in the minds of these modern, mechanized tourists is seen in the journal musings of Nathan Hubbell upon his safe arrival at Queenstown in 1889. He wrote:

One is saddened to think of the bottom of the mighty ocean. Thousands of human beings are buried there. What a vast charnel-house! How many ships slumber beneath the restless wave!—the *President, Arctic, Oregon,* and a long list besides. How many homes have been blasted. How many hearts have been broken. . . . And yet annually, thousands sail over these waters thoughtlessly, carelessly . . . while the laugh, the jest, the wine cup, and the merry dance go on.[103]

16

The Birth of Tourism

"Plentiful . . . as flies at a sugar barrel," remarked Curtis Guild of the hordes of American tourists in Britain during the summer of 1888, "wandering through England's castles and abbeys."[1] Anybody in the United States "who had any surplus money came to England every summer to spend it," declared the American lawyer-politician Chauncey Depew to a British audience, and "afterwards the English actors and lecturers came over to the United States and took what was left."[2]

Before long the tourists themselves would complain of their own numbers. "Americans are everywhere," groaned one of them disgustedly, "and in greater numbers than ever before."[3] Journalist Theron Crawford reported that "it is only through visits to the interior places of England that you obtain some correct knowledge of the perfect army of American travelers here. In London they are swallowed up, but out there they are in the great majority . . . at the leading hotels."[4] Since so many of the American travelers were women in mourning, unaccompanied by men, Mary Wills asked herself: "Have they come to assuage grief, or has the death of a substantial pater familias furnished them with the means of enjoyment?"[5]

William Dean Howells found his favorite Liverpool hotel so "swarmed and buzzed" with his countrymen that he could "scarcely get to the office window to plead for a room."[6] In a letter to Henry Cabot Lodge back in Boston Henry Adams complained in 1880, "America is all here!"[7] The American tour of Britain, now almost without exception a part of the larger trip to "Yurrop," in the final decades of the century had narrowed itself down to visits to the enduring trinity of Stratford-on-Avon, Warwick Castle, and the Kenilworth Castle ruins; stops at Chatsworth and Haddon Hall; a quick spin through the Lake District; a brief foray into "Scott-land"; a once-over-lightly tour of the Lakes of Killarney, followed by a quick trip up to the Giants' Causeway; and, last but not least, a sojourn in London. Although these pilgrims still followed an old, familiar trail, they were now summer "vacationers" and completed it in a much shorter time. Even tour eschewers, traveling alone or with their own private courier who functioned as a combination guide, majordomo and, troubleshooter, were pressed by time, or pressed themselves.

In her little book *Rapid Transit Abroad,* published in 1879, Evelyn R. Stetson proposed to demonstrate to her readers "how many places can be visited, and how many marvels of art and nature admired, and how much delight experienced . . . during a summer vacation of three months." Time's winged chariot hurried Evelyn and her companions at a breathless pace from place to place, and her account finally compresses itself into a litany of "hurry" phrases. In one place she writes, "[T]ime is precious and we must be up and doing." And "we have not time to listen to the whole of her story," she says of the guide at Warwick Castle, as off they rush by carriage for "a glimpse of Kenilworth." Rushing out to Chatsworth, they "hurry from room to room" only to find that they "have lingered here beyond the time allowed," and the feet of their horses "fairly fly as they bear us to Haddon Hall, but there is only time to see the exterior." And for this they had forgone luncheon at the famed Peacock Inn at Rowsley, near Chatsworth, "fairly begrudging the time for rest and refreshment." Back in London, finally, they "are now so accustomed to making use of every moment" that they decide one hour at the British Museum before lunch is better than no time at all, and at least they get to view the Elgin Marbles. Their frantic pace on one day so exhausts them that they dispatch their dinner "with all possible haste" so as to fall into bed and be asleep by eight o'clock to rest up for the next day.[8]

For tour groups the pace was almost as relentless. The party led by Dr. Eben Tourjée of Boston in the summer of 1879, following his success of the previous year, was described in detail in separate books by three of its members—Adelaide Harrington, Burr Polk, and James McClay—no doubt imitating the effort of Luther Holden who wrote up the first tour a year previous.[9] Arrangements for these tours were by Henry Gaze and Son, rather than Cook, and the overall effect is that of an army on the march, tied to an inexorable "printed program" and plagued by the old army psychology of "hurry up and wait." For a cost of $500 the 1879 party covered over 9,000 miles in eighty-five days, including the 3,000 miles of sea travel.[10] The party included 313 members, who were broken up on their arrival in Britain into four smaller groups of about seventy-five each.[11] Even so, they were stared at as they moved about Great Britain. Arriving at Glasgow, they were driven to the Grand Hotel, where a crowd gathered to view them. "One of our party overheard one Scotsman say to another, 'What's the matter here?' 'O, a thousand Americans have just come!' "[12] At Edinburgh, too, Adelaide Harrington observed that the group was stared at as if an invading army. Even before they finished "doing" that city, she also noted that "here on the very threshold of our tour, the exhaustion attendant upon sightseeing is already making a sad inroad upon sentiment and enthusiasm." As they pushed on, phrases like "we were due," "we had no time for," and "the few hours the exigencies of the excursion allowed us" creep ever more into her account. Some idea of the pace of these early tours, not unlike those of today, is seen when she writes that in "thirty-six hours, we had sailed over Lochs Katrine and Lomond, rode through the Trossachs, visited Abbotsford and Stirling, and taken our farewell of Edinburgh."[13] Burr Polk was feeling the pressure as well. "So much has been crowded into so short a space I find it impossible to realize that it has been less than four days since we landed," he wrote on leaving the Scottish capital.[14]

When this 1879 Tourjée Party left Scotland and headed south, they found themselves sitting up all night in the train and then lining up for an outdoor breakfast at Kenilworth, because "the Queen and Castle Hotel was not equal to such a crowd." A similar army-style meal awaited them at Stratford where "those of us who could not get under the roof of Washington Irving's inn, the Red Horse, were provided with dinner in the adjacent bowling alley."[15] Polk was not much impressed with Stratford. "Of all the funny-looking places we have seen" he wrote, "Stratford beat the list." Their view of the celebrated ruins at Kenilworth did not excite him, either. "I have been into that line so much already since coming here. Two or three rooms," he added, "are filled with relics, all of which are duly inventoried and entered into more than a hundred notebooks."[16]

Reflecting their relentless pace, Mrs. Harrington wrote, "[O]n, on we ride, utilizing every moment of our stay."[17] In London finally, for three days they were whirled about the great city in carriages and "went hurriedly through the museums," seeing "pictures in the National Gallery something like one sees the country as he speeds through it in a railroad car. At St. Paul's and Westminster we groped about . . . [and] of course we jammed into the House of Lords," reported Polk.[18]

Some of the less pleasant aspects of mass tourism manifested themselves even in these early days: such as travelers too ignorant or exhausted, or both, to know or care whether they were in Westminster Abbey or St. Paul's Cathedral; or the woman who remarked that she didn't see what there was worth "trotting so far to see" at Holyrood Palace;[19] tourists shuffling resignedly through the Shakespeare house, "some of whom, I verily believe," wrote James McClay of Hartford, Conn., "hardly knew whether Shakespeare was a king or a bootblack."[20] An elderly Ohioan on one tour was heard to remark that "one place is as good as another."[21]

At the end of two months, back in Britain from the Continent and preparing for the voyage home aboard the *Circassia*, Mrs. Harrington wrote wonderingly in her overflowing notebook. "For the first hour in two months I was in perfect repose; not a moment of that time had there been opportunity for aught but wonder, admiration, or solicitude for rest; we had, as it were . . . been revolving the mechanism of a huge kaleidoscope which brought to view an endless succession of varying scenes, keeping mind and body stretched to the highest tension."[22] Safe at home again in Vicksburg, Mississippi, Burr Polk said that it was not until then he realized the magnitude of their tour. Recalling their conductor, Mr. E. McQueen Gray, "our interpreter, guide, cashier and companion," Polk wrote that "in all he was royal! I doubt if a better man could have been selected . . . remarkably patient with our troublesome party . . . never out of humor at things . . . it seemed to me would have annoyed a saint."[23] McClay summed up his experience, indicating that the prospectus might have thrown "a glamor over some portions that the reality failed to give, but we are generally satisfied that we have had more than the worth of our money."[24] Tours were here to stay, despite the disillusionment that inevitably set in as they grew in popularity and number. Having once experienced the pressures of mass travel, some travelers advised others against the packaged tour. "I would not join an excursion party," a fellow clergyman advised the Reverend William Davis in 1880. "You are tied down to cast-iron rules, must move with the caravan, and save but little if anything."[25] Other travelers, possibly more sturdy and less concerned about the loss of privacy and individuality inherent in the package tour, continued to recommend excursions, especially Cook's, even to the point of dedicating their books to that entrepreneur—as did the Reverend Samuel Watson of Memphis, a member of the original 1873 "Party." Watson wrote: "To Mr. Thomas Cook, Sr., of London, to whose liberality and kindness the Educational Party are much indebted for favors beyond their agreement." Watson further recommended Cook's to all travelers, assuring them that "there are not enough of these Cooks yet to spoil the broth."[26]

Eliza Connor—as did several other early Cook's tourists—dedicated her book, *E. A. Abroad,* to her traveling companions: "To the 'Cookies' composing the vacation party of 1882 this volume is dedicated with sunny remembrances of one and all." Added Miss Connor, "it is really a great system of travel. The Cooks keep their word to the traveler strictly and are to be entirely recommended to those who wish to see much in a little time. To Americans of moderate means who must see Europe hurriedly or not at all, I consider these 'Tours' a great boon." It was a marvelous way for lone women to travel, she continued, with all the "fuss and bother about tickets, seats in compartments, baggage, and the rows with cabmen and hotel-keepers taken off [one's] shoulders." Recording the itinerary of her group up in Scotland, she remarked, "[W]e have seen more . . . than persons wholly ignorant of the country could have done in any other way in the same length of time." So pleased were they with their conductor, Mr. Frank Clark, that they took up a collection and presented him with a farewell gift of "a handsome gold watch and chain."[27] How patient and personable must these tour "conductors" have been!

Nevertheless, in these accounts of mass travel one cannot escape the mounting references to speed, haste, pressure, and fatigue. Phrases like "necessarily hurried" appear with reference to famous historical spots, along with "in our haste," and "only a cursory inspection." One independent traveler clocked the visit of a group of his countrymen at Muckross Abbey, in Ireland, to be fourteen minutes altogether.[28]

As his numbers multiplied, the individual compelled to travel by excursion party began to sense that he was missing out on the status and freedom of the independent traveler. "Where is the chance for one to distinguish himself as a traveler," asked William Falkner in 1883, "when everybody else is on the tramp?"[29] Almost half a century earlier Hezekiah Wright had actually written a similar complaint. "Now that everyone travels," he wrote in 1838, "travelling is consequently no longer fashionable."[30] In 1877 Curtis Guild remarked that he had seen American parties abroad unfit for foreign travel. "The cheap excursion system has enabled a large number of this class of travellers to visit Europe; and although not denying for a moment that it has enabled many worthy and well-educated persons of limited means an opportunity for foreign travel and sight-seeing," which they might never have been able to enjoy otherwise, he nonetheless deplored some of the specimens he had run across in his own travels—

men from western New York who couldn't tell you the height of Niagara Falls; an Illinois farmer who had never been in any city in his life but Indianapolis, and that only twice. . . . Great tall fellows, with mourning-clothed fingernails, who chewed tobacco and spat on the floors of cathedrals, and were the very types of characters which English writers have described in their books of travel on America as representatives of our country.[31]

Independent travelers noted and felt the effects on hotel service of these large groups that "sent the help altogether out of their wits" trying to feed, house, and otherwise administer to the army-scale requirements of the group tour.[32] The tour groups, moreover, were a further source of despair for the help since they did not tip, or "fee," well—if at all, apparently in the belief that "affectionate adieux were sufficient," observed Henry Holloway.[33]

The "jaded" and "worn" condition of his countrymen embarked on these fast tours was noted by journalist Theron Crawford, observing them in London. "The majority come over as a matter of education. Many cannot afford to come twice, and once here they feel in duty bound to work almost day and night at that hardest of all kinds of work, sight-seeing."[34] Another newsman, James Matthews, was asked in 1866 by a Briton why he tried to cover so much ground in a single summer. "I reminded him that Americans had to travel three or four thousand miles before they reached Europe," Matthews wrote, "and as many more to return. Having journeyed so far, and not expecting to make such a trip very soon again, they must see all they can in the time afforded them. Unless Americans spend their holidays at home they cannot do their traveling in a leisurely way. My friend was good enough to say he had not looked at it that way before, and that there was some method in our madness after all."[35]

Inevitably, it became the habit of increasingly class-conscious Americans, especially those with sufficient money and leisure to travel on their own, to sneer at the group tourists. Art devotee Adelaide Hall of Chicago indicated her disdain for "a party of tourists, probably 'Cookies', rushing through the rooms of the National Gallery in London, glancing at the pictures, evidently for the sole purpose of saying, 'I have done the National Gallery.' "[36] Lily Rust of Washington, traveling leisurely with her mother in 1903, wrote in her journal that "the sight of a tourist in the distance means death to any artistic sensations and thrills on my part."[37] Laura Collins complained about those from her country "who go about in groups and everybody seems to recognize them as Americans."[38] William Dean Howells, on a summer afternoon just before the start of World War I, referred to the "preposterous" spectacle of hordes of visitors, many of them American, about 13,000 each year, it was said, arriving at Stratford-on-Avon "in huge motor-omnibus loads, and by carriage, and automobile, and [even] on foot."[39]

Some of these Americans, on balance a small minority, still looked on their tour of Great Britain, even in these last decades of the nineteenth century, as an opportunity to settle old scores of resentment against "the parent nation" and to display their patriotism by going about noisily denigrating the very antiquities and natural wonders they had come so far to see. Francis Sessions returned to Columbus, Ohio, in the late 1880s, firmly convinced that "the old State House .... our Hospital for the Insane . . . and all of our public buildings—the Idiot Asylum and those for the Blind, Deaf and Dumb, the Ohio State University and the Penitentiary . . . considering their cost, [were] equal for style of architecture, to any in the world."[40] An American teenager judged the Gobelin tapestry she

Lily Lawrence Rust, American traveler, 1903. "The sight of a tourist in the distance means death to any artistic sensations and thrills on my part," she wrote in her journal of the Yankee hordes abroad at the turn of the century.

viewed at Chatsworth "not nearly as nice as our modern carpeting . . . of course it was much better looking a century or two ago."[41] And a Floridian who published his book anonymously, speaking of Britain, declared that "the whole country should be turned over to a receiver."[42] Bostonian Levina Urbino overheard a California mother, who had "not found any fruit fit to eat in all Europe," assuring her five-year-old champagne-sipping son that he was "better than any emperor or prince because he was an American."[43]

Other Yankee chauvinists showed the flag by harassing the guides, cicerones, or other minions who crossed their paths. For sheer stupidity few could equal William Falkner and his friends on their excursion to Windsor Castle in 1883. First, there was the hapless London ticket agent who must be humbled because he could not supply tourist information regarding the town and castle of Windsor as he supplied their railway tickets. Once at the castle, a guardian was offered "a shilling to dance a jig on the grave of the villainous old wife-killer, Henry VIII," and Falkner was miffed when informed that "that sort of amusement was wholly out of style now." Apparently Falkner believed, as one other

American traveler of the period insisted, that "every Englishman is for sale."[44]

Next, after having complained all over Britain about the small "fees" or tips expected everywhere for humble but vital services, Falkner was further annoyed when the elderly guide conducting them through the castle's apartments refused a gratuity. "Hooknose," as they had dubbed him, replied, " 'Hi beg pardon, Hi ham not hallowed to haccept fees for hexibiting 'er Majesty's hapartments.' 'Could you honor me with your company at dinner this evening?' said Dick." With a low bow, the old man declined. Dick "took off his hat and made a comical bow. 'Then give my respects to your grandma and be a good boy yourself!' Hooknose," continued Falkner, "seemed puzzled as to whether Dick was making sport of him or not. " 'Well,' exclaimed a female member of the party, 'I am happy to find that all the fools in the world don't live in the United States.' 'I guess they have no insane asylums here,' drily remarked another lady. 'Their lunatics are all ranging at large.' Human nature is the same all over the earth," declared Falkner, "and the only difference I see is that many of the English are full of egotism." At dinner that evening, before their return to London, "Dick mimicked the waiter so successfully," according to Falkner, "as to make him believe it was his natural way of speaking; indeed, the waiter took him for a brother Englishman."[45]

Many Americans liked to complain about how much more slowly transactions of various sorts were managed in Britain, but this complaint did not apply to their guides in historic buildings. "He is anything but slow," said Sam Fiske of the typical British guide, "and annihilates time and space in a way to make railways and electric telegraphs hide their diminished heads. With him a thousand years are as but as a quarter of an hour; and a whole empire full of poets, statesmen and heroes, only a five-minute's walk. Having pocketed the shillings, or six pences, the object is to get rid of us in the shortest possible time to be ready for the next pocket of change."[46] Ella Thompson concluded that many of these cathedral vergers had "pickled themselves in brandy against the damp. A blind person could easily follow them by the sense of smell."[47]

Usually the poor guides bore stoically with the quirks and humors of their Yankee clients, and seldom is there an example of any sort of retort to incivilities. One such occurred at Stirling Castle in 1888, related an onlooker, when an obnoxious American traveler, "whose self-consciousness and egotism were in reverse ratio to the dimensions of his body, was quieted, at least momentarily, when the guide suddenly dropped on him, like a candle snuffer, an enormous old hat reputed to have belonged to Oliver Cromwell. He looked," wrote his countryman, "like an ant carrying off an egg larger than itself."[48]

The American travelers almost uniformly resented having to pay entrance fees to cathedrals and castles, and one complained that, "if Heaven were under English management, an entrance fee of one shilling—neither more nor less—would be demanded."[49] Advising future travelers of what to expect, Hemstreet warned in the seventies that "the expenses of sight-seeing are by the shilling a item. The shillings fly easily, and the English can poultice them out of the visitor about as well as any people in the world."[50]

What most roused the ire of traveling Yankees was the system of "feeing," or tipping, which apparently had not yet taken deep root in the United States. "The practice of feeing servants at hotels and on lines of travel is a practice which I hope may never be introduced into our country," John Mitchell had written back in 1843.[51] William Hichborn of Boston would complain in 1897, however, of "the detestable custom of feeing that is in vogue all over Europe and is beginning to prevail to some extent in [our] country, which I think is un-American, to say the least. If there is anything that a Yankee wants to know, it is how much he has got to pay and what he is going to get when he makes a bargain."[52]

Several of the pilgrims refer to a legendary fellow-countryman who, home-ward bound, from the bridge of his Liverpool steamer, addressed the crowded wharf: "If there is any man, woman or child on this island to whom I have not yet given a shilling, now is the time to speak!"[53]

In any event, the Americans met this custom head-on all through the century and reacted in their various ways. "England seems to have been built on pennies," snorted one traveler. "They are asked for at every turn."[54] Lou Beauchamp grumped in 1896: "Suffice it to say it costs a penny to open your mouth in London, and 'tuppence' to keep it open. You can't get out of a cab, or your hotel, or into or out of the theater, without shedding pennies like a duck sheds water."[55]

Emma Willard had resigned herself gracefully to the custom back in the 1830s, and so did historian Reuben Thwaites in the 1890's. "It is best to submit to it with philosophic patience," he advised, "as it cannot be avoided." Then he added, "[O]ne becomes reconciled . . . when it brings service . . . so different from that to be met within an American village tavern."[56]

In the century's first decade Silliman had made a similar observation that the small cost of feeing was more than made up for by the civil and attentive service it provided, cheerfully rendered.[57] William Nevin reminded readers that "the sums are very small, and you get a great deal for them, a willing, perfect, and kindly service you do not get in our country at all."[58]

No one devised as ugly a protest against the feeing system as author Henry Morford, who bragged about his treatment of the hostler at a country inn when the latter uttered the customary reminder, "Please Sir, remember the hostler. . . . Gentlemen *always* remember the hostler." Morford's response was to bring his cane down suddenly on the driver's head, "leading him to 'drive on' with such suddenness as threw the hostler down between the wheels and ran over him, my last sight of him revealing some rolling and howling hobnails and a smock frock in the middle of the road." Satisfied, Morford headed back to London, reflecting that "I had seen Runnymede a few hours before—wherein and whereat monarchy received one of its early lessons: I had been the humble means, at the neighboring Wheat-Sheaf, of teaching one milder lesson to the new and worse monarchy of all Great Britain, *servant begging!*"[59]

For travelers unwilling to go quite as far as Henry Morford in running down things British, complaining itself now developed into a veritable art form: complaints about the table d'hote meals at hotels, for example. "Too tedious and time-consuming," fumed Burr Polk. "Not enough freedom about it. They stuff you with things contained in the limited bill of fare. It is that or nothing." He also ranted about having to wait for others to consume the various courses. "You sit there and wait and gnash your teeth till all the others are through." If British traveler-writers had complained of Americans "pitchforking" their food down their gullets, now Americans would retaliate about slow food service in Great Britain.[60]

Hotel rooms were cold and inadequately heated, they also grumbled. Doors and windows were left open at all hours as if deliberately to chill the guests. "We were all half freezing as we have been much of the time since arriving in England," reported one tourist. "The people of the country don't think it is cold . . . [and] are dressed in summer clothing, and don't wear or carry wraps."[61] This was in June. "It was warmer outdoors than within," recalled another shivering Yankee. "After walking about in the warm air, you are chilled by the interiors of the buildings."[62]

The use of candles for lighting in the bedrooms further irritated Americans accustomed to gas lighting in their bedrooms as well as the public rooms. Some took to carrying extra candles of their own, while others hung onto used "ends" to add to their illumination at night. "When one pays from twenty to thirty cents for an indifferent candle, this is pretty often practiced," observed Dr. Sinclair Tousey.[63] Banker Claudius Patten said that he was told by an English hotel-keeper that "none of their English customers would tolerate for a night in their sleeping chambers the gaslights so common in all our public houses. They deem it unhealthy."[64] Travel writer Curtis Guild claimed that candles were just one more way for inn- and hotelkeepers to make money off the traveler.[65]

Other travelers, like Orrin Hubbell of Elkhart, Indiana, found insupportable the lack of elevators, "which an American deems an essential feature of any good hotel."[66] John Higinbotham refused a room above the second floor of the Warwick Arms as there was no lift to waft him aloft.[67] There were also complaints by Americans about the lack of American rocking chairs in British hotels, the lack of newsstands in the lobbies, and the fact that British hotels often were run by women to whom American males, doubtless conditioned by their wives, were afraid to complain.

Luggage handling in Britain was another source of anxiety to Americans accustomed to their system of "checking baggage through." First of all, they had to learn to call their baggage "luggage," which annoyed many. Next, they had to learn to trust the efficient porters who loaded and unloaded luggage for travelers at their stops. "It is a wonder that some enterprising Yankee does not come here and establish one of the baggage transfer companies for which our country is renowned; he would have no competition," wrote Annie Wolf in 1878.[68] Josephine Tyler coined the term "baggagia" for "the wear and worry over baggage," a malady from which "I have suffered much."[69] The Yankee travelers found it hard to trust the porters and to stifle their anxiety lest someone walk off with their luggage. Actually, there were no complaints in this connection, but, as one traveler observed, "[O]ne cannot help thinking what a harvest some expert railroad thief of the West could reap in Great Britain."[70]

The size of British currency was another problem. "My pockets were so full of silver and their ugly copper pennies," complained Burr Polk, "that my suspenders would hardly bear the great weight."[71] The "Honorable William A. Braman of Ohio" deplored "the conservatism of the English in some respects," particularly their currency, which was "very annoying" to American tourists. "If their

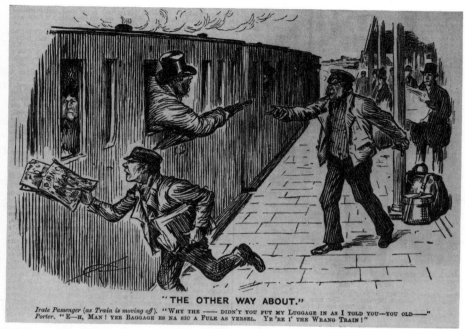

"THE OTHER WAY ABOUT."

Irate Passenger (as Train is moving off). "Why the —— didn't you put my Luggage in as I told you—you old——"
Porter. "E—h, Man! yer Baggage es na sic a Fule as yersel. Ye 're i' the Wrang Train!"

Anxiety over their luggage plagued the American traveler accustomed to "checking baggage through" and unused to relying on porters to do this for them. *Punch,* **vol. 95, December 1, 1888, p. 255.** *Courtesy the Library of Congress.*

currency was less cumbrous and more readily comprehended, it would be much better for all concerned."[72]

Since the Americans were always complaining of feeling cold, their thirst for ice water, which led to a virtual cultural clash, seemed incomprehensible to many Britons. Cyclist Reuben Thwaites and his wife overheard two servants at a country inn discussing this odd Yankee trait.

I' heern Bill, the waiter, a'tellin' o' Cook as 'ow 'e knowed 'em for 'Mericans immedjate, for the young missus ordered on a pitcher o' cold wahter at breakfas'—and that's 'Merican every time 'e says; and 'e owght to know, as 'e's served towrists oop in Wyles, where they set a joog o' wahter on every mornin' for breakfas', there's so many 'Mericans as comes that wye. They drinks wahter wi' their victuals, and says "pitcher" w'en they means "joog".[73]

Even old Dr. Holmes got in on the ice water act. "You will surely die eating such cold stuff," an Englishwoman warned him.[74] "Ice water is seldom found," complained William Hemstreet, "and a bartender will assure you that his soda water is 'cold' because in a cool place 'under the counter' "[75] A woman tourist concluded that "the Yankee ice pitcher, kept well-filled, is an unknown article here."[76]

"I cannot soon forget the astonishment with which an Englishman looked upon my little boy of ten," wrote Claudius Patten, "who at the Cunard steamer's table would have his glass of cold water. He said to me he did not see how I could let the little fellow pour such stuff into his stomach along with his dinner."[77] Another traveler said that he asked for a glass of water with his meal. "The waiter shouted my request up the dumb waiter in a very loud voice, and after an interval of several minutes, came back and reported there was not a drop in the house."[78] Francis Sessions claimed that a distinguished professor of Trinity College, Cambridge, informed him, "I never drank water in my life."[79]

John Higinbotham listed the Empire Hotel at Bath as the one hotel in England where water is served without fuss.[80] But the Arundel Hotel, just off London's Strand, in recognition of the water problem for American guests, proudly advertised its "free" water cooler "especially provided for Americans and their

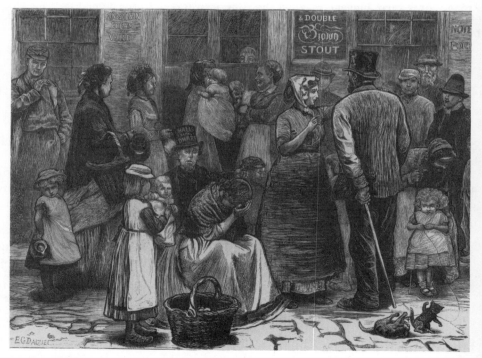

"Sunday Afternoon 1 P.M.: Waiting for the Public House to Open." Americans purported to be shocked by the amount of drinking they saw, even by women. *The Graphic*, vol. IV, January 10, 1874, p. 41. *Courtesy the Library of Congress.*

families."[81] Unfortunately, not all the Americans found their way to that spot. Journalist Joel Cook, on August 19, 1878, saw his letter published in the *Times* of London in which he complained that, having been traveling "for about a month past in the United Kingdom," [he had] frequently been "put to sad straits to get a drink of water . . . The Americans notice the want of this convenience more than anything else," he informed the British public at large.[82]

Many of them being teetotalers, American travelers had much to say concerning the lack of temperance in Britain. "People do not know how to drink water," declared the Reverend Samuel Mutchmore in 1887.

> It is tabooed in society. Ice . . . is unknown to the vast multitudes, and what is more, they do not care for it. The majority drink nothing but preparations. Coffee and tea at meals, whiskies, brandies, malts, wines, lemonades—indeed every conceivable concoction. . . . A man will confound the servants in an English hotel in asking for ice water, and all the guests by drinking it. It is not their idea of the eternal fitness of things to drink water.[83]

Nathaniel Hawthorne had earlier commented on the "bitter ale, which is like mother's milk to an Englishman, and soon grows equally acceptable to his American cousin."[84] Maybe to Hawthorne—but not to most of his countrymen.

American clergyman John Codman had been stunned in 1835 to see "decanters of wine on . . . the platform" and horrified to be offered wine by the sexton as a refreshment after preaching.[85] Richard McCormick was scarcely able "to make some of my religious acquaintances believe that in the United States it is demanded in the covenants of many of the churches that the members shall conform to principles of the strictest total abstinence."[86] Mrs. L. C. Lane was astonished to see "very respectable-looking women on their way from church, prayer-book in hand, entering . . . a bar."[87] David Locke concluded that "one-half of England is engaged in manufacturing beer for the other half."[88]

"Keep your eye upon the drinking question wherever you go," Pastor Theodore Cuyler of Brooklyn's Lafayette Avenue Church was advised by his parishioners in 1881 as he embarked.[89] Emerson had marveled in 1848: "What rivers of wine are drunk in all England daily!"[90] Matters had changed but little, apparently. Stern paragraphs were written by visiting Americans on evidences of alcoholism in the laboring classes, and horrendous pictures of glittering "gin palaces" were painted for American readers. Stopping at the "McGilvray Hotel—a temperance house," in Edinburgh in the nineties, Janet Collins surveyed that city's drinking habits and called on the temperance folk to "Rise in majesty as in martyr days and strike at the root as did Knox that of Romanism!"[91] As a symbol of the evils of drink among the London poor, Henry James recalled his glimpse of "a horrible old woman in a smokey bonnet, lying prone in a puddle of whiskey! She seemed to assume a kind of symbolic significance," he wrote, "and almost frightened me."[92]

For their part, Britons were often puzzled at the abstemiousness of their American guests. "Are you a teetotaler? meets the American at every turn, if he has any social relations with the English," observed Caroline Sheldon in 1904. "I was indeed a *tea*-totaller," she wrote, "for I drank more tea in those two weeks than in all the previous years of my mortal pilgrimage; and came near being a nervous wreck in consequence."[93] Mrs. Stowe had found herself, back in 1853, having to explain frequently to her aristocratic and sophisticated hosts that she and her clergyman-husband, Calvin, were indeed both teetotalers by conviction, but that "in America *all* clergymen were tee-totallers, of course."[94] She apparently had written off the Episcopalians. Three years earlier at Oxford her saintly brother, the famous Brooklyn preacher, was the object of "a knowing laugh when I declined beer and wine, as articles that I never employed. A thing more utterly inconceivable than a deliberate rejection of good wine and beer could not be told to an Oxford butler."[95] Visiting with English friends in the sixties, Mrs. A. E. Newman was shocked to find *four* glasses at each plate, "which in turn were filled with wine and liquors."[96]

Noble Prentis of Kansas observed that in 1877 "total abstinence is getting along very slowly in England," adding that "at the rate of present progress, I should judge that about twenty-thousand years would be required for the Independent Order of Good Templars to acquire a good and sufficient foothold."[97] About 1890 Baptist minister Walter Whittle visited the "Great Assembly Hall" mission operated by Fred Charrington, a son of the famous brewer who, having undergone a religious conversion, and seeing the effects of drink on the poor of the East End, gave up the brewery business, and founded his mission which required total abstinence of its members. "His Sunday audiences range from 4,000 to 5,000," marveled Whittle, adding like a good Baptist, "he is strictly an immersionist!"[98]

Before long their own travel authorities and advisers began to chide Americans for their complaining, rudeness to servants, loud talking, undisciplined children, irreverence in churches and cathedrals, and general boasting about the superiority of everything at home. "Some of the Americans who visit Europe are such odd personages," remarked Frank Stockton in his book *Personally Conducted,* of 1890, a combination travel narrative and guide book,

> that it is not to be wondered at if they give the people they meet a queer idea of our nation. Some of these are very fond of boasting that they come from a part of our country where currants are as large as grapes, grapes as big as plums, plums the size of peaches, peaches like melons, melons as big as great clothes-baskets and other things to match. Others complain if they cannot have ice-water and griddle-cakes in every European city they visit; while others again are continually growling and grumbling because waiters and drivers expect small fees, not considering that at home they not only pay very much *more* at hotels, and for carriage hire, but sometimes are expected to give fees which are ten times as much as the poor people of Europe are accustomed to receive.[99]

Up in the Highlands of Scotland one summer a little country woman took care of Iowan Julia Hallam, who found Loch Achray disappointing. " 'What a little bit of a lake! In my country it would hardly be considered large enough to name,' " she announced to her fellow travelers. " 'I hear they have everything on a grand scale in that countree,' " responded the female Scot who overheard her. On this same excursion Mrs. Hallam felt it necessary to inform another Scot that she was an American. " 'Ah, madam, you did not need to tell me that; I knew you were an American as soon as I saw you,' " was his reply. The odd thing is that Mrs. Hallam reports these little encounters without a shade of embarrassment.[100]

"Why is it," asked Ehrmann Nada—a secretary at the United States legation during the seventies—in his *Americans Abroad,*

that Americans look so much worse abroad than at home? The truth is, I suppose, that we see a worse class than we see at home, or see more of them, or that we see them under circumstances which are not in their favor. As I have before said, any foreigner is seen at a disadvantage in a country not his own. He is especially at a disadvantage, if he lacks social education. He is amid circumstances to which he is not accustomed, and if their is any vulgarity in him it is sure to come out.[101]

"Can't we do anything to keep such people at home?" asked Rudolph Williams in 1894, after watching a little group of American "oil heiresses" up in the Highlands, argue for forty-five minutes with a luckless Scottish coach driver regarding his fee.[102]

Sad to say, it was the American women who were the worst offenders in this respect—far more so than their male counterparts. There is a continual, carping, querulous tone in so many commentaries by American women in the later decades of the century that one comes to the conclusion that they must have been very wearing as traveling companions. Did they catch the malady, perhaps, from Sophia Hawthorne— from reading her *Notes in England and Italy,* published in 1870, which reveals what can only be called a case of "the cutes"? She delighted, for example, in doing a poor hardworking railway porter out of his tip, going against her husband's wish in so doing. She also boasted of her little technique by which she drove other travelers from public conveyances. "We were happy as usual in having the carriage to ourselves," she wrote concerning their trip from Peterborough to Nottingham. "Once a gentleman came into our private boudoir, and after sitting a few minutes, seemed to be conscious of intruding into domestic sanctities, and left us again for which I was much obliged to him." On another occasion she feigned illness to dupe a verger into leading her to a better seat at York Cathedral, leaving her husband in the rear. Always she preferred to explore by closed carriage, "so one can have the prospect without the dust," and she resented her husband's desire to wander as a pedestrian. "Papa, you know, hates to drive and prefers to wander off by himself on foot."[103]

A number of women bragged of their rudeness to minions endeavoring to please them, as did Miss L. L. Rees and her companions on their overnight visit to the Red Horse Inn at Stratford-on-Avon. When the waiter brought them the fabled "scepter" of Washington Irving for their inspection, an item sacred to most Americans, they laughed at him as he drew it from its "red-flannel scabbard" and informed him that they had "no reverence for these inanimate objects."[104] One "gorgeously-and wonderfully arrayed Western dame" was overheard, by a countryman, informing the rector of Stratford's Trinity Church, who was "showing her attention. . . that she had been 'a gooddle around an' seen a good many places', but, [as] for a place to live in, she had 'seen nawthin' like Louyville in Kaintucky!' "[105]

Henry Adams's, wife, Marion, although entertained graciously by countless hospitable Britons, was forever finding fault with all sorts of things, such as: the Englishwomen's "taste" in clothes; a countess with "dirty collars and sleeves"; cold country houses; "an offensive baronet who took me down and made sneering remarks about America. I laid him out stiff"; Browning—"not exciting and I don't hanker to see him again—heavy and utterly uninteresting"; Lady Salisbury, [who has] "the manners of a discouraged cook"; the ghastliness of "an English table d'hote where the British female airs her charms"; and even the meager refreshments served by Dean Stanley, of the Abbey, who "skipped about in small clothes and silk stockings, with big paste shoe buckles and a broad crimson ribbon round his neck [looking] like a hungry little gray rat."[106]

One American husband had to stand by while his wife lectured a pretty young woman at a church fair at Warwick on the evils of lotteries, when the latter tried to sell her a raffle ticket for money for church restoration. " 'I happen to share this prejudice, as you may term it, of my country people,' " the Yankee matron proudly announced. " 'And you really think it wrong?' persisted the English lady eagerly, 'wrong to raffle when the aim is so good a one?' 'Yes, we object to the principle involved!' " declared the American. When she rejoined her embarrassed husband he informed her that she had been fussing "for the last half hour with her Grace, the Countess of Warwick."[107] Why is it, Caroline Sheldon wondered, that "the American traveler always feels he ought to be a missionary."[108]

When they weren't complaining about the Englishwomen's taste in clothes, the weather, the food, the cold, the service, or the lack of ice water, American women fumed because they were not deferred to as they were accustomed to be at home. "The inferior female sex appears to me to be sat upon and suppressed in almost every way in England," observed Eliza Connor in 1882.[109] Mrs. Kirkland had made a similar observation thirty years before. "The English seem heartily to have adopted Miss Martineau's maxim that a woman has no right to expect or accept any attention or advantage on account of her sex."[110] The women particularly resented not being given seats on buses and steamers. "Mr. P. made an appeal to some men, who refused without hesitation, appearing to think our expectations were impertinent," complained Catherine Sedgwick in 1841.[111]

"In no other country but America do women receive the courtesy their sex requires," fussed Miss L. L. Rees, boasting one minute that she and her companions were traveling without male escort and the next expecting gallant attentions from gentlemen all along the way. "I do not mean to imply that in our travels we met with any insult whatsoever," she admitted, "but the deference and respect to which we have been accustomed was lacking."[112] Miss Connor of Ohio remarked: "Did we thank the Lord we were American women, with husbands, lovers, brothers, as the case might be, all belonging to that universal Yankee Nation? Maybe we didn't!" She missed "the ways of our gentlemen at home," she said.[113] "My own countrymen," Grace Greenwood had gushed back in 1852, "how inexpressibly proud I feel of them for their generous kindness, the chivalric gallantry, which everywhere mark their manner toward women, in whatever character or guise she appeals to them."[114] One young American woman admitted, however, that, when it came to "good looks and style, courtly manners and taste in costumes," she would have to give precedence to the English gentlemen.[115]

The different balance between the sexes of the two nations was analyzed by Price Collier, at the turn of the century, in his book *England and the English from an American Point of View*, which can be compared for its shrewd insights with Emerson's earlier *English Traits*. "Society is so patently, even impertinently, for the women in America," Collier wrote,

> that to the American it is with some awe that he sees even social matters dominated by and adjusted to, the convenience and even to the whims of the men here. One may say humbly, and with apologies to his countrywomen, that this masculine dominance is not altogether a failure. It is perhaps old-fashioned, and due also to the refined feminine influences of one's past and present surroundings, but it never seems quite as though the social adjustment of things is right when woman becomes conspicuous, and certainly not right or wise when she becomes the target for the camera and the paragraph. . . .The English woman knows that tradition, the law, and Society, demand of her that she shall make a home for a man; the American woman has been led astray by the force of circumstance into thinking that her first duty is to make a place for herself.[116]

Samuel Young, goodness knows, had seen the whole thing taking shape back in mid-century, as he compared American women with their British counterparts, and he sounded a warning to his countrymen. In Britain, he observed,

> the husband is, as he should be, Number 1. Now, this is not so with us. The contrast strikes me more forcibly abroad, where I have met several American families in every one of which the "grey mare was the better horse." Our little girls, too, of fourteen and sixteen years of age, put themselves forward in the hotels and other public places. . .and hardly wait to be spoken to first. There is a soft spot in the head or heart of the American. Let him tread with caution: Herodotus tells us of a people in Egypt where the women subdued the men, and compelled them to perform all the household offices, while they managed the out-of-door business, and all the affairs of state. And yet Horace Greeley and other ugly old feminines, are continually crying out for Women's Rights: Now, I say, let the press from Maine to California, raise a new banner and inscribe upon it "Men's Rights:" Americans: Look your peril boldly in the face!!! Let us gird up our loins and be up and stirring!!! Liberty or death.[117]

That traveling with their women required considerable patience is hinted at by a number of the pilgrims. John Latrobe sat down and reckoned how much more he might have seen and done without his womenfolk. "Traveling alone, a gentleman may do much more than was done on this occasion," he concluded.[118]

Once American males heard the soft, pleasant voices of Englishwomen, they were embarrassed by what William Dean Howells termed "the cat-bird twang of so many of our women."[119] "The soft and gentle cadences of English speech, in low life no less than high," admitted one American, "shame the nervous, high-strung utterances of us. . .across the sea."[120] Caroline Sheldon identified her own countrywomen by their "high, metallic buzzing," she wrote.[121] "Strident tones projected well through the nose apprised me that the Traveling American had arrived and was on duty" was the way one Yankee characterized the loud-mouthed tourist who showed up everywhere on their itinerary.[122] "As much as we love our country. . .we must record that after hearing the lady's voice and noting the lack of discipline with the children, we murmured 'Americans' and resigned ourselves," wrote another traveler of a similar case.[123]

"I had not been in their company five minutes when I was pierced through from ear to ear," groaned Richard White, observing some ladies from his country touring England in a group. "They seemed to be talking in italics, to be emphasizing every word, as if they would thrust it into my ears, whether I would or not."[124] At the theater an elderly and somewhat deaf Englishwoman whispered innocently to Eliza Connor, seated next to her, concerning a noisy female across the aisle: "She must be an American because she speaks so loudly."[125]

Dr. Rodney Glisan, in England to attend the International Medical Congress in London in August 1881, realized, as had Andrew Jackson Downing three decades before, that the American girl could learn a lot from her British cousins about attractive feminine qualities, among them her voice and manner of speech. "The average American girl . . . who takes her first trip to Europe is looked upon as a kind of savage," he explained, "and is considered a target for all sorts of fun and satire. She is described as a fresh Yankee, who has never before been out of her Boston or New York. She may be pretty, have a dazzling complexion, bright eyes, handsome figure, and an easy carriage; but her harsh and loud voice, and nasal twang set . . . the nerves in a flutter."[126]

"I rather fear," confided Loretta Post in her journal, "that some of our party, by loud talk, brought upon us the censure so often deservedly given us by foreigners. Their more quiet manners and softer tones of voice are well worthy of our imitation."[127] The Women's Rest Tour Association of Boston, among all their other practical advice for female travelers, had something to say in this regard. "Independent as you may be, do not scorn to imitate one grace of the English woman, be she duchess or chambermaid—her soft, low voice, that excellence which no American woman has attained in its infinitude of sweetness. Listen to it, delight in it, and *copy* it if you can."[128] One suspects that this was the experienced president of the association, Julia Ward Howe, speaking. Young Frederick Law Olmsted, too, had noticed the more agreeable speech of the British women—"a rich, musical tone. . . . I wonder that beauty of speech is not more thought of as accomplishment," he mused. "It is surely capable of great cultivation, and should not be forgotten in education."[129]

Cultural Shrines

Setting out on their pilgrimages around the country, most Americans in these years still took the trains, which differed so much from theirs at home. "The first experience of an American on a British railroad is an event," declared Union booster John Forney in 1867, "and mine was not exceptional." He praised the system of buying tickets before boarding, which cut down on both disorder and congestion; the civility and efficiency of the employees; the dignity and privacy of the compartments; and the smooth roadbeds that provided a comfortable ride even at such high rates of speed as "thirty miles an hour." The negative reaction of American females to being locked in their compartment by the conductor between the stops Forney attributed to their having read of "Müller's horrible murder of an inoffensive passenger a few years ago."[1] In 1878 Annie Wolf still fretted over "the *accidental* occurrence of travelers becoming too closely allied while confined in these flying prisons. There lingers in my mind," she worried, "recollections of a catastrophe that transpired in one of these carriages . . . which created a vivacious gossip on both sides of the Atlantic."[2]

Dr. Rodney Glisan warned in 1887 as to "the danger of being shut up in one of these small divisions at night with a disagreeable, perhaps, murderous companion. Helpless females have been insulted, and many persons robbed and murdered in these lonely compartments," he advised his readers earnestly.[3] The Reverend Zachary Taylor Sweeney "objected very seriously," he said, "as every American does, to the abridgment of our liberties in locking us in the cars, which are entered from the side."[4]

Some of the American men were more concerned for the health and safety of the train guard exposed to the weather and the dangers of "the board ten inches wide, along the side of the cars, on which he walks, holding to an iron rail screwed to the side," an arrangement perhaps nautical in origin but obviously designed to "keep him nimble . . . or to give him ready access to the passengers locked up in the carriages if any of them should get into a fight, or attempt to frighten or injure helpless women."[5]

As of old, the Americans' first move on leaving Liverpool, was to head for Chester "for a little comfortable medievalism," as William Dean Howells put it.[6] "Americans know Chester better than most other old towns in England," Dr. Oliver Holmes judged.

It has a mouldy old cathedral, an old wall, partly Roman, strange old houses with overhanging upper floors, which makes sheltered sidewalks and dark basements. When one sees an old house in New England with the second floor projecting a foot or two beyond the wall of the ground floor, the country boy will tell him that "them haouses was built so th't th' folks upstairs could shoot the Injins when they was tryin' to git threew th' door or int' th' winder." There are plenty of such houses all over England where there are no "Injins" to shoot, but the story adds interest to the somewhat lean traditions of our rather dreary past, and it is hardly worth while to disturb it.[7]

"The brave little walls of Chester" was how Henry James referred to the ancient wall encircling the city, with its walkway permitting one to stroll the circumference of the town whose streets he termed "a perfect feast of crookedness."[8] Dr. Holmes found Chester "wonderfully beautiful and interesting." The old cathedral he thought

particularly mouldy, and in fact, too high-flavored with antiquity. I could not help comparing some of the ancient cathedrals and abbey churches to so many old cheeses. They have a tough gray rind and a rich interior, which find food and lodging for numerous tenants who live and die under their shelter or shadow—lowly servitors some of them, portly dignitaries others, humble, holy ministers of religion many, I doubt not,—larvae of angels, who will get their wings by and by.[9]

The grounds of Eaton Hall, the traditional first exposure of Americans to ducal magnificence, now occupied "a larger space than . . . the District of Columbia," so Colonel Forney informed his readers, "and nearly as large as that included in all the boundaries of the consolidated city of Philadelphia."[10] Gone are the detailed references to romantic Gothic Revival architecture; they are replaced by comments instead on monumental splendor and the duke's fabulous income. All the years of building and rebuilding had produced what many travelers now considered an enormous architectural hash. The construction work, however, had benefited the locals. "Makes trade, you know," Joel Cook was reminded in 1878.[11] Dr. Holmes termed it "a palace, high-roofed, marble-columned, vast, magnificent, everything but homelike."[12] Youthful Lenamay Green of Nashville solemnly assured her readers that the duke's income was "two pounds, five shillings *a minute!*"[13]

Birmingham in these years was merely a place one passed through en route to Stratford-on-Avon and London, although a few words might be devoted to it by an occasional tourist. "She haunts us from the cradle to the grave," observed an Ohioan at the turn of the century. "She supplies us with the spoon that first brings our infant lips into acquaintance with pap, and she provides the dismal furniture which is affixed to our coffins."[14]

Chatsworth, always high on American lists, had by 1863, declared Elihu Burritt, become "lion number three, according to the American ranking of the historical edifices and localities of England. Stratford-on-Avon, Westminster Abbey and Chatsworth are the three representative celebrities which our travelers think they must visit, if they would see the life of England's ages from the best stand-points. And this is the order in which they rank them."[15]

"Governments and joint stock companies," wrote Burritt, "may erect and fill, with a world of utilities and curiosities of ancient and modern times, British Museums, National Galleries, Crystal Palaces, and Polytechnic Institutions; but not one of these," the American maintained, "can compete with one private mind, taste and will concentrated upon one great work for a lifetime." There was something of all the human types of endeavor to be seen at Chatsworth, observed Burritt. "It is the parlor pier glass of the present century. . . . The architecture, sculpture, carving, paintings, engravings, furniture, libraries, conservatories, flowers, shrubberies and rockeries, all bear and honor the fingerprints of modern taste and art."[16] Chatsworth, declared a tourist in 1878, is "one of the great show-houses of the realm." He claimed to have heard, however, that the present duke "is not enamored of this white elephant his ancestors have left him to maintain."[17]

"All the Americans go to Kenilworth, and to Warwick Castle, and to Stratford," exclaimed a handsome Englishwoman conversing with Richard Grant White on a train in the seventies. "I must go there," she added; "I have never been!"[18] William Rideing describes Yankee tourists in the nineties still scurrying about this sacred circuit "with guidebooks tucked under their arms, and their satchels swelled by new souvenirs of travel in the shape of photographs or paperweights and inkpots. . . . Yesterday . . . it was the Customhouse and the landing-stage at Liverpool," Rideing continued. "Since then they have been to Chester. . . . Today they are debating how they shall apportion their time so that they may be in London tomorrow."[19] Thirty years earlier a tourist covering this trinity of tourist shrines in a single day considered it "a good day's work though it was only sight-seeing," adding, "I know very well that we ought to spend a week instead of a day exploring such places. But what is one to do when his time is as limited as mine?"[20] This cry was heard more and more as the decades wore on and such visits were reduced to mere hours.

"We went to Stratford-on-Avon," wrote Lucy Dudley on July 18, 1895, "where all good Americans go; and it is said their patronage aids materially to support the town."[21] Another American declared that "England never discovered Stratford; Washington Irving did, and it is made altogether what it is by the tribute *we* pay to the Bard of Avon."[22] Well-heeled Americans, not being herded through in droves, still made the effort to stay overnight at the Red Horse Inn, and Orrin Hubbell of Ohio quoted Irving's essay for his readers of the 1890s. Mary Terhune [author Marion Harland] on being shown the old poker in 1877, remembered reading Nathaniel Willis's article thirty years earlier in "a bound volume of the New York Mirror," adding that "what we read in those days we digested!"[23]

Journalist Theron Crawford, referring in the eighties to the hordes of his countrymen who made Stratford their mecca, believed that there was no

more disappointing place to visit in all England. It is one of the few places that does not correspond in any degree to one's anticipations. The town is uninteresting. It has no picturesque features. It has a very modern look, and the majority of the houses are ugly, unornamented brick. The greater number of the streets present the hard, glaring appearance of hurriedly finished villages of the far West. The town is permeated with Shakespeare's history and name. His fame apparently affords the principal livelihood for the inhabitants.[24]

Far less emotional responses were aroused in these late-nineteenth-century Yankee visitors to the birthplace of "the bard." One labeled the house "a dingy and decaying enclosure,"[25] while another thought the town itself "a duty to visit and a pleasure to leave."[26] The scholarly anglophile Richard Grant White found it "the rawest, most uninteresting place that I had seen since my foot first touched British soil although," he added, he was kindly shown about the town by the mayor himself, "an intelligent gentleman of pleasant manners."[27] Howells wondered if the armies of Yankees visiting Stratford annually in the years just before World War I were not driven by some inexpressible urge to make "a tacit atonement there for the Baconian heresy which our nation invented."[28] If they had read Hawthorne's *Our Old Home,* as so many American travelers had, they knew all about poor old Delia Bacon to whom that author devoted so many pages of his account of his own visit to Stratford-on-Avon in the fifties. In his chapter entitled "Recollections of a Gifted Woman" he described both Miss Bacon and her obsession that the plays of Shakespeare were actually written by a committee of three—Bacon, Raleigh, and Spenser—and used as vehicles to express liberal concepts otherwise denied expression in their day.

"Uncommonly tall" was Delia Bacon, with "a striking and expressive face; dark hair, dark eyes, which shone with an inward light as soon as she began to speak; and, by-and-by, a color came into her cheeks and made her almost young. . . . Unquestionably she was a monomaniac," Hawthorne concluded. "These over-mastering ideas about the authorship of Shakespere's [sic] plays, and the deep political philosophy concealed beneath the surface of them, had completely thrown her off balance; but at the same time they had wonderfully developed her intellect, and made her what she otherwise could not have become."[29]

"All that Miss Bacon now remained in England for," recalled Hawthorne, "indeed, the object for which she had come hither, and which had kept her here for three years past—was to obtain possession of these material and unquestionable proofs of the authenticity of her theory." Miss Bacon believed that in a hollow space under Shakespeare's gravestone these documents lay hidden, wrote Hawthorne, and "began to haunt the church like a ghost." Her lengthy tome explaining her theory—*The Philosophy of the Plays of Shakespeare Unfolded* (1857)—went largely unread. In due time, Hawthorne said, he received a letter from Stratford's mayor informing him that Miss Bacon was afflicted with insanity, and "in a lucid interval she had referred to me, as a person who had some knowledge of her family affairs. What she may have suffered before her intellect gave way," Hawthorne wrote, "we had better not try to imagine."[30]

"If any community ever owed a statue to the honour of a benefactor for money value received, the Kenilworthies owe one to Sir Walter Scott," observed Elihu Burritt in 1868. "The principal source of their income is derived from their vested interest in Scott's *Kenilworth,* not in the real castle walls. Take away that famous novel, and, with all the authenticated history that remains attached to them, not one in five visitors they now attract would walk around them with admiration . . . they are more a monument to the genius of the great novelist than to the memory of Elizabeth and the Earl of Leicester."[31]

"I'm sure I shall never be happy until I own a ruin like Kenilworth," enthused young Lilian Leland in 1890, taking a few hours off from her *Woman's Journey*

Kenilworth Castle ruins in 1897. "A very tame lion indeed," remarked Henry James of this once highly popular American tourist objective. *Courtesy the Library of Congress.*

around the World to visit that site. "I adore 'ru-uns' as my fellow countrymen call them."[32] No more, however, did romantic young men like William Dana make trips by moonlight to indulge their fantasies in the shadows of the crumbling stones. "As a ruin, Kenilworth is eminently satisfactory," judged a "Cookie" matter-of-factly.[33] "The castle is literally a ruin and nothing more," reported John Latrobe, "and one looks in vain for something to recall a single passage of the novel."[34] Travelers now found the premises infested with insistent hawkers. "We had to shake ourselves free from the briery hold of women who assaulted us with petitions to buy unripe fruit, photographs, and *Kenilworth Guides*," remarked a visitor in the eighties.[35] "We were disappointed in this ruin," observed celebrity hound James Hoyt in 1871, "and I will not further allude to it."[36] Kenilworth was losing its magic—"a very tame lion" indeed Henry James termed it by the century's end.[37]

Visitors at Warwick Castle still complained of being hurried through the grand apartments. Annie Wolf was shown around in the seventies "by the old Janitress, who acts as a sort of lady abbess, or, as I have heard her called, 'jailoress', of the old pile. She looks like one of the weird sisters who met Macbeth upon the heath. . . . This woman, who must be at least eighty, told us that she had been retained by the Neville family since her childhood; and for ever so many years she has day after day repeated the stories of Guy of Warwick, and sounded the vast metal 'porridge pot'."[38]

Mary Terhune, on her Warwick tour, declared that

we seldom met with a more satisfactory specimen in this line than the antique servitor that kept the lodge of Warwick Castle. She wore a black gown, short-waisted and short-skirted, a large cape of the same stuff, and what Dickens had taught us to call a "mortified" black bonnet of an exaggerated type. . . . Entering the lodge hastily, after the young woman who admitted us had begun cataloguing the curiosities collected there, she put her aside with a sweep of her bony arm, and an angry, gutteral "Ach!" and began the solemnly circumstantial relation she must have rehearsed a thousand times.[39]

A decade later, Louise Robinson found, instead of this old lady, "red and gold uniformed Guards . . . pacing up and down the gravelled walks" and was shown through "in a most stately manner" by a "Grand Mogul" whose "backbone was surely made of iron." When he did not readily repeat a description at her request, she informed him, so she says, that " 'You are here for the purpose of explaining; will you please tell me the story of [the] table again.'. . . The man changed his superior attitude," Miss Robinson wrote with satisfaction, "and from that [sic] on through the entire castle he gave me his devoted attention."[40] A visitor in 1904 claimed that her group was "driven through the castle by a red-uniformed soldier whose general appearance and behavior suggest those of a loquacious lobster, and although the rate of speed at which the traveller progresses is like that of a pea through a pop-gun, . . . it is always possible to enjoy the garden and park at leisure."[41] "The bonniest sight" for Louise Moulton, visiting Warwick Castle in the eighties, was her glimpse of the young countess herself at an upper window, "with her two little children leaning against her knees, looking down, with an idle, yet not uninterested curiosity, at the strangers within her gates."[42]

At Stonehenge in 1871 "a little infirm, old man popped out from behind the stones and began his story of the place," recalled Elizabeth Peake. "He has spent forty-one years of his life here. I asked him if he did not find it very lonesome. . . . Oh, no, quiet was conducive to study . . . besides he reads a great deal. Americans gave him our newspapers, and he was for the North all through the war. I promised myself he should have all the papers at our hotel for saying so."[43]

In 1891 his successor, a Mr. Judd, would greet the Americans—ready with his camera to record their visit as well as guard the stones themselves and recite the history of the place. The cycling Thwaites found him asleep in an armchair on their arrival. "Just as we had fairly risen to the proper mental attitude of true pilgrims, our musings were rudely broken in upon by the arrival of . . . two or three carriage loads of tourists . . . among them some Americans,—you always know them a quarter of a mile away."[44]

Tourist visits to Oxford tended now to be quick and cursory. Many descriptions bear the mark of the guidebook rather than of the eye, and stops seem to have been made primarily during those months when few students were about and those chiefly mousing about the libraries. A traveler in the eighties observed that "we stopped over at Oxford long enough to take a walk through the colleges and churches, and enjoy a drive through her pretty streets. Large numbers of embryo statesmen, priests and poets are learning to smoke cigars and handle boat-oars here."[45]

Unlike most tourists, Charles Wood actually "enjoyed the honor of dining in University with the Fellows" on the night of the boat races near the close of the summer term. "Exciting for those who look calmly on from the banks or the barges," he decided, "but what must they be for the men in the boats!"[46] Not even Oxford could charm that grim anglophobe from Ohio, the self-styled "Hon. Wm. A. Braman." He found everything "black and grim," complaining that the "ancient walls are beginning to crumble, and there was a spooky appearance and an air of desolation in its multitude of halls. There was no college campus in sight."[47]

Most tourist comments on Cambridge also tended now to be equally superficial—simply remarks of travelers passing through. In the eighties P. B. Cogswell recommended it as "a pleasant town in which to spend leisure time" and directed his readers to "a very pleasant home at No. 15 Upper Woburn Place, kept by Mrs. Wright. It is more than a boarding house; it is an English home for Americans. . . . Like Oxford, Cambridge has a large number of college buildings. . . . The same ground plan of architecture is maintained . . . enclosed courts and archways—which gives the buildings a quaint appearance."[48] James Hoyt boasted of seeing in the Trinity College library "a book of which but one other copy is extant, entitled *The Passionate Pilgrime* (a book of poems) by William Shakespeare."[49]

The Lake District attracted the Americans in these years not so much for its scenic beauty as for its many literary associations—which so largely determined these American travel itineraries in Britain, particularly in the second half of the century, when travelers came for romantic escape rather than their onetime professional tours and social surveys.

"I cannot tell, as I look back, whether my interest in the English lakes has been most largely literary or scenic," observed William Gage after spending the summer of 1884 here.

I think the blending of the two has been their perfect charm; for I do not think that, in all their beauty, they so far transcend our Lake George and Winnepesaukee as to be worth crossing the Atlantic to see. But in this little tract, which you can traverse in a day's ride, lie the homes of Tennyson, Ruskin, Wordsworth, Coleridge, Southey, Faber, Professor Wilson, Bishop Watson, DeQuincey, Hartley Coleridge, Miss Martineau, Dr. Arnold, and many others.

Indeed, you cannot journey for an hour in any part of the lake country, but you pass either the home of some man equally known to Englishmen and Americans, or some scene which the pen of Southey or Wordsworth or DeQuincey has made famous. I have gone through all the local poems of Wordsworth since being here, and they have been a revelation; for it was he who, most of all, caught the beauty of these landscapes.

He added that "throngs of tourists go trooping by in July and August," an observation borne out by other tourists who found an American flag floating over their hotel and "the traffic in souvenirs and in travelers unceasing day and night."[50] A. Vandoren Honeyman complained at the turn of the century of "the rush and push of ingoing and outgoing tourists," with peace all but destroyed by "jostling and busy parties arriving hourly; all is hurly-burly and confusion."[51] How unlike Orville Dewey's "walk to Grassmere Lake to see it after sunset" with Wordsworth—"that loveliest of all scenes I ever witnessed on earth."[52]

Still, the Yankee pilgrims made their way to the cathedral at York, although Elizabeth Peake, visiting in 1871, admitted that "it has so often been described that I will only say it met my expectations." She was much amused as their guide called their attention to the carving of the head of an ape in one of the stalls, remarking, " 'We call that Darwin.' " She also distinguished herself by rescuing "a small boy, about four years old, with his head caught between the bars of a railing."[53] Claudius Patten attended the annual service of the Royal Society for the Prevention of Cruelty to Animals on May 29, 1882, along with "a great swarm of English boys belonging to some charity foundation in York." His descent from the tower of the cathedral was something he would never forget, as it coincided with the ascent of these eager children:

> They were forcing their way through the darkness and dust, completely occupying the old stone steps. Gradually they became wedged in with the party . . . descending, and a perfect jam was the result. I was in the heart of the throng, and for a while, actually feared that some of us would be suffocated . . . . Nothing but the pluck and vigor of the little English rascals, who had gotten us into the scrape, helped us out of it. They finally butted and bored their way to daylight at the top . . . . I came out of the hole at the bottom, feeling as if I had been dragged through a dirty chimney.

As for all those stairs, he concluded, "few tourists must ever care to force their way up them a second time."[54]

For most Americans in these last decades of the nineteenth century, Edinburgh was but a blur in their hurried tour of the Scott country, although some of them still worked hard to recapture something of the old magic. William Stevenson in 1881 now found himself doubting the authenticity of the Rizzio bloodstain at Holyrood, which had "so wonderfully impressed [his] youthful imagination . . . just thirty-five years ago."[55] Lucy Culler in 1882 actually hiked up to the summit of Arthur's Seat, the volcanic mount overlooking the ancient city, since "several scenes of *The Heart of Midlothian* were laid there," and at the top she was surprised to find not poetic thrills but a couple of Edinburgh ladies "with tablecloths spread on the ground, covered with cakes, buns, lemonade, gingerbread, etc., for sale."[56]

Baptist minister Walter Whittle in the 1880s toted with him *The Heart of Midlothian, Rob Roy, The Lady of the Lake, The Lay of the Last Minstrel,* and *Marmion* in his already heavy luggage. "When I become very tired . . . I spread myself out on the soft side of some projecting rock, high on the mountain side, and there, while resting, I alternately feast my eager eyes . . . or read." The Scott magic, although fading, still held many travelers in its spell. So many monuments to great men did Whittle find in Edinburgh that he decided he had better "leave here tomorrow before they put up a monument to me."[57]

Casting about for something novel to write about rather than provide more descriptions of poverty in Edinburgh's "old town," Helen Hunt Jackson came up with the Newhaven fishwives in their "short, full, blue cloth petticoats . . . white blouses and gay kerchiefs; big, long-sleeved cloaks of the same blue cloth . . . the married women with white caps, standing up stiff and straight in a point on top of the head." They carried great loads of fish, "that it taxes a man's strength merely to lift . . . [in] two big wicker-work creels, one above the other . . . on their broad shoulders, and held in place by a stout leather strap passing round their foreheads."[58]

Edinburgh's serious approach to Sunday, and to religion in general, elicited a comment from William Wilberforce Nevin in 1879. Noting "a curious, raw-boned theological cast to the Scotch popular mind which crops out everywhere," he concluded that "in Edinburgh they do not seem to have gotten over the Reformation yet, and are still fighting it out with polemic treatises and news-paper articles."[59] Benjamin Bausman, himself a preacher, warned his readers that "a Sunday in Scotland gives one much to think about."[60]

The Highland kilt still offended the modesty of many American puritans, like the Reverend Morton Wharton, who, in 1884, called the garb "simply barbar-ous."[61] The music of the pipes was, if anything worse, according to Catherine Dyer who quoted Scott to the effect that Highlanders reach the highest point of happiness when twenty-four bagpipe players are assembled together in a small room, all playing at the same time different tunes.[62] The ubiquitous "Usque-baugh" (water of life), or whiskey, continued to offend the Yankee teetotalers as well. In the seventies Mary Wills was shocked to be offered a lunch by a respectable family, consisting of

bread, cheese, Scotch whisky, brandy and wine, and the gray-haired man who presided reverently asked God to bless what was spread before us, and then proceeded to mix "toddy" for his daughters . . . . Here they prescribe liquor when you are sick and when you are well, for cold and for heat, for fatigue or lack of spirits, on account of the damp climate, to cure nervousness, and to induce sleep, which excuses may all be summed up in one phrase: they use it freely because they like it.[63]

It was one thing to read of mist and rain in the novels of Scott in an overheated American parlor but quite another to ride for miles "in open wagons along the skirts of lochs, and there wasn't an hour of the time that the rain didn't pour," according to Eliza Connor. "The Scotch mist which wets an Englishman to the skin drowns an American, blots him out completely," she concluded.[64] "On a wild afternoon," seated atop an open coach where everyone had raised his

Tourists up in Scotland—bored, tired, damp, cold, and all because of Sir Walter Scott.
The Graphic, vol. VIII, September 13, 1873, p. 237. *Courtesy the Library of Congress.*

umbrella, recalled James Hoyt, "the drip of the umbrella protecting me would fall in the lap, or neck, or possibly face, of my neighbor in front; and his drip, with due impartiality would favor me, and so likewise through the crowd. Nevertheless, on that stage coach, in the scurrying storms of the Scotch Highlands," he recalled, "there never was a better-natured set of tourists. Each one, while being patiently soaked, was intent upon persuading his fellow, that all was as well as could be; and so we mutually accommodated each other, till we reached the welcome Trossachs Hotel."[65]

"I believe it always does rain in these mountain defiles," concluded E. L. Temple at the turn of the century.[66] "Only a Scotch mist," E. R. Hendrix said his driver assured his thoroughly soaked passengers.[67] "So many umbrellas carried water away from heads aboard Lucy Culler's coach that they found their respective shoulders turned into "eaves troughs," she wrote.[68] Coming over on the boat with her, Miss Connor remembered, was "an ancient mariner whom we dubbed Captain Cuttle. He was an American citizen, who started in life. . .a Scot, and he was returning to his native land after an absence of more than a generation. He looked at the shores of bonny Scotland, muddy, rainy, and gloomy, and raised both hands. 'Aweel, aweel,' said he, 'it was rainin' when I left Glasgie, forty years ago, and it's rainin' noo; I suppose it's been rainin' ever since.' "[69]

The trip through the Trossachs or "Lady of the Lake" region now took but a day in large "wagonettes," forerunners of the tourist coach, or bus, of today. "These coaches are made especially for tourists," reported Burr Polk.

There is a low, box-like covered body into which whatever baggage there may be is carried, and across the top of this are four seats, including that of the driver, each capable of comfortably seating four persons, three seats facing to the front, that behind the driver, facing to the rear. They are very strong and are drawn by splendid horses, generally four to each, between the two lakes, though the one I got upon, had only two, which gave the gentlemen of the party the privilege of walking to the summit of the mountain. I did not regret it. My Colorado experience made it light work, albeit I wore my overcoat, the pockets of which were stuffed with something less than a ton of guidebooks, rubber shoes belonging to the ladies of the party and other trinkets too tedious to mention.[70]

Drivers of these conveyances still specialized in reciting or reading long passages from *The Lady of the Lake,* which no doubt charmed their passengers into better gratuities, and tourists followed their route with close attention. "Guide books were in requisition," wrote Miss Peake, "and Scott's *Lady of the Lake* also, and everyone was reading and pointing out the places as we passed them."[71] Just as at Kenilworth, Scott's romantic fiction still served as guide.

There were frequent references now to swarms of tourists, many of them Americans, so many that the hotel at Inversnaid on Loch Lomond routinely flew the American flag. "Thousands of people walk about and scatter gold," wrote Rudolph Williams, "and laugh while they ride through Lochs Lomond and Katrine . . . the proof of the adage of the greatness of the pen."[72]

"I was rather disappointed in the Trossachs," decided Miss Lilian Leland of this brief segment of her journalistic round-the-world tour. "I had been told in

Loch Katrine at the turn of the century showing the trim little steamer that swooshed visitors across the loch once the domain of strong-armed rowers who recited Scott's poetry. *Courtesy the Library of Congress.*

England that I should see the loveliest scenery in the world. The Trossachs are low, bare and ungainly. Most of it was very ordinary; prettier than the dry cornstalk plains of Ohio and Illinois to be sure," she admitted, "but not pretty enough to set the world on fire."[73] Back in 1851 her countryman, Andrew Dickinson, less jaded, had declared that he "would not give those two glorious days in the Highlands for a hundred fashionable trips to Saratoga." He filled a small bottle "with the crystal water of Loch Katrine" and brought it home to America.[74]

Still, the American tourists came, even after the turn of the century. About 1905 Jesse Johnson sat on top of a stage in "a perfect downpour. . .in cheerful, almost joyous mood"—exchanging snatches of Scott's poetry with the elderly Englishman on his right, and, like the thousands of his countrymen before him, paying his tribute to the genius of Scott, the "Wizard of the North," who had populated "these great mountains, glens, lakes and streams" with his immortal beings.[75]

The Burns Cottage, in the period following the American Civil War, was in the charge of an Englishman, Thomas Moreley, who had himself fought in that war in the 113th Regiment of the Pennsylvania Volunteers and also survived a spell in Richmond's infamous Libby Prison; he had his commission hung on the wall to prove all this.[76] He was also a veteran of Balaklava. Helen Hunt Jackson reported that "he does not love the Scotch people. 'I would not give the Americans for all the Scotch ever born,' he says, and is disposed to speak with unjust satire of their apparent love of Burns, which he ascribes to a perception of his recognition by the rest of the world and a shamefaced desire not to seem behindhand in paying tribute to him. 'Oh, they let me to think much of him,' he said. 'It's money in their pockets.' "[77] Visiting the cottage in the seventies, Loretta Post found that "the hawkers quite disturb the poetic spell."[78]

Like many of her countrymen, Mrs. Jackson paid a call on Burns's two nieces, the Misses Begg, who recalled for her a few anecdotes from the poet's life and assured her that his intemperate habits "had been greatly exaggerated."[79] Leonard Morrison described the pleasure with which visiting Americans were received in his day by the one remaining Miss Begg. " 'Scotsmen,' when speaking of her uncle, she said, 'would commence by apologizing for his faults. Americans said nothing about them.' "[80]

Few took the trouble, as Mrs. Jackson did, to seek out the gloomy little rooms in which the poverty-stricken, ailing Burns died in 1796. " 'They say there was a great lot o' papers up here when he died,' " the servant girl said who showed her the way up. " 'But nobody knew what become of them. Now that he's so much thought aboot, I wonder his widow did not keep them. But, ye know, the poor thing was just comin' to be ill; that was the last thing he wrote when he knew he was dyin', for someone to come and stay with her; and I dare say she was in such a sewither she did not know about anything.' "[81]

The struggle to seat oneself for a moment in the chair of Sir Walter Scott's study at Abbotsford continued. "I had leave of the wooden guide to seat myself for a few moments," wrote Margaret Preston in the eighties.[82] "I took a seat in this chair, viewed the interesting mementoes around, proud as a Jew sitting in Moses' seat," wrote a clergyman.[83] But by 1895 the rules had changed again. And poor Edgar Magness, trying for a quick furtive plop, "did not long enjoy the honor. The attendant quickly caught my eye and recalled me to my feet again."[84]

During the Civil War Elihu Burritt, the American peace-temperance-abolition crusader, had been disturbed to find at Abbottsford "the initials 'U.S.A.' and 'C.S.A.'. . .chasing each other up and down the pages of the visitors' register. . . . If they represented the dissolution of a great political fabric," he decided, at least "they meant union here. . .a common-homage gift to the memory of the Writer of Abbotsford."[85]

Unlike William Dana, with his penchant for moonlight visits to ruins, most tourists in these decades had to settle for brief daytime stops at even the most sacred Scott shrines such as Melrose Abbey. William Stevenson in the eighties was not unhappy. "Indeed, my youthful fancy had been so wrought upon by the weird and terrible things which occurred in these aisles in Scott's *Lay of the Last Minstrel*," he wrote, "that a moonlight visit to the haunted spot would have tested my courage severely. I had in Edinburgh provided myself with a copy of the poem, and found the second canto good reading in the abbey."[86]

A few travelers in these years were even getting out into the Western Isles, or Hebrides, off Scotland's west coast, if only to make the day trip, still being done to this day, out to the sacred Isle of Iona, starting from Oban and sailing around the Isle of Mull with a brief stop at Fingal's Cave on the way. In the nineteenth century the Gaelic-speaking boatmen actually risked their lives landing boatloads of tourists among these treacherous rocks at the cave and then getting them safely off again. "The sailors are provided with hooks and short poles which they use with great dexterity in guarding the boat from being driven against the rocks by the mighty surge that ebbs and flows round Fingal's Cave," wrote George Williams in 1866.[87] Few tourists looked with any real attention at the hard-scrabble life of the Islanders, although one or two mention buying pebbles and shells from scrawny, ragged moppets as mementoes of Iona.[88]

The London-based American artist Joseph Pennell and his wife Elizabeth did look and told what they saw in a series of articles in *Harper's Magazine*, later published as a book in 1889 entitled *Our Journey to the Hebrides*. They had, they claimed, seen what "has seldom been seen by other travelers." Instead of focusing on the romances of Scott, they had concentrated "on the immediate reasons for the present condition of the Western Highlanders and Islanders," which they termed a "condition of absolute wretchedness and semi-starvation." Most Americans, they said, saw the Highlands "as they are in the stupid romance of Scott or in the sickly sentiment of Landseer, or as a mere pleasure ground for tourists and sportsmen." The tourists in the fast-moving wagonettes and steamers did not realize, asserted the Pennells, that "this land which holiday-makers have come to look upon as their own, is the saddest on God's earth." The poverty, unemployment, and hopelessness of the region they summed up in a picture of an old man in a tam-o'-shanter seated before a decaying cottage, "his head bent low, his clasped hands falling between his knees," while "a few miles away, men in a fortnight throw away on their fishing more than these people can make in years. Scotch landlords rent their wild, uncultivated acres for fabulous sums, while villages like this grow desolate."[89]

The eminent Presbyterian clergyman Samuel Mutchmore, observing the plight of the Gaels, both Scottish and Irish, at the turn of the century was moved to remark that "the English government has gone daft over the absurd notion that the Celt cannot govern himself. Government is not a gift peculiar to any class," he maintained. "Any class of men are able to rule if God calls them to it. The Celt," he concluded, "has been treated much after the style of the North American Indian, based on the idea that 'the only good Indian is the dead Indian.' "[90]

"When an American goes to Ireland," remarked Junius Browne in 1871, "it seems very much as if he were visiting his own country. He sees the same faces, hears the same voices, notices the same peculiarities with which he has been familiar from his childhood. Barring the externals, Dublin becomes New York; Cork, Boston; Galway, Cincinnati; and Limerick, St. Louis. He does not find, as he may have expected, the indigenous Irish different from the transplanted article."[91] Such was the result of the mass nineteenth-century migration from Ireland to the United States. "This looks like home," remarked Rudolph Williams of Chicago in 1894.[92]

Sadder thoughts pressed in on other American travelers. "Ireland depressed us," wrote Mary Wills, "as a world deserted by all save a few left to beg and show the country to strangers. And yet there is a sort of justice in the matter when you consider how many annually flock to our shores to attend to our domestic and industrial interests, while we traverse so many weary miles to see the land they have quitted."[93] Another traveler observed that "the priests are the best-dressed and the best-fed people in Ireland. The young men enlist, join the constabulary, or go to America; there is nothing else to do."[94]

"The poorer classes look as if hope had left them forever," observed Dr. Sinclair Tousey in 1868. An old laborer with whom he spoke had two sons in America, both of whom had "joined a Massachusetts regiment" during the Civil War; "in fact, everyone you talk with in Ireland has a relative or friend in America."[95] About this same time Charles Poston assured his readers that, while not all the Irish had yet left for America, *they are coming!*"[96]

Ireland in the second half of the century—with certain areas long since having become overworked tourist meccas and little else—was haunted ground for Americans whose own country continued to receive Irish immigrants by the boatload. Everywhere an American went he was met with questions concerning long-lost relatives and friends, employment opportunities, and expenses, and also was subjected frequently to petty extortions, "because you are all rich." Passing through port cities and railway stations, they observed many a tearful parting between parents and their children setting out for the United States or entire families saying farewell to relatives as they prepared to board ships "already swarming with emigrants," ready to put out to sea. "Three thousand sailed from this port [of Queenstown] alone last week," reported traveler J. H. Bates in May of 1889, "mostly young men and women, a few of middle age, and fewer still of aged, robust in health, and, as it seemed to me, more pleased than sad at . . . leaving a land which promises so little to their future."[97] Observing this same phenomenon, Elizabeth Wetmore wrote in 1890: "I gaze at these sturdy young men and women, and I wonder how soon they will be New York aldermen, and mayors of Chicago; how soon these rosy girls in their queer, bunchy, provincial gowns will be leaders of Washington society and dressed by Worth."[98]

The three main tourist objectives in Ireland in the late decades of the nineteenth century were Blarney Castle near Cork, the Lakes of Killarney in the southwest, and the Giants' Causeway in the north. Those travelers planning a stop in Ireland usually first disembarked at Queenstown, today called by its original name, Cobh, instead of landing at Liverpool—a decision they sometimes regretted when descended upon by "the excited rabble of beggars and car men" lying in wait for them. "As soon as an American steamer is telegraphed," Rideing told his readers in the nineties, "it is known among the thatched cottages on the hillside by some rapid but mysterious agency. When the passenger lands he is confused by the importunities to buy and to give."[99] Back in 1851 Benjamin Moran had written that "the beggars of Queenstown clung to us like wax . . . half-starved, bare-footed . . . so filthy and covered with vermin as to make me shudder to think of them for days afterward."[100]

"They are more persistent than a swarm of blue-tail flies and stick closer than sheep ticks," William Hemstreet warned in 1875.[101] The women flattered the tourists outrageously, calling all the ladies "pretty" and all the men "lady-killers" and the like. Dr. William Taylor was much amused to hear his fat male companion praised for "the shapely rotundity of his body and the symmetrical massiveness of his head." They were followed for blocks, but when the expected donation was not forthcoming the flattery turned to scorn. " 'Down't ye axe the ould divil inny mowre. His hid an' his billy's too big to hiv innything good in 'em!' " an old crone advised her companions at last.[102] Another tourist in the eighties pronounced Queenstown "one of the dirtiest and most forbidding places I have ever seen, with but one crowning advantage. It is exactly suited to the purpose for which it was designed. It is a good place to emigrate from." He had tried hard, he wrote, to comfort a young man on the train with him who had "wept bitterly" after saying good-bye to his aged parents at the station—probably forever.[103]

The average tourist was soon on his or her way out of Queenstown, en route for Cork, there to perform his or her duty to the Blarney Stone. There seems to have been some confusion as to "the real" and a substitute stone, but in any event thousands of Yankees endured considerable stretching and projecting of their bodies over an open drop of about one hundred feet, all the while being held by the ankles, according to traveler-writer, William Hemstreet.[104] Thomas Rees and a friend joined in assisting a youthful countryman in his obsession to kiss the stone and were alarmed as he "kicked and scrambled and twisted like an eel until he almost got away from us. Finally he smacked the stone and yelled for us to pull him up which we did with great alacrity."[105] Little Amy Smith claimed that a female member of their party performed the same feat in 1865, while those below "were aghast to see half the figure of a lady projecting over the high crumbling old wall to reach the battlement containing the stone."[106]

"We, of course, had to *do* the Lakes of Killarney," wrote the Reverend Mutchmore in 1887. "There would be no respect for an American who did not make this far-famed pilgrimage. Ignorance is the hand-maid to all such endeavors," he warned future travelers. "The first part of the journey is delightful. . . . The round trip is about thirty miles, seven of which are made in a carriage. But as we near the mountains which stand defying approach, we see that the only pass between these frowning fortresses must be passed on horseback, and here the trials of the tourist's life begin."[107]

"It is impossible to estimate the multitude of men, children, and especially women, who live chiefly as beasts of prey and almost drive the desperate traveler into the water, where alone he can be quit of them," observed Harvard's Andrew Peabody in the sixties of his Killarney pilgrimage.

> Some have ponies to let; some bugles to blow [for the echoes]. Then there are numerous vendors of bogwood ornaments, and of articles manufactured from the wood of the arbutus. There are blind men with wives to hold their hats; and legless men with children to run after pennies; and idiots who, incapable of learning anything else, are adepts in the science of mendicancy. The women bring out goat's milk and *mountain-dew* (the Hibernian euphemism for whiskey) and run along with their bottles as fast as the car or pony can go at full speed, always so civil and good-natured that you cannot speak rudely to them.[108]

Retreat was impossible, for these women and children were able to run for miles. "One woman followed us four miles," Mutchmore recalled, "going as fast as two good horses could jog. Her face was the color of mahogany, her feet bare, but hard as a horse's hoof. When the driver told her she was wasting her time, she replied that this was her way of earning a living, and she did not give up until someone gave her a shilling."[109]

"Women tried, and kept trying to sell us woolen stockings," wrote Rudolph Williams, "telling us to encourage home industry. Others told us we should do something for the poor of Ireland, as America was the place where all are rich." On being told that he was "clean out of change," one woman offered, so he said, to change a sovereign for him.[110] " 'Shure, ye'll be goin' back to Ameriky where there is plenty,' " pleaded an old woman to John Higinbotham, " 'and ye'll niver miss a penny for poor Mary Sullivan here in the Black Valley.' "[111]

At the so-called cottage of "Kate Kearney," immortalized by the poet Moore in his song "Sweet Innisfallen," travelers were importuned by "Kate" or one of her many "descendants" to buy goat's milk or whiskey along with her photograph. "You run a gauntlet," observed Alexander McKenzie at Killarney in the eighties. "The first fact which is made apparent is that all people live on the traveler . . . there is no escape."[112] Two decades later a traveler reported that, "if you do not wish to buy, they hang onto your stirrups. If you are polite in your refusals, they are persistent. If you are firm, they grow abusive. Such a day! The town of Killarney once worked for a living and had iron smelters and foundries; but now it has tasted the joys of 'easy money,' and its fifty-five hundred people depend on tourists for a livelihood."[113] Observed another visiting Yankee: "I was a tourist and an American and was thus a legitimate object of plunder. As there were four of them, and only one of me, I fed them all."[114]

Their brief stops at Dublin in these later years provide cursory descriptions of architecture and not much else. "Most tourists visit Dublin to see the buildings," observed Joel Cook in 1878.[115] Hotels and tours by jaunting car—"a sort of Irish joke on wheels," as one tourist put it—are described. There are still plenty of

Irish cabman and newly arrived Yankee tourist about to be overcharged for his ride because "you are all rich." *Punch,* **vol. 70, January 22, 1876, p. 20.** *Courtesy the Library of Congress.*

references to the quick Irish wit often used to put a bumptious Yankee tourist in his place. One smart aleck, observing large numbers of poor women going barefoot, asked his driver, " 'What kind of shoes have those women got on?' 'Those are made of bareskin, sir,' " he was told quick as a flash.[116] A visitor from Ohio, criticizing some fruit offered for sale by an old woman, remarked, " 'I suppose you think those melons of yours are large, but we have apples in Kansas that would beat them for size.' " Fixing a beady eye on her superior, she replied, " 'Go along wid yez; I don't want to be bothered wid a man that don't know melons from gooseberries!' "[117] Another traveler, annoyed by a beggar woman, at last gave in when she called to him: " 'May ye ride in a fine carriage, and the mud o' yer wheels splash in the face of yer inimies—though I know ye haven't inny!' "[118]

It was different up in the North, even as it had been back in the fifties when Randal MacGavock said that one "feels as if he were transported into another land among a different race of people. Here there is comparatively no beggary or misery; the lands are better cultivated, the houses of the peasantry more comfortable, and the towns present a more thrifty and business-like appearance."[119] Belfast was still surrounded by fields full of bleaching linen "giving the appearance of a winter scene after a heavy fall of snow." Belfast demonstrated thrift, prosperity, and work, compared with Dublin, most Yankees thought. "A cheerful place, and its dwellings have a comfortable, prosperous appearance," remarked Charles Taylor in 1899. "The city is full of the vigor and bustle of an American town."[120] There were other influences at work there as well, Leonard Morrison had discovered on his arrival there just a decade earlier. He arrived in Belfast on the 199th anniversary of the Battle of the Boyne—July 12, 1889. "The Orangemen were out in force" with wildly beating drums, and skirling bagpipes—at least 150,000 in the crowd. "The greatest force, vindictiveness and spite, were manifested in many things which I observed," wrote Morrison, himself of Scots-Irish origin. Neither side, the Irish Catholics or the Scots-Irish Protestants, displayed the common sense and charity needed, he concluded, adding, "What fools these mortals be!"[121]

The object of the American travelers' interest in northern Ireland was not Belfast, of course, although they usually bought considerable linen goods there, but the nearby Giants' Causeway where as many as a thousand tourists a day were known to visit in the 1890s. "Well worth the inconvenience and expense of a visit," pronounced Loring Converse of the strange, hexagonal-shaped basalt columns said to have been the walkway between Ireland and Scotland of a long-ago race of Celtic giants. Thus he contradicted Dr. Johnson who, back in the eighteenth century, had pronounced those same stones " 'worth seeing . . . but not worth going to see.' "[122]

Charles Williams, the youthful, impecunious wanderer of the sixties, had been much impressed by the information and civility possessed by his equally youthful guide at the Causeway. "Having seen all the prominent features of this great curiosity," wrote Charles, "I handed my guide sixpence, with the remark that I regretted not being able to give more, but my finances being very low, it was necessary to make my donations small. True to the instincts of his country, both in blarney and wit, he replied, 'Oh, sir, an' this is enough, an' I'd rather go round wi' th' likes o' you for nothing than with a *gentleman'*, mark the emphasis, 'for a shilling.' " Not to be "entirely outdone in courtesy," wrote young Williams, "I replied, 'and will you please, sir, to give me your name, for I may publish an account of this visit, and if so, your name shall go to the public as my guide.' 'Faith, sir, indade I will,' says he. 'My name is Archie Fall.' "[123]

Half a century later J. V. Higinbotham and friends were "hardly off the car at the Causeway until we are surrounded by guides. We pick number seven as the most energetic and intelligent and do not regret our choice," wrote Higinbotham. "We are assured that we are fortunate in finding the Atlantic so smooth, and are easily persuaded to take the long boat ride . . . past the northernmost point of the Causeway." At one point their guide informed them that they were in a direct line with New York, adding that " 'if this weather would hold, sir, I could take you all the way to America.' " He had spent, he said, one winter of his life in Glasgow, "but the crowds worried him, and so he came back to County Antrim and its beautiful scenery. He said that there are people within five miles of the Causeway who have never seen it nor the tramway leading to it." Higinbotham asked the guide his name as they parted. " 'My name is Archie Fall, sir,' " he said.[124]

18

Celebrity Hunting

In the nineteenth century's later decades the fast-paced American tourists lacked time for those leisurely visits—properly arranged through letters of introduction—with Britain's leading achievers in science, literature, and the arts that were once so enjoyed and proudly recounted by their predecessors. Many travelers still were eager, however, to record in their travel books at least brief "pen portraits" or "pen sketches," as they called them, of famous Britons, and these travelers were capable of going to considerable lengths, some of them, to achieve this end.

Certain travelers began bagging their game while still on the Atlantic. "As I sit writing in the saloon, the genial face of Mr. Dickens peeps in," wrote Catherine Dyer, aboard the *Russia* in the sixties, seated before her journal. Five days later she nabbed him. "Had a pleasant conversation with Mr. Dickens, who has been suffering much from his lame foot," she wrote. "He says, playfully, that he has 'read himself off his legs,' but speaks warmly of his 'delightful visit' to our beloved land, and of the great improvements and changes since his former visit." Dickens chatted with her, she claimed, about the English train accident that had left him "extremely nervous." She was, moreover, "struck with his devout manner during the religious services yesterday, and the earnestness of his responses in the beautiful liturgy of the Church of England."[1]

Methodist Bishop Gilbert Haven, upon arriving in Britain, trained his sight on the elusive poet Alfred Tennyson. "I had loaded my gun," Haven wrote,

for the purpose of bringing down this shyest of game. It missed, as was not unlikely, with so poor a marksman. A card accompanied a note, stating in few words my nationality, admiration, and desire for a brief interview. approach the door, inquire if Mr. Tennyson is at home, and am answered in the affirmative. I requested the lad to hand him the note, and soon receive . . . the less agreeable conclusion that Mr. Tennyson is not in. Who was right, the boy or the mistress, I had no means of learning.

Stung by this rebuff, Haven not only licked his wound in print but also got his revenge. "Perhaps that 'American' was the reason of my failure—his aristocratic sympathies making him repellent of too great familiarity with the representative of ideas that he prefers to sing rather then to practice; for quite a worshipper of titles is the author of 'Locksley Hall', 'Lady Clara Vere de Vere', and 'Maud. Perhaps he was not really in; and most likely . . . though in," Haven admitted

350

more realistically, "he disliked being pen-and-inked by this unknown wandering gamester from foreign shores."[2]

Other "wandering gamesters," less sensitive than Haven to the feelings of their prey, went much further. The poet, essayist, and critic Matthew Arnold was methodically tracked to earth one summer afternoon in 1871 by the Brooklyn pastor, James Hoyt, and his companion. "We are inquiring pilgrims, pulling many a doorbell," wrote Hoyt. " 'Is it here', we ask, 'where Dr. Arnold lived?' and uniformly we are told, 'It is further on,' until finally turning into a lane on our left . . . in full view before us, Matthew Arnold, eldest son of the Doctor, and himself a writer of note, is seen playing croquet on the lawn, with his wife and a gentleman." His companion paused, but not Hoyt, who said, " 'Go on, and tell your errand as an American admirer and eulogist of the father. You will not be thought rude, but will be welcomed; for human nature has always a susceptible side to such approaches!' " The two intruders were, according to Hoyt, greeted with "unaffected and manly blandness," given leave to enter the garden and go around the house, but obviously not invited inside nor to stay for tea. Hoyt was satisfied, however; he had taken his scalp. "We went round the grounds," he wrote, "looking in at the windows of the house, and getting impressions of the sunny and beautiful interior, adorned as the most cultured literary tastes would direct."[3]

The prize for sheer, all-around effrontery must go to Henry Morford, that self-advertised chastiser of hostlers and vandalizer of cathedrals, who literally cornered the novelist Anthony Trollope by leaping aboard a moving train and forcing his way into the compartment of the helpless author. " 'Yes, Mr. Trollope is in that train just starting for Cambridge,' " Morford was told by a trainman, unaware of what was to follow. "He pointed out to me the face of the author [who was] sitting alone on one seat of a first-class carriage . . . . In far less time than it takes to relate," bragged Henry, "I had sprung to the handle of the door (the train already in pretty rapid motion), discovered that the door was not locked, swung it open and myself around it . . . and with a fortunate display of gymnastic power of which I am not often guilty, drew to the door behind me and came down with a bump upon one of the seats." Trollope's reaction was either that of a man stunned or one possessed of unusual calm and civility or some combination of all three; for he not only conversed politely with the intruder but helped to straighten out matters when the conductor came through and discovered that the intruder was an American stowaway.[4]

Trains apparently had some sort of stimulating effect on Morford, for on another occasion, finding himself in a second-class compartment with a tall, handsome, bronzed Irish recruiting sergeant of middle age, who was conducting "five, ill-dressed hawbucks" to be inducted into Her Majesty's service, Morford began at once to try to dissuade the recruits from enlisting. "I found myself descanting on the material glory of the New World . . . and the folly of any man remaining in England who could raise the money to emigrate," recalled Henry, " 'Boys, you don't look, to me, as if you had much in the world or many ties to bind you to England. If you will take my advice, you will get out of it as fast as possible and make your way to America.' " Morford also felt "called upon" to misrepresent himself as a Union army veteran. When Sergeant Holihan at last had enough, he spoke up. " 'You are a bould man . . . whether you wint wid Sherman to the say or not . . . thrying to coax half-a-dozen of Her Majesty's boys for the red coats to desert, in an English railway carriage widin sixty miles o' Lunnon, and under the very noses of two Recruitin' Sergeants! Wud you give me your name, sir, Major, I mane, to lay up among me little curiosities?' "[5]

Brontë country was apparently too far off the beaten tourist path for most nineteenth-century travelers, but a few echoes of the three enchanted sisters, Charlotte, Emily, and Anne, were captured by Professor James Hoppin of Yale. He made the pilgrimage to the parsonage at Haworth up in Yorkshire where he met their elderly father, Parson Brontë, who "was induced to invite me to his house, though he saw very little company, because he learned I was an American, and he thought much of America." They talked primarily of religion, Hoppin reported, but at length old Brontë showed him the parlor "where his daughters used to sit and write. There was Charlotte's portrait, with those large, dark eyes, square impending brow, and sad, unsmiling mouth. Branwell Brontë's medallion likeness hung opposite; and Thackeray's portrait, 'looking past her' as she said, was on the front wall. Her books still lay on the table. There was a Bible of Emily's, and a much-worn copy of Mrs. Gaskell's 'Mary Barton'." This room, wrote Hoppin, "had rather a pleasant look; but its furnishing was simple to severity and its only ornament was a little bunch of broom-grass on the table. . . . In the afternoon I heard Mr. Brontë preach from Job iii, 17: 'There the wicked cease from troubling; and the weary be at rest.' It was the simple, extemporaneous talk of an aged pastor to his people, spoken . . . right out of that old graveyard. . . . On the whole," Professor Hoppin concluded, "my Haworth visit was a serious and sobering one."[6]

Miss Angela Burdett-Coutts—heiress of the famed London banking family, who as a young woman, had quietly assisted Victoria's debt-ridden mother, the Duchess of Kent, and then gone on to a lifetime career of private philanthropy in association with Lord Shaftesbury—had been caught in a little candid portrait by Henry Martyn Field in 1858. "That lady with a long red nose, who sits near the stage, at Mr. Dickens' feet," Field observed, "is Miss Burdett-Coutts, the richest heiress in England—a lady who is very plain, but who makes up for want of beauty by being very good. She is full of charitable deeds."[7] Dr. Rodney Glisan, attending the International Medical Congress in 1881, was among the one hundred fifty guests invited out to her home, Holly Lodge, "where most elaborate preparations" were made in the way of music and luncheon for the entertainment of her guests, driven inside, alas, by rain. Now a baroness and married to a much-younger-than-herself American husband, who had been her secretary, she appeared "quite young for a lady of seventy," Glisan thought, adding that "she adroitly warded off all attempts on the part of guests at compliment for the blessing her charities had conferred upon the thousands of her race."[8]

An associate in philanthropy of both Lord Shaftesbury and Miss Burdett-Coutts, was the American, George Peabody, who had made a fortune in London and poured some £500,000 of his wealth back into good works, particularly into housing, most of which still stands today, modernized and well maintained, in the great metropolis. In 1867 Colonel Forney visited Peabody Square, Islington, to see for himself the results of the American's philanthropy, and he was much impressed with these model tenement blocks for working-class families. He found great care given to light and ventilation, rubbish disposal, running water, and in every tenement were free laundries with "wringing machines and drying lofts." Forney noted, too, the care given to cupboards, shelving and fireplaces, each with "a boiler and oven. But what gratifies the tenants, perhaps more than any other part of the arrangements," he wrote, "are the ample and airy spaces which serve as play-grounds for their children, where they are always under their mothers' eyes and safe from . . . passing carriages and laden carts." The modern visitor to Westminster Abbey will find these three nineteenth-century philanthropists cozily commemorated together near the main entrance at the foot of the nave: Lord Shaftesbury's tall form in a statue just to the left as one enters, and the Baroness Burdett-Coutts and George Peabody, whose body rested in the Abbey before being carried home to America, aboard H.M.S. *Monarch* in 1870, in tablets nearby in the floor.[9]

John Bright, M.P., a special favorite of Americans because of his pro-Union stand during the Civil War, as seen in the attention paid him by politican John Forney, had been observed by Samuel Prime, in the fifties, speaking in the House of Commons concerning Britain's relationship with the United States. Reported Prime,

> He spoke of the great danger of provoking hostilities with the United States of America, "a power", he said, "now equal to your own," and he predicted that if Great Britain should attempt to enforce her doctrine of "the right of search" in an American vessel, there would be war between the two countries in less than a year. He then inquired if the government had taken any steps toward securing a good understanding with the United States on this subject.[10]

Traveling with ex-President Ulysses S. Grant on his round-the-world tour in 1877, journalist J. F. Packard referred to Bright as a "Quaker, reformer, liberal leader and outspoken friend of the Union in its dark days," just as had Colonel Forney.[11] "Indeed," Forney remarked of Bright, "he deserves the title of the champion of American liberty in the British Parliament. There has never been a moment when he has doubted or turned his back in the support of genuine republican principles."[12] George Walton Williams, a wealthy American businessman, was less enthusiastic, saying that "he is what we should call in the United States a political demagogue." Nevertheless, Williams added, "I like his republican and temperance principles. Mr. Bright is a fine specimen of a John Bull, and looks as if he enjoyed good beef and plum puddings."[13]

Disraeli received harsh treatment, for the most part, at the hands of American observers. In 1851 the Reverend Arthur Cleveland Coxe depicted him as "a jaunty and rather flashy young man, with black ringlets twisted about a face quite devoid of elevated expression. . . . One feels that he cannot be confided in and that he is a mere adventurer." Then the clergyman was at least candid enough to reveal what probably lay beneath many of these derogatory descriptions. "That he is a Jew is a great bar to his advancement, although he is a Jewish Christian."[14] A few years later, another traveler observed Disraeli locked in debate with Lord Palmerston and detected, so he claimed, "an undertone of Mephistophilian sneering running through all his speech. It sounds almost demoniacal; so constant, so intense is the scorn. . . . How Palmerston can sit so drowsily under this stinging sarcasm is marvelous. He hears every word; he feels every word; yet he sleeps on."[15] Perhaps the kindest treatment Disraeli received was at mid-century at the hands of that aristocratic, southern belle, whose sojourn in Britain included even an introduction to the queen at a private royal ball. Meeting Disraeli at a party at the home of Lord and Lady Manners, Octavia LeVert recorded in her journal her impression of a "strongly-marked Hebrew face" and then went on to express her pleasure in his "bright and sparkling conversation."[16]

Lord Palmerston, whose understandable inability as prime minister to perceive which side would eventually win the American Civil War put relations between the United States and Britain at such risk, was studied by a postwar visitor to the House of Commons.

> His *sang-froid* is extraordinary even in a Briton. It is not the coolness of a fluent orator, for he is anything but fluent. It is not the sparkling jets of a ready debater, though in these he is not lacking. It is simply the imperturbability of the man . . . prepared for every emergency that his antagonists can create. His is not merely cool; he is adroit. . . . His friends and foes grow nervous beside his unchanging calmness. "What's the overthrow of my administration?" he seems to say. "Mere bagatelle."[17]

Maunsell Field had noticed this same quality in Palmerston, whom he saw sitting with "his hat drawn over his eyes. Occasionally, he would jump up suddenly, and go off into the wine-room for a glass of sherry, or into the lobby for a chat; but while he sat in the House, he never moved or spoke until he arose to close the debate."[18]

"Gladstone," Prime had prophesied in 1855, "is the coming man in England. With a transparency of language that is beautiful to observe," wrote Prime, "he makes the driest financial . . . matters almost entertaining to his hearers, and when pressed in debate, he displays such fluency, elegance, and energy of expression, as to make him one of the most captivating of public speakers."[19] From this point, when Gladstone was in his forties, until his death in 1898, there are frequent references in American travelers' accounts to that English statesman whom they loved to praise for what they called his "un-Englishness." One wrote of his resemblance to "an American in his looks, speech and appearance. . . . He does not appear an Englishman."[20] Observed the sharp-tongued Kate Field, journalist and devoted promoter of the Shakespeare Memorial at Stratford-on-Avon: "He looks like Webster, shaved down and diluted."[21]

William Henry Rideing joined swarms of visitors to Gladstone's home at Hawarden, near Chester, which by the 1890s had virtually assumed the characteristics of a political shrine where "entire excursion trains from cities as distant as London, Birmingham, and Bristol" arrived with whole families and their picnic lunches to be eaten on the grounds of the estate. There the only prohibition was against the cutting of "the trees or shrubs, which have suffered much in times past from the knives of the relic hunters."[22]

Gladstone, now eighty-five, attributed much of his fascination simply to his longevity. " 'You see', he told Rideing, " 'the people are always interested in an old man, and I believe that no other man at my time of life has been a leader of his party, though there have been older men in Parliament.' " Continuing his walk about the grounds with his American visitor, Gladstone predicted his own political demise. " 'I know myself, with such eyes, ears, and years, to be politically dead,' he said, 'though I doubt if the world believes it.' " At one point, Rideing recalled, the old man pointed out a thick, brown cloud on the horizon. "That cloud is the smoke of Liverpool, where he was born; and as we face it, there is a minute or two of silence, which for us, and probably for him too, opens a long vista of memories."[23]

Near the end of the old statesman's life another of his Yankee admirers bribed an attendant to gain a stance near an exit the "Grand Old Man" would presumably take on leaving the House of Commons. "I step out from the throng," wrote Charles Taylor, "and extend my hand, saying, 'I am an American who wishes to shake the hand of the man who has fought a brave battle.' The proud old face looks pleasantly into mine; his hand meets mine with a cordial grasp, and replying that he is glad to meet an American, Gladstone passes on."[24]

In the fifties, eager young Americans like Bayard Taylor had sought out political refugees in Britain such as Kossuth, "serious if not sad, though he still spoke of Hungary with a desperate hope", and Mazzini (whom he visited along with James Russell Lowell), who seemed "as if exhausted . . . yet spoke of Italy with enthusiasm and faith."[25] Of the young Americans visiting these early-day "freedom fighters" in exile, only Henry Tuckerman seems to have sensed the pathos of the political refugee, a figure soon to become far more common as history marched into the twentieth century. Tuckerman perceived the effects of enforced idleness, poverty, the shabby lodgings, the loss of identity and political power, and, above all, the terrible loneliness. "How many noble spirits have tasted this bitter cup. . . . The foreigner is ever apart in London. . . . England nobly gives asylum to the life, but not to the soul of the refugee; she is, with casual exceptions, true to national hospitality; but it is the aegis of her laws, and not the embrace of her sympathy, which she casts around the hunted stranger."[26]

In 1880, a young American journalist in Britain on holiday, John Swinton, sought out another of Britain's famed refugees: "One of the most remarkable men of the day," Swinton wrote of his subject,

who has played an inscrutable but puissant part in the revolutionary politics of the last forty years. . . . A man without desire for show or fame, caring nothing for the fanfaronade of life or the pretense of power, without haste and without rest, a man of strong, broad, elevated mind, full of far-reaching projects, logical methods, and practical aims, he has stood and yet stands behind more of the earthquakes which have convulsed nations and destroyed thrones, and do now menace and appall crowned heads and established frauds, than any other man in Europe. . . . He has been expelled from half the countries of Europe, proscribed in nearly all of them, and for thirty years past has found refuge in London.[27]

Swinton tracked his quarry to Ramsgate, the seashore resort for Londoners, and "there I found him in his cottage, with his family of two generations. The saintly-faced, sweet-voiced, graceful woman who welcomed me at the door, was evidently the mistress of the house. And is this massive-headed, generous-featured, courtly, kindly man of sixty, with the bushy masses of long, revelling gray hair, Karl Marx?" It was, and as the old man talked the young one listened. "It was evident that this man, of whom so little is seen or heard, is deep in the times, and that from the Neva to the Seine, from the Urals to the Pyrenees, his hand is at work preparing for the new advent," prophesied the young American.[28]

As the evening wore on the two walked down to the shore, there to join Marx's wife, their two daughters, their sons-in-law, and the children, where throngs of after-dinner strollers promenaded along the beach. As darkness came on, the youngsters were carried off to bed, and in the ensuing quiet the young journalist angled for the appropriate quote from the old man for the book taking shape in his mind. Eyeing Marx in the gathering gloom, young Swinton asked the question, *"What is?"* Recalled the youthful writer, "[I]t seemed as though his mind were inverted for a moment while he looked upon the roaring sea in front and the restless multitude upon the beach. *'What is?'* I had inquired, to which, in deep and solemn tone, he replied, 'STRUGGLE!' "[29]

Pen pictures of Victoria, who finally emerged a little from the long seclusion she imposed on herself following the death of her beloved Albert, were, in these later decades, based on her limited-in-number and carefully-arranged public appearances. One of these, the dedication of the Albert Hall, completed in 1871, proved that she could still charm a crowd when she put her mind to it.

"The building was crowded to its utmost," recalled Adam Badeau of the American legation. "The Queen walked down the vast amphitheatre to what may be called the stage, preceded by great dignitaries and accompanied by the Prince and Princess of Wales. When she turned to face the multitude, eight thousand people were standing in her honor, and the cheers were deafening. And then," Badeau continued,

> there came across her features an expression which it is hardly possible to describe; her face fairly shone with gratification at the loyalty of her people and motherly affection for them in return. She courtesied again and again, lower and lower, exactly like a great actress playing a queen. . . . But of all the famous mistresses of the stage that I have seen . . . none ever surpassed in grace or dignity, at the proudest moments of her mimicry, this real sovereign, acknowledging absolute homage.[30]

When Victoria made another formal public appearance, this time on February 27, 1872, at the Royal Thanksgiving Service at St. Paul's Cathedral, to mark the recovery of the Prince of Wales from typhoid, the queen was eyed by journalist Kate Field, who boasted to her readers that she was one of eight out of four hundred Americans besieging their legation for tickets who obtained "the desired entree."[31]

"The Queen is exceedingly plain," sniped Miss Field. "Her sons are not in the least good-looking; the Prince of Wales appears to better advantage than he has for some time, for the reason that he is thinner and his face has lost its redness." Labeling this event "the Great Raree Show," she decided that "the Boston Peace

Jubilee of 1869 was so magnificently superior . . . as to blot the Thanksgiving out of my memory."[32]

"The Queen has become very stout, and the fair hair is turning gray," observed Theodore Cuyler, spotting Victoria out in her carriage in Hyde Park in 1881. "The royalest thing about her," he concluded gallantly, "is her pure, kind, exemplary womanhood."[33] Observing the queen at the opening of Parliament in this period, journalist Louise Moulton declared that "one would never has guessed she was a queen but for her good clothes and the fuss they were making about her."[34] In 1887 Victoria had another chance to demonstrate that she could still handle a crowd when she consented to appear at a private performance of the Buffalo Bill Cody Wild West Show, which wowed London in the summer of her Golden Jubilee year. When the American flag was borne into the arena by a horseman, the Queen "rose from her seat and bowed deeply and impressively towards the banner" at which the whole party rose, the ladies bowed, the Generals saluted, and the English noblemen took off their hats. "Then, we couldn't help it," wrote Cody, "there arose such a genuine, heart-stirring American yell from our company as seemed to shake the sky. It was a great event." Victoria then solemnly shook hands with many of the Indians in the company as if this was the normal thing to do, petted two little papooses "handed up for her inspection," acting not unlike the young queen of long ago, meeting George Catlin's bewildered Indians at Windsor Castle, with Albert at her side.[35]

Victoria went through the celebrations marking her fifty years on the throne with a grace reminiscent of that she exhibited when she was a happy young woman at the side of her handsome Prince Albert. London rocked with noise of every description from early morning on that day itself, June 21, recalled the Reverend Samuel Mutchmore: artillery, steam whistles from the river, bells, chimes, singing, and clamor. "Bands in quick succession traversed the streets; bagpipes, accordions, mouth-organs, violins and harps, jew's-harps and penny trumpets, drums; songs by sailors on the crafts, on the streets, in the drinking-houses were heard; busses, cabs and street-cars passed along filled with men and women shouting 'God Save the Queen!' " Such immense, patient, good-natured waiting crowds had never been seen before by the Americans present. Some Londoners stood all day, from six in the morning, for a view. "As far as the eye could reach, even the walls were festooned with life; men and women stood in windows, filled balconies, men hung from the sides of walls, clung to . . . rods, hung to turnbuckles, stood on the frames of awnings, climbed to the pinnacles and roofs of the Abbey, sat on the sharp points of the high fences on the wall around the Abbey. The police could not club them off, or if they did it was so that they might climb up again. . . . Men hung to the iron rungs in the mouths of the lion heads projecting from walls and gates."[36]

"Men hired out their backs and shoulders for a shilling for five minutes to hold up the Zaccheuses of the multitude," continued Mutchmore. "The roofs everywhere groaned under the enthusiastic life bent on seeing the Queen. . . . In all that crowd of nearly two million people, waiting in that intense heat and weariness for their Queen," marveled the American, "there was no disorder or drunken demonstration. Men and women were fainting and were carried off by

Golden Jubilee Procession: June 21, 1887. Queen Victoria's carriage passes through Trafalgar Square. *Illustrated London News,* **June 25, 1887, p. 709.** *Courtesy the Library of Congress.*

the police on stretchers; not less than one hundred such cases were within our own observation."[37]

Not until nearly afternoon were the trumpets of the heralds heard announcing the coming of the Queen, wrote Walter Whittle. "The shout is taken up . . . by a thousand times a thousand voices. . . . The enthusiastic cries come rolling down the avenue like waves of the ocean. It strikes the fibers of every heart. The electric current flashes along the whole line—every man feels the shock."[38] It was two o'clock when the object of all this patient waiting through the weary hours came into sight. "Her appearance was dignified but cheerful," wrote Mutchmore. "She had for the first time since the death of the Prince-Consort taken from her person every sign of mourning and widowhood. It was a Jubilee to her people. . . . A more handsome woman at the age of sixty-nine cannot be found on either hemisphere."[39] Orrin Hubbell of Indiana long remembered seeing the "large bonfires in honor of the fiftieth anniversary of the Queen's accession," as his vessel, the *Ethiopia,* neared the Irish coast."[40]

In the years that followed, Victoria came to be one of the great attractions in all of Britain for American tourists. No longer did they, like young Benjamin Silliman a century earlier, apologize for their "pardonable curiosity"; they indulged it to the full. "We had a strong desire to see Queen Victoria," confessed Janet Collins. And see her they did at Windsor, "fresh and rosy-looking," being driven down the hill to her railway car. "She shied a little," recalled Mrs. Collins, "as the handsome horses swept a curve in the street, giving us a good view of her royal person. She may have been frightened at the prancing horses, or she may have been conscious that curious eyes were fastened upon her."[41]

To view "their German Majesties," the Emperor William and his wife—there on a visit to his grandmother, Queen Victoria, in the 1890s—Julia Dorr and her friends extended their stay in Windsor. "As they passed me so close that I could have touched them," Julia wrote, "the Emperor and Empress were talking and laughing like any common Darby and Joan, while they obviously took in all about them with quick, observant eyes. He wore the splendid uniform of his regiment. He has a fine, strong and thoughtful face, a face that attracts and impresses one; and with his powerful figure and martial bearing, he looked that day the embodiment of manly health and vigor."[42] Robert Young also noted one of these imperial German visits. "Remarkable for his unflagging industry and attention to business," said Young of Wilhelm, "if war comes, he holds himself ready to lead his army."[43] Neither of these two Americans could have known that these visits of Victoria's sword-rattling grandson were embarrassing to the royal family and that the British ambassador had been instructed to pass along this information to the German government.[44]

Delegations of visiting American professional, business, or fraternal organizations were sometimes informally welcomed at Windsor in these years with matters so arranged that the aged queen's carriage could roll up at an opportune moment, during her afternoon drive, to greet the gathering before they were ushered into the orangery for refreshments. For the representatives of the International Railway Congress and their wives, visiting on July 6, 1895, these refreshments consisted of "sandwiches, cakes, grapes, gooseberries, strawberries, cherry ice, orangeade, lemonade, claret cup, tea, and coffee."[45] The queen, reported William Hichborn of Boston, when she greeted the members of the Ancient and Honorable Artillery Company of Boston and their wives in the summer of 1896, remarked to them in her still melodic voice: "I hope you and your lady relatives had a pleasant voyage, and I am glad to see you here."[46]

At the time of Victoria's Diamond Jubilee in 1897, marking her sixty years as queen, visiting Americans lost entirely whatever inhibitions and reservations they might once have had concerning Britain's institution of monarchy. It was as if they saw Victoria as a kind of grandmother to the English-speaking people and perhaps even regretted not having her for their own. In order to see the royal procession one American, according to Richard Harding Davis, rented a house for a week in Piccadilly for ten thousand dollars. Certain less wealthy and more gullible would-be celebrants fell victim, even before they got out of Liverpool, to sharpers who sold them "beautifully-colored tickets that called for places which existed only on paper . . . one man paying two hundred and fifty dollars for two seats for which he may still be looking." In the Savoy restaurant one evening the

Diamond Jubilee: June 28th, 1897. Queen Victoria's carriage leaving Paddington
Station on her arrival in London for the celebration of her sixty years on the throne.
Courtesy the Library of Congress.

orchestra suddenly struck up the British national anthem, Davis recalled, and men and women from all over the world, including many Americans, "rose from their chairs and cheered and waved napkins, and remained standing until the music ended and while their dinners grew cold."[47]

On the great day itself, the old queen's carriage brought her to the foot of the steps of St. Paul's, which she was no longer able to climb because of her lameness. "The Stars and Stripes waved in every block, and there was no more hearty cheering than that which came from the tens of thousands of American citizens as an expression of their respect," wrote the American General Nelson Miles.[48] At the close of the brief prayer service held in front of the great cathedral, Victoria was seen to smile even as "she nodded and bowed her head . . . and winked away the tears."[49]

With much of the same "pardonable curiosity" with which youthful Benjamin Silliman had eyed the queen's grandfather a century earlier, young Wilbur Fauley, intent on *Seeing Europe on Sixty Dollars* in accord with his book's title, waited for Queen Victoria to return from one of her afternoon carriage drives at Windsor near the end of her long life and reign. "Here was an empress passing my way, in a little black bonnet tied under her chin," he thought with amazement as her carriage drew near. "I raised my hat and bowed, and the Queen smiled and nodded her head. I was much puffed up," admitted Wilbur, "at being noticed by a queen!"[50]

19

Relic Gathering

American tourists had long been known for their relic-gathering propensities. Cooper had found that out in the 1830s when he asked the verger in Westminster Abbey about the missing head of George Washington on the bas relief adorning the tomb of Major André and was told, "[*S*]*ome American* has done it, no doubt!"[1] By the waning decades of the century Americans were notorious for their theft of "real" souvenirs of the literary and historical shrines they visited. "Our countrymen are keener on the scent for historical relics than any other class of visitors to England," the Reverend Theodore Cuyler of Brooklyn told his readers in 1882.[2]

Commercial souvenirs such as cups, seals, ornamental boxes and paperweights, jewelry, prints, and even the newly invented "stereoscopic views" failed to satisfy the Yankee thirst for genuine historical relics appropriated by the pilgrim himself at the shrine of his veneration. What they wanted was a great man's pen, such as the one Mrs. Kirkland pinched from the desk of Charles Dickens or the one Lydia Sigourney almost spirited away from Lord Brougham. She would have had it, too, except that he suddenly snatched it up again and began writing.[3] These acquisitive travelers lusted after a stone actually stood on, a cup drunk from, a flower planted by, a knob turned by, or even just a fragment of an article once used by, or of a house once lived in by the object of their homage. Thus Methodist minister Wilbur Fisk had been enchanted back in the thirties with a chip from the rafter of John Bunyan's house, a quick try-on of "an old preaching gown of Wesley's, now almost in shreds," and a battered cup from the home of Francis Asbury.[4] Many years later another Methodist preacher handed over a shilling to a sexton in London's Bunhill Fields burying ground for a scrap of a clay pipe dug up in the vicinity of Wesley's grave.[5]

The collection of these earthly treasures often resulted in burdens so cumbersome that the pilgrims had trouble toting them onto the ship for the voyage home. Dr. William Taylor in 1871 judged his own "inestimable collection of weeds, lumps of rock, brickbats, etc.," at more than a peck, "closer to a peck and a half or two pecks."[6] In the relic hunters' own minds their trophies were modest enough—a sprig of ivy here, a few flowers there, a fragment of stone from a cottage floor, a snip of fabric, perhaps even the finger of an effigy in a cathedral. The cumulative effect, however, of this century-long orgy of picking, plucking, snipping, chipping, clipping, poking, and pawing leads one to marvel that there is anything left to see in the twentieth century. While the pilgrims were busily appropriating bits of the past for themselves, it occurred to only a few that they might be destroying it for future generations.

One who perceived the effects of this indiscriminate relic hunting was Junius Browne. Viewing the desolate ruins of Kenilworth Castle about 1870, he found them more of a ruin than he expected. "What Cromwell's soldiers left, sightseers have sought to rifle," he wrote. "They have hacked the ruins and pulled out the bricks to such an extent that entire portions of walls have fallen down; and those still standing require the support of heavy timbers. What a mania is this of relic hunters," groaned Browne. "To gratify their vulgar curiosity they spare nothing. . . . They are the modern Vandals, and without the excuse of the old barbarians; they wish their culture to be an apology for their ravages."[7] Just as Sophia Hawthorne had insisted that "papa," as she called the ever-patient Nathaniel, pull a stone from the old Alloway Kirk as a relic for her, so she had to have a branch from Burns's "Lousy Thorn," which "papa cut of out of love for the poet."[8] Charles Butler said that his English friends, at the turn of the century, told him "the Yankees would carry away all England if it was possible."[9]

So detailed are the American relic hunters' own accounts of their industry that one finally must conclude that this reputation was wholly deserved. Many seemed to consider their depredations not only perfectly justifiable but cute and clever as well. "We Americans are great on getting souvenirs wherever we go," boasted Lou Beauchamp in 1896 in connection with his visit to Holyrood Palace in Edinburgh, where his party of tourists was shown a table just set for an official dinner. "Had it not been for the guards every few feet," admitted Beauchamp, "half the tableware would have been minus."[10]

Confided William Hemstreet, the travel writer, "I have pinched off pieces of St. Paul's Church and Westminster Abbey with my thumb and finger," adding by way of rationalization, "in some out-of-the-way, dilapidated place which already needed repairing."[11] In 1874 lawyer John Bender of Indiana craved a chip of Queen Mary's [Tudor] chair at Winchester Cathedral "to preserve as a memorial of our visit," but he wisely concluded that "solemn reflection convinced us that if every impudent American were allowed to do as he pleases with these old relics, they would soon lose their interest, if not become invisible to the naked eye." Instead, he contented himself with "a small bit of common glass hanging loose in one of the windows at nearby St. Cross Hospital, which we appropriated and have carefully preserved."[12]

Pilgrim William Falkner, who so distinguished himself with his boorish behavior at Windsor Castle, staged an even more dramatic confrontation at the Shakespeare cottage at Stratford-on-Avon between himself and the elderly female cicerone in charge. He must have been proud of it, for he himself describes it in detail.

" 'Please don't take that,' " begged the ancient female clad in black alpaca, showing Falkner and his party about the poet's birthplace. "I was endeavoring," he explains to his readers, "to pluck a little fragment of the rock from the hearth." Foiled at this, Falkner next attacked "an old wooden button fastened to a door-post with a rusty screw. It was nearly worn through by constant use. 'How often was this old button turned by the fingers of the great bard?' " he asked himself. " 'What harm,' " thought Falkner, " 'can there be to take a little insignificant bit of timber that could be of no use to anybody? None. Then I'll watch for an opportunity to steal it!' " He already had it in his pocket a few moments later when the sharp-eyed old lady caught him again. " 'I beg your pardon, sir, you must put that button back from whence you took it. I have orders not to let anything go,' " she said. Falkner did as he was asked, and, after a brief, forbidden plop on Shakespeare's purported armchair he finally had to leave "without having been able to filch anything."[13]

Chipping and clipping at the Shakespeare cottage began early in its history as a tourist attraction. As early as 1782 Elkanah Watson reported seeing rings and bracelets made from its woodwork and furnishings.[14] In 1860 Bayard Taylor was told of a party of schoolgirls who made off "with a large square block of the mantelpiece" after having begged to be left alone for a few minutes of meditation in the poet's alleged birth chamber.[15] In 1879 Burr Polk saw so much evidence "of the vandals who had been here before us, much of the woodwork chipped away by the knives of relic-hunters," he proposed the enclosure of "the entire building with a strong case [and a] regiment of honest soldiers to guard it."[16] One of these knife-wielders had been one of his own countrymen, William Dana, who boasted in 1843 of having "severed with my penknife a splinter from the massive oaken mantle-tree, apparently coeval with the house, which I preserve as a relic."[17]

In contrast to the 1830s, when visitors to Stonehenge were actually encouraged to chip souvenirs off the mighty monoliths with the aid of a mallet hung there for that purpose, by the 1890s the premises were guarded against such vandalism by an elderly man who also photographed tourists to augment his meager income. Reuben Thwaites mentions such a guardian, although not by name. It was probably a Mr. Judd, according to the pedestrian pilgrim Clifton Johnson, who chatted with him at some length in 1898. "One American has told Mr. Judd that he would give a million dollars for this lot of stones if he could get the privilege of removing them. He would set them up on American soil in or near some large city, build a fence around them, charge admission, and advertise it as the eighth wonder of the world. This speculator from across the sea told the Stonehenge photographer he thought it would make a grand, good show." The afternoon sun was getting low at this point, Johnson recalled, and "presently Mr. F. H. Judd gathered up his belongings, caught his horse, hitched it to his wagon and bade me good evening."[18]

One of the most persistent of all these nineteenth-century Yankee souvenir hunters was Henry Morford, that earnest exponent of republican government who had "taught a lesson" to the poor hostler at the Wheat-Sheaf Inn near Runnymede. After trying out various bribes on the elderly male custodian at the King Charles Tower on the Roman-Medieval wall at Chester, Morford finally secured "the coveted square inch of Roman pavement" he desired, as well as, he boasted, "carte blanche to knock off as many pieces of the old wall as I thought I could carry."[19]

Morford performed equally well at Westminster Abbey. There, he admitted, "the Vandal was strong within me as it is in most Americans, and the desire to knock off the nose of an alabaster cherub or the toe of an oaken Baron of the Crusades and carry it away as a relic might have overpowered me if the old

THE GOVERNOR, EN GRANDE TENUE.

Vandal Henry Morford found his "low-crowned tourist hat of felt" the ideal place to "hide one's plunder," i.e., his stolen souvenirs. *From the author's collection.*

verger had not kept watch upon *me*, of all the queue he was showing around—very much as if someone had suggested that I, so heavy in other regards, was *light-fingered*." But this intuitive caution on the verger's part did not deter Morford for very long. "I found my little opportunity directly," he bragged to his readers, "and perpetrated my little theft. I acknowledge the fact with the candor of the detected criminal."[20] Such vandalism in the Abbey today is reportedly virtually nonexistent, although the small printed cards that identify the various tombs and effigies have a habit of disappearing rather quickly.[21]

Morford followed up his raid on the Abbey with similar forays all over Britain. Wherever he went he got into fracases with vergers who wished him to remove his hat. Whether or not they sensed his looting propensities is a moot question, but Morford confided to his readers, as a matter of fact, that he had found his "low-crowned tourist hat of felt" indeed the ideal place to "hide one's plunder."[22]

Morford never does reveal exactly what he purloined or vandalized at Westminster Abbey, but he is quite specific about his trophies from the Tower of London, modest though they were. "It was a very slight tangible memorial which I could bring away with me; for the cannon were heavy, and the armor clumsy, and the jewels were preposterously guarded," he complained. "Besides the little pebble from the scaffold stone on Tower Green, I could only secure a flint which I pried out of the Flint Tower at the expense of a knife blade . . . the astounded 'beefeater' informing me that he should 'notify the War office, an American having commenced prying down the Tower of London with his jack-knife'."[23]

Not even the great stone masses of Ireland's Giants' Causeway were safe from these Yankee relic hunters. Clara Tadlock would have loved to take home one of those rocks "but found them rather heavy." She was told the story of one of her countrymen who had hired men to row him out in the night, where he succeeded in lifting a mass of rock and was rowed away again before being discovered.[24]

Less effort was required to snip off pieces of fabric of various sorts. At home, Americans all but demolished Mrs. Lincoln's window curtains following her refurbishing of the White House after her elevation to First Lady, just as visitors today have performed some minor miracles of souvenir-gathering at Washington's newest tourist attraction, the Kennedy Center. The nineteenth-century counterparts of these "collectors" were obsessed by the lining of Napoleon's carriage on display at Madame Tussaud's. William Cord, traveling in 1883 with his Knights Templar group from Chicago, had his heart set on a snip of fabric from that carriage upholstery. An extra coin, he had been told, permitted him to seat himself for a moment in the vehicle of the glorious Bonaparte. "The cloth of the carriage seat was already much torn," Cord perceived, "and while the writer would never have dreamed of committing an act of vandalism, in order to obtain the coveted relic, he thought he would watch the opportunity and secure a small piece of cloth. He dexterously removed a small piece of blue cloth," admitted Cord, speaking of himself in the third person. "But, alas! for the fruition of all human hopes, the coveted relic, which was carefully put away in the writer's pocket-book, had mysteriously disappeared by the following morning."[25] Nathaniel Hawthorne also had a similar experience some decades earlier when he cut off "one little bit, no bigger than a finger-nail . . . of a woefully tattered and utterly faded banner . . . absolutely falling to pieces" in an old church in

Oxfordshire. Like Cord, he had placed the rotting silk in his wallet, only to find later that it had turned to dust.[26]

In lieu of chipping stone or snipping fabric, other pilgrims settled for pawing, poking, or otherwise manhandling the ancient or precious objects they had come so far to see. James Hoyt deplored the "poor quality" of the stone used by the medieval builders at Oxford. "Why, in some places," he discovered, "I could push the end of my umbrella right into the decaying walls and pillars as though they had been sand and lime!"[27] And yet some of these tourists were outraged when asked to deposit their canes and umbrellas for safekeeping on entering museums, galleries, and "stately homes."

Asked by his guide at the Tower of London please not to handle the exhibits, John Bender found the urge "irresistible" and "thus could not help lifting the axe and feeling the block" on display. Later he wondered why it was he, of all his group who was selected to be locked up for a few minutes in Sir Walter Raleigh's cell as "a joke."[28]

"Pawer" par excellence was Curtis Guild, traveling in 1867 and sending letters home to the *Boston Commercial Bulletin*. Guild obviously prided himself on tugging at every ancient flag, brandishing every old sword, and ringing every bell that fell within his reach. "It was interesting for me to grasp with my sacrilegious American hand one of the colors borne by a British regiment in America during the war of the Revolution," he wrote of the old battle flags in Chester Cathedral. Seizing an ancient sword "visitors were not allowed to handle" at Rosslyn Castle, he boasted of waving it above his head to the disgust of his guide. At York he was shown a huge old Saxon cup the verger "permits sacrilegious Yankees like myself to press their lips to its brim." Just as well; he'd have done it anyway. Guild's star performance was at Oxford's Christ Church College, where he climbed the gate tower to see the famous bell, "Great Tom"; and, having been told the bell was so hung that the lightest pull would sound it, he waited until "the porter's back was turned to give a smart tug to the rope which swung invitingly towards my hand. The pull elicted a great boom of bell metal like a musical artillery discharge," he wrote, adding that "the custodian did not seem desirous of prolonging my visit."[29]

Plopping in the chairs of the great was another popular pastime, after the manner of assaults upon Scott's study chair. Almost everybody imitated their youthful idol Bayard Taylor, who in 1844 took a brief turn in the Coronation Chair in Westminster Abbey, where he "sat down and rested in it without ceremony."[30] E. L. Temple recorded a furtive sit-down in Her Majesty's chair in St. George's Chapel at Windsor Castle.[31] And even the usually civil and respectful Elizabeth Peake defied a guard in the House of Lords chamber, "when he wasn't looking," to rest her aching feet momentarily by lighting on the bench of a lord.[32] Little wonder that by 1882 the alcove bed in the old Burns cottage at Ayr bore a card requesting "visitors *not* to jump into the bed."[33]

Women tourists worked at getting "peeks," whenever it was possible, of family members at the great, stately houses they visited. Mrs. Adelaide Hall, the Chicago art fancier, informed her readers that she had spied the Duke and Duchess of Marlborough, when she toured Blenheim Palace, "at luncheon in another apartment. The Duchess," claimed Mrs. Hall, "was attired in a negligee of blue satin and white lace, and the servants wore powdered wigs and knee breeches."[34] When Mrs. A. E. Newman could not talk her way into Queen Victoria's private estate, Osborne, on the Isle of Wight—not even by telling the porter "we were from America, and this was the only opportunity we would have"—she was content to be allowed by a gardener at least to peer into the grounds through a gate and was charmed with the gift of "a little bouquet and a fuchsia nicely growing in a flower pot."[35]

Sometimes it seemed as if the Americans thought that they could buy up everything in sight. Besides the million-dollar offer for Stonehenge, there were said to be substantial offers from P. T. Barnum himself for the Shakespeare cottage at Stratford, and one party from Illinois in 1892 announced their desire to buy the cottage for £3,000 and ship it to Chicago, according to the Reverend William Meloy, pastor of the First United Presbyterian Church of that city.[36]

Fantastic offers were made by devout Methodists for relics of their founder, John Wesley, seen even today in his home near the famed City Road Chapel where he preached in London. For the huge old blue and white teapot, made and presented by Josiah Wedgwood and used by Wesley and his preachers, "Cyrus W. Field has made a standing offer of $2500 . . . and Mr. Peck of the firm of Peck and Snyder in New York has recently offered $5,000 for the relic without avail," marveled the Reverend Nathan Hubbell in 1889.[37] The old pot, still on exhibit in a glass case at the Wesley house, bears the famous little grace: "Be present at our table, Lord; Be here and everywhere ador'd; These creatures bless and grant that we may feast in Paradice [sic] with thee."

"An ardent American professor once tried to buy the door to the room Coleridge used for his study, and only the lack of money prevented him from attempting to buy all the doors, indeed the whole house with them, and packing them off to America," reported Professor Moses Coit Tyler.[38] The custodian at the Anne Hathaway cottage near Stratford told a visitor that she had been offered $2,000 for an old mahogany bedstead there.[39] At Carisbrooke Castle on the Isle of Wight a close eye was kept on the old donkey in the wheel who pumped up water from the well for thirsty tourists—lest some eager Yankee kidnap *him* for a souvenir as well, it was said.[40]

With equal vigor some Americans applied themselves to Britain's lush vegetation—leaves, petals, whole flowers, cuttings from vines, and plants, as well as assorted twigs and branches. So busily did they pursue their harvest in the days before their own customs prevented the importation of foreign vegetation that their collective accounts of their activities leave us with the impression of a gigantic human reaper cutting, snipping, uprooting, clipping, and mowing everything in its path. Sophia Hawthorne, with her penchant for vegetable matter—perhaps best exhibited at Newstead Abbey, where she finally realized that she was being watched as she cruised about the garden—possibly set the pace.[41] In any event, J. M. Loring busied himself at Stratford plucking "one of each" of every wildflower in a meadow near the town, and he also tore "fresh, green ivy leaves from the wall near the gate of the porch to the church."[42] An Ohio woman acquired an unusual vegetable memento by simply stealing a wreath off Charles Dickens's memorial in Westminster Abbey. At Hampton Court various American ladies tried for "cuttings" from the gigantic grape vine that grew there, invariably being informed, " 'O, no, not for any money. I might make my fortune quickly if I accepted all the bribes offered me; but, you see, it belongs to the Queen' "—this from the elderly gardener on guard.[43]

An insight into the psychology of these uninhibited, happy reapers is provided by David Semple in his own 1878 account of how he and members of his party behaved on the grounds of a private estate in Ireland. Ignoring the signs forbidding visitors to "pull flowers or leaves," these tourists went about busily "pulling an ivy leaf here, a sprig of heather there, a bit of shamrock, occasionally a pretty flower until our pockets were overflowing, and resorted to filling our hats; knowing full well that we were American sovereigns, and compelled to no law save that of etiquette to lift our hats to any foreign potentate, landed proprietor or aristocracy of any kind."[44]

Entire plants sometimes made it back to the New World, there to take root in that harsher clime. Mrs. Sigourney enjoyed her clump of daisies from the meadow at Runnymede for several years until they were accidentally rooted up by a careless gardener.[45] Fannie Tyler accumulated so much greenery in a single day that she had to "slip out after dinner to buy penny crocks in which to plant today's cuttings."[46] Despising virtually everything in the British Isles except the London omnibus, Braman of Ohio in 1900 finally turned sentimental in Ireland and dug up a piece of sod from the grave of St. Finian. It died.[47]

If the American pilgrim could not carry home pieces of Britain with him, he could at least leave something of himself behind—besides his money—so some of them seemed to reason: thus the mania for signing names and carving initials. An exception was editor Charles Linskill who declared, "I may say here that I did not write my name once, on my tour, in a public, famous, or conspicuous place. It is a forlorn, sentimental gesture productive of no good."[48] Few shared this opinion. At Stratford, for example, so many were the American names in the register provided for that purpose that American visitors were wont to hunt for the names of friends or acquaintances even as they signed their own. In 1892 Lucy Williams, who had already commented in her book about the "better," more modest behavior of British moppets, wryly observed that there was little doubt as to the nationality of the child who signed herself: "Winifred Blake and parents."[49]

The signing of names went far beyond the albums provided. Many pilgrims craved a far more intimate association with history than that. Beyond any doubt, the most favored signature spot in all of Britain, for Americans at least, consisted of the walls of that tiny room in which Shakespeare is said to have been born. By 1825 these walls were already "entirely covered over with the names of visitants among whom are numbered kings and dignitaries of all descriptions," Nathaniel Carter had noted back in 1825.[50] By 1850 "in some portions of the room," observed the Reverend Henry Ward Beecher, "the signatures overlay each other two or three deep."[51] Another visitor in the same period reported that "the ceiling and walls are so filled that the appearance from the middle of the room is that of a large spider's web."[52]

"The walls are obscured by ten thousands names of scribblers," William Furniss had noticed at mid-century. "How few reflect, when gratifying their own vanity under a specious tribute to the dramatist, that the flies of summer may

The Coronation Chairs in the Abbey. If not guarded, the tourists would doubtless "carry hoff the chairs haltogether," a verger informed Joel Cook in 1878. *From the author's collection*.

also drop their own insignificant ciphers, and burst the bubble of such ephemeral immortality."[53] Most pilgrims did not indulge in such thoughts and went right on signing—including Samuel Young, who was advised "to write small" and also directed to a space about "two inches from the floor where I added my name to those of the other pilgrims."[54] Observing "all these writings that abound on castle walls, columns and towers, bridges, turnstiles, etc.," Mrs. William Backhouse concluded that "it is but one form of giving natural expression to the desire for an eternity of existence."[55]

Those for whom mere autographing was not enough went in for carving upon wood or stone. "One prize imbecile had actually cut letters deep into an alabaster monument at Salisbury," John Higinbotham discovered, concluding that "it must have taken him an hour to do it."[56] Susan Wallace, wife of General Lew Wallace, soldier, politician, and author of *Ben Hur,* found names and dates even on the faces of effigies in Westminster Abbey.[57] Joel Cook asked "a lynx-eyed verger" at the Abbey whose names were carved on the Coronation Chairs. " 'Hennybody's; heverybody's,' he replied, 'but they hain't doing it hennymore.' Then he told me that if that particular portion of the Abbey were not closely guarded, the public would probably 'carry hoff the chairs haltogether.' "[58] The famed journalist Richard Harding Davis, who was disturbed at the sight of noisy young American girls racing about the corridors of London hotels, also expressed the hope that all his countrymen would not be judged "by the American who scratches his name over cathedrals when the verger isn't looking."[59] As early as 1832 Zachariah Allen had reported seeing many of the trees on the banks of the Avon beside Warwick Castle deeply scored with initials, one of these carvings exhibiting "the name and place of residence of a fellow countryman."[60]

Even the winsome Welshman William Whyte, returning for a visit to his homeland in 1867 after becoming successful in America, was not immune to the disease. He succumbed to the impulse at one shrine to Robert Burns, the "Auld Brig o' Doon" at Ayr, "recently much restored" but still "covered with thousands of names and initials rudely carved." He gave in and confessed, "I availed myself of the opportunity of adding mine to the list, choosing for the purpose the tenth or centre stone on the right hand side going towards Maybole."[61]

Out-and-out trespassing was also looked on as an "inalienable right" by some American tourists, such as the Reverend William Pratt Breed in 1884. The American carries this right "abroad with him," trumpeted the preacher, "and as a tourist it is no small part of his happiness to see things *ad libitum.*" With this conviction in mind, he and his party drove boldly into the grounds of Holland House near London, proud of this "specimen of American impudence" and mightily amused at the poor gatekeeper's "indignant amazement."[62]

A most unusual relic collector was a young lady from Chicago at the turn of the century, whose little obsession satisfied her collecting urge and at the same time caused less harm to property and plant life than the activities of so many of her fellow Americans. Wilbur Fauley spotted her performing "some mysterious act which had to do with Mr. Rudyard Kipling's coat-tail and a signet-ring. We had seen this young person approach the author when his back was turned, and touch the end of his coat with the ring. She might have been a feminine anarchist for all we knew, lighting the fuse of a concealed bomb. The incident passed unnoticed on the part of Mr. Kipling. Later came the explanation," Fauley wrote.

"You see this ring," she began. "Well, it was a present from my maw on, well, my last birthday, and I call it my Prominent People Ring. It's far easier to touch prominent people with this ring when they're not looking than to go through a lot of red tape for their autographs. I'm on my way home now on a trip around the world, and you bet your life I've been busy with this ring. A list of names goes with it, and when I get back to Chicago, I'll show *it* as a souvenir."[63]

The introduction of photography no doubt did much to cut down on this mania for tangible relics or souvenirs, for now the traveler could carry home actual photos of what he had seen with which to remember his trip and also to impress stay-at-homes. Visiting Holyrood Palace in 1865, G. H. Mathews sensed the importance of the camera as he watched a photographer at his work.

Strange things happen in these latter days when people can sit quietly in their parlors at home, and yet see the mountains, and castles, and old abbeys of far-distant lands. There is something singular in the thought that these haunts of history are being represented upon pictured cards, to be transmitted to all parts of the world, by an art which was (when these old castles stood in all their glory) undiscovered and undreamed of! In the very room in which stood the veritable bed upon which Queen Mary reposed, we bought card photographs representing that room and its contents, perfectly, even to the tapestry hangings on the wall and the hole in the door opening into the secret passage. . . . And so it was, go where we might, an opportunity was offered us of carrying away not only an image in the mind's eye, but accurate representations of those objects upon which others as well as ourselves might look, and from the view receive pleasure and instruction.[64]

In that same year little Amy Smith was also busily buying "what I buy everywhere—stereoscopic views."[65] And in 1903 Lily Rust of Washington purchased "card photos" of each locale described in her meticulously handwritten journal, carefully placing and pasting them so as to illustrate her text.[66] In 1891 Reuben Thwaites looked forward to the time "when we shall have color in our Kodak views, not mere lifeless shadows."[67]

A few pilgrims, not suffering quite so much from the compulsion to return with tangible mementos of their travels, instead performed various little rituals to mark their visits at historic shrines. In 1871 good-natured Elizabeth Peake, one of the most appealing of the female travelers throughout the century, stood patiently before the tomb of Shakespeare in Trinity Church at Stratford while a young compatriot read a nine-stanza poem he had composed in the poet's honor. He promised to send Elizabeth a copy if she would include it in her book. He did; and she did. The final stanza reads:

> I leave thee to thy slumbers; I must go
>   Back to the struggles of my adverse lot,
> To feel the nameless agonies that flow
>   From a cold world that understands me not.

Greater than I may linger on this spot,
  Of many a language and of many a shore;
Some other bard of loftier mind may raise
  A song more sweet, more lasting in thy praise;
  But none can love thee more![68]

Twenty years later on this same spot another little tourist drama unfolded and was observed with astonishment by Edgar Magness. A young female American approached the sacred place and demonstrated her own unique expression of appreciation "by executing, while the custodian's back was turned, a mild cancan on the poet's grave!"[69]

20

New Modes of Travel

To restore some measure of status, exclusivity, and dignity to travel—once the domain of a favored few but now possible for lesser mortals as well—new and unusual modes of travel had to be devised or old ones revived. Out of this need came the fashionable "walking tour" of Great Britain, bicycle tours, "coaching," and, finally, the motor tour.

Ever since 1844 when young Bayard Taylor made his famous two-year pedestrian tour of Britain and the Continent for $500, which he wrote up under the title *Views Afoot,* the fancy of America's young had been filled with romantic visions of tramping about, like Taylor, in a linen smock with leather belt, slouch hat, boots, knapsack and pilgrim staff—just as he pictured himself in a print at the front of his book. In later years the author admitted that he "did not venture to anticipate that the work would become permanently popular." He himself had been inspired both to travel and to write "when as a boy of ten years I read Willis's *Pencillings By The Way* as they appeared from week to week in the country newspaper. In my fifteenth year," recalled Taylor also, "a little book entitled *The Tourist in Europe* by Mr. George P. Putnam fell into my hands." This was, of course, the young Yankee puritan who had had such fun in the "kissing ring" at the rowdy Greenwich Fair in 1836.[1]

Short on funds, Taylor chose the vagabond approach for his wanderings, paying ten dollars for "second-class" accommodations on the *Oxford,* a merchant ship—which turned out to be "a small space amidships, flanked with bales of cotton, and fitted up with temporary berths of rough planks." In addition to the dark, cramped quarters, Taylor and his six fellow passengers were kept awake at night by "the singing and howling" of a group of Indians en route to London to join George Catlin's "Indian Collection" at the Egyptian Hall in London. The Indians, wrote Taylor, kept time by "slapping their hands violently on their bare breasts" as they sang and helped in many other ways "to relieve the tedium of the voyage." Once in London, Taylor visited the exhibit and was instantly recognized "by our old friends, the Iowas, particularly Blister-Feet who often used to walk a line on deck with me at sea."[2]

Bayard Taylor concluded his book with practical words of advice to future young wanderers desiring to take "the same romantic journey." He advised his readers that they must be content to "sleep on hard beds, and partake of coarse fare; to undergo rudeness at times from . . . the porters of palaces and galleries; or to travel for hours in rain and storm without finding a shelter. The knapsack will at first be heavy upon the shoulders," he warned, and "the feet will be sore, and the limbs weary . . . [but] what at first was borne as a hardship became at last an enjoyment."[3] There are frequent references to Taylor's book in the accounts of later travelers. E. L. Temple observed at the turn of the century that he had longed to visit Europe ever since reading Taylor "more than a generation ago."[4]

The *Footpath and Highway* wanderings of Benjamin Moran through Britain in 1851-52, "chiefly performed on foot amid the pressure of many difficulties," admitted him to the brotherhood. "The wayside cottage was a home to him," Moran wrote of himself in the third person, "and the wayfarer was his brother and equal. His pencillings and sketches were partly communicated to American journals, that the proceeds might aid him on his way, but were chiefly preserved for the gratification of a few near and dear to him."[5] Both Taylor and Moran ended up in the diplomatic service, no doubt enriched by their youthful travels.

In the 1860s another youthful adventurer, Elihu Burritt, the self-educated Connecticut blacksmith, chose hiking "in order to become more thoroughly acquainted with the country and the people than I could by any other mode of traveling. For . . . ten years I was nearly the whole time in Great Britain, travelling from one end of the kingdom to the other."[6] Burritt's famous "walks" included those through the Black Country (the industrial region) and "its green borderland"; from London to Land's End and back; and up to John O'Groat's and back.

The travel accounts of these young men from the 1840s onward provide an interesting and unusual first-hand, detailed collection of observations of British industry, agriculture, and the cultural life of the period. It was no idle boast on their part, as Moran put it, that lonely rambles provide a view of a foreign country gained in to other way. "Railway travelling, as yet," declared Burritt, "takes everything at a disadvantage; it does not front on nature, or art, or the common conditions and industries of men in town or country . . . . It presents everything the wrong side-out . . . . How unnatural, and more, almost profane and inhuman, is the fiery locomotive of the Iron Horse through these densely-peopled towns!"[7]

In 1861 Charles Williams also based his travels on these models although, as he pointed out, "a disability" prevented his traveling on foot; thus he was "under the necessity of always going by public conveyance." Nevertheless, Williams toured for seven months, including eleven weeks in London itself, for $220, which covered his passage across the Atlantic as well as his expenses in Britain. He moved about in the "penny-a-mile," so-called "parliamentary trains," open to the weather; and he stayed at "model lodging houses" in the principal cities, where he could scrape together his own meals and enjoy a rough bed and even facilities for bathing at low cost. Urging other young men to follow his example, Williams wrote: "Thus I passed among the countless millions of Britain, unknowing and unknown, leading a "two-penny life as to the outward but reveling in scenes of spiritual glory and feasting at intellectual banquets which the wealth of a Rothschild would not have enabled me to enjoy with a keener zest." As an amateur astronomer Williams reported that his greatest adventure was his entrance into the famed Greenwich Observatory, "relentlessly closed against all who come not armed with the magic of a name." At first turned away, he sat down and wrote an appeal to "George B. Airy, the Astronomer Royal, not daring even to hope for a reply." Not only did he receive a reply, but he was allowed to enter and study the wonders of the great observatory to his heart's content. "I shall long cherish a grateful recollection of the generous kindness of the Astronomer Royal in admitting me to this building, which of all others I have had the greatest desire to visit, even from the time when an intense love of astronomy first took possession of my youthful mind," wrote the young American. "Thanks, thanks to George B. Airy!"[8]

The so-called "parliamentary trains" some of the younger, more adventurous, and impecunious travelers rode—"which the Government requires all companies to run once a day," as Andrew Dickinson wrote at mid-century—provided them an insight into the lives and character of humble Britons they perhaps could have gained in no other way.[9] Usually uncovered, these cars brought people together "like so many sheep going to market." Aboard one of these cars, a traveler came upon an elderly American woman, "fresh from Yankeeland, who was grievously teased for the general benefit; but Aunt Jonathan, although indifferently furnished with teeth, had an effective tongue; and Mister Bull, in most of the bouts, came off second best."[10]

George Alfred Townsend, the youthful Civil War artist-correspondent—whose plans to lecture on the war to British audiences in the early sixties came to naught—published in 1870 a fictionalized account of a pedestrian tour of

Third Class

The so-called "Parliamentary Train"—low fares for the poor "like so many sheep going to market." *Illustrated London News,* **May 22, 1847, p. 328.** *From the author's collection.*

Britain, obviously satirical, beginning with a horrendous crossing in the steerage. Obviously intending to deromanticize the "tramp tour," Townsend has his hero, once on his feet in the countryside, badgered, insulted, robbed, and generally finding his walking tour "the hardest work" he has ever done. Townsend's young hero claims that "the most shocking *view afoot,*" he had at any time was once when he took off his shoes and saw his bare skin cut and bloody and dusty. He would have given," he says, "half his money for a seat in a passing stagecoach."[11]

Despite such adventures, real or imaginary, the walking tour mystique continued to attract young American males, including even a Texan, Albert Maverick, who walked the 203 miles from Liverpool to London in 1876. Maverick also was drawn to the growing bicycle craze and suffered considerable injury to his person trying to learn to ride his machine. Emerging from the hospital at Dover, he gave up cycling altogether, declaring, "I have changed my mind. I don't want a bicycle," to the salesman who had instructed him in its use, adding, "I will pay all trouble or damage."[12]

The most enthusiastic nineteenth-century account of a bicycle tour of England—which is today quite the vogue all over again—is that of Reuben Thwaites. With his wife, Thwaites spent part of the summer of 1891 "coursing along English highways and byways, and lovingly touching elbows with English rural life." He recommended the cycle as the freest and most independent mode of travel. "It enables one to meander at will, to linger or fly as fancy dictates. By no other conveyance is one so independent in action, so free from care, or so thoroughly in communion with folk and nature." He compared his peaceful, quiet arrival with his wife at Stonehenge with that of carriageloads of tourists brought out from Salisbury like so many herds of sheep. Part of the cyclists' tour had to be made in the conventional manner, "in stuffy compartments, in ill-smelling cabins," which, he wrote, made them "sigh for the freedom of our cycles. . . . Railways, coaches, and steamboats had thenceforth but little attraction. . . . We have come to regard our cycling experience of six weeks as of far more value than our six months of conventional traveling," declared historian Thwaites.[13]

The great cycling vogue lasted several decades. No doubt Albert Chandler's *A Bicycle Tour in England and Wales*—based on a series of articles first published in *Bicycling World* in 1881 about a trip made during the summer of 1879—did much to encourage Thwaites and others like him. Chandler described types of "wheels" and suitable clothing, suggested travel routes, and even explained the rules of the road in Britain—in detail. For those fearing to cycle through the streets of London itself, he pointed out that the bicycle "can easily be carried in a hansom by standing it between the dasher and your seat; it just fits it."[14] In 1887 a member of the Massachusetts Bicycle Club, Thomas Stevens, outdid everybody by going, and by writing, *Around the World on a Bicycle.*

Traveling genteelly in 1896 by carriage out in the English countryside, Adelaide Hall observed "many cyclers, for wheelmen are not slow to take advantage of the picturesque country roads of England."[15] In 1910 John Higinbotham saw "cyclists, both male and female, pedal past us decorously."[16] One female American was "glad the popularity of these machines has not waned

"Only he who has tried it can appreciate the independence of a walking tour," observed Lee Meriwether. *Illustrated London News,* August 15, 1874, p. 145. *Courtesy the Library of Congress.*

here as it has in the United States. Motor-cars are plenty, but they are beyond the reach of travellers like our party; we are glad that we learned to ride wheels. . . . The bicycle is a great blessing," concluded Josephine Tozier in 1904.[17]

The walking tour soon revived once more in reaction to the bicycle craze—the sort of flip-flop so often observed in social history. Lee Meriwether self-consciously "donned the blouse and hobnailed shoes of a workman" to spend a year on a "tramp trip" in the eighties which he recommended as superior to a bicycle tour. "The bicycle might go faster," wrote young Meriwether, "but [the traveler] would see less. Leave your cycle at home and walk. . . . Only he who has tried it can appreciate the independence of a walking tour."[18] Recalling Elihu Burritt's "alluring title," *A Walk from London to John O' Groats,* banker Claudius Patten made a spring walking tour of England in the eighties. "I am not a great walker," admitted Patten, "yet I often made my thirty miles a day in England with ease, without the slightest overweariness. . . . There was something in the atmosphere of the island . . . more stimulating to out-of-door traveling," he wrote.

I today count no places visited by me in England that I did not walk into, walk through, and walk out of. . . . The glory of the walker is his independence, his perfect freedom, and *abandon*. He can go anywhere, stop anywhere, and do as he pleases. He can make closer observation, more completely "do" a place, and altogether become better acquainted with countries, cities, or towns, by walking through them, than by seeing them in any other way.[19]

A female walker, Alice Brown, believed that "to walk is to truly live," but she also learned that, after hiking all day, "you seem to be walking still"—even in sleep.[20]

Walking tours were not always quite as romantic as participants depicted them. Artist Joseph Pennell and his wife, gamely trudging through the Highlands of Scotland in 1888, found that their "knapsacks weighed like lead, and did not grow lighter; each mile seemed interminable. . . . This was the more provoking, because with every step the way grew lovelier."[21]

Some of these youthful wanderers endeavored to add the adventure of a steerage crossing to their "tramp tour," as did Frederick Stokes and a group of pals all of them students* at Yale in 1878. Wearing their newly purchased "famous never-get-dirty shirts which made the late A. T. Stewart's fortune," they embarked. Their travel agent had promised to introduce them to the captain of the ship as "eccentric millionaires and to see to it that we were allowed the freedom of the whole ship." Once aboard, this boon failed to materialize, and the young men found themselves, just like the other steerage inmates, arranging their "kits" consisting of "a rude straw mattress and pillow, tin cup, pan, spoon, knife and fork, also a bed quilt." They spent their first night at sea "smoking and singing college songs," and only the next day, when seasickness fastened its grip on them, did they realize what they were in for. The highlight of their voyage was the determination of a psychotic passenger to set the ship afire, as Stokes later recounted in his book *College Tramps*.[22] For several years travel writers had been warning young men of limited means to avoid the steerage at any cost, "for the money thus saved," as Moses Sweetser wrote in the 1870s, "can never make compensation for the hardships endured." Sweetser went on to describe "a young theological student who was made so dangerously ill by the steerage air that he was unable to commence his travels on the other side for several weeks."[23]

There was yet another glamorous and romantic way to escape the mad rush and mechanization of group travel in the final decades of the century: "coaching"—a lively revival of the stagecoach, which long ago had carried traveling Americans, to their surprised delight, all over England with a degree of comfort, speed, and efficiency unknown in their own country, until, of course, the coaches were put out of existence by the burgeoning British rail systems.

"The railways and the bicycle have more speed," admitted A. V. Honeyman near the turn of the century—himself a veteran of over a thousand miles of "coaching" through England—in an account of his experiences entitled *Bright Days in Merrie England*. But, he added, "let us on the threshold of the twentieth century, take it more easy and prolong the ecstasies of the journey."[24]

The "coaching" revival had begun with wealthy and titled Britons who acquired beautifully appointed stagecoaches, which they called "drags," and themselves formed organizations to foster and promote their hobby. The famous Four-in-Hand Club, for example, held meets in Hyde Park, which were by

The old coaching days revived. Americans were picked up at their "monster hotels" in Trafalgar Square and whirled out into the English countryside for the day, with dinner at a village inn. *The Graphic*, vol. VII, May 24, 1873, p. 481. *Courtesy the Library of Congress.*

1880, according to journalist Louise Moulton, always "great events in London. She noted how "throngs assemble in the Park to see the sight. Nothing could be finer in its way. The drivers are the first gentlemen in the kingdom. The turnouts are the most perfect affairs which combined money and good taste can procure. They meet at noon in Hyde Park, and then drive off to some appointed rendezvous, a score of miles away."[25]

Some of these amateur "coachmen" revived actual, old-time stagecoach routes operating them on a regular basis all through the summer months, starting May 1. Some, as of old, left from the White Horse Cellar in Piccadilly, by the period Hatchett's Hotel. Others, catering to the growing desire of foreigners especially Americans—to see the countryside from atop a coach began starting out from Northumberland Avenue, at the doors of the huge, new tourist hotels, the Grand, the Metropole, and the Victoria—today dingy office buildings looking out on Trafalgar Square.[26]

These coach trips were usually one-day affairs, with a good dinner at a comfortable country inn making the turn-around point for the excursion. One of the earliest descriptions of one of these amateur coach lines is by the American politician John Pendleton Kennedy, who, sometime in 1867 or 1868, while on his European trip, drove down to Brighton with the Duke of Beaufort himself in the role of coachman. "He takes the whip and box himself and drives the coach the whole way through, almost every day," wrote Kennedy, noting how people gathered to stand and stare at this "prodigy of a nobleman" at his work.[27]

" 'Four-in-hand' stage-coaching in England is something more than a rich man's amusement," William Nevin assured his readers in 1879; "it is an institution. It is the assertion of a national and class tradition, and when an English gentleman assumes charge for a season of a coachline, it is looked on as a patriotic act." The stage line from Oxford via London to Cambridge, Nevin reported, was "owned and driven by a gentleman of the County, Captain B. His line of road is one hundred and twenty miles, and his coach stable is stocked with just one hundred and twenty horses. He drives this entire route in one day, returning the next, and resting only on Sunday. . . . for a season of some five months each year." This gentleman had, according to Nevin,

perfected every arrangement of detail in his enterprise, and both the safety and pleasure of his passengers were looked after with scrupulous regard. He carried with him three servants, a guard, a valet, and a relay driver in case of emergency. While everything was thus provided to support and sustain him and keep him in good condition, he personally did the work of driving, and it was one whose magnitude and steadiness would, I think, appall most American gentlemen. It was not a party or an excursion, recollect, or a spurt, but regular daily work, in wet weather and fine—this year nearly every day wet, and carried on often without even the relief of a congenial companion.

Here was the only way, concluded Nevin, "to see the English stage-coach in all its glory—the struggling survival of the eighteenth century. This is a historic study, and alone is a picture worth coming to England for."[28] One recalls Joe Walton, the professional coachman who was described in so much detail by Calvin Colton half a century earlier.

For sheer excitement the departure and arrival of these coaches topped anything Civil War veteran Nevin could remember. He had, he said, seen "battles forced in a flash . . . a council of officers with defeat all around them . . . answering with solemn defiance a summons to surrender . . . half a dozen army corps deploying in their massed battalions in silence onto a field of history." But, he insisted, "I have never seen anything half so impressive, so utterly and overwhelmingly imposing, as the arrival or departure of a swell English coach-and-four in front of an old-fashioned country inn."[29]

In 1895 William Rideing reported

seventeen coaches were running, the nearest destination being Hampton Court, sixteen miles away, and the farthest, Oxford, fifty-five miles. The starting-place for nearly all of them is Northumberland Avenue, in front of the Americanized hotels of that neighborhood; and the hour is between ten and eleven. . . . The greatest show on earth is London, and one of its prettiest "features" is the departure of the coaches. . . . A smartly-dressed crowd is there to see it. Preceded by the musical winding of horns, which rise above the noise of cabs, 'buses, and carriages, the coaches turn into the magnificent avenue from the Embankment, or from Trafalgar Square. . . . They are party-colored, and lettered on the boot and on the panels with the names of the towns and villages they pass through. There is an inside . . . but the blinds are down, for nobody ever wants to be inside. Outside, there are seats for thirteen, including the box-seat, the privileged position, for which a larger fare is charged.

Just as in the old days, passengers wanted the seat beside the driver and now willingly paid an extra shilling for it.[30]

Continued Rideing,

Everything is clean, fresh and shining. . . . The horses are frisky, and in splendid condition; and as they wheel round, and pull up at the door of the hotel, cutting in between hansoms and other vehicles, it is easy to see the coachman is a master of his art. The guard is like a tulip in his scarlet coat, with its silver or gold facings; but his appearance and his skill with the long brass horn, are not his only recommendations. He can handle the ribbons almost as well as the driver does, and is factotum not only to him but the passengers. Now he is at the horses' heads, or diving under their bellies, putting a final touch to the harness, and then bestowing mackintoshes and wraps in the interior, sticks and umbrellas in the basket, or handing the ladies up to their seats where their gay bonnets, parasols, and bouquets bloom as a garden.[31]

"The coachman," went on Rideing,

in a long drab jean, or box-cloth driving coat, reaching to his ankles, overlooks it all, with the eye of a skipper of a double topsail ship. . . . A score of details are on his mind. . . . A brass carriage clock is secured to the dashboard, under the driver's eye, for unpunctuality is a cardinal sin, and at the appointed hour, neither a minute earlier, or a minute later, he mounts the box, tucks himself in his apron, and is off, the leaders lifting themselves up out of sheer joy, and the guard wreathing his horn like a thread of gold through the noise of the town.

Rideing sounds very much like lively Alexander MacKenzie, setting out aboard an actual stagecoach over a half a century earlier. "That coaching is a pleasure accessible to the public," Rideing continued, "is due to the appreciation of the art of driving by rich men and amateur coachmen. The old mail-coaches ceased running with the advent of railways in 1840; and, out of twenty-seven in service up to that year, not one was left."[32]

"Each coach has its own name," continued Rideing, describing the "coaching" revival.

It is usually the namesake of a predecessor in the old coaching days. Thus, the Brighton coach is the *Comet;* the Oxford coach, the *Age;* the Box-Hill coach, the *Rocket;* the Virginia Water coach, the *Old Times;* and the Guildford coach, the *New Times.* Then there are an *Excelsior,* a *Wonder,* a *Magnet,* a *Venture,* a *Vivid,* a *Perseverance,* and two *Telegraphs.* Altogether, seventeen coaches were running last summer, an average sufficient to show how strong the revival is; for even before the railways . . . there were only twenty-seven mail coaches to and from London. . . . Seated on a box-seat on such a summer's morning as June often bestows on England the sorriest pessimist must feel that life is not long enough.[33]

And all along the route, in slow places, the little English children turned out, reviving the custom of their grandparents' day, thrusting up bouquets of flowers, fastened to sticks—running alongside trying to sell them for a penny, just as Joshua White had seen them doing over half a century before.

Dr. John B. Gough, a British emigrant to the United States, having returned for a visit to his homeland in later life, claimed to have talked with a onetime coachman from the old days. "The innkeepers, coach-proprietors, hostlers, and coachmen made common cause against the rail," wrote Gough.

"Ah!" said one of the last stage-coachmen,—giving a history of his opposition and final surrender, "ah, sir, I did my utmost to oppose 'um. I vas von of the last to give in. I kep' a-losing day arter day. I drove a coach the last day with an old voman and a carpet-bag hinside and some hempty trunks on the top. I vas determined to 'ave some passengers, so I took my vife and children 'cos nobody else vouldn't go. Ve vas game to the last, but ve guv in. The landlord of this 'ere 'ouse vas an austerious man. He use' to hobserve that he honly vished a railway committee vould dine hat 'is 'ouse,—he'd pizen 'em all; and he vould, too, sir! Lor, sir, see vat ve've come to, all along of the rail! Vy, sir, I've been werry popular, I have. I've been drownded in 'thank yers' from ladies for never letting anybody step through their bandboxes. Vy, sir, the chamber-maids use' to smile hat me, the dogs vagged their blessed tails and barked ven I come. But hit's all over now, sir, and the gemman that kep' this 'ere 'ouse takes tickets at a railroad station now, poor fellow! And the chambermaids makes scalding 'ot tea be'ind a ma'ogany counter for people as 'as no time to drink it in. Ah, vell, sir, 'ow ve do run be'ind in this world surely!"[34]

Tourists with more money and time and a greater desire for exclusivity hired coaches and drivers for long trips and were driven on private tours of their own choosing. Such a tour was the famous seven-week coach trip in 1881 from Brighton to Inverness, in Scotland, chartered by the fabled Andrew Carnegie. Among his passengers were the Matthew Arnolds, the James G. Blaines, and a couple of Gladstones. His account was entitled *An American Four-in-Hand in Britain.* Three years later a friend of Carnegie, John Champlin, made a similar excursion, dedicating his *Chronicle of the Coach*—an account of a trip from London to Ilfracombe—to Carnegie. Later travelers would boast of having secured the services of Mr. Carnegie's driver, or coachman, Mr. George Punton.[35]

Finally, even the novelty of "coaching" wore off, and, when Anna Bowman Dodd and her husband sought something new and different for a countryside tour at the turn of the century, they put down the suggestion of a friend, "[O]f course you'll coach it," with their proposal to travel "in a much humbler fashion than from the throne-like elevation of a coach." Thus they outlined their plan for a six-week tour of cathedral towns with a hired horse and trap.[36]

The Dodds' route took them to Chichester, Winchester, Salisbury, Bath, Wells, Glastonbury, and Exeter, stopping at country inns along the way. "Don't do it

"To see the country and find out how people live, and explore out-of-the-way places, . . . one must go by automobile," declared Herbert Gunnison in 1905. *From the author's collection.*

LOOKING ACROSS THIRLMERE AT HELVELLYN

A DELIGHTFUL HALT BESIDE A BORDER CASTLE

again—don't tell them we are Americans; it makes us so conspicuous," Mrs. Dodd begged her husband on leaving one of these inns where she thought they had been stared at. "They are always expecting us to do something queer." Her patient husband responded, "That is the reason I do mention it. I want them to see we *don't* do anything queer."[37]

In these waning years of the nineteenth century, which had seen so many changes, yet another phenomenon made its appearance—one which would revolutionize human life in ways undreamed of. In future years, as philosophers would try to determine the causes of great social and economic problems, such as the decay of the cities, some would name the automobile. In any event, it brought a new dimension to traveling.

"The stage-coach and the four-in-hand are things of the past," American Herbert Gunnison announced in 1905. "Bicycling for tourists has about had its day," he continued, and "railway trains will do for those who wish to see the cities and to follow in the old, beaten tracks of travel, but to see the country and find out how the people live and explore out-of-the-way places which even Baedeker has not found, one must go by automobile!"[38]

"It is said," Gunnison reported, "that more Americans went to Europe last summer than in any previous year. A great many took automobiles with them; some purchased them abroad, while others hired machines . . . . Automobiling was one of the chief topics of conversation on shipboard," he added, and "when we reached Liverpool . . . ex-Mayor Grant of New York found his large touring Panhard waiting for him at the dock, and with his wife and children began his trip that evening by going to Chester. Hugh J. Chisholm Jr., also found his Mercedes touring car waiting . . . and with his father and mother began his trip the following morning." Gunnison and his companion made their own "four-day ride" through Britain's countryside in a hired "10–12 horsepower Argyll made in Glasgow."[39]

Gunnison's account is unbearably dull, mainly because all the details described by earlier travelers by coach, rail, foot, and bicycle are missing, as is any real contact with people of the country. He himself records the dismay of the landlord at the Red Horse Inn at Stratford, "once a great place for coaching parties, but now the motor takes the place of the four-in-hand . . . . When a party drove up with horses it usually meant a night and two or three meals. Now the majority of automobilists take a meal and are off to the next place, or run back to London."[40]

Promising to show his readers "how in a trip of five thousand miles, occupying about fifty days in actual traveling time, I covered much of the most beautiful country in England and Scotland and visited a large proportion of the most interesting and historic places in the kingdom," Thomas D. Murphy produced his *British Highways and Byways from a Motor Car* in 1908. The motor car is "always ready when you are ready, subservient to your whim to visit some inaccessible old ruin, flying over the broad main highways, or winding . . . the unfrequented country byways. . . . The country hotel keeper in Britain is just waking up to the importance of motor travel. Already most of the hotels are prepared to take care of this class of tourists. . . . It is generally assumed," Murphy warned his readers, "that a man who is in possession of an automobile is able to pay his bills, and charges and fees are exacted in accordance with this idea." Murphy found twenty-five miles an hour far too fast to permit enjoyment of the English countryside and even worried about speed traps. At Netley they were nabbed by a local constable for leaving their vehicle "standing on a public walk," but the captain waived prosecution, Murphy reported, pointing out that "some of the people in Netley were prejudiced against motors and no doubt were annoyed by the numerous tourists. . . . He said that the motor car was detested by many people . . . but it had come to stay and forbearance and common sense were needed on the part of the motorist and the public generally." Murphy recommended an open car. "Plenty of waterproof coats and coverings answer the purpose very well," he advised, "and the open air is much pleasanter than being cooped up in a closed vehicle." As with Gunnison's account there is far more attention to mileage and the automobile itself than to people or places. The traveler was covering more ground faster—but seeing and experiencing less.[41]

Somewhat more interesting is the account of a six-week motor tour by Robert and Elizabeth Shackleton in the summer of 1913, entitled *Four on a Tour in England*. There are repeated references in this book to the motorist's temptation to make haste and think of "how many miles he must still make that day." The motorist, warned the Shackletons, "must never let a sense of haste disturb him." But even in their concern there seems to be the admission that this was exactly the effect automobile travel had on its practitioners. Their tour, starting in Wales, carried them down into Cornwall and then east to Canterbury, then north up into Scotland and finally to the Lake District. At Boston the Shackletons suffered a minor mishap when "an English motorist rounded a market wagon, in that swift and careless way that we have noticed with so many English motorists, and rammed in under our mudguard. . . . Fortunately, the local constable declared that "he had all the damage, to the great glee of the bystanders and ourselves."[42]

All along their peaceful route that summer of 1913 the Shackletons observed encampments of soldiers and other evidences of military activity. Passing through Monmouth of a Sunday morning, they watched a military formation of six hundred young men marching behind a band to church, "and in a little while we heard their six hundred voices joining tremendously in 'God Save the King!' " Stopping at Stonehenge on Salisbury Plain, the Americans saw off in the distance "lines and lines of tents for regiments camping there . . . and in the gathering gloom their pickets and sentries."[43]

Arriving at Oxford one evening, they noticed that "every house in the square, indeed, every house we passed in getting there, seemed given over to quiet young men seated on cushions on the window-sills, with knees drawn up and decorously reading in the soft evening light; or, if perchance there was one sill without its student, his cushion was still there."[44] For us now, knowing what we know, a shadow hangs over this faded picture of quiet young Englishmen peacefully reading in that soft summer evening light in 1913.

Back in London, other Americans tourists had noticed on a newsstand in the Strand, near the Savoy Hotel, a sign that read: "How to Fight Germany. Read John Bull!"[45]

London

" ' 'Ere comes Hamerica!' " Yankee tourist William Croffut overheard one Londoner remark to another in the summer of 1882, as the native eyed him and his companions emerging from their hotel for a day of sightseeing in the world's largest city.[1] "Circuitous, somber and vast—a fog-ridden, far-reaching prison of stone"—so London seemed to this American. "Its wilderness highway we ramble alone—alone among millions."[2] Journalist Theron Crawford noticed that "in London one does not obtain any idea of the number of American visitors to England, [for] they are swallowed up and lost in the throngs of that great centre of the world."[3]

Professor Milton Terry of Ohio had always longed to see London more than any other city in the world, he admitted in the nineties. "Its great sights and treasures were familiar to me from pictures and from reading. I knew just where I wanted to go," he wrote, "and just how to get there. I had long been prepared for this, and now my hour had come!"[4]

Despite this book-bred familiarity of so many Americans, the great feast of London—which one traveler swore he could both smell and taste while still aboard a train half an hour out—proved as overwhelming to Yankee visitors near the end of the century as at the beginning it had to Benjamin Silliman and his contemporaries. "If London could be cut up . . . and taken in twelve separate, distinct doses, the effect might perhaps be pleasant and healthful," Samuel Fiske had written home to *The Springfield Republican* back in the fifties, "but as it is, all together, swallowed whole, it nearly kills one."[5] His countrymen in later decades would share his conviction.

Speaking as a son of Kansas in 1877, Noble Prentis told his readers that "the City proper, as everyone is supposed to know, is a small spot in London comprising between three and four thousand acres; but from that center London has spread like a prairie fire until it is simply a county covered with houses."[6]

"London is not a city but an empire," declared another stunned Yankee in the seventies, "a nation in itself, a province of brick and mortar, a maze of streets and houses and pleasure parks, the metropolis not of one land, but of the entire globe."[7] Even with a map—like Silliman so long ago—Rudolph Williams, with his street guide bought for two shillings from W. H. Smith at No. 186 in the Strand, had difficulty navigating London in the nineties. "London is beyond me," he groaned, "and ever will be. New York, Chicago, and Philadelphia I can com-

London c. 1900—the "City"—showing the Bank of England in the background. London's "bigness" overwhelmed many an American tourist. *The Graphic,* vol. XXXVI, October 15, 1887, p. 437. *Courtesy the Library of Congress.*

prehend, can carry them geographically in my mind, but London, no. We seem to be in the middle of a world that is all city."[8]

Standing at the end of London Bridge in 1879, where Dr. John Corson had stood in 1846, Adelaide Harrington viewed a similar scene. "It seems as if half the men and horses of the nation were fighting to see which could get into London quickest. . . . The jam at the junction of [New York's] Park Row and Broadway in comparison is as the Falls of Tivoli to Niagara. And there . . . in that wedged mass of man, brute, and vehicle, was a market wagon of vegetables, surmounted by a woman eating a lunch as unconcernedly as though in the corner of a country field!"[9]

"So dense is the travel on the main thoroughfares," wrote P. L. Groome in a letter home to North Carolina in 1889, "that it is often difficult to leave a store for want of a place, but once in, one is moved along almost involuntarily."[10] Not only did Londoners walk much faster than New Yorkers, Elizabeth Peake concluded; they walked more—and "inexpressibly stronger," with even the

London Bridge. "It seemed as if half the men and horses of the nation were fighting to see which could get into London first," wrote Adelaide Harrington. *Illustrated London News,* **November 16, 1872.** *Courtesy the Library of Congress.*

women swinging their arms and striding along with vigor—a characteristic the American in London notices even today. "The carriages, hansoms, and cabs are driven much faster here than in New York," Miss Peake added.[11] The Americans also had to learn, as Richard Grant White pointed out, that in England, "he who walks is expected to give place to him who rides and to him who drives."[12]

"Who are they all, and where are they all going, and whence have they come?" Henry James asked himself one lovely summer evening as he watched the ebb and flow of traffic all around him in London.[13] It was the same question old Wilbur Fisk had posed half a century before.

Into the mind of naturalist John Burroughs came the figure of "a great human anthill," just as it had to the mind of Hiram Fuller in the fifties. "See the great steam highways, leading to all points of the compass," wrote Burroughs in the eighties.

> See the myriads swarming, jostling each other in the streets, and overflowing all the surrounding country. See the under-ground tunnels and galleries and the overground viaducts; see the activity and the supplies, the whole earth the hunting ground of these insects and rustling with their multitudinous stir. One

may be pardoned, in the presence of such an enormous aggregate of humanity as London shows, for thinking of insects. . . . How the throngs stream on interminably, the streets like river-beds, full to their banks! One hardly notices the units—he sees only the black tide. He loses himself, and is borne along through the galleries and passages to the underground railway, and is swept forward like a drop in the sea. I used to make frequent trips to the country, or seek out some empty nook in St. Paul's to come to my senses.[14]

Depression fastened on many their first night in the great formicary—especially if they were travelling alone. "Got to London last night at eleven o'clock," wrote Dr. Clement Pearson about 1880. "Reader, have you ever been in London? If not, imagine yourself in an African desert, or a Western prairie, in the middle of the night. Though there are people enough . . . still you feel much like a lost dog."[15] Richard White "never felt so lonely, so cut off from my family and home."[16]

Youthful Kate Murphy gave up and went to bed early on her first night in London. "It was the first day I had traveled alone, and it was pouring rain when I went to bed. I cried myself to sleep, I was so tired and nervous; the sense of forlornness and helplessness was horrible. . .the depressed feeling of that first night passed away," she admitted later, and "London grew on me." But all the while she was still aware "what a small mite I was in the great surging mass of humanity."[17] Mused George Williams: "How sad and lonely it made me feel as I gazed on millions of human beings not one knowing or caring a fig for me. . . . I was convinced that Charleston, the 'Old City by the Sea', was quite large enough for me."[18]

Nevertheless, soon enough all the American visitors were out tearing around on London's great network of public transport. "Though London is so immense, we can go from place to place with but little inconvenience since 'rapid transit' is here carried to utmost perfection," enthused Morton Wharton of Atlanta in 1884. "Cabs, hackney coaches, omnibuses, tramways, over and underground railways, and steamboats afford all the accomodation the countless thousands of the metropolis require."[19] James Converse did not believe that "the Thames steamers deserve all the abuse they receive," he wrote in 1877. "It is true that they are without awnings . . . that the passenger is dampened and smoked . . . yet they are swift, noiseless, make their landings easily and quickly and there is little waiting."[20]

American women still took to the sporty, private little hansoms. "We spend our days in Hansom cabs," wrote Louise Moulton in 1881, and her description of the little two-wheeled vehicle differs little from that of Mrs. Newman's two decades earlier except that white-lettered advertisements now appear on the dashboard. "One day we inform the world of Day and Martin's blacking," observed Miss Moulton. "Another time we celebrate the wonders wrought by Johnson's troches; yet again we kindly advise people where to get their false teeth. But never mind, we are seeing London, and there is no way to do it so well as by a hansom."[21] A few years later traveler-writer Morris Phillips described such added amenities to the London hansom as thick rubber tires and interior fittings that included "a holder for lighted cigars, a box of matches, a small bevelled mirror on either side of the cab, and a swinging rubber bulb attached to a rubber

A London "Gondola." "We spend our days in Hansom Cabs," observed Louise Moulton. *Illustrated London News,* **April 19, 1890, p. 492.** *Courtesy the Library of Congress.*

tube with a whistle at the end. You lightly press the bulb, and in this way whistle to the cabbie on top, who hears the summons above the roar of the streets and responds by opening his trap door in the roof to receive instructions."[22]

American men still preferred the catbird seat aboard the top deck of the London omnibus. "To see life in London, when I am not with Mrs. B.," wrote James A. Bradley in 1882, "I ride a good deal on top of the omnibus."[23] That drivers of these great buses exhibited something of the authority and panache of the old stagecoach pilots is evident in Phillips's description.

The driver is generally a jolly, red-faced fellow and very smartly dressed, especially on Sunday. He then always wears a "top-hat", in winter it is of black silk, in summer a pearl-gray felt. His coat is often a double-breasted drab cassimere, and in the top buttonhole of the left lapel is a large and loud nose-gay. A showy scarf and a pair of heavy, tan-colored driving gloves complete his costume. He makes quite a picture as he sits on the box, with a leather strap across his waist which holds him securely on the seat, and a black leather apron to protect the lower part of his body from wind and rain. He carries a showy whip with a very long and loose thong, with the end of which he can pick a fly from the ear of his leader.[24]

"The drivers are an institution," wrote P. B. Cogswell in 1880, "rarely leaving their boxes when driving, even for drinks which are handed to them from convenient corners by bar-tenders who know their weaknesses and wants." [25] An Ohioan advised, "Pump your driver to your heart's content. When limbered up he is a fund of information, an encyclopedia eclipsing all guide books."[26] James Rusling considered it "a fine thing to climb to the top of one of these great omnibuses, and go sailing through the streets of London. There is no better place to study English life and character, and to see great London."[27]

One American who had been long enough in England to know of the fantastically dressed dummies the children devise for Guy Fawkes celebrations was much amused by an encounter between a bus driver and the gorgeously red-coated and gold-laced coachman seated on a royal equipage that had

"To see life in London . . . I ride a good deal on top of the omnibus," wrote James A. Bradley. *From the author's collection.*

Top of the Bus. "Pump your driver . . . he is a fund of information . . . eclipsing all guide books," advised William Braman. *Punch*, vol. 78, March 13, 1880, p. 119. *Courtesy the Library of Congress*.

Motorized omnibus c. 1910. Still "no better place to study English life and character, and to see great London," advised J.S. Rusling. *From the author's collection.*

blocked a great mass of traffic. Looking contemptuously down from his high seat, the bus driver called out, " 'Urry up, Guy Fowkes!' " to the great embarrassment of "that pampered menial" causing him to turn "purple with helpless rage to the delighted enjoyment of other drivers within earshot."[28]

When sampling London's underground about 1868—a novel experience for them—American visitors emerged with various reactions. John Latrobe decided to give it a try

after several journeys from the Langham Hotel to the City through the Strand, Fleet Street and Ludgate Hill in cabs. . . . I descended a handsome stairway, found myself on a platform well lighted with gas on one side of the track. On either hand was the mouth of a tunnel. Presently, there was a rumble as of distant thunder, which grew louder and louder; and then, following the glare of its own lamp, came the engine and its train differing in no wise from any other engine and train.

The writer was disappointed. "It was to be nothing but going through a tunnel after all, save that it was more disagreeable than the longest tunnel the writer had ever passed through." He emerged "with a taste of sulphur on his lips, a weight upon his chest, a difficulty of breathing . . . and with a firm determination to

Westminster Abbey, c. 1900, showing visitors headed for the entrance, omnibus at left, and hansom cabs in the foreground. *Courtesy the Library of Congress.*

encounter ten jams on Ludgate Hill rather than make another trip on the underground rail of London."[29] A decade later, however, in 1878, journalist Joel Cook devoted an entire chapter to London's underground railway. "To an American," he wrote, it is "one of the great sights of the city." He also found the system so swift and efficient that "I have seldom used any other vehicle in going about. Whatever direction, or whatever great building I desired to reach, the most convenient route was sure to be the Underground Railway."[30]

An estimated 200,000 of her compatriots were in London during the summer of 1895, according to Mary Krout of Chicago. They could be "counted by scores along Piccadilly, thronging the shops in Oxford and Regent streets, and wandering through the National Gallery, St. Paul's and Westminster."[31] Thus, setting out on their tourist rounds in these final decades of the century, Americans had to beat their way through hordes of other Americans all doing the same thing.

Susan Wallace, wife of General Lew Wallace, author of *Ben Hur,* considered her two days spent exploring Westminster Abbey well worth her stormy passage across the Atlantic, during which she had apparently suffered mightily. On Sunday, September 25, 1881, she attended the memorial service for President Garfield, at last taken by death eighty days after his assassin's attack. "The crowd began to gather early," recalled Mrs. Wallace,

> a crowd of mourners, mostly in black, till the immense place was thronged. . . . The anthem written for the funeral of the Duke of Wellington, introducing the magnificent *Dead March* in Saul . . . was given, and the vast assemblage bowed as with one impulse under the rolling waves of sound. With deep emotion, Canon Duckworth read from the thirty-ninth Psalm . . . and as the eloquent Dean proceeded, tears fell like rain, and every American present felt

Tower of London c. 1900. "No man can listen to these tales of blood without being impressed . . . that the world is growing better," decided a tourist at the turn of the century. *From the author's collection.*

The execution block in the Tower of London. " 'Ef 'eed lived, 'eed never 'ave lost 'is 'ead,' " said a guide to Edward Thwing. *The Graphic,* vol. IV, December 30, 1871, p. 632. *Courtesy the Library of Congress.*

a fresh strengthening of the bond which binds all English-speaking people . . . and so in Westminster Abbey we held the funeral service of our chief, James A. Garfield.[32]

A few Americans, still intent on twisting the tail of the lion at every opportunity, remained resolutely unimpressed by the Abbey or anything in it. "It is a mass of monuments, statues, and busts, memorials to the dead buried there and elsewhere," declared lawyer Charles Collins. "The days when Irving and the sentimentalists gushed over this edifice are past. Like all other *sepulchral showplaces,* rushed over by tourists, it no longer impresses you. The usual beggars, trinket-sellers, and peddlers of catalogues besiege you at the doors."[33]

"The beauty of the Abbey has long vanished," asserted another of these turn-of-the-century goodwill ambassadors, Ohio's "Hon. Wm. A. Braman," who declared that "its architecture was never pleasing, and I doubt if the old structure was ever accused of being symmetrical or comely. Its grimy walls are in streaks assuming an inky blackness, and the rapid deterioration of the marble is causing much solicitude. There is an awe-inspiring gloom pervading the vast recesses of this great sepulchre that is anything but cheerful."[34]

In 1885, Josephine Tyler complained: "I do not recall any woman in the marble rolls of Westminster Abbey, because of the gift of genius. Not even Mrs. Browning has a name in the Poets' Corner. But never mind! When the British people discover a female Shakespeare, it will be time to erect another Abbey, no doubt."[35]

So crowded was the Tower of London on the day of James Bates's visit in 1889 that he found it "hard to absorb its somber essence thronged with sightseers and bustling with various activities and signs of modern life."[36] Another found the guides' spiels especially interesting because of their "Cockney speech" and listened attentively to their "dignified but loquacious warder" orating about a "Devereaux, or somebody else who fell under royal wrath" that began with "the perfectly safe remark, 'Ef 'eed lived, 'eed never 'ave lost 'is 'ed' "—followed by " 'now then, 'ere is the silly-brated Toledo blades, werry pretty. Over yer 'eds the wall is sixteen feet thick. Show yer yaller tickets, please.' "[37]

Poor consumptive Agnes Claflin, on her way to her grave in Rome, got to see the Tower first, "which has been my wonderment all my life." She found it all too much for her tired pen to describe in her journal that night, and she resolved instead to bring cards home to show her family what she could not depict.[38]

During one of the dynamite scares in 1884, Lilian Leland, on her round-the-world tour, found the Tower barred to visitors but finally gained admission through a letter she obtained from the American consul.[39] Several years later another pilgrim observed the contents of "satchels" being examined at the Houses of Parliament. " 'Oh, we have to look out for dynamite,' " replied the policeman in answer to his query.[40] Lou Beauchamp's wife, "the duchess," was quite put out at having to relinquish her "hand satchel" before being admitted to those same premises. "England is a great nation," Beauchamp snorted, "but she trembles today in her very capital at the sight of a little woman with a shopping bundle in her hand. Bully for free America, where we aren't afraid of anything but the other fellows getting another term in Washington."[41]

"The dynamite scare, being at its height, every one of our trunks was mercilessly explored," wrote V. M. Potter in this same period; "handkerchiefs unfolded, tiny boxes emptied, and such confusion wrought with our luggage that we might almost have fancied ourselves arch-conspirators."[42] A young American male was put out at having his revolver taken from him on landing in Ireland, Clara Tadlock observed. " 'They are not allowed to be used in this counthry,' " the customs officer declared in a severely magisterial tone. 'If you want that article, you may perhaps get it tomorra by applying at the Custom House, and presenting to them . . . well, you'll see tomorra' and he turned away."[43]

Actually, American awareness of all the "Fenian" agitation commenced directly after the Civil War. "The Fenian excitement has produced considerable indignation, if not consternation in Government circles," reported Colonel Forney in 1867, "and travelers by land and water are sometimes roughly overhauled as they enter the disaffected sections of this island. More than one

Dynamite Terrorism in London in the eighties. "They shiver and call 'police' when an Irishman passes with a lunch or tin can," snorted Lee Meriwether. *Illustrated London News,* June 7, 1884, p. 545. *Courtesy the Library of Congress.*

American has had to submit to a rigid inspection as he stepped from the deck of a Cunard or Inman steamer upon Irish soil." Philanthropist George Peabody joined with Captain Judkins to vouch for a Mr. Dougherty of Philadelphia on board the *Scotia*, who was not exactly welcomed on reaching the soil of his ancestors.[44] Widow Martha Coston, zealously promoting her husband's maritime signal rockets, endured much embarrassment on one of her trips when a careless purser allowed her box of sample signals to be stored with her personal luggage. "A friend had to exercise all his kindness and bribery to get me out of this scrape," she admitted.[45]

By the 1880s the fear was at the door of the British Museum itself. Lee Meriwether noted the sign at the entrance: "No bags, parcels, or coats carried over the arm allowed in the building until they have been carefully searched by the police." The American professed amazement at this "wonderful timidity" of the Britons. "They shiver and call 'police' when an Irishman passes with a lunch or a tin can."[46]

Despite these sneers at British concern for the public safety in the face of the dynamite terrorism, American admiration for the London police still poured forth. In 1889 Nathan Hubbell allayed fears of Yankee tourists by assuring them that "secret but persevering efforts are still being made by the London police to ferret out 'Jack the Ripper.' Justice is on the track of the most blood-thirsty assassin of modern times, and sooner or later his arrest will follow."[47] On his way back to his hotel in Trafalgar Square at the turn of the century, J. F. Rusling observed policemen handling a large peace demonstration of fifty thousand people against the Boer War. War advocates drowned out the speakers, and the atmosphere was "electric with patriotism and battle," reported Rusling. To protect the speakers when they finished, Rusling noticed how the big, tall policemen "formed a wedge, and putting the speakers in the middle marched them quickly out of the crowd and into a neighboring hotel," whence they disappeared to their homes. "The London police," Rusling concluded, "are an honor and credit to the city."[48]

"**The London police are an honor and a credit to the city**," thought J.F. Rusling, a sentiment shared by all the American visitors. *The Graphic*, vol. VI, December 21, 1872, p. 589. *Courtesy the Library of Congress.*

The British Museum c. 1900. A visit here impressed Dr. Oliver Wendell Holmes with "the fathomless abyss of our own ignorance." *From the author's collection.*

Despite bomb scares and actual incidents, Americans still flocked to the British Museum. Old Dr. Holmes told the visitor how *not* to see the great treasure house of Britain. "When he has a spare hour at his disposal, let him drop in at the Museum and wander among its books and its various collections. He will know as much about it as the fly that buzzes in at one window and out another. . . . There is one lesson to be got from a visit of an hour or two to the British Museum,— namely, the fathomless abyss of our own ignorance." This he followed with his own prescription for seeing "the dry-as-dust galleries," as less appreciative William Cord of Chicago referred to the museum.[49] "Take lodgings next door," advised Dr. Holmes, "in a garret, if you cannot afford anything better,—and pass all your days at the Museum during the whole period of your natural life. At three score years and ten you will have some faint conception . . . of this great British institution."[50]

Young Alfred Townsend, fresh from reporting the Civil War and trying a career of lecturing and writing in England, found that his "author's ticket to the British Museum put the whole world so close around me that I could touch it everywhere. I never entered the noble rotunda of that vast collection," he recalled, "without an emotion of littleness and awe."[51] Mrs. E. A. Forbes, a visitor in the same period, was a bit ruffled to find that, although given an "order of admission to this speechless room," the reading room, she was, as a female she claimed, "permitted to advance only to the bar just within the entrance—a significant utterance of the reputation of the sisterhood on the score of silence."[52]

For many of the tourists their museum visit proved more a matter of duty than pleasure. "Museums are always a bore," wrote one young woman, "but of course we must go."[53] Another traveler called the museum "the traditional refuge of tourists from rain,"[54] and a young man admitted somewhat grudgingly that "this rather beats Barnum's."[55] Other travelers enlivened their visit with some personal contact with the museum's treasures. James F. Rusling was pleased when a staff member verified "the Museum's claim of having a copy of every modern book printed by producing two of my own."[56] In 1871 Elizabeth Peake "became so interested in looking at old manuscripts that I told the others to go on and not wait for me." Before she was through, she had applied for and received permission to look at a version of the Domesday Book "in modern Latin." Asked by an official why she wished to examine it, she replied, " 'First because it is such a famous book; and secondly, to see if my name is in it.' He laughed, and after

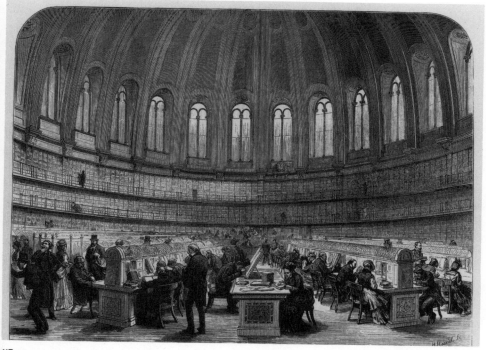

"I never entered the noble rotunda . . . without an emotion of littleness and awe," remembered George Alfred Townsend of the British Museum. *The Graphic*, vol. XI, January 16, 1875, p. 60. *Courtesy the Library of Congress.*

The familiar view of St. Paul's dome from Fleet Street, c. 1900. Note Cheshire Cheese
tavern sign (at left) designating Dr. Johnson's old haunt—still a tourist objective for
Americans of today. *From the author's collection.*

some further compliments, I was shown into the Reading Room, a chair was
given me, and the book was brought."[57]

Still smarting, as were many Unionists after the Civil War, over Britain's
official stance toward their cause, Dr. William Taylor was annoyed in 1868, to
find in the ornithological department of the museum, "a feathered monster
ostentatiously labeled 'Great American Turkey-Buzzard', perched up and fixed
off with the identical sweep of wing and cock of head with which our artists love
to give to their portraitures of the Fowl of Freedom. I do not suppose," opined
Dr. Taylor, "that anybody can fail to see in this another British outrage.
Something ought to be done about it; and I hope that . . . Senator Sumner will
include it in his *Alabama* account along with the blood and treasure and sweat . . .
in his comprehensive bill of charges against Great Britain." Was Taylor joking?
One would like to think so, but he does sound very stern.[58]

St. Paul's Cathedral still drew its flocks of Americans but with fewer diatribes
now on the fees charged, fewer complaints on the martial emphasis of the
memorials, and less fussing by ladies about dust and dirt as well. Poor tired
Adelaide Harrington left the hard-pressed and weary members of her "Dr.
Tourjée Party" behind at the hotel in 1879 and dragged herself and her heavy

skirts to the top of the dome, just like sailor Alexander MacKenzie many years before her. There she, too, marveled at the vast expanses of London stretched out below her on all sides and recalled Samuel Goodrich's "Peter Parley" book on London that, in her childhood, had first fired her interest in the "city which every American hopes to live long enough to behold." Now, weary and worn-out, here she was at last. "Standing here in the Golden Gallery of St. Paul's, just below the Ball and Cross . . . four hundred feet above the level of London Bridge, something of the old-time spell comes over me."[59]

Knight Templar William Cord of Chicago realized in 1883 that one could learn more about London from this vantage point, on a clear day at least, even though "the wind blew something like a Western cyclone," than by looking at maps and traversing its streets for six months. Taking one long last look, he prepared to descend to the world below. "The manifold beauties of the scene make you forget yourself for a time being. Then you give one 'last, long, lingering look' around, clamber down the six hundred steps, which you have mounted with such fatigue, look hastily back at the heroic figures which embellish the body of the church . . . and regretfully pass out . . . into the busy city, almost at one stride; and you have left this noble mausoleum of many of England's greatest—perhaps, forever."[60]

Attending a vesper service at St. Paul's in the eighties Mary McMurphy of Wisconsin enjoyed a peculiar experience as the fog had penetrated the great cathedral to such an extent that they could not see objects ten feet away:

The misty cloud had entered the Cathedral . . . and the lights were like stars glimmering in the dim distance, and the white-robed priests moving slowly to and fro were shadowy, ghost-like shapes that had only a semblance to beings corporeal. . . . When the able Canon, whose form could be indistinctly marked, began to speak from the pulpit, in rich full tones, it was like the voice of inspiration from out the clouds. The effect was startling. A breathless silence held the vast concourse of people whose presence was *felt*, not *seen*. . . . And as we slowly left the church, passing from the dim whiteness within to the dense blackness without, there was indeed darkness everywhere. An impenetrable, mysterious, ghostly envelope surrounded everything. We left the carriage near Westminster Bridge when suddenly the fog, like wreaths of dense smoke, rolled upward and was dissipated in the higher air. The golden rays of the setting sun shone directly upon the Parliament buildings, making a brilliant picture in high lights and deep shadows.[61]

"But how to get in?" asked Bostonian Louise Robinson, standing outside the Houses of Parliament one day in 1889. Tickets of admission were required, and she had not had time yet to present her letter of introduction from a mutual friend to the American minister. Like many other Americans in this period, she was soon introduced to the "system" by which an Irish M.P. would willingly secure admission for a visiting Yankee. She sent in her card to the member suggested by the attendant, "with Boston, U.S.A." inscribed on the corner, "which we find is a good place to hail from," and she later decided this might have had something to do with her cordial greeting from "a small, pleasant-faced gentleman who immediately extended his hand with words of welcome as if we were expected guests." Before he was through, he had them installed behind the

Houses of Parliament, c. 1900. "But how to get in?" Being from Boston helped, Louise Robinson discovered. *From the author's collection.*

famous grill in the seragliolike "Ladies Gallery." Recording their experience in her journal that evening, Miss Robinson decided that, while she still believed "the manners of a Massachusetts legislative body superior in dignity to those of . . . the House of Commons, *who* under the gilded dome on Beacon Hill would give himself as much trouble to entertain a strange English lady, as our Member took upon himself to entertain us!"[62]

Having smarted under satirical descriptions of their Congress during the first half of the century, the Americans had long sniped vigorously at all that went on in the House of Commons, getting their own back for the ridicule concerning overflowing spittoons, feet up on chairs, and backwoods manners in general. Now they reserved their carping principally for the Westminster architecture, some predicting its decay within fifty years under the assault of London's coal smoke and remarking endlessly on the "unsuitability" of the Gothic for government buildings. The women had a special gripe, however, and Ella Thompson got quickly to it in her description of her visit to the House of Commons. It was that famous "Ladies Gallery" enclosed with its gilded latticework or grating, where women are permitted to hear "without being seen."[63] It reminded her, she said, of the slave quarters of some Turkish sultan's palace. This gallery was denigrated by many American women visitors, accustomed as they were to far more deference at home even in the halls of Congress, where, in large, open galleries they could sit on display to show off new gowns and bonnets and even exchange admiring glances and notes with bemused legislators on the floor below.

Perhaps the ultimate swipe at Westminster came from an expected quarter, the anglophobic "Hon. Wm. A. Braman of Ohio" himself. "The entire structure, roofs, cornices, in fact, every nook and corner was firmly in the possession of the birds," he discovered. Furthermore, Parliament was not even in session on the day of his visit, and he was convinced that "those dignified landmarks who stood on guard, swelled with their own importance, reveled in our disappointment."[64]

Christ's Hospital still attracted American visitors to its public suppers, and most tourists enjoyed the familiar glimpses of the boys darting about London streets in their quaint garb—always bareheaded. "Like the Shakers in the United States," wrote one observer, "they are dressed in a quaint costume belonging to ancient days."[65] Another thought that "they look very funny in their old-fashioned rig," which "gave so much the look of a juvenile priesthood, and so elongated and solemnized their slender figures that their childish gaiety seemed curiously inappropriate." Mrs. E. A. Forbes was also much impressed by the supper she attended in "a long stately room" where eighteen tables were laid. "And along these tables the boys clustered, like bees about a hive," for their dinner followed by the ancient bread and beer ritual.[66]

Greenwich Hospital no longer functioned as a quiet harbor for ancient mariners after 1865, and there were far fewer visits to the Royal Hospital for army veterans in Chelsea. Americans had little time for old soldiers in these years, or perhaps they now had too many old soldiers of their own at home—veterans of their bloody Civil War.

A favorite excursion mecca outside London in these waning years of the nineteenth century was Windsor Castle, some of its attraction for them stemming no doubt from the fact that it was a much-lived-in residence of the aging Queen Victoria, once called "The Widow of Windsor" during her long years of seclusion following the death of her beloved Albert. Also, it was simply a great show of royal splendor for these visiting republicans and ideal for a day's outing. The more anglophobic visitors also enjoyed this opportunity to deprecate the institution of the monarchy. "It takes a great deal of fuss to run royalty," remarked P. B. Cogswell, "as well as hard cash, and we wonder that sensible Englishmen consider the sport worth the candle."[67]

Impressed one day in the eighties with the happy mood of Londoners and their children out at Windsor for a day's pleasure, Margaret Preston observed "how good-naturedly the epauletted officials" reacted to "the wails and pipings of this squadron of infantry. And when the same crowd pressed through the doors of St. George's Chapel where English royalty is wed and buried, we wondered if such a phalanx of screaming babyhood in our Capitol at Washington would be so smiled upon by the porters. It gave us an idea of free and equal rights in this monarchial land," wrote Mrs. Preston, "to see these poor mothers seat themselves on a bench just outside the small chapel in which the Queen has placed a beautiful recumbent figure of Prince Albert, and proceed without any show of offended modesty, to give the babies their dinner!"[68]

Rotten Row, Hyde Park, c. 1900. "All London may be seen ... high and low, rich and poor, tradesmen and lords, childhood and old age, and all life in between these extremes," wrote Samuel Mutchmore of London's parks. *From the author's collection.*

London's parks continued to elicit admiration from Americans, not so much now for the brilliant parades of horseflesh, fashion and beauty, as for the vast, open spaces themselves resting like blessings in the midst of the world's greatest city. "The parks," wrote an American near the end of the century, "are where that great Leviathan, the London populace, comes up to breathe, darting back again into the deep waters of the crowded stream; then rising here each day to catch a breath of the pure and vital air of heaven. Nothing is more surprising to an American, accustomed to the narrow and contracted squares of his own cities than these great spaces, open to the sky in such a metropolis as London."[69] The Americans were also impressed that the parks were open to everybody, and that in them "all London may be seen, high and low, rich and poor, tradesmen and lords, childhood and old age, and all life in between these extremes."[70]

Elizabeth Peake was charmed by the custom of cows tied to the railing in St. James's Park, with "heaps of mown grass lying before them as they were milked into cups, and the milk sold for the young brought to the Park in their baby wagons for that purpose."[71]

Fascinated by the scene at Speakers' Corner in Hyde Park on a Sunday afternoon in the 1880s, one American tourist recorded the variety of interests and opinion expressed there. First, he found "a group of standing worshipers. They had a portable organ and were singing hymns; then a crowd being harangued by an Internationalist, a man who denounced all institutions and government; within a hundred feet was another crowd hearing a man preach on the duty of repentance; then an atheist who was eliciting the greatest response of all from his listeners; and near this a temperance speaker."[72]

Referring to London's phenomenal growth, Elihu Burritt noted in the sixties its steady absorption of all nearby small towns and villages. "But London is not wolfish," observed the American. "It takes them in gently while they are asleep, and lets them sleep on as if nothing had happened. It lets them stand where they stood before, only not alone as then."[73] And the Britons zealously maintained their playing grounds and parks, he noticed, despite their increasing urbanization.

Among "whole droves of littler 'lions' roaring for their turn," as tourist Charles Wood put it in the eighties, was the famed wax museum of Madame Tussaud.[74] One American lady who resolutely did not care for much else in London termed the waxworks "the oddest and most entirely unique place for a stranger to visit in London."[75] One of her countrymen, who was enthusiastic about almost everything else in Britain, labeled it "an abomination, a hall of humbugs."[76] Many Americans complained that their own Civil War generals in particular, but also their presidents and politicians, were poorly depicted. This was done on purpose, so onetime Postmaster General Horatio King believed. He took it upon himself to seek out the proprietors of Madame Tussaud's and "earnestly protested against burlesquing our modern statesmen, warriors and divines in such a shocking manner."[77] Another tourist was mightily impressed that a felon, "hanged in London only the day before," was already on exhibition in wax.[78] Like visitors to this day, many were fooled by "policemen," "attendants," and other "visitors" who, when one started to apologize for bumping into them, turned out to be creatures of wax.

Buckingham Palace, today so mobbed by tourists to see the changing of the guard, is barely mentioned by the nineteenth-century travelers. To them it was simply another royal residence and not a very interesting one at that. "It has never dazzled Americans with its beauty," remarked Mr. Braman, "and would be a poor rival for any one of a hundred residences which might be selected in New York. The addition of some trees and grass would make it much more homelike."[79]

The Albert Memorial in Hyde Park was called by Mark Twain "the most generously humorous idea I have met in this grave land."[80] It had, of course, to be seen by all the tourists and duly praised, or denigrated, according to the eye and taste of the beholder. Lucy Culler thought that "it excels anything in the form of a monument that we saw anywhere—the most sumptuous!"[81] Canon John Harris Knowles of Chicago pronounced it "the apotheosis of wifely devotion."[82] Others were less laudatory. "Poor man," wrote Caroline Sheldon, "doomed to sit for ages under this ugly canopy."[83] Another termed it "a fitting pyramid in which to bury a sacred cow."[84] Richard Grant White had called it, in a Boston magazine article, "the most obtrusively offensive monument in London."

Charing Cross Hotel c. 1900. Much frequented by Americans because of the American Exchange which provided them with currency exchange services, cashed their checks, kept a registrar of Americans in London, carried their country's newspapers, and served as a meeting place. *From the author's collection.*

But William Stevenson sharply disagreed with him, thinking it a fitting memorial "to a pure and upright man."[85] Perhaps Twain was closer to the truth when he finally concluded that it was "the brightest, freshest, loveliest bit of gigantic jewelry in all this battered and blackened old city."[86]

The traditional British fondness for animals and flowers was noted even in the great city. About 1900 Hiram Fuller found the church of St. Clement Danes "in mourning for" a lost and obviously cherished cat. "Placards written in a trembling hand on note paper with a black border, and fastened to the iron pickets, announced the 'Tom Cat', as strayed or stolen, and proffered a reward of five shillings 'without questions' for his return!"[87] Like a young man in the fifties who had noticed the Londoners' taste for flowers, one of Fuller's countrymen in the eighties made a similar observation, but he found it "incongruous that the lovely flowers of the meadows, fields and gardens of England were in the dirty hands of a gang of flower women and girls who were ready to chaff each other in the most rude, and often indecent manner, and ready also to cheat the traveler who

Northumberland House in Trafalgar Square. "That last ragged remnant of feudal magnificence in London," as Richard White described it, was torn down in 1874 to make way for tourist hotels. *From the author's collection.*

Trafalgar Square c. 1900, showing the huge hotels for which Northumberland House was sacrificed: the Grand, the Metropole, and the Victoria. Morley's Hotel, now passé, still huddles at the left, soon to be replaced by South Africa House. *From the author's collection.*

Viewed from Charing Cross, the Grand Building, an office block in Trafalgar Square today. In the final decades of the nineteenth century, this was the hotel "Grand," much favored by visiting Americans. Having been saved from the fate of old Northumberland House, which once stood there, the "Grand" is undergoing rehabilitation. Note the jogger in the foreground. Photo by Dan Cruikshank. *From the author's collection.*

lingered among them in search of a supply of the treasures of joy and beauty in which they dealt"—no admirer of Eliza Doolittle here![88]

Trafalgar Square had always been familiar ground to Americans because of its nearness to many of the "lions" of London they most wished to see, but also because of the hotels in the vicinity. In the early days of the century many had put up at the Golden Cross, immortalized by Charles Dickens as the coaching inn from which Mr. Pickwick and his friends set out on their adventures with Alfred Jingle. Later the favorite American haunt was Morley's Hotel. Just after the Civil War the posh new Langham was very much "in," followed by the Grosvenor, the St. Pancras, the Westminster Palace, and the Charing Cross Hotel. Then, starting in the eighties, Americans began to put up at those huge, newly built tourist beehives, the Grand, the Metropole, and the Victoria, clustered at the southeast corner of Trafalgar Square where the lovely old Jacobean Northumberland House had been pulled down to make way for them. R. G. White regarded sadly what remained of its foundations in 1876, mourning the loss of "that last ragged remnant of feudal magnificence in London."[89] Back in 1835 Alexander Mac-Kenzie had almost been run down by a brewer's cart as he stood gazing up at one of London's landmarks, the Percy family lion perched on the roof of that ancient house.[90]

Americans followed the British vogue of denigrating Trafalgar Square. Henry James termed it a "grimy desert."[91] Noble Prentis growled about Landseer's "beastly lions" crouching at the foot of Nelson's column.[92] Often the column itself was faulted for being too tall to permit a proper view of the brave little admiral forever on duty at its top. Still, as did Londoners themselves, the Americans liked to stand and stare in the great open space of the square and marvel, just as they do today, at some of the fiercest traffic in the world. "It is two or three Broadways concentrated into one," remarked a New Yorker, "and the gymnastics required to get safely across that Square, or any of the streets that flow into or out of it, are sometimes trying and often ludicrous."[93] Standing bemused in the square on an August evening in the seventies, Ehrmann Nadal of the American legation heard all around him "the desolate roar of the city. The granite column seemed borne upward and to swim in the air, and Nelson from its summit looked far away to Egypt and the Nile."[94]

For years before World War I a traditional feature of the square was the recruiting sergeants, whose hunting ground was the stretch of pavement between the National Gallery and the Portrait Gallery just behind it to the right. "Here you may see the recruiting sergeants peacocking up and down," wrote E. V. Lucas, "flicking their legs with their little canes, throwing out their fine chests, and personifying with all their might the allurements of the lordliest life on earth. One has to watch but a very short time to see a shy youth, tired of being an errand boy or grocer's assistant, grab at the bait; when off they go to the barracks behind the National Gallery to complete the business."[95] The "business," as Lucas called it, is still carried on in the same vicinity, but today in a modest storefront office near the foot of the Strand.

"It is a common opinion that the reign of Victoria has been a peaceful one," observed American historian Moses Coit Tyler, writing in the sixties, "but the truth is, there has scarcely been a day since she ascended the throne that she has not had a war or two on her hands. There was the Canada war, the Syrian war, the Afghanistan war, the Scinde and Moultan war, two Punjaub wars, two Kaffir wars, the Assam war, the Burma war, three Chinese wars, the Persian war, the Russian war, the Japan war, unnumbered New Zealand wars, the Bhootan war, the wars internal to India and to Ceylon, the wars in West Africa and in South America."[96]

Even after their own deadly Civil War, with its one million fatalities from both combat and disease, Americans still were impressed at the evidences they saw of the cost of empire. "There is not a church or cathedral. . .that the tourist visits in Great Britain, but that he reads the bloody catalogue of victims of England's glory," remarked Curtis Guild, ". . .noble young soldiers of twenty-two and twenty years and even younger, who have fallen 'victims to Chinese treachery', 'perished in a typhoon in the Indian Ocean', 'been massacred in India', 'lost at sea', 'killed in the Crimea', . . ."[97] Wrote another Yankee, "[T]here is not an old parish church in England that does not contain memorials of English soldiers who died in Spain, Belgium, in India, in America, everywhere."[98] William Wilberforce Nevin, himself a Civil War veteran, standing in St. Paul's in 1879, watched a little group of "young sergeants, proud of their early chevrons. . .poring earnestly over the names of some poor, unknown ship-boys who in a great naval action went down nobly, standing to their duty as grandly and faithfully as admiral or general." They were on their way to the African War, Nevin realized, "and I knew that the real service of this cathedral would be offered some day in silence on the battlefields of Zululand."[99]

At the Agricultural Hall in Islington in the 1880s journalist Theron Crawford one day watched a display of daring horsemanship by "strong, wiry, active, and splendid-looking young fellows . . . all non-commissioned officers." Much attention went to the handling of field pieces. "The rapidity with which all the field pieces can be fired, and the murderous efficacy of the improved Gatlings, and the rapidity with which soldiers can discharge their breech-loaders," concluded the American, "show that . . . a war between any of the great powers would be of necessity a very bloody and a very brief one."[100]

Shopping at London's famous luxury emporiums consumed even more time in these years. For a decade or so after the Civil War men saved the cost of a steamship ticket, or so they thought, by laying in a stock of clothing to last for several years. "They used to come over with handbags or valises, holding just enough for the trip," wrote Thomas Knox, "and go back with trunks filled with new clothing which they had worn sufficiently to enable them to go through the custom-house without paying duties."[101] Joel Cook watched women en route home "trailing their new dresses over the decks all through the voyage to make them look old."[102] Francis Sessions saw women "in their silks and splendid suits; with cloaks of seal-skin and velvet, although it was only September. Such an array of diamonds and precious stones I never had witnessed before. The gentlemen also had on their new suits and overcoats, and a better-dressed company never landed in New York."[103]

Dr. Terhune had observed the frantic shopping of some of his countrymen and countrywomen and recalled in particular a Cincinnati mother and her daughter reading a letter from home. " 'Maria, the buggy business is picking up ... that is good news for us.' 'Maw, I'm going to have that diamond ring for sure, now.' And from the look on Maw's face, I am sure Maria got her ring."[104]

Some of these eager shoppers, especially the women, fussed at "the slow plodding fashion of doing things" in London shops, one of them declaring that "it made us long for some of our American briskness."[105] Curtis Guild, however, advised Yankee travelers that "shopping in London is, on the whole, more satisfactory than in any other city in Europe, from the fact that all respectable shop-keepers believe in the value of reputation, and where competition is so close, wisely believe it will not pay to imperil their business by any dishonest act." He praised also the high quality of English clothing, shoes, and most other goods as well.[106]

At the turn of the century, during the Boer War, Esther Davenport of Buffalo was ecstatic over the bargains she found in London shops.

With the war in Africa and half the gentry in mourning, Regent and Oxford Streets have been running over, all summer, with all sorts of unused finery, which is to be had at one-third its original cost. . . . Such window shows of

Regent Street c. 1900. Esther Davenport found it "running over, all summer, with all sorts of unused finery" which she bought up. Londoners were in mourning for their dead in the Boer War. *From the author's collection.*

jewelry, laces, fabrics, mantles, and dresses, such novelties in gloves, fans and parasols, such labyrinths of things for women to wear and trim their houses with surely can be shown nowhere else on earth, excepting always Buffalo![107]

Rich American women, even those who would be classified merely as visitors rather than residents, now fought to be presented at the British court, believing it "a considerable distinction," although Ehrmann Nadal, a secretary at the legation, assured his readers that "it has entirely ceased to have any social significance whatever in England."[108] Maybe none in England, but what about New York or Chicago? An American woman, even without "connections," could achieve the distinction, journalist Elizabeth Banks claimed, if she were able "to pay out between £4,000 and £5,000 for 'a season' in London, introductions into the best society, and a presentation at Court."[109]

Despite such negative judgments, society matrons like the mighty Mrs. Mackin, so thrilled to have bowed with Mrs. Cornelius Vanderbilt, considered it the duty of the American ambassador to arrange such important matters for them. During the 1890s between "four and five hundred" such applications would arrive for the four presentations at each of perhaps three Courts to be held, according to journalist George Smalley. In this period he also recalled how one "eminent statesman, arriving after Levées and Drawing-rooms were over, desired a secretary to arrange that he and his family should take tea with the Queen at Windsor Castle."[110]

The mixed delight and disapproval with which some of the earlier puritan pilgrims sampled the entertainment of London was almost a thing of the past by the 1880s. Now, reported Crawford, they flocked to London theaters to view "the Kendals, Henry Irving, Ellen Terry, the Bancrofts, Bernard Beere, Mrs. Beerbohm-Tree, Charles Wyndham and Toole." They fussed at having to pay for programs but reveled in the bars and refreshment rooms they did not have at home. Men boasted of having taken in racy shows at the Empire and Alhambra in Leicester Square, and Crawford describes Piccadilly Circus in these years as "the slave market of London, where women are as openly and publicly bought and sold as in the slave marts of Constantinople."[111] Several decades earlier there had been references to two "dancing saloons," the Assembly Room and the Argyll, [also spelled Argyle by other writers] where brisk nightlife prevailed. "It is not unusual to see at the Argyll, just when the dancing is at its wildest," observed Ehrmann Nadal, "...the really honest traveler from America—a Sunday school teacher, likely ... looking on with a countenance expressive of edification and enlightenment."[112] There are also veiled references to the "Judge and Jury Club," also in Leicester Square, specializing in lewd performances, "verbal filth, physical vulgarity ... the display of almost nude women ... and orgies behind the scene after the performance."[113] Perhaps this was a carry-over of the "Judge and Jury" show referred to by young Melville back in 1849, which he visited in Bow Street, terming the performance "exceedingly diverting but not superlatively moral."[114] Family tourist parties, of course, flocked to the rebuilt Crystal Palace, now a pleasure dome in Sydenham, which William Stevenson, attending the Methodist Ecumenical Conference in London in 1881, pronounced "the cheapest and best place of amusement in London."[115]

Those earnest, fact-finding tours of mid-century American visitors were now replaced by what can only be called callous "slumming" expeditions. "Our landlord," wrote Francis Sessions in one of his letters home to the *Daily Ohio State Journal* of Columbus in the 1880s, "asked us to accompany him to a different scene from those we had witnessed during the day." So, after a day of conventional sightseeing, and leaving their wives behind at the hotel, "we were divested of watches, money and jewelry, and started out to see the 'slums' of London. Such squalor and poverty were heart-rending," he wrote, "but the saddest sight was at the drinking places. There were more women drinking and drunk than men, and they were altogether the most boisterous and belligerent."[116] The busy Dr. Edward Thwing was thrilled to be able to tell his readers that he had attended a meeting "among a company of robbers and prostitutes whom it would not be safe to meet under ordinary circumstances." The high spot of such evening entertainment as this was a visit to a "genuine" opium den:

We climbed to the smoke-room by a crooked, rickety staircase. Ragged papers are pasted over cracked and broken window-panes; cobwebs and filth abound. Little do they care who come hither to drown their senses in the intoxication of opium. There lies an Arab; his face is black but between his parted lips, teeth shine white as ivory. . . . I was glad to get a breath of air outside, poor as that was, and I was ill all the night following.[117]

Americans still observed and commented on the poverty they saw in London but not with the same air of horror and indignation as in earlier years. Perhaps they were beginning to see something of this in their own great urban centers. They were more likely now to admire the jaunty spirit of Londoners, especially that of the children. One evening, walking out not far from the St. Pancras Hotel, Noble Prentis of Kansas came on a scene of wild delight as a group of children, attracted by the music of a hand organ, gathered to dance. "The babies were gathered up anywhere, by the arm, by the leg, by the neck, by the heels . . . it was a whirlpool of tangled hair, little bare legs, glittering eyes, white teeth, and rags."[118] Richard White said that he came "again and again upon little groups of children dancing in dingy courts upon damp pavement. It might be drizzling rain, although not enough to wash their faces, yet they, poor, hatless, shoeless, breakfastless creatures, danced and danced merrily without other music than that of their own little pipes."[119] Martha Coston never forgot the little street urchin who peered into her carriage to admire her fine feathers, as she waited in the long line of vehicles for her presentation at court in the sixties. Such inspections of these grand ladies were a regular pastime for poor London children. "Look which way I could, I encountered a myriad of eyes, and finally was feign to fix my own steadfastly on the buttons of the coachman's great-coat," recalled Mrs. Coston, "while I tried to appear oblivious. My dignity tottered for a moment when an exceedingly small and exceedingly dirty boy, crooking his bony little fingers into the shape of a binocular, exclaimed, 'Oh, my h'eye!' "[120]

Even tart-tongued journalist Kate Field was kind to the Londoners, for, after cussing both the weather and the climate, she declared, " 'I like London . . . I like it because of the people.' "[121] Dr. William Taylor, writing in 1868, was amused, so he said, at all the space given over the previous three decades by his compatriots in their books to the vice and virtues of London.

Children of London dancing in the street—"poor, shoeless, breakfastless creatures," as Richard White described them, but full of the joy of life. *The English Illustrated Magazine,* **vol. 2, 1884–85, p. 609.** *Courtesy the Library of Congress.*

The social contrasts have also been thoroughly talked about. Some writers moralize with great power upon the vast difference that intervenes here between the top and the bottom rounds of the ladder of life—a marvellous thing which they appear to have realized for the first time on arriving in London. For my part, I did not have to come to the great city to realize this. I can see it plainly enough in my own little town. I have known, I think, from my childhood, that very rich folks are better off than very poor ones. . . . Of a truth, London has its penury and its wealth, its disgraces and its glories, its abasements and exaltations, its pains and pleasures, its woes and joys, like every other spot on this Hell-cursed, Heaven-blessed earth.[122]

That tireless, unflappable, professional Presbyterian pilgrim Janet Collins, who spent most of her time up in Scotland locating scenes of religious martyrdom of the Covenanters and specializing in "bottle-shaped dungeons," also had something to say about this hypocritical American preoccupation with British poverty and social inequality:

We of America manifest great impatience at the existing state of things in the British Isles; but we forget to clear our own skirts. We have the Indian and the negro on our hands. What of them? We cannot shift responsibility in their case. They have belonged to the soil for hundreds of years and, as a class, they are still oppressed, downtrodden, hated, the light of knowledge withheld, robbed, scorned, and almost every indignity heaped upon them.[123]

"Most people who come here are very much disappointed if they do not at once meet with all the experiences common to London life," observed Theron Crawford in one of his dispatches to the *New York World* in the 1880s. "I have often heard American visitors to London say that they wished they could experience a real London fog."[124] Unless they visited London during the summer months, as of course more and more Americans came to do in the years of mass tourism, there was still plenty of opportunity to enjoy fog in London from November on, when the soft coal smoke issued from the millions of chimney pots to combine with certain weather and temperature conditions and thus smother the great city in a thick, impenetrable blanket.

Fog might seem picturesque at first to a visiting Yankee, but not when it reached the point where it actually penetrated their rooms. "It was a filthy brown, almost a greasy black, the hue of mendicant monks," wrote Margaret Wright in 1897, "and its odor was—well, it was, if possible, even worse than a begging friar's. The drawing room seemed full of smoke, sewer gas weighted the air, the lighted chandelier struggled ineffectually to lessen the gloom. . . . This was November in London."[125]

Seated in the little parlor of their London lodgings in the same period, Mrs. L. C. Lane and her companion found the light actually growing dimmer as the day wore on. By noon they were "obliged to give up reading altogether. At one o'clock the house was so pervaded with smoke that half-way across our sitting room we could not clearly discern each other's faces, nor the color of each other's clothing. . . . Since three o'clock," she added, "it has been gradually lessening."[126] Journalist Leander Richardson recalled a night at the Savoy Theatre when he could not see the stage from his seat in the balcony.[127]

Dutifully visiting Bunhill Fields burial ground one foggy Autumn morning, YMCA representative Charles Butler took refuge in the little City Road Chapel of John Wesley across the way. "The fog seemed to fill every nook and corner of the chapel," he noticed. " 'This is a fearful fog,' I said to an old Londoner in the Chapel. 'Eh, my word,' he replied, 'but this is light to some we 'ave. Sometimes it is so thick that all traffic has to stop, and I 'ave known people who 'ave not been able to find their way 'ome.' "[128] Entering London via Windsor by train in 1877, Noble Prentis observed over the city a pall of "blue smoke like that which rolls away from a battlefield when the day is won and lost."[129] In London on the eve of World War I, George Hills found similar conditions still prevailing in the three worst months of winter. People were stuffing their ears and nostrils with cotton, he reported, and some were "displaying that remarkably British institution, a mouth filter or sieve, strapped on like a dog-muzzle and designed to prevent the breathing of microbes, germs and other pollywogs of the air. The fog and filter go hand in hand in Merrie England."[130]

"It has always been assumed that dirt and smoke are necessary evils in manufacturing towns," Andrew Carnegie observed in 1881,

"In London you thank Heaven when the sun shines, and say nothing when it does not," concluded Stephen Fiske. *Punch*, vol. 95, August 11, 1888, p. 71. *Courtesy the Library of Congress.*

but the next generation will probably wonder how men could be induced to live under such disagreeable conditions. Many of us will live to see all the fuel which is now used in so thriftless a way converted into clean gas before it is fed to the furnaces, and thus consumed without poisoning the atmosphere with smoke, which involves at the same time so great a loss of carbon. Birmingham and Pittsburgh will some day rejoice in unsullied skies, and even London will be a clean city.[131]

It would be over seventy years before the latter would come true, with the development of technology and the passage of legislation.

London's drizzle, which had so long ago driven rain-soaked Alexander Mac Kenzie to purchase and tote an umbrella, had the same effect on Stephen Fiske in 1868:

My first purchase in England was an umbrella. One soon learns to love the fog and rain as characteristics of London, and would as soon see the City deprived of St. Paul's as of these pecularities. The fact is, that you pay no more attention to bad weather in London than to the noise of the vehicles. It is a thing to be anticipated, and to miss if you are deprived of it. . . . In London you thank Heaven when the sun shines, and say nothing when it does not.[132]

Young Charles Williams had hoped to take his English umbrella home as a memento of his journeying in Britain. It had "sheltered me from the dripping rains of London, and been my constant attendant through her parks, gardens and her thoroughfares. I had carried it over the downs of Wiltshire to the ruins of Stonehenge, through the beautiful land of Wales, and the enchanting scenes of the Emerald Isle." Alas, his wish was not to be fulfilled, for the umbrella was stolen from him in a railway station. His one consolation was its battered condition, which would probably cause the broken ribs to "droop helplessly round his rascally head."[133]

If the fog and rain did not bother these Yankee sojourners in London, the omnipresent soot was more likely to. "White marble statues may be beautiful in Athens and Paris," wrote James Converse, "but they are hideous in smoky London. Wellington and Nelson, and all the others, how one does long to wash their faces for them. . . . How mortified the admirals, generals, bishops, and nobles would be if they could only see the condition of their faces, their hands and their coats in Westminster Abbey and St. Paul's Cathedral! . . . London smoke makes these heroes look like coal miners!"[134]

Even the ancient Elgin Marbles in the British Museum "are nearly black," complained a visitor in the late nineties.[135] Eliza Connor, usually quick to denigrate things British, found London "ugly and gigantic, but not nearly so smoky and sooty as Cincinnati," her home town.[136]

The effect of rain coursing down the surfaces of London's soot-blackened monuments and structures was thought strangely beautiful by one American with an artistic eye, who saw them as "heavily shaded engravings," or like "India Ink sketches shaded from pale gray to almost black."[137] Henry James perceived a certain romantic beauty in some of London's "winter effects" caused by fog, soot, and rain, "not intrinsically sweet" but which somehow "touch the chords of memory and even the fount of tears; as for instance the front of the British Museum on a black afternoon . . . The romance . . . arises," he concluded, "from the general lamplight," which imparted "something of a cheer of red lights in a storm," and "the sense of the misty halls within where all the treasures lie."[138]

Many Americans were far less concerned with what the soot was doing to London's structures than its effects upon their persons. Unafflicted, for the most part, with the American female traveler's propensity for complaint, Elizabeth Peake nevertheless observed that "anyone who could invent a method of consuming the smoke of London should be knighted upon the spot. I can neither walk nor ride without getting begrimed. Particles of sooty smoke settle on my face, and, as the water is hard, I find it difficult to keep off. I am sure I could wear a collar and cuffs a week at home, and they would not be as much soiled as in one-half day here."[139]

At least one American husband pointed out to his wife that the women of London had wisely adapted themselves to prevailing circumstances in London, and "hence, dark dresses are much more common among ladies than with us when they go into the streets to walk for business or recreation."[140] A Floridian, however, shunned any such measures as stout shoes and sensible clothes, preferring to complain that "it was disgusting. You soil your clothes; you cannot touch anything without soiling your hands or your gloves."[141]

Despite rain and soot, Londoners of the middle and upper classes, probably those with the proper facilities and servants to make it possible, maintained an astonishing degree of personal and general cleanliness—more so than people at home, some Americans decided. "Amidst all the smoke and filth of the city," recalled Dr. George Loring the newly-appointed American minister to Portugal, in 1889, "I was struck with the neatness of the people. Every man who pretended to wear a shirt wore a clean one. Clean boots, clothes, cravats were conspicuous everywhere. The servants, with their white collars and neck-cloths and black coats . . . the clean table-cloths in the eating-houses, the clean floors and walls, and the clean, well-arranged shops, bade defiance to the smoky air and . . . dripping sky."[142]

The cleanliness of the streets themselves, observed by travelers at mid-century, still prevailed. "I have never, in any city in the United States, or in Europe, found the streets so clean and so well paved as in London . . . not only the leading avenues . . . but every side street and every little back street. . . . I am confident," declared banker Claudius Patten in the eighties, "that London streets are kept in a far smoother and cleaner condition than are the streets of Boston and New York, notwithstanding the enormous traffic and travel that encumbers them."[143] Theron Crawford made the same observation, adding that "it is the public sentiment of London that keeps its streets so clean. In the lowest quarter the streets are as clean as in the best quarters of New York."[144] Upon his arrival back in America, in 1881, James Scripps decided that "New York looks very dirty in contrast with the cities we have seen abroad."[145]

Londoners were then still dependent on horses as the primary means of locomotive power. The problem of horse droppings was neatly solved by the "scavenger boys," as one tourist called them. There is "a force of street workers in London, under city pay, of boys from the age of fourteen to sixteen years, who are termed 'street slippers' in the local vocabulary," observed Patten.

> These little fellows, who are about the age and general style of the London boot-blacks, are paid wages of nine pence a day or so; and their special duty is to keep the streets clear of the filth made by the horses. Each boy carries in his hand a small broom and a small box; and the rapid, lively manner in which they dart among the flying teams and saddle horses, and whisk into their boxes the manure of the street, rightly entitles them to the name of "slippers". The contents of the little boxes are emptied into larger boxes at regular intervals along the streets. These . . . are emptied daily of their contents, by city wagons . . . and sold to farmers.[146]

Marveling at the agility of these same boys, William Hichborn, near the end of the century, observed them "located about one hundred feet apart through all the principal streets. . . . They dodged in between teams and carriages on their hands and knees and seemed to be as spry as cats."[147] These boys, whose official name was "Street Orderly Boys," wore little white jackets, rough corduroy trousers, a cap with a brass badge and number. They worked from eight to five, with a half hour off for lunch and a brief rest in mid-afternoon when traffic slowed for a time. According to a London journalist J. D. Symon, writing in the *English Illustrated Magazine* in 1898, their pay was nine shillings a week—"really much better than many more 'genteel' occupations. 'And after work?' I asked them. 'What then?' 'Why,' said the urchins eagerly anticipating the stroke of five, 'Why, then, sir, we *play!*' "[148]

Still a novelty to visiting Americans were London's crossing sweepers. In the 1890s journalist Elizabeth Banks counted fourteen of them during her walk from Oxford Circus to Charing Cross, and for their services she distributed a total of twelve pence and a ha'penny. To gain material for articles Elizabeth was ready to try anything; among other occupations, including that of housemaid, laundry worker, and sweatshop seamstress, she had a go at both crossing sweeping and flower selling. In two articles, both published in the *English Illustrated Magazine,* she confessed to finding the jobs more arduous than they appeared and also to meeting a degree of hostility from the minions whose meager living these jobs provided. "I hold that the sweep is not a beggar," she concluded when she finished her experiment, "but a man of business, however humble his line of operations may be." She achieved similar respect for the tough, tireless creatures who worked as "flower girls," like the Eliza Doolittle Shaw depicted in *Pygmalion.*[149]

"Buskers," street musicians and entertainers, continued to surprise American visitors "as something quite foreign . . . which we hardly expected to have seen in the streets of London, but rather supposed to be confined to vivacious Italy," as artist-illustrator Felix Darley wrote. "Sometimes we were regaled by an exhibition of 'ground and lofty tumbling' on an outspread carpet, or charmed by a band of wind instruments, or a female ballad-singer. . . . Now we have a learned monkey who discharges a gun . . . at another time the redoubtable Punch and his life-long associate, Judy . . . again, a band of Ethiopian minstrels in their striped unmentionables and long-tailed blue" [coats].[150] Still the "screevers," or sidewalk artists, made their appearance, as a visitor noted in 1889. "Often one sees a boy or man with colored crayons making beautiful pictures on the smooth stones of the sidewalk. You cannot but pause to admire them, stretching for many yards, and often the product of real genius. You will soon see in large letters: 'Will you not contribute to aid a poor ambitious youth?' "[151]

The English capacity for enjoying a holiday continued to astonish these Yankee products of the Protestant work ethic. "They give themselves up to enjoyment much more than we do," an American clergyman observed back at mid-century. "Here at home it is all 'get, get'; but there, the desire to enjoy prevails."[152] In London, observed Stephen Fiske nearly two decades later,

"the number of working-days is practically only four and a half. First, Sunday has to be deducted from the week; then the labouring-classes do not care to labour on blue Monday; then the Saturday half-holiday must be subtracted; and what with Volunteer parades, Crystal Palace fêtes, public receptions, Reform demonstrations, military and naval reviews, Lord Mayors' Shows, Good Friday, Christmas, and other religious holidays, great cricket-matches, the Derby, the University boat races, and many other metropolitan festivals, the Londoners contrive to secure at least another half a day of relaxation per week on the average. They are the same sort of pleasure-loving people as their ancestors, who used to dance around bon-fires in the narrow streets of the old city, and play at quintain before the lords and ladies at Smithfield. The games have changed, but not the popular disposition.[153]

"They give themselves up to enjoyment much more than we do," observed **Daniel Eddy** of Londoners and the English people in general. *The Graphic,* vol. IV, September 9, 1871, p. 252. *Courtesy the Library of Congress.*

"No American, unless he be a sporting man, ever goes to the Derby twice," warned journalist David Ross Locke—otherwise known as Petroleum V. Nasby—in 1881, speaking of one of nineteenth-century London's great holidays. "It is necessary to go once to see it, but once is quite enough. It is a sight to see three hundred thousand people in one mass, but it is not a pleasant thing to realize the fact that two-thirds or more of their number are under the influence of liquor ... and went there with no other idea."[154] Horace Greeley had resolutely stayed away in 1851 because of "all the Gambling, Intoxication and Licentiousness" he knew would be there.[155] But most Americans went to the derby if they could manage it, and, if they let themselves, had a very good time.

In the eighties and nineties many Americans, even Henry James, made the journey out to the derby on the tops of hired coaches decorated with American flags and carrying huge hampers stuffed with "sandwiches, boiled eggs, lobster salad, cheese cakes, bottles of ale, bottles of lemonade, a bottle of milk, oranges and champagne"—which is what Elizabeth Peake's contained, at any rate.[156] Theron Crawford called it "really an overgrown picnic ... a day of holiday making, and the scenes on Epsom Downs are those to be found at any great country fair in England on a pleasant day, multiplied many times over." The sight of the American flag, he observed, was always a signal for the minstrels to strike up Yankee Doodle, and for small boys along the road to cry, " 'Chuck out your rolling coppers!' "[157] Elizabeth Peake, returning to London from the derby on May 25, 1871, in the massive crowds thronging the way spotted "a young soldier with one leg standing beside the roadside. I threw him the biggest orange I had," she recalled, "and he, fearful that some who were walking near him might get it, threw down both crutches and hopped till he caught it. The fun seemed to grow more 'fast and furious' the nearer we came to London," she wrote. And "just before entering the city, the Prince of Wales, with postillions and outriders, dashed by us. We reached our hotel a little before sunset, perfectly satisfied with Darby-day."[158]

"Tourists have rummaged London from end to end," wrote an American near the end of the century, "yet it still interests and fills the stranger with astonishment. The more he knows of it, the more he wishes to know."[159]

"How can they expect us to 'do' all this?" asked Charles Wood. "There is so much to be seen."[160] Almost as if answering him, old Dr. Holmes wrote: "No

Return from Epsom on Derby Day. "The fun seemed to grow more 'fast and furious' the nearer we came to London," observed Elizabeth Peake in 1871. They were passed by the Prince of Wales! *Illustrated London News,* **June 3, 1854, p. 512.** *Courtesy the Library of Congress.*

person can be said to know London. The most that anyone can claim is that he knows something of it."[161]

"We find ourselves in love with London," confessed Louise Moulton, a lady who had begun her stay in the great city with complaints about dim lights, no rocking chairs, and open fires "that burn your nose and freeze your back."[162] Packing her trunk in the Westminster Palace Hotel—a great favorite of Americans, just across from the Abbey itself—little Annie Wolf took time to write of London in her journal in March 1878, "I wonder if I shall ever see it all again?"[163]

"The greatest wonder that England has to show the wanderer from the other side of the sea is London," wrote Henry Martyn Field in 1875; "not the Tower, nor Westminster Abbey, nor the Houses of Parliament, but London itself. . . . London is to the modern world what Rome was to the ancient world—the centre to which come all races of men from the ends of the earth. To 'take it all in' is something which no man ever did, or can!"[164]

Not all Americans would go as far as Henry James in his love of London. Then again, many of them would. "The capital of the human race happens to be British," thought James. "Surely every other people would have it theirs if they could. . . . The sense of life is greatest there."[165]

22

The British Sabbath

"Sunday in London is almost as sedate as Sunday in Philadelphia," observed Colonel John Forney of the typical late nineteenth-century Sabbath in that city.[1] The visiting Americans livened it up, however, by taking in on that day one of the most important tourist objectives, or "lions," in London during the second half of the century. The Reverend Charles Spurgeon, a self-made Baptist preacher, was sought after by these Yankee pilgrims almost as if he were a Protestant pope. Their accounts of visits to the Metropolitan Tabernacle of this "British Beecher," as some of them referred to him, are innumerable, repetitious, frequently fulsome, and yet in the end undeniably impressive. Obviously, this short, square, toothy, bustling, crowd-manipulating preacher supplied some article vital to the spiritual diet of these visiting Americans as well as to his own loyal London parishioners. "His name has become a household word throughout Europe and America," wrote the Reverend Walter Whittle.[2]

"No preacher in England since Edward Irving," declared the American pastor Henry Field, brother of David Dudley Field and Cyrus W. Field, "has had such popularity as Mr. Spurgeon. He is one of the lions of London—who since his appearance in the field has roared so loudly as to make all nations hear, and every stranger who wishes to 'do' the sights of this Babylon, must, for once at least, see and hear him."[3] Methodist Bishop Gilbert Haven, who, along with a number of other skeptics, confessed to "a previous prejudice against him," also fell under the spell once he heard him speak. "He is a very remarkable man," concluded Haven, "the greatest preacher, I think, I have ever heard."[4]

Spurgeon had begun his career as a sort of religious prodigy, attaining the pastorate of London's New Park Street Baptist Chapel at nineteen. From that moment on his preaching drew ever larger crowds, necessitating in 1855 the hiring of Exeter Hall in the Strand to accommodate them and then the larger Surrey Music Hall across the Thames. Cabbies, spotting the human tide moving toward the bridges on Sunday, would call out to prospective fares, "Over the river to Charlie?'"[5] By this time Spurgeon was preaching, including both morning and evening services, to about ten thousand people each Sabbath.

In 1861 Spurgeon completed the building of his own huge Metropolitan Tabernacle across the river, near the famous landmark the Elephant and Castle—once a famous coaching stop and travel center and today just another London traffic rotary—at a cost of almost $140,000, with "every cent [of it] paid before the first hallelujah was sung," reported one of his Yankee admirers.[6] This

"Every cent of it paid for before the first hallelujah was sung," remarked Thomas
Handford of Spurgeon's Tabernacle. *Illustrated London News,* **April 6, 1861, p. 319.**
Courtesy the Library of Congress.

immense, neo-Grecian structure, capable of holding up to seven thousand
worshipers, was usually filled to capacity; and the faithful, including countless
American tourists, queued early for seats. "He draws like a blister plaster,"
snorted "Free Thinker" De Robigne Mortimer Bennett enviously.[7] One American remembered seeing crowds gathering on a wet Sunday, "people hurrying
through the rain in every direction, the whole region seeming black with
umbrellas."[8] Strangers, asking omnibus drivers if they stopped at the Elephant
and Castle, were told automatically, "We go right by Spurgeon's; set you down at
the door."

Visitors willing to slip a "special offering" of a shilling into an envelope, and
this included most tourists, were admitted early through a side door. One who
would not, and thus took his chances with the crowd, was the Reverend
Benjamin Bausman, who suddenly found himself swept through the door "by a
rushing crowd in a most ungraceful and undevout style and landed on a window
sill in one of the galleries . . . such a congregation as we had, I never saw before
indoors."[9]

"Mr. Spurgeon's Tabernacle has about twice the seating capacity of Plymouth

Church," noted Mrs. Harrington, making the inevitable comparison with the Reverend Henry Ward Beecher's installation back home in Brooklyn.[10] The tabernacle, wrote Burr Polk, "very much resembles a theater with three tiers, except that the upper two run all the way around the house, while at the lower one, where a stage would be, runs out a platform for the choir, and above this, not extending so far out, is another platform which serves as a pulpit. A plain railing runs around both of these, the pulpit itself being a plain table. . . . There is no ornamentation about the building."[11]

Spurgeon's charisma was analyzed by many a Yankee observer. "A born actor," claimed Bausman.[12] "Utterly free . . . from the tricks of the stage," judged John Kennedy, who had "expected to find an actor."[13]

Spurgeon is frequently described as "hurrying" up to his pulpit and always as being very punctual. "Exactly at the hour," wrote one observer, "Mr. Spurgeon stepped quickly on the platform."[14] No one ever called Spurgeon handsome. "Common looking," judged one young lady.[15] "Short, fat, round-faced and good-natured looking," wrote the Reverend Joseph Cross.[16] "Fond of roast beef, plump and well fed," was the Reverend Bausman's description.[17] "A short, stoutish, solid man with much of the appearance of a substantial farmer," wrote another.[18] Mary Wills found him more "a religious exhorter than a logical thinker" and decided also that his protruding teeth "render the expression of his mouth unpleasant." She noticed the famous American evangelists, "Messrs. Moody and Sankey, among the number, they taking no part, however, in the exercises."[19]

When Spurgeon began to speak, however, all such considerations were apparently forgotten. "His countenance is radiant, spiritual, and wonderfully vivid in its play and in its prompt adaptation to the thought he utters," declared the noted author and cleric, the Reverend Andrew Peabody of Harvard, in 1868. "His voice is the finest I ever heard."[20] According to all accounts, Spurgeon's greatest asset was a remarkably clear voice which, together with the good acoustics of the tabernacle, carried his message to every ear of the thousands gathered to hear him. "His clear voice rings every syllable through the entire building; a voice used in a natural tone, without the least perceptible exertion," remarked Bausman.[21] Junius Browne observed, "I was as far off as anyone in the congregation, and I did not miss a syllable."[22] Together with audibility, Spurgeon apparently combined plain language, fluency, and an interesting regional pronunciation of words like "mood" which he rhymed with "good," and "Lord" which he pronounced "Lard," according to one of his listeners.[23]

There are frequent references to Spurgeon's "lapses into vulgar expressions, common even to coarseness," as Cross indicated.[24] One searches in vain for an example until prim Mary Terhune who, after expressing her hesitance "to record a sentence that shocked me to disgust as being not only in atrocious taste and an unfortunate figure of speech, but . . . [also] irreverent," shared with her readers the following quote from out of the mouth of the preacher. "If we are not filled," declared the Reverend Spurgeon, "if we are not filled, it is because we do not hang upon and suck at those blessed breasts of God's promises as we might and should do."[25]

It was not difficult for the American visitors to quote from and even recapitu-

The Reverend Charles Haddon Spurgeon, called by some "The Protestant Pope". *The Graphic,* vol. XLV, February 6, 1892, p. 169. *Courtesy the Library of Congress.*

late parts of sermons for their readers, as some of them did, for they were taken down in shorthand "by as many as nine quill-drivers at a time," as one traveler observed, and then reported in the newspapers and printed up as tracts.[26] Spurgeon's sermons appeared to be virtually extemporaneous. One viewer thought that he observed "a small piece of paper" in the preacher's fist.[27] Another believed that Spurgeon spoke "entirely without notes."[28] The Reverend Theodore Cuyler of Brooklyn, on a visit to Spurgeon at his villa in Sydenham in the 1880s, settled the matter when the famous preacher confessed that he "never selected a text until the close of Saturday, after which he devotes a half hour to arranging his heads or divisions, jotting them down on a small bit of paper. Two of these which he gave to me are written on the back of letter envelopes," wrote Cuyler. "He said he would rather be hung than to attempt to write a sermon and that he never pre-composed a single sentence before entering the pulpit."[29]

The simplicity of Spurgeon's subject matter, based four-square on the *Bible,* dealing primarily with sin and the duty of each individual to battle it in his own mind and heart, apparently precluded the need for scholarly notes. "His sermon was perfectly transparent," wrote Bausman. "No nibbling at disputed questions of theology, nothing equivocal. Not much to excite future reflection or investigation, no points that he left his hearers to analyze or untangle. The dish had just enough nourishment for the occasion."[30] Spurgeon's colorful examples, lifted directly from everyday life and contemporary events, further reinforced the interest of his listeners. One American recalled Spurgeon's saying, during one of his latter-day illnesses: "The Master has handled me roughly, but I rejoice to follow him. I would rather be a dog following Jesus than be the devil's darling."[31] Even William Falkner, who tended to denigrate most everything British, responded to Spurgeon. "Sometimes I would imagine this man could see and read my very thoughts," wrote Falkner who had come to scoff but remained to pray. "There was a shrinkage of two hundred percent in my self-conceit in the short space of one hour."[32]

While not neglecting his own parishioners, Spurgeon seems to have played up to his many American visitors. For one thing, eager to hear him speak, they were very quick to fill the little envelopes handed out at the door for contributions, which gained them early admission and good seats. Frequently, he called attention to the presence of Americans in the audience, and he was always gracious to those who sought him out for introductions after the service. One traveler wrote: "After communion we went up to shake hands and found him a really pleasant, jovial, warm-hearted man, 'glad to see everybody from America', who, with a warm grasp of the hand said, 'God bless you my brothers, and take you all back home in safety.' "[33] Lucy Culler, herself the wife of a clergyman, was shocked at "the audacity of an American lady who, no sooner had the benediction been pronounced, ... was up in the pulpit soliciting Mr. Spurgeon's autograph. Think of it!"[34] A North Carolina clergyman, P. L. Groome, introduced himself to Spurgeon with the remark that he felt he had seen one of the greatest men who ever lived. To this Spurgeon smiled and said, " 'Well, you have seen a great somebody indeed!' "[35]

Part of the mutual attraction between Spurgeon and his American admirers perhaps stemmed from his anti-Establishment attitude, which appealed to the more chauvinistic tourists. In 1879 James McClay quoted Spurgeon as saying that "England has waged two unjust wars in which there could be no glory, for it was the strong fighting the weak. Out upon the policy that makes people call England the growlers and snarlers among nations. England is today shedding innocent blood without just cause. Surely, the curse must follow, yes, it is at hand. Call this political or not, it is true. Do what you will with it, I have said it." Commented McClay further: "I fancy it would hardly do for one of our clergymen to meddle with politics as freely as Spurgeon did today. He echoes public sentiment, however, for they think here among the most intelligent classes that the Zulu War was unnecessary and was badly managed. They seem to consider Lord Beaconsfield what we should call a demagogue."[36] On that same occasion Spurgeon was heard not only to excoriate Britain's imperial policy which "brought so many wars upon their hands," but also to assert that it had "invaded domains they had no right to, and that Great Britain, in that respect, was no better than a thief or robber, using those very words," reported Burr Polk with astonishment.[37]

"The radicalism of the man" was how Salon Thacher of Kansas referred in 1883 to the spirit of the preacher as revealed "in his petition for the Queen, being qualified with 'as we are bound to do'; while that for the United States was without explanation, and overflowing with good feeling."[38]

Only a handful of Americans reacted to Spurgeon with a negative response altogether. One young woman referred to his "use of claptraps to gain attention."[39] Joseph Battell simply pronounced him "an elaborate failure."[40] William Brawley, the battered young Confederate veteran with one arm but two good eyes for the ladies, later a well-known Charleston judge, called Spurgeon "this famous humbug."[41]

Beginning in the early seventies there were steadily increasing references to the ailment that sapped Spurgeon's vitality and finally ended his life at the age of fifty-eight. Commonly alluded to as "gout," the condition caused him to limp rather than bustle up to his pulpit as of old; to rest his leg on a chair seat as he spoke; and to be seen "moving stiffly in the pulpit as if he feared the awakening of slumbering pain."[42] Finally, there are repeated references to cancellation of appearances, to the great disappointment of visiting Americans who had counted on seeing him as one of the great London "lions." In 1892 Robert Young of Nashville reported that "Mr. Spurgeon appears to be nearing his end. . . . Messages of sympathy are wired from all parts of the Christian world. The Primate of the Church of England has visited him. The Archdeacon of London has eulogized him from the pulpit of St. Paul's Cathedral."[43] A few short years after Spurgeon's death, Peter Hamilton revisited the tabernacle where so many had flocked to hear Spurgeon in his prime, and for a moment he recalled "the sleepy-looking man whom I once heard preach there a good, plain sermon. I remember that he accented Deuteronomy on the fourth syllable and earnestly prayed for rain."[44] Dr. George Maughs of St. Louis would remember Spurgeon as an earnest crusader against doctrines of men like Comte, Spencer and Darwin.[45] In 1888 the Reverend Zachary Taylor Sweeney declared that Charles Spurgeon was "more familiar to Americans than any other living Englishman . . . and for nearly thirty years has drawn and held the largest audience in the world." Sweeney maintained, moreover, that the preacher had never become "puffed up by his marvelous success" nor "disposed to become the Baptist Pope," as detractors had claimed.[46]

Despite its primary emphasis on the traditional liturgy, the Church of England in this period also possessed crowd-drawing preachers. In the seventies throngs queued every Sunday at St. Paul's to hear Canon Liddon, and the mad rush when the doors were opened astonished Elizabeth Peake in 1871. "No sooner was the door opened," she recalled, "than a general foot-race commenced; such rushing and pushing I never saw in my life but once, and that was in Barnum's old museum."[47] On Sunday afternoons at Westminster Abbey Dean Stanley would preach, as one American described it, "to a living sea of heads stretching out every broad aisle as far as the voice will reach. The wave of his audience even overflows the generous provision of the seats and surges up and over the tombs of the historic dead. On the confines of the seated congregation throng dark clouds of standing listeners, ever moving restlessly for some point of vantage."[48] One traveler recalled that her husband had to stand throughout an entire service in the Abbey while she perched on "a projection of a marble monument about six inches wide."[49] Stanley apparently read his sermons, but one American concluded that this did not matter, as "it is the exquisite English of these sermons and their gentle spirit which draws all London and all the world of travel to hear them."[50]

Dean Stanley's unfailing kindness to American visitors is recorded in many accounts of personally conducted tours of the Abbey about which he knew so much. Small, white-haired, and "with wrinkles that spoke of age," there was nevertheless "something in his manner that seemed to savor of perpetual youth," recalled one American after Stanley's death. "He came forward and shook hands with such a sweet, gentle smile of welcome that no one but the Fenian who wrote threatening letters during his last illness, could have resisted its charm."[51] In the official history of the Abbey, *A House of Kings,* Dean Stanley is credited with having done much to make the Abbey a great national monument for the public. Stanley would have liked it to have been open free every day of the year but recognized the need to charge for admission to the Royal Chapels in order to pay the staff needed to guard the building. "Then, as now," so goes the text, ". . . protection was required against 'mischievous boys,' eccentric or crazy persons, and relic hunters."[52]

The Reverend Theodore Cuyler, pastor of the Lafayette Avenue church in Brooklyn, attended Stanley's funeral. "The crowd in the Abbey was prodigious," he recalled.

Many of the guests climbed on the monuments. . . . The heir to the throne marched in and occupied the pew of his old tutor, who was lying in the coffin before him. . . . By the foot of the coffin the most conspicuous figure was William E. Gladstone. . . . The Dean had been to me a very kind and beloved friend. I had broken bread with him in his hospitable home. I had enjoyed with him a memorable visit to the Jerusalem Chamber; and on his last day in America he had gone with me to Greenwood Cemetery and had asked me to conduct him to the grave of Dr. Edward Robinson, and to the spot where slumbers my own loved child.[53]

Canon Farrar, Stanley's successor, drew equally large crowds. "A great crowd stood for nearly half an hour before the doors of the Abbey," reported Charles Wood, "waiting with as much patience as possible for their opening. The moment the bolts were drawn, a mass of pushing, crowding, elbowing human beings rushed through the aisles, some over the backs of the pews into the most advantageously located seats ... Could they have been Episcopalians?" he wondered.[54] Eliza Connor could not get close enough to hear much of Farrar's sermon. "I caught little more than one sentence clearly, but that one, uttered in the deep, musical tones of Canon Farrar, was worth going to Westminster Abbey to hear. I shall never forget it: 'The world,' he said, 'is no worse now than it has been for centuries. In some respects, it is better today than it ever was before.' "[55]

An interesting result of the special consideration with which American Episcopal bishops and priests were treated by their brethren of the Church of England was pointed out by Joel Cook. After visits with the Archbishop of Canterbury at Lambeth Palace, the American clergy sometimes emerged speaking of the Anglican church as "the nursing mother" and with a penchant for gaiters. "So many American clergymen are in England," reported Cook in the summer of 1878, "particularly of the Episcopal Church, whose great conference has just closed, that many pulpits are being filled with my countrymen, and at the two great churches of London, St. Paul's Cathedral and Westminster Abbey, American bishops preached the sermons yesterday. In England," Cook pointed out, "a Bishop is always a 'lord bishop,' so that on making the inquiry at St. Paul's I was informed that the 'Lord Bishop of Nebraska' was preaching the sermon, and was given a printed notice announcing that 'the Lord Bishop of Pittsburgh' would preach ... next Sunday."[56] All this English "pomp and circumstance" went to the heads of some of these Yankee clerics, according to Adam Badeau of the United States legation, and they were seen to acquire "breeches and aprons," like those worn by their English counterparts, "to wear to dinner."[57]

American evangelicals, such as Baptists, Methodists, and Presbyterians, reacted much in the manner of their predecessors at mid-century to evidences of "Puseyism" or "Ritualism" in the Anglican church. "The candles, tapers, and an illuminated cross" at St. Paul's, complained a visitor in 1880, "made the service seem like a Roman Catholic performance, despite Canon Liddon's masterly sermon."[58] Another tourist considered the choral service at the Temple "very Romish."[59]

Those evangelical Protestants who really wanted to suffer martyrdom and to share the experience with their readers, took themselves to London's St. Alban's, "the famous ritualistic church," where they gazed horrified on the "attempt to appropriate the useless trappings of Romanism in order to produce a dramatic effect," including incense, genuflecting, and the sign of the cross "all shockingly overdone," complained John Pendleton Kennedy, prominent American politician and onetime secretary of the navy.[60] At St. Andrew's, in Wells Street, reported Ella Thompson, "the Protestantism is so very 'high' as to be clean out of sight."[61]

Boston's famed convert to Roman Catholicism, Father George Foxcroft Haskins, on the other hand, was delighted at the progress that Ritualism was making. "The defenders of Ritualism ... are in earnest ... determined ... brave ... they mean to stand. Such men *ought* to be CATHOLICS, and I believe, will be; they cannot long be content with imitation."[62]

The Reverend Charles Spurgeon had had something to say about "this spread of idolatry over the land," observed Junius Browne, and in one of his prayers he asked for "redemption from foreign influences of Popery and Ritualism which is the same thing."[63]

So aware of the boatloads of Irish emigrants headed for the United States were the Americans—and so quick were they to blame all of Ireland's troubles on the Catholic Church—that one must conclude that they were haunted by the growth of that religion in their own country, which they still liked to think of as a Protestant nation. "Where Protestantism prevails, the people are intelligent and thrifty," observed an American traveler in Ireland in the seventies. Of the rest of the country, he added, "it is all the reverse under Romanism, which is the curse of the country."[64] Presbyterian Janet Collins was quite disturbed when she and her companion were taken for Catholics in Ireland by a hotel "runner" leading them to his establishment. Pointing out a large church under construction, he remarked proudly that considerable American money was going into its building. " 'That's what's the matter with you,' " snapped Mrs. Collins. " 'You build these fine churches and starve in idleness and expect others to help you out.' "[65]

"The multitudes are ignorant, degraded Papists," pronounced Henry Day, prominent American corporation lawyer, in 1872.

A system that makes the Virgin Mary or the priest a god, that palliates injustice, fraud, and falsehood, that turns truth into fables and closes the book of knowledge,—such a system of religion will ever debase a people. Give Ireland a Protestant religion, and how quick would parental training and education change the whole character of the people—and a splendid people they would be! The native talent, wit, and ardor of the Irish people, when once elevated, would make a remarkable nation as Burke, Grattan, O'Connell and Wellington well prove. Parliament would at once introduce the compulsory common-school system into Ireland, as they have already into Scotland, if the Irish would stand it; but they will not; and why? Because the priest will not allow it. Their religion forbids it.[66]

In any event, these primarily white Anglo-Saxon Protestant American travelers seemed to take comfort in the might and power of the great, officially Protestant nation ruled by Victoria. The religious picture might be changing back home, but here in England Catholics were less in evidence and still obviously "in their place."

Another aspect of religion in nineteenth-century Britain, oddly enough, called forth considerable negative comment from American travelers: the Salvation Army. Visiting in York in 1885, William Gage was appalled to find in the same city as that great cathedral "a great following of these noisy Salvationists,—a strong proof that the English Church, with all its beauty and taste, has not touched the dregs of the people!" The singing, beating of drums, accordions, loud cornets, and trumpets, all in a military style, gave great offence to prim puritans from America. "As I see the excited women who march in their ranks, and the rough and ill-dressed men who lead . . . I am filled at once with disgust and pity," wrote Gage.[67] "Some of its advertisements seem almost sacrilegious to a refined Christian person," observed preacher's wife Lucy Culler, although her

General William Booth, founder of the Salvation Army, was "cool as a statue in the midst of his noisy and enthusiastic followers," observed Robert Young. *The Graphic*, vol. XLIII, January 3, 1891, p. 1.

husband went to a Salvation Army meeting at Congress Hall in London in 1882 "to learn something of its workings."[68]

A coaching party at Ilfracombe in the eighties was shocked by "the clash of a brass band . . . in the public streets in moral England on Sunday! . . . . Such a profanation of the day would not be permitted even in New York," declared John Champlin, Carnegie's friend. Referring to the Army as "a nineteenth century anachronism," Champlin

> gazed at the solemn farce with as much curiosity as he would have bestowed on the procession of Juggernaut. Perhaps he ought to say . . . Juggernaut in *England,* for the outings of the bloody god within his own heathen jurisdiction would be far less remarkable than are the parades of the Salvation Army in a civilized Christian land [with] this warlike masquerading . . . the leader with a black cloth cap . . . and a red woolen shirt and black trousers. . . . Young women in black dresses . . . red jackets, and all had a piece of red ribbon around the bonnet or hat. . . . At a signal from their leader they pounded their tambourines and shouted "Halleloo!" . . . with an energy worthy of a better cause,

remarked this observer caustically.[69]

Another visitor noticed a similar scene in Liverpool, where "a flabby bass-drum and a consumptive brass horn, accompanied by a wheezing fife, were making a most fearful noise, while a motley crowd of men, women, and yelling boys marched after them. All were singing, though everyone appeared to be running a separate concert. . . . If that's the army that the cause of Christ has to depend on for support, it's a ruined community for certain," declared the American.[70] These ragged, noisy gatherings of Britain's poor in the streets of her cities did not, obviously, measure up to those middle-class standards of "respectability" with which most of these nineteenth-century Americans identified their own Protestant religion at home.

Only occasionally does one of them unbend to express any understanding or approval. "The Salvationists," insisted Charles Taylor, "have by their indefatigable labors reclaimed thousands of these men and women from their lives of sin and misery. You will meet these untiring workers everywhere, exhorting, praying, pleading with fallen humanity. . . . They fear nothing, knowing that their cause is God's cause."[71] Bishop Phillips Brooks of Massachusetts attended an "All Night With Jesus" rally in London in May 1883. Observing the ill-fed, ill-clad enthusiasts, he found it "noisy and unpleasant, but there was nothing very bad about it, and I am not sure it might not do good to somebody."[72] General William Booth himself, the founder of the Army, was described by another traveler who attended one of his services in London "as an old gentleman (with an immense beard), who puts on quiet airs, and seems cool as a statue in the midst of his noisy and enthusiastic followers."[73]

Still, the Salvationists' unbridled, lower-class fervor continued to rile American travelers, including one who was setting out atop a coach with a small party of tourists for a bit of quiet sightseeing on a *Sunday* afternoon up in Scotland. They should have known better. Fixing her blazing eyes on one gentleman in particular, a fire-breathing Salvation Army Lassie accosted him. " 'Do you know that you are going straight to hell and damnation?' " she demanded. " 'No!' " protested the red and embarrassed Yankee. " 'I am going to see the Forth Bridge!' "[74]

Kindness to strangers from abroad appears to be a virtue with the English. This sentiment I can fully corroborate by personal experience, never having found twenty days of greater pleasure in my life, than were spent in England.
—John Bender, *A Hoosier's Experience in Western Europe,* 1874

Conclusion

Preparing to embark on his last voyage in 1886, Dr. Oliver Wendell Holmes looked back over his long life (1809–1894) as physician and author, a life that virtually spanned the nineteenth century.

> With regard to the changes in the general conditions of society and the advance in human knowledge, think for one moment what fifty years have done! . . . Ocean steamers, the railroads that spread themselves like cobwebs over the civilized and half-civilized portions of the earth; the telegraph and the telephone, the photograph and the spectroscope . . . the electric light . . . the friction match. . . . anaesthesia . . . the later conclusions of geology . . . the fully developed law of the correlation of forces . . . the cell doctrine . . . the revolutionary apocalypse of Darwinism. All this change in the aspects, position, beliefs, of humanity since the date of my own graduation from college! . . . I ought to consider myself highly favored to have lived through such a half century,

concluded the little doctor.[1]

This same enthusiasm, pride, self-respect, energy, curiosity, sense of wonder, and faith in the future of mankind breathes from the pages of almost all these nineteenth-century travelers whose adventures make up this book. They considered themselves and their experiences important and worth recording, their individual responses and reactions of value and worth preserving. We have seen how, in the early decades of the century, they sought earnestly to sort out their identity as Americans, citizens of a new nation—just as toward the end of the century they worked at reestablishing the old roots and seemingly reassuring themselves of the durability of their Anglo-Saxon heritage. At all times they looked for their own past that they had left behind in the mother country. By the century's end it was as if, like Janus, on one side they looked wistfully back at a past gone forever, while on the other side they hopefully faced the future—although not without some anxiety over the great and unceasing changes they perceived in their society.

A persistent theme crops up in the reminiscences of these nineteenth-century Americans in, of all places, their accounts of their visits to the Tower of London. Gazing on the strange weapons in the armory, peering into fearful places of confinement, and shuddering at instruments of torture, Octavia LeVert, of Mobile, Alabama, for one, was moved to remark at mid-century: "I thanked the good God that those dark days have vanished before the clear light of civilization."[2]

"No man can listen to these tales of blood without being impressed with the fact that the world is growing better," declared another American near the

century's end. "Human life has . . . become much more sacred . . . human right
are better guarded . . . humanity has broadened, deepened, and become more
intense."[3] These typical expressions of nineteenth-century optimism, elicited in a
setting redolent of man's inhumanity to man, were echoed by many other
travelers, and they now sound curiously quaint to us in the twentieth century
with all our new and improved ways to make fellow creatures suffer.

"You are reminded of the startling difference between the days in which such
wrongs were committed," remarked politician John Forney just after the Civil
War, "and the triumphs of a higher civilization, when Englishmen, however
proud of all that is honorable in the past, do not hesitate to labor for a better
condition of things in the future."[4] Visiting the Tower in the seventies J. J. Smith
found "that though much . . . within its walls is sad, it is nevertheless pleasant to
see how glorious is the present compared with the past. We live in a better age
than did our ancestors."[5]

"I cross the drawbridge," wrote William Stevenson on leaving the Tower in
1881, "stepping again into the world of the nineteenth century, and try to realize
I am within a mile of the busiest business centre of the commercial world of
today; and brushing away my dreams of the dim and shadowy past, I thank God
that during all these centuries the world has been growing better."[6] Declared
New Hampshireman Leonard Morrison: "The future is big with hope, radiant
with promise. Every American has reason for gratitude his home is beneath
American skies, and that over him is the protecting banner of the wise and great
Republic." As for the American people, he said, "if they are not a happy and
prosperous people, the fault is in . . . themselves."[7]

Something of this same hopeful spirit colors all the more serious observations
of the American traveler in England; and underneath all their complaints and
invidious comparisons, their Yankee pride, rivalry, and chauvinism, and despite
recurrent political differences, they found much in the old parent nation to love
and to cherish as their historical and cultural heritage.

"The two countries are so much alike and yet so different," observed Stephen
Fiske in 1869,

> that at every step there is something new to learn—something to imitate—
> something to avoid. In some respects, the Americans are centuries in advance
> of the English people; in others, we Transatlantic folks, compared with the
> English, are barbarians. If I were forced to sum up the characteristics of the
> two nations in a single sentence, I should say that the English are too fond of
> retaining old ideas because they are old, and that the Americans are too fond
> of adopting new ideas because they are new. Too much Conservatism *versus*
> too much rapid Progress—this is England and America in a nut-shell.[8]

How energetically the Americans applied themselves to comparisons, studying
everything in sight and contrasting it with what they knew at home. A British
literary critic has said that the nineteenth-century American visitor in Britain
appears to have been searching for "a negative definition of himself" and thus
was actually "intent on making England cogently, dramatically different from
the United States"—depicting it "as a land of comic hyperbole, perpetually
fogbound, snobbish, lazy."[9] One will see that this is not quite accurate if one has
the chance to read widely and deeply in the vast accumulation of American

commentary by writers both noted and obscure, both professional and amateur, and from a variety of backgrounds. All through the century there can be seen appreciation and admiration—often approaching love—of Britain and the British way of life in these American accounts, save for those few written as obvious polemic tracts around the middle of the century.

Hardly had they stepped wearily off their ships at Liverpool, when they began to savor the contrasts between Britain and America. "It is difficult for an American in England to avoid comparisons," Mrs. Kirkland pointed out at mid-century. "These begin as soon as we land, when the first thing that strikes us is the plain, substantial air of everything."[10] A traveler a decade earlier observed that "here everything appears on a great and grand scale. All seems to carry an air of stability: iron lamp, bridge, gallery, piazza, gate posts, and almost everything for which we use heavy timber, is there substituted by iron. The houses are built to shelter the heads of ten generations yet to come."[11]

"You are scarcely landed on the shores of England, before you are struck by the solidity and durability of everything around you.... The houses, the furniture, the public buildings, even the people, seem built to last.... And what beasts of burden!" marveled Orville Horwitz. "The English draught horses are young mastodons!"[12]

In the summer of 1877 Kansan Noble Prentis wrote home to the *Topeka Commonwealth* about "the enormous strength and solidity of everything." In Liverpool he observed

the pavements of great stones; the warehouses which look as if they had stood for all time and were ready for eternity ... the enormous amount of brass-work everywhere; and the big knockers on the doors, which would break in an American door. Everything is in the same proportion, horses as big as elephants, shod with high-corked shoes, hauling a load for a small locomotive, go clanking up and down the rocky ways; and omnibuses are rolling about, drawn by three horses abreast; and the street car, lately introduced, is a huge, lumbering contrivance with a circular stairway for people to climb up on top—for English people love to ride outside in the rain.[13]

"The greatness of England extends even to these little things," Prentis continued,

but the fierce pride of this people, their unconquerable bull-dog courage in war, is commemorated everywhere in great works. The docks, the like of which exist nowhere else, bear the names of Waterloo, Trafalgar, and Nelson. Wellington looks afar from the top of an enormous pillar, and Nelson is everywhere in stone and bronze.... The public buildings are enormous, all of stone, and built to last forever. I should imagine that no sensible earthquake would presume to attack them.... And yet they call this a *new* town.[14]

When it came to the interiors of buildings in Britain, Eliza Connor in the eighties remarked that "there is an exquisite finish about everything.... Nothing here is left half done. Even the furniture is satisfactory. Doors shut and bolt, and the knobs do not come off in your hands. Will my native land ever be like that? Not in my time, I'm afraid."[15]

The next impressions of recently arrived Americans in Britain usually had to do with the climate and the countryside, as they moved out of Liverpool by stagecoach or train, or on foot or bicycle, traditionally visiting Chester before heading for Shakespeare country and thence to London.

"Punch has discovered a burlesque emblem for all nationalities," wrote Henry Tuckerman in 1852. "The most appropriate for England . . . would be a tea kettle and an umbrella—one being the universal indoor cordial, and the other the great external necessity of the climate."[16] Remarked another traveler, "[T]he first thing to do on landing is to marry an umbrella, and never to separate from it on any incompatibility whatever!"[17]

Over for the Great Exhibition in 1851, and depressed by the lack of bright sun, Horace Greeley warned that, "if the day of your embarkation be fair, take a long earnest gaze at the sun, so that you will know him again when you return. They have something they call the sun over here which they show occasionally, but it looks more like a boiled turnip than it does like its American namesake. Yet they cheer us with the assurance that there *will be* real sunshine here by-and-by."[18] Elizabeth Peake told her readers that "you would go nowhere in England if you stopped for the rain. Indeed it has rained every few hours since we have been in London."[19] Harriet Beecher Stowe concluded that "this constant drizzle is good for ivies, hawthorns and ladies' complexions . . . but it certainly is very bad for tourists."[20]

The longer they stayed, however, the more the Americans came to realize that the moist climate of the British Isles was responsible for the loveliness of the countryside. "Nature waters her English plants whenever she happens to think of it," observed Ella Thompson, "and without the least calculation when she did it last; and they repay her bounty with an intense greenness and thick luxuriance, as if every separate leaf had its own polishing."[21]

"People may complain of the humid climate of England, and curse the umbrella which must accompany them whenever they walk out; but when the sun does shine, it shines upon a scene of beautiful fertility unequalled elsewhere in the world," declared Charles Fairbanks.[22] Some of the travelers even came to appreciate the role played by Britain's climate in creating the luminous quality of the light. "The abundance of moisture in the air gives, I think," wrote James Clarke in mid-century, "a most picturesque effect to all objects. All things have a silvery or pearly gray tint. Sharp outlines melt away. You see the atmosphere itself, like a liquid ocean, rolling between you and the object, and not as a transparent medium."[23] Even the English sunlight was different, another traveler decided. "The fine golden light fell like a shower upon the land . . . that delicate, vague, misty veil of light, which imparts to all English landscape a certain aqueous quality."[24]

"England is incomparably the most beautiful country in the world!" enthused Samuel Goodrich in 1857. "The sun . . . is not so hot, the air is not so highly perfumed, the buzz of the insects is not so intense. Everything is more tranquil. With us, all nature, during summer, appears to be in haste, as if its time was short—as if it feared the coming frost. In England, on the contrary, there seems to be a confidence in the seasons . . . each and all attaining their perfection at leisure."[25] England, wrote Joshua White in the century's first decade, "may indeed be said to resemble a great garden, of which the roads are the gravel walks."[26]

Heman Humphrey, president of Amherst College, accustomed to the changeable rigors of the seasons in western Massachusetts, was convinced beyond all doubt that Britain's climate was not only more pleasant but more healthful as well. "To the extremes of heat and cold, which are so trying here, they are not liable," he wrote in the 1830s.[27] Theron Crawford found British summers especially "agreeable" to Americans. "There is no day in an English summer which approaches even in a remote degree to the sweltering heat of July and August days of our northern cities."[28]

Britain's more temperate climate and lack of extremes in temperature indeed had their effect upon the temperament of her people, the Americans concluded. "The climate is not so *wasting* as ours," observed Samuel Young.[29] "Even such violent exercise as playing at ball may be indulged in with safety and pleasure, at a season of the year when in America the heat is almost intolerable," remarked Benjamin Silliman.[30] Henry Tuckerman was convinced, moreover, that Britain's cool, temperate climate, with all those gray skies and soft rain was positively conducive to "brain work," and thus he attributed much of that nation's prodigious literary output to the withdrawal "to an arm-chair and the sight of curtains and a fire."[31]

American naturalist John Burroughs considered the English climate

a kind of prolonged May, and a vernal lustiness and raciness are characteristic of all the prevailing forms. Life is rank and full. Reproducton is easy. There is plenty of sap, plenty of blood. . . . We can almost hear the cattle ripping off the lush grass in the fields. One feels as if he could eat the grass himself. It is a pastoral paradise. . . . Nature has grown mellow under these humid skies, as in our fiercer climate, she grows harsh and severe. . . . England is like the margin of a spring-run, near its source—always green, always cool, always moist, comparatively free from frost in winter and from drought in summer. The spring-run to which it owes this character is the Gulf Stream which brings out of the pit of the southern ocean what the fountain brings out of the bowels of the earth—a uniform temperature, low, but constant; a fog in winter, a cloud in summer. . . . Cloud evolved, cloud-enveloped, cloud-protected, it fills the eye of the American traveler with a vision of greenness such as he has never before dreamed of; a greenness born of perpetual May, tender, untarnished, ever-renewed. . . . Never was such a restful land to the eye, especially to the American eye.[32]

"The English grass retains its verdure, and even roses continue to bloom in the open air throughout the winter," observed Fanny Hall with amazement in 1836.[33] Echoing her many decades later, Margaret Wright assured her readers that "England lends herself most exquisitely to passionate pilgrimages, even in winter."[34] When Louise Robinson questioned an English gardener at Leamington concerning his lush green lawn, assuring him that Americans also tended and watered theirs but not always with the same result, he replied with a smile, "You forget, Madame, that we have watered ours for centuries."[35]

"One chief condition of my enjoyment was the weather," recalled Nathaniel Hawthorne of his seven-year residence in Britain.

During my first year in England, residing in perhaps the most uncongenial part of the kingdom, I could never be quite comfortable without a fire on the hearth; in the second twelvemonth, beginning to get acclimatized, I became sensible of an austere friendliness, shy but sometimes almost tender, in the veiled, shadowy, seldom-smiling summer; and in the succeeding years— whether that I had renewed my fibre with English beef and . . . ale, or whatever the cause—I grew content with winter and especially in love with summer, desiring little more for happiness than merely to breathe and bask.[36]

The English summer, he concluded, was the weather of Paradise itself.

"The English summer-day," discovered Hawthorne, "has positively no beginning, and no end. When you awake at any reasonable hour, the sun is already shining through the curtains; you live through unnumbered hours of Sabbath quietude . . . and at length you become conscious that it is bedtime again, while there is still enough daylight in the sky to make the pages of your book distinctly legible. Night, if there be any such season, hangs down a transparent veil through which the by-gone day beholds its successor. . . . Tomorrow is born before Yesterday is dead."[37]

The neatness of the countryside also enchanted these American travelers. "Certain characteristics here are very reminiscent of Japan," wrote the well-traveled Elizabeth Wetmore, referring to "the neatness and completeness of everything."[38] Samuel Fiske found Britain "the only country in the world that is all finished, perfectly complete, with the scaffoldings taken down and the rubbish picked up. There are no odds and ends lying around loose, no out of the way corners where the work has been slighted, nothing anywhere but will bear the closest inspection."[39] Charles Fairbanks thought that "the whole country looks as if it had been swept and dusted that morning."[40]

"Nothing struck me so forcibly as peculiar to the lower classes in England, or won me more in their favor, than their love of flowers," wrote a pedestrian traveler in the 1870s. "Go where I would, in the abode of the poorest farm laborer, through the back streets of little country towns, where the houses were hovels, grimier and gloomier than any cottage I entered, I saw flowers. Sometimes it was a single flower that could have cost nothing, set in an old, broken tea-pot or other shard of earthenware; but it was there and it was put in the window, and plainly was prized and tended."[41]

Octavia LeVert had noticed the same trait back at mid-century. "Nearly all the houses, it matters not how humble, have their little gardens, and even in the most thronged and tumultuous . . . city, flowers are in all the windows. Even in the wretched dwellings of the poor, they are seen growing in broken cups and old boxes . . . a love for the beautiful which not even poverty could destroy."[42]

In the Edinburgh slums Helen Hunt Jackson spied "a little fern growing in a pot" in a window nine stories up from the ground. "It was a tiny thing, but my eye fell on it. . . . Outside the window it stood on a perilously narrow ledge. . . . It seemed the brave signal of a forlorn hope, of a dauntless, besieged soul that would never surrender."[43]

On visiting author Mary Russell Mitford in 1839 at her cottage in the village of Swallowfield, near Reading, Catherine Sedgwick remembered most of all that lady's flowers. " 'I must show you my geraniums while it is light,' " Miss Mitford exclaimed to her American visitor. " 'I love them next to my father.' And they were indeed treated like petted children. . . . Oh, that I could give some of my countrywomen a vision of this little paradise of flowers that they might learn how *taste and industry,* and an earnest love and study of the art of garden-culture, might triumph over small space and small means," wrote Mrs. Sedgwick.[44]

The Briton's love of nature was summed up for one American, the bumptious Henry Morford, no less, in the effort made by an English friend to treat him to the song of the skylark, which he had never heard. " 'You have not yet *heard* an English skylark?' asked his host at a London club late one evening. 'Then, by George, you *shall* . . . if there is one to be found, and I think there is, in the meadows of Kent!' Pulling out his watch, he observed, 'It is nearly two. The day will break in an hour. Come along,' " he said to his American guest, " 'and any two of you other wretches who believe in displaying British institutions.' "[45]

After a drive of an hour or so, they pulled up in a meadow on the bank of the Thames, somewhere near Walton-on-Thames, Morford thought. An English member of the little company remarked that he did not believe a lark had been heard there "since the time of Henry the Seventh," but the host of the expedition had more faith. "Only a moment later," recalled Morford, "some twenty or thirty feet from us . . . there was a slight whirr not much louder than the fluttering of a young bird in the nest—followed by a chirp that began to be a trill as it ascended. The body from which it came was so small," observed Morford,

that it seemed only a pellet, and no idea could be formed of its appearance as it shot skyward almost perpendicularly. But if the eye caught little or nothing, the ear had that crowning rapture for which it had so long waited. No words can quite describe it, as to its place among bird-songs. It did not seem, after the first instant, to be chirped, but literally poured out—flowing like a stream of tiny melody. . . . The song of the skylark would be comparatively insignificant if heard at the ordinary bird-song level: it is as it fades away and yet retains its trenchant quality in the far upper air, that the admiration grows to wonder that wonder to something approaching adoration. Higher, higher, higher, it ascended, the strained eyes still looking up . . . from the thrownback heads. . . . Higher, higher, still higher, and yet within hearing—sweeter, fainter, and yet more joyous as the very gates of morning may have been approached in the bold upward flight—where indeed wert thou, oh English skylark, when the last faint tinkle of thy bird-soul, poured out in dropping, rippling melody died away upon the fainting sense, and we all drew breath once more and returned to that lower earth.[46]

The Britons' love of a holiday amazed their puritanical American cousins. "Nowhere in America do they make a holiday for the mere sake of having an outing as the English do," observed an American onlooker. "They are willing to stop work and shut up shop at any time that a van for a rural picnic or an excursion ticket for anywhere falls in their way. This fondness for holidays and for the open air is a national characteristic."[47] Even hard-driving Andrew Carnegie perceived that his adopted countrymen and countrywomen might learn something from the Britons on this score. "We decided that the Americans were the saddest-looking race we had seen," he wrote during his summer coaching tour in 1881.

Life is so terribly earnest here [the U.S.]. Ambition spurs us all on, from him
who handles the spade to him who employs thousands. We know no rest. It is
different in the older lands—men rest oftener and enjoy more of what life has
to give. The young Republic has some things to teach the parent land, but the
elder has an important lesson to teach the younger in this respect. In this
world we must learn not to lay up our treasures, but to enjoy them day by day,
as we travel the path we never return to.[48]

"To describe all of the pictures of an English holiday would require a special
volume," decided Theron Crawford in the summer of 1887. At Epping Forest
several miles beyond Hampstead Heath, he had observed thousands of people
out on picnics one summer afternoon.

Along the line of every country road were picnic parties. Groups were
gathered in upon every corner where shade and green grass were to be found.
There was also to be found on every turn, a British workman fast asleep upon
his face. The trains that run to the seashore were loaded almost to suffocation.
At least half a million people were carried down . . . during this holiday time.
At the Crystal Palace there were 30,000. At the Wild West Show there were
40,000 during the day, but it is useless to try and give with mere figures any idea
of the outpouring of the public when one of these great days has come.[49]

Henry James, too, commented on this English trait. "A large appetite for
holidays, the ability not only to take them, but to know what to do with them," he
observed, "is a sign of a robust people, and judged by this measure, we
Americans are sadly inexpert."[50]

In 1895 American sportsman Caspar Whitney surveyed all the popular British
sports he once believed the Briton must have taken up in order "to keep his
blood from congealing," until he realized that a love of sport was "bred in the
bone." The Englishman, he observed, "inhales a sporting atmosphere from the
day he is old enough to trundle a cricket ball on the village common." Americans
had been too busy building a nation, and now must learn how to play, he
believed. In Britain, he observed, "there is something going on all the time,
winter and summer:" fox-hunting, rowing, foot-ball, both university and working men's clubs, cycling, cricket and golf. Britain is "a nation of sports lovers,"
declared Whitney,

from "me lord" that follows the hounds, to the very coster-monger racing his
whippets. . . . The American sportsman marvels at this enormous general
participation in all sport, just as he stares in wonder at the pheasants he may
see feeding in fields as peacefully as barn fowls—and quite as indifferent to
onlookers—or plentifully stocking the poulterers' shops in London; or, if he
happens to hail from New York, he is amazed at having violets for one penny
(two cents) a bunch offered him along Piccadilly.[51]

"Almost all travelers have remarked the extreme neatness and great attention
to comfort, in the houses of the English," remarked Joshua White in 1810, "and I
must add my testimony to others who have gone before me."[52] White had, as a
matter of fact, struck a note that would be sounded by most travelers who came
after him. "The English," decided Mrs. Sigourney, were "experts in the science
of home-comfort which seems better understood in the Mother Land than in any

other [country] which I have critically examined."[53] Henry Colman, who went in and out of so many English homes in the forties, listed as the primary characteristics of English housekeeping "neatness, punctuality, order, quiet and comfort . . . the order such that nothing ever seems to be out of place; the quiet delightful."[54]

"Comfort. How well the English understand it, I learn more and more every day," observed Mrs. George Bancroft, wife of the American minister, in 1847.[55] "Comfort is truly an English word," remarked John W. Corson in 1846.[56] "The English understand the arts of comfort better than we do," echoed Caroline Kirkland in 1849, "at least their domestic habits are more rational and homelike." The Britons used and enjoyed all their parlors and sitting rooms, she observed, not setting aside for entertaining empty rooms "piled with unmeaning splendours, and shining in unused and unusable neatness."[57] David Bartlett wrote at mid-century that "the art of housekeeping is carried to perfection in England. The quietness and smoothness with which the routine of domestic duties glides along, astonishes the American who is accustomed to noise and hurry, voracity and fretfulness, as the accompaniment to 'household joys.' "[58]

Harriet Beecher Stowe, too, concluded that "in England the matter of coziness and home comfort has been so studied, and matured, and reduced to system, that they really have it in their power to effect more, towards making their guests comfortable, than perhaps any other people."[59] An American art student in England recalled that "an Englishman once said to me, while in Rome, that Italians had no word expressing home or comfort. 'Home! Comfort!' he exclaimed, smacking his lips, as if he tasted them. 'They are the most beautiful words in our language!' "[60]

The more perceptive travelers quickly became aware that much of this comfort and domestic serenity stemmed from the unstinting efforts of faithful and efficient servants. Mrs. Stowe wrote enviously of her English hostesses,

They do not fade their cheeks lying awake nights ruminating the awful question who shall do the washing next week, or who shall take the chambermaid's place, who is going to be married, or that of the cook who has signified her intention of parting with the mistress. Their hospitality is never embarrassed by the consideration that their whole kitchen may desert at the moment that their guests arrive. They are not obliged to choose between washing their own dishes, or having their cut glass, silver, and china left to the mercies of a foreigner, who has never done anything but field work.[61]

"In Britain," observed Henry Colman, "servants are trained to be servants, and expect to live and die servants."[62] And Mrs. Sigourney wrote that

each one is at his post, in the neatest costume, ready to maintain the clockwork regularity of the establishment . . . . They are happy in their station, and in the respect which attends the faithful discharge of their duties. They consider servitude no mark of disgrace, and sometimes continue with their employers ten, fifteen, or twenty years, or throughout their whole lives . . . . The mistress of a family, thus sustained, has opportunity for the better points of her character to expand, and leisure to modify that of her children, as well as to enjoy the friends who partake of her hospitality.[63]

"One thing that charms American visitors, especially ladies from the northern states who have been tormented almost out of their senses by Irish peasants who pretend to serve them as servants at home," observed Bostonian Curtis Guild in the seventies, "is the admirable service in these English homes. All appears to move without a jar, the servants, to use an American expression, 'run the house'."[64] The English servants, moreover, performed their duties with an ease of manner, observed R. G. White, "very uncommon in the Hibernian maid-servant of America."[65]

Male visitors remarked on the quality of service in England generally. "One of the first things that strikes the American stranger ... is the attention and deference he receives from those classes of the people whose business it is to minister to his comfort—from innkeepers, proprietors, and drivers of coaches, waiters, porters, etc.,—servants of all descriptions," reported Orville Dewey in the thirties. They are "looking to you for a gratuity, it is true," he admitted, "but it is a fair compact; and degrading to neither party."[66] So impressed was he by the waiters at the famed Adelphi Hotel in Liverpool in the seventies that Benjamin Bausman was embarrassed to be served by them. "Intelligent, dignified, grave-looking gentlemen, all dressed in the finest black with white cravats ... [looking like] learned and eminent divines."[67] Unlike her fellow Americans who earlier had condemned Britain's class system that provided this efficient and willing servant class, Anna Dodd frankly admitted in the 1880s that she enjoyed a society "where there is somebody left in the class below you who is willing, for a consideration, to wait on you!"[68]

Scarcely were the Americans off their ships at Liverpool when they noticed what appeared to be the look of greater health and vigor of the English people. "My first and last observations and inquiries served to confirm that first impression," remarked Heman Humphrey in the thirties.[69] "We have nothing like the aspect of health that prevails here," remarked Orville Dewey in the same period, noticing "the solid, substantial, rotund, rubicund appearance of all classes. We are, in comparison, a thin, delicate-faced people. We are, I am sometimes tempted to say, a nation of invalids in comparison."[70] Two decades later Mrs. Stowe also remarked that "indeed, this air of health is one of the most striking things when one lands in England."[71] In the seventies a traveler observed that "the English look remarkably healthy. Both sexes seem to retain the flush and vigor of health far beyond the meridian of life."[72]

London businessmen were quite different from their American counterparts, concluded Alexander MacKenzie in the 1830s. "In Wall-street the same sort of men would look lean, hungry, unquiet; their hands grasping bonds, stock certificates, and promissory notes would tremble like a gambler with his last decisive card, as they might be seen crossing the street in a hop and jump, darting like lightning." British businessmen were decidedly "fuller, fatter, more rosy, more deliberate, and more staid. They seemed very intent indeed in the pursuit of gain, but by no means so impatient."[73]

Perceiving this same difference in facial expression, posture, and overall appearance near the end of the century, Richard Grant White wondered as to its origin. "The toil and struggle of life is harder in England," he reasoned.

Poor men are more driven by necessity; rich men think more; among all classes, except the frivolous part of the aristocracy (not a large class), there is more mental strain, more real anxiety, than we know here, where all the material conditions of life are easier, and where there is less care for political and social matters. Why, then, this difference of look? I am inclined to think it is due, in some measure, to difference of climate. . . . Briefly, I think that an expression of anxiety is given to "the American" face by an effort to resist the irritating effect of our sun and wind. . . . Americans who reside in England for a few years generally lose, in great measure, if not entirely, the look in question.[74]

Humphrey, decades earlier, pondering this same question, also acknowledged the effect of climate but further observed that the English took far more outdoor exercise than the Americans, either out of necessity or for pleasure, dressed more sensibly, especially the women, suffered less of the type of nervous and mental excitement caused by the competitiveness of American life, and, finally, *"they eat a great deal slower"*. The rapid gobbling of their meals by Americans, so commented upon by British travelers in America, was, he decided, a prime cause of their tension and related infirmities.[75]

"There is more truth than fiction in the remark that we eat fast, drink fast, work fast, and die fast," concluded successful businessman William Whyte, the Welshman who had migrated to the United States and risen to a position of prominence with the Anchor Line.[76] The Americans still continued to complain, however, about the slow service in English hotel dining rooms and the "dragging out" of their meals through carefully defined courses. "An Englishman eats what he orders as fast as anybody else," insisted George Wilkes in 1851, "but he consumes two-thirds of his time in waiting to get it, and what he does not waste in this way, he lengthens out by sitting over his ale and wine, after his dinner is devoured."[77]

"We rush to the table as if eating was an affair to be dispatched in the shortest time possible," admitted author Samuel Goodrich in the fifties.

The Englishman, on the contrary, arranges his business for his dinner; he prepares his mind for it; he sets himself to the table, and adjusts his legs beneath it; he unfolds his napkin and lays it in his lap, or tucks a corner within his waistcoat . . . he finally qualifies himself the better to enjoy it by taking a loving survey of the good things before him and the good friends around him. He begins leisurely, as if feeling that Providence smiles upon him, and he would acknowledge its bounties by prolonging the enjoyment of them. As he proceeds, he spices his gratification by sips of wine, exchanges of compliments with the ladies and convivial chat, right and left, with his neighbors. . . . The victory is, at last, substantially won: all that remains is to to capture the pies, cakes, tarts, ices, creams, fruits, etc., which is usually done with a running artillery of light wit. Conversation ensues. . . . An hour is past, and the ladies retire. The Gentlemen fill their glasses, and offer them a parting toast; then they drink "The Queen", and give themselves up to social enjoyment.[78]

In addition to eating more slowly, the Britons were *always* eating, observed Alexander MacKenzie and he thought well worth imitating this "sensible custom . . . of going always armed with eatables to sustain their energies and keep alive their enthusiasm. The pleasures and excitement of a journey, the rapture which is kindled by the contemplation of fine scenery, or the ecstasy with which the soul is moved by the triumphs of music at a festival or an oratorio, are never allowed to be diminished by the inward discomfort of an empty stomach."[79]

American preachers, who, as one of their own number observed, tended to be "lean, pale, cadaverous-looking clergymen who glide like specters into their pulpits," were pleased, some of them, at least, to see the part that "meat and drink" played at British religious convocations.[80] The ladies provided "ham, bread and butter, cake, tea, etc.," for a missionary meeting attended by the Reverend Wilbur Fisk in 1831, and he remarked "how the whole was well calculated to promote Christian social intercourse, and to interweave our sympathies with the hallowed cause which had brought us together."[81] English clergymen were robust, observed the Reverend Daniel Eddy, and "looked as well able to hold the plough . . . as to write a sermon."[82]

It was "the cold and damp," concluded R. G. White,

> that makes the Englishman so capable of food and drink. Nothing is more impressive about him than his diligence in this respect. He never neglects an opportunity. Hearty breakfast at nine o'clock; luncheon at half past one or two, at which there is a hot joint and cold bird pies, with wine and beer; at five o'clock, tea . . . with thin bread and butter; dinner at eight, serious business; sherry and biscuits or sandwiches at eleven, as you take your bedroom candle. At home it would have killed me in a month; there I throve upon it mightily.[83]

The greater dignity, along with more physical vigor, of the elderly also impressed most Americans. Harriet Beecher Stowe, being lionized at a dinner in London, said:

> I could not help thinking as I looked around on so many men whom I had heard of historically all my life, how very much less they bear the marks of age than men who have been connected a similar length of time with the movements of our own country. This appearance of youthfulness and alertness has a constantly deceptive influence upon one in England. I cannot realize that people are as old as history states them to be. . . . Generally speaking, our working minds seem to wear out their bodies faster; perhaps because our climate is more stimulating; more, perhaps from the intense stimulus of our political *régime*, which never leaves anything long at rest.[84]

Hawthorne, too, noted that in England "Old-Age comes forth more cheerfully and genially into the sunshine, than among ourselves, where the rush, stir, bustle, and irreverent energy of youth are so preponderant that the poor forlorn grandsires begin to doubt whether they have a right to breathe in such a world any longer, and so hide their silvery heads in solitude."[85] Dr. William Gibson observed the same phenomenon and decided that elderly Englishmen and women retained their "place" by refusing "to be elbowed out, and thus, actually preserved their health and good looks, instead of sinking into mopes and drones."[86]

British children came off with high marks from the American travelers, who tended to worry about all the little bare legs they saw but marveled at how "the English children . . . are much better trained than ours; conducting themselves like little gentlemen and ladies, and not dragging their weak and affectionate parents around as if *they* were the children. In the training of youth," concluded

Samuel Young at mid-century, "we are behind the rest of the world. Our easy government is, doubtless, partly the cause why our little boys and girls are considered of so much importance."[87]

Mrs. Kirkland thought the English far more skilled in caring "for the physique of children. They feed them with the simplest possible food," she discovered, "and are astonished when they hear that our young folks share the rich, heavy, high-seasoned dishes of their parents. Oat-meal porridge is considered a suitable breakfast for infant royalty itself; and a simple dinner at one o'clock the proper thing for children whose parents dine sumptuously at seven."[88]

Much impressed with the pleasant behavior of her landlord's children at a country inn, Lucy Williams listened closely as he explained his theory of child rearing. " 'You tyke a young vine hand you cut hit hand train hit, hand hit will go whatever way you want hit,' " he said. " 'But if you wait till hit grows hup, you cahn't do nothing with hit. A child that does not hobey his parents his a trouble to heverybody, and a mortification to hits parents.' "[89] Lydia Sigourney, too, approved the simple foods and outdoor exercise regimen of British children along with the discipline to which they were subjected. "Subordination, the privilege of childhood, is better secured to them" than it is to American children, she observed. "Their little minds are not fevered with doubt whether they are to rule or be ruled. The sentiment of respect, constantly cherished within them, is a sedative principle, and contributes to serenity."[90]

The women of Britain underwent a close inspection by the American males and emerged with flying colors as did the British children. "Comparisons are odious," admitted David Bartlett at mid-century, but these "are noble women! . . . red-cheeked, of stout muscle and nimble gait, of fine health and appetite."[91] MacKenzie also had noted earlier that they were "plump and comely, their complexions universally good."[92]

"How comes it?" asked Mrs. Stowe,

> that our married ladies dwindle, fade, and grow thin—that their noses incline to sharpness and their elbows to angularity, just as at the same time of life when their island sisters round out into a comfortable and becoming amplitude and fulness? If it is the fog and the sea coal, why, then, I am afraid we shall never come up with them. But perhaps there may be other causes why a country which starts out with some of the most beautiful girls in the world produces so few beautiful women.

She was speaking of her countrywomen. "Have not our close, stove-heated rooms something to do with it? Have not the immense amount of hot biscuits, hot corn cakes, and other compounds got up with the acrid poison of saleratus, something to do with it? Above all, has not our climate, with its alternate extremes of heat and cold, a tendency to induce habits of indoor indolence?"[93]

Octavia LeVert noticed that Englishwomen spent "many hours" each day in the open air, walking and riding.[94] American men noticed this also and approved its effects in the rosy cheeks, vitality, and good nature they admired in the Englishwomen. "They retain their beauty to a much later period, also, than our American fair ones," observed Fanny Hall. "An Englishwoman is hardly reckoned past the prime of her beauty at thirty-five; while an American lady of the same age is considered quite passé."[95] Hiram Fuller declared that he had "never before seen so large a collection of fresh, fine, rosy-looking women."[96] One young female American admitted, as she surveyed the maids in her hotel up in Scotland, that "our American epidermis reminded us rather of cold roast potato-skin."[97]

Going on the defensive, American female travelers often pronounced the dress of their British cousins "dowdy," charged them with having large hands and feet, and made fun of their shoes. It was the sturdy outer wear of these women, however, that made all their healthful exercise possible, one American husband realized. "We see no frippery or finery here in the railway carriage," commented Hiram Fuller, "and silks and satins in the street are apt to excite rather uncomplimentary suspicions of the wearers."[98] An American physician, noting the greater physical vigor of women in Britain, remarked that "the walking shoes of an English lady would astonish an American belle out of all the senses she happened to possess. The English lady evidently thinks a stout figure, a good-sized arm, and a massive hand and foot, no deformities; consequently, she is not obliged to compress her waist into the circumference of a bracelet, or torture her feet with small shoes."[99] The Englishwomen going out to walk, Fanny Hall informed her American readers,

> put on substantial, thick, solid shoes; and if the streets are wet, pattens; while they wrap their persons in shawls, or, if the weather is cold, in warm fur capes. . . . Probably the humidity and equable temperature of the climate have some influence in preserving their bloom and beauty; and something, too, I imagine, is attributable to their habit of taking much exercise in the open air. The English ladies are great walkers, nothing being more common than for them to walk ten or twelve miles per day.[100]

"One half of the consumption cases among the American women," Fuller pointed out, "are owing to the wafer-soled shoes, which render walking both difficult and dangerous. And so they sit pining in satin chairs in over-heated rooms, sucking cough candy, and waiting for the doctor, and his shadow, the undertaker; while these buxom English beauties are tramping about in their water-proof boots, or darting through the lanes and parks in their saddles. To appear delicate or lackadaisical," he added, referring to the nineteenth-century American female's vogue for poor health, "is no part of an Englishwoman's ambition. Health and vigor of body and mind are considered of primary importance, not only for comfort's sake, but as the most essential qualifications for satisfactorily performing the duties of wives and mothers. And they dress, and eat, and exercise accordingly."[101]

This admiration of the American male for Englishwomen was not based on their physical qualities alone, but also on an innate attitude of "deference to manhood," as Richard White put it, which apparently many of them found lacking in their own countrywomen. "I should call England the Paradise of Men," enthused White, "for there the world is made for them; and women are happy in making it so."[102] Yankee men observed lower-class wives actually buttering their husband's bread. "An American husband might eat dry bread forever if he were unwilling to butter it for himself," snorted one traveler, who also noticed the women filling their husband's pipes and pouring out their ale. "Englishwomen belonging to what are called the lower classes are evidently the servants of men; while in America the men are as evidently the servants of the women."[103]

A tough, self-reliant confidence underscored all this feminine deference to the male, certain observers noted. Nathaniel Wheaton had been astonished back in the thirties in London to see a slender, well-dressed lady actually spring under the horses to rescue a poor woman and her child who had been knocked down by a coach—"a gratifying instance of female intrepidity."[104] Other Americans observed how so many Englishwomen worked outside their homes with no apparent loss of "femininity." In 1863, Mrs. E. A. Forbes was astonished to find "women in nearly all the booking offices of hotels; they are the best book-keepers in shops; they fill positions as housekeepers, and discharge, with propriety, many offices we bestow upon men."[105] Visitors later in the century also remarked on women tending shops, virtually running hotels, and manning telegraph offices, with none of their "womanliness" impaired. "A consciousness of womanhood combined with a feeling of modest but very firm self-respect" was how White saw these working women of Britain in their "black serge or alpaca" dresses.[106]

Charles Poston, who traveled with Colonel Forney on his post-Civil War peregrinations, was so captivated by one particular Englishwoman—"the lady proprietress of the Peacock Inn at Rowley"—that he vowed that "if I should ever be unfortunate in my speculations in America, like Mark Tapley and Martin Chuzzlewit, I shall go back to England and marry that buxom widow and ever afterwards live in peace."[107]

The unfailing civility of the British people was so different from the attitude of the Americans, who "seem to carry the Declaration of Independence in their pockets, and regard the least degree of urbanity which may possibly be construed into obsequiousness, a breach of the Constitution," as William Austin observed in 1802.[108] The British civility was experienced throughout the nineteenth century by traveling Yankees. "If you are run over in London, they 'beg your pardon'," William Wells Brown, the fugitive slave, observed; "if they run over you in New York you are laughed at; in London, if your hat is knocked off, it is picked up and handed to you; if in New York, you must pick it up yourself."[109]

"We were, upon all occasions," declared Orville Horwitz in 1853, "even when we had no claim to attention, treated with the utmost politeness in England. . . . there is no European, whose courtesy, or whose sense of politeness, or whose hospitality equals that of an Englishman."[110] In the sixties Gilbert Haven said that he had "never met persons more anxious to please. Ask your way, and they will go far out of theirs to show it to you."[111] George Wilkes experienced "a sterling politeness which cannot be exceeded by that of any other people in the world."[112]

The respect of Americans for the London police remained high, as travelers continued to compare those tall, quiet "servants of the people" with officers "drafted from the political 'heelers' of New York or Chicago," as William Rideing wrote in the nineties. Above all, he praised the self-control and forbearance of the London policemen.

They don't rush in and club every head within reach, but use moral suasion before they try any other force. I have seen one of these model officers standing alone in a threatening crowd of disorderly people, and not reply to threat with threat, but patiently endeavoring to have them "move on" . . . On Lord Mayor's Day, or at some other public celebration . . . I have been forced to admire their good humor as the crowd, becoming restive, has made bold attempts to break bounds. . . . The big, full-chested fellows have stood shoulder-to-shoulder, and held back the mass behind them as by a wall. There was no clubbing, no bullying; and continuing to hold their position against all the impatient pushing, the policemen, or "Bobbies", as they are commonly called, have smiled triumphantly, and perhaps jokingly taunted the besiegers with their failure.

"Watching them," Rideing went on, "an American looker-on must have thought how different it would have been in New York,—how much aggressive ferocity there would have been, how many dazed and bleeding heads." Comparing the twenty- to thirty-dollar-a-week American policeman's salary with the Briton's seven, he concluded, "there surely cannot be any scarcity of Christian virtues in a country where fortitude and valor are purchaseable at so low a price."[113] James E. Scripps, editor of the *Detroit Evening News,* wrote about 1880 that

there is in Great Britain but a mere fraction of the lawlessness and criminality that we are exposed to at home. I presume that the laws are more rigidly enforced than with us, for in almost any part of London ladies can be out up to a late hour in the evening unattended; no householder ever for a moment worries himself about burglars; no one ever dares to claim another party's baggage on the railway platform . . . room doors at hotels are rarely locked during the day . . . and murderous assaults are scarcely, if at all, more numerous than cold-blooded, willful murders, which, of course, is a phase of crime that no laws or penalties can check. Dishonesty is severely dealt with in England, whether it be the case of the boy who pilfers an apple, or the bank teller who misuses the funds with which he is entrusted. That assaults are less numerous than with us, is perhaps, owing in large measure to the restrictions placed upon the carrying of firearms of any sort. To carry a gun or pistol without a license is a serious offense.[114]

In this same decade Eudora South was assured by a youthful Scot that he would like to visit America—"but not to stay. It's so dangerous there. If a man gets a spite at you, he will slip up on you and shoot you down anytime, and nobody says a word."[115]

Yet with all this self-restraint and order, the Britons were in some ways more free than themselves, some Americans perceived—at least with respect to self-expression. Joshua White observed about 1810, "[T]he liberty with which the people write on affairs of government, is an evidence that they are not kept in that awe of the 'powers that be' which is commonly supposed on the American side of the Atlantic."[116] The black Abolitionist, William Brown, perceived that "not even in our own beloved America can the man who feels himself oppressed speak as he can in Great Britain."[117] Anglophobe extraordinaire George Hills paid an unintentional tribute to this aspect of British life in his antisocialist rant, written just before World War I, concerning the degree of political expression permitted in London. "If you object to royalty or the Government, if you disapprove of law and order or the English Church, if you have ideas of your own that conflict ever so directly with prevailing conditions and customs—even if you happen to be a suffragette—you are at perfect liberty to go to Hyde Park, get on a barrel, gather a crowd, and preach anything you like from atheism to treason, so long as you do not injure the *grass!*" He was appalled at groups of marchers bearing banners with "such inflammatory inscriptions as 'Down With Capitalism', 'Socialism Forever', 'The Coming Revolution', 'We Are the Workers Whose Blood Supports Capital', 'Death To the Upper Class', 'We Don't Ask Bread; We Want Work', 'Free Distribution of Wealth', and followed by eighty great barges full of children waving small red flags and singing Socialist songs" on their way to Hyde Park guided, protected, and with watching crowds kept in order all along the way by the patient London police.[118]

Although some Americans carped at certain manifestations of the British love of tradition and old customs, generally speaking it was "antiquity" in all its forms they had come to see. "Nothing charms the American traveler more than the relics of old times," Mrs. Kirkland assured her readers at mid-century,[119] and Professor Milton Terry stated that he went abroad especially "to see *old* things."[120] Tuckerman advised his readers that "the transatlantic pilgrim naturally craves the hoary emblems of the ages."[121] Hawthorne had earlier noted this Yankee fondness for antiquity, his relish for the picturesque, and his emotional attitude at historic shrines. It would diminish as he stayed on. "But while you are still new in the Old Country, it thrills you with strange emotion to think that this little church . . . stood for ages under the Catholic faith, and has not materially changed since Wickcliffe's days, and that it looked as gray now as in Bloody Mary's time, and that Cromwell's troopers broke off the noses of those same gargoyles that are now grinning in your face."[122] Emerging from a little shop in Warwick in 1867, Curtis Guild thought "how staid, and quaint, and curious these stand-still old English towns, clinging to their customs half a century old, seem to us restless, uneasy and progressive Yankees!"[123]

"In America, Time is a destroying radical," observed Noble Prentis of Kansas; "in England an easy conservative. With us nothing will ever be old; in England, few things seem young or new."[124] Andrew Peabody of Harvard remarked on the tendency in Britain to preserve. "No token of antiquity that can be preserved is obliterated. Restoration is preferred to renovation. An old building is not disused so long as it admits of occupancy; nor is a dilapidated member of a building removed simply because it is untenantable."[125] Orville Dewey had realized in the thirties that what charmed Americans most about Britain was its very "antiquity," this sense of the past their ancestors had left behind when they left for the New World. "The sublimity of ages is about you at every step, and you feel your connection with past races of men, in a way that you are not naturally led to do in a country where there are no monuments of the past."[126]

Americans were always asking, to the amusement of Britons, if things were "old," and each came to realize that the other's sense of age was quite different. "An American visitor," related Goldwin Smith, "pointing to a black-looking pile, asked his host if that building was not very old. 'Oh, no,' was the reply, 'its color deceives you; it has not been built much more than two hundred years.' "[127] Old buildings had a unique odor tantalizing to American noses, Hawthorne observed one morning as he awoke in the Black Swan at Lichfield, conscious that "the musty odor of a bygone century was in my nostrils—a faint, elusive smell, of which I never had any conception before crossing the Atlantic." Another time he spoke of "a musty fragrance of antiquity, such as I have smelt in a seldom-opened London church." On one occasion it was too much even for this antiquarian, "the aged, musty smell with which old Chester first made me acquainted, and which goes far to cure an American of his excessive predeliction for antique residences."[128]

Comments on the British character flew thick and fast whenever Americans chanced to meet by themselves. "After bowing and shaking hands," wrote Henry Field in 1858, "the first question they ask each other is, 'What do you think of the English?' Each answers according to his own experience." A friend of Field's, the Reverend William H. Channing of Boston, who had spent five years preaching to a Unitarian congregation in Liverpool, told him that "he did not think he understood them so well as he did when he first came to England five years before! I commend this answer," concluded Field, "to those who are so prompt and even flippant in their judgment of a great people. If a man of so much intelligence, and with such excellent opportunities of seeing the better class of English society, has to confess himself perplexed in trying to comprehend the English character, a stranger who has been but a few weeks in the country had better be modest in expressing his opinion."[129]

Not all American travelers were as cautious as Field, however, and opinions on this British "character" flew thick and fast. Some thought them "haughty"; others termed this merely their innate pride and self-confidence in being British. A small handful considered Britons brusque and ill-mannered; the majority found them, like pilgrim Gilbert Haven, "remarkable for their kindness and honesty."[130] A young American art student, who had studied in both London and Rome, wrote of the British in 1855: "From the highest to the lowest, each possesses a self-respect, a true nobility; insult a low Italian, and he thrusts a knife into your back; deeply offend an English 'Cad' [omnibus conductor], and stopping for a moment his monotonous cry of 'Going hup 'oburn 'ill?', he jumps down from his little shelf behind the omnibus, and quietly offers in fair and honorable combat to 'Punch your heye hout!' "[131]

Some Americans complained that British servants and shop clerks were too servile while others praised the unaccustomed courtesy and efficiency with which they were served. A few travelers still harped on the British "caste system," terming it outrageous, but others, like Mrs. Forbes, admitted that they enjoyed "the unfailing well-bred courtesy of equals, and the unfailing respectful civility of inferiors."[132] Written in 1863, this seems to reveal a growing sense of "caste" in America itself.

As if summing up this ambivalent American attitude toward Britons at mid-century, and perhaps even beyond, the crusty Horace Greeley himself had something positive to say. "I do not wholly like these cold and stately English, yet I think I am not blind to their many sterling qualities." First of all, he found them "eminently *industrious*," testifying that "I have seen no country in which the proportion of idlers is smaller . . . Work is the general rule." As a judge at the

Great Exhibition in 1851 Greeley, was, of course, seeing the British work ethic at its height. He acknowledged their methodical ways and praised their economy. "You never see a lighted candle set down carelessly and left to burn an hour or two . . . as is so common with us; if you leave one burning, some one speedily comes and quietly extinguishes the flame." He found the British also superbly practical in all things. "When the portly and well-to-do Briton vociferates 'God Save The Queen!' with intense enthusiasm," said Mr. Greeley, "he means 'God save my estates, my rents, my shares, my consols, my expectations.' . . . The poor like the Queen personally, and like to gaze at royal pageantry; but they are not fanatically loyal." Greeley thought the British grave, "their manner of expressing themselves literal and prosaic; the American tendency to hyperbole and exaggeration grates harshly on their ears."[133]

Greeley jibed at the Britons' gravity—"awkward at a frolic as a bear at a dance,"—and charged them with having "a sharp eye to business" at all times. "Yet," he concluded,

> the better qualities in the English character decidedly preponderate . . . . This people love justice, manly dealing, fair play; and although I think the shop-keeping attitude is unfavorable to this tendency, it has not effaced it. The English have too much pride to be tricky or shabby, even in the essentially corrupting relation of buyer and seller. And, the Englishman who may be repulsive in his out-of-door intercourse or spirally inclined in his dealings, is generally tender and truthful in his home . . . . The quiet comfort and heartfelt warmth of an English fireside must be felt to be appreciated.[134]

This theme of hospitality, of which Mr. Greeley's English hearth might stand as the symbol, runs throughout all American travelers' accounts during the nineteenth century. Joshua White commented on it in the first decade. "Hospitality has been most liberally extended to me," wrote the Georgian, "and I am forced to declare that since I have been in the kingdom, I have seen much more of it than I have in a section of that country where I drew my earliest breath, was educated and reared; or among a people whom I knew much better."[135]

"There is no hospitality like that of an Englishman, when you have crossed his threshold," wrote Samuel Goodrich at mid-century.

> Everywhere else he will annoy you . . . . He will rebuff you, if sitting at his side in a locomotive, you ask a question by way of provoking a little conversation; he will get the advantage of you in trade, if he can; he carries at his back a load of prejudices, like that of Christian in *Pilgrim's Progress,* and instead of seeking to get rid of them, he is always striving to increase his collection. If he becomes a diplomat, his great business is to meddle in everybody's affairs; if an editor, he is only happy in proportion as he can say annoying and irritating things. And yet, catch this same John Bull at home, and his crusty, crocodile armor falls off, and he is the very best fellow in the world—liberal, hearty, sincere— the perfection of a gentleman.[136]

Over and over again these American travelers return to their theme of the Briton's kindness to the stranger within his gates. "It is very singular how kind an individual Englishman will almost invariably be to an individual American," observed Nathaniel Hawthorne, "without ever bating a jot of his prejudice against the American character in the lump."[137] Maunsell B. Field said he discovered that "an American is always favored. They hardly look on him as a foreigner. I have frequently heard this phrase, 'Oh, there were two or three Americans and half a dozen foreigners.' "[138]

Like good deeds in a naughty world, examples of kindness to travelers from the United States dot the pages of these books throughout the century. English friends rallied around poor Emma Willard when her companion died of "typhus" during their trip to England, assisting during the illness itself and then even opening up a family vault, at a cost of £30, for the burial. "The English are endeared to me by the kindness which I have received from so many individuals on this melancholy occasion," wrote Mrs. Willard. "And England itself will be to me what it has never been before."[139]

A widow with two small children, arriving alone in Britain in 1853 and endeavoring to promote the maritime signal rockets of her deceased husband, Martha Coston never forgot the kindness shown her when she found herself short of cash at a railway ticket window and the banks closed:

> The clerk asked, "Madam, how much have you?" I quickly emptied my purse; he counted the money and said, "that is all right. I will give you my card with the amount still due written on the back, and when you reach London, you can send it on in stamps." As he spoke, he put some change back in my purse "for the comforts," he added, "that you will be sure to need on your way." It was, to be sure, only a matter of a few shillings, but if it had been a thousand pounds I should not have been more grateful. That one act wiped out all my prejudices against the English . . . and my first act in London was to write him a grateful note enclosing the stamps.[140]

In the same period Andrew Dickinson remembered "an English lady who prepared many little articles of diet" for him during his severe shipboard illness on his way across the Atlantic in 1851. Then at Chester he was shown the city and invited home for dinner by a citizen of whom he had merely asked directions.[141]

At Hampton Court Samuel Prime, who arrived to find the palace closed to sightseers, was taken in hand by one of the residents of the "grace and favor" apartments. "It will give me great pleasure to walk with you through the palace; the porters are all away, but if I can get the keys we will be our own porters, and take our own time." Prime was brought home to dinner by his unexpected guide, and "the rest of the day was spent at his hospitable board. In America we have thought our English brethren selfish," Prime told his readers, "cold and disinclined to open their hearts to strangers, especially those from our country. I have not found it so. A gentleman is always kind. But few are so kind in any land as he to whom I was indebted for one of my most agreeable days in England."[142]

At Canterbury in 1884 Presbyterian minister William Breed was observed peering through a locked gate leading to "the ruins of the old Augustinian monastery" when an ecclesiastical gentleman offered to show him around. "For a half hour or more we enjoyed the company of our unknown friend," wrote Breed, "who led us into many nooks and corners of that old ruin, imparting information and pointing out objects to us of curious interest." Breed was then invited to the home of his guide, who proved to be "a Right Reverend Bishop of the Church of England." Breed does not give the bishop's name but adds that "if he should visit Philadelphia one of these days, he shall have a cordial welcome to our West Spruce Street church Presbyterian pulpit!"[143]

After the American Minister Lowell told them that he could do nothing for them concerning "the sixteen seats in the ladies' gallery" in the House of Commons, youthful Mary Louise Ninde and a friend, touring together in the eighties determined to see Parliament in session and sought out the office of "Sir William Knollys, Usher of the Black Rod, who had special charge of the ladies' gallery." Within a few minutes the two young ladies had the desired permit in hand and soon found themselves seated in the Speaker's private gallery, near "Mrs. Brand, the Speaker's wife, in a long silk dress and flashing diamonds." She pointed out the politicians of note and told them that "the Irish members are so tiresome, nobody stays to hear them."[144]

"In England," declared George Williams of Charleston, "you can find everything that can contribute to the happiness of man."[145] And one of many Americans who did was the cantankerous lawyer John Bender of Plymouth, Indiana—who embarked aboard the *Russia* in 1874, according to his own account, because of "a nervous disease which threatened to become troublesome to manage, whereupon a change of climate was recommended." His trip was, from the very start, fraught with strife,—fights over tickets and accommodations; harangues on board ship at Britons in which he attacked "the objectionable features" of their system of government; followed by general dissatisfaction with everything he saw upon his arrival in London. "I saw no building that would equal in magnitude and beauty the new telegraph office in New York or the Palmer House in Chicago," snorted Bender. "The buildings are densely packed . . . and if we except the cathedral, churches, and some public buildings, they are inferior to those in some of our American cities. . . . Most of the streets and lanes are like a serpent's tail." Then, after paying his respects to the Tower of London, he insisted on being conducted to "a ballet" at the Alhambra, one of London's racier "nightspots" in this period. He there comported himself in such a manner that his youthful guide was sufficiently embarrassed to leave early, after informing Bender, " 'We are [being] watched. . . . We must go!' "[146] Bender was then sent back to his hotel alone in a hansom.

Nevertheless, the Indiana lawyer completed his trip, and as he settled down he began to enjoy himself, while not forgetting to keep his diary up. Arriving home several months later, he summed up his adventures in Britain with the maxim that "kindness to strangers appears to be a virtue with the English."

> View them near, at home, where all their
>   pride is placed,
> And there, their hospitable fires burn clear.

"This sentiment I can fully corroborate by personal experience," testified lawyer Bender, "never having found twenty days of greater pleasure in my life, than were spent in England."[147] It was as if he were demonstrating William Winter's belief in England's power to "charm" and to "soothe" and also his conviction that "the man who could not be happy in England—insofar, at least, as happiness depends upon external objects and influences—could not reasonably expect to be happy anywhere."[148]

Surely one of the most amiable and open-hearted pilgrims of the century was William Hichborn of Boston—an official of the Navy Yard—who made his month-long pilgrimage to Britain in the summer of 1896 with the Ancient and Honorable Artillery Company of Boston, which was royally received and entertained by the Honourable Artillery Company of London. No American enjoyed and appreciated his trip to Britain more, and Hichborn's testimony at the end of his book is symbolic of the self-confidence, national pride, and progressive outlook of most of these pilgrims-in-reverse of the nineteenth century.

Coming back home to America, Hichborn spent considerable time down in the steerage chatting with the Irish immigrants and befriending in particular a young mother traveling alone with her children. To her little ones he brought "some oranges and knick-knacks" by way of comfort, but he found himself wondering: "I could not help soliloquizing what made them come, suffering all the privations of a sea voyage, to a land of strangers." Happily, the father was waiting for them on the wharf in East Boston when they landed, and Hichborn saw them reunited as a family on Friday, July 31, 1896.[149]

"I was soon on deck," wrote Hichborn of that morning when he entered Boston harbor,

> there to behold once more the headlands of my native city, the State House, the Bunker Hill Monument,—under whose shadow for more than sixty years I had lived and slept without ever thinking of visiting a foreign shore till on this occasion,—the Navy Yard, where for so many years I had been in and out, and where it seemed to me every foot of its soil my feet had sometime pressed. . . . At two o'clock I was at my home, 27 Trenton Street, glad that I went and twice glad to be home again. I would not call it back . . . for double what it cost. I was glad I took my wife along with me. . . . The next day, Saturday, August 1st, the anniversary of my sixty-sixth birthday, I took charge of the Construction Department of the Boston Navy Yard as General Foreman, Acting Naval Constructor, and resumed the duties I had left to go.[150]

"While I am an American, and all that it implies," wrote Hichborn, "I feel proud of my English ancestry. . . . I have faith in my country, its flag and its destiny. . . . I believe that God has made of one blood all nations of men to dwell in peace on all the face of the earth. I believe that the trend of all things is onward and upward; that humanity, the rights of man, and his equal chance in the battle of life, are well under way to recognition." And that his own special pilgrimage had meaning there was absolutely no doubt in the mind of Boston's William Hichborn. "History will cause the visit of the Ancients to London to live forever, and it will be sung in song, and told in story, long after everyone who participated therein shall have become dust and been forgotten."[151]

"It takes passionate pilgrims, vague aliens, and other disinherited persons to appreciate the 'points' of this admirable country," declared Henry James, the quintessential anglophile, who extended his own devotion even to the point of seeking British citizenship at the time of World War I, and who is today honored in the Poets' Corner of Westminster Abbey.[152] "Only Henry James was really content with the country," concluded a London critic not long ago in a review of an anthology featuring considerable querulous American commentary on Great Britain, "and in the best, most enterprisingly American fashion, he had invented the England he lived in,—it was the most elaborate of all his fictions."[153]

Nineteenth-century American commentary on Britain was often ambivalent, as we have seen, but far from primarily negative or querulous. Perhaps the reviewer was nearer the truth on the second count. Most Americans, even down to this latter day, as a result of their reading, films, and now television, invent their own Britain before they ever see it.

"You Americans know better than we do where certain odd places are located," a London policeman remarked to one American not long ago. "You often ask for places we've not heard of—you've done so much reading, it seems." The same remark was made to lawyer Erastus Benedict, an American tourist over a century ago: "You read so much more."[154] But, with the aid of their little pocket directories, the patient "Bobbies"—as the Americans still like to call them—invariably do their level best to aid the traveler.

No more do wide-eyed Americans come to Britain to marvel at science and technology far in advance of their own, nor to track down her authors and leading politicians. Very much a thing of the past is their obsession with Sir Walter Scott, and they long ago ceased worrying about their national identity.

Something of the old affinity, however, still endures. Almost one and a half million American visitors arrive in Britain each year, many of them imitating in many ways, quite unconsciously, their predecessors of the nineteenth century. Even today an occasional lone American pilgrim is seen huddled in the Poets' Corner of Westminster Abbey, "looking mournful and thinking up quotations" from his literary heritage, while hordes of Japanese, German, and French tour groups, dutiful but uncomprehending, ebb and flow around him. Occasionally the dedicated Sherlock Holmes buff is spotted stalking furtively up and down busy Baker Street, searching longingly for the legendary 221B; and frantic Fleet Street still poses problems for those many Yankee pilgrims seeking the small alley that leads them into Dr. Johnson's old brick house in Gough Square.

Americans continue to insist on making the pilgrimage to Stratford-on-Avon, now in even larger "omnibus-motor loads" than Howells complained of, only to find that Shakespeare is not there but rather in their own heads and hearts. Standing in the great cathedral at Canterbury, thinking of Chaucer's pilgrims, many an American comes to the quiet realization that he himself is but one of their number.

Some Americans newly arrived in Britain still complain of the rain and damp, and then perversely expect ice water with their meals. One or two will actually express disappointment at not finding any fog in London, but all are impressed still by the quiet, helpful policemen.

Certain Americans, those steeped in English literature, admit even today to experiencing the old nineteenth-century sensation of déjà vu expressed by Nathaniel Hawthorne—that odd feeling of returning to an "old home."

As Emerson's friend Orville Dewey asked almost a century and a half ago: "What is the traveller but a pilgrim of the heart, the imagination, the memory?"[155]

Notes

Introduction

1. Frederick Law Olmsted, *Walks and Talks of an American Farmer in England* (1852; reprint ed., Ann Arbor, Mich.: University of Michigan Press, 1967), pp. 89–90.

2. Ibid.

3. Stephen Spender, *Love-Hate Relations: English and American Sensibilities* (New York: Vintage Books, 1975), pp. xv–xvi.

4. *The Graphic* 1 (1869): 12 (an unsigned review of a book by G. M. Towles entitled *American Society* [London: Chapman and Hall, 1869]).

5. Allan Nevins, *American Social History as Recorded by British Travellers* (New York: Holt, 1923; reprint ed., Augustus M. Kelley, 1969), p. 556.

6. John E. Edwards, *Random Sketches and Notes of European Travel in 1856* (New York: Harper & Brothers, 1857), p. 1.

7. Spender, *Love-Hate Relations*, p. 5.

✓8. James Fenimore Cooper, *Gleanings in Europe. By an American*, 2 vols. 1837; (New York: Oxford University Press, 1930; reprint ed. Kraus Reprint Co., 1970), 2:380.

9. Reuben C. Thwaites, *Our Cycling Tour in England, from Canterbury to Dartmoor Forest and Back by Way of Bath, Oxford, and the Thames Valley* (Chicago: McClurg, 1892), p. viii.

10. Horace Greeley, *Glances at Europe: In a Series of Letters from Great Britain, France, Italy, Switzerland, etc., during the Summer of 1851* (New York: DeWitt & Davenport, 1851), p. 21.

11. Charles Williams, *Old World Scenes* (Pittsburgh, Pa.: Haven, 1867), advertisement.

12. *Dictionary of American Biography*, (New York: Charles Scribner's Sons, 1960), Vol. IX–Part 1, pp. 314–16.

13. Moses F. Sweetser, *Europe for $2.00 a Day: A Few Notes for the Assistance of Tourists of Moderate Means, with some Personal Reminiscences of Travel* (Boston: Osgood, 1875), p. 107.

14. Eliza A. Connor, *E. A. Abroad: A Summer in Europe* (Cincinnati, Ohio: W. E. Dibble & Co., 1883), p. v.

15. Roderick MacLeish, "Enigmatic Us," *Washington Post*, 2 August 1975.

16. Robert E. Spiller, *The American in England during the First Half Century of Independence* (New York: Henry Holt & Co., 1926), pp. viii–ix.

17. O. R. Burchard, *Two Months in Europe; a Record of a Summer Vacation Abroad* (Syracuse, N.Y.: Davis, Bardeen & Co., 1879), p. 1.

18. John P. Donelan, *My Trip to France* (New York: Dunnigan, 1857), p. vi.

19. Eugene Vetromile, *Travels in Europe, Egypt, Arabia, Petraea, Palestine and Syria* (New York: Sadlier, 1871), p. 13.

20. Spiller, *The American in England*, p. 392.

21. William A. Braman, *Glimpses of Europe* (Cleveland, Ohio: J. B. Savage, 1901), p. 39.

22. Isaac A. Jewett, *Passages in Foreign Travel*, 2 vols. (Boston: Charles C. Little & James Brown, 1838), 1:5–6.

23. Quoted by Moses Coit Tyler in *Glimpses of England; Social, Political, Literary* (New York & London: G. P. Putnam's Sons, 1898), p. 109.

24. John Mitchell, *Notes From Over Sea; Consisting of Observations Made in Europe in the Years 1843 and 1844*, 2 vols. (New York: Gates & Stedman, 1845), 1: 204.

25. John H. B. Latrobe, *Hints for Six Months in Europe; Being the Programme of a Tour through Parts of France, Italy, Austria, Saxony, Prussia, the Tyrol, Switzerland, Holland, Belgium, England and Scotland in the Summer of 1868* (Philadelphia: Lippincott, 1869), p. 338.

26. Richard G. White, *England Without and Within* (Boston: Houghton, Mifflin, 1881), p. 2–5.

✓ 27. Elkanah Watson, *Men and Times of the Revolution, or, Memoirs of Elkanah Watson, including Journals of Travel in Europe and America from 1777 to 1842* (New York: Dana, 1856), pp. 176–78.

28. Samuel G. Goodrich, *A Pictorial History of England* (Philadelphia: E. H. Butler Company, 1871), p. 11.

29. Stephen H. Tyng, *Recollections of England* (London: Bagster, 1847), p. 165.

30. James F. Rusling, *European Days and Ways* (Cincinnati: Jennings & Pye, 1902), p. 326.

31. Sara Jeanette Duncan, *An American Girl in London* (New York: Appleton, 1891), p. 153.

32. Ehrmann Syme Nadal, *Impressions of London Social Life* (New York: Scribner, Armstrong & Company, 1875), p. 142.

33. George P. Putnam, *The Tourist in Europe* (New York: Wiley & Putnam, 1838), pp. 107–8. Putnam is quoting an unsigned review of the *Great Metropolis* in the *North American Review*.

34. Noble L. Prentis, *A Kansan Abroad* (Topeka, Kans.: Martin, 1878), p. 135.

35. Curtis Guild, *Over the Ocean; or, Sights and Scenes in Foreign Lands* (Boston: Lee & Shepard, 1871), pp. 137–38.

36. *Old Sights with New Eyes*, "By a Yankee," intro. Robert Baird, D.D. (New York: M. W. Dodd, 1854), p. 20.

✓ 37. Nathaniel Hawthorne, *Our Old Home: A Series of English Sketches* (1863; Columbus, Ohio: Ohio State University Press, 1970), pp. 63–64.

38. George H. Calvert. *First Years in Europe* (Boston: William V. Spencer, 1866), p. 16.

39. William A. Drew, *Glimpses and Gatherings during a Voyage and Visit to London and the Great Exhibition in the Summer of 1851* (Augusta, Me.: Homan & Manley, 1852), p. 318.

40. Thurlow Weed, *Letters from Europe and the West Indies, 1843–1852* (Albany, N.Y.: Weed, Parsons and Company, 1866), p. 107.

41. Charles S. Stewart, *Sketches of Society in Great Britain and Ireland*, 2 vols. (Philadelphia: Carey, Lea & Blanchard, 1834), 1:81.

42. Mary H. Wills, *A Summer in Europe* (Philadelphia: J. B. Lippincott, 1876), p. 30.

✓ 43. Benjamin Silliman, *A Journal of Travels in England, Holland and Scotland, and of Two Passages over the Atlantic, in the Years 1805 and 1806*, 2 vols. (New York: Bruce, 1810), 1:239.

44. John W. Higinbotham, *Three Weeks in the British Isles* (Chicago: Reilly & Britton, 1911), p. 120.

45. Nathaniel Parker Willis, *Pencillings by the Way*, 3 vols. (London: T. Werner Laurie, Ltd., 1844), 3:506–7.

46. Charles Wood. *Saunterings in Europe* (New York: Randolph, 1882), p. 14.

47. Thwaites, *Our Cycling Tour in England*, p. 16.

Part I

Chapter 1

✓ 1. Margaret Fuller Ossoli, *At Home and Abroad: or, Things and Thoughts in America and Europe* (Boston: Crosby, Nichols and Company, 1856), pp. 205–51.

2. Ibid., p. 251.

3. Ibid., p. 252.

4. Benjamin Silliman, *A Journal of Travels in England, Holland and Scotland, and of Two Passages over the Atlantic in the Years 1805 and 1806*, 2 vols. (New York: Bruce, 1810), 2:371.

✓ 5. Joseph Ballard, *England in 1815 as Seen by a Young Boston Merchant* (Boston and New York: Houghton, Mifflin, 1913), pp. 172–73.

6. Emma H. Willard, *Journal and Letters, From Florence and Great-Britain* (Troy, N.Y.: Tuttle, 1833), p. 384.

7. William H. Seward, *Autobiography of William H. Seward from 1801 to 1834*, ed. Frederick Seward (New York: Appleton, 1877), p. 110.

8. *Dictionary of American Biography*. Ed. Allen Johnson. New York: Charles Scribner's Sons, 1927, 28, 29, 36. vol. IV, p. 259. See also *Dictionary of National Biography*. Ed. Sir Leslie Stephen and Sir Sidney Lee. Oxford: Oxford University Press, 1917, vol. II, p. 156. *re:* Gibson's mentor, the famed British surgeon, Sir Charles Bell, who went "in 1815 to Brussels to treat the wounded of Waterloo." It seems likely that Gibson accompanied Bell.

✓9. Heman Humphrey, *Great Britain, France and Belgium: A Short Tour in 1835*, 2 vols. (New York: Harper & Brothers, 1838). 1:237, 83, 84.

10. Calvin Colton, *Four Years in Great Britain, 1831–1835* (New York: Harper & Brothers, 1836), p. 172.

11. Wilbur Fisk, *Travels on the Continent of Europe* (New York: Harper, 1838), pp. 558, 630.

12. Nathaniel S. Wheaton, *A Journal of a Residence during Several Months in London; Including Excursions through Various Parts of England; and a Short Tour in France and Scotland; in the Years 1823 and 1824* (Hartford, Conn.: Huntington, 1830), pp. 161–62.

13. James Fenimore Cooper, *Gleanings in Europe. By an American*, 2 vols. 1837 (New York: Oxford University Press, 1930, reprint ed. Kraus Reprint Co., 1970), preface to 1930 edition, by Robert E. Spiller. 2:xxii.

14. Robert E. Spiller, *The American in England during the First Half Century of Independence* (New York: Henry Holt & Co., 1926), pp. 364–65.

15. Bayard Taylor, *Views Afoot; or, Europe as Seen with Knapsack and Staff* (New York: G. P. Putnam, 1859), p. 17.

16. Hezekiah H. Wright, *Desultory Reminiscences of a Tour through Germany, Switzerland and France. By an American* (Boston: Ticknor, 1838), p. 342.

17. Ibid., p. 347.

18. Ralph Waldo Emerson, *English Traits* (Boston: Phillips, Sampson and Company, 1856), p. 41.

19. Wright, *Desultory Reminiscences*, pp. 343–44.

Chapter 2

1. Andrew Carnegie, *An American Four-in-Hand in Britain* (New York: Scribner's, 1883), p. 12.

✓2. Nathaniel S. Wheaton, *A Journal of a Residence during Several Months in London; Including Excursions through Various Parts of England; and a Short Tour in France and Scotland; in the Years 1823 and 1824* (Hartford, Conn.: Huntington, 1830), p. 15.

3. James F. Clarke, *Eleven Weeks in Europe; And What May Be Seen in That Time* (Boston: Ticknor, Reed & Fields, 1852), p. 12.

4. Zachariah Allen, *The Practical Tourist; or, Sketches of the State of the Useful Arts, and of Society, Scenery, etc. etc., in Great Britain, France and Holland*, 2 vols. (Providence, R.I.: Beckwith, 1832), 2:409.

5. George P. Putnam, *The Tourist in Europe* (New York: Wiley & Putnam, 1838), p. 73.

6. Robert J. Breckinridge, *Memoranda of Foreign Travel: Containing Notices of a Pilgrimage through Some of the Principal States of Western Europe* (Baltimore, Md.: D. Owen & Son, 1845), pp. 8–9.

7. Allen, *The Practical Tourist*, 2:410.

8. Clarke, *Eleven Weeks in Europe*, p. 4.

9. Allen, *The Practical Tourist*, 2:409.

10. Fanny W. Hall, *Rambles in Europe; or, A Tour through France, Italy, Switzerland, and Great Britain, and Ireland in 1836*, 2 vols. (New York: French, 1838), 2:231.

✓11. Jacob Green, *Notes of a Traveller, during a Tour through England, France and Switzerland, in 1828*, 3 vols. (New York: Carvill, 1830), 1:45–46.

12. George Rapelje, *A Narrative of Excursions, Voyages and Travels Performed at Different Periods in America, Europe, Asia and Africa* (New York: West & Trow, 1834), p. 413.

13. Randal W. MacGavock, *A Tennessean Abroad; or, Letters from Europe, Africa, and Asia* (New York: Redfield, 1854), p. 13.

14. Dean Dudley, *Pictures of Life in England and America; Prose and Poetry* (Boston: French, 1851), p. 11.

15. Alexander Slidell MacKenzie, *The American in England*, 2 vols. (New York: Harper & Brothers, 1835), 1:39.

16. William H. Taylor, M.D. *The Book of Travels of a Doctor of Physic* (Philadelphia: Lippincott, 1871), p. 372.

17. John Griscom, *A Year in Europe, Comprising a Journal of Observations in England, Scotland, Ireland, France, Switzerland, the North of Italy, and Holland in 1818 and 1819*, 2 vols. (New York: Collins, 1823), 1:16.

18. Calvin Colton, *Four Years in Great Britain, 1831–1835* (New York: Harper & Brothers, 1836), p. 23.

19. John Jay Smith, *A Summer's Jaunt across the Water: Including Visits to England, Ireland, Scotland, France, Switzerland, Germany, Belgium, etc.,* 2 vols. (Philadelphia: Moore, 1846), 1:24.

20. Colton, *Four Years in Great Britain,* pp. 29–30.

21. Joseph Ballard, *England in 1815 as Seen by a Young Boston Merchant* (Boston and New York: Houghton, Mifflin Co., 1913), p. 7.

22. Breckinridge, *Memoranda of Foreign Travel,* p. 11.

23. Hall, *Rambles in Europe,* 2:237.

24. William H. Seward, *Autobiography of William H. Seward from 1801 to 1834,* ed. Frederick Seward (New York: Appleton, 1877), p. 104.

25. Smith, *A Summer's Jaunt across the Water,* 1:25–26.

26. Breckinridge, *Memoranda of Foreign Travel,* p. 15.

27. Green, *Notes of a Traveller,* 1:20–21.

28. Wheaton, *Journal of a Residence,* p. 21.

29. Cornelius C. Felton, *Familiar Letters From Europe* (Boston: Ticknor & Fields, 1865), p. 2.

30. Ballard, *England in 1815,* p. 4.

31. Allen, *The Practical Tourist,* 1:17.

32. Oliver Wendell Holmes, *Our Hundred Days in Europe* (Boston and New York: Houghton, Mifflin, 1887), pp. 16, 22.

33. Benjamin Silliman, *A Journal of Travels in England, Holland and Scotland, and of Two Passages over the Atlantic, in the Years 1805 and 1806,* 2 vols. (New York: Bruce, 1810), 1:18–19.

34. Ibid., 1:22–23.

35. Edward Dawson, *Benedict's Wanderings* (New York: George H. Richmond & Co., 1873), pp. 80–82.

36. Wheaton, *Journal of a Residence,* pp. 502–20.

37. Green, *Notes of a Traveller,* 1:13.

38. Zadock Thompson, *Journal of a Trip to London, Paris, and the Great Exhibition in 1851* (Burlington, Vt.: Nichols & Warren, 1852), p. 14.

39. George Catlin, *Catlin's Notes of Eight Years' Travel and Residence in Europe, with His North American Collection,* 2 vols. (New York: the author, 1848), 1:2–3.

40. Rapelje, *A Narrative of Excursions,* p. 410.

41. Felton, *Familiar Letters from Europe,* p. 5.

42. Samuel I. Prime, *Travels in Europe and the East; A Year in England, Scotland, Ireland, Wales, France, Belgium, Holland, Germany, Austria, Italy, Greece, Turkey, Syria, Palestine and Egypt,* 2 vols. (New York: Harper, 1855), 1:27–28.

43. Heman Humphrey, *Great Britain, France and Belgium: A Short Tour in 1835,* 2 vols. (New York: Harper & Brothers, 1838), 1:13.

44. Sarah M. Burnham, *Pleasant Memories of Foreign Travel* (Boston: Bradlee Whidden, 1896), p. 4.

45. Silliman, *A Journal of Travels,* 1:29.

46. Green, *Notes of a Traveller,* 1:66.

47. Samuel G. Goodrich, *Recollections of a Lifetime; or, Men and Things I Have Seen: in a Series of Familiar Letters to a Friend, Historical, Biographical, Anecdotal, and Descriptive,* 2 vols. (New York and Auburn: Miller, Orton & Co., 1857), 1:162.

48. Breckinridge, *Memoranda of Foreign Travel,* p. 31.

49. Putnam, *The Tourist in Europe,* p. 79.

50. Colton, *Four Years in Great Britain,* p. 42.

51. Silliman, *A Journal of Travels,* 1:47.

52. Griscom, *A Year in Europe,* 1:25.

53. Wheaton, *Journal of a Residence,* p. 25.

54. Silliman, *A Journal of Travels,* 1:34–35.

55. Charles S. Stewart, *Sketches of Society in Great Britain and Ireland,* 2 vols. (Philadelphia: Carey, Lea & Blanchard, 1834) 1:205.

√ 56. Orville Dewey, *The Old World and the New; or, A Journal of Reflections and Observations Made on a Tour in Europe,* 2 vols. (New York: Harper & Bros., 1836), 1:24–26.

57. Ballard, *England in 1815,* p. 166.

√ 58. Nathaniel H. Carter, *Letters From Europe, Comprising the Journal of a Tour through Ireland,*

England, Scotland, France, Italy, and Switzerland in the Years 1825–6–7, 2 vols. (New York: G. & C. & H. Carvill, 1829), 1:75.

59. Lily Lawrence Rust, *Hand-written Journal.* Pages unnumbered. 3 vols. 1903.

60. Stewart, *Sketches of Society,* 1:35.

61. Fisk, *Travels on the Continent,* pp. 499, 501.

62. Green, *Notes of Traveller,* 1:100–101.

Chapter 3

✓ 1. Calvin Colton, *Four Years in Great Britain, 1831–1835* (New York: Harper & Brothers, 1836), p. 53.

✓2. Alexander Slidell MacKenzie, *The American in England,* 2 vols. (New York: Harper & Brothers, 1835), 1:63.

3. Ibid., 1:63–64.

4. Ibid., 1:127–28.

✓ 5. Nathaniel S. Wheaton, *A Journal of a Residence during Several months in London; Including Excursions through Various Parts of England; and a Short Tour in France and Scotland; in the Years 1823 and 1824* (Hartford, Conn.: Huntington, 1830), p. 102.

✓ 6. Joshua E. White, *Letters on England: Comprising Descriptive Scenes; with Remarks on the State of Society, Domestic Economy, Habits of the People, and Condition of the Manufacturing Classes Generally,* 2 vols. (Philadelphia: Carey, 1816), 1:4–5.

7. Joseph Ballard, *England in 1815 as Seen by a Young Boston Merchant* (Boston and New York: Houghton, Mifflin, Co., 1913), p. 67.

8. Wheaton, *Journal of a Residence,* pp. 111–12.

9. William Gibson, M.D., *Rambles in Europe in 1839; With Sketches of Prominent Surgeons, Physicians, Medical Schools, Hospitals, Literary Personages, Scenery, etc.* (Philadelphia: Lea & Blanchard, 1841), p. 308.

10. Benjamin Silliman, *A Journal of Travels in England; Holland and Scotland, and of Two Passages over the Atlantic, in the Years 1805 and 1806,* 2 vols. (New York: Bruce, 1810), 2:123.

11. Jacob Green, *Notes of a Traveller, during a Tour through England, France and Switzerland, in 1828,* 3 vols. (New York: Carvill, 1830), 1:121.

✓ 12. Heman Humphrey, *Great Britain, France and Belgium: A Short Tour in 1835,* 2 vols. (New York: Harper & Brothers, 1838), 1:23.

13. Colton, *Four Years in Great Britain,* p. 268.

14. Humphrey, *Great Britain,* 1:25.

15. MacKenzie, *The American in England,* 1:131, 2:185.

16. Jacob Abbott, *A Summer in Scotland* (New York: Harper, 1848), p. 63.

17. Emma H. Willard, *Journal and Letters, From France and Great-Britain* (Troy, N.Y.: Tuttle, 1833), p. 338.

18. Silliman, *A Journal of Travels,* 2:29.

19. Washington Irving, *The Sketchbook of Geoffrey Crayon, Gentleman* (New York: G. P. Putnam & Co., 1854), pp. 247, 325–26.

20. Colton, *Four Years in Great Britain,* p. 62.

21. Nathaniel H. Carter, *Letters From Europe, Comprising the Journal of a Tour through Ireland, England, Scotland, France, Italy, and Switzerland in the Years 1825–6–7,* 2 vols. (New York: G. & C. & H. Carvill, 1829), 1:171–72.

✓22. Henry B. McLellan, *Journal of a Residence in Scotland, and a Tour through England, France, Germany, Switzerland and Italy* (Boston: Allen & Ticknor, 1834), p. 110.

23. Colton, *Four Years in Great Britain,* pp. 44–48.

✓ 24. Isaac A. Jewett, *Passages in Foreign Travel,* 2 vols. (Boston: Charles C. Little & James Brown, 1838), 1:51.

25. Ibid., 1:53, 56, 59, 62.

26. Caroline M. Kirkland, *Holidays Abroad; or, Europe from the West,* 2 vols. (New York: Baker and Scribner, 1849), 1:43.

✓27. Henry Colman, *European Life and Manners: In Familiar Letters to Friends,* 2 vols. (Boston: Charles C. Little & James Brown, 1849), 2:412–13.

28. Zachariah Allen, *The Practical Tourist; or, Sketches of the State of the Useful Arts, and of Society, Scenery, etc. etc., in Great Britain, France and Holland,* 2 vols. (Providence, R.I.: Beckwith, 1832), 1:71.

29. Ballard, *England in 1815,* pp. 84–85, 69.

30. Ibid., pp. 20–21.

31. Wilbur Fisk, *Travels on the Continent of Europe* (New York: Harper, 1838), pp. 676–77, 605.

32. Allen, *The Practical Tourist,* 1:128–29.

33. Ibid., 1:148–50, 152.

34. Humphrey, *Great Britain,* 1:136.

35. Fisk, *Travels on the Continent,* pp. 680–81.

36. Fanny W. Hall, *Rambles in Europe; or, A Tour through France, Italy, Switzerland, Great Britain, and Ireland in 1836,* 2 vols. (New York: French, 1838), 2:172.

37. Green, *Notes of a Traveller,* 1:160–61.

38. Fisk, *Travels on the Continent,* p. 504.

39. Ibid., p. 605.

40. Ballard, *England in 1815,* p. 158.

41. Humphrey, *Great Britain,* 1:230–32.

42. Samuel Curwen, *Journal and Letters of the Late Samuel Curwen,* ed. George A. Ward (New York: C. S. Francis & Co., 1842), p. 135.

43. Carter, *Letters from Europe,* 1:229.

✓ 44. Margaret Fuller Ossoli, *At Home and Abroad: or, Things and Thoughts in America and Europe* (Boston: Crosby, Nichols, and Company, 1856), p. 164.

45. Ballard, *England in 1815,* p. 15.

46. Allen, *The Practical Tourist,* 1:153.

47. White, *Letters on England,* 2:216–17, 218.

48. Green, *Notes of a Traveller,* 2:137.

49. Colman, *European Life and Manners,* 1:309–10.

50. Ibid., 1:155, 324.

51. Ibid., 1:320.

52. Ibid.

✓ 53. Frederick Law Olmsted, *Walks and Talks of an American Farmer in England* (1852; reprint, ed. Ann Arbor, Mich.: University of Michigan Press, 1967), Preface, pp. xv–xvi.

54. Ibid., pp. 236–38.

55. Ibid., p. 310.

56. Silliman, *A Journal of Travels,* 1:124–26.

57. Wheaton, *A Journal of Residence,* p. 256.

58. Silliman, 2:224, 236.

59. Ibid., 2:238–39.

60. Ibid., 2:239.

61. Gibson, *Rambles in Europe,* pp. ix, 35.

62. Ibid., pp. 39–40.

63. Ibid., p. 42.

64. Ibid., pp. 136–37, 140.

Chapter 4

1. Quoted by Edward L. Temple in *Old World Memories,* 2 vols. (Boston: Page, 1899), 1:119.

✓ 2. George Ticknor, *Life, Letters and Journals of George Ticknor,* 2 vols. (Boston: Osgood, 1876), 1:287–88, 432.

3. Orville Dewey, *The Old World and the New; or, A Journal of Reflections and Observations Made on a Tour in Europe,* 2 vols. (New York: Harper & Bros., 1836), 1:91–92, 94.

4. Margaret Fuller Ossoli, *At Home and Abroad: or, Things and Thoughts in America and Europe* (Boston: Crosby, Nichols, and Company; 1856), p. 132.

✓5. George H. Calvert, *Scenes and Thoughts in Europe. By an American* (New York: Wiley & Putnam, 1846), p. 2.

6. Orlando W. Wight, *Peoples and Countries Visited in a Winding Journey around the World* (Detroit, Mich.: Raynor & Taylor, 1888), p. 20.

✓7. Nathaniel H. Carter, *Letters from Europe, Comprising the Journal of a Tour through Ireland, England, Scotland, France, Italy, and Switzerland in the Years 1825–6–7*, 2 vols. (New York: G. & C. & H. Carvill, 1829), 1:95.

8. Dewey, *The Old World and the New*, 1:102–3.

9. Carter, *Letters from Europe*, 1:96.

10. Samuel S. Cox, *A Buckeye Abroad: or, Wanderings in Europe and the Orient* (New York: G. P. Putnam, 1852), p. 431.

11. Richard C. McCormick, *St. Paul's to St. Sophia; or, Sketchings in Europe* (New York: Sheldon, 1860), pp. 156–57.

✓12. Benjamin Moran, *The Footpath and Highway: or, Wanderings of an American in Great Britain in 1851 and '52* (Philadelphia: Lippincott, Grambo and Co., 1853), pp. 71–72.

13. Andrew McFarland, M.D., *The Escape, or, Loiterings amid the Scenes of Song and Story* (Boston: Mussey, 1851), p. 61.

✓14. Sophia A. Hawthorne, *Notes in England and Italy* (New York: Putnam, 1870), pp. 90, 102.

15. Joel Cook, *A Holiday Tour in Europe, Described in a Series of Letters for the Public Ledger during the Summer and Autumn of 1878* (Philadelphia: J. B. Lippincott Co., 1879), p. 85.

16. Dewey, *The Old World and the New*, 1:106–7.

17. Andrew Jackson Downing, *Rural Essays* (New York: Leavitt & Allen, 1855), p. 512.

18. Zachariah Allen, *The Practical Tourist; or, Sketches of the State of the Useful Arts, and of Society, Scenery, etc. etc., in Great Britain, France and Holland*, 2 vols. (Providence, R.I.: Beckwith, 1832), 1:279.

✓19. Charles S. Stewart, *Sketches of Society in Great Britain and Ireland*, 2 vols. (Philadelphia: Carey, Lea & Blanchard, 1834), 2:56–57.

20. Sir Walter Scott, "The Lay of the Last Minstrel", in his *Poetical Works* (London: Oxford University Press, 1904), Canto Second, no. xi, ll. 1–12, p. 10.

21. Hawthorne, *Notes in England and Italy*, p. 25.

22. Andrew Dickinson, *My First Visit to Europe; or, Sketches of Society, Scenery, and Antiquities in England, Wales, Ireland, Scotland, and France* (New York: George P. Putnam, 1851), pp. 105–6.

23. Caroline M. Kirkland, *Holidays Abroad; or, Europe from the West*, 2 vols. (New York: Baker and Scribner, 1849), 1:30.

24. Cox, *A Buckeye Abroad*, p. 423.

25. Benjamin Silliman, *A Journal of Travels in England, Holland and Scotland, and of Two Passages over the Atlantic, in the Years 1805 and 1806*, 2 vols. (New York: Bruce, 1810), 2:278, 299.

26. Ibid., 2:345–46.

27. Dewey, *The Old World and the New*, 1:61.

28. Silliman, *A Journal of Travels*, 2:277.

29. Carter, *Letters from Europe*, 1:250.

✓30. Fanny W. Hall, *Rambles in Europe; or, A Tour through France, Italy, Switzerland, and Great Britain, and Ireland in 1836*, 2 vols. (New York: French, 1838), 2:200

31. Ibid., 2:194–95.

✓32. John A. Clark, *Glimpses of the Old World, or, Excursions on the Continent and in Great Britain*, 2 vols. (London: Samuel Bagster and Sons, 1840), 2: 332–33.

33. Dickinson, *My First Visit to Europe*, pp. 67, 69.

34. Moran, *Footpath and Highway*, pp. 185–86.

35. Nathaniel Hawthorne, *The English Notebooks*, ed. Randall Stewart (New York: Russell & Russell, Inc., 1962), p. 336.

36. Samuel Young, *A Wall-Street Bear in Europe, With His Familiar Foreign Journal of a Tour through Portions of England, Scotland, France, and Italy* (New York: S. Young, Jr., privately printed 1855), p. 194.

37. John Mitchell, *Notes From Over Sea; Consisting of Observations Made in Europe in the Years 1843 and 1844*, 2 vols. (New York: Gates & Stedman, 1845), 1:124–25.

✓38. Bayard Taylor, *Views Afoot; or, Europe as Seen with Knapsack and Staff* (New York: G. P. Putnam, 1859), p. 66.

39. Ralph Waldo Emerson, *English Traits* (Boston: Phillips, Sampson, and Company 1856), pp. 254–55.

40. George P. Putnam, *The Tourist in Europe* (New York: Wiley & Putnam, 1838), p. 131.

41. Henry Colman, *European Life and Manners: In Familiar Letters to Friends*, 2 vols. (Boston: Charles C. Little & James Brown, 1849), 1:86.

42. Washington Irving, *The Works of Washington Irving*, 15 vols. (New York: G. P. Putnam & Co., 1854), 9:245.

43. William Gibson, M.D., *Rambles in Europe in 1839; With Sketches of Prominent Surgeons, Physicians, Medical Schools, Hospitals, Literary Personages, Scenery, etc.* (Philadelphia: Lea & Blanchard, 1841), pp. 186–88.

44. Carter, *Letters from Europe*, 1:287.

45. Calvin Colton, *Four Years in Great Britain, 1831–1835* (New York: Harper & Brothers, 1836), p. 208.

46. Allen, *The Practical Tourist*, 2:345–46.

47. Dewey, *The Old World and the New*, 1:67.

48. Silliman, *A Journal of Travels*, 2:317.

49. Dewey, *The Old World and the New*, 1:61.

50. Colton, *Four Years in Great Britain*, p. 209.

51. Taylor, *Views Afoot*, p. 52.

52. Henry P. Tappan, *A Step from the New World to the Old, and Back Again; With Thoughts on the Good and Evil in Both*, 2 vols. (New York: Appleton, 1852), 1:235, 214–15.

53. Mitchell, *Notes from Over Sea*, 1:96–97.

54. Harriet Beecher Stowe, *Sunny Memories of Foreign Lands*, 2 vols. (Boston: Phillips, Sampson and Company, 1854), 1:69.

55. Samuel G. Goodrich, *Recollections of a Lifetime; or, Men and Things I Have Seen: in a Series of Familiar Letters to a Friend, Historical, Biographical, Anecdotal, and Descriptive*, 2 vols. (New York and Auburn: Miller, Orton & Co., 1857), 2:175–76.

56. Edward Everett, *The Mount Vernon Papers* (New York: D. Appleton & Co., 1860), pp. 118, 121–22, 143.

57. Stewart, *Sketches of Society*, 1:77.

58. Henry B. McLellan, *Journal of a Residence in Scotland, and a Tour through England, France, Germany, Switzerland and Italy* (Boston: Allen & Ticknor, 1834), p. 225.

59. Dewey, *The Old World and the New*, 1:74.

60. Gibson, *Rambles in Europe*, p. 130.

61. Ossoli, *At Home and Abroad*, p. 137.

62. Charles F. Greville, *The Greville Memoirs*, 2 vols. (New York: Appleton, 1885–87), 2:408–9.

63. Cox, *A Buckeye Abroad*, p. 414.

64. Moran, *Footpath and Highway*, p. 195.

65. Cox, *A Buckeye Abroad*, p. 415.

66. Mrs. A. E. Newman [Evangeline], *European Leaflets for Young Ladies* (New York: John F. Baldwin, 1861), p. 185.

67. Taylor, *Views Afoot*, pp. 66–67.

68. Tappan, *A Step from the Old World*, 1:208.

69. Grace Greenwood, *Haps and Mishaps of a Tour in Europe* (Boston: Ticknor, Reed & Fields, 1854), p. 134.

70. Scott, "The Lay of the Last Minstrel," Canto Second, ll. 1–3.

71. Colman, *European Life and Manners*, 1:79.

72. Moran, *Footpath and Highway*, pp. 199–200.

73. Jacob Abbott, *A Summer in Scotland* (New York: Harper, 1848), p. 190.

74. Taylor, *Views Afoot*, p. 53.

75. William Cullen Bryant, *Letters of a Traveller; or, Notes of Things Seen in Europe and America* (New York: George P. Putnam, 1850), p. 409.

76. Andrew Bigelow, *Leaves From a Journal; or, Sketches of Rambles in Some Parts of North Britain and Ireland, Chiefly in the Year 1817* (Boston: Wells & Lilly, 1821), p. 33.

77. Carter, *Letters from Europe*, 1:331–32, 349.

78. Moran, *Footpath and Highway*, pp. 170–71.

79. Elkanah Watson, *Men and Times of the Revolution, or, Memoirs of Elkanah Watson, Including Journals of Travel in Europe and America from 1777 to 1842* (New York: Dana, 1856), p. 154.

80. Silliman, *A Journal of Travels,* 1:122–23.

81. Joseph Ballard, *England in 1815 as Seen by a Young Boston Merchant* (Boston & New York: Houghton, Mifflin, Co., 1913), p. 157.

✔ 82. Washington Irving, *The Sketchbook of Geoffrey Crayon, Gentleman,* (New York: G. P. Putnam & Co., 1854), pp. 325–26.

83. Young, *A Wall-Street Bear in Europe,* p. 181.

84. Stephen C. Massett, *"Drifting About"; or, What "Jeems Pipes of Pipesville," Saw-and-Did* (New York: Carleton, 1863), p. 184.

85. Irving, *Sketchbook,* p. 326, 333.

86. Stewart, *Sketches of Society,* 1:81.

87. Carter, *Letters from Europe,* 1:361–62.

✔ 88. George Putnam, *The Tourist in Europe* (New York: Wiley & Putnam, 1838), pp. 86–87.

89. Henry Ward Beecher, *Star Papers; or, Experiences of Art and Nature* (New York: Derby, 1855), pp. 23–25.

✔ 90. Nathaniel Parker Willis, *Famous Persons and Places* (New York: Scribner, 1854), pp. 282–83.

91. Nathaniel Hawthorne, *Our Old Home: A Series of English Sketches* (1863; Columbus, Ohio: Ohio State University Press, 1970), p. 99.

92. Quoted in Stewart, *Sketches of Society,* 1:72.

93. Ibid., 1:73–74.

94. Allen, *The Practical Tourist,* 1:82.

✔ 95. Robert J. Breckinridge, *Memoranda of Foreign Travel: Containing Notices of a Pilgrimage through some of the Principal States of Western Europe* (Baltimore, Md.: D. Owen & Son, 1845), pp. 56–57.

96. John H. B. Latrobe, *Hints for Six Months in Europe; Being the Programme of a Tour through Parts of France, Italy, Austria, Saxony, Prussia, the Tyrol, Switzerland, Holland, Belgium, England and Scotland in the Summer of 1868* (Philadelphia: Lippincott, 1869), p. 342.

97. Randal W. MacGavock, *A Tennessean Abroad; or, Letters from Europe, Africa, and Asia* (New York: Redfield, 1854), p. 36.

98. Putnam, *The Tourist in Europe,* pp. 83–85.

99. Downing, *Rural Essays,* pp. 475–76.

100. Beecher, *Star Papers,* p. 18.

101. James F. Clarke, *Eleven Weeks in Europe; and What May Be Seen in That Time* (Boston: Ticknor, Reed & Fields, 1852), p. 54.

102. Putnam, *The Tourist in Europe,* pp. 85–86.

103. Dewey, *The Old World and the New,* 1:117–18.

104. Stewart, *Sketches of Society,* 1:67.

✔ 105. William Coombs Dana, *A Transatlantic Tour: Comprising Travels in Great Britain, France, Holland, Belgium, Germany, Switzerland and Italy* (Philadelphia: Perkins & Purves, 1845), p. 24.

106. Kirkland, *Holidays Abroad,* 1:39.

107. Beecher, *Star Papers,* pp. 14–17.

108. Greenwood, *Haps and Mishaps,* p. 27.

109. Jacob Green, *Notes of a Traveller, during a Tour through England, France and Switzerland, in 1828,* 3 vols. (New York: Carvill, 1830), 1:178.

110. Dana, *A Transatlantic Tour,* p. 46.

111. Samuel Curwen, *Journal and Letters of the Late Samuel Curwen,* ed. George A. Ward (New York: C. S. Francis & Co., 1842), p. 137.

112. Allen, *The Practical Tourist,* 1:326.

113. McLellan, *Journal of a Residence,* p. 336.

114. Abigail Adams, *Letters of Mrs. Adams, the Wife of John Adams* (Boston: Little & Brown, 1840), pp. 312, 314–15.

115. Watson, *Men and Times,* pp. 172–73.

116. Silliman, *A Journal of Travels,* 2:20–21.

117. George Rapelje, *A Narrative of Excursions, Voyages and Travels Performed at Different Periods in America, Europe, Asia, and Africa* (New York: West & Trow, 1834), p. 79.

118. Green, *Notes of a Traveller,* 1:91.

119. John Griscom, *A Year in Europe, Comprising a Journal of Observations in England, Scotland, Ireland, France, Switzerland, the North of Italy, and Holland, in 1818 and 1819*, 2 vols. (New York: Collins, 1823), 1:237.

120. Nathaniel S. Wheaton, *A Journal of a Residence during Several Months in London; Including Excursions through Various Parts of England; and a Short Tour in France and Scotland; in the Years 1823 and 1824* (Hartford, Conn.: Huntington, 1830), pp. 331–32.

121. Alexander Slidell MacKenzie, *The American in England*, 2 vols. (New York: Harper & Brothers, 1835), 2:166, 168–69, 172.

122. Heman Humphrey, *Great Britain, France and Belgium: A Short Tour in 1835*, 2 vols. (New York: Harper & Brothers, 1838), 1:160–62.

Chapter 5

1. Henry B. McLellan, *Journal of a Residence in Scotland, and a Tour through England, France, Germany, Switzerland and Italy* (Boston: Allen & Ticknor, 1834), p. 228.

2. Benjamin Silliman, *A Journal of Travels in England, Holland and Scotland, and of Two Passages over the Atlantic, in the Years 1805 and 1806*, 2 vols. (New York: Bruce, 1810), 1:133–34.

3. Joshua E. White, *Letters on England: Comprising Descriptive Scenes; with Remarks on the State of Society, Domestic Economy; Habits of the People, and Condition of the Manufacturing Classes Generally*, 2 vols. (Philadelphia: Carey, 1816), 1:264–65.

4. James F. Clarke, *Eleven Weeks in Europe; and What May Be Seen in That Time* (Boston: Ticknor, Reed & Fields, 1852), p. 59.

5. Henry Colman, *European Life and Manners: In Familiar Letters to Friends*, 2 vols. (Boston: Charles C. Little & James Brown, 1849), 1:196.

6. Joseph Battell, *The Yankee Boy from Home* (New York: John F. Trow, Printer, 1863), p. 204.

7. Wilbur Fisk, *Travels on the Continent of Europe* (New York: Harper, 1838), p. 510.

8. Colman, *European Life and Manners*, 1:3–4.

✓ 9. Isaac A. Jewett, *Passages in Foreign Travel*, 2 vols. (Boston: Charles C. Little & James Brown, 1838), 1:10.

10. Alexander Slidell MacKenzie, *The American in England*, 2 vols. (New York: Harper & Brothers, 1835), 2:74–75.

11. White, *Letters on England*, 1:260–62.

12. MacKenzie, *The American in England*, 2:56.

13. Jewett, *Passages in Foreign Travel*, 1:9–10.

14. MacKenzie, *The American in England*, 2:71, 73.

15. Mark Trafton, *Rambles in Europe: In a Series of Familiar Letters* (Boston: Peirce, 1852), p. 72.

16. Silliman, *A Journal of Travels*, 1:156.

17. Nathaniel H. Carter, *Letters from Europe, Comprising the Journal of a Tour through Ireland, England, Scotland, France, Italy, and Switzerland in the Years 1825–6–7*, 2 vols. (New York: G. & C. & H. Carvill, 1829), 1:133.

✓ 18. James Fenimore Cooper, *Gleanings in Europe. By an American*, 2 vols., 1837 (New York: Oxford University Press, 1930; reprint ed. Kraus Reprint Co., 1970), 2:38.

19. Carter, *Letters from Europe*, 1:133.

20. Mordecai M. Noah, *Travels in England, France, Spain and the Barbary Coast in the Years 1813–14 and 1815* (New York: Kirk & Mercein, 1819), p. 36.

21. Emma H. Willard, *Journal and Letters, from France and Great-Britain* (Troy, N.Y.: Tuttle, 1833), pp. 292–93.

22. Zachariah Allen, *The Practical Tourist; or, Sketches of the State of the Useful Arts, and of Society, Scenery, etc. etc., in Great Britain, France and Holland*, 2 vols. (Providence, R.I.: Beckwith, 1832), 1:262.

23. Silliman, *A Journal of Travels*, 1:140–41, 147, 152.

24. Nathaniel S. Wheaton, *A Journal of a Residence during Several Months in London; Including Excursions through Various Parts of England; and a Short Tour in France and Scotland; in the Years 1823 and 1824* (Hartford, Conn.: Huntington, 1830), p. 124.

✓ 25. James F. Clarke, *Eleven Weeks in Europe: and What May Be Seen in That Time* (Boston: Ticknor, Reed & Fields, 1852), pp. 165–66.

26. MacKenzie, *The American in England*, 2:67–68.

27. Jacob Green, *Notes of a Traveller, during a Tour through England, France and Switzerland, in 1828*, 3 vols. (New York: Carvill, 1830), 2:273–74.

28. Samuel I. Prime, *Travels in Europe and the East; A Year in England, Scotland, Ireland, Wales, France, Belgium, Holland, Germany, Austria, Italy, Greece, Turkey, Syria, Palestine and Egypt*, 2 vols. (New York, Harper, 1855), 1:90.

29. Wheaton, *Journal of a Residence*, p. 122.

30. Carter, *Letters from Europe*, 1:127.

31. Wheaton, *Journal of a Residence*, p. 123.

32. George Rapelje, *A Narrative of Excursions, Voyages, and Travels Performed at Different Periods in America, Europe, Asia, and Africa* (New York: West & Trow, 1834), p. 43.

33. MacKenzie, *The American in England*, 1:222.

34. Green, *Notes of a Traveller*, 1:202–3.

35. George P. Putnam, *The Tourist in Europe* (New York: Wiley & Putnam, 1838), p. 95.

36. MacKenzie, *The American in England*, 1:225, 228–29.

37. Ibid., 1:231–32.

38. Ibid., 1:234–36.

39. *Old Sights with New Eyes*, "By a Yankee," intro. Robert Baird, D.D. (New York: M. W. Dodd, 1854), p. 55.

40. Stephen H. Tyng, *Recollections of England* (London: Bagster, 1847), pp. 222–23.

41. Rapelje, *A Narrative of Excursions*, pp. 89–90.

42. Colman, *European Life and Manners*, 1:23.

43. Tyng, *Recollections of England*, 224–25.

44. Allen, *The Practical Tourist*, 1:294.

45. Green, *Notes of a Traveller*, 2:4–5, 19.

46. McLellan, *Journal of a Residence*, p. 229.

47. Calvin Colton, *Four Years in Great Britain, 1831–1835* (New York: Harper & Brothers, 1836, pp. 101–2, 114–15.

48. MacKenzie, *The American in England*, 2:51–53.

49. Fanny W. Hall, *Rambles in Europe; or, A Tour through France, Italy, Switzerland, and Great Britain, and Ireland, in 1836*, 2 vols. (New York: French, 1838), 2:139.

50. Heman Humphrey, *Great Britain, France and Belgium: A Short Tour in 1835*, 2 vols. (New York: Harper & Brothers, 1838), 1:88–89.

51. Charles S. Stewart, *Sketches of Society in Great Britain and Ireland*, 2 vols. (Philadelphia: Carey, Lea & Blanchard, 1834), 2:166.

52. Silliman, *A Journal of Travels*, 1:223, 225.

53. William Austin, *Letters from London Written during the Years 1802 and 1803* (Boston: Pelham, 1804), p. 139.

54. Silliman, *A Journal of Travels*, 1:277–28, 230.

55. Cooper, *Gleanings*, 1:130–32.

56. William H. Seward, *Autobiography of William H. Seward from 1801 to 1834*, ed. Frederick Seward (New York: Appleton, 1877), pp. 113–14.

57. Wheaton, *Journal of a Residence*, pp. 185–86.

58. MacKenzie, *The American in England*, 2:167–68.

59. Wheaton, *Journal of a Residence*, p. 218.

60. Putnam, *The Tourist in Europe*, pp. 100–101.

61. Humphrey, *Great Britain*, 1:80–81.

62. Hall, *Rambles in Europe*, 2:147.

63. Silliman, *A Journal of Travels*, 1:330–31.

64. Abigail Adams, *Letters of Mrs. Adams, the Wife of John Adams* (Boston: Little & Brown, 1840), p. 179.

65. Ibid., p. 180.

66. Silliman, *A Journal of Travels*, 1:319.

67. William A. Drew, *Glimpses and Gatherings during a Voyage and Visit to London and the Great Exhibition in the Summer of 1851* (Augusta, Me.: Homan & Manley, 1852), pp. 162–64.

68. William Coombs Dana, *A Transatlantic Tour: Comprising Travels in Great Britain, France, Holland, Belgium, Germany, Switzerland, and Italy* (Philadelphia: Perkins & Purves, 1845), p. 73.

✓ 69. Grant Thorburn, *Men and Manners in Great Britain: A Bone to Gnaw on for the Trollopes, Fidlers, &c.* (New York: Wiley & Long, 1834), p. 39.

✓70. Calvin Colton, *Four Years in Great Britain, 1831–1835* (New York: Harper & Brothers, 1836), pp. 117–18.

71. Silliman, *A Journal of Travels,* 1:263–65.

72. Stewart, *Sketches of Society,* 1:151–52.

73. Colton, *Four Years in Great Britain,* pp. 118–19, 121, 123.

74. Willard, *Journal and Letters,* p. 305.

✓ 75. Lydia H. Sigourney, *Pleasant Memories of Pleasant Lands* (Boston: Munroe, 1842), pp. 301–2.

76. Silliman, *A Journal of Travels,* 1:294.

77. Humphrey, *Great Britain,* 1:100.

78. Joseph Ballard, *England in 1815 as Seen by a Young Boston Merchant* (Boston & New York: Houghton, Mifflin, Co., 1913), pp. 44–45.

79. Humphrey, *Great Britain,* 1:98–99, 104.

80. Silliman, *A Journal of Travels,* 1:238.

81. Nathaniel Hawthorne, *Our Old Home: A Series of English Sketches* (1863; Columbus, Ohio: Ohio State University Press, 1970), p. 257.

82. Humphrey, *Great Britain,* 1:74–75, 86.

83. Thorburn, *Men and Manners,* pp. 159–60.

✓84. Samuel G. Goodrich, *Recollections of a Lifetime; or, Men and Things I Have Seen: in a Series of Familar Letters to a Friend, Historical, Biographical, Anecdotal, and Descriptive,* 2 vols. (New York & Auburn: Miller, Orton, & Co., 1857), 2:240–41.

85. Stewart, *Sketches of Society,* 1:181.

86. Humphrey, *Great Britain,* 1:33, 38–39, 41.

87. Carter, *Letters from Europe,* 1:370–71.

88. MacKenzie, *The American in England,* 2:35–36.

89. Green, *Notes of a Traveller,* 2:25–26.

90. Silliman, *A Journal of Travels,* 1:254–55.

91. Stewart, *Sketches of Society,* 1:144–45.

92. Ballard, *England in 1815,* p. 36.

93. Silliman, *A Journal of Travels,* 1:217–222.

94. Green, *Notes of a Traveller,* 1:288.

95. Putnam, *The Tourist in Europe,* p. 104.

96. Orville Dewey, *The Old World and the New; or, A Journal of Reflections and Observations Made on a Tour in Europe,* 2 vols. (New York: Harper & Bros., 1836), 2:245–46.

97. Silliman, *A Journal of Travels,* 1:337–40; 2:9–10.

98. John Griscom, *A Year in Europe, Comprising a Journal of Observations in England, Scotland, Ireland, France, Switzerland, the North of Italy, and Holland, in 1818 and 1819,* 2 vols. (New York: Collins, 1823), 1:153.

99. Austin, *Letters from London,* p. 247.

✓100. George Ticknor, *Life, Letters and Journals of George Ticknor,* 2 vols. (Boston: Osgood, 1876), 1:59–60.

✓101. Nathaniel Parker Willis, *Pencillings by the Way,* 3 vols. (London: T. Werner Laurie, Ltd., 1844), 3:424–26.

102. Green, *Notes of a Traveller,* 1:245, 260–61.

103. Griscom, *A Year in Europe,* 1:148–51.

104. Silliman, *A Journal of Travels,* 2:13–15.

105. Ibid., 1:164–65.

106. Ticknor, *Life, Letters, and Journals,* 1:63.

107. Aaron Burr, *The Private Journal of Aaron Burr,* ed. Matthew L. Davis (New York: Harper & Bros., 1838), p. 113.

108. William Gibson, M.D. *Rambles in Europe in 1839; With Sketches of Prominent Surgeons, Physicians, Medical Schools, Hospitals, Literary Personages, Scenery, etc.* (Philadelphia: Lea & Blanchard, 1841), p. 182.

109. Margaret Fuller Ossoli, *At Home and Abroad: or, Things and Thoughts in America and Europe* (Boston: Crosby, Nichols, and Company, 1856), p. 174.

110. Wheaton, *Journal of a Residence*, p. 156.

111. Ticknor, *Life, Letters, and Journals*, 1:297.

112. Hawthorne, *Our Old Home*, p. 263.

113. Willard, *Journal and Letters*, pp. 307–10.

114. Griscom, *A Year in Europe*, 1:379–80.

✓115. Ralph Waldo Emerson, *The Heart of Emerson's Journals*, ed. Bliss Perry (Boston and New York: Houghton Mifflin Co., 1926), p. 230.

116. Colman, *European Life and Manners*, 2:402.

117. Willard, *Journal and Letters*, pp. 311–12.

118. Silliman, *A Journal of Travels*, 1:191, 194.

119. Ballard, *England in 1815*, p. 55.

120. Stewart, *Sketches of Society*, 1:114.

121. Willard, *Journal and Letters*, p. 329.

✓122. Oliver Wendell Holmes, *Our Hundred Days in Europe* (Boston and New York: Houghton, Mifflin, Co., 1887), pp. 7–8.

123. Willis, *Pencillings by the Way*, 3:423.

124. Putnam, *The Tourist in Europe*, pp. 89–90.

125. Henry Wikoff, *The Reminiscences of an Idler* (New York: Fords, Howard & Hulbert, 1880), pp. 407–8.

126. Clarke, *Eleven Weeks in Europe*, pp. 220–21.

127. MacKenzie, *The American in England*, 1:102, 107.

128. Fisk, *Travels on the Continent*, p. 525.

129. Humphrey, *Great Britain*, 1:110–11.

130. Richard Rush, *Residence at the Court of London. . .* (Philadelphia: Lippincott, 1872), p. 336.

131. Carter, *Letters from Europe*, 1:373.

132. Wheaton, *Journal of a Residence*, p. 56.

133. MacKenzie, *The American in England*, 2:101–2.

134. Ballard, *England in 1815*, p. 142.

135. White, *Letters on England*, 1:3.

136. Green, *Notes of a Traveller*, 1:250.

137. White, *Letters on England*, 1:5.

138. Wheaton, *Journal of a Residence*, p. 161.

139. Humphrey, *Great Britain*, 1:25.

140. Willard, *Journal and Letters*, p. 339.

141. Silliman, *A Journal of Travels*, 1:65.

142. Ibid., 1:242–43.

143. MacKenzie, *The American in England*, 1:171–72.

144. Wheaton, *Journal of a Residence*, p. 223.

145. Arthur Cleveland Coxe, *Impressions of England; or, Sketches of English Scenery and Society* (New York: Dana & Co., 1856), p. 70.

146. Rapelje, *A Narrative of Excursions*, p. 50.

147. Mark Trafton, *Rambles in Europe: In a Series of Familiar Letters* (Boston: Peirce, 1852), pp. 61–62.

148. Colman, *European Life and Manners*, 2:61.

149. MacKenzie, *The American in England*, 2:73–74.

150. Jewett, *Passages in Foreign Travel*, 1:75.

151. Ibid., 1:76.

152. MacKenzie, *The American in England*, 1:172–73.

153. Jewett, *Passages in Foreign Travel*, 1:75–76.

154. Ibid., 1:74–75.

155. Silliman, *A Journal of Travels*, 1:245–46.

156. Wheaton, *Journal of a Residence*, p. 33.

157. Thorburn, *Men and Manners*, p. 32.

158. Fisk, *Travels on the Continent*, pp. 516–17.

159. Green, *Notes of a Traveller*, 2:47–48.

160. Noah, *Travels in England*, p. 54.

Chapter 6

1. Benjamin Silliman, *A Journal of Travels in England, Holland and Scotland, and of Two Passages over the Atlantic, in the Years 1805 and 1806*, 2 vols. (New York: Bruce, 1810), 1:286, 324.

2. Ibid., 2:119, 207–8.

3. Nathaniel Hawthorne, *Our Old Home: A Series of English Sketches* (1863; Columbus, Ohio: Ohio State University Press, 1970), pp. 233-34.

✓4. Joseph Ballard, *England in 1815 as Seen by a Young Boston Merchant* (Boston & New York: Houghton, Mifflin, Co., 1913), pp. 115–117.

5. Ibid., p. 148.

✓ 6. Robert J. Breckinridge, *Memoranda of Foreign Travel: Containing Notices of A Pilgrimage through Some of the Principal States of Western Europe* (Baltimore, Md.: D. Owen & Son, 1845), Chapter 17, pp. 140–50.

✓ 7. Charles S. Stewart, *Sketches of Society in Great Britain and Ireland*, 2 vols. (Philadelphia: Carey, Lea & Blanchard, 1834), 1:16.

8. Ibid., 1:52–53.

9. Ibid., 1:169–71.

✓ 10. Alexander Slidell MacKenzie, *The American in England*, 2 vols. (New York: Harper & Brothers, 1835), 2:109–10.

11. Ibid., 2:110–11.

12. Ibid., 2:111–13.

13. Ibid., 2:114–15.

14. Heman Humphrey, *Great Britain, France and Belgium: a Short Tour in 1835*, 2 vols. (New York: Harper & Brothers, 1838), 1:231.

15. Wilbur Fisk, *Travels on the Continent of Europe* (New York: Harper, 1838), p. 680.

16. Humphrey, *Great Britain*, 1:234.

17. William Austin, *Letters from London Written during the Years 1802 and 1803* (Boston: Pelham, 1804), pp. 62–63.

18. MacKenzie, *The American in England*, 1:197–198.

19. Ibid., 1:198–99; 2: 21–2.

20. Henry Colman, *European Life and Manners: in Familiar Letters to Friends*, 2 vols. (Boston: Charles C. Little & James Brown, 1849), 1:90–94.

21. Zachariah Allen, *The Practical Tourist; or, Sketches of the State of the Useful Arts, and of Society, Scenery, etc. etc., in Great Britain, France and Holland*, 2 vols. (Providence, R.I.: Beckwith, 1832), 1:78; Austin, *Letters from London*, p. 87.

22. Humphrey, *Great Britain*, 1:182.

23. MacKenzie, *The American in England*, 1:197.

24. Joshua E. White, *Letters on England: Comprising Descriptive Scenes; with Remarks on the State of Society, Domestic Economy; Habits of the People, and Condition of the Manufacturing Classes Generally*, 2 vols. (Philadelphia: Carey, 1816), 1:24–25.

25. Silliman, *A Journal of Travels*, 1:216–17.

✓26. Isaac A. Jewett, *Passages in Foreign Travel*, 2 vols. (Boston: Charles C. Little & James Brown, 1838), 1:45–46.

27. Austin, *Letters from London*, pp. 170–171.

28. Thurlow Weed, *Letters from Europe and the West Indies, 1843–1852* (Albany, N.Y.: Weed, Parsons, and Company, 1866), p. 242.

✓ 29. Abigail Adams, *Letters of Mrs. Adams, the Wife of John Adams* (Boston: Little & Brown, 1840), p. 172.

30. Austin, *Letters from London*, p. 176.

31. MacKenzie, *The American in England*, 1:113.

32. Allen, *The Practical Tourist*, 1:304–6.

33. Austin, *Letters from London*, p. 169.

34. Fisk, *Travels on the Continent*, p. 609.

35. Stewart, *Sketches of Society*, 1:230–31, 264–65.

36. John Griscom, *A Year in Europe, Comprising a Journal of Observations in England, Scotland, Ireland, France, Switzerland, the North of Italy, and Holland, in 1818 and 1819*, 2 vols. (New York: Collins, 1823), 1:183.

37. Allen, *The Practical Tourist,* 1:331.

38. William A. Drew, *Glimpses and Gatherings during a Voyage and Visit to London and the Great Exhibition in the Summer of 1851* (Augusta, Me.: Homan & Manley, 1852), p. 403.

39. Zadock Thompson, *Journal of a Trip to London, Paris, and the Great Exhibition in 1851* (Burlington, Vt.: Nichols & Warren, 1852), p. 10.

40. Fanny W. Hall, *Rambles in Europe; or, A Tour through France, Italy, Switzerland, and Great Britain, and Ireland, in 1836,* 2 vols. (New York: French, 1838), 2:235–36, 245.

Part II

Chapter 7

1. Ralph Waldo Emerson, *The Selected Writings of Ralph Waldo Emerson*, ed. Brooks Atkinson (New York: The Modern Library, 1940), p. 8.

2. George M. Dallas, *A Series of Letters from London Written during 1856, 1857, 1858, 1859, and 1860* (Philadelphia: Lippincott, 1869), pp. 61, 166.

3. Margaret J. Sweat, *Highways of Travel; or, A Summer in Europe* (Boston: Walker, Wise, and Company, 1859), p. 1.

4. Samuel S. Cox, *A Buckeye Abroad: or, Wanderings in Europe and the Orient* (New York: G. P. Putnam, 1852), preface, p. 1.

5. John W. Corson, *Loiterings in Europe; or, Sketches of Travel in France, Belgium, Switzerland, Italy, Austria, Prussia, Great Britain and Ireland* (New York: Harper & Bros., 1848), p. 279.

6. Benjamin Moran, *The Footpath and Highway; or, Wanderings of an American in Great Britain in 1851 and '52* (Philadelphia: Lippincott, Grambo and Co., 1853), preface, p. 1.

7. Rev. John Overton Choules, D.D., *The Cruise of the Steam Yacht* North Star (London: James Blackwood, 1854), preface, p. vi.

8. Orville Horwitz, *Brushwood Picked Up on the Continent; or, Last Summer's Trip to the Old World* (Philadelphia: Lippincott, Grambo & Co., 1855), pp. 32–33.

9. Hiram Fuller, *Sparks from a Locomotive* (New York: Derby & Jackson, 1859), p. 123.

10. John E. Edwards, *Random Sketches and Notes of European Travel in 1856* (New York: Harper & Brothers, 1857), preface, p. 4.

11. Robert J. Breckinridge, *Memoranda of Foreign Travel: Containing Notices of a Pilgrimage through Some of the Principal States of Western Europe* (Baltimore, Md.: D. Owen & Son, 1845), p. 34.

12. Frank C. Bowen, *A Century of Atlantic Travel . . .* (Boston: Little, Brown, 1930), p. 38.

13. Ibid., pp. 38–39, 50.

14. Ibid., pp. 56–57.

15. Ibid., p. 54.

16. Charles D. Poston, *Europe in the Summer-Time* (Washington, D.C.:M'Gill & Witherow, 1868), pp. 7–8.

17. Moses F. Sweetser, *Europe for $2.00 a Day: A Few Notes for the Assistance of Tourists of Moderate Means, with Some Personal Reminiscences of Travel* (Boston: Osgood, 1875), pp. 40–41.

18. May Alcott Nieriker, *Studying Art Abroad and How to Do It Cheaply* (Boston: Roberts, 1879), p. 10.

19. Noble L. Prentis, *A Kansan Abroad* (Topeka, Kans.: Martin, 1878), p. 6.

20. Breckinridge, *Memoranda of Foreign Travel,* p. 8.

21. Bowen, *A Century of Atlantic Travel,* p. 18.

22. Horace Greeley, *Glances at Europe: In a Series of Letters from Great Britain, France, Italy, Switzerland, etc, during the Summer of 1851* (New York: Dewitt & Davenport, 1851), pp. 12–15.

23. William A. Drew, *Glimpses and Gatherings during a Voyage and Visit to London and the Great Exhibition in the Summer of 1851* (Augusta, Me.: Homan & Manley, 1852), p. 112.

24. Ibid., pp. 112–13.

25. Ibid., p. 200.

26. Ralph Waldo Emerson, *English Traits* (Boston: Phillips, Sampson and Company, 1856), p. 33.

27. George S. Fisher, *Notes by the Wayside* (New York: Derby & Jackson, 1858), p. 26.

28. John H. Tobitt, *What I Heard in Europe during the "American Excitement" . . .* (New York: H. M. Tobitt, 1864), p. 15.

✓ 29. Walter Channing, M.D., *A Physician's Vacation; or, A Summer in Europe* (Boston: Ticknor & Fields, 1856), pp. 4–5.

30. Fisher, *Notes by the Wayside*, p. 33.

31. Channing, *A Physician's Vacation*, pp. 18–19.

32. Charles B. Fairbanks, *Aguecheek* (Boston: Shepard, Clark & Brown, 1859), p. 11.

33. Grace Greenwood, *Haps and Mishaps of a Tour in Europe* (Boston: Ticknor, Reed & Fields, 1854), p. 1.

✓34. Harriet Beecher Stowe, *Sunny Memories of Foreign Lands*, 2 vols. (Boston: Phillips, Sampson and Company, 1854), 1:6.

35. Ibid., 1:6–9.

36. Martha J. Coston, *A Signal Success; The Work and Travels of Mrs. Martha J. Coston: An Autobiography*, (Philadelphia: J. B. Lippincott Company, 1886), p. 57.

37. Stowe, *Sunny Memories*, 1:3–6.

38. Louis J. Frazee, *The Medical Student in Europe* (Maysville, Ky.: Collins, 1849), p. 29.

39. Joel Cook, *A Holiday Tour in Europe. Described in a Series of Letters for the Public Ledger during the Summer and Autumn of 1878* (Philadelphia: J. B. Lippincott Co., 1879), pp. 10–11.

40. William C. Falkner, *Rapid Ramblings in Europe* (Philadelphia: J. B. Lippincott, Co., 1884), p. 50.

41. Clement Pearson, M.D., *A Journal of Travels in Europe during the Summer of 1881* (Washington, D.C.: Judd & Detweiler, 1885), p. 11.

✓ 42. Beverly Carradine, *A Journey to Palestine* (St. Louis, Mo.: C. B. Woodward Printing & Book Mfg. Co., 1891), p. 32.

43. Prentis, *A Kansan Abroad*, p. 124.

44. William F. Cody, *Story of the Wild West and Camp-fire Chats by Buffalo Bill . . . Including a Description of Buffalo Bill's Conquests in England with His Wild West Exhibition* (Philadelphia & Chicago: Historical Pub. Co., 1888), p. 704.

45. Albert Maverick, *A Maverick Abroad*, ed. James S. Maverick. (San Antonio, Tex.: Principia Press of Trinity University, 1965), p. 15.

46. Samuel Young, *A Wall-Street Bear in Europe, with His Familiar Foreign Journal of a Tour through Portions of England, Scotland, France and Italy* (New York: S. Young, Jr., privately printed, 1855), p. 227.

47. Samuel A. Mutchmore, *A Visit of Japheth to Shem and Ham* (New York:Carter, 1889), pp. 9–10.

48. Julia Ward Howe, *Reminiscences, 1819-1899* (Boston and New York: Houghton, Mifflin, 1899), pp. 89, 91.

49. Mrs. E. D. Wallace, *A Woman's Experiences in Europe; Including England, France, Germany and Italy* (New York: Appleton, 1872), p. 23.

50. Pearson, *A Journal of Travels*, p. 11.

51. Young, *A Wall-Street Bear in Europe*, p. 6.

52. Carradine, *Journey to Palestine*, p. 34.

53. Channing, *A Physician's Vacation*, p. 25.

54. Walter A. Whittle, *A Baptist Abroad; or, Travels and Adventures in Europe and All Bible Lands* (New York: Hill, 1890), p. 34.

55. George Wilkes, *Europe in a Hurry* (New York: Long, 1853), p. 7.

56. Randal W. MacGavock, *A Tennessean Abroad; or, Letters from Europe, Africa, and Asia* (New York: Redfield, 1854), p. 14.

57. Rodney Glisan, M.D., *Two Years in Europe* (New York and London: Putnam, 1887), p. 2.

58. Mrs. S. R. Urbino, *An American Woman in Europe; The Journal of Two Years and a Half Sojourn in Germany, Switzerland, France, and Italy* (Boston: Lee & Shepard, 1869), pp. 10–11.

59. Jacob Abbott, *A Summer in Scotland* (New York: Harper, 1848), pp. 20–21.

60. Henry Morford, *Over-Sea; or, England, France and Scotland As Seen by a Live American* (New York: Hilton, 1867), p. 34.

61. Edward Thomson, *Letters from Europe: Being Notes of a Tour through England, France, and Switzerland* (Cincinnati, Ohio: L. Swormstedt & A. Poe, 1856), pp. 29–30.

62. Channing, *A Physician's Vacation*, pp. 6–7.

63. Thurlow Weed, *Letters from Europe and the West Indies, 1843–1852* (Albany, N.Y.: Weed, Parsons and Company, 1866), p. 408.

64. Augustus Hoppin, *Crossing the Atlantic* (Boston: Osgood, 1872), p. 5.

65. Wilkes, *Europe in a Hurry,* p. 5.

66. Thomson, *Letters from Europe,* pp. 30–31.

67. Thomas Rees, *Sixty Days in Europe: What I Saw There* (Springfield, Ill.: State Register Co., 1908), p. 20.

68. Carradine, *Journey to Palestine,* p. 447.

69. Charles H. Haesler, M.D., *Across the Atlantic* (Philadelphia: Peterson, 1868), p. 42.

70. Pearson, *A Journal of Travels,* p. 173.

71. David R. Locke [Petroleum V. Nasby], *Nasby in Exile; or, Six Months of Travel in England, Ireland, Scotland, France, Germany, Switzerland and Belgium, with Many Things Not of Travel* (Toledo and Boston: Locke Publishing Co., 1882), pp. 21–22.

72. Moran, *Footpath and Highway,* pp. 21–22.

73. Charles Williams, *Old World Scenes* (Pittsburgh, Pa.: Haven, 1867), p. 261.

74. Fairbanks, *Aguecheek,* p. 12.

75. William Hutton, *Twelve Thousand Miles over Land and Sea* (Philadelphia: Grant, Faires & Rodgers, 1878), p. 180.

76. Burr H. Polk, *The Big American Caravan in Europe* (Evansvile: Journal Co., 1879), p. 10.

77. James S. McClay, *Style-O!-Graphic Pens and Funny Pencillings in Europe* (Hartford, Conn.: Phoenix, 1881), p. 11.

78. Joseph Cross, D.D. *The American Pastor in Europe* (London: Bentley, 1860), pp. 3–4.

79. Caroline M. Kirkland, *Holidays Abroad; or, Europe from the West,* 2 vols. (New York: Baker and Scribner, 1849), 1: 330.

80. Wilbur O. Davidson, *Over the Sea, And What I Saw* (Cincinnati, Ohio: Cranston & Stowe, 1885), p. 23.

81. William H. Taylor, M.D., *The Book of Travels of a Doctor of Physic* (Philadelphia: Lippincott, 1871), p. 372.

82. Abbott, *A Summer in Scotland,* pp. 38–39.

83. Fisher, *Notes by the Wayside,* p. 21.

84. Edwards, *Random Sketches,* p. 22.

85. John A. Clark, *Glimpses of the Old World; or, Excursions on the Continent and in Great Britain,* 2 vols. (London: Samuel Bagster and Sons, 1840), 2; 463.

86. William P. Davis, *Across the Sea* (Trenton, N.J.: John L. Murray, 1889), p. 39.

87. Francis C. Sessions, *On the Wing through Europe* (Columbus, Ohio: H. W. Derby and Co., 1880), p. 5.

88. Morford, *Over-Sea,* p. 51.

89. Thomson, *Letters from Europe,* p. 175.

90. Phoebe W. Palmer, *Four Years in the Old World; Comprising the Travels, Incidents, and Evangelistic Labors of Dr. and Mrs. Palmer in England, Ireland, Scotland and Wales* (New York: Foster and Palmer, Jr., 1866), p. 20.

91. Breckinridge, *Memoranda of Foreign Travel,* p. 13.

92. Thomson, *Letters from Europe,* pp. 174–75.

93. Nicholas Murray, *Men and Things as I Saw Them in Europe* (New York: Harper, 1853), pp. 11–13.

94. Orlando W. Wight, *Peoples and Countries Visited in a Winding Journey around the World* (Detroit, Mich.: Raynor & Taylor, 1888), pp. 17–18.

95. Cross, *The American Pastor in Europe,* p. 3.

96. Margaret Fuller Ossoli, *At Home and Abroad: or, Things and Thoughts in America and Europe* (Boston: Crosby, Nichols and Company, 1856) p. 120.

97. Charles H. Collins, *From Highland Hills to an Emperor's Tomb* (Cincinnati, Ohio: Robert Clarke & Co., 1886), p. 71.

98. Morford, *Over-Sea,* p. 31.

99. Alexander Slidell MacKenzie, *The American in England,* 2 vols. (New York: Harper & Brothers, 1835), 1:37.

100. Joel T. Headley, *Rambles and Sketches* (New York: Taylor, 1850), p. 193.

101. William Wells Brown, *The American Fugitive in Europe; Sketches of Places and People Abroad* (Boston: Jewett; New York: Sheldon, Lamport & Blakeman, 1855), p. 310.

102. Headley, *Rambles and Sketches,* pp. 194–95.

103. Ossoli, *At Home and Abroad,* pp. 120–21.

104. Edwards, *Random Sketches,* pp. 19–20, 29–30.

105. Ibid., pp. 30–32.

106. G. H. Mathews, *Diary of a Summer in Europe, 1865* (New York: Marsh, 1866), p. 107.

107. John W. Forney, *Letters from Europe* (Philadelphia: Peterson, 1867), p. 22.

108. Mrs. E. A. Forbes, *A Woman's First Impressions of Europe; Being Wayside Sketches Made during a Short Tour in the Year 1863* (New York: Derby & Miller, 1865), p. 347.

109. Edwards, *Random Sketches,* p. 30.

110. Dean Dudley, *Pictures of Life in England and America; Prose and Poetry* (Boston: French, 1851), p. 152.

111. Forbes, *A Woman's First Impressions,* p. 12.

112. Cross, *The American Pastor in Europe,* p. 4.

113. Dudley, *Pictures of Life,* p. 16.

114. Kirkland, *Holidays Abroad,* 1: 17–18, 52.

115. Howe, *Reminiscences,* p. 90.

116. Abbott, *A Summer in Scotland,* p. 23.

117. Henry P. Tappan, *A Step from the New World to the Old, and Back Again: With Thoughts on the Good and Evil in Both,* 2 vols. (New York: Appleton, 1852), 1:24.

118. Channing, *A Physician's Vacation,* pp. 10–11.

119. Wilkes, *Europe in a Hurry,* p. 6.

120. Weed, *Letters from Europe,* p. 410.

121. Cross, *The American Pastor in Europe,* p. 419.

122. Herman Melville, *Journal of a Visit to London and the Continent,* ed. Eleanor Melville Metcalf (Cambridge, Mass.: Harvard University Press, 1948), p. 7.

123. Arthur Cleveland Coxe, *Impressions of England; or, Sketches of English Scenery and Society* (New York: Dana & Co., 1856), p. 2.

124. Coston, *A Signal Success,* p. 114.

125. Kirkland, *Holidays Abroad,* 1:10.

126. Elias H. Derby, *Two Months Abroad, or, a Trip to England, France, Baden, Prussia, and Belgium. In August and September, 1843* (Boston: Redding & Co., 1844), p. 5.

127. Polk, *The Big American Caravan,* p. 11.

128. Daniel C. Eddy, *Europa: or, Scenes and Society in England, France, Italy, and Switzerland* (Boston: Bradley, Dayton, & Co., 1859), pp. 486–87.

129. James M. Hoyt, *Glances on the Wing at Foreign Lands* (Cleveland, Ohio: Fairbanks, Benedict & Co., 1872). p.259.

130. Urbino, *An American Woman in Europe,* p. 9.

131. Henry B. McLellan, *Journal of a Residence in Scotland, and a Tour through England, France, Germany, Switzerland and Italy* (Boston: Allen & Ticknor, 1834), p. 86.

132. Clarke, *Glimpses of the Old World,* p. 465.

133. Mathews, *Diary of a Summer in Europe,* pp. 5–6.

134. Charles C. Fulton, *Europe Viewed through American Spectacles* (Philadelphia: Lippincott, 1874), p. 306.

135. Lydia H. Sigourney, *Pleasant Memories of Pleasant Lands* (Boston: Munroe, 1842), pp. 372–75.

136. Zadock Thompson, *Journal of a Trip to London, Paris, and the Great Exhibition in 1851* (Burlington, Vt.: Nichols & Warren, 1852), pp. 124–26.

137. William A. Braman, *Glimpses of Europe* (Cleveland, Ohio: J. B. Savage, 1901), pp. 209–10.

138. James N. Matthews, *My Holiday; How I Spent It: Being Some Rough Notes of a Trip to Europe and Back, in the Summer of 1866* (New York: Hurd & Houghton, 1867), pp. 247–48.

139. Morford, *Over-Sea,* p. 53.

140. Mark Trafton, *Rambles in Europe: In a Series of Familiar Letters* (Boston: Peirce, 1852), p. 374.

141. George W. Hills, *John Bull, Limited* (Philadelphia: Privately printed, 1918), p. 80.

142. Abbott, *A Summer in Scotland,* p. 49.

143. Brown, *The American Fugitive in Europe,* p. 40.

Chapter 8

1. Theodore B. Witmer, *Wild Oats Sown Abroad; or, On and Off Soundings; Being Leaves from a Private Journal; by a Gentleman of Leisure* (Philadelphia: Peterson, 1853), p. 21.

2. Henry James, *Essays in London and Elsewhere* (New York: Harper & Bros., 1893), p. 4.

3. Charles B. Fairbanks, *Aguecheek* (Boston: Shepard, Clark & Brown,1859), pp. 28–29.

4. Ibid., p. 29.

5. John E. Edwards, *Random Sketches and Notes of European Travel in 1856* (New York: Harper & Brothers, 1857), p. 34.

6. Nathaniel Hawthorne, *Our Old Home: A Series of English Sketches* (1863; Columbus, Ohio: Ohio State University Press, 1970), p. 215.

7. John W. Corson, *Loiterings in Europe; or, Sketches of Travel in France, Belgium, Switzerland, Italy, Austria, Prussia, Great Britain and Ireland* (New York: Harper & Bros., 1848), p. 268.

8. Ibid.

9. Joel Headley, *Rambles and Sketches* (New York: Taylor, 1850), p. 135.

10. Thurlow Weed, *Letters from Europe and the West Indies, 1843–1852* (Albany, N.Y.: Weed, Parsons and Company, 1866), p. 69.

11. Elias H. Derby, *Two Months Abroad; or, A Trip to England, France, Baden, Prussia, and Belgium. In August and September, 1843* (Boston: Redding & Co., 1844), pp. 9–10.

12. Henry Morford, *Over-Sea; or England, France and Scotland as Seen by a Live American* (New York: Hilton, 1867), p. 76.

13. George Wilkes, *Europe in a Hurry* (New York: Long, 1853), pp. 78–79.

14. Ibid., p. 80.

15. Caroline M. Kirkland, *Holidays Abroad; or, Europe from the West*, 2 vols. (New York: Baker and Scribner, 1849), 1:312–13.

16. William Cullen Bryant, *Letters of a Traveller; or, Notes of Things Seen in Europe and America* (New York: George P. Putnam, 1850), pp. 170–71.

17. Fairbanks, *Aguecheek*, pp. 26–27.

18. David V. G. Bartlett, *What I Saw in London; or, Men and Things in the Great Metropolis* (New York: C. M. Saxton, Barker & Co., 1861), pp. 79–80.

19. George W. Hills, *John Bull, Limited* (Philadelphia: Privately printed, 1918), pp. 20–21.

20. Noble L. Prentis, *A Kansan Abroad* (Topeka, Kans.: Martin, 1878), p. 49.

21. Headley, *Rambles and Sketches*, p. 144.

22. *Punch* 9 (1845):178.

23. Mark Trafton, *Rambles in Europe: In a Series of Familiar Letters* (Boston: Peirce, 1852), pp. 100–107.

24. Horace Greeley, *Glances at Europe: In a Series of Letters from Great Britain, France, Italy, Switzerland, etc., during the Summer of 1851* (New York: DeWitt & Davenport, 1851), p. 78.

25. Hawthorne, *Our Old Home*, p. 253.

26. Alonzo Tripp, *Crests from the Ocean-World; or, Experiences in a Voyage to Europe* (Boston: Whittemore, Niles & Hall, 1855), p. 364.

27. Wilkes, *Europe in a Hurry*, p. 105.

28. Trafton, *Rambles in Europe*, p. 64.

29. Julia Ward Howe, *From the Oak to the Olive; A Plain Record of a Pleasant Journey* (Boston: Lee & Shepard, 1868), p. 24.

30. Wilbur Fisk, *Travels on the Continent of Europe* (New York: Harper, 1838), p. 526.

31. John W. Forney, *Letters from Europe* (Philadelphia: Peterson, 1867), p. 296.

32. Trafton, *Rambles in Europe*, pp. 75–79.

33. Kirkland, *Holidays Abroad*, 1:56-57.

34. Stephen H. Tyng, *Recollections of England* (London: Bagster, 1847), p. 224.

35. John P. Kennedy, *At Home and Abroad, Including a Journal in Europe, 1867–68* (New York: Putnam, 1872), p. 392.

36. William A. Drew, *Glimpses and Gatherings during a Voyage and Visit to London and the Great Exhibition in the Summer of 1851* (Augusta, Me.: Homan & Manley, 1852), pp. 246–48.

37. Henry Maney, *Memories over the Water; or, Stray Thoughts on a Long Stroll* (Nashville, Tenn.: Toon, Nelson & Co., 1854), p. 52.

38. Headley, *Rambles and Sketches,* p. 168.

39. Weed, *Letters from Europe,* p. 93.

40. Octavia W. LeVert, *Souvenirs of Travel* (New York and Mobile: Goetzel, 1857), p. 44.

✓ 41. Edward Thomson, *Letters from Europe: Being Notes of a Tour through England, France, and Switzerland* (Cincinnati, Ohio: L. Swormstedt & A. Poe, 1856), p. 120.

✓ 42. Samuel S. Cox, *A Buckeye Abroad: or, Wanderings in Europe and the Orient* (New York: G. P. Putnam, 1852), p. 365.

✓ 43. Arthur Cleveland Coxe, *Impressions of England; or, Sketches of English Scenery and Society* (New York: Dana & Co., 1856), p. 114.

44. *Punch* 2 (1842): 183.

45. Forney, *Letters from Europe,* p. 327.

46. Kirkland, *Holidays Abroad,* 1:62–63.

47. Grace Greenwood, *Haps and Mishaps of a Tour in Europe* (Boston: Ticknor, Reed & Fields, 1854), p. 33.

48. Maunsell B. Field, *Memories of Many Men and of Some Women: Being Personal Recollections of Emperors, Kings, Queens, Princes, Presidents, Statesmen, Authors, and Artists, at Home and Abroad during the Last Thirty Years* (New York: Harper, 1874), p. 45.

49. Andrew Jackson Downing, *Rural Essays* (New York: Leavitt & Allen, 1855), pp. 489–91.

50. Kirkland, *Holidays Abroad,* 1:70–71.

51. George H. Mathews, *Diary of a Summer in Europe, 1865* (New York: Marsh, 1866), p. 64.

52. Ella W. Thompson, *Beaten Paths: or, A Woman's Vacation* (Boston: Lee & Shepard, 1874), pp. 88–89.

53. Greeley, *Glances at Europe,* p. 67.

54. Downing, *Rural Essays,* pp. 547–57.

55. Ibid., p. 550.

56. Randal W. MacGavock, *A Tennessean Abroad; or, Letters from Europe, Africa, and Asia* (New York: Redfield, 1854), p. 69.

57. Bartlett, *What I Saw in London,* pp. 34, 38, 135.

58. Coxe, *Impressions of England,* pp. 73–74.

59. Witmer, *Wild Oats Sown Abroad,* pp. 22–23.

60. Henry T. Tuckerman, *A Month in England* (New York: Redfield, 1853), p. 134.

✓ 61. Rev. John O. Choules, D. D. *Young Americans Abroad: or, Vacation in Europe; The Results of a Tour through Great Britain, France, Holland, Belgium, Germany and Switzerland* (Boston: Gould & Lincoln, 1852), pp. 96–97.

62. Kirkland, *Holidays Abroad,* 1:77.

63. Quoted by Edward Wagenknecht in *Washington Irving: Moderation Displayed* (New York: Oxford University Press, 1962), p. 93.

✓ 64. Quoted by Herman Melville in *Journal of a Visit to London and the Continent,* ed. Eleanor Melville Metcalf (Cambridge, Mass.: Harvard University Press, 1948), p. 124.

65. Richard C. McCormick, *St. Paul's to St. Sophia; or, Sketchings in Europe* (New York: Sheldon, 1860), p. 126.

66. James F. Clarke, *Eleven Weeks in Europe: And What May Be Seen in That Time* (Boston: Ticknor, Reed & Fields, 1852), p. 78.

67. Cornelius C. Felton, *Familiar Letters from Europe* (Boston: Ticknor & Fields, 1865), p. 32.

68. Harriet Beecher Stowe, *Sunny Memories of Foreign Lands,* 2 vols. (Boston: Phillips, Sampson and Company, 1854), 1:321.

69. James W. Wall, *Foreign Etchings . . .* (Burlington, N.J.: Atkinson, 1856), p. 69.

70. Julia Ward Howe, *Reminiscences, 1819–1899* (Boston and New York: Houghton, Mifflin, 1899), p. 99.

71. Kirkland, *Holidays Abroad,* 1:74.

72. Greenwood, *Haps and Mishaps,* pp. 48–49.

73. Stephen C. Massett, *"Drifting About," or, What "Jeems Pipes of Pipesville", Saw-and-Did.* (New York: Carleton, 1863), p. 349.

74. Henry M. Field, *Summer Pictures: From Copenhagen to Venice* (New York: Sheldon, 1859), p. 30.

75. Catherine M. Sedgwick, *Letters from Abroad to Kindred at Home,* 2 vols. (New York: Harper, 1841), 1:92–93.

76. Greenwood, *Haps and Mishaps,* p. 49.

77. Margaret Fuller Ossoli, *At Home and Abroad: or, Things and Thoughts in America and Europe* (Boston: Crosby, Nichols, and Company, 1856), p. 134.

78. Bayard Taylor, *At Home and Abroad: a Sketch-Book of Life, Scenery, and Men* (New York: Putnam, 1860), p. 444.

79. Hiram Fuller, *Sparks from a Locomotive* (New York: Derby & Jackson, 1859), p. 173.

80. Drew, *Glimpses and Gatherings,* p. 239.

81. Dean Dudley, *Pictures of Life in England and America; Prose and Poetry* (Boston: French, 1851), p. 103.

82. William Wells Brown, *The American Fugitive in Europe; Sketches of Places and People Abroad* (Boston: Jewett; New York: Sheldon, Lamport & Blakeman, 1855), p. 46.

83. Dudley, *Pictures of Life,* p. 103.

84. Cox, *A Buckeye Abroad,* p. 41.

85. Mrs. A. E. Newman [Evangeline], *European Leaflets for Young Ladies* (New York: John F. Baldwin, 1861), p. 145.

86. Phoebe W. Palmer, *Four Years in the Old World: Comprising the Travels, Incidents, and Evangelistic Labors of Dr. and Mrs. Palmer in England, Ireland, Scotland and Wales* (New York: Foster & Palmer, Jr., 1866), p. 535.

87. Agnes E. Claflin, *From Shore to Shore: A Journey of Nineteen Years* (Cambridge, Mass.: Riverside Press, 1873), p. 154.

88. Brown, *American Fugitive,* p. 118.

89. Ibid.

90. Ibid., pp. 118–19.

91. Melville, *Journal of a Visit,* p. 49.

92. Margaret J. Sweat, *Highways of Travel; or, A Summer in Europe* (Boston: Walker, Wise, and Company, 1859), pp. 302, 327–28.

93. John P. Durbin, *Observations in Europe, Principally in France and Great Britain,* 2 vols. (New York: Harper, 1844), 2:259.

94. Brown, *American Fugitive,* pp. 211–12.

95. Hugh Miller, *First Impressions of England and Its People* (Boston: Gould & Lincoln, 1857), p. 272.

96. Trafton, *Rambles in Europe,* p. 76.

97. Beverly Carradine, *A Journey to Palestine* (St. Louis, Mo.: C. B. Woodward Printing & Book Mfg. Co., 1891), p. 113.

98. Choules, *Young Americans Abroad,* p. 369.

99. Ibid., p. 370.

100. Tyng, *Recollections of England,* pp. 87–88.

Chapter 9

1. Stephen Spender, *Love-Hate Relations: English and American Sensibilities* (New York: Vintage Books, 1975), p. 4.

2. Allan Nevins, *American Social History as Recorded by British Travellers* (New York: Holt, 1923; Augustus M. Kelley, reprint ed., 1969), pp. 556–68.

3. Benjamin Silliman, *A Journal of Travels in England, Holland and Scotland, and of Two Passages over the Atlantic, in the Years 1805 and 1806,* 2 vols. (New York: Bruce, 1810), 2:349–51.

4. Joshua E. White, *Letters on England: Comprising Descriptive Scenes; With Remarks on the State of Society, Domestic Economy; Habits of the People, and Condition of the Manufacturing Classes Generally,* 2 vols. (Philadelphia: Carey, 1816), 1:64.

5. George Ticknor, *Life, Letters and Journals of George Ticknor,* 2 vols. (Boston: Osgood, 1876), 1:424–425.

6. Jane L. Mesick, *The English Traveller in America, 1785–1835.* (1922; reprint ed. Westport, Conn.: Greenwood Press, 1970), pp. 271–72.

7. Quoted by H. L. Mencken in *The American Language,* 4th ed. (New York: Alfred A. Knopf, 1965), p. 13.

8. Washington Irving, *The Sketchbook of Geoffrey Crayon, Gentleman* (New York: G. P. Putnam & Co., 1854), p. 69.

9. Emma H. Willard, *Journal and Letters, from France and Great-Britain* (Troy, N.Y.: Tuttle, 1833), p. 313.

10. Alexander Slidell MacKenzie, *The American in England,* 2 vols. (New York: Harper & Brothers, 1835), preface, pp. x–xii.

11. Heman Humphrey, *Great Britain, France and Belgium: A Short Tour in 1835,* 2 vols. (New York: Harper & Brothers, 1838), 1:172.

12. Henry B. McLellan, *Journal of a Residence in Scotland, and a Tour through England, France, Germany, Switzerland and Italy* (Boston: Allen & Ticknor, 1834), preface, p. ix.

13. Allan Nevins, *America through British Eyes* (New York: Oxford University Press, 1948), pp. 79ff.

14. Basil Hall, *Travels in North America in the Years 1827–1828,* 3 vols. (London: Simpkins & Marshall, 1829), preface, pp. iii–iv.

15. Ibid., 3:226.

16. Jared Sparks, *The Life and Writings of Jared Sparks,* ed. Herbert D. Adams, 2 vols. (Boston: Houghton, Mifflin, 1893), 2:61.

17. Matthew F. Ward, *English Items: or, Microscopic Views of England and Englishmen* (New York: Appleton, 1853), p. 109.

18. Quoted in Mesick, *The English Traveller,* p. 291.

19. Irving, *The Sketchbook,* p. 90.

20. Samuel G. Goodrich, *Recollections of a Lifetime; or, Men and Things I Have Seen: in a Series of Familiar Letters to a Friend, Historical, Biographical, Anecdotal, and Descriptive,* 2 vols. (New York & Auburn: Miller, Orton & Co., 1857), 2:358.

21. Thurlow Weed, *Letters from Europe and the West Indies, 1843–1852* (Albany, N.Y.: Weed, Parsons and Company, 1866), p. 79.

22. Thomas C. Haliburton, *The Letter Bag of the Great Western; or, Life in a Steamer* (Halifax, Nova Scotia: Joseph Howe, 1840), pp. 87–88.

23. Grant Thorburn, *Men and Manners in Great Britain: A Bone to Gnaw on for the Trollopes, Fidlers, &c.* (New York: Wiley & Long, 1834), p. 53.

24. Quoted in Mesick, *The English Traveller,* p. 298; *Quarterly Review* 54:408.

25. Quoted in Nevins, *America Through British Eyes,* pp. 257–58.

26. Ibid., p. 258.

27. Ibid., p. 260.

28. Oliver P. Hiller, *English and Scottish Sketches, By an American* (Boston: Clapp, 1857), pp. 191–97.

29. Ward, *English Items,* pp. 86–87.

30. Orville Dewey, *The Old World and the New; or, A Journal of Reflections and Observations Made on a Tour in Europe,* 2 vols. (New York: Harper & Bros., 1836), 1:323.

31. Ward, *English Items,* pp. 98–99, 132–33.

32. Samuel Young, *A Wall-Street Bear in Europe, with His Familiar Foreign Journal of a Tour through Portions of England, Scotland, France and Italy* (New York: S. Young, Jr., privately printed, 1855), p. 209.

33. George F. Train, *Spread-Eagleism* (New York: Derby & Jackson, 1859), p. 106.

34. Ibid., pp. 106–7.

35. Henry T. Tuckerman, *America and her Commentators* (New York: Augustus M. Kelley, 1970 reprint), p. 253.

36. Ibid., pp. 281, 291–92.

37. Samuel I. Prime, *Travels in Europe and the East; a Year in England, Scotland, Ireland, Wales, France, Belgium, Holland, Germany, Austria, Italy, Greece, Turkey, Syria, Palestine and Egypt,* 2 vols. (New York: Harper, 1855), 1:101.

38. James Fenimore Cooper, *Gleanings in Europe. By an American,* 2 vols. 1837. (New York: Oxford University Press, 1930; reprint ed. Kraus Reprint Co., 1970), 2:353–55.

39. McLellan, *Journal of a Residence,* p. 353.

40. John Mitchell, *Notes from Over Sea; Consisting of Observations Made in Europe in the Years 1843 and 1844,* 2 vols. (New York: Gates & Stedman, 1845), 1:321.

41. Frederick Law Olmsted, *Walks and Talks of an American Farmer in England* (1852; reprint ed. Ann Arbor, Mich.: University of Michigan Press, 1967), p. 166.

42. Charles S. Stewart, *Sketches of Society in Great Britain and Ireland,* 2 vols. (Philadelphia: Carey, Lea & Blanchard, 1834), 1:214.

43. Catherine M. Sedgwick, *Letters from Abroad to Kindred at Home,* 2 vols. (New York: Harper, 1841), 1:14–20.

✓44. Bayard Taylor, *At Home and Abroad: A Sketch-Book of Life, Scenery, and Men* (New York: Putnam, 1860), p. 40.

✓45. David V. G. Bartlett, *What I Saw in London; Or, Men and Things in the Great Metropolis* (New York: C. M. Saxton, Barker & Co., 1861), p. 71.

Chapter 10

1. Henry B. McLellan, *Journal of a Residence in Scotland, and a Tour through England, France, Germany, Switzerland and Italy* (Boston: Allen & Ticknor, 1834), p. 144.

2. Dean Dudley, *Social and Political Aspects of England and the Continent: A Series of Letters* (Boston: Printed for the author, 1862), p. 79.

3. John Mitchell, *Notes from Over Sea; Consisting of Observations Made in Europe in the Years 1843 and 1844,* 2 vols. (New York: Gates & Stedman, 1845), 1:324.

4. Ibid., 1:204.

✓5. Henry P. Tappan, *A Step from the New World to the Old, and Back Again: With Thoughts on the Good and Evil in Both,* 2 vols. (New York: Appleton, 1852), 1:123.

6. George P. Putnam, *The Tourist in Europe* (New York: Wiley & Putnam, 1838), pp. 134–35.

7. John P. Durbin, *Observations in Europe, Principally in France and Great Britain,* 2 vols. (New York: Harper, 1844), 2:309.

8. Mitchell, *Notes from Over Sea,* 1:61.

9. Caroline M. Kirkland, *Holidays Abroad: or, Europe from the West,* 2 vols. (New York: Baker and Scribner, 1849), 1:305–6.

10. Tappan, *A Step from the New World,* 1:123, 125, 126.

11. Stephen W. Sears, ed., *The Horizon History of the British Empire* (New York: American Heritage Publishing Co., Inc., 1973), p. 180.

12. Mitchell, *Notes from Over Sea.* 1:324.

13. Tappan, *A Step from the New World,* 1:128.

14. Ibid., 1:128–30, 133.

15. Samuel I. Prime, *Travels in Europe and the East; a Year in England, Scotland, Ireland, Wales, France, Belgium, Holland, Germany, Austria, Italy, Greece, Turkey, Syria, Palestine and Egypt,* 2 vols. (New York: Harper, 1855), 1:122, 137.

16. Mitchell, *Notes from Over Sea,* 1:328.

17. Ibid.

18. E. K. Washington, *Echoes of Europe: or, World Pictures of Travel* (Philadelphia: Challen, 1860), pp. 209–10.

19. Henry Maney, *Memories over the Water; or, Stray Thoughts on a Long Stroll* (Nashville, Tenn.: Toon, Nelson & Co., 1854), p. 38.

20. John Timbs, *Curiosities of London* (London: John Camden Hotten, 1867), p. 334.

✓ 21. Henry Colman, *European Life and Manners: In Familiar Letters to Friends,* 2 vols. (Boston: Charles C. Little & James Brown, 1849), 2:99–100.

22. William H. Seward, *Autobiography of William H. Seward, from 1801 to 1834,* ed. Frederick Seward (New York: Appleton, 1877), p. 114.

23. Daniel C. Eddy, *Europa: or, Scenes and Society in England, France, Italy, and Switzerland* (Boston: Bradley, Dayton & Co., 1859), pp. 172–73.

24. Ibid., p. 174.

25. Randal W. MacGavock, *A Tennessean Abroad; or, Letters from Europe, Africa, and Asia* (New York: Redfield, 1854), p. 63.

26. Harriet Beecher Stowe, *Sunny Memories of Foreign Lands,* 2 vols. (Boston: Phillips, Sampson and Company, 1854), 1:148.

✓27. William Wells Brown, *The American Fugitive in Europe; Sketches of Places and People Abroad* (Boston, Jewett; New York, Sheldon, Lamport & Blakeman, 1855), pp. 29–32.

28. Ibid., p. 140.

29. Ibid., pp. 140–41.

30. Ibid., pp. 216–17.

31. Ibid., p. 303.

32. Ibid., pp. 312–13.

✓ 33. Horace Greeley, *Glances at Europe: In a Series of Letters from Great Britain, France, Italy, Switzerland, etc., during the Summer of 1851* (New York: Dewitt & Davenport, 1851), pp. 79–80.

34. Ibid., p. 80.

35. Ibid., pp. 81–82.

36. Richard C. McCormick, *St. Paul's to St. Sophia; or, Sketchings in Europe* (New York: Sheldon, 1860), p. 85.

37. Greeley, *Glances at Europe*, pp. 84–85.

38. Ibid., pp. 85–86.

39. Eddy, *Europa*, p. 174.

40. William Gibson, M.D., *Rambles in Europe in 1839; With Sketches of Prominent Surgeons, Physicians, Medical Schools, Hospitals, Literary Personages, Scenery, etc.* (Philadelphia: Lea & Blanchard, 1841), pp. 275–76.

41. Greeley, *Glances at Europe*, p. 86.

42. Charles H. Collins, *From Highland Hills to an Emperor's Tomb* (Cincinnati, Ohio: Robert Clarke & Co., 1886), p. 284.

43. William Ware, *Sketches of European Capitals* (Boston: Phillips, Sampson & Co., 1851), pp. 295–97.

44. David V. G. Bartlett, *What I Saw in London; or, Men and Things in the Great Metropolis* (New York: C. M. Saxton, Barker & Co., 1861), p. 317.

✓ 45. Benjamin Moran, *The Footpath and Highway: or, Wanderings of an American in Great Britain in 1851 and '52* (Philadelphia: Lippincott, Grambo & Co., 1853), p. 124.

46. Kirkland, *Holidays Abroad*, 1:303–4.

47. Grace Greenwood, *Haps and Mishaps of a Tour in Europe* (Boston: Ticknor, Reed & Fields, 1854), p. 6.

48. Thomas C. Upham, *Letters Esthetic, Social and Moral, Written from Europe, Egypt, and Palestine* (Brunswick, Me.: Griffin, 1855), pp. 32–33.

49. *Dictionary of American Biography*, Ed. by Allen Johnson. New York: Charles Scribner's Sons, 1927, 28, 29, 36. 9:117.

50. Henry T. Tuckerman, *A Month in England* (New York: Redfield, 1853), pp. 118–19.

51. Ibid., pp. 119–20.

52. Eddy, *Europa*, p. 176.

53. Tuckerman, *A Month in England*, pp. 121–25.

54. Ibid., pp. 126–27.

55. Elihu Burritt, *A Walk from London to Land's End and Back, with Notes by the Way* (London: Low & Marston, 1865), p. 4.

56. Stowe, *Sunny Memories*, 1:18–19.

57. Ibid., 1:xvi–lxiv.

58. Ibid., 1:73.

59. Ibid., 1:138.

60. Ibid., 1:221.

61. Ibid., 1:100.

62. Ibid., 1:239.

63. Ibid., 1:259–60.

64. Ibid., 1:261–65.

65. Ibid., 2:14–15.

66. Ibid., 1:267.

67. George W. Williams, *Sketches of Travel in the Old and New World* (Charleston, S.C.: Walker, Evans & Cogswell, 1871), p. 278.

68. Stowe, *Sunny Memories*, 1:276–77.

69. Ibid., 2:120–21.

70. Ibid., 2:83.

71. Ibid., 2:84.

72. Ibid., 2:84–86.

73. Henry B. Stanton, *Random Recollections* (New York: Macgowan & Slipper, Printers, 1886), p. 45.

74. Stowe, *Sunny Memories*, 1:268–69.

75. Ibid., 1:269–71, 272.

76. Ibid., 1:287–90.

77. Ibid., 1:290–91.

78. Ibid., 1:292.

79. Ibid., 1:298–99.

80. *Dictionary American Biography*, 9:118.

81. Stowe, *Sunny Memories*, 1:302.

82. Ibid., 1:302–13.

83. Joseph Pennell and Elizabeth Robins Pennell, *Our Journey to the Hebrides* (New York: Harper, 1889), pp. 170–71.

84. Mitchell, *Notes from Over Sea*, 1:118–19.

Chapter 11

1. John H. Barrows, *A World Pilgrimage* (Chicago: A. C. McClurg & Co., 1897), p. 176.

2. Henry T. Tuckerman, *A Month in England* (New York: Redfield, 1853), p. 75.

3. Gilbert Haven, *The Pilgrim's Wallet; or, Scraps of Travel Gathered in England, France and Germany* (New York: Carlton & Porter, 1866), pp. 188–89.

4. Hugh Miller, *First Impressions of England and Its People* (Boston: Gould & Lincoln, 1857), p. 377.

5. Henry Colman, *European Life and Manners: In Familiar Letters to Friends*, 2 vols. (Boston: Charles C. Little & James Brown, 1849), 1:100, 164–65.

6. Ibid., 1:159.

7. George Wilkes, *Europe in a Hurry* (New York: Long, 1853), p. 125.

8. Ibid.

9. Nathaniel Hawthorne, *Our Old Home: A Series of English Sketches* (1863; Columbus, Ohio: Ohio State University Press, 1970), pp. 281-2, 287, 283, 288.

10. Stephen C. Massett, *"Drifting About"; or, What "Jeems Pipes of Pipesville", Saw-and-Did* (New York: Carleton, 1863), p. 179.

11. Joel T. Headley, *Rambles and Sketches* (New York: Taylor, 1850), pp. 146–47.

12. William Cullen Bryant, *Letters of a Traveller: or, Notes of Things Seen in Europe and America* (New York: George P. Putnam, 1850), p. 172.

13. Alonzo Tripp, *Crests from the Ocean-World; or, Experiences in a Voyage to Europe* (Boston: Whittemore, Niles & Hall, 1855), p. 359.

14. Tuckerman, *A Month in England*, p. 222.

15. Hiram Fuller, *Sparks from a Locomotive* (New York: Derby & Jackson, 1859), p. 185.

16. Ibid., pp. 186–88.

17. Herman Melville, *Journal of a Visit to London and the Continent*, ed. Eleanor Melville Metcalf (Cambridge, Mass.: Harvard University Press, 1948), p. 40.

18. William A. Brawley, *The Journal of William A. Brawley, 1864–1865*, ed. Francis Poe Brawley (Charlottesville, Va., 1970), p. 48.

19. Sinclair Tousey, *Papers from over the Water; A Series of Letters from Europe* (New York: American News Co., 1869), p. 183.

20. Theodore B. Witmer, *Wild Oats Sown Abroad; or, On and Off Soundings; Being Leaves from a Private Journal; by a Gentleman of Leisure* (Philadelphia: Peterson, 1853), p. 23.

21. Andrew McFarland, M.D., *The Escape, or, Loiterings amid the Scenes of Song and Story* (Boston: Mussey, 1851), p. 14.

22. Henry M. Field, *Summer Pictures: From Copenhagen to Venice* (New York: Sheldon, 1859), p. 79.

23. Melville, *Journal of a Visit*, p. 30.

24. Dean Dudley, *Social and Political Aspects of England and the Continent: A Series of Letters* (Boston: Printed for the author, 1862), p. 45.

25. Massett, *"Drifting About,"* pp. 351–52.

26. Ibid., p. 352.

27. Julia Ward Howe, *Reminiscences, 1819–1899* (Boston and New York: Houghton, Mifflin, 1899), p. 108.

28. Wilkes, *Europe in a Hurry*, p. 53.

29. Ibid., pp. 53–54.

30. Ibid., pp. 54–55.

31. Ibid., p. 59.

32. Ibid., pp. 49–51.

33. Warren Isham, *The Mud Cabin; or, The Character and Tendency of British Institutions* (New York: Appleton, 1853), preface.

34. Ibid., pp. 76, 134.

35. Ibid., pp. 149, 150–51, 155–57, 199.

36. Ibid., pp. 303–4, 309, 312.

37. Stephen H. Tyng, *Recollections of England* (London: Bagster, 1847), pp. 263–64.

38. Jacob Abbott, *A Summer in Scotland* (New York: Harper, 1848), pp. 100–102.

39. Ibid., pp. 103–7.

40. Ibid., pp. 108–9.

41. John P. Durbin, *Observations in Europe, Principally in France and Great Britain*, 2 vols. (New York: Harper, 1844), 2: 137-38.

42. Daniel C. Eddy, *Europa: or, Scenes and Society in England, France, Italy, and Switzerland* (Boston: Bradley, Dayton & Co., 1859), pp. 46–47.

43. Charles B. Fairbanks, *Aguecheek* (Boston: Shepard, Clark & Brown, 1859), pp. 184–86.

44. Abbott, *A Summer in Scotland*, pp. 324–26.

45. George S. Fisher, *Notes by the Wayside* (New York: Derby & Jackson, 1858), pp. 21–22.

46. Benjamin Silliman, *A Journal of Travels in England, Holland and Scotland, and of Two Passages over the Atlantic, in the Years 1805 and 1806*, 2 vols. (New York: Bruce, 1810), 1:47.

47. Nathaniel H. Carter, *Letters from Europe, Comprising the Journal of a Tour through Ireland, England, Scotland, France, Italy, and Switzerland in the Years 1825–6–7*, 2 vols. (New York: G. & C. & H. Carvill, 1829), 1:27.

48. Orville Dewey, *The Old World and the New; or, A Journal of Reflections and Observations Made on a Tour in Europe*, 2 vols. (New York: Harper & Bros., 1836), 1:37–42.

49. Ibid., 1:43–45.

50. Andrew Bigelow, *Leaves from a Journal: or, Sketches of Rambles in Some Parts of North Britain and Ireland, Chiefly in the Year 1817* (Boston: Wells & Lilly, 1821), p. 124.

51. Wilbur Fisk, *Travels on the Continent of Europe* (New York: Harper, 1838), p. 624.

52. Colman, *European Life and Manners*, 1:259–60.

53. Ibid., 1:268.

54. Ibid., 1:268–69.

55. Ibid., 2:13.

56. Ibid.

57. Fanny W. Hall, *Rambles in Europe; or, A Tour through France, Italy, Switzerland, and Great Britain, and Ireland, in 1836*, 2 vols. (New York: French, 1838), 2:217–18.

58. William Wells Brown, *The American Fugitive in Europe; Sketches of Places and People Abroad* (Boston: Jewett; New York: Sheldon, Lamport & Blakeman, 1855), p. 44.

59. Andrew Dickinson, *My First Visit to Europe; or, Sketches of Society, Scenery, and Antiquities in England, Wales, Ireland, Scotland, and France* (New York: George P. Putnam, 1851), pp. 48–49.

60. Asenath Nicholson, *Lights and Shades of Ireland* (London: Houlston & Stoneman, 1850), p. 224.

61. Ibid., pp. 219–20.

62. Ibid., pp. 274, 272, 223.

63. Ibid., p. 237.

64. John Mitchell, *Notes from Over Sea; Consisting of Observations Made in Europe in the Years 1843 and 1844*, 2 vols. (New York: Gates & Stedman, 1845), 1:212–14.

65. Hawthorne, *Our Old Home*, p. 309.

66. Ralph Waldo Emerson, *The Heart of Emerson's Journals*, ed. Bliss Perry (Boston and New York: Houghton Mifflin Co., 1926), p. 228.

67. Elizabeth Davis Bancroft (Mrs. George Bancroft), *Letters from England: 1846–1849* (New York: Charles Scribner's Sons, 1904), pp. 175–76.

✓ 68. Maunsell B. Field, *Memories of Many Men and of Some Women: Being Personal Recollections of Emperors, Kings, Queens, Princes, Presidents, Statesmen, Authors, and Artists, at Home and Abroad during the Last Thirty Years* (New York: Harper, 1874), pp. 40–42.

69. Ibid., p. 42.

70. Bancroft, *Letters from England*, p. 177.

71. Field, *Memories of Many Men*, pp. 43–44.

72. Bancroft, *Letters from England*, p. 182.

73. Colman, *European Life and Manners*, 2:386–88; 392.

74. Caroline M. Kirkland, *Holidays Abroad; or, Europe from the West*, 2 vols. (New York: Baker and Scribner, 1849), 1:72.

75. Field, *Memories of Many Men*, p. 141.

76. Quoted by Eric de Mare in *London 1851: The Year of the Great Exhibition* (London: J. M. Dent, Ltd, 1973), p. 2.

Chapter 12

✓ 1. William A. Drew, *Glimpses and Gatherings during a Voyage and Visit to London and the Great Exhibition in the Summer of 1851* (Augusta, Me.: Homan & Manley, 1852), pp. 198, 336.

✓ 2. Horace Greeley, *Glances at Europe: In a Series of Letters from Great Britain, France, Italy, Switzerland, etc., during the Summer of 1851* (New York: DeWitt & Davenport, 1851), p. 21.

✓ 3. Benjamin Moran, *The Footpath and Highway: or, Wanderings of an American in Great Britain in 1851 and '52* (Philadelphia: Lippincott, Grambo, and Co., 1853), p. 109.

4. Benjamin Silliman, *A Visit to Europe in 1851*, 2 vols. (New York: George P. Putnam, 1853), 2:421–22.

5. William Wells Brown, *The American Fugitive in Europe; Sketches of Places and People Abroad* (Boston: Jewett; New York: Sheldon, Lamport & Blakeman, 1855), pp. 195–96.

6. John M. Brinnin, *The Sway of the Grand Saloon* (New York: Delacorte Press, 1971), p. 489.

7. George Wilkes, *Europe in a Hurry* (New York: Long, 1853), p. 40.

8. Drew, *Glimpses and Gatherings*, p. 322.

9. Zadock Thompson, *Journal of a Trip to London, Paris, and the Great Exhibition in 1851* (Burlington, Vt.: Nichols & Warren, 1852), p. 137.

10. Drew, *Glimpses and Gatherings*, p. 317.

✓ 11. Arthur Cleveland Coxe, *Impressions of England; or, Sketches of English Scenery and Society* (New York: Dana & Co. 1856), p. 65.

12. Drew, *Glimpses and Gatherings*, p. 195.

13. David F. Dorr, *A Colored Man around the World; By a Quadroon* (Cleveland, Ohio: Printed for the author, 1858), p. 22.

14. Caroline M. Kirkland, *Holidays Abroad; or, Europe from the West*, 2 vols. (New York: Baker and Scribner, 1849), 1: 96.

15. Edward Thomson, *Letters from Europe: Being Notes of a Tour through England, France, and Switzerland* (Cincinnati, Ohio: J. Swormstedt & A. Poe, 1856), p. 94.

16. Ralph Keeler, *Vagabond Adventures* (Boston: Fields, Osgood, & Co., 1870), p. 231.

17. Mark Trafton, *Rambles in Europe: In a Series of Familiar Letters* (Boston: Peirce, 1852), p. 90.

18. Drew, *Glimpses and Gatherings*, pp. 279, 198.

19. Moran, *Footpath and Highway*, p. 110.

20. Silliman, *A Visit to Europe*, 2:420.

21. Brown, *American Fugitive*, p. 194.

22. Moran, *Footpath and Highway*, p. 111.

23. Greeley, *Glances at Europe*, pp. 19, 24.

24. Thompson, *Journal of a Trip*, pp. 140–41.

25. Ibid., p. 141.

26. Henry Colman, *European Life and Manners: In Familiar Letters to Friends*, 2 vols. (Boston: Charles C. Little & James Brown, 1849), 1:45.

27. Andrew Jackson Downing, *Rural Essays* (New York: Leavitt & Allen, 1855), p. 506.

28. Coxe, *Impressions of England*, pp. 68–69.

29. Drew, *Glimpses and Gatherings*, p. 321.

30. Samuel S. Cox, *A Buckeye Abroad: or, Wanderings in Europe and the Orient* (New York: G. P. Putnam, 1852), p. 31.

31. Greeley, *Glances at Europe*, p. 30.

32. Dorr, *A Colored Man*, p. 20.

33. Brown, *American Fugitive*, pp. 204–5.

34. David V. G. Bartlett, *What I Saw in London; or, Men and Things in the Great Metropolis* (New York: C. M. Saxton, Barker & Co., 1861), p. 318.

35. Ibid., p. 319.

36. Rev. John Overton Choules, D. D. *Young Americans Abroad: or, Vacation in Europe; The Results of a Tour through Great Britain, France, Holland, Belgium, Germany and Switzerland* (Boston: Gould & Lincoln, 1852), pp. 98–99.

37. Ibid., pp. 99–100.

38. Aaron S. Willington, *A Summer's Tour in Europe, in 1851, in a Series of Letters Addressed to the Editors of the Charleston Courier* (Charleston, S. C.: Walker & James, 1852), p. 21.

39. Ibid.

40. Greeley, *Glances at Europe*, pp. 20–21.

41. Ibid., pp. 21–23.

42. Cox, *A Buckeye Abroad*, pp. 66–67.

43. Bartlett, *What I Saw in London*, p. 136.

44. Coxe, *Impressions of England*, pp. 43, 64.

45. Ibid., p. 65.

46. Ibid., p. 64.

47. Eric de Mare, *London 1851: The Year of the Great Exhibition* (London: J. M. Dent, Ltd, 1973), pages not numbered, appears same page as illus. no. 67.

48. Cox, *A Buckeye Abroad*, p. 34.

49. Drew, *Glimpses and Gatherings*, pp. 349, 370.

50. Ibid., pp. 349–55.

51. Bartlett, *What I Saw in London*, p. 321.

52. Drew, *Glimpses and Gatherings*, pp. 344, 356.

53. Greeley, *Glances at Europe*, p. 32.

54. Dorr, *A Colored Man*, p. 19.

55. Greeley, *Glances at Europe*, p. 32.

56. Randal W. MacGavock, *A Tennessean Abroad; or, Letters from Europe, Africa, and Asia* (New York: Redfield, 1854), pp. 44–45.

57. Ibid., p. 45.

58. Choules, *Young Americans Abroad*, p. 105.

59. Drew, *Glimpses and Gatherings*, p. 329.

60. Thompson, *Journal of a Trip*, p. 67.

61. Cox, *A Buckeye Abroad*, p. 38.

62. Drew, *Glimpses and Gatherings*, p. 325.

63. *New York Times* 1, no. 36 (October 29, 1851): 2.

64. Dorr, *A Colored Man*, p. 19.

65. Silliman, *A Visit to Europe*, 2:422–24.

66. Quoted in the *New York Times* 1, no. 7 (September 25, 1851): 4.

67. *The National Cyclopaedia of American Biography* (New York: James T. White & Company, 1933), vol. xxiii, pp. 336–37.

68. Bartlett, *What I Saw in London*, p. 324.

69. Greeley, *Glances at Europe*, p. 287.

70. Ibid., pp. 387–89.

71. Quoted in the *New York Times* 1, no. 25 (October 16, 1851): 4.

72. *New York Times* 1, no. 36 (October 29, 1851): 2.

73. Ibid., no. 7 (September 25, 1851): 1.

74. Drew, *Glimpses and Gatherings*, pp. 372–73.

75. MacGavock, *A Tennessean Abroad*, pp. 46–47.

76. Daniel C. Eddy, *Europa: or, Scenes and Society in England, France, Italy, and Switzerland* (Boston: Bradley, Dayton & Co., 1859), pp. 100–101.

77. Drew, *Glimpses and Gatherings,* pp. 357–58.

78. Ibid., p. 358.

79. Thomson, *Letters from Europe,* p. 129.

80. Moran, *Footpath and Highway,* p. 109.

81. Cox, *A Buckeye Abroad,* p. 30.

82. Greeley, *Glances at Europe,* pp. 23, 36–37.

83. Bartlett, *What I Saw in London,* pp. 323–24.

84. Coxe, *Impressions of England,* p. 70.

85. Cox, *A Buckeye Abroad,* p. 6.

86. Moran, *Footpath and Highway,* pp. 111–12.

87. Ibid., p. 112.

Chapter 13

1. George M. Dallas, *Diary of George Mifflin Dallas while United States Minister to Russia, 1837 to 1839, and to England, 1856 to 1861,* ed. Susan Dallas (Philadelphia: Lippincott, 1892) pp. 442–43.

2. Ibid., p. 443.

3. Quoted in Stephen Fiske, *English Photographs, by an American* (London: Tinsley Brothers, 1869), p. 277.

4. John P. Kennedy, *At Home and Abroad, Including a Journal in Europe, 1867–68* (New York: Putnam, 1872), p. 351.

5. *The New Encyclopaedia Britannica.* Micropaedia. (U.S.A.: Encyclopedia Brittanica, 1978), 15th Edition. Vol. I, pp. 180–81.

6. John M. Forbes, *Letters and Recollections of John Murray Forbes,* ed. Sarah Forbes Hughes, 2 vols. (Boston and New York: Houghton, Mifflin, 1899), 1:9.

7. Quoted in Ernest Samuels, *The Young Henry Adams* (Cambridge, Mass.: Harvard University Press, 1948), p. 100.

8. Dean Dudley, *Social and Political Aspects of England and the Continent: A Series of Letters* (Boston: Printed for the author, 1862), p. 101.

9. Moses Coit Tyler, *Glimpses of England; Social, Political, Literary* (New York & London: G. P. Putnam's Sons, 1898), p. 65

10. George F. Train, *Train's Great Speeches in England on Slavery and Emancipation, Delivered in London, on March 12th and 13th, 1862* (Philadelphia: T. B. Peterson & Brothers, 1862), p. 25.

11. Hugh Brogan, *The American Civil War:* Extracts from *The Times* 1860–1865, ed. Hugh Brogan (London: Times Books, 1975), pp. xiv–xviii.

12. Ibid., p. xviii.

13. Ernest Samuels, *The Young Henry Adams* (Cambridge, Mass.: Harvard University Press, 1948), p. 108.

14. Charles Williams, *Old World Scenes* (Pittsburgh, Pa.: Haven, 1867), p. 241.

15. Ibid., pp. 242–43.

16. Ibid., pp. 244–46.

17. Ibid., pp. 247–48.

18. Ibid., p. 248.

19. Phoebe W. Palmer, *Four Years in the Old World; Comprising the Travels, Incidents, and Evangelistic Labors of Dr. and Mrs. Palmer in England, Ireland, Scotland and Wales* (New York: Foster & Palmer, Jr., 1866), pp. 498–99.

20. Ibid., p. 499–500.

21. Ibid., p. 500–501.

22. John L. Peyton, *The American Crisis; or, Pages from the Notebook of a State Agent during the Civil War,* 2 vols. (London, Saunders, Otley and Co., 1867), 2:73–74, 101.

23. Palmer, *Four Years in the Old World,* pp. 647–48.

24. Elihu Burritt, *A Walk from London to Land's End and Back, with Notes by the Way* (London: Low & Marston, 1865), pp. 226–227.

25. George A. Townsend, *Campaigns of a Non-Combatant, and His Romaunt Abroad during the War* (New York: Blelock, 1866), pp. 277, 284.

26. Joseph Battell, *The Yankee Boy from Home* (New York: John F. Trow, Printer, 1863), pp. 205–6, 208, 222.

27. John H. Tobitt, *What I Heard in Europe during the "American Excitement"* (New York: H. M. Tobitt, 1864), p. 17.

28. Ibid., pp. 51–57.

29. Ibid., p. 88.

30. Ibid., pp. 132, 131.

31. Forbes, *Letters and Recollections*, 1:17–18, 9.

32. Ibid., 1:36.

33. Ibid., 1:18.

34. Stephen Fiske, *English Photographs, by an American* (London: Tinsley Brothers, 1869), preface, p. x.

35. Ibid., p. 279.

36. Ibid., pp. 280, 282–83, 290.

37. Thomas J. Clayton, *Rambles and Reflections; Europe from Biscay to the Black Sea and from Aetna to the North Cape with Glimpses at Asia, Africa, America, and the Islands of the Sea* (Chester, Pa.: Press of the Delaware Co. *Republican*, 1892), p. 25.

38. James R. Lowell, *My Study Windows.* "On a Certain Condescension in Foreigners" (New York: AMS Press, 1971), pp. 77–78, 80–81.

Part III

Chapter 14

1. *New York Times* 14 (June 1, 1866): 4.

2. Charles D. Poston, *Europe in the Summer-Time* (Washington, D. C.: M'Gill & Witherow, 1868), p. 7.

3. John L. Peyton, *Rambling Reminiscences of a Residence Abroad. England—Guernsey* (Staunton, Va.: Yost, 1888), p. 144.

4. Ernest Samuels, *The Young Henry Adams* (Cambridge, Mass.: Harvard University Press, 1948, p. 126.

5. James M. Hoppin, *Old England: Its Scenery, Art, and People* (New York: Hurd and Houghton, 1867), preface, pp. iii–iv.

6. Ibid., pp. 149–50.

7. James M. Hoyt, *Glances on the Wing at Foreign Lands* (Cleveland, Ohio: Fairbanks, Benedict & Co., 1872), p. 11.

8. Henry Morford, *Over-sea; or, England, France and Scotland As Seen by a Live American* (New York: Hilton, 1867), pp. 152, 71, 354.

9. James N. Matthews, *My Holiday; How I Spent It: Being Some Rough Notes of a Trip to Europe and Back, in the Summer of 1866* (New York: Hurd & Houghton, 1867), p. 211.

10. John W. Forney, *Letters from Europe* (Philadelphia: Peterson, 1867), pp. 36–37.

11. Ibid., p. 79.

12. Ibid., pp. 72–74.

13. Ibid., p. 75.

14. Ibid., p. 53.

15. Ibid., pp. 54–55.

16. Ibid., pp. 83–84.

17. Ibid., p. 373.

18. Ibid., p. 83.

19. Ibid., pp. 372, 376.

20. Mrs. Mary H. Wills, *A Summer in Europe* (Philadelphia: J. B. Lippincott, 1876), pp. 69–70.

21. Robert E. Spiller, *The American in England during the First Half Century of Independence* (New York: Henry Holt & Co., 1926), p. 385.

22. Theron C. Crawford, *English Life* (New York: Lovell, 1889), p. 169.

23. Hezekiah H. Wright, *Desultory Reminiscences of a Tour through Germany, Switzerland and France. By an American* (Boston: Ticknor, 1838), p. 342.

24. Stephen Spender, *Love-Hate Relations: English and American Sensibilities* (New York: Vintage Books, 1975), p. 5.

25. William A. Braman, *Glimpses of Europe* (Cleveland, Ohio: J. B. Savage, 1901), p. 204.

26. Thomas Bailey Aldrich, *Poems,* in *The Works of Thomas Bailey Aldrich,* vol. 2 (New York: AHS Press, Inc., 1970): 71–72.

27. William Hemstreet, *The Economical European Tourist: A Journalist's Three Months Abroad for $430, Including Ireland, Scotland, England, France, Switzerland, Italy, Austria, Prussia* (New York: S. W. Green, Printer, 1875), p. 227.

28. Richard G. White, *England Without and Within* (Boston: Houghton, Mifflin, 1881), pp. 11–12.

29. Gilbert Haven, *The Pilgrim's Wallet; or, Scraps of Travel Gathered in England, France and Germany* (New York: Carlton & Porter, 1866), p. 268.

30. Beverly Carradine, *A Journey to Palestine* (St. Louis, Mo.: C. B. Woodward Printing & Book Mfg. Co., 1891), p. 19.

31. O. R. Burchard, *Two Months in Europe; a Record of a Summer Vacation Abroad* (Syracuse, N.Y.: Davis, Bardeen & Co., 1879) p. 6.

32. James B. Pond, *A Summer in England with Henry Ward Beecher* (New York: Howard & Hulbert, 1887), pp. 9–10.

33. Benjamin Walker, *Aboard and Abroad; Vacation Notes, in Ten Letters, Originally Published in the Lowell Daily Courier* (Lowell, Mass.: Courier Press, 1889), p. 11.

34. Daniel F. Beatty, *In Foreign Lands* (Washington, N.J.: D. F. Beatty, 1878), pp. 3, 97.

35. White, *England Without and Within,* pp. 1, 164–65.

36. Mrs. Lucy Yeend Culler, *Europe through a Woman's Eye* (Philadelphia: Lutheran Publication Society, 1883), pp. 187, 225.

37. Stephen C. Massett, *"Drifting About"; or What "Jeems Pipes of Pipesville", Saw-and-Did* (New York: Carleton, 1863), p. 190.

38. William Peberdy, *Extracts from the Journal of My Trip to Europe* (Willimantic, Conn.: Home Press, 1889), pp. 21–23.

39. William E. Whyte, *O'er the Atlantic; or, A Journal of a Voyage to and from Europe* (New York: American News Co., 1870), p. 91.

40. Charles D. Linskill, *Travels in Lands beyond the Sea* (Wilkes-Barre, Pa.: Baur, 1888), p. 99.

41. James F. Rusling, *European Days and Ways* (Cincinnati, Ohio: Jennings & Pye, 1902), pp. 341–45.

42. Edward P. Thwing, M.D. *Outdoor Life in Europe; or, Sketches of Seven Summers Abroad* (New York: Hurst, 1888), p. 48.

43. George W. Williams, *Sketches of Travel in the Old and New World* (Charleston, S.C.: Walker, Evans & Cogswell, 1871), p. 308.

44. Leonard A. Morrison, *Rambles in Europe: In Ireland, Scotland, England, Belgium, Germany, Switzerland, and France.* (Boston: Cupples, Upham & Co. 1887). p. 199.

45. Kate A. Murphy, *Trials and Triumphs of a Summer Vacation* (New York: Michael Sullivan, 1886), pp. 9, 72.

46. Nicholas Murray, *Men and Things as I Saw Them in Europe* (New York: Harper, 1853), p. 255.

47. Oliver Wendell Holmes, *Our Hundred Days in Europe* (Boston and New York: Houghton, Mifflin, 1887), pp. 165–67, 169–72, 176, 39, 282.

48. Mrs. E. A. Forbes, *A Woman's First Impressions of Europe; Being Wayside Sketches Made during a Short Tour in the Year 1863* (New York: Derby & Miller, 1865), pp. 106–7.

49. Agnes E. Claflin, *From Shore to Shore: A Journey of Nineteen Years* (Cambridge, Mass.: Riverside Press, 1873), p. 139.

50. John S. Bender, *A Hoosier's Experience in Western Europe, With Notes on the Way* (Plymouth, Ind.: Published for the author, 1880), p. 28.

51. Kate Field, *Hap-Hazard* (Boston: Osgood, 1873), pp. 173, 177.

52. Sarah Maria Aloisa (Britton) Spottiswood Mackin, *A Society Woman on Two Continents* (New York and London: Transatlantic, 1896), pp. 120–24.

53. *Program of Cook's Second Educational Tour* (New York: Cook, Son and Jenkins, 1874), pp. 3–4.

54. *Programs and Itineraries of Cook's Grand Excursions to Europe* (London and New York: Thomas Cook & Son, 1880), p. 3.

55. Mackin, *A Society Woman,* introduction, p. 1.

56. Mary Elizabeth Blake, *A Summer Holiday Tour in Europe* (Boston: Lee and Shepard, 1890), p. 1.

57. Hiram Fuller, *Ten Days Abroad* (New York: School News Co. 1901), p. 136.

✓ 58. Mrs. E. H. Thompson, *From the Thames to the Trossachs: Impressions of Travel in England and Scotland.* The Epworth League Readings for 1890–91 (New York: Hunt & Eaton, 1890), introduction, p. 1.

59. *Old Sights with New Eyes, "By a Yankee,"* intro. Robert Baird, D.D. (New York: M. W. Dodd, 1854), p. 358.

60. Randal W. MacGavock, *A Tennessean Abroad; or, Letters from Europe, Africa, and Asia* (New York: Redfield, 1854), p. 57.

61. Bender, *A Hoosier's Experience*, p. 87.

62. Beatty, *In Foreign Lands*, p. 80.

63. Zachary Taylor Sweeney, *Under Ten Flags; An Historical Pilgrimage* (Cincinnati, Ohio: Standard, 1888), p. 24.

64. Hemstreet, *Economical European Tourist*, p. 12.

65. Womens' Rest Tour Association, *A Summer in England: A Handbook for Use of American Women* (Boston: Beacon, 1896), pp. 57–60.

66. May Alcott Nieriker, *Studying Art Abroad, and How to Do it Cheaply* (Boston: Roberts, 1879), pp. 8–9.

67. Moses F. Sweetser, *Europe for $2.00 a Day: A Few Notes for the Assistance of Tourists of Moderate Means, with Some Personal Reminiscences of Travel* (Boston: Osgood, 1875), pp. 30–31.

68. James S. McClay, *Style-O!-Graphic Pens and Funny Pencillings in Europe* (Hartford, Conn.: Phoenix, 1881), p. 68.

Chapter 15

1. Henry Adams, *The Letters of Henry Adams*, 2 vols., ed. Chauncey Worthington Ford (Boston and New York: Houghton, Mifflin, 1930), 2:6.

2. William H. Rideing, *At Hawarden with Mr. Gladstone, and Other Transatlantic Experiences* (New York and Boston: Crowell, 1896), pp. 232–33.

3. William H. Rideing, *Luxury At Sea* (Boston: Peter & Son, 1890), p. 15.

4. Ibid., pp. 11–14.

5. Rideing, *At Hawarden*, pp. 227–34.

6. Rideing, *Luxury At Sea*, pp. 16–18.

7. Ibid., pp. 18–19.

8. Ibid., pp. 4–6; 15.

9. Ibid., pp. 23–25.

10. Moses F. Sweetser, *Europe for $2.00 a Day: A Few Notes for the Assistance of Tourists of Moderate Means, with Some Personal Reminiscences of Travel* (Boston: Osgood, 1875), pp. 40–42.

11. Noble L. Prentis, *A Kansan Abroad* (Topeka, Kans.: Martin, 1878), pp. 5–6.

12. Theodore L. Cuyler, *From the Nile to Norway and Homeward* (New York: Robert Carter & Bros., 1882), p. 16.

13. Benjamin R. Curtis, *Dottings Round the Circle* (Boston: Osgood, 1876), p. 328.

14. May Alcott Nieriker, *Studying Art Abroad, and How to Do it Cheaply* (Boston: Roberts, 1879), p. 10.

✓ 15. William Dean Howells, *Seven English Cities* (New York: Harper, 1909), p. 11.

16. George M. Beard, M.D., *A Practical Treatise on Seasickness* (New York: E. B. Treat, 1880), pp. iii, 30–58.

✓ 17. Phoebe W. Palmer, *Four Years in the Old World; Comprising the Travels, Incidents, and Evangelistic Labors of Dr. and Mrs. Palmer in England, Ireland, Scotland and Wales* (New York: Foster & Palmer, Jr., 1866), pp. 14–15.

✓ 18. James M. Bailey, *England from a Back Window; With Views of Scotland and Ireland* (Boston: Lee & Shepard, 1879), p. 10.

19. Charles D. Linskill, *Travels in Lands beyond the Sea* (Wilkes-Barre, Pa.: Baur, 1888), p. 57.

20. Lou J. Beauchamp, *What the Duchess and I Saw in Europe* (Hamilton, Ohio: Brown & Whitaker, 1896), pp. 10–13.

21. Mrs. Lucy Yeend Culler, *Europe through a Woman's Eye* (Philadelphia: Lutheran Publication Society, 1883), p. 2.

22. Eudora L. South, *Wayside Notes and Fireside Thoughts* (St. Louis, Mo.: Burns, 1884), pp. 20, 33–34.

23. William T. Meloy, *Wanderings in Europe* (Chicago: LaMonte, O'Donnell & Co., 1892), pp. 12–13.

24. Women's Rest Tour Association, *A Summer in England: A Handbook for Use of American Women* (Boston: Beacon, 1896), pp. 9–10.

25. Thomas W. Knox, *How to Travel; Hints, Advice and Suggestions to Travellers by Land and Sea All over the Globe* (New York: G. P. Putnam's Sons, 1887), p. 56.

26. William Hemstreet, *The Economical European Tourist . . .* (New York: S. W. Green, Printer. 1875), p. 25.

27. Knox, *How to Travel*, pp. 38–39.

28. Ella W. Thompson, *Beaten Paths: or, A Woman's Vacation* (Boston: Lee & Shepard, 1874), p. 12.

29. Eliza A. Connor, *E. A. Abroad: A Summer in Europe* (Cincinnati, Ohio: W. E. Dibble & Co., 1883), pp. 11–12.

30. Francis C. Sessions, *On the Wing through Europe* (Columbus, Ohio: H. W. Derby & Co., 1880), p. 3.

31. Beverly Carradine, *A Journey to Palestine* (St. Louis, Mo.: C. B. Woodward Printing & Book Mfg. Co., 1891), p. 35.

32. Mrs. W. G. Rose, *Travels in Europe and Northern Africa* (Cleveland, Ohio: The Whitworth Bros., Co., 1901). p. 11.

33. Jesse Johnson, *Glimpses of Europe; A Series of Letters Written from Abroad to the Standard Union of Brooklyn, New York* (New York: The Grafton Press, 1906), p. 5.

34. Miss L. L. Rees, *We Four: Where We Went and What We Saw in Europe* (Philadelphia: Lippincott, 1880), pp. 14–15.

35. Florence Trail, *My Journal in Foreign Lands* (Baltimore: W. S. Stock & Co., 1884), p. 5.

36. Joseph Cross, D.D., *The American Pastor in Europe* (London: Bentley, 1860), p. 5.

37. Zachary Taylor Sweeney, *Under Ten flags; An Historical Pilgrimage* (Cincinnati, Ohio: Standard, 1888), pp. 3–4.

38. Adeline Trafton, *An American Girl Abroad* (Boston: Lee & Shepard, 1872), p. 21.

39. South, *Wayside Notes*, p. 29.

40. Thomas J. Clayton, *Rambles and Reflections; Europe from Biscay to the Black Sea and from Aetna to the North Cape with Glimpses at Asia, Africa, America, and the Islands of the Sea* (Chester, Pa.: Press of the Delaware Co. *Republican*, 1892), p. 1.

41. Knox, *How to Travel*, p. 69.

✓42. Leonard A. Morrison, *Rambles in Europe: In Ireland, Scotland, England, Belgium, Germany, Switzerland, and France* (Boston: Cupples, Upham & Co., 1887), pp. 24–27.

43. Edgar Magness, *Tramp Tales of Europe through the Tyrolean and Swiss Alps and the Italian Lake Region* (Buffalo, N.Y.: Charles Wells Moulton, 1895), p. 17.

44. Joel Cook, *A Holiday Tour in Europe. Described in a Series of Letters for the Public Ledger during the Summer and Autumn of 1878* (Philadelphia: J. B. Lippincott Co., 1879), p. 13.

45. James M. Hoyt, *Glances on the Wing at Foreign Lands* (Cleveland, Ohio: Fairbanks, Benedict & Co., 1872), p. 255.

46. James A. Bradley, *Across the Atlantic; A Series of Descriptive Letters to the Asbury Park Journal* (Asbury Park, N.J.: John L. Coffin, 1884), p. 6.

47. William P. Breed, *Aboard and Abroad, in 1884* (New York: Funk & Wagnalls, 1885), p. 157.

48. Mary E. Sherwood, *Here and There and Everywhere; Reminiscences* (Chicago and New York: Stone, 1898), p. 209.

49. Julia P. Wilson, *Leaves from My Diary* (Norwalk, Conn.: Gardner, 1900), p. 132.

50. South, *Wayside Notes*, p. 20.

51. Adelaide S. Hall, *Two Women Abroad* (Chicago: Monarch Book Company, 1898), pp. 20–21.

52. William A. Braman, *Glimpses of Europe* (Cleveland, Ohio: J. B. Savage, 1901), p. 206.

53. Wilson, *Leaves from My Diary*, p. 9.

54. Edward L. Temple, *Old World Memories*, 2 vols. (Boston: Page, 1899), 1:16.

55. Marion Adams, *The Letters of Mrs. Henry Adams*, ed. Ward Theron (Boston: Little, Brown & Co., 1936), p. 15.

56. Fannie A. Tyler, *Home Letters from over the Sea* (Boston: Williams, 1883), pp. 335–36.

57. Morton B. Wharton, *European Notes; or, What I Saw in the Old World* (Atlanta, Ga.: James P. Harrison & Co., 1884), p. 360.

58. E. K. Washington, *Echoes of Europe: or, World Pictures of Travel* (Philadelphia: Challen, 1860), pp. 691–92.

59. Charles D. Poston, *Europe in the Summer-Time* (Washington: M'Gill & Witherow, 1868), p. 97.

60. DeRobigne Mortimer Bennett, *A Truth Seeker around the World; A Series of Letters Written while Making a Tour of the Globe* (New York: D. M. Bennett, 1882), pp. 22–23.

61. William C. Falkner, *Rapid Ramblings in Europe* (Philadelphia: J. B. Lippincott Co., 1884), pp. 57–58.

62. South, *Wayside Notes*, pp. 465–66.

63. Temple, *Old World Memories*, 1:304.

64. William Hutton, *Twelve Thousand Miles over Land and Sea* (Philadelphia: Grant, Faires & Rodgers, 1878), p. 19.

65. William Hichborn, *Trip of the Ancients . . .* (Malden, Mass.: G. E. Dunbar, 1897), p. 21.

66. Frederick A. Stokes, *College Tramps; A Narrative of the Adventures of a Party of Yale Students . . .* (New York: Carleton, 1880), pp. 29–30.

67. Theron C. Crawford, *English Life* (New York: Lovell, 1889), pp. 152–53.

68. Curtis Guild, *Abroad Again: or, Fresh Forays in Foreign Fields* (Boston: Lee & Shepard, 1877), p. 37.

69. Henry Morford, *Over-Sea; or, England, France and Scotland As Seen by a Live American* (New York: Hilton, 1867), p. 25.

70. Lily Lawrence Rust, *Hand-written journal*. Pages unnumbered. 3 vols. 1903.

71. Linskill, *Travels*, pp. 44–45.

72. Hoyt, *Glances on the Wing*, p. 16.

73. Temple, *Old World Memories*, 1:18.

74. Charles Wood, *Saunterings in Europe* (New York: Randolph, 1882), pp. 1–5.

75. Benjamin Bausman, *Wayside Gleanings in Europe* (Philadelphia: Reformed Church Publication Board, 1875), p. 11.

76. John Burroughs, *Fresh Fields* (Boston: Houghton, Mifflin, & Co., 1885), pp. 290–91.

77. James N. Matthews, *My Holiday; How I Spent It: Being Some Rough Notes of a Trip to Europe and Back, in the Summer of 1866* (New York: Hurd & Houghton, 1867), pp. 254–55.

78. Noble L. Prentis, *A Kansan Abroad* (Topeka, Kans.: Martin, 1878), p. 7.

79. Charles C. Fulton, *Europe Viewed through American Spectacles* (Philadelphia: Lippincott, 1874), p. 301.

80. Adelaide L. Harrington, *The Afterglow of European Travel* (Boston: Lothrop, 1882), p. 294.

81. George W. Hills, *John Bull, Limited* (Philadelphia: Privately printed, 1918), p. 12.

82. Laura G. Collins, *By-gone Tourist Days: Letters of Travel* (Cincinnati, Ohio: Robert Clarke & Co., 1900), p. 2.

83. John H. Barrows, *A World Pilgrimage* (Chicago: A. C. McClurg & Co., 1897), p. 174.

84. Breed, *Aboard and Abroad*, p. 11.

85. Burr H. Polk, *The Big American Caravan in Europe* (Evansvile: Journal Co., 1879), pp. 10–11.

86. Henry Maney, *Memories over the Water; or, Stray Thoughts on a Long Stroll* (Nashville, Tenn.: Toon, Nelson & Co., 1854), p. 31.

87. O. R. Burchard, *Two Months in Europe; A Record of a Summer Vacation Abroad* (Syracuse, N.Y.: Davis, Bardeen & Co., 1879), pp. 7–8.

88. Clement Pearson, M.D., *A Journal of Travels in Europe during the Summer of 1880* (Washington, D.C.: Judd & Detweiler, 1885), p. 170.

89. *Punch* 99 (October 18, 1890): 183.

90. Conner, *E. A. Abroad*, pp. 364–66.

91. Ibid., pp. 366–69.

92. Ibid., pp. 370–72.

93. Fulton, *Europe Viewed*, p. 306.

94. Poston, *Europe in the Summertime*, p. 8.

95. William P. Davis, *Across the Sea* (Trenton, N.J.: John L. Murray, 1889), pp. 24–34.

96. Henry C. Holloway, *A New Path across an Old Field* (Philadelphia: Lutheran Publication Society, 1886), p. 301.

97. Peter J. Hamilton, *Rambles in Historic Lands; Travels in Belgium, Germany, Switzerland, Italy, France and England* (New York: Putnam, 1893), pp. 7–8.

98. Prentis, *A Kansan Abroad,* p. 11.

99. George W. Williams, *Sketches of Travel in the Old and New World* (Charleston, S.C.: Walker, Evans & Cogswell, 1871), p. 311.

100. Sherwood, *Here and There,* p. 210.

101. James H. Bates, *Notes of Foreign Travel* (New York: Burr Printing House, 1891), p. 8.

102. William Dean Howells, *Seven English Cities* (New York and London: Harper, 1909), p. 10.

103. Nathan Hubbell, *My Journey to Jerusalem, Including Travels in England, Scotland, Ireland, France, Belgium, Germany, Holland, Switzerland, Italy, Greece, Turkey, Palestine, and Egypt* (New York: Hunt & Eaton, 1890), p. 16.

Chapter 16

1. Curtis Guild, *Britons and Muscovites, or Traits of Two Empires* (Boston: Lee & Shepard, 1888), p. 1.

2. Theron C. Crawford, *English Life* (New York: Lovell, 1889), p. 167.

3. Francis C. Sessions, *On the Wing through Europe* (Columbus, Ohio: Derby & Co., 1880), p. 97.

4. Crawford, *English Life,* p. 167.

5. Mary H. Wills, *A Summer in Europe* (Philadelphia: J. B. Lippincott, 1876), p. 31.

6. William Dean Howells, *Seven English Cities* (New York: Harper, 1909), p. 4.

7. Henry Adams, *The Letters of Henry Adams,* 2 vols., ed. Chauncey Worthington Ford (Boston and New York: Houghton, Mifflin, 1930), 1:325.

8. Evelyn R. Stetson, *Rapid Transit Abroad* (New York: James Miller, 1879), preface (no p. no.); pp. 51, 52–54, 55–57.

9. Luther L. Holden, *A Summer Jaunt through the Old World: Record of an Excursion Made to and through Europe, by the Tourjée Educational Party of 1878* (Boston: Lee & Shepard, 1879).

10. James S. McClay, *Style-O!-Graphic Pens and Funny Pencillings in Europe* (Hartford, Conn.: Phoenix, 1881), pp. 111–12.

11. Burr H. Polk, *The Big American Caravan in Europe* (Evansvile, Journal Co., 1879), p. 5.

12. McClay, *Style-O!-Graphic Pens,* appendix, p. 4.

13. Adelaide L. Harrington, *The Afterglow of European Travel* (Boston: Lothrop, 1882), pp. 16–17, 24, 9, 26.

14. Polk, *Big American Caravan,* p. 32.

15. Harrington, *The Afterglow,* pp. 26, 31.

16. Polk, *Big American Caravan,* pp. 34–35.

17. Harrington, *The Afterglow,* p. 16.

18. Polk, *Big American Caravan,* p. 39.

19. Ibid., p. 24.

20. McClay, *Style-O!-Graphic Pens,* appendix, p. 6.

21. William Stevenson, *Sights and Scenes in Europe: or, Pencillings by the Way in England, Scotland, Ireland, France, Switzerland, Germany and Belgium, during a Short Tour in the Summer and Autumn of 1881* (Flint, Mich.: M. S. Elmore & Co., 1882), p. 261.

22. Harrington, *The Afterglow,* p. 293.

23. Polk, *Big American Caravan,* p. 174.

24. McClay, *Style-O!-Graphic Pens,* pp. 111–12.

25. William P. Davis, *Across the Sea* (Trenton, N.J.: John L. Murray, 1889), p. 13.

26. Samuel Watson, *A Memphian's Trip to Europe with Cook's Educational Party* (Nashville, Tenn.: Southern Methodist Publishing House, 1874), dedication, pp. 3, 350.

27. Eliza A. Connor, *E. A. Abroad: A Summer in Europe* (Cincinnati, Ohio: W. E. Dibble & Co., 1883), pp. 355–56, 36.

28. J. S. Cantwell, *Thirty Days over the Sea; A Holiday Ramble in the Old World* (Cincinnati, Ohio: Williamson & Cantwell, 1873), p. 53.

29. William C. Falkner, *Rapid Ramblings in Europe* (Philadelphia: J. B. Lippincott, 1884), p. 15.

30. Hezekiah H. Wright, *Desultory Reminiscences of a Tour through Germany, Switzerland and France. By an American* (Boston: Ticknor, 1838), p. 339.

✓31. Curtis Guild, *Abroad Again; or, Fresh Forays in Foreign Fields* (Boston: Lee & Shepard, 1877), pp. 19–20.

✓32. Elizabeth Peake, *Pen Pictures of Europe; When and How We Went, and What We Saw during a Seventeen Month's Tour* (Philadelphia: Lippincott, 1874), p. 115.

33. Henry C. Holloway, *A New Path across an Old Field* (Philadelphia: Lutheran Publication Society, 1886), p. 286.

34. Crawford, *English Life*, p. 157.

35. James N. Matthews, *My Holiday; How I Spent It: Being Some Rough Notes of a Trip to Europe and Back, in the Summer of 1866* (New York: Hurd & Houghton, 1867), pp. 265–66.

36. Adelaide S. Hall, *Two Women Abroad* (Chicago: Monarch Book Company, 1898), p. 467.

37. Lily Lawrence Rust, *Hand-written journal*. Pages unnumbered. 3 vols. 1903.

38. Laura G. Collins, *By-gone Tourist Days: Letters of Travel* (Cincinnati, Ohio: Robert Clarke & Co., 1900), p. 19.

✓39. William Dean Howells, *Seen and Unseen at Stratford-on-Avon* (New York and London: Harper, 1914), p. 102.

40. Francis C. Sessions, *On the Wing through Europe* (Columbus, Ohio: H. W. Derby & Co., 1880), pp. 296–97.

41. Amy G. Smith and Mary E. Smith, *Letters from Europe: 1865–1866*, ed. David Saunders Clarke (Washington, D.C.: Library of Congress, 1948), p. 18.

42. *Diary of My Itinerary of Sixty Days across the Water* (St. Augustine, Fla., 1904), p. 38.

43. Mrs. S. R. Urbino, *An American Woman in Europe; The Journal of Two Years and a Half Sojourn in Germany, Switzerland, France, and Italy* (Boston: Lee & Shepard, 1869), p. 334.

44. Falkner, *Rapid Ramblings*, pp. 540–41.

45. Ibid., pp. 547, 550.

46. Samuel W. Fiske, *Mr. Dunn Browne's Experiences in Foreign Parts* (Boston: Jewett, 1857), p. 22.

47. Ella W. Thompson, *Beaten Paths: or, A Woman's Vacation* (Boston: Lee & Shepard, 1874), p. 69.

48. Orlando W. Wight, *Peoples and Countries Visited in a Winding Journey around the World* (Detroit, Mich.: Raynor & Taylor, 1888), pp. 24–25.

49. Noble L. Prentis, *A Kansan Abroad* (Topeka, Kans.: Martin, 1878), p. 42.

50. William Hemstreet, *The Economical European Tourist . . .* (New York: S. W. Green, Printer, 1875), p. 89.

51. John Mitchell, *Notes from Over Sea; Consisting of Observations Made in Europe in the years 1843 and 1844*, 2 vols. (New York: Gates & Stedman, 1845), 1:311.

52. William Hichborn, *Trip to the Ancients . . .* (Malden, Mass.: G. E. Dunbar, 1897), p. 111.

✓53. William W. Nevin, *Vignettes of Travel: Some Comparative Sketches in England and Italy* (Philadelphia: Lippincott, 1881), p. 443.

54. Lucy B. Dudley, *Letters to Ruth* (New York and Boston: Gilson, 1896), p. 57.

55. Lou J. Beauchamp, *What the Duchess and I Saw in Europe* (Hamilton, Ohio: Brown & Whitaker, 1896), p. 38.

56. Reuben G. Thwaites, *Our Cycling Tour in England, from Canterbury to Dartmoor Forest and Back by Way of Bath, Oxford and the Thames Valley* (Chicago: McClurg, 1892), pp. 184, 128.

57. Benjamin Silliman, *A Journal of Travels in England, Holland and Scotland, and of Two Passages over the Atlantic, in the Years 1805 and 1806*, 2 vols. (New York: Bruce, 1810), 1:65.

58. Nevin, *Vignettes of Travel*, p. 442.

✓59. Henry Morford, *Over-Sea: or, England, France and Scotland As Seen by a Live American* (New York: Hilton, 1867), pp. 122–23.

60. Polk, *Big American Caravan*, p. 167.

61. Rudolph Williams, *Europe from May to December* (Chicago: Weeks, 1895), p. 43.

✓62. John W. Higinbotham, *Three Weeks in the British Isles* (Chicago: Reilly & Britton, 1911), p. 81.

63. Sinclair Tousey, *Papers from over the Water; a Series of Letters from Europe* (New York: American News Co., 1869), p. 204.

64. Claudius B. Patten, *England as Seen by an American Banker; Notes of a Pedestrian Tour* (Boston: Lothrop, 1885), p. 261.

65. Curtis Guild, *Over the Ocean; or, Sights and Scenes in Foreign Lands* (Boston: Lee & Shepard, 1871), p. 139.

66. Orrin Z. Hubbell, *A University Tramp* (Elkhart, Ind.: G. W. Butler, 1889), p. 16.

67. Higinbotham, *Three Weeks,* p. 88.

68. Annie S. Wolf, *Pictures and Portraits of Foreign Travel* (Philadelphia: Claxton, 1881), p. 15.

✓69. Josephine Tyler, *Waymarks; or, Sola in Europe* (New York and Chicago: Brentano, 1885), p. 5.

70. Leonard A. Morrison, *Rambles in Europe: In Ireland, Scotland, England, Belgium, Germany, Switzerland, and France* (Boston: Cupples, Upham & Co., 1887), p. 34.

71. Polk, *Big American Caravan,* p. 17.

72. William A. Braman, *Glimpses of Europe* (Cleveland, Ohio: J. B. Savage, 1901), p. 159.

73. Thwaites, *Our Cycling Tour,* p. 18.

74. Oliver Wendell Holmes, *Our Hundred Days in Europe* (Boston and New York: Houghton, Mifflin, 1887), p. 42.

75. Hemstreet, *Economical European Tourist,* p. 81.

76. Louise B. Robinson, *A Bundle of Letters from over the Sea* (Boston: J. G. Cupples Company, 1890), p. 30.

77. Patten, *England,* p. 125.

78. James B. Converse, *A Summer Vacation: Sketches and Thoughts Abroad in the Summer of 1877* (Louisville, Ky.: Converse & Co., 1878), pp. 179–80.

79. Sessions, *On the Wing,* p. 234.

80. Higinbotham, *Three Weeks,* p. 70.

81. Old advertisement in author's possession.

82. Joel Cook, *A Holiday Tour in Europe. Described in a Series of Letters for the Public Ledger during the Summer and Autumn of 1878* (Philadelphia: J. B. Lippincott Co., 1879), p. 125.

83. Samuel A. Mutchmore, *A Visit to Japheth to Shem and Ham* (New York: Carter, 1889), p. 159.

84. Nathaniel Hawthorne, *Our Old Home: A Series of English Sketches,* (1863; Columbus, Ohio: Ohio State University Press, 1970), p. 190.

85. John Codman, D.D., *A Narrative of a Visit to England* (Boston: Perkins & Marvin, 1836), pp. 146–47.

86. Richard C. McCormick, *St. Paul's to St. Sophia; or, Sketchings in Europe* (New York: Sheldon, 1860), p. 49.

87. Mrs. L. C. Lane, *Letters of Travel* (San Francisco, Calif.: Bancroft, 1886), p. 79.

88. David R. Locke [Petroleum V. Nasby], *Nasby in Exile; or, Six Months of Travel in England, Ireland, Scotland, France, Germany, Switzerland and Belgium, with Many Things Not of Travel* (Toledo and Boston: Locke Publishing Co., 1882), p. 77.

89. Theodore L. Cuyler, *From the Nile to Norway and Homeward* (New York: Robert Carter & Bros., 1882), p. 309.

90. Ralph Waldo Emerson, *The Heart of Emerson's Journals,* ed. Bliss Perry (Boston and New York: Houghton Mifflin Co., 1926), p. 237.

91. Mrs. N. J. H. Collins [Janet], *Reminiscences; or, A Few Glimpses from over the Sea* (Philadelphia: Collins & Co., 1891), p. 176.

✓92. Henry James, *English Hours* (Boston and New York: Houghton, Mifflin, 1905), p. 131.

93. Caroline Sheldon, *Princess and Pilgrim in England* (Washington, D.C.: Lincoln, 1904), p. 199.

94. Harriet Beecher Stowe, *Sunny Memories of Foreign Lands,* 2 vols. (Boston: Phillips, Sampson and Company, 1854), 1:273.

96. Mrs. A. E. Newman [Evangeline], *European Leaflets for Young Ladies* (New York: John F. 47.

96. Mrs. A. E. Newman, [Evangeline] *European Leaflets for Young Ladies* (New York: John F. Baldwin, 1861), p. 109.

97. Prentis, *A Kansan Abroad,* p. 28.

98. Walter A. Whittle, *A Baptist Abroad; or, Travels and Adventures in Europe and All Bible Lands* (New York: Hill, 1890), pp. 113–14.

✓ 99. Frank R. Stockton, *Personally Conducted* (New York: Charles Scribner's Sons, 1890), pp. 229–30.

100. Julia C. Hallam, *The Story of a European Tour* (Sioux City, Iowa, 1900), pp. 294–95.

✓ 101. Ehrmann Syme Nadal, *Impressions of London Social Life* (New York: Scribner, Armstrong & Company, 1875), pp. 212, 191–92.

102. Williams, *Europe from May to December,* pp. 133–4.

✓ 103. Sophia A. Hawthorne, *Notes in England and Italy* (New York: Putnam, 1870), pp. 106, 85–86, 26, 86, 67.

104. Miss L. L. Rees, *We Four: Where We Went and What We Saw in Europe* (Philadelphia: Lippincott, 1880), p. 277.

105. Richard G. White, *England Without and Within* (Boston: Houghton, Mifflin, 1881), p. 529.

106. Marion Adams, *The Letters of Mrs. Henry Adams*, ed. Ward Theron (Boston: Little, Brown & Co., 1936), pp. 148, 150, 151, 118, 151, 151–2, 167, 118–19.

107. Margaret J. Preston, *A Handful of Monographs, Continental and English* (New York: Randolph, 1886), pp. 120–24.

108. Sheldon, *Princess and Pilgrim*, p. 216.

109. Connor, *E. A. Abroad*, p. 63.

110. Caroline M. Kirkland, *Holidays Abroad; or, Europe from the West*, 2 vols. (New York: Baker and Scribner, 1849), 1:320.

111. Catherine M. Sedgwick, *Letters from Abroad to Kindred at Home*, 2 vols. (New York: Harper, 1841), 1: 69.

112. Rees, *We Four*, p. 32.

113. Connor, *E. A. Abroad*, p. 18.

114. Grace Greenwood, *Haps and Mishaps of a Tour in Europe* (Boston: Ticknor, Reed & Fields, 1854), pp. 72–73.

115. Robinson, *A Bundle of Letters*, p. 44.

✓116. Price Collier, *England and the English from an American Point of View* (New York: Scribner's, 1909), pp. 374–77.

✓117. Samuel Young, *A Wall-Street Bear in Europe, with His Familiar Foreign Journal of a Tour through Portions of England, Scotland, France, and Italy* (New York: S. Young, Jr., privately printed, 1855), pp. 203–4.

118. John H. B. Latrobe, *Hints for Six Months in Europe; Being the Programme of a Tour through Parts of France, Italy, Austria, Saxony, Prussia, the Tyrol, Switzerland, Holland, Belgium, England and Scotland in the Summer of 1868* (Philadelphia: Lippincott, 1869), p. 374.

119. William Dean Howells, *Seen and Unseen at Stratford-on-Avon* (New York and London: Harper, 1914), p. 67.

120. Edward L. Temple, *Old World Memories*, 2 vols. (Boston: Page, 1899), 1:164.

121. Sheldon, *Princess and Pilgrim*, p. 188.

✓122. Mary V. Terhune [Marion Harland], *Loiterings in Pleasant Paths* (New York: Scribner's, 1880), p. 58.

123. Higinbotham, *Three Weeks*, p. 293.

124. White, *England Without and Within*, pp. 234–35.

125. Connor, *E. A. Abroad*, p. 70.

126. Rodney Glisan, M.D., *Two Years in Europe* (New York and London: Putnam, 1887), p. 397.

127. Loretta J. Post, *Scenes in Europe; or, Observations by an Amateur Artist* (Cincinnati, Ohio: Hitchcock & Walden, 1874), p. 62.

128. Women's Rest Tour Association, *A Summer in England: A Handbook for Use of American Women* (Boston: Beacon, 1896), p. 54.

129. Frederick Law Olmsted, *Walks and Talks of an American Farmer in England* (1852; reprint ed., Ann Arbor, Mich.: University of Michigan Press, 1967) p. 66.

Chapter 17

1. John W. Forney, *Letters from Europe* (Philadelphia: Peterson, 1867), pp. 38–41.

2. Annie S. Wolf, *Pictures and Portraits of Foreign Travel* (Philadelphia: Claxton, 1881), p. 19.

3. Rodney Glisan, M.D., *Two Years in Europe* (New York and London: Putnam, 1887), p. 20.

4. Zachary Taylor Sweeney, *Under Ten Flags; An Historical Pilgrimage* (Cincinnati, Ohio: Standard, 1888), p. 10.

5. Samuel A. Mutchmore, *A Visit of Japheth to Shem and Ham* (New York: Carter, 1889), p. 154.

✓6. William Dean Howells, *London Films* (New York and London: Harper, 1905), p. 271.

✓7. Oliver Wendell Holmes, *Our Hundred Days in Europe* (Boston and New York: Houghton, Mifflin, 1887), pp. 27–28.

8. Henry James, *English Hours* (Boston and New York: Houghton, Mifflin, 1905), pp. 62, 65.

9. Holmes, *Our Hundred Days,* pp. 28–29.

10. Forney, *Letters from Europe,* p. 332.

11. Joel Cook, *A Holiday Tour in Europe. Described in a Series of Letters for the Public Ledger during the Summer and Autumn of 1878* (Philadelphia: J. B. Lippincott Co., 1879), p. 33.

12. Holmes, *Our Hundred Days,* p. 30.

13. Lenamay Green, *A Girl's Journey through Europe, Egypt, and the Holy Land* (Nashville, Tenn.: Publishing House of the M. E. Church, South, 1889), p. 383.

✓14. William A. Braman, *Glimpses of Europe* (Cleveland, Ohio: J. B. Savage, 1901), p. 178.

✓15. Elihu Burritt, *A Walk from London to John O'Groat's; With Notes by the Way* (London: Sampson, Low & Marston, 1864), pp. 293–94.

16. Ibid., pp. 297–99.

17. Cook, *A Holiday Tour,* pp. 86, 88.

18. Richard G. White, *England Without and Within* (Boston: Houghton, Mifflin, 1881), p. 225.

✓19. William H. Rideing, *In the Land of Lorna Doone and Other Pleasurable Excursions in England* (New York and Boston: Crowell, 1895), pp. 145–46.

20. James N. Matthews, *My Holiday; How I Spent It: Being Some Rough Notes of a Trip to Europe and Back, in the Summer of 1866* (New York: Hurd & Houghton, 1867), p. 214.

21. Lucy B. Dudley, *Letters to Ruth* (New York and Boston: Gilson, 1896), p. 55.

✓22. A. Vandoren Honeyman, *Bright Days in Merrie England* (Plainfield, N.J.: Honeyman & Co., 1901), p. 38.

✓23. Mary V. Terhune [Marion Harland], *Loiterings in Pleasant Paths* (New York: Scribner's, 1880), p. 80.

24. Theron C. Crawford, *English Life* (New York: Lovell, 1889), pp. 174–75.

25. Braman, *Glimpses of Europe,* p. 171.

26. Noble L. Prentis, *A Kansan Abroad* (Topeka, Kans.: Martin, 1878), p. 32.

27. White, *England Without and Within,* pp. 517, 524.

✓28. William Dean Howells, *Seen and Unseen at Stratford-on-Avon* (New York and London: Harper, 1914), p. 90.

29. Nathaniel Hawthorne, *Our Old Home: A Series of English Sketches* (1863; Columbus, Ohio: Ohio State University Press, 1970), pp. 105–6.

30. Ibid., pp. 107, 110, 115.

✓31. Elihu Burritt, *Walks in the Black Country and Its Green Border-land* (London: Sampson, Low, Son, and Marston, 1868), p. 206.

32. Lilian Leland, *Traveling Alone: A Woman's Journey around the World* (New York: American News Co., 1890), p. 288.

33. Adelaide L. Harrington, *The Afterglow of European Travel* (Boston: Lothrop, 1882), p. 28.

34. John H. B. Latrobe, *Hints for Six Months in Europe; Being the Programme of a Tour through Parts of France, Italy, Austria, Saxony, Prussia, the Tyrol, Switzerland, Holland, Belgium, England, and Scotland in the Summer of 1868.* (Philadelphia: Lippincott, 1869), p. 342.

35. Terhune, *Loiterings in Pleasant Paths,* p. 85.

36. James M. Hoyt, *Glances on the Wing at Foreign Lands* (Cleveland, Ohio: Fairbanks, Benedict & Co., 1872), p. 180.

37. James, *English Hours,* p. 199.

38. Wolf, *Pictures and Portraits,* p. 65.

39. Terhune, *Loiterings in Pleasant Paths,* p. 54.

40. Louise B. Robinson, *A Bundle of Letters from over the Sea* (Boston: J. G. Cupples Company, 1890), pp. 25–26.

41. Caroline Sheldon, *Princess and Pilgrim in England* (Washington, D.C.: Lincoln, 1904), p. 110.

42. Louise C. Moulton, *Random Rambles* (Boston: Roberts, 1881), pp. 160–61.

43. Elizabeth Peake, *Pen Pictures of Europe; When and How We Went, and What We Saw during a Seventeen Month's Tour* (Philadelphia: Lippincott, 1874), pp. 55–57.

✓44. Reuben G. Thwaites, *Our Cycling Tour in England, from Canterbury to Dartmoor Forest and Back by Way of Bath, Oxford and the Thames Valley* (Chicago: McClurg, 1892), p. 147.

45. William C. Falkner, *Rapid Ramblings in Europe* (Philadelphia: J. B. Lippincott, 1884), p. 96.

46. Charles Wood, *Saunterings in Europe* (New York: Randolph, 1882), pp. 315–16.

47. Braman, *Glimpses of Europe,* p. 163.

48. Peter B. Cogswell, *Glints from over the Water* (Concord, N.H.: Public Press Association, 1880), p. 381.

49. Hoyt, *Glances on the Wing*, p. 116.

50. William L. Gage, *A Leisurely Journey* (Boston: Lothrop, 1886), pp. 2–3.

51. Honeyman, *Bright Days*, p. 376.

52. Orville Dewey, *The Old World and the New; or, A Journal of Reflections and Observations Made on a Tour in Europe*, 2 vols. (New York: Harper & Bros., 1836), 1:94.

53. Peake, *Pen Pictures of Europe*, pp. 82–83.

54. Claudius B. Patten, *England as Seen by an American Banker; Notes of a Pedestrian Tour* (Boston: Lothrop, 1885), pp. 110–13.

55. William Stevenson, *Sights and Scenes in Europe: or, Pencillings by the Way in England, Scotland, Ireland, France, Switzerland, Germany and Belgium, during a Short Tour in the Summer and Autumn of 1881* (Flint, Mich.: M. S. Elmore & Co., 1882), p. 44.

56. Mrs. Lucy Yeend Culler, *Europe through a Woman's Eye* (Philadelphia: Lutheran Publication Society, 1883), p. 202.

57. Walter A. Whittle, *A Baptist Abroad; or, Travels and Adventures in Europe and All Bible Lands* (New York: Hill, 1890), pp. 68–69, 50.

58. Helen Hunt Jackson, *Glimpses of Three Coasts* (Boston: Roberts, 1886), p. 187.

59. William W. Nevin, *Vignettes of Travel: Some Comparative Sketches in England and Italy* (Philadelphia: Lippincott, 1881), p. 235.

60. Benjamin Bausman, *Wayside Gleanings in Europe* (Philadelphia: Reformed Church Publication Board, 1875), p. 42.

61. Morton B. Wharton, *European Notes; or, What I Saw in the Old World* (Atlanta, Ga.: James P. Harrison & Co., 1884), p. 338.

62. Catherine C. Dyer, *Sunny Days Abroad; or, The Old World Seen with Young Eyes* (New York: Whittaker, 1873), p. 245.

63. Mary H. Wills, *A Summer in Europe* (Philadelphia: J. B. Lippincott, 1876), pp. 166–67.

64. Eliza A. Connor, *E. A. Abroad: A Summer in Europe* (Cincinnati, Ohio: W. E. Dibble & Co., 1883), p. 25.

65. Hoyt, *Glances on the Wing*, pp. 159–60.

66. Edward L. Temple, *Old World Memories*, 2 vols. (Boston: Page, 1899), 1:155.

67. Eugene R. Hendrix, *Around the World* (Nashville, Tenn.: A. H. Redford, 1878), p. 588.

68. Culler, *Europe*, pp. 215–16.

69. Connor, *E. A. Abroad*, p. 24.

70. Burr H. Polk, *The Big American Caravan in Europe* (Evansvile: Journal Co., 1879) p. 21.

71. Peake, *Pen Pictures*, p. 577.

72. Rudolph Williams, *Europe from May to December* (Chicago: Weeks, 1895), pp. 183–84.

73. Leland, *Traveling Alone*, p. 293.

74. Andrew Dickinson, *My First Visit to Europe; or, Sketches of Society, Scenery, and Antiquities in England, Wales, Ireland, Scotland, and France* (New York: George P. Putnam, 1851), p. 65, 59.

75. Jesse Johnson, *Glimpses of Europe; A Series of Letters Written from Abroad to the Standard Union of Brooklyn, N. Y.* (New York: The Grafton Press, 1906), pp. 37–39.

76. Miss L. L. Rees, *We Four: Where We Went and What We Saw in Europe* (Philadelphia: Lippincott, 1880), p. 228.

77. Jackson, *Glimpses of Three Coasts*, p. 167.

78. Loretta J. Post, *Scenes in Europe; or, Observations by an Amateur Artist* (Cincinnati, Ohio: Hitchcock & Walden, 1874), p. 111.

79. Jackson, *Glimpses of Three Coasts*, pp. 170–71.

80. Leonard A. Morrison, *Rambles in Europe: In Ireland, Scotland, England, Belgium, Germany, Switzerland, and France* (Boston: Cupples, Upham & Co., 1887), p. 104.

81. Jackson, *Glimpses of Three Coasts*, p. 173.

82. Margaret J. Preston, *A Handful of Monographs, Continental and English* (New York: Randolph, 1886), p. 156.

83. Wharton, *European Notes*, p. 352.

84. Edgar Magness, *Tramp Tales of Europe through the Tyrolean and Swiss Alps and the Italian Lake Region* (Buffalo, N.Y.: Charles Wells Moulton, 1895), p. 24.

85. Elihu Burritt, *A Walk from London to John O'Groat's; With Notes by the Way* (London: Sampson, Low & Marston, 1864), p. 348.

86. Stevenson, *Sights and Scenes in Europe,* pp. 53–54.

87. George W. Williams, *Sketches of Travel in the Old and New World* (Charleston, S.C.: Walker, Evans & Cogswell, 1871), p. 296.

88. James B. Converse, *A Summer Vacation: Sketches and Thoughts Abroad in the Summer of 1877* (Louisville, Ky.: Converse & Co., 1878), p. 51.

89. Joseph Pennell and Elizabeth Robins Pennell, *Our Journey to the Hebrides* (New York: Harper, 1889), pp. vi, xiv, 34–35.

90. Mutchmore, *Visit of Japheth,* p. 41.

91. Junius H. Browne, *Sights and Sensations in Europe; Sketches of Travel and Adventure in England, France, Spain, Germany, etc., with an Account of Places and Persons Prominent in the Franco-German War* (Hartford, Conn.: American Publishing Co., 1871), p. 80.

92. Rudolph Williams, *Europe from May to December,* p. 104.

93. Wills, *A Summer in Europe,* p. 19.

94. Elias S. Hutchinson, *Two Weeks in Europe* (Washington, D.C.: Paret, 1885), p. 24.

95. Sinclair Tousey, *Papers from over the Water; A Series of Letters from Europe* (New York: American News Co., 1869), p. 192.

96. Charles D. Poston, *Europe in the Summer-Time* (Washington, D.C.: M'Gill & Witherow, 1868), p. 89.

97. James H. Bates, *Notes of Foreign Travel* (New York: Burr Printing House, 1891), p. 7.

98. Mrs. Elizabeth B. Wetmore, *A Flying Trip around the World* (New York: Harper, 1891), p. 199.

99. William H. Rideing, *At Hawarden with Mr. Gladstone, and Other Transatlantic Experiences* (New York and Boston: Crowell, 1896), pp. 47–48.

100. Benjamin Moran, *The Footpath and Highway: or, Wanderings of an American in Great Britain in 1851 and '52* (Philadelphia: Lippincott, Grambo and Co., 1853), p. 27.

101. William Hemstreet, *The Economical European Tourist* (New York: S. W. Green, Printer, 1875), p. 27.

102. William H. Taylor, M.D., *The Book of Travels of a Doctor of Physic* (Philadelphia: Lippincott, 1871), p. 361.

103. Wharton, *European Notes,* pp. 357, 360.

104. Hemstreet, *Economical European Tourist,* pp. 32–33.

105. Thomas Rees, *Sixty Days in Europe: What I Saw There* (Springfield, Ill.: State Register Co., 1908), p. 430.

106. Amy G. Smith and Mary E. Smith, *Letters from Europe: 1865–1866,* ed. David Saunders Clarke (Washington, D.C.: Library of Congress, 1948), p. 3.

107. Mutchmore, *Visit of Japheth,* p. 34.

108. Andrew P. Peabody, *Reminiscences of European Travel* (New York: Hurd & Houghton, 1868), pp. 58–59.

109. Mutchmore, *Visit of Japheth,* p. 34.

110. Rudolph Williams, *Europe from May to December,* p. 117.

111. John W. Higinbotham, *Three Weeks in the British Isles* (Chicago: Reilly & Britton, 1911), p. 271.

112. Alexander McKenzie, *Some Things Abroad* (Boston: Lothrop, 1887), pp. 13–14.

113. Higinbotham, *Three Weeks,* pp. 271, 267.

114. Morrison, *Rambles in Europe,* p. 83.

115. Cook, *A Holiday Tour,* p. 38.

116. Francis C. Sessions, *On the Wing through Europe* (Columbus, Ohio: H. W. Derby & Co., 1880), p. 8.

117. Braman, *Glimpses of Europe,* p. 203.

118. Henry M. Field, *From the Lakes of Killarney to the Golden Horn* (New York: Scribner's, 1898), p. 17.

119. Randal W. MacGavock, *A Tennessean Abroad; or, Letters from Europe, Africa, and Asia* (New York: Redfield, 1854), p. 90.

120. Charles M. Taylor, *Odd Bits of Travel with Brush and Camera* (Philadelphia: George W. Jacobs & Co., 1900), p. 204.

121. Leonard A. Morrison, *Among the Scotch-Irish: And a Tour in Seven Countries, in Ireland, Wales, England, Scotland, France, Switzerland, and Italy* (Boston: Damrell & Upham, 1891), pp. 51–52.

122. Loring Converse, *Notes of What I Saw and How I Saw It* (Bucyrus, Ohio: Forum Steam Printing House, 1882), p. 391.

123. Charles Williams, *Old World Scenes* (Pittsburgh, Pa.: Haven, 1867), p. 148.

124. Higinbotham, *Three Weeks,* pp. 203–5, 222–23.

Chapter 18

1. Catherine C. Dyer, *Sunny Days Abroad; or, The Old World Seen with Young Eyes* (New York: Whittaker, 1873), pp. 11–12.

2. Gilbert Haven, *The Pilgrim's Wallet; or, Scraps of Travel Gathered in England, France and Germany* (New York: Carlton & Porter, 1866), pp. 210–11.

3. James M. Hoyt, *Glances on the Wing at Foreign Lands* (Cleveland, Ohio: Fairbanks, Benedict & Co., 1872), pp. 177–78.

4. Henry Morford, *Over-Sea; or, England, France and Scotland As Seen by a Live American* (New York: Hilton, 1867), pp. 133–34.

5. Ibid., pp. 105–8.

6. James M. Hoppin, *Old England: Its Scenery, Art, and People* (New York: Hurd & Houghton, 1867), pp. 236–39.

7. Henry M. Field, *Summer Pictures: from Copenhagen to Venice* (New York: Sheldon, 1859), p. 29.

8. Rodney Glisan, M.D., *Two Years in Europe* (New York and London: Putnam, 1887), p. 44.

9. John W. Forney, *Letters from Europe* (Philadelphia: Peterson, 1867), pp. 62–65.

10. Samuel I. Prime, *Travels in Europe and the East; a Year in Scotland, Ireland, Wales, France, Belgium, Holland, Germany, Austria, Italy, Greece, Turkey, Syria, Palestine and Egypt,* 2 vols. (New York: Harper, 1855), 1:102.

11. J. F. Packard, *Grant's Tour around the World; with Incidents of His Journey through England, Ireland, Scotland, France, Spain, Germany, Austria, Italy, Belgium, Switzerland, Russia, Egypt, India, China, Japan, ETC.* (Philadelphia: Flint, 1880), p. 61.

12. Forney, *Letters from Europe,* pp. 72–73.

13. George W. Williams, *Sketches of Travel in the Old and New World* (Charleston, S.C.: Walker, Evans & Cogswell, 1871), p. 307.

14. Arthur Cleveland Coxe, *Impressions of England; or, Sketches of English Scenery and Society* (New York: Dana & Co., 1856), pp. 90–91.

15. Haven, *The Pilgrim's Wallet,* pp. 182–83.

16. Octavia W. LeVert, *Souvenirs of Travel* (New York and Mobile: Goetzel, 1857), p. 27.

17. Haven, *The Pilgrim's Wallet,* p. 181.

18. Maunsell B. Field, *Memories of Many Men and of Some Women: Being Personal Recollections of Emperors, Kings, Queens, Princes, Presidents, Statesmen, Authors, and Artists, at Home and Abroad during the Last Thirty Years* (New York: Harper, 1874), pp. 147–48.

19. Prime, *Travels in Europe,* 1:103–4.

20. Leonard A. Morrison, *Rambles in Europe: In Ireland, Scotland, England, Belgium, Germany, Switzerland, and France* (Boston: Cupples, Upham & Co., 1887), p. 291.

21. Kate Field, *Hap-Hazard* (Boston: Osgood, 1873), p. 114.

22. William H. Rideing, *At Hawarden with Mr. Gladstone, and Other Transatlantic Experiences* (New York and Boston: Crowell, 1896), pp. 7–8.

23. Ibid., pp. 8–10, 12–13.

24. Charles M. Taylor, *Odd Bits of Travel with Brush and Camera* (Philadelphia: George W. Jacobs & Co., 1900), p. 67.

25. Bayard Taylor, *At Home and Abroad: A Sketch-Book of Life, Scenery, and Men* (New York: Putnam, 1860), pp. 438–39.

26. Henry T. Tuckerman, *A Month in England* (New York: Redfield, 1853), pp. 223–25.

27. John Swinton, *John Swinton's Travels: Current Views and Notes of Forty Days in France and England* (New York: Carleton, 1880), pp. 41–42.

28. Ibid., pp. 42–43.

29. Ibid., pp. 44–45.

30. Adam Badeau, *Aristocracy in England* (New York: Harper & Bros., 1886), pp. 15–16.

31. Field, *Memories of Many Men*, pp. 136–37.

32. Ibid., pp. 146, 148.

33. Theodore L. Cuyler, *From the Nile to Norway and Homeward* (New York: Robert Carter & Bros., 1882), pp. 275–76.

34. Louise C. Moulton, *Random Rambles* (Boston: Roberts, 1881), p. 19.

35. William F. Cody, *Story of the Wild West and Campfire Chats, by Buffalo Bill . . . Including a Description of Buffalo Bill's Conquests in England with His Wild West Exhibition* (Philadelphia & Chicago: Historical Publishing Co., 1888), pp. 735–38.

36. Samuel A. Mutchmore, *A Visit of Japheth to Shem and Ham* (New York: Carter, 1889), pp. 63–34.

37. Ibid., p. 64.

38. Walter A. Whittle, *A Baptist Abroad; or, Travels and Adventures in Europe and All Bible Lands* (New York: Hill, 1890), p. 103.

39. Mutchmore, *Visit of Japheth*, p. 66.

40. Orrin Z. Hubbell, *A University Tramp* (Elkhart, Ind.: G. W. Butler, 1889), p. 8.

41. Mrs. N. J. H. Collins [Janet], *Reminiscences; or, A Few Glimpses from over the Sea* (Philadelphia: Collins & Co., 1891), p. 46.

42. Julia C. Dorr, *"The Flower of England's Face"; Sketches of English Travel* (New York: Macmillan Co., 1895), p. 87.

43. Robert A. Young, *Sketchy Pages of Foreign Travel* (Nashville, Tenn.: Publishing House of the Methodist Episcopal Church, 1892), p. 152.

44. Elizabeth Longford, *Queen Victoria: Born to Succeed* (New York: Harper & Row, 1964), p. 522.

45. Lucy B. Dudley, *Letters to Ruth* (New York and Boston: Gilson, 1896), pp. 32–33.

46. William Hichborn, *Trip of the Ancients . . .* (Malden, Mass.: G. E. Dunbar, 1897), pp. 44–45.

47. Richard Harding Davis, *A Year from a Reporter's Notebook* (New York: Harper & Bros., 1898), pp. 263–64, 269–70.

48. General Nelson A. Miles, *Military Europe; a Narrative of Personal Observations and Personal Experience* (New York: Doubleday & McClure, 1898), pp. 59–60.

49. Davis, *A Year*, p. 305.

50. Wilbur F. Fauley, *Seeing Europe on Sixty Dollars* (New York: Fitzgerald, 1901), p. 89.

Chapter 19

1. James Fenimore Cooper, *Gleanings in Europe. By an American*, 2 vols. (1837; New York: Oxford University Press, 1930; reprint ed. Kraus Reprint Co., 1970), 2:38.

2. Theodore L. Cuyler, *From the Nile to Norway and Homeward* (New York: Robert Carter & Bros., 1882), p. 327.

3. Lydia H. Sigourney, *Pleasant Memories of Pleasant Lands* (Boston: Munroe, 1842), pp. 348–49.

4. Wilbur Fisk, *Travels on the Continent of Europe* (New York: Harper, 1838), pp. 560, 619, 606.

5. Morton B. Wharton, *European Notes; or, What I Saw in the Old World* (Atlanta, Ga.: James P. Harrison & Co., 1884), p. 26.

6. William H. Taylor, M.D., *The Book of Travels of a Doctor of Physic* (Philadelphia: Lippincott, 1871), p. 346.

7. Junius H. Browne, *Sights and Sensations in Europe; Sketches of Travel and Adventure in England, France, Spain, Germany, etc., with an Account of Places and Persons Prominent in the Franco-German War* (Hartford, Conn.: American Publishing Co., 1871), p. 59.

8. Sophia A. Hawthorne, *Notes in England and Italy* (New York: Putnam, 1870), pp. 143, p. 131.

9. Charles Butler, *A Bachelor's Rambles through the British Isles* (Camden, N.J.: Louis B. Cox, 1895), p. 238.

10. Lou J. Beauchamp, *What the Duchess and I Saw in Europe* (Hamilton, Ohio: Brown & Whitaker, 1896), p. 30.

11. William Hemstreet, *The Economical European Tourist . . .* (New York: S. W. Green, Printer, 1875), p. 81.

12. John S. Bender, *A Hoosier's Experience in Western Europe, with Notes on the Way* (Plymouth, Ind.: Published for the author, 1880), pp. 112–13.

13. William C. Falkner, *Rapid Ramblings in Europe* (Philadelphia: J. B. Lippincott, 1884), pp. 78–81.

14. Elkanah Watson, *Men and Times of the Revolution, or, Memoirs of Elkanah Watson, Including Journals of Travel in Europe and America from 1777 to 1842* (New York: Dana, 1856), p. 154.

15. Bayard Taylor, *At Home and Abroad: A Sketch-Book of Life, Scenery, and Men* (New York: Putnam, 1860), p. 61.

16. Burr H. Polk, *The Big American Caravan in Europe* (Evansvile: Journal Co., 1879), p. 35.

✓17. William Coombs Dana, *A Transatlantic Tour: Comprising Travels in Great Britain, France, Holland, Belgium, Germany, Switzerland and Italy* (Philadelphia: Perkins & Purves, 1845), p. 33.

18. Clifton Johnson, *Among English Hedgerows* (New York: Macmillan Co., 1899), p. 251.

✓19. Henry Morford, *Over-Sea; or, England, France and Scotland As Seen by a Live American* (New York: Hilton, 1867), p. 156.

20. Ibid., p. 171.

21. Related to author by N. H. MacMichael, Keeper of the Muniments, Westminster Abbey.

22. Morford, *Over-Sea*, p. 179.

23. Ibid., pp. 194–95.

24. Clara M. Tadlock, *Bohemian Days: A Narrative of a Journey around the World* (New York: Alden, 1889), pp. 58–59.

✓25. William H. Cord, *A Knight Templar Abroad; or, Reminiscences of Travel beyond the Sea* (St. Louis, Mo.: John Burns, 1885), pp. 78–79.

26. Nathaniel Hawthorne, *Our Old Home: A Series of English Sketches*, (1863; Columbus, Ohio: Ohio State University Press, 1970), p. 184.

27. James M. Hoyt, *Glances on the Wing at Foreign Lands* (Cleveland, Ohio: Fairbanks, Benedict & Co., 1872), p. 100.

28. Bender, *A Hoosier's Experience*, pp. 135–36.

29. Curtis Guild, *Over the Ocean; or, Sights and Scenes in Foreign Lands* (Boston: Lee & Shepard, 1871), pp. 26, 94, 142.

30. Bayard Taylor, *Views Afoot: or, Europe Seen with Knapsack and Staff* (New York: G. P. Putnam, 1859), p. 84.

31. Edward L. Temple, *Old World Memories*, 2 vols. (Boston: Page, 1899), 1:67.

32. Elizabeth Peake, *Pen Pictures of Europe; When and How We Went, and What We Saw during a Seventeen Month's Tour* (Philadelphia: Lippincott, 1874), p. 21.

33. William Stevenson, *Sights and Scenes in Europe: or, Pencillings by the Way in England, Scotland, Ireland, France, Switzerland, Germany, and Belgium, during a Short Tour in the Summer and Autumn of 1881* (Flint, Mich.: M. S. Elmore & Co., 1882), p. 26.

34. Adelaide S. Hall, *Two Women Abroad* (Chicago: Monarch Book Company, 1898), p. 494.

35. Mrs. A. E. Newman [Evangeline], *European Leaflets for Young Ladies* (New York: John F. Baldwin, 1861), pp. 33–34.

✓36. William T. Meloy, *Wanderings in Europe* (Chicago: LaMonte, O'Donnell & Co., 1892), p. 34.

37. Nathan Hubbell, *My Journey to Jerusalem, Including Travels in England, Scotland, Ireland, France, Belgium, Germany, Holland, Switzerland, Italy, Greece, Turkey, Palestine, and Egypt* (New York: Hunt & Eaton, 1890), p. 37.

38. Moses Coit Tyler, *Glimpses of England; Social, Political, Literary* (New York and London: G. P. Putnam's Sons, 1898), p. 218.

39. Hoyt, *Glances on the Wing*, p. 184.

40. *The English Illustrated Magazine* (London: Macmillan & Co., 1884–1906), 23 (1900): 443.

41. Sophia A. Hawthorne, *Notes in England*, p. 102.

42. James M. Loring, *The Old World through New World Eyes* (St. Louis, Mo.: R. B. Crossman, 1904), p. 97.

43. Mrs. William Parker, *Wandering Thoughts and Wandering Steps*. By a Philadelphia lady. (Philadelphia: J. B. Lippincott & Co., 1880), pp. 238–39.

44. David W. Semple, *Crusading with Knights Templar, under the Banners of Allegheny Commandery No. 35, Allegheny City, Pa., during 1878* (Pittsburgh, Pa., Bennett, 1879), p. 117.

45. Sigourney, *Pleasant Memories*, pp. 359–60.

46. Fannie A. Tyler, *Home Letters from over the Sea* (Boston: Williams, 1883), p. 327.

✓47. William A. Braman, *Glimpses of Europe* (Cleveland, Ohio: J. B. Savage, 1901), p. 195.

✓48. Charles D. Linskill, *Travels in Lands beyond the Sea* (Wilkes-Barre, Pa.: Baur, 1888), p. 372.

49. Lucy L. Williams, *A Too Short Vacation* (Philadelphia: Lippincott, 1892), p. 60.

50. Nathaniel H. Carter, *Letters from Europe, Comprising the Journal of a Tour through Ireland, England, Scotland, France, Italy, and Switzerland in the Years 1825–6–7*, 2 vols. (New York: G. & C. & H. Carvill, 1829), 1:162.

✓51. Henry Ward Beecher, *Star Papers; or, Experiences of Art and Nature* (New York: Derby, 1855), p. 25.

52. James W. Wall, *Foreign Etchings . . .* (Burlington, N.J.: Atkinson, 1856), p. 105.

53. William Furniss, *Landvoieglee: or, Views across the Sea* (Philadelphia: D. Appleton & Company, 1850), p. 25.

54. Samuel Young, *A Wall-Street Bear in Europe, with His Familiar Foreign Journal of a Tour through Portions of England, Scotland, France, and Italy* (New York: S. Young, Jr., Privately printed, 1855), p. 184.

55. Mrs. M. Backhouse, *Holiday Wanderings* (London: Blanchard & Sons, 1868), p. 34.

56. John W. Higinbotham, *Three Weeks in the British Isles* (Chicago: Reilly & Britton, 1911), p. 68.

57. Susan A. Wallace, *Along the Bosphorus and Other Sketches* (New York and Chicago: Rand, McNally, 1898), p. 314.

58. Joel Cook, *A Holiday Tour in Europe; Described in a Series of Letters for the Public Ledger during the Summer and Autumn of 1878* (Philadelphia: J. B. Lippincott Co., 1879), p. 99.

59. Richard Harding Davis, *Our English Cousins* (New York: Harper, 1894), p. 210.

60. Zachariah Allen, *The Practical Tourist; or, Sketches of the State of the Useful Arts, and of Society, Scenery, etc. etc., in Great Britain, France and Holland*, 2 vols. (Providence, R.I.: Beckwith, 1832), 1:83.

61. William E. Whyte, *O'er the Atlantic; or, A Journal of a Voyage to and from Europe* (New York: American News Co., 1870), p. 249.

62. William P. Breed, *Aboard and Abroad, in 1884* (New York: Funk & Wagnalls, 1885), pp. 46–48.

63. Wilbur F. Fauley, *Seeing Europe on Sixty Dollars* (New York: Fitzgerald, 1901), pp. 100–101.

✓64. G.H. Mathews, *Diary of a Summer in Europe, 1865* (New York: Marsh, 1866), pp. 75–76.

65. Amy G. and Mary E. Smith, *Letters from Europe 1865–1866*, ed. David Saunders Clarke (Washington, D.C.: Library of Congress, 1948), p. 14.

66. Lily Lawrence Rust, Hand-written journal. Pages unnumbered. 3 vols. 1903.

67. Reuben G. Thwaites, *Our Cycling Tour in England, from Canterbury to Dartmoor Forest and Back by Way of Bath, Oxford, and the Thames Valley* (Chicago: McClurg, 1892), p. 189.

68. Peake, *Pen Pictures*, pp. 568–70.

69. Edgar Magness, *Tramp Tales of Europe through the Tyrolean and Swiss Alps and the Italian Lake Region* (Buffalo, N.Y.: Charles Wells Moulton, 1895), pp. 92–93.

Chapter 20

1. Bayard Taylor, *Views Afoot; or, Europe Seen with Knapsack and Staff* (New York: G.P Putnam, 1859), preface, pp. vii, 17–18.

2. Ibid., pp. 22–23, 27, 85–86.

3. Ibid., pp. 495, 498.

4. Edward L. Temple, *Old World Memories*, 2 vols. (Boston: Page, 1899), 1:3.

5. Benjamin Moran, *The Footpath and Highway: or, Wanderings of an American in Great Britain in 1851 and '52*. (Philadelphia: Lippincott, Grambo and Co., 1853), preface, pp. vi–vii.

6. Elihu Burritt, *A Walk from London to John O'Groat's; With Notes by the Way* (London: Sampson, Low & Marston, 1864), preface, p.i.

7. Ibid., pp. 1–2.

8. Charles Williams, *Old World Scenes* (Pittsburgh, Pa.: Haven, 1867), p. 269; preface, p. viii; pp. 270–71, 97–101.

✓9. Andrew Dickinson, *My First Visit to Europe; or, Sketches of Society, Scenery, and Antiquities in England, Wales, Ireland, Scotland, and France* (New York: George P. Putnam, 1851), pp. 108–9.

10. Hugh Miller, *First Impressions of England and Its People* (Boston: Gould & Lincoln, 1857), pp. 366–67.

11. George A. Townsend, *Lost Abroad* (Hartford, Conn.: Betts, 1870), p. 59.

✓12. Albert Maverick, *A Maverick Abroad*, ed. James S. Maverick (San Antonio, Tex.: Principia Press of Trinity University, 1965), p. 85.

13. Reuben G. Thwaites, *Our Cycling Tour in England, from Canterbury to Dartmoor Forest and Back by Way of Bath, Oxford, and the Thames Valley* (Chicago: McClurg, 1892), preface, pp. vii–viii; pp. 147, 308–9.

14. Alfred Dupont Chandler, *A Bicycle Tour in England and Wales; Made in 1879, by the President, Alfred D. Chandler, and Captain John C. Sharp, Jr., of the Suffolk Bicycle Club, of Boston, Mass.* (Boston: A. Williams & Co., 1881), p. 49.

15. Adelaide S. Hall, *Two Women Abroad* (Chicago: Monarch Book Company, 1898), p. 498.

16. John W. Higinbotham, *Three Weeks in the British Isles* (Chicago: Reilly & Britton, 1911), p. 189.

17. Josephine Tozier, *Among English Inns: The Story of a Pilgrimage to Characteristic Spots of Rural England* (Boston: L. C. Page, 1904), p. 24.

18. Lee Meriwether, *A Tramp Trip: How to See Europe on Fifty Cents a Day* (New York: Harper, 1887), preface, p. 1; pp. 8, 268.

19. Claudius B. Patten, *England As Seen by an American Banker; Notes of a Pedestrian Tour* (Boston: Lothrop, 1885), pp. 6, 1–2.

20. Alice Brown, *By Oak and Thorn: A Record of English Days* (Boston: Houghton, Mifflin & Co., 1896), p. 219, p. 226.

21. Joseph Pennell and Elizabeth Robins Pennell, *Our Journey to the Hebrides* (New York: Harper, 1889), p. 13.

22. Frederick A. Stokes, *College Tramps; A Narrative of the Adventures of a Party of Yale Students . . .* (New York: Carleton, 1880), pp. 24–26, 29–30.

23. Moses F. Sweetser, *Europe for $2.00 a Day: A Few Notes for the Assistance of Tourists of Moderate Means, with Some Personal Reminiscences of Travel* (Boston: Osgood, 1875), p. 38.

24. A. Vandoren Honeyman, *Bright Days in Merrie England* (Plainfield, N.J.: Honeyman & Co.. 1901), p. 6.

25. Louise C. Moulton, *Random Rambles* (Boston: Roberts, 1881), p. 122.

26. William H. Rideing, *In the Land of Lorna Doone and Other Pleasurable Excursions in England* (New York and Boston: Crowell, 1895), p. 77.

27. John P. Kennedy, *At Home and Abroad, Including a Journal in Europe, 1867–1868* (New York: Putnam, 1872), p. 349.

28. William W. Nevin, *Vignettes of Travel: Some Comparative Sketches in England and Italy* (Philadelphia: Lippincott, 1881), pp. 56–58.

29. Ibid., pp. 60–61.

30. Rideing, *In the Land of Lorna Doone*, pp. 76–78.

31. Ibid., pp. 78–79.

32. Ibid., pp. 79–80.

33. Ibid., pp. 80–81, 90–91.

34. John B. Gough, *Sunlight and Shadow; or, Gleanings from My Life Work.* (Hartford, Conn.:Worthington, 1880), pp. 170–71.

35. James H. Bates, *Notes of Foreign Travel* (New York: Burr Printing House, 1891), p. 68.

36. Anna Bowman Dodd, *Cathedral Days: a Tour in Southern England* (Boston: Little, Brown, and Company, 1899), pp. 9–10.

37. Ibid., p. 124.

38. Herbert F. Gunnison, *Two Americans in a Motor Car; Touring in Europe* (Brooklyn, N.Y.: Brooklyn Daily Eagle, 1905), p. 7.

39. Ibid., pp. 7–10.

40. Ibid., pp. 29–30.

41. Thomas D. Murphy, *British Highways and Byways from a Motor Car* (Boston: L. C. Page & Co., 1908), pp. 5–6, 8–9, 57, 129, 268–69, 298.

42. Robert Shackleton, *Touring Great Britain* (Philadelphia: Penn Publishing Company, 1926), pp. 216, 228.

43. Ibid., pp. 87–88; p. 148.

44. Ibid., p. 199.

45. A. W. Hart., *The Quick Traveler,* privately printed, 1912, p. 53.

Chapter 21

1. William A. Croffut, *A Mid-Summer Lark* (New York: Holt, 1883), p. 78.

2. Ibid., pp. 49–50.

3. Theron C. Crawford, *English Life* (New York: Lovell, 1889), p. 167.

4. Milton S. Terry, *Rambles in the Old World* (Cincinnati, Ohio: Cranston & Curts, 1894), p. 291.

5. Samuel W. Fiske, *Mr. Dunn Browne's Experiences in Foreign Parts* (Boston: Jewett, 1857), pp. 19–20.

6. Noble L. Prentis, *A Kansan Abroad* (Topeka, Kans.: Martin, 1878), p. 46.

7. James B. Converse, *A Summer Vacation: Sketches and Thoughts Abroad in the Summer of 1877* (Louisville, Ky.: Converse & Co., 1878), p. 76.

8. Rudolph Williams, *Europe from May to December* (Chicago: Weeks, 1895), p. 61.

9. Adelaide L. Harrington, *The Afterglow of European Travel* (Boston: Lothrop, 1882), p. 283.

10. P. L. Groome, *Rambles of a Southerner in Three Continents; Containing Graphic Descriptions of the Peoples Living along the Line of His Travels* (Greensboro, N.C.: Thomas Bros., 1891), p. 306.

11. Elizabeth Peake, *Pen Pictures of Europe; When and How We Went, and What We Saw during a Seventeen Month's Tour* (Philadelphia: Lippincott, 1874), p. 29.

12. Richard G. White, *England Without and Within* (Boston: Houghton, Mifflin, 1881), p. 320.

13. Henry James, *English Hours* (Boston and New York: Houghton, Mifflin, 1905), p. 47.

14. John Burroughs, *Fresh Fields* (Boston: Houghton, Mifflin & Co., 1885), pp. 199–200.

15. Clement Pearson, M.D., *A Journal of Travels in Europe during the Summer of 1885* (Washington, D.C.: Judd & Detweiler, 1885), p. 31.

16. White, *England Without and Within*, p. 62.

17. Kate A. Murphy, *Trials and Triumphs of a Summer Vacation* (New York: Michael Sullivan, 1886), p. 24.

18. George W. Williams, *Sketches of Travel in the Old and New World* (Charleston, S.C.: Walker, Evans & Cogswell, 1871), p. 312.

19. Morton B. Wharton, *European Notes; or, What I Saw in the Old World* (Atlanta, Ga.: James P. Harrison & Co., 1884), p. 52.

20. Converse, *A Summer Vacation*, pp. 77–78.

21. Louise C. Moulton, *Random Rambles* (Boston: Roberts, 1881), pp. 11–12.

22. Morris Phillips, *Abroad and at Home: Practical Hints for Tourists* (New York: Brentano's, 1892), pp. 13–14.

23. James A. Bradley, *Across the Atlantic; A Series of Descriptive Letters to the Asbury Park Journal* (Asbury Park, N.J.: John L. Coffin, 1884), p. 13.

24. Phillips, *Abroad and at Home*, p. 19.

25. Peter B. Cogswell, *Glints from over the Water* (Concord, N.H.: Public Press Association, 1880), p. 350.

26. William A. Braman, *Glimpses of Europe* (Cleveland, Ohio: J. B. Savage, 1901), pp. 37–38.

27. James F. Rusling, *European Days and Ways* (Cincinnati, Ohio: Jennings & Pye, 1902), p. 362.

28. George W. Hills, *John Bull, Limited* (Philadelphia: Privately printed, 1918), p. 21.

29. John H. B. Latrobe, *Hints for Six Months in Europe; Being the Programme of a Tour through Parts of France, Italy, Austria, Saxony, Prussia, the Tyrol, Switzerland, Holland, Belgium, England and Scotland in the Summer of 1868* (Philadelphia: Lippincott, 1869), p. 339.

30. Joel Cook, *A Holiday Tour in Europe. Described in a Series of Letters for the Public Ledger during the Summer and Autumn of 1878* (Philadelphia: J. B. Lippincott, Co., 1879), pp. 100, 103.

31. Mary H. Krout, *A Looker-On in London* (New York: Dodd, Mead, 1899), p. 5.

32. Susan A. Wallace, *Along the Bosphorus and Other Sketches* (New York and Chicago: Rand, McNally, 1898), pp. 306, 374–76.

33. Charles H. Collins, *From Highland Hills to an Emperor's Tomb* (Cincinnati, Ohio: Robert Clarke & Co., 1886), p. 241.

34. Braman, *Glimpses of Europe*, p. 39.

35. Josephine Tyler, *Waymarks; or, Sola in Europe.* (New York and Chicago: Brentano, 1885), p. 8.

36. James H. Bates, *Notes of Foreign Travel* (New York: Burr Printing House, 1891), pp. 108–9.

37. Edward P. Thwing, M.D., *Out-door Life in Europe: or, Sketches of Seven Summers Abroad* (New York: Hurst, 1888), p. 66.

✓38. Agnes E. Claflin, *From Shore to Shore: A Journey of Nineteen Years* (Cambridge, Mass.: Riverside Press, 1873), p. 137.

39. Lilian Leland, *Traveling Alone: A Woman's Journey around the World* (New York: American News Co., 1890), pp. 280, 282–83.

40. Leonard A. Morrison, *Rambles in Europe: In Ireland, Scotland, England, Belgium, Germany, Switzerland, and France* (Boston: Cupples, Upham & Co., 1887), p. 287.

41. Lou J. Beauchamp, *What the Duchess and I Saw in Europe* (Hamilton, Ohio: Brown & Whitaker, 1896), pp. 36–37.

42. V. M. Potter, *To Europe on a Stretcher* (New York: Dutton, 1890), pp. 39–40.

✓43. Clara M. Tadlock, *Bohemian Days: A Narrative of a Journey around the World* (New York: Alden, 1889), p. 15.

44. John W. Forney, *Letters from Europe* (Philadelphia: Peterson, 1867), p. 25.

45. Martha J. Coston, *A Signal Success; the Work and Travels of Mrs. Martha J. Coston: an Autobiography* (Philadelphia: Lippincott Company, 1886), p. 58.

✓46. Lee Meriwether, *A Tramp Trip: How to See Europe on Fifty Cents a Day* (New York: Harper, 1887), pp. 258–59.

✓47. Nathan Hubbell, *My Journey to Jerusalem, Including Travels in England, Scotland, Ireland, France, Belgium, Germany, Holland, Switzerland, Italy, Greece, Turkey, Palestine, and Egypt* (New York: Hunt & Eaton, 1890), p. 44.

48. Rusling, *European Days and Ways*, p. 366.

49. William H. Cord, *A Knight Templar Abroad; or, Reminiscences of Travel beyond the Sea* (St. Louis, Mo.: John Burns, 1885), p. 408.

✓50. Oliver Wendell Holmes, *Our Hundred Days in Europe* (Boston and New York: Houghton, Mifflin, 1887), pp. 231–34.

51. George A. Townsend, *Campaigns of a Non-Combatant, and His Romaunt Abroad during the War* (New York: Blelock, 1866), pp. 293–94.

52. Mrs. E. A. Forbes, *A Woman's First Impressions of Europe; Being Wayside Sketches Made during a Short Tour in the Year 1863* (New York: Derby & Miller, 1865), p. 117.

53. Claflin, *From Shore to Shore*, p. 155.

54. Croffut, *A Mid-Summer Lark*, p. 56.

55. Samuel Young, *A Wall-Street Bear in Europe, with His Familiar Foreign Journal of a Tour through Portions of England, Scotland, France, and Italy* (New York: S. Young, Jr., privately printed, 1855), p. 175.

56. Rusling, *European Days and Ways*, p. 364.

57. Peake, *Pen Pictures*, pp. 23–24.

✓58. William H. Taylor, M.D., *The Book of Travels of a Doctor of Physic* (Philadelphia: Lippincott, 1871), p. 351.

59. Harrington, *Afterglow*, p. 37.

60. Cord, *A Knight Templar Abroad*, p. 104.

✓61. Mary L. McMurphy, *Only Glimpses* (Racine, Wis.: Advocate Steam Print, 1887), pp. 139–40.

62. Louise B. Robinson, *A Bundle of Letters from over the Sea* (Boston: J. G. Cupples Company, 1890), pp. 44–48.

63. Ella W. Thompson, *Beaten Paths: or, A Woman's Vacation* (Boston: Lee & Shepard, 1874), pp. 74–75.

64. Braman, *Glimpses of Europe*, pp. 48–49.

65. Claudius B. Patten, *England As Seen by an American Banker; Notes of a Pedestrian Tour* (Boston: Lothrop, 1885), p. 277.

66. Forbes, *A Woman's First Impressions*, pp. 328–29.

67. Cogswell, *Glints from over the Water*, p. 344.

68. Margaret J. Preston, *A Handful of Monographs, Continental and English* (New York: Randolph, 1886), p. 226.

69. James W. Wall, *Foreign Etchings* (Burlington, N. J.: Atkinson, 1856), p. 66.

70. Samuel A. Mutchmore, *A Visit of Japheth to Shem and Ham* (New York: Carter, 1889), p. 99.

71. Peake, *Pen Pictures*, p. 18.

72. Mutchmore, *Visit of Japheth*, pp. 100–107.

73. Elihu Burritt, *A Walk from London to Land's End and Back, With Notes by the Way* (London: Low & Marston, 1865), p. 5.

74. Charles Wood, *Saunterings in Europe* (New York: Randolph, 1882), p. 278.

75. Margaret J. Sweat, *Highways of Travel; or, A Summer in Europe* (Boston: Walker, Wise, and Company, 1859), p. 316.

76. Benjamin Moran, *The Footpath and Highway: or, Wanderings of an American in Great Britain in 1851 and '52* (Philadelphia: Lippincott, Grambo and Co., 1853), p. 218.

77. Horatio King, *Sketches of Travel* (Washington, D.C.: Adams, 1878), pp. 54–55.

78. Charles D. Linskill, *Travels in Lands beyond the Sea* (Wilkes-Barre, Pa.: Baur, 1888), p. 155.

79. Braman, *Glimpses of Europe*, p. 47.

80. Samuel L. Clemens [Mark Twain], *Letters from the Earth*, "From an English Notebook," (New York: Harper & Row, 1962), p. 138.

81. Mrs. Lucy Yeend Culler, *Europe through a Woman's Eye* (Philadelphia: Lutheran Publication Society, 1883), p. 158.

82. John H. Knowles, *To England and Back* (Chicago: McClurg, 1892), pp. 73–74.

83. Caroline Sheldon, *Princess and Pilgrim in England* (Washington, D.C.: Lincoln, 1904), p. 184.

84. Thompson, *Beaten Paths*, p. 58.

85. William Stevenson, *Sights and Scenes in Europe: or, Pencillings by the Way, in England, Scotland, Ireland, France, Switzerland, Germany and Belgium, during a Short Tour in the Summer and Autumn of 1881*, (Flint, Mich.: M. S. Elmore & Co., 1882), pp. 67–68.

86. Clemens, *Letters from the Earth*, p. 137.

87. Hiram Fuller, *Ten Days Abroad* (New York: School News Co., 1901), p. 53.

88. Patten, *England As Seen . . .*, p. 267.

89. White, *England Without and Within*, p. 78.

90. Alexander Slidell MacKenzie, *The American in England*, 2 vols. (New York: Harper & Brothers, 1835), 2:104–06.

91. James, *English Hours*, p. 21.

92. Prentis, *A Kansan Abroad*, p. 62.

93. William P. Breed, *Aboard and Abroad in 1884* (New York: Funk & Wagnalls, 1885), pp. 150–51.

94. Ehrmann Syme Nadal, *Impressions of London Social Life* (New York: Scribner, Armstrong & Co., 1875), pp. 161–62.

95. E. V. Lucas, *A Wanderer in London* (New York: Macmillan Co., 1906), p. 84.

96. Moses Coit Tyler, *Glimpses of England; Social, Political, Literary* (New York & London: G. P. Putnam's Sons, 1898), p. 214.

97. Curtis Guild, *Over the Ocean; or, Sights and Scenes in Foreign Lands* (Boston: Lee & Shepard, 1871), p. 96.

98. Prentis, *A Kansan Abroad*, p. 23.

99. William W. Nevin, *Vignettes of Travel: Some Comparative Sketches in England and Italy* (Philadelphia: Lippincott, 1881), p. 14.

100. Crawford, *English Life*, pp. 147–50.

101. Thomas W. Knox, *The Boy Travellers in Great Britain and Ireland* (New York: Harper & Bros., 1891), p. 122.

102. Cook, *A Holiday Tour*, p. 299.

103. Francis C. Sessions, *On the Wing through Europe* (Columbus, Ohio: H. W. Derby & Co., 1880), pp. 295–96.

104. William L. Terhune, *My Friend, the Captain; or, Two Yankees in Europe: a Descriptive Story of a Tour of Europe* (New York: Dillingham, 1898), p. 45.

105. Mary L. Ninde, *We Two Alone in Europe* (Chicago: A. C. McClurg & Company, 1897), p. 13.

106. Curtis Guild, *Abroad Again; or, Fresh Forays in Foreign Fields* (Boston: Lee & Shepard, 1877), p. 11.

107. Esther C. Davenport, *Going on Me Own* (Buffalo, N. Y.: Matthews-Northrup Co., 1900), p. 93.

108. Nadal, *Impressions*, p. 110.

109. Elizabeth L. Banks, *Campaigns of Curiosity: Journalistic Adventures of an American Girl in London* (Chicago and New York: F. Tennyson Neely, 1894), p. 108.

110. George W. Smalley, *Anglo-American Memories* (New York: Putnam's, 1911), pp. 198–99.

111. Crawford, *English Life*, pp. 120–25.

112. Nadal, *Impressions*, p. 215.

113. Stephen Fiske, *English Photographs, by an American* (London: Tinsley Brothers, 1869), pp. 173–4.

114. Herman Melville, *Journal of a Visit to London and the Continent,* ed. Eleanor Melville Metcalf (Cambridge, Mass.: Harvard University Press, 1948), p. 29.

115. Stevenson, *Sights and Scenes,* p. 256.

116. Sessions, *On the Wing,* p. 92.

117. Thwing, *Outdoor Life in Europe,* pp. 69–71.

118. Prentis, *A Kansan Abroad,* p. 52.

119. White, *England Without and Within,* p. 271.

120. Coston, *A Signal Success,* p. 122.

121. Kate Field, *Hap-Hazard* (Boston: Osgood, 1873), p. 240.

122. Taylor, *The Book of Travels,* p. 356.

123. Mrs. N. J. H. Collins [Janet], *Reminiscences; or, A Few Glimpses from over the Sea* (Philadelphia: Collins & Co., 1891), p. 247.

124. Crawford, *English Life,* p. 11.

125. Margaret B. Wright, *Hired Furnished; Being Certain Economical Housekeeping Adventures in England* (Boston: Roberts, 1897), p. 1.

126. Mrs. L. C. Lane, *Letters of Travel* (San Francisco, Calif.: Bancroft, 1886), p. 82.

127. Leander Richardson, *The Dark City; or, Customs of the Cockneys* (Boston: Doyle & Whittle, 1886), pp. 23–24.

128. Charles J. Butler, *A Yankee Bachelor Abroad* (Charles J. Butler, 1901), p. 302.

129. Prentis, *A Kansan Abroad,* p. 45.

130. Hills, *John Bull, Limited,* p. 184.

131. Andrew Carnegie, *An American Four-in-Hand in Britain* (New York: Scribner's, 1883), p. 150.

132. Fiske, *English Photographs,* p. 57.

133. Charles Williams, *Old World Scenes* (Pittsburgh, Pa.: Haven, 1867), pp. 238–39.

134. Converse, *A Summer Vacation,* pp. 184, 82.

135. Adelaide S. Hall, *Two Women Abroad* (Chicago: Monarch Book Company, 1898), p. 465.

136. Connor, *E. A. Abroad,* pp. 66–67.

137. Tyler, *Waymarks,* p. 9.

138. James, *English Hours,* pp. 32–33.

139. Peake, *Pen Pictures,* p. 27.

140. Wilbur Fisk, *Travels on the Continent of Europe* (New York: Harper, 1838), p. 525.

141. *Diary of My Itinerary of Sixty Days Across the Water* (St. Augustine, Fla.: 1904), p. 32.

142. George B. Loring, *A Year in Portugal* (New York and London: Putnam's, 1891), pp. 2–3.

143. Patten, *England,* p. 253.

144. Crawford, *English Life,* pp. 8–9.

145. James E. Scripps, *Five Months Abroad; or, The Observations and Experiences of an Editor in Europe* (Detroit, Mich.: Dickerson, 1882), p. 452.

146. Patten, *England As Seen . . . ,* pp. 255–56.

147. William Hichborn, *Trip of the Ancients . . .* (Malden, Mass.: G. E. Dunbar, 1897), p. 75.

148. *The English Illustrated Magazine* (London: Macmillan & Co., 1884–1906), 20, no. 183 (December 1898): 306–7.

149. Banks, *Campaigns of Curiosity,* p. 129.

150. Felix O. C. Darley, *Pen and Pencil Sketches in Europe* (Boston: Estes & Lauriat, 1890), pp. 25–26.

151. Groome, *Rambles of a Southerner,* p. 326.

152. Daniel C. Eddy, *Europa: or, Scenes and Society in England, France, Italy, and Switzerland* (Boston: Bradley, Dayton & Co., 1859), p. 157.

153. Stephen Fiske, *English Photographs,* pp. 147–48.

154. David R. Locke [Petroleum V. Nasby], *Nasby in Exile; or, Six Months of Travel in England, Ireland, Scotland, France, Germany, Switzerland and Belgium, with Many Things Not of Travel* (Toledo and Boston: Locke Publishing Co., 1882), pp. 75–76.

155. Horace Greeley, *Glances at Europe: In a Series of Letters from Great Britain, France, Italy, Switzerland, etc. during the Summer of 1851* (New York: Dewitt & Davenport, 1851), p. 69.

156. Peake, *Pen Pictures,* p. 41.

157. Crawford, *English Life,* pp. 14–17.

158. Peake, *Pen Pictures,* p. 42.

✓159. John L. Peyton, *Rambling Reminiscences of a Residence abroad. England—Guernsey* (Staunton, Va.: Yost, 1888), p. 2.

160. Wood, *Saunterings in Europe,* p. 278.

161. Holmes, *Our Hundred Days,* p. 245.

162. Moulton, *Random Rambles,* p. 11.

163. Annie S. Wolf, *Pictures and Portraits of Foreign Travel* (Philadelphia: Claxton, 1881), p. 77.

✓ 164. Henry M. Field, *From the Lakes of Killarney to the Golden Horn* (New York: Scribner's, 1898), p. 28.

165. James, *English Hours,* p. 13.

Chapter 22

1. John W. Forney, *Letters from Europe* (Philadelphia: Peterson, 1867), p. 69.

2. Walter A. Whittle, *A Baptist Abroad; or, Travels and Adventures in Europe and All Bible Lands* (New York: Hill, 1890), p. 120.

3. Henry M. Field, *Summer Pictures: From Copenhagen to Venice* (New York: Sheldon, 1859), p. 47.

4. Gilbert Haven, *The Pilgrim's Wallet; or, Scraps of Travel Gathered in England, France and Germany* (New York: Carlton & Porter, 1866), p. 174.

5. Richard E. Day, *The Shadow of the Broad Brim* (Philadelphia and Boston: Judson Press, 1934), pp. 93–97.

6. Thomas W. Handford, *Spurgeon: Episodes and Anecdotes from His Busy Life* (Chicago: W. B. Conkey & Co., 1894), p. 38.

7. DeRobigne Mortimer Bennett, *A Truth Seeker around the World; A Series of Letters Written while Making a Tour of the Globe* (New York: D. M. Bennett, 1882), p. 406.

8. Morton B. Wharton, *European Notes; or, What I Saw in the Old World* (Atlanta, Ga.: James P. Harrison & Co., 1884), p. 28.

9. Benjamin Bausman, *Wayside Gleanings in Europe* (Philadelphia: Reformed Church Publication Board, 1875), p. 99.

10. Adelaide L. Harrington, *The Afterglow of European Travel* (Boston: Lothrop, 1882), p. 200.

11. Burr H. Polk, *The Big American Caravan in Europe* (Evansvile: Journal Co., 1879), p. 36.

12. Bausman, *Wayside Gleanings,* p. 100.

13. John P. Kennedy, *At Home and Abroad, Including a Journal in Europe, 1867–68* (New York: Putnam, 1872), p. 395.

14. William Stevenson, *Sights and Scenes in Europe: or, Pencillings by the Way in England, Scotland, Ireland, France, Switzerland, Germany and Belgium, during a Short Tour in the Summer and Autumn of 1881* (Flint, Mich.: M. S. Elmore & Co., 1882), p. 225.

15. Agnes E. Claflin, *From Shore to Shore: A Journal of Nineteen Years* (Cambridge, Mass.: Riverside Press, 1873), p. 413.

16. Joseph Cross, D. D., *The American Pastor in Europe* (London: Bentley, 1860), p. 26.

17. Bausman, *Wayside Gleanings,* p. 99.

18. James H. Bates, *Notes of Foreign Travel* (New York: Burr Printing House, 1891), p. 104.

19. Mary H. Wills, *A Summer in Europe* (Philadelphia: J. B. Lippincott, 1876), pp. 59–60.

20. Andrew P. Peabody, *Reminiscences of European Travel* (New York: Hurd & Houghton, 1868), pp. 21–22.

21. Bausman, *Wayside Gleanings,* p. 99.

22. Junius H. Browne, *Sights and Sensations in Europe; Sketches of Travel and Adventure in England, France, Spain, Germany, etc., with an Account of Places and Persons Prominent in the Franco-German War* (Hartford, Conn.: American Publishing Co., 1871), p. 40.

23. Mary V. Terhune [Marion Harland], *Loiterings in Pleasant Paths* (New York: Scribner's, 1880), pp. 33–34.

24. Cross, *The American Pastor,* p. 28.

25. Terhune, *Loiterings in Pleasant Paths,* p. 35.

26. William C. Falkner, *Rapid Ramblings in Europe* (Philadelphia: J. B. Lippincott, 1884), p. 524.

27. Peter B. Cogswell, *Glints from over the Water* (Concord, N.H.: Public Press Association, 1880), pp. 342–43.

28. Francis C. Sessions, *On the Wing through Europe* (Columbus, Ohio: H. W. Derby & Co., 1880), p. 96.

29. Theodore L. Cuyler, *From the Nile to Norway and Homeward* (New York: Robert Carter & Bros., 1822), pp. 289–90.

30. Bausman, *Wayside Gleanings,* p. 101.

31. James M. Hoyt, *Glances on the Wing at Foreign Lands* (Cleveland, Ohio: Fairbanks, Benedict & Co., 1872), p. 54.

32. Falkner, *Rapid Ramblings,* p. 525.

33. Samuel Watson, *A Memphian's Trip to Europe with Cook's Educational Party* (Nashville, Tenn.: Southern Methodist Publishing House, 1872), p. 320.

34. Mrs. Lucy Yeend Culler, *Europe Through a Woman's Eye* (Philadelphia: Lutheran Publication Society, 1833), p. 167.

35. P. L. Groome, *Rambles of a Southerner in Three Continents; Containing Graphic Descriptions of the Peoples Living along the Line of His Travels* (Greensboro, N.C.: Thomas Bros., 1891), p. 320.

36. James S. McClay, *Style-O!-Graphic Pens and Funny Pencillings in Europe* (Hartford, Conn.: Phoenix, 1881), p. 24.

37. Polk, *Big American Caravan,* p. 37.

38. Salon Otis Thacher, *What I Saw in Europe* (Topeka, Kans.: Kansas Publishing House, 1883), p. 124.

39. Miss L. L. Rees, *We Four: Where We Went and What We Saw in Europe* (Philadelphia: Lippincott, 1880), p. 289.

40. Joseph Battell, *The Yankee Boy from Home* (New York: John F. Trow, Printer, 1863), p. 219.

41. William A. Brawley, *The Journal of William A. Brawley, 1864–1865,* ed. Francis Poe Brawley (Charlottesville, Va.: 1970), p. 41.

42. Beverly Carradine, *A Journey to Palestine* (St. Louis, Mo.: C. B. Woodward Printing & Book Mfg. Co., 1891), p. 92.

43. Robert A. Young, *Sketchy Pages of Foreign Travel* (Nashville, Tenn.: Publishing House of the Methodist Episcopal Church, 1892), p. 153.

44. Peter J. Hamilton, *Rambles in Historic Lands; Travels in Belgium, Germany, Switzerland, Italy, France and England* (New York: Putnam, 1893), p. 269.

45. George M. B. Maughs, M.D., *Souvernirs of Travel* (St. Louis, Mo.: Farris, Smith & Co., 1887), pp. 339–40.

46. Zachary Taylor Sweeney, *Under Ten Flags; An Historical Pilgrimage* (Cincinnati, Ohio: Standard, 1888), pp. 27–28.

47. Elizabeth Peake, *Pen Pictures of Europe; When and How We Went, and What We Saw during a Seventeen Month's Tour* (Philadelphia: Lippincott, 1874), pp. 18–19.

48. William W. Nevin, *Vignettes of Travel: Some Comparative Sketches in England and Italy* (Philadelphia: Lippincott, 1881), p. 175.

49. Culler, *Europe Through a Woman's Eye,* p. 150.

50. Nevin, *Vignettes of Travel,* p. 175.

51. Charles Wood, *Saunterings in Europe* (New York: Randolph, 1882), p. 286.

52. Edward Carpenter, ed., *A House of Kings* (London: Westminster Abbey Bookshop, 1969), p. 307.

53. Cuyler, *From the Nile to Norway,* pp. 296–98.

54. Wood, *Saunterings in Europe,* p. 22.

55. Eliza A. Connor, *E. A. Abroad; A Summer in Europe* (Cincinnati, Ohio: W. E. Dibble & Co., 1883), p. 71.

56. Joel Cook, *A Holiday Tour in Europe. Described in a Series of Letters for the Public Ledger during the Summer and Autumn of 1878* (Philadelphia: J. B. Lippincott Co., 1879), p. 94.

57. Adam Badeau, *Aristocracy in England* (New York: Harper & Bros., 1886), p. 213.

58. William P. Davis, *Across the Sea* (Trenton, N.J.: John L. Murray, 1889), p. 288.

59. Fannie A. Tyler, *Home Letters from over the Sea* (Boston: Williams, 1883), p. 249.

60. Kennedy, *At Home and Abroad,* pp. 346–47.

61. Ella W. Thompson, *Beaten Paths: or, A Woman's Vacation* (Boston: Lee & Shepard, 1874), p. 91.

✓ 62. George F. Haskins, *Six Weeks Abroad in Ireland, England and Belgium* (Boston: Patrick Donahoe, 1872), p. 133.

63. Browne, *Sights and Sensations,* p. 41.

64. Sylvanus D. Phelps, *The Holy Land, with Glimpses of Europe and Egypt* (New Haven, Conn.: Chatfield, 1872), p. 21.

65. Mrs. N. J. H. Collins [Janet], *Reminiscences; or, A Few Glimpses from over the Sea* (Philadelphia: Collins & Co., 1891), pp. 289–90.

✓ 66. Henry Day, *A Lawyer Abroad* (New York: Robert Carter and Brothers, 1874), pp. 10–11.

✓ 67. William L. Gage, *A Leisurely Journey* (Boston: Lothrop, 1886), p. 17.

68. Culler, *Europe through a Woman's Eye,* pp. 167–68.

✓ 69. John D. Champlin, *Chronicle of the Coach: Charing Cross to Ilafracombe* (New York: Scribner's, 1886), pp. 292–95.

70. Falkner, *Rapid Ramblings,* pp. 63–64.

✓ 71. Charles M. Taylor, *Odd Bits of Travel with Brush and Camera* (Philadelphia: George W. Jacobs, 1900), p. 33.

72. Phillips Brooks, *Letters of Travel* (New York: E. P. Dutton & Co., 1893), p. 293.

73. Young, *Sketchy Pages,* p. 148.

74. Charles M. Taylor, *The British Isles through an Opera Glass* (Philadelphia: George W. Jacobs, 1899), p. 293.

Conclusion

1. Oliver Wendell Holmes, *Our Hundred Days in Europe* (Boston and New York: Houghton, Mifflin, 1887), pp. 2–11.

2. Octavia W. LeVert, *Souvenirs of Travel* (New York and Mobile: Goetzel, 1857), p. 42.

3. William A. Braman, *Glimpses of Europe* (Cleveland, Ohio: J. B. Savage, 1901), p. 42.

4. John W. Forney, *Letters from Europe* (Philadelphia: Peterson, 1867), p. 312.

5. J. J. Smith, D.D., *The Wonders of the East; or, The Record of a Journey through Europe, Egypt, and the Holy Land* (New York: Goodenough, 1873), p. 54.

6. William Stevenson, *Sights and Scenes in Europe; or, Pencillings by the Way in England, Scotland, Ireland, France, Switzerland, Germany and Belgium, during a Short Tour in the Summer and Autumn of 1881* (Flint, Mich.: M. S. Elmore & Co., 1882), p. 122.

7. Leonard A. Morrison, *Rambles in Europe: In Ireland, Scotland, England, Belgium, Germany, Switzerland, and France* (Boston: Cupples, Upham & Co., 1887), p. 351.

✓ 8. Stephen Fiske, *English Photographs, by an American* (London: Tinsley Brothers, 1869), pp. 93–94.

9. Jonathan Raban. "Fog-Bound in England." *Sunday Times Weekly Review.* September 8, 1974, p. 38.

10. Caroline M. Kirkland, *Holidays Abroad; or, Europe from the West,* 2 vols. (New York: Baker and Scribner, 1849), 1:311.

11. Grant Thorburn, *Men and Manners in Great Britain: A Bone to Gnaw on for the Trollopes and Fidlers, &c.* (New York: Wiley & Long, 1834), p. 35.

12. Orville Horwitz, *Brushwood Picked Up on the Continent; or, Last Summer's Trip to the Old World* (Philadelphia: Lippincott, Grambo & Co., 1855), p. 19.

✓ 13. Noble L. Prentis, *A Kansan Abroad* (Topeka, Kans.: Martin, 1878), p. 12.

14. Ibid., p. 12–13.

15. Eliza A. Connor, *E. A. Abroad: A Summer in Europe* (Cincinnati, Ohio: W. E. Dibble & Co., 1883), p. 31.

16. Henry T. Tuckerman, *A Month in England* (New York: Redfield, 1853), p. 240.

17. Ella W. Thompson, *Beaten Paths: or, A Woman's Vacation* (Boston: Lee & Shepard, 1874), p. 21.

18. Horace Greeley, *Glances at Europe: In a Series of Letters from Great Britain, France, Italy, Switzerland, etc., during the Summer of 1851* (New York: DeWitt & Davenport, 1851), p. 46.

19. Elizabeth Peake, *Pen Pictures of Europe; When and How We Went, and What We Saw during a Seventeen Month's Tour* (Philadelphia: Lippincott, 1874), p. 565.

20. Harriet Beecher Stowe, *Sunny Memories of Foreign Lands,* 2 vols., (Boston: Phillips, Sampson and Company, 1854), 1:198.

21. Thompson, *Beaten Paths*, p. 21.

22. Charles B. Fairbanks, *Aguecheek* (Boston: Shepard, Clark & Brown, 1859), p. 23.

23. James F. Clarke, *Eleven Weeks in Europe; And What May Be Seen in That Time* (Boston: Ticknor, Reed & Fields, 1852), pp. 80–81.

24. Anna Bowman Dodd, *Cathedral Days: A Tour in Southern England* (Boston: Little, Brown, and Company, 1889), p. 248, 43.

25. Samuel G. Goodrich, *Recollections of a Lifetime; or, Men and Things I Have Seen: In a Series of Familiar Letters to a Friend, Historical, Biographical, Anecdotal, and Descriptive*, 2 vols. (New York & Auburn: Miller, Orton & Co., 1857), 2:212–13.

26. Joshua E. White, *Letters on England: Comprising Descriptive Scenes; With Remarks on the State of Society, Domestic Economy; Habits of the People, and Condition of the Manufacturing Classes Generally*, 2 vols. (Philadelphia: Carey, 1816), 1:234.

27. Heman Humphrey, *Great Britain, France and Belgium: A Short Tour in 1835*, 2 vols. (New York: Harper & Brothers, 1838), 1:164.

28. Theron C. Crawford, *English Life* (New York: Lovell, 1889), p. 11.

29. Samuel Young, *A Wall-Street Bear in Europe, with His Familiar Foreign Journal of a Tour through Portions of England, Scotland, France, and Italy* (New York: S. Young, Jr., privately printed, 1855), p. 173.

30. Benjamin Silliman, *A Journal of Travels in England, Holland and Scotland, and of Two Passages over the Atlantic, in the Years 1805 and 1806*, 2 vols. (New York: Bruce, 1810), 1:253.

31. Tuckerman, *A Month in England*, pp. 65–66, 22, 31.

32. John Burroughs, *Fresh Fields* (Boston: Houghton, Mifflin & Co., 1885), pp. 201, 5, 9, 22, 31.

33. Fanny W. Hall, *Rambles in Europe; or, a Tour through France, Italy, Switzerland, and Great Britain, and Ireland, in 1836*, 2 vols. (New York: French, 1838), 2:142.

34. Margaret B. Wright, *Hired Furnished; Being Certain Economical Housekeeping Adventures in England* (Boston: Roberts, 1897), preface, p. viii.

35. Louise B. Robinson, *A Bundle of Letters from over the Sea* (Boston: J. G. Cupples Company, 1890), p. 62.

36. Nathaniel Hawthorne, *Our Old Home: A Series of English Sketches* (1863; Columbus, Ohio: Ohio State University Press, 1970), pp. 217–18.

37. Ibid., pp. 218–19.

38. Mrs. Elizabeth B. Wetmore, *A Flying Trip around the World* (New York: Harper, 1891), p. 194.

39. Samuel W. Fiske, *Mr. Dunn Browne's Experiences in Foreign Parts* (Boston: Jewett, 1857), p. 261.

40. Fairbanks, *Aguecheek*, p. 23.

41. Richard G. White, *England Without and Within* (Boston: Houghton Mifflin, 1881), p. 183.

42. LeVert, *Souvenirs of Travel*, p. 53.

43. Helen Hunt Jackson, *Glimpses of Three Coasts* (Boston: Roberts, 1886), p. 184.

44. Catherine M. Sedgwick, *Letters from Abroad to Kindred at Home*, 2 vols. (New York: Harper, 1841), 1:47.

45. Henry Morford, *Over-sea; or, England, France and Scotland As Seen by a Live American* (New York: Hilton, 1867), pp. 144–45.

46. Ibid., pp. 146–47.

47. Stephen Fiske, *English Photographs*, pp, 148–50.

48. Andrew Carnegie, *An American Four-in-Hand in Britain* (New York: Scribner's, 1883), p. 149.

49. Crawford, *English Life*, p. 165.

50. Henry James, *English Hours* (Boston and New York: Houghton, Mifflin, 1905), p. 129.

51. Caspar Whitney, *A Sporting Pilgrimage; Riding to Hounds, Golf, Rowing, Football, Club and University Athletics; Studies in English Sport, Past and Present* (New York: Harper, 1895), pp. 1, 13, 4–7.

52. Joshua White, *Letters on England*, p. 22.

53. Lydia H. Sigourney, *Pleasant Memories of Pleasant Lands* (Boston: Munroe, 1842), p. 314.

54. Henry Colman, *European Life and Manners: In Familiar Letters to Friends*, 2 vols. (Boston: Charles C. Little & James Brown, 1849), 2:35.

55. Elizabeth Davis Bancroft (Mrs. George Bancroft), *Letters from England: 1846–1849* (New York: Charles Scribner's Sons, 1904), p. 45.

56. John W. Corson, *Loiterings in Europe; or, Sketches in France, Belgium, Switzerland, Italy, Austria, Prussia, Great Britain and Ireland* (New York: Harper & Bros., 1848), p. 271.

57. Kirkland, *Holidays Abroad,* 1:327.

58. David V. G. Bartlett, *What I Saw in London; or, Men and Things in the Great Metropolis* (New York: C. M. Saxton, Barker & Co., 1861), p. 311.

59. Stowe, *Sunny Memories,* 1:20.

60. *The Rambles and Reveries of an Art Student in Europe* (Philadelphia: Thomas T. Watts, 1855), p. 7.

61. Stowe, *Sunny Memories,* 1:22.

62. Colman, *European Life and Manners,* 2:35–36.

63. Sigourney, *Pleasant Memories,* pp. 314–15.

64. Curtis Guild, *Abroad Again; or, Fresh Forays in Foreign Fields* (Boston: Lee & Shepard, 1877), p. 91.

65. Richard White, *England Without and Within,* p. 103.

66. Orville Dewey, *The Old World and the New; or, A Journal of Reflections and Observations Made on a Tour in Europe,* 2 vols. (New York: Harper & Bros., 1836), 1:22–23.

67. Benjamin Bausman, *Wayside Gleanings in Europe* (Philadelphia: Reformed Church Publication Board, 1875), p. 9.

68. Dodd, *Cathedral Days,* pp. 70–71.

69. Humphrey, *Great Britain,* 1:163.

70. Dewey, *The Old World,* 1:126.

71. Stowe, *Sunny Memories,* 1:19.

72. Bausman, *Wayside Gleanings,* p. 103.

73. Alexander Slidell MacKenzie, *The American in England,* 2 vols. (New York: Harper & Brothers, 1835), 2:11–12.

74. Richard White, *England Without and Within,* pp. 19–20, 21.

75. Humphrey, *Great Britain,* 1:165–69.

76. William E. Whyte, *O'er the Atlantic; or, A Journal of a Voyage to and from Europe* (New York: American News Co., 1870), p. 282.

77. George Wilkes, *Europe in a Hurry* (New York: Long, 1853), pp. 29–30.

78. Goodrich, *Recollections of a Lifetime,* 2:187–88.

79. MacKenzie, *The American in England,* 1:79.

80. Daniel C. Eddy, *Europa: or, Scenes and Society in England, France, Italy, and Switzerland* (Boston: Bradley, Dayton, & Co., 1859), p. 58.

81. Wilbur Fisk, *Travels on the Continent of Europe* (New York: Harper, 1838), p. 562.

82. Eddy, *Europa,* p. 58.

83. Richard White, *England Without and Within,* p. 31.

84. Stowe, *Sunny Memories,* 1:293.

85. Hawthorne, *Our Old Home,* p. 165.

86. William Gibson, M.D., *Rambles in Europe in 1839; With Sketches of Prominent Surgeons, Physicians, Medical Schools, Hospitals, Literary Personages, Scenery, etc.* (Philadelphia: Lea & Blanchard, 1841), p. 181.

87. Young, *A Wall-Street Bear,* p. 223.

88. Kirkland, *Holidays Abroad,* 1:98.

89. Lucy L. Williams, *A Too Short Vacation* (Philadelphia: Lippincott, 1892), pp. 64–65.

90. Sigourney, *Pleasant Memories,* p. 362.

91. Bartlett, *What I Saw in London,* pp. 91–92.

92. MacKenzie, *The American in England,* 2:199–200.

93. Stowe, *Sunny Memories,* 2:21.

94. LeVert, *Souvenirs of Travel,* p. 70.

95. Hall, *Rambles in Europe,* p. 152.

96. Hiram Fuller, *Sparks from a Locomotive* (New York: Derby & Jackson, 1859), p. 101.

97. Connor, *E. A. Abroad,* p. 25.

98. Fuller, *Sparks from a Locomotive,* p. 118.

99. Andrew McFarland, M.D., *The escape, or, Loiterings amid the Scenes of Story and Song* (Boston: Mussey, 1851), p. 40.

100. Hall, *Rambles in Europe,* p. 152.

101. Fuller, *Sparks from a Locomotive,* p. 120.

102. Richard White, *England Without and Within,* p. 207.

103. Stephen Fiske, *English Photographs*, pp. 169–70.

104. Nathaniel S. Wheaton, *A Journal of a Residence during Several Months in London; Including Excursions through Various Parts of England; and a Short Tour in France and Scotland; in the Years 1823 and 1824* (Hartford, Conn.: Huntington, 1830), p. 190.

105. Mrs. E. A. Forbes, *A Woman's First Impressions of Europe; Being Wayside Sketches Made during a Short Tour in the Year 1863* (New York: Derby & Miller, 1865), p. 344.

106. Richard White, *England Without and Within*, p. 229.

107. Charles D. Poston, *Europe in the Summer-Time* (Washington, D.C.: M'Gill & Witherow, 1868), p. 76.

108. William Austin, *Letters from London Written during the Years 1802 and 1803* (Boston: Pelham, 1804), p. 39.

109. William Wells Brown, *The American Fugitive in Europe; Sketches of Places and People Abroad* (Boston: Jewett; New York: Sheldon, Lamport & Blakeman, 1855), p. 53.

110. Horwitz, *Brushwood*, pp. 25–26.

111. Gilbert Haven, *The Pilgrim's Wallet; or, Scraps of Travel Gathered in England, France and Germany* (New York: Carlton & Porter, 1866), p. 267.

112. Wilkes, *Europe in a Hurry*, p. 32.

113. William H. Rideing, *At Hawarden with Mr. Gladstone, and Other Transatlantic Experiences* (New York and Boston: Crowell, 1896), pp. 179–82.

114. James E. Scripps, *Five Months Abroad; or, The Observations and Experiences of an Editor in Europe* (Detroit, Mich.: Dickerson, 1882), pp. 450–51.

115. Eudora L. South, *Wayside Notes and Fireside Thoughts* (St. Louis, Mo.: Burns, 1884), p. 64.

116. Joshua White, *Letters on England*, p. 236.

117. Brown, *The American Fugitive*, p. 139.

118. George W. Hills, *John Bull, Limited* (Philadelphia: Privately printed, 1918), pp. 88–89.

119. Kirkland, *Holidays Abroad*, 1:30.

120. Milton S. Terry, *Rambles in the Old World* (Cincinnati, Ohio: Cranston & Curts, 1894), p. 11.

121. Tuckerman, *A Month in England*, p. 8.

122. Hawthorne, *Our Old Home*, pp. 58–59.

123. Curtis Guild, *Over the Ocean; or, Sights and Scenes in Foreign Lands* (Boston: Lee & Shepard, 1871), p. 132.

124. Prentis, *A Kansan Abroad*, p. 143.

125. Andrew P. Peabody, *Reminiscences of European Travel* (New York: Hurd & Houghton, 1868), pp. 4–5.

126. Dewey, *The Old World*, 1:60.

127. Goldwin Smith, *A Trip to England* (New York and London: Macmillan and Company, 1895), p. 48.

128. Hawthorne, *Our Old Home*, pp. 120–21, 142, 98.

129. Henry M. Field, *Summer Pictures: From Copenhagen to Venice* (New York: Sheldon, 1859), pp. 66–67.

130. Haven, *The Pilgrim's Wallet*, p. 267.

131. *Rambles and Reveries*, pp. 7–8.

132. Forbes, *A Woman's First Impressions*, pp. 118–19.

133. Greeley, *Glances at Europe*, pp. 340–42.

134. Ibid., pp. 342, 346–47.

135. Joshua White, *Letters on England*, p. 160.

136. Goodrich, *Recollections of a Lifetime*, p. 219.

137. Hawthorne, *Our Old Home*, p. 318.

138. Maunsell B. Field, *Memories of Many Men and of Some Women: Being Personal Recollections of Emperors, Kings, Queens, Princes, Presidents, Statesmen, Authors, and Artists, at Home and Abroad during the Last Thirty Years* (New York: Harper, 1874), pp. 137–38.

139. Emma H. Willard, *Journal and Letters, From France and Great-Britain* (Troy, N.Y.: Tuttle, 1833), pp. 286–90.

140. Martha J. Coston, *A Signal Success; The Work and Travels of Mrs. Martha J. Coston: An Autobiography* (Philadelphia: J. B. Lippincott Co., 1886), pp. 59–60.

141. Andrew Dickinson, *My First Visit to Europe; or, Sketches of Society, Scenery, and Antiquities in England, Wales, Ireland, Scotland, and France* (New York: George P. Putnam, 1851), pp. 6, 25.

142. Samuel I. Prime, *Travels in Europe and the East; A Year in England, Scotland, Ireland, Wales, France, Belgium, Holland, Germany, Austria, Italy, Greece, Turkey, Syria, Palestine and Egypt,* 2 vols. (New York: Harper, 1855), 1: 81–85.

143. William P. Breed, *Aboard and Abroad, in 1884* (New York: Funk & Wagnalls, 1885), pp. 103–5.

144. Mary L. Ninde, *We Two Alone in Europe* (Chicago: A. C. McClurg & Company, 1897), pp. 23–28.

145. George W. Williams, *Sketches of Travel in the Old and New World* (Charleston, S.C.: Walker, Evans & Cogswell, 1871), p. 317.

146. John S. Bender, *A Hoosier's Experience in Western Europe, with Notes on the Way* (Plymouth, Ind.: Published for the author, 1880), introduction, p. 28; pp. 61, 80, 79, 90, 139–41.

147. Ibid., p. 219.

148. William Winter, *The Trip to England* (New York: Lee & Shepard, 1879), pp. 84, 18.

149. William Hichborn, *Trip of the Ancients . . .* (Malden, Mass.: G. E. Dunbar, 1897), p. 116.

150. Ibid., pp. 127–28.

151. Ibid., pp. 133, 139, 47.

152. James, *English Hours,* p. 76.

153. Jonathan Raban, "Fog-Bound in England," p. 38.

154. Erastus C. Benedict, *A Run through Europe* (New York: D. Appleton & Co., 1860), p. 40.

155. Dewey, *The Old World,* 1:88.

Bibliography

Abbott, Jacob. *A Summer in Scotland.* New York: Harper, 1848.

Adams, Abigail. *Letters of Mrs. Adams, the Wife of John Adams.* Boston: Little & Brown, 1840.

Adams, Henry. *The Letters of Henry Adams.* 2 vols. Edited by Chauncey Worthington Ford. New York: Houghton, Mifflin, 1930.

Adams, Marion. *The Letters of Mrs. Henry Adams.* Edited by Ward Theron. Boston: Little, Brown & Co., 1936.

Aldrich, Thomas Bailey. *Poems in the Works of Thomas Bailey Aldrich.* vol. 2. New York: AHS Press, 1970.

Allen, Zachariah. *The Practical Tourist; or, Sketches of the State of the Useful Arts, and of Society, Scenery, etc. etc., in Great Britain, France and Holland.* 2 vols. Providence, R.I.: Beckwith, 1832.

Austin, William. *Letters from London Written during the Years 1802 and 1803.* Boston: Pelham, 1804.

Backhouse, Mrs. M. *Holiday Wanderings.* London: Blanchard & Sons, 1868.

Badeau, Adam. *Aristocracy in England.* New York: Harper & Bros., 1886.

Bailey, James M. *England from a Back Window; With Views of Scotland and Ireland.* Boston: Lee & Shepard, 1879.

Ballard, Joseph. *England in 1815 As Seen by a Young Boston Merchant.* Boston and New York: Houghton, Mifflin, 1913.

Bancroft, Elizabeth Davis (Mrs. George Bancroft). *Letters from England: 1846–1849.* New York: Charles Scribner's Sons, 1904.

Banks, Elizabeth L. *Campaigns of Curiosity: Journalistic Adventures of an American Girl in London.* Chicago and New York: F. Tennyson Neely, 1894.

Barrows, John H. *A World Pilgrimage.* Chicago: A. C. McClurg & Co., 1897.

Bartlett, David V. G. *What I Saw in London; or, Men and Things in the Great Metropolis.* New York: C. M. Saxton, Barker & Co., 1861.

Bates, James H. *Notes of Foreign Travel.* New York: Burr Printing House, 1891.

Battell, Joseph. *The Yankee Boy from Home.* New York: John F. Trow, Printer, 1863.

Bausman, Benjamin. *Wayside Gleanings in Europe.* Philadelphia: Reformed Church Publication Board, 1875.

Beard, George M., M.D. *A Practical Treatise on Seasickness.* New York: E. B. Treat, 1880.

Beatty, Daniel F. *In Foreign Lands.* Washington, N.J.: D. F. Beatty, 1878.

Beauchamp, Lou J. *What the Duchess and I Saw in Europe.* Hamilton, Ohio: Brown & Whitaker, 1896.

Beecher, Henry Ward. *Star Papers; or, Experiences of Art and Nature.* New York: Derby, 1855.

Bender, John S. *A Hoosier's Experience in Western Europe, With Notes on the Way.* Plymouth, Ind.: published for the author, 1880.

Benedict, Erastus C. *A Run through Europe.* New York: D. Appleton & Co., 1860.

Bennett, DeRobigne Mortimer. *A Truth Seeker around the World; A Series of Letters Written while Making a Tour of the Globe.* New York: D. M. Bennett, 1882.

Bigelow, Andrew. *Leaves From a Journal: or, Sketches of Rambles in Some Parts of North Britain and Ireland, Chiefly in the Year 1817.* Boston: Wells & Lilly, 1821.

Blake, Mary Elizabeth. *A Summer Holiday Tour in Europe.* Boston: Lee and Shepard, 1890.

Bowen, Frank C. *A Century of Atlantic Travel.* Boston: Little, Brown, 1930.

Bradley, James A. *Across the Atlantic; A Series of Descriptive Letters to the Asbury Park Journal.* Asbury Park, N.J.: John L. Coffin, 1884.

Braman, William A. *Glimpses of Europe.* Cleveland, Ohio: J. B. Savage, 1901.

Brawley, William A. *The Journal of William A. Brawley, 1864–1865.* Edited by Francis Poe Brawley. Charlottesville, Va., 1970.

Breckinridge, Robert J. *Memoranda of Foreign Travel: Containing Notices of a Pilgrimage through Some of the Principal States of Western Europe.* Baltimore, Md.: D. Owen & Son, 1845.

Breed, William P. *Aboard and Abroad, in 1884.* New York: Funk & Wagnalls, 1885.

Brinnin, John M. *The Sway of the Grand Saloon.* New York: Delacorte Press, 1971.

Brogan, Hugh. *The American Civil War: Extracts from The Times 1860–1865.* Edited by Hugh Brogan. London: Times Books, 1975.

Brooks, Phillips. *Letters of Travel.* New York: E. P. Dutton & Co., 1893.

Brown, Alice. *By Oak and Thorn: A Record of English Days.* Boston: Houghton, Mifflin & Co., 1896.

Brown, William Wells. *The American Fugitive in Europe; Sketches of Places and People Abroad.* Boston: Jewett; New York: Sheldon, Lamport & Blakeman, 1855.

Browne, Junius H. *Sights and Sensations in Europe; Sketches of Travel and Adventure in England, France, Spain, Germany, etc., With an Account of Places and Persons Prominent in the Franco-German War.* Hartford, Conn.: American Publishing Co., 1871.

Bryant, William Cullen. *Letters of a Traveller; or, Notes of Things Seen in Europe and America.* New York: George P. Putnam, 1850.

Burchard, O. R. *Two Months in Europe; A Record of a Summer Vacation Abroad.* Syracuse, N.Y.: Davis, Bardeen & Co., 1879.

Burnham, Sarah M. *Pleasant Memories of Foreign Travel.* Boston: Bradlee, Whidden, 1896.

Burr, Aaron. *The Private Journal of Aaron Burr.* Edited by Matthew L. Davis. New York: Harper & Bros., 1838.

Burritt, Elihu. *A Walk from London to John O'Groats; with Notes by the Way.* London: Sampson, Low & Marston, 1864.

Burritt, Elihu. *A Walk from London to Land's End and Back, with Notes by the Way.* London: Low & Marston, 1865.

Burritt, Elihu. *Walks in the Black Country and Its Green Border-land.* London: Sampson, Low, Son, and Marston, 1868.

Burroughs, John. *Fresh Fields.* Boston: Houghton, Mifflin & Co., 1885.

Butler, Charles J. *A Bachelor's Rambles through the British Isles.* Camden, N.J.: Louis B. Cox, 1895.

Butler, Charles J. *A Yankee Bachelor Abroad.* Charles J. Butler, 1901.

Calvert, George H. *First Years in Europe.* Boston: William V. Spencer, 1866.

Calvert, George H. *Scenes and Thoughts in Europe. By an American.* New York: Wiley & Putnam, 1846.

Cantwell, J. S. *Thirty Days over the Sea; A Holiday Ramble in the Old World.* Cincinnati, Ohio: Williamson & Cantwell, 1873.

Carnegie, Andrew. *An American Four-in-Hand in Britain.* New York: Scribner's, 1883.

Carpenter, Edward., ed. *A House of Kings.* London: Westminster Abbey Bookshop, 1966.

Carradine, Beverly. *A Journey to Palestine* St. Louis, Mo: C. B. Woodward Printing & Book Mfg. Co., 1891.

Carter, Nathaniel H. *Letters From Europe, Comprising the Journal of a Tour through Ireland, England, Scotland, France, Italy, and Switzerland in the Years 1825–6–7.* 2 vols. New York: G. & C. & H. Carvill, 1829.

Catlin, George. *Catlin's Notes of Eight Years' Travel and Residence in Europe, With His North American Collection.* 2 vols. New York: the author, 1848.

Champlin, John D. *Chronicle of the Coach: Charing Cross to Ilfracombe.* New York: Scribner's, 1886.

Chandler, Alfred Dupont. *A Bicycle Tour in England and Wales; Made in 1879, by the President, Alfred D. Chandler, and Captain John C. Sharp, Jr., of the Suffolk Bicycle Club, of Boston, Mass.* Boston: A. Williams & Co., 1881.

Channing, Walter, M.D. *A Physician's Vacation; or, A Summer in Europe.* Boston: Ticknor & Fields, 1856.

Choules, Rev. John Overton, D.D. *The Cruise of the Steam Yacht North Star.* London: James Blackwood, 1854.

Choules, Rev. John Overton, D.D. *Young Americans Abroad: or, Vacation in Europe; the Results of a Tour through Great Britain, France, Holland, Belgium, Germany and Switzerland.* Boston: Gould & Lincoln, 1852.

Claflin, Agnes E. *From Shore to Shore: A Journey of Nineteen Years.* Cambridge, Mass.: Riverside Press, 1873.

Clark, John A. *Glimpses of the Old World; or, Excursions on the Continent and in Great Britain.* 2 vols. London: Samuel Bagster and Sons, 1840.

Clarke, James F. *Eleven Weeks in Europe; and What May Be Seen in That Time.* Boston: Ticknor, Reed & Fields, 1i52.

Clayton, Thomas J. *Rambles and Reflections; Europe from Biscay to the Black Sea and from Aetna to the North Cape with Glimpses at Asia, Africa, America, and the Islands of the Sea.* Chester, Pa.: Press of the Delaware Co. *Republican,* 1892.

Clemens, Samuel L. [Mark Twain]. *Letters from the Earth.* "From an English Notebook." New York: Harper & Row, 1962.

Codman, John, D.D. *A Narrative of a Visit to England.* Boston: Perkins & Marvin, 1836.

Cody, William F. *Story of the Wild West and Camp-fire Chats, by Buffalo Bill.* Philadelphia and Chicago: Historical Pub. Co., 1888.

Cogswell, Peter B. *Glints from over the Water.* Concord, N.H.: Public Press Association, 1880.

Collier, Price. *England and the English from an American Point of View.* New York: Scribner's, 1909.

Collins, Charles H. *From Highland Hills to an Emperor's Tomb.* Cincinnati, Ohio: Robert Clarke & Co., 1886.

Collins, Laura G. *By-gone Tourist Days: Letters of Travel.* Cincinnati, Ohio: Robert Clarke & Co., 1900.

Collins, Mrs. N. J. H. [Janet]. *Reminiscences; or, A Few Glimpses from over the Sea.* Philadelphia: Collins & Co., 1891.

Colman, Henry. *European Life and Manners: In Familiar Letters to Friends.* 2 vols. Boston: Charles C. Little & James Brown, 1849.

Colton, Calvin. *Four Years in Great Britain, 1831–1835.* New York: Harper & Brothers, 1836.

Connor, Eliza A. *E. A. Abroad: A Summer in Europe.* Cincinnati, Ohio: W. E. Dibble & Co., 1883.

Converse, James B. *A Summer Vacation: Sketches and Thoughts Abroad in the Summer of 1877.* Louisville, Ky.: Converse & Co., 1878.

Converse, Loring. *Notes of What I Saw and How I Saw It.* Bucyrus, Ohio: Forum Steam Printing House, 1882.

Cook, Joel. *A Holiday Tour in Europe. Described in a Series of Letters for the Public Ledger during the Summer and Autumn of 1878.* Philadelphia: J. B. Lippincott Co., 1879.

Cooper, James Fenimore. *Gleanings in Europe. By an American.* 2 vols. 1837; New York: Oxford University Press, 1930; reprint ed. Kraus Reprint Co., 1970. [Preface to 1930 ed. Robert E. Spiller.]

Cord, William H. *A Knight Templar Abroad; or, Reminiscences of Travel beyond the Sea.* St. Louis, Mo.: John Burns, 1885.

Corson, John W. *Loiterings in Europe: or, Sketches of Travel in France, Belgium, Switzerland, Italy, Austria, Prussia, Great Britain and Ireland.* New York: Harper & Bros., 1848.

Coston, Martha J. *A Signal Success; The Work and Travels of Mrs. Martha J. Coston: An Autobiography.* Philadelphia: J. B. Lippincott Company, 1886.

Cox, Samuel S. *A Buckeye Abroad: or, Wanderings in Europe and the Orient.* New York: G. P. Putnam, 1852.

Coxe, Arthur Cleveland. *Impressions of England; or, Sketches of English Scenery and Society.* New York: Dana & Co., 1856.

Crawford, Theron C. *English Life.* New York: Lovell, 1889.

Croffut, William A. *A Mid-Summer Lark.* New York: Holt, 1883.

Cross, Joseph, D.D. *The American Pastor in Europe.* London: Bentley, 1860.

Culler, Mrs. Lucy Yeend. *Europe Through a Woman's Eye.* Philadelphia: Lutheran Publication Society, 1883.

Curtis, Benjamin R. *Dottings Round the Circle.* Boston: Osgood, 1876.

Curwen, Samuel, *Journal and Letters of the Late Samuel Curwen.* Edited by George A. Ward. New York: C. S. Francis & Co., 1842.

Cuyler, Theodore L. *From the Nile to Norway and Homeward.* New York: Robert Carter & Bros., 1882.

Dallas, George M. *Diary of George Mifflin Dallas while United States Minister to Russia, 1837 to 1839, and to England, 1856 to 1861.* Edited by Susan Dallas. Philadelphia: Lippincott, 1892.

Dallas, George M. *A Series of Letters Written from London during 1856, 1857, 1858, 1859, and 1860.* Philadelphia: Lippincott, 1869.

Dana, William Coombs. *A Transatlantic Tour: Comprising Travels in Great Britain, France, Holland, Belgium, Germany, Switzerland and Italy.* Philadelphia: Perkins & Purves, 1845.

Darley, Felix O. C. *Pen and Pencil Sketches in Europe.* Boston: Estes & Lauriat, 1890.

Davenport, Esther C. *Going on Me Own.* Buffalo, N.Y.: Matthews-Northrup Co., 1900.

Davidson, Wilbur O. *Over the Sea; And What I Saw.* Cincinnati, Ohio: Cranston & Stowe, 1885.

Davis, Richard Harding. *Our English Cousins.* New York: Harper, 1894.

Davis, Richard Harding. *A Year from a Reporter's Notebook.* New York: Harper & Bros., 1898.

Davis, William P. *Across the Sea.* Trenton, N.J.: John L. Murray, 1889.

Dawson, Edward. *Benedict's Wanderings.* New York: George H. Richmond & Co., 1873.

Day, Henry. *A Lawyer Abroad.* New York: Robert Carter and Brothers, 1874.

Day, Richard E. *The Shadow of the Broad Brim.* Philadelphia and Boston: Judson Press, 1934.

de Mare, Eric. *London 1851: The Year of the Great Exhibition.* London: J. M. Dent, Ltd., 1973.

Derby, Elias H. *Two Months Abroad; or, A Trip to England, France, Baden, Prussia, and Belgium. In August and September, 1843.* Boston: Redding & Co., 1844.

Dewey, Orville. *The Old World and the New; or, A Journal of Reflections and Observations Made on a Tour in Europe.* 2 vols. New York: Harper & Bros., 1836.

Diary of My Itinerary of Sixty Days across the Water. St. Augustine, Fla., 1904.

Dickinson, Andrew. *My First Visit to Europe; or, Sketches of Society, Scenery, and Antiquities in England, Wales, Ireland, Scotland, and France.* New York: George P. Putnam, 1851.

Dictionary of American Biography. Edited by Allen Johnson. New York: Charles Scribner's Sons, 1927–1936.

The Dictionary of National Biography. Edited by Sir Leslie Stephen and Sir Sidney Lee. Oxford: Oxford University Press, 1917.

Dodd, Anna Bowman. *Cathedral Days: A Tour in Southern England.* Boston: Little, Brown, and Company, 1899.

Donelan, John P. *My Trip to France.* New York: Dunnigan, 1857.

Dorr, David F. *A Colored Man around the World; By a Quadroon.* Cleveland, Ohio: printed for the author, 1858.

Dorr, Julia C. *"The Flower of England's Face"; Sketches of English Travel.* New York: Macmillan Co., 1895.

Downing, Andrew Jackson. *Rural Essays.* New York: Leavitt & Allen, 1855.

Drew, William A. *Glimpses and Gatherings during a Voyage and Visit to London and the Great Exhibition in the Summer of 1851.* Augusta, Me.: Homan & Manley, 1852.

Dudley, Dean. *Pictures of Life in England and America; Prose and Poetry.* Boston: French, 1851.

Dudley, Dean. *Social and Political Aspects of England and the Continent: A Series of Letters.* Boston: printed for the author, 1862.

Dudley, Lucy B. *Letters to Ruth.* New York and Boston: Gilson, 1896.

Duncan, Sara Jeanette. *An American Girl in London.* New York: Appleton, 1891.

Durbin, John P. *Observations in Europe, Principally in France and Great Britain.* 2 vols. New York: Harper, 1844.

Dyer, Catherine C. *Sunny Days Abroad; or, the Old World Seen with Young Eyes.* New York: Whittaker, 1873.

Eddy, Daniel C. *Europa: or, Scenes and Society in England, France, Italy, and Switzerland.* Boston: Bradley, Dayton & Co., 1859.

Edwards, John E. *Random Sketches and Notes of European Travel in 1856.* New York: Harper & Brothers, 1857.

Emerson, Ralph Waldo. *English Traits.* Boston: Phillips, Sampson and Company, 1856.

Emerson, Ralph Waldo. *The Heart of Emerson's Journals.* Edited by Bliss Perry. Boston and New York: Houghton Mifflin Co., 1926.

Emerson, Ralph Waldo. *The Selected Writings of Ralph Waldo Emerson.* Edited by Brooks Atkinson. New York: Modern Library, 1940.

The English Illustrated Magazine. London: Macmillan & Co., 1884–1906. No. 183. December, 1898.

Everett, Edward. *The Mount Vernon Papers.* New York: D. Appleton & Co., 1860.

Fairbanks, Charles B. *Aguecheek.* Boston: Shepard, Clark & Brown, 1859.

Falkner, William C. *Rapid Ramblings in Europe.* Philadelphia: J. B. Lippincott Co., 1884.

Fauley, Wilbur F. *Seeing Europe on Sixty Dollars.* New York: Fitzgerald, 1901.

Felton, Cornelius C. *Familiar Letters from Europe.* Boston: Ticknor & Fields, 1865.

Field, Henry M. *From the Lakes of Killarney to the Golden Horn.* New York: Scribner's, 1898.

Field, Henry M. *Summer Pictures: from Copenhagen to Venice.* New York: Sheldon, 1859.

Field, Kate. *Hap-Hazard.* Boston: Osgood, 1873.

Field, Maunsell B. *Memories of Many Men and of Some Women: Being Personal Recollections of Emperors, Kings, Queens, Princes, Presidents, Statesmen, Authors, and Artists, at Home and Abroad during the Last Thirty Years.* New York: Harper, 1874.

Fisher, George S. *Notes by the Wayside.* New York: Derby & Jackson, 1858.

Fisk, Wilbur, *Travels on the Continent of Europe.* New York: Harper, 1838.

Fiske, Samuel W. *Mr. Dunn Browne's Experiences in Foreign Parts.* Boston: Jewett, 1857.

Fiske, Stephen. *English Photographs, by an American.* London: Tinsley Brothers, 1869.

Forbes, Mrs. E. A. *A Woman's First Impressions of Europe; Being Wayside Sketches Made during a Short Tour in the Year 1863.* New York: Derby & Miller, 1865.

Forbes, John M. *Letters and Recollections of John Murray Forbes.* Edited by Sarah Forbes Hughes. 2 vols. Boston and New York: Houghton, Mifflin, 1899.

Forney, John W. *Letters from Europe.* Philadelphia: Peterson, 1867.

Frazee, Louis J. *The Medical Student in Europe.* Maysville, Ky.: Collins, 1849.

Fuller, Hiram. *Sparks from a Locomotive.* New York: Derby & Jackson, 1859.

Fuller, Hiram, *Ten Days Abroad.* New York: School News Co., 1901.

Fulton, Charles C. *Europe Viewed through American Spectacles.* Philadelphia: Lippincott, 1874.

Furniss, William. *Landvoieglee: or, Views across the Sea.* Philadelphia: D. Appleton & Company, 1850.

Gage, William L. *A Leisurely Journey.* Boston: Lothrop, 1886.

Gibson, William M.D. *Rambles in Europe in 1839; With Sketches of Prominent Surgeons, Physicians, Medical Schools, Hospitals, Literary Personages, Scenery, etc.* Philadelphia: Lea & Blanchard, 1841.

Glisan, Rodney, M.D. *Two Years in Europe*. New York and London: Putnam, 1887.

Goodrich, Samuel G. *A Pictorial History of England*. Philadelphia: E. H. Butler Company, 1871.

Goodrich, Samuel G. *Recollections of a Lifetime; or, Men and Things I Have Seen: in a Series of Familiar Letters to a Friend, Historical, Biographical, Anecdotal, and Descriptive*. 2 vols. New York & Auburn: Miller, Orton & Co., 1857.

Gough, John B. *Sunlight and Shadow; or, Gleanings from My Life Work*. Hartford, Conn.: Worthington, 1880.

The Graphic. London: Chapman and Hall, 1869–1903, vol. 1, 1869.

Greeley, Horace. *Glances at Europe: In a Series of Letters from Great Britain, France, Italy, Switzerland, etc., during the Summer of 1851*. New York: DeWitt & Davenport, 1851.

Green, Jacob. *Notes of a Traveller, during a Tour through England, France and Switzerland, in 1828*. 3 vols. New York: Carvill, 1830.

Green, Lenamay. *A Girl's Journey through Europe, Egypt, and the Holy Land*. Nashville, Tenn.: Publishing House of the M.E. Church, South, 1889.

Greenwood, Grace. *Haps and Mishaps of a Tour in Europe*. Boston: Ticknor, Reed & Fields, 1854.

Greville, Charles F. *The Greville Memoirs*. 2 vols. New York: Appleton, 1885–7.

Griscom, John. *A Year in Europe, Comprising a Journal of Observations in England, Scotland, Ireland, France, Switzerland, the North of Italy, and Holland, in 1818 and 1819*. 2 vols. New York: Collins, 1823.

Groome, P. L. *Rambles of a Southerner in Three Continents; Containing Graphic Descriptions of the Peoples Living along the Line of His Travels*. Greensboro, N.C.: Thomas Bros., 1891.

Guild, Curtis. *Abroad Again; or, Fresh Forays in Foreign Fields*. Boston: Lee & Shepard, 1877.

Guild, Curtis. *Britons and Muscovites, or Traits of Two Empires*. Boston: Lee & Shepard, 1888.

Guild, Curtis. *Over the Ocean; or, Sights and Scenes in Foreign Lands*. Boston: Lee & Shepard, 1871.

Gunnison, Herbert F. *Two Americans in a Motor Car; Touring in Europe*. Brooklyn, N.Y.: Brooklyn Daily Eagle, 1905.

Haesler, Charles H., M.D. *Across the Atlantic*. Philadelphia: Peterson, 1868.

Haliburton, Thomas C. *The Letter Bag of the Great Western; or, Life in a Steamer*. Halifax, Nova Scotia: Joseph Howe, 1840.

Hall, Adelaide S. *Two Women Abroad*. Chicago: Monarch Book Company, 1898.

Hall, Basil. *Travels in North America in the Years 1827–1828*. 3 vols. London: Simpkins & Marshall, 1829.

Hall, Fanny W. *Rambles in Europe; or, A Tour through France, Italy, Switzerland, and Great Britain, and Ireland, in 1836*. 2 vols. New York: French, 1838.

Hallam, Julia C. *The Story of a European Tour*. Sioux City, Ia., 1900.

Hamilton, Peter J. *Rambles in Historic Lands; Travels in Belgium, Germany, Switzerland, Italy, France and England*. New York: Putnam, 1893.

Handford, Thomas W. *Spurgeon: Episodes and Anecdotes from His Busy Life*. Chicago: W. B. Conkey & Co., 1894.

Harrington, Adelaide L. *The Afterglow of European Travel*. Boston: Lothrop, 1882.

Hart, A. W. *The Quick Traveler*. Privately printed, 1912.

Haskins, George F. *Six Weeks Abroad in Ireland, England and Belgium*. Boston: Patrick Donahoe, 1872.

Haven, Gilbert. *The Pilgrim's Wallet; or, Scraps of Travel Gathered in England, France and Germany*. New York: Carlton & Porter, 1866.

Hawthorne, Nathaniel. *The English Notebooks*. Edited by Randall Stewart. New York: Russell & Russell, Inc., 1962.

Hawthorne, Nathaniel. *Our Old Home: A Series of English Sketches*. 1863; Columbus, Ohio: Ohio State University Press, 1970.

Hawthorne, Sophia A. *Notes in England and Italy*. New York: Putnam, 1870.

Headley, Joel T. *Rambles and Sketches*. New York: Taylor, 1850.

Hemstreet, William. *The Economical European Tourist: A Journalist's Three Months Abroad for $430, Including Ireland, Scotland, England, France, Switzerland, Italy, Austria, Prussia*. New York: S.W. Green, Printer, 1875.

Hendrix, Eugene R. *Around the World*. Nashville, Tenn.: A.H. Redford, 1878.

Hichborn, William. *Trip of the Ancients; A Memoir of Events, Personal Experiences, and Impressions Received on the Visit of the Ancient and Honorable Artillery Company of Boston to the Honourable Artillery Company of London in the Summer of 1896*. Malden, Mass.: G.E. Dunbar, 1897.

Higinbotham, John W. *Three Weeks in the British Isles*. Chicago: Reilly & Britton, 1911.

Hiller, Oliver P. *English and Scottish Sketches, By an American*. Boston: Clapp, 1857.

Hills, George W. *John Bull, Limited*. Philadelphia: privately printed, 1918.

Holden, Luther L. *A Summer Jaunt through the Old World: Record of an Excursion Made to and through Europe, by the Tourjée Educational Party of 1878*. Boston: Lee & Shepard, 1879.

Holloway, Henry C. *A New Path across an Old Field*. Philadelphia: Lutheran Publication Society, 1886.

Holmes, Oliver Wendell. *Our Hundred Days in Europe*. Boston and New York: Houghton, Mifflin, 1887.

Honeyman, A. Vandoren. *Bright Days in Merrie England*. Plainfield, N.J.: Honeyman & Co., 1901.

Hoppin, Augustus. *Crossing the Atlantic*. Boston: Osgood, 1872.

Hoppin, James M. *Old England: Its Scenery, Art, and People*. New York: Hurd and Houghton, 1867.

Horwitz, Orville. *Brushwood Picked Up on the Continent; or, Last Summer's Trip to the Old World*. Philadelphia: Lippincott, Grambo & Co., 1855.

Howe, Julia Ward. *From the Oak to the Olive; A Plain Record of a Pleasant Journey*. Boston: Lee & Shepard, 1868.

Howe, Julia Ward. *Reminiscences, 1819–1899*. Boston and New York: Houghton, Mifflin, 1899.

Howells, William Dean. *London Films*. New York and London: Harper, 1905.

Howells, William Dean. *Seen and Unseen at Stratford-on-Avon*. New York and London: Harper, 1914.

Howells, William Dean. *Seven English Cities*. New York: Harper, 1909.

Hoyt, James M. *Glances on the Wing at Foreign Lands*. Cleveland, Ohio: Fairbanks, Benedict & Co., 1872.

Hubbell, Nathan. *My Journey to Jerusalem, Including Travels in England, Scotland, Ireland, France, Belgium, Germany, Holland, Switzerland, Italy, Greece, Turkey, Palestine, and Egypt*. New York: Hunt & Eaton, 1890.

Hubbell, Orrin Z. *A University Tramp*. Elkhart, Ind.: G. W. Butler, 1889.

Humphrey, Heman. *Great Britain, France and Belgium: A Short Tour in 1835*. 2 vols. New York: Harper & Brothers, 1838.

Hutchinson, Elias S. *Two Weeks in Europe*. Washington, D.C.: Paret, 1885.

Hutton, William. *Twelve Thousand Miles over Land and Sea*. Philadelphia: Grant, Faires & Rodgers, 1878.

Illustrated London News. London: 1842–.

Irving, Washington. *The Sketchbook of Geoffrey Crayon, Gentleman*. New York: G. P. Putnam & Co., 1854.

Irving, Washington. *The Works of Washington Irving*. 15 vols. New York: G. P. Putnam & Co., 1854.

Isham, Warren. *The Mud Cabin; or, The Character and Tendency of British Institutions*. New York: Appleton, 1853.

Jackson, Helen Hunt. *Glimpses of Three Coasts*. Boston: Roberts, 1886.

James, Henry. *English Hours*. Boston and New York: Houghton, Mifflin, 1905.

James, Henry. *Essays in London and Elsewhere*. New York: Harper & Bros., 1893.

Jewett, Isaac A. *Passages in Foreign Travel*. 2 vols. Boston: Charles C. Little & James Brown, 1838.

Johnson, Clifton. *Among English Hedgerows*. New York: Macmillan Co., 1899.

Johnson, Jesse. *Glimpses of Europe; A Series of Letters Written from Abroad to the Standard Union of Brooklyn, New York*. New York: Grafton Press, 1906.

Keeler, Ralph. *Vagabond Adventures*. Boston: Fields, Osgood, & Co., 1870.

Kennedy, John P. *At Home and Abroad, Including a Journal in Europe, 1867–68*. New York: Putnam, 1872.

King, Horatio, *Sketches of Travel*. Washington, D.C.: Adams, 1878.

Kirkland, Caroline M. *Holidays Abroad; or, Europe from the West*. 2 vols. New York: Baker and Scribner, 1849.

Knowles, John H. *To England and Back*. Chicago: McClurg, 1892.

Knox, Thomas W. *The Boy Travellers in Great Britain and Ireland*. New York: Harper & Bros., 1891.

Knox, Thomas W. *How to Travel; Hints, Advice and Suggestions to Travellers by Land and Sea All over the Globe*. New York: G.P. Putnam's Sons, 1887.

Krout, Mary H. *A Looker-on in London*. New York: Dodd, Mead, 1899.

Lane, Mrs. L.C. *Letters of Travel*. San Francisco, Calif.: Bancroft, 1886.

Latrobe, John H.B. *Hints for Six Months in Europe; Being the Programme of a Tour through Parts of France, Italy, Austria, Saxony, Prussia, the Tyrol, Switzerland, Holland, Belgium, England and Scotland in the Summer of 1868*. Philadelphia: Lippincott, 1869.

Leland, Lilian. *Traveling Alone: A Woman's Journey around the World*. New York: American News Co., 1890.

LeVert, Octavia W. *Souvenirs of Travel*. New York and Mobile: Goetzel, 1857.

Linskill, Charles D. *Travels in Lands beyond the Sea*. Wilkes-Barre, Pa.: Baur, 1888.

Locke, David R. [Petroleum V. Nasby]. *Nasby in Exile; or, Six Months of Travel in England, Ireland, Scotland, France, Germany, Switzerland and Belgium, with Many Things Not of Travel*. Toledo and Boston: Locke Publishing Co., 1882.

Longford, Elizabeth. *Queen Victoria: Born to Succeed*. New York: Harper & Row, 1964.

Loring, George B., M.D. *A Year in Portugal.* New York: G. P. Putnam's Sons, 1891.

Loring, James M. *The Old World through New World Eyes.* St. Louis, Mo.: R.B. Crossman, 1904.

Lowell, James Russell. *My Study Windows.* "On a Certain Condescension in Foreigners." New York: AMS Press, 1971.

Lucas, E.V. *A Wanderer in London.* New York: Macmillan Co., 1906.

McClay, James S. *Style-O!-Graphic Pens and Funny Pencillings in Europe.* Hartford, Conn.: Phoenix, 1881.

McCormick, Richard C. *St. Paul's to St. Sophia; or, Sketchings in Europe.* New York: Sheldon, 1860.

McFarland, Andrew, M.D. *The Escape, or, Loiterings amid the Scenes of Song and Story.* Boston: Mussey, 1851.

MacGavock, Randal W. *A Tennessean Abroad; or, Letters from Europe, Africa, and Asia.* New York: Redfield, 1854.

McKenzie, Alexander. *Some Things Abroad.* Boston: Lothrop, 1887.

MacKenzie, Alexander Slidell. *The American in England.* 2 vols. New York: Harper & Brothers, 1835.

Mackin, Sarah Maria Aloisa (Britton) Spottiswood. *A Society Woman on Two Continents.* New York and London: Transatlantic, 1896.

MacLeish, Roderick. "Enigmatic Us," *Washington Post,* 2 August, 1975.

McLellan, Henry B. *Journal of a Residence in Scotland, and a Tour through England, France, Germany, Switzerland and Italy.* Boston: Allen & Ticknor, 1834.

McMurphy, Mary L. *Only Glimpses.* Racine, Wis.: Advocate Steam Print, 1887.

Magness, Edgar. *Tramp Tales of Europe through the Tyrolean and Swiss Alps and the Italian Lake Region.* Buffalo, N.Y.: Charles Wells Moulton, 1895.

Maney, Henry. *Memories over the Water; or, Stray Thoughts on a Long Stroll.* Nashville, Tenn.: Toon, Nelson & Co., 1854.

Massett, Stephen C. *"Drifting About"; or, What "Jeems Pipes of Pipesville", Saw-and-Did.* New York: Carleton, 1863.

Mathews, G.H. *Diary of a Summer in Europe, 1865.* New York: Marsh, 1866.

Matthews, James N. *My Holiday; How I Spent It: Being Some Rough Notes of a Trip to Europe and Back, in the Summer of 1866.* New York: Hurd & Houghton, 1867.

Maughs, George M.B., M.D. *Souvenirs of Travel.* St. Louis, Mo.: Farris, Smith & Co., 1887.

Maverick, Albert. *A Maverick Abroad.* Edited by James S. Maverick. San Antonio, Tex.: Principia Press of Trinity University, 1965.

Mayhew, Henry. *London Labour and the London Poor.* London: Griffin, Bohn, and Company, 1861–62.

Meloy, William T. *Wanderings in Europe.* Chicago: LaMonte, O'Donnell & Co., 1892.

Melville, Herman. *Journal of a Visit to London and the Continent.* Edited by Eleanor Melville Metcalf. Cambridge, Mass.: Harvard University Press, 1948.

Mencken, Henry L. *The American Language.* 4th ed. New York: Alfred A. Knopf, 1965.

Meriwether, Lee. *A Tramp Trip: How to See Europe on Fifty Cents a Day.* New York: Harper, 1887.

Mesick, Jane L. *The English Traveller in America, 1785–1835.* 1922; reprint ed. Westport, Conn.: Greenwood Press, 1970.

Miles, General Nelson A. *Military Europe; a Narrative of Personal Observations and Personal Experience.* New York: Doubleday & McClure, 1898.

Miller, Hugh. *First Impressions of England and Its People.* Boston: Gould & Lincoln, 1857.

Mitchell, John, *Notes From Over Sea; Consisting of Observations Made in Europe in the Years 1843 and 1844.* 2 vols. New York: Gates & Stedman, 1845.

Moran, Benjamin. *The Footpath and Highway: or, Wanderings of an American in Great Britain in 1851 and '52* Philadelphia: Lippincott, Grambo and Co., 1853.

Morford, Henry. *Over-Sea; or, England, France and Scotland As Seen by a Live American.* New York: Hilton, 1867.

Morford, Henry. *Morford's Short-Trip Guide to Europe.* New York: Lee, Shepard & Dillingham, 1874.

Morrison, Leonard A. *Among the Scotch-Irish: and a Tour in Seven Countries, in Ireland, Wales, England, Scotland, France, Switzerland, and Italy.* Boston: Damrell & Upham, 1891.

Morrison, Leonard A. *Rambles in Europe: In Ireland, Scotland, England, Belgium, Germany, Switzerland, and France.* Boston: Cupples, Upham & Co., 1887.

Moulton, Louise C. *Random Rambles.* Boston: Roberts, 1881.

Murphy, Kate A. *Trials and Triumphs of a Summer Vacation.* New York: Michael Sullivan, 1886.

Murphy, Thomas D. *British Highways and Byways from a Motor Car.* Boston: L. C. Page & Co., 1908.

Murray, Nicholas. *Men and Things as I Saw Them in Europe.* New York: Harper, 1853.

Mutchmore, Samuel A. *A Visit of Japheth to Shem and Ham.* New York: Carter, 1889.

Nadal, Ehrmann Syme. *Impressions of London Social Life.* New York: Scribner, Armstrong & Company, 1875.

The National Cyclopaedia of American Biography. New York: James T. White & Company, 1921.

Nevin, William W. *Vignettes of Travel: Some Comparative Sketches in England and Italy.* Philadelphia: Lippincott, 1881.

Nevins, Allan. *America through British Eyes.* New York: Oxford University Press, 1948.

Nevins, Allan. *American Social History as Recorded by British Travellers.* New York: Holt, 1923; reprint ed. Augustus M. Kelley, 1969.

Newman, Mrs. A. E. [Evangeline]. *European Leaflets for Young Ladies.* New York: John F. Baldwin, 1861.

Nicholson, Asenath. *Lights and Shades of Ireland.* London: Houlston & Stoneman, 1850.

Nieriker, May Alcott. *Studying Art Abroad, and How to Do It Cheaply.* Boston: Roberts, 1879.

Ninde, Mary L. *We Two Alone in Europe.* Chicago: A. C. McClurg & Company, 1897.

Noah, Mordecai M. *Travels in England, France, Spain and the Barbary States in the Years 1813–14 and 1815.* New York: Kirk & Mercein, 1819.

Old Sights with New Eyes, "By a Yankee," intro. Robert Baird, D.D. New York: M. W. Dodd, 1854.

Olmsted, Frederick Law. *Walks and Talks of an American Farmer in England.* 1852; reprint ed. Ann Arbor, Mich.: University of Michigan Press, 1967.

Ossoli, Margaret Fuller. *At Home and Abroad: or, Things and Thoughts in America and Europe*. Boston: Crosby, Nichols, and Company, 1856.

Packard, J. F. *Grant's Tour around the World; with Incidents of His Journey through England, Ireland, Scotland, France, Spain, Germany, Austria, Italy, Belgium, Switzerland, Russia, Egypt, India, China, Japan, ETC*. Philadelphia: Flint, 1880.

Palmer, Phoebe W. *Four Years in the Old World; Comprising the Travels, Incidents, and Evangelistic Labors of Dr. and Mrs. Palmer in England, Ireland, Scotland and Wales*. New York: Foster & Palmer, Jr., 1866.

Parker, Mrs. William. *Wandering Thoughts and Wandering Steps. By a Philadelphia lady*. Philadelphia: J.B. Lippincott & Co., 1880.

Patten, Claudius B. *England As Seen by an American Banker; Notes of a Pedestrian Tour*. Boston: Lothrop, 1885.

Peabody, Andrew P. *Reminiscences of European Travel*. New York: Hurd & Houghton, 1868.

Peake, Elizabeth. *Pen Pictures of Europe; When and How We Went, and What We Saw during a Seventeen Month's Tour*. Philadelphia: Lippincott, 1874.

Pearson, Clement, M.D. *A Journal of Travels in Europe during the Summer of 1881*. Washington, D.C.: Judd & Detweiler, 1885.

Peberdy, William. *Extracts from the Journal of My Trip to Europe*. Willimantic, Conn.: Home Press, 1889.

Pennell, Joseph and Elizabeth Robins Pennell. *Our Journey to the Hebrides*. New York: Harper, 1889.

Peyton, John L. *The American Crisis; or, Pages from the Notebook of a State Agent during the Civil War*. 2 vols. London: Saunders, Otley and Co., 1867.

Peyton, John L. *Rambling Reminiscences of a Residence Abroad. England-Guernsey*. Staunton, Va.: Yost, 1888.

Phelps, Sylvanus D. *The Holy Land, with Glimpses of Europe and Egypt*. New Haven, Conn.: Chatfield, 1872.

Phillips, Morris. *Abroad and at Home: Practical Hints for Tourists*. New York: Brentano's, 1892.

Polk, Burr H. *The Big American Caravan in Europe*. Evansvile: Journal Co., 1879.

Pond, James B. *A Summer in England with Henry Ward Beecher*. New York: Howard & Hulbert, 1887.

Post, Loretta J. *Scenes in Europe; or, Observations by an Amateur Artist*. Cincinnati, Ohio: Hitchcock & Walden, 1874.

Poston, Charles D. *Europe in the Summer-Time*. Washington, D.C.: M'Gill & Witherow, 1868.

Potter, V. M. *To Europe on a Stretcher*. New York: Dutton, 1890.

Prentis, Noble L. *A Kansan Abroad*. Topeka, Kans: Martin, 1878.

Preston, Margaret J. *A Handful of Monographs, Continental and English*. New York: Randolph, 1886.

Prime, Samuel I. *Travels in Europe and the East; A Year in England, Scotland, Ireland, Wales, France, Belgium, Holland, Germany, Austria, Italy, Greece, Turkey, Syria, Palestine and Egypt*. 2 vols. New York: Harper, 1855.

Program of Cook's Second Educational Tour. New York: Cook, Son and Jenkins, 1874.

Programs and Itineraries of Cook's Grand Excursions to Europe. London and New York: Thomas Cook & Son, 1880.

Punch. London: published for the proprietors, 1841–99 (October 18, 1890):183.

Putnam, George P. *The Tourist in Europe.* New York: Wiley & Putnam, 1838.

Raban, Jonathan. *Sunday Times* (London) *Weekly Review.* September 8, 1974, p. 38.

The Rambles and Reveries of an Art Student in Europe. Philadelphia:Thomas T. Watts, 1855.

Rapelje, George. *A Narrative of Excursions, Voyages and Travels Performed at Different Periods in America, Europe, Asia, and Africa.* New York: West & Trow, 1834.

Rees, Miss L.L. *We Four: Where We Went and What We Saw in Europe.* Philadelphia: Lippincott, 1880.

Rees, Thomas, *Sixty Days in Europe: What I Saw There.* Springfield, Ill.: State Register Co., 1908.

Richardson, Leander. *The Dark City; or, Customs of the Cockneys.* Boston: Doyle & Whittle, 1886.

Rideing, William H. *At Hawarden with Mr. Gladstone, and Other Transatlantic Experiences.* New York and Boston: Crowell, 1896.

Rideing, William H. *In the Land of Lorna Doone and Other Pleasureable Excursions in England.* New York and Boston: Crowell, 1895.

Rideing, William H. *Luxury at Sea.* Boston: Peter & Son, 1890.

Robinson, Louise B. *A Bundle of Letters from over the Sea.* Boston: J.G. Cupples Company, 1890.

Rose, Mrs. W. G. *Travels in Europe and Northern Africa.* Cleveland, Ohio: Whitworth Bros., 1901.

Rush, Richard. *Residence at the Court of London.* Philadelphia: Lippincott, 1872.

Rusling, James F. *European Days and Ways.* Cincinnati, Ohio: Jennings & Pye, 1902.

Rust, Lily Lawrence. Hand-written Journal. Pages unnumbered. 3 vols. 1903.

Samuels, Ernest. *The Young Henry Adams.* Cambridge, Mass.: Harvard University Press, 1948.

Scott, Sir Walter. "The Lay of the Last Minstrel," in his *Poetical Works.* London: Oxford University Press, 1904.

Scripps, James E. *Five Months Abroad; or, The Observations and Experiences of an Editor in Europe.* Detroit, Mich.: Dickerson, 1882.

Sears, Stephen W., ed. *The Horizon History of the British Empire.* New York: American Heritage Publishing Co., 1973.

Sedgwick, Catherine M. *Letters from Abroad to Kindred at Home.* 2 vols. New York: Harper, 1841.

Semple, David W. *Crusading with Knights Templar, under the Banners of Allegheny Commandery No. 35, Allegheny City, Pa., during 1878.* Pittsburgh, Pa.: Bennett, 1879.

Sessions, Francis C. *On the Wing through Europe.* Columbus, Ohio: H. W. Derby & Co., 1880.

Seward, William H. *Autobiography of William H. Seward from 1801 to 1834.* Edited by Frederick Seward. New York: Appleton, 1877.

Shackleton, Robert. *Touring Great Britain.* Philadelphia: Penn Publishing Company, 1926.

Sheldon, Caroline. *Princess and Pilgrim in England.* Washington, D.C.: Lincoln, 1904.

Sherwood, Mary E. *Here and There and Everywhere; Reminiscences*. Chicago and New York: Stone, 1898.

Sigourney, Lydia H. *Pleasant Memories of Pleasant Lands*. Boston: Munroe, 1842.

Silliman, Benjamin. *A Journal of Travels in England, Holland and Scotland, and of Two Passages over the Atlantic, in the Years 1805 and 1806*. 2 vols. New York: Bruce, 1810.

Silliman, Benjamin. *A Visit to Europe in 1851*. 2 vols. New York: George P. Putnam, 1853.

Smalley, George W. *Anglo-American Memories*. New York, Putnam's, 1911.

Smith, Amy G. and Mary E. Smith. *Letters from Europe: 1865–1866*. Edited by David Saunders Clarke. Washington, D.C.: Library of Congress, 1948.

Smith, Goldwin. *A Trip to England*. New York and London: Macmillan and Company, 1895.

Smith, John Jay. *A Summer's Jaunt across the Water: Including Visits to England, Ireland, Scotland, France, Switzerland, Germany, Belgium, etc.* 2. vols. Philadelphia: Moore, 1846.

Smith, J. J., D. D. *The Wonders of the East; or, The Record of a Journey through Europe, Egypt, and the Holy Land*. New York: Goodenough, 1873.

South, Eudora L. *Wayside Notes and Fireside Thoughts*. St. Louis, Mo.: Burns, 1884.

Sparks, Jared. *The Life and Writings of Jared Sparks*. Edited by Herbert D. Adams. 2 vols. Boston: Houghton, Mifflin, 1893.

Spender, Stephen. *Love-Hate Relations: English and American Sensibilities*. New York: Vintage Books, 1975.

Spiller, Robert E. *The American in England during the First Half Century of Independence*. New York: Henry Holt & Co., 1926.

Stanton, Henry B. *Random Recollections*. New York: Macgowan & Slipper, Printers, 1886.

Stetson, Evelyn R. *Rapid Transit Abroad*. New York: James Miller, 1879.

Stevenson, William. *Sights and Scenes in Europe: or, Pencillings by the Way in England, Scotland, Ireland, France, Switzerland, Germany and Belgium, during a Short Tour in the Summer and Autumn of 1881*. Flint, Mich.: M. S. Elmore & Co., 1882.

Stewart, Charles S. *Sketches of Society in Great Britain and Ireland*. 2 vols. Philadelphia: Carey, Lea & Blanchard, 1834.

Stockton, Frank R. *Personally Conducted*. New York: Charles Scribner's Sons, 1890.

Stokes, Frederick A. *College Tramps; A Narrative of the Adventures of a Party of Yale Students during a Summer Vacation in Europe with Knapsack and Alpenstock, and the Incidents of a Voyage to Rotterdam and Return, Taken in Steerage*. New York: Carleton, 1880.

Stowe, Harriet Beecher. *Sunny Memories of Foreign Lands*. 2 vols. Boston: Phillips, Sampson and Company, 1854.

Sweat, Margaret J. *Highways of Travel; or, A Summer in Europe*. Boston: Walker, Wise, and Company, 1859.

Sweeney, Zachary Taylor. *Under Ten Flags; An Historical Pilgrimage*. Cincinnati, Ohio: Standard, 1888.

Sweetser, Moses F. *Europe for $2.00 a Day: A Few Notes for the Assistance of Tourists of Moderate Means, with Some Personal Reminiscences of Travel*. Boston: Osgood, 1875.

Swinton, John. *John Swinton's Travels: Current Views and Notes of Forty Days in France and England.* New York: Carleton, 1880.

Tadlock, Clara M. *Bohemian Days: A Narrative of a Journey around the World.* New York: Alden, 1889.

Tappan, Henry P. *A Step from the New World to the Old, and Back Again: With Thoughts on the Good and Evil in Both.* 2 vols. New York: Appleton, 1852.

Taylor, Bayard. *At Home and Abroad: a Sketch-Book of Life, Scenery, and Men.* New York: Putnam, 1860.

Taylor, Bayard. *Views Afoot; or, Europe as Seen with Knapsack and Staff.* New York: G. P. Putnam, 1859.

Taylor, Charles M. *The British Isles through an Opera Glass.* Philadelphia: George W. Jacobs, 1899.

Taylor, Charles M. *Odd Bits of Travel with Brush and Camera.* Philadelphia: George W. Jacobs, 1900.

Taylor, William H., M.D. *The Book of Travels of a Doctor of Physic.* Philadelphia: Lippincott, 1871.

Temple, Edward L. *Old World Memories.* 2 vols. Boston: Page, 1899.

Terhune, Mary V. [Marion Harland]. *Loiterings in Pleasant Paths.* New York: Scribner's, 1880.

Terhune, William L. *My Friend, the Captain; or, Two Yankees in Europe: a Descriptive Story of a Tour of Europe.* New York: Dillingham, 1898.

Terry, Milton S. *Rambles in the Old World.* Cincinnati, Ohio: Cranston & Curts, 1894.

Thacher, Salon Otis. *What I Saw in Europe.* Topeka, Kans: Kansas Publishing House, 1883.

Thompson, Mrs. E. H. *From the Thames to the Trossachs: Impressions of Travel in England and Scotland.* The Epworth League Readings for 1890–91. New York: Hunt & Eaton, 1890.

Thompson, Ella W. *Beaten Paths: or, A Woman's Vacation.* Boston: Lee & Shepard, 1874.

Thompson, Zadock. *Journal of a Trip to London, Paris, and the Great Exhibition in 1851.* Burlington, Vt.: Nichols & Warren, 1852.

Thomson, Edward. *Letters from Europe: Being Notes of a Tour through England, France, and Switzerland.* Cincinnati, Ohio: L. Swormstedt & A. Poe, 1856.

Thorburn, Grant. *Men and Manners in Great Britain: A Bone to Gnaw on for the Trollopes, Fidlers, &c.* New York: Wiley & Long, 1834.

Thwaites, Reuben G. *Our Cycling Tour in England, from Canterbury to Dartmoor Forest and Back by Way of Bath, Oxford, and the Thames Valley.* Chicago: McClurg, 1892.

Thwing, Edward P., M.D. *Out-door Life in Europe; or, Sketches of Seven Summers Abroad.* New York: Hurst, 1888.

Ticknor, George. *Life, Letters and Journals of George Ticknor.* 2 vols. Boston: Osgood, 1876.

Timbs, John. *Curiosities of London.* London: John Camden Hotten, 1867.

Tobitt, John H. *What I Heard in Europe during the "American Excitement."* New York: H. M. Tobitt, 1864.

Tousey, Sinclair. *Papers from over the Water; A Series of Letters from Europe.* New York: American News Co., 1869.

Townsend, George A. *Campaigns of a Non-Combatant, and His Romaunt Abroad during the War.* New York: Blelock, 1866.

Townsend, George A. *Lost Abroad.* Hartford, Conn.: Betts, 1870.

Tozier, Josephine. *Among English Inns: The Story of a Pilgrimage to Characteristic Spots of Rural England.* Boston: L.C. Page, 1904.

Trafton, Adeline. *An American Girl Abroad.* Boston: Lee & Shepard, 1872.

Trafton, Mark. *Rambles in Europe: In a Series of Familiar Letters.* Boston: Peirce, 1852.

Trail, Florence. *My Journal in Foreign Lands.* Baltimore, Md.: W.S. Stock & Co., 1884.

Train, George F. *Spread-Eagleism.* New York: Derby & Jackson, 1859.

Train, George F. *Train's Great Speeches in England on Slavery and Emancipation, Delivered in London, on March 12th and 13th, 1862.* Philadelphia: T.B. Peterson & Brothers, 1862.

Tripp, Alonzo. *Crests from the Ocean-World; or, Experiences in a Voyage to Europe.* Boston: Whittemore, Niles & Hall, 1855.

Tuckerman, Henry T. *America and Her Commentators.* 1864. Reprint ed. New York: Augustus M. Kelley, 1970.

Tuckerman, Henry T. *A Month in England.* New York: Redfield, 1853.

Tyler, Fannie A. *Home Letters from over the Sea.* Boston: Williams, 1883.

Tyler, Josephine. *Waymarks; or, Sola in Europe.* New York and Chicago: Brentano, 1885.

Tyler, Moses Coit. *Glimpses of England; Social, Political, Literary.* New York and London: G.P. Putnam's Sons, 1898.

Tyng, Stephen H. *Recollections of England.* London: Bagster, 1847.

Upham, Thomas C. *Letters Esthetic, Social and Moral, Written from Europe, Egypt, and Palestine.* Brunswick, Me.: Griffin, 1855.

Urbino, Mrs. S.R. *An American Woman in Europe; The Journal of Two Years and a Half Sojourn in Germany, Switzerland, France, and Italy.* Boston: Lee and Shepard, 1869.

Vetromile, Eugene. *Travels in Europe, Egypt, Arabia, Petraea, Palestine and Syria.* New York: Sadlier, 1871.

Wagenknecht, Edward. *Washington Irving: Moderation Displayed.* New York: Oxford University Press, 1962.

Walker, Benjamin. *Aboard and Abroad; Vacation Notes, in Ten Letters, Originally Published in the Lowell Daily Courier.* Lowell, Mass.: Courier Press, 1889.

Wall, James W. *Foreign Etchings.* Burlington, N.J.: Atkinson, 1856.

Wallace, Mrs. E.D. *A Woman's Experiences in Europe; Including England, France, Germany and Italy.* New York: Appleton, 1872.

Wallace, Susan A. *Along the Bosphorus and Other Sketches.* New York and Chicago: Rand, McNally, 1898.

Ward, Matthew F. *English Items: or, Microscopic Views of England and Englishmen.* New York: Appleton, 1853.

Ware, William. *Sketches of European Capitals.* Boston: Phillips, Sampson & Co., 1851.

Washington, E.K. *Echoes of Europe: or, World Pictures of Travel.* Philadelphia: Challen, 1860.

Watson, Elkanah. *Men and Times of the Revolution, or, Memoirs of Elkanah Watson, Including Journals of Travel in Europe and America from 1777 to 1842.* New York: Dana, 1856.

Watson, Samuel. *A Memphian's Trip to Europe with Cook's Educational Party.* Nashville, Tenn.: Southern Methodist Publishing House, 1874.

Weed, Thurlow. *Letters From Europe and the West Indies, 1843–1852.* Albany, N.Y.: Weed, Parsons and Company, 1866.

Wetmore, Mrs. Elizabeth B. *A Flying Trip Around the World.* New York: Harper, 1891.

Wharton, Morton B. *European Notes; or, What I Saw in the Old World.* Atlanta, Ga.: James P. Harrison & Co., 1884.

Wheaton, Nathaniel S. *A Journal of a Residence during Several Months in London; Including Excursions through Various Parts of England; and a Short Tour in France and Scotland; in the Years 1823 and 1824.* Hartford, Conn.: Huntington, 1830.

White, Joshua E. *Letters on England: Comprising Descriptive Scenes; with Remarks on the State of Society, Domestic Economy; Habits of the People, and Condition of the Manufacturing Classes Generally.* 2 vols. Philadelphia: Carey, 1816.

White, Richard G. *England Without and Within.* Boston: Houghton, Mifflin, 1881.

Whitney, Caspar. *A Sporting Pilgrimage; Riding to Hounds, Golf, Rowing, Football, Club and University Athletics; Studies in English Sport, Past and Present.* New York: Harper, 1895.

Whittle, Walter A. *A Baptist Abroad; or, Travels and Adventures in Europe and All Bible Lands.* New York: Hill, 1890.

Whyte, William E. *O'er the Atlantic; or, A Journal of a Voyage to and from Europe.* New York: American News Co., 1870.

Wight, Orlando W. *Peoples and Countries in a Winding Journey around the World.* Detroit, Mich.: Raynor & Taylor, 1888.

Wikoff, Henry. *The Reminiscences of an Idler.* New York: Fords, Howard & Hulbert, 1880.

Wilkes, George. *Europe in a Hurry.* New York: Long, 1853.

Willard, Emma H. *Journal and Letters, From France and Great-Britain.* Troy, N.Y.: Tuttle, 1833.

Williams, Charles. *Old World Scenes.* Pittsburgh, Pa.: Haven, 1867.

Williams, George W. *Sketches of Travel in the Old and New World.* Charleston, S.C.: Walker, Evans & Cogswell, 1871.

Williams, Lucy L. *A Too Short Vacation.* Philadelphia: Lippincott, 1892.

Williams, Rudolph. *Europe from May to December.* Chicago: Weeks, 1895.

Willington, Aaron S. *A Summer's Tour in Europe, in 1851, in a Series of Letters Addressed to the Editors of the Charleston Courier.* Charleston, S.C.: Walker & James, 1852.

Willis, Nathaniel Parker. *Famous Persons and Places.* New York: Scribner, 1854.

Willis, Nathaniel Parker. *Pencillings by the Way.* 3 vols. London: T. Werner Laurie, Ltd., 1844.

Wills, Mary H. *A Summer in Europe.* Philadelphia: J.B. Lippincott, 1876.

Wilson, Julia P. *Leaves from My Diary.* Norwalk, Conn.: Gardner, 1900.

Winter, William. *The Trip to England.* New York: Lee & Shepard, 1879.

Witmer, Theodore B. *Wild Oats Sown Abroad; or, On and Off Soundings; Being Leaves from a Private Journal; by a Gentleman of Leisure.* Philadelphia: Peterson, 1853.

Wolf, Annie S. *Pictures and Portraits of Foreign Travel.* Philadelphia: Claxton, 1881.

Women's Rest Tour Association. *A Summer in England: A Handbook for Use of American Women.* Boston: Beacon, 1896.

Wood, Charles. *Saunterings in Europe.* New York: Randolph, 1882.

Wright, Hezekiah H. *Desultory Reminiscences of a Tour through Germany, Switzerland and France. By an American.* Boston: Ticknor, 1838.

Wright, Margaret B. *Hired Furnished; Being Certain Economical Housekeeping Adventures in England.* Boston: Roberts, 1897.

Young, Robert A. *Sketchy Pages of Foreign Travel.* Nashville, Tenn.: Publishing House of the Methodist Episcopal Church, 1892.

Young, Samuel. *A Wall-Street Bear in Europe, with His Familiar Foreign Journal of a Tour through Portions of England, Scotland, France, and Italy.* New York: S. Young, Jr., privately printed, 1855.

Index